The GNU C Library Reference Manual

Sandra Loosemore
with
Richard M. Stallman, Roland McGrath, and Andrew Oram

Edition 0.07 DRAFT

last updated 21 May 1996

for version 1.09 Beta

Copyright © 1993, '94, '95, '96 Free Software Foundation, Inc.

Published by the Free Software Foundation
59 Temple Place – Suite 330,
Boston, MA 02111-1307 USA
Printed copies are available for $50 each.
ISBN 1-882114-53-1

Permission is granted to make and distribute verbatim copies of this manual provided the copyright notice and this permission notice are preserved on all copies.

Permission is granted to copy and distribute modified versions of this manual under the conditions for verbatim copying, provided also that the section entitled "GNU Library General Public License" is included exactly as in the original, and provided that the entire resulting derived work is distributed under the terms of a permission notice identical to this one.

Permission is granted to copy and distribute translations of this manual into another language, under the above conditions for modified versions, except that the text of the translation of the section entitled "GNU Library General Public License" must be approved for accuracy by the Foundation.

The GNU C Library Reference Manual

Short Contents

1	Introduction	1
2	Error Reporting	13
3	Memory Allocation	27
4	Character Handling	55
5	String and Array Utilities	59
6	Input/Output Overview	75
7	Input/Output on Streams	83
8	Low-Level Input/Output	139
9	File System Interface	169
10	Pipes and FIFOs	201
11	Sockets	207
12	Low-Level Terminal Interface	255
13	Mathematics	281
14	Low-Level Arithmetic Functions	289
15	Searching and Sorting	299
16	Pattern Matching	305
17	Date and Time	321
18	Extended Characters	345
19	Locales and Internationalization	357
20	Non-Local Exits	367
21	Signal Handling	371
22	Process Startup and Termination	425
23	Processes	443
24	Job Control	457
25	Users and Groups	479
26	System Information	495
27	System Configuration Parameters	499
Appendix A	C Language Facilities in the Library	515
Appendix B	Summary of Library Facilities	533
Appendix C	Library Maintenance	621
Appendix D	GNU LIBRARY GENERAL PUBLIC LICENSE	639
Concept Index		649
Type Index		659
Function and Macro Index		661
Variable and Constant Macro Index		667
Program and File Index		673

Table of Contents

1 Introduction ... 1
- 1.1 Getting Started ... 1
- 1.2 Standards and Portability ... 1
  - 1.2.1 ANSI C ... 2
  - 1.2.2 POSIX (The Portable Operating System Interface) ... 2
  - 1.2.3 Berkeley Unix ... 3
  - 1.2.4 SVID (The System V Interface Description) ... 3
- 1.3 Using the Library ... 4
  - 1.3.1 Header Files ... 4
  - 1.3.2 Macro Definitions of Functions ... 5
  - 1.3.3 Reserved Names ... 6
  - 1.3.4 Feature Test Macros ... 8
- 1.4 Roadmap to the Manual ... 10

2 Error Reporting ... 13
- 2.1 Checking for Errors ... 13
- 2.2 Error Codes ... 14
- 2.3 Error Messages ... 23

3 Memory Allocation ... 27
- 3.1 Dynamic Memory Allocation Concepts ... 27
- 3.2 Dynamic Allocation and C ... 27
- 3.3 Unconstrained Allocation ... 28
  - 3.3.1 Basic Storage Allocation ... 28
  - 3.3.2 Examples of `malloc` ... 29
  - 3.3.3 Freeing Memory Allocated with `malloc` ... 30
  - 3.3.4 Changing the Size of a Block ... 31
  - 3.3.5 Allocating Cleared Space ... 32
  - 3.3.6 Efficiency Considerations for `malloc` ... 32
  - 3.3.7 Allocating Aligned Memory Blocks ... 33
  - 3.3.8 Heap Consistency Checking ... 33
  - 3.3.9 Storage Allocation Hooks ... 35
  - 3.3.10 Statistics for Storage Allocation with `malloc` ... 36
  - 3.3.11 Summary of `malloc`-Related Functions ... 37
- 3.4 Obstacks ... 38
  - 3.4.1 Creating Obstacks ... 38
  - 3.4.2 Preparing for Using Obstacks ... 39
  - 3.4.3 Allocation in an Obstack ... 40
  - 3.4.4 Freeing Objects in an Obstack ... 41
  - 3.4.5 Obstack Functions and Macros ... 41

		3.4.6	Growing Objects	42
		3.4.7	Extra Fast Growing Objects	44
		3.4.8	Status of an Obstack..........................	45
		3.4.9	Alignment of Data in Obstacks	46
		3.4.10	Obstack Chunks.............................	46
		3.4.11	Summary of Obstack Functions................	47
	3.5	Automatic Storage with Variable Size.....................		49
		3.5.1	`alloca` Example...............................	50
		3.5.2	Advantages of `alloca`..........................	50
		3.5.3	Disadvantages of `alloca`	51
		3.5.4	GNU C Variable-Size Arrays	51
	3.6	Relocating Allocator......................................		52
		3.6.1	Concepts of Relocating Allocation	52
		3.6.2	Allocating and Freeing Relocatable Blocks........	52
	3.7	Memory Usage Warnings		53

4 Character Handling 55
    4.1 Classification of Characters 55
    4.2 Case Conversion 57

5 String and Array Utilities 59
    5.1 Representation of Strings 59
    5.2 String and Array Conventions............................ 60
    5.3 String Length 61
    5.4 Copying and Concatenation.............................. 61
    5.5 String/Array Comparison................................ 65
    5.6 Collation Functions...................................... 67
    5.7 Search Functions.. 70
    5.8 Finding Tokens in a String............................... 72

6 Input/Output Overview 75
    6.1 Input/Output Concepts.................................. 75
        6.1.1 Streams and File Descriptors 75
        6.1.2 File Position 77
    6.2 File Names 77
        6.2.1 Directories 78
        6.2.2 File Name Resolution 78
        6.2.3 File Name Errors 79
        6.2.4 Portability of File Names...................... 80

7 Input/Output on Streams 83

- 7.1 Streams 83
- 7.2 Standard Streams 83
- 7.3 Opening Streams 84
- 7.4 Closing Streams 86
- 7.5 Simple Output by Characters or Lines 87
- 7.6 Character Input 88
- 7.7 Line-Oriented Input 89
- 7.8 Unreading 91
  - 7.8.1 What Unreading Means 92
  - 7.8.2 Using `ungetc` To Do Unreading 92
- 7.9 Block Input/Output 93
- 7.10 Formatted Output 94
  - 7.10.1 Formatted Output Basics 94
  - 7.10.2 Output Conversion Syntax 95
  - 7.10.3 Table of Output Conversions 97
  - 7.10.4 Integer Conversions 98
  - 7.10.5 Floating-Point Conversions 100
  - 7.10.6 Other Output Conversions 101
  - 7.10.7 Formatted Output Functions 103
  - 7.10.8 Dynamically Allocating Formatted Output 104
  - 7.10.9 Variable Arguments Output Functions 105
  - 7.10.10 Parsing a Template String 107
  - 7.10.11 Example of Parsing a Template String 109
- 7.11 Customizing `printf` 110
  - 7.11.1 Registering New Conversions 111
  - 7.11.2 Conversion Specifier Options 111
  - 7.11.3 Defining the Output Handler 113
  - 7.11.4 `printf` Extension Example 114
- 7.12 Formatted Input 115
  - 7.12.1 Formatted Input Basics 115
  - 7.12.2 Input Conversion Syntax 116
  - 7.12.3 Table of Input Conversions 117
  - 7.12.4 Numeric Input Conversions 118
  - 7.12.5 String Input Conversions 120
  - 7.12.6 Dynamically Allocating String Conversions 121
  - 7.12.7 Other Input Conversions 122
  - 7.12.8 Formatted Input Functions 123
  - 7.12.9 Variable Arguments Input Functions 123
- 7.13 End-Of-File and Errors 124
- 7.14 Text and Binary Streams 125
- 7.15 File Positioning 126
- 7.16 Portable File-Position Functions 127
- 7.17 Stream Buffering 129
  - 7.17.1 Buffering Concepts 129

		7.17.2	Flushing Buffers...............................	130
		7.17.3	Controlling Which Kind of Buffering..........	130
	7.18	Other Kinds of Streams		132
		7.18.1	String Streams	132
		7.18.2	Obstack Streams	135
		7.18.3	Programming Your Own Custom Streams	136
			7.18.3.1 Custom Streams and Cookies	136
			7.18.3.2 Custom Stream Hook Functions......	137

8 Low-Level Input/Output 139

8.1	Opening and Closing Files	139
8.2	Input and Output Primitives...........................	141
8.3	Setting the File Position of a Descriptor	144
8.4	Descriptors and Streams	147
8.5	Dangers of Mixing Streams and Descriptors	148
	8.5.1 Linked Channels...............................	148
	8.5.2 Independent Channels	149
	8.5.3 Cleaning Streams..............................	149
8.6	Waiting for Input or Output	150
8.7	Control Operations on Files...........................	153
8.8	Duplicating Descriptors................................	154
8.9	File Descriptor Flags	156
8.10	File Status Flags.....................................	158
	8.10.1 File Access Modes	158
	8.10.2 Open-time Flags.............................	159
	8.10.3 I/O Operating Modes........................	161
	8.10.4 Getting and Setting File Status Flags	162
8.11	File Locks	164
8.12	Interrupt-Driven Input	167

9 File System Interface 169

9.1	Working Directory	169
9.2	Accessing Directories	171
	9.2.1 Format of a Directory Entry...................	171
	9.2.2 Opening a Directory Stream...................	172
	9.2.3 Reading and Closing a Directory Stream	173
	9.2.4 Simple Program to List a Directory	174
	9.2.5 Random Access in a Directory Stream..........	174
9.3	Hard Links	175
9.4	Symbolic Links	176
9.5	Deleting Files..	178
9.6	Renaming Files	179
9.7	Creating Directories	180
9.8	File Attributes	181

	9.8.1	What the File Attribute Values Mean 181
	9.8.2	Reading the Attributes of a File 184
	9.8.3	Testing the Type of a File 185
	9.8.4	File Owner 186
	9.8.5	The Mode Bits for Access Permission 188
	9.8.6	How Your Access to a File is Decided 190
	9.8.7	Assigning File Permissions 190
	9.8.8	Testing Permission to Access a File 192
	9.8.9	File Times 194
9.9	Making Special Files 196
9.10	Temporary Files 197

10 Pipes and FIFOs 201
10.1 Creating a Pipe 201
10.2 Pipe to a Subprocess 203
10.3 FIFO Special Files 204
10.4 Atomicity of Pipe I/O 205

11 Sockets 207
11.1 Socket Concepts 207
11.2 Communication Styles 208
11.3 Socket Addresses 209
11.3.1 Address Formats 210
11.3.2 Setting the Address of a Socket 211
11.3.3 Reading the Address of a Socket 212
11.4 The File Namespace 212
11.4.1 File Namespace Concepts 212
11.4.2 Details of File Namespace 213
11.4.3 Example of File-Namespace Sockets 214
11.5 The Internet Namespace 215
11.5.1 Internet Socket Address Format 215
11.5.2 Host Addresses 216
11.5.2.1 Internet Host Addresses 216
11.5.2.2 Host Address Data Type 217
11.5.2.3 Host Address Functions 218
11.5.2.4 Host Names 219
11.5.3 Internet Ports 222
11.5.4 The Services Database 222
11.5.5 Byte Order Conversion 224
11.5.6 Protocols Database 225
11.5.7 Internet Socket Example 226
11.6 Other Namespaces 228
11.7 Opening and Closing Sockets 228
11.7.1 Creating a Socket 228

		11.7.2	Closing a Socket	229
		11.7.3	Socket Pairs	229
	11.8	Using Sockets with Connections		230
		11.8.1	Making a Connection	231
		11.8.2	Listening for Connections	232
		11.8.3	Accepting Connections	233
		11.8.4	Who is Connected to Me?	234
		11.8.5	Transferring Data	234
			11.8.5.1 Sending Data	235
			11.8.5.2 Receiving Data	236
			11.8.5.3 Socket Data Options	236
		11.8.6	Byte Stream Socket Example	237
		11.8.7	Byte Stream Connection Server Example	238
		11.8.8	Out-of-Band Data	240
	11.9	Datagram Socket Operations		243
		11.9.1	Sending Datagrams	244
		11.9.2	Receiving Datagrams	244
		11.9.3	Datagram Socket Example	245
		11.9.4	Example of Reading Datagrams	246
	11.10	The `inetd` Daemon		247
		11.10.1	`inetd` Servers	248
		11.10.2	Configuring `inetd`	248
	11.11	Socket Options		249
		11.11.1	Socket Option Functions	249
		11.11.2	Socket-Level Options	250
	11.12	Networks Database		252

12 Low-Level Terminal Interface 255

	12.1	Identifying Terminals		255
	12.2	I/O Queues		255
	12.3	Two Styles of Input: Canonical or Not		256
	12.4	Terminal Modes		257
		12.4.1	Terminal Mode Data Types	257
		12.4.2	Terminal Mode Functions	258
		12.4.3	Setting Terminal Modes Properly	260
		12.4.4	Input Modes	261
		12.4.5	Output Modes	263
		12.4.6	Control Modes	264
		12.4.7	Local Modes	266
		12.4.8	Line Speed	268
		12.4.9	Special Characters	270
			12.4.9.1 Characters for Input Editing	271
			12.4.9.2 Characters that Cause Signals	272
			12.4.9.3 Special Characters for Flow Control	274
			12.4.9.4 Other Special Characters	274

		12.4.10 Noncanonical Input 275
	12.5	Line Control Functions 277
	12.6	Noncanonical Mode Example 279

13 Mathematics 281

13.1	Domain and Range Errors 281
13.2	Trigonometric Functions 282
13.3	Inverse Trigonometric Functions 282
13.4	Exponentiation and Logarithms 283
13.5	Hyperbolic Functions 285
13.6	Pseudo-Random Numbers 285
	13.6.1 ANSI C Random Number Functions 286
	13.6.2 BSD Random Number Functions 287

14 Low-Level Arithmetic Functions 289

14.1	"Not a Number" Values 289
14.2	Predicates on Floats 289
14.3	Absolute Value 290
14.4	Normalization Functions 291
14.5	Rounding and Remainder Functions 292
14.6	Integer Division 293
14.7	Parsing of Numbers 294
	14.7.1 Parsing of Integers 294
	14.7.2 Parsing of Floats 296

15 Searching and Sorting 299

15.1	Defining the Comparison Function 299
15.2	Array Search Function 299
15.3	Array Sort Function 300
15.4	Searching and Sorting Example 301

16 Pattern Matching 305

16.1	Wildcard Matching 305
16.2	Globbing 306
	16.2.1 Calling `glob` 306
	16.2.2 Flags for Globbing 308
16.3	Regular Expression Matching 309
	16.3.1 POSIX Regular Expression Compilation 309
	16.3.2 Flags for POSIX Regular Expressions 311
	16.3.3 Matching a Compiled POSIX Regular Expression 312
	16.3.4 Match Results with Subexpressions 313
	16.3.5 Complications in Subexpression Matching 314
	16.3.6 POSIX Regexp Matching Cleanup 314

		16.4	Shell-Style Word Expansion............................ 315
			16.4.1 The Stages of Word Expansion 316
			16.4.2 Calling `wordexp`............................. 316
			16.4.3 Flags for Word Expansion..................... 318
			16.4.4 `wordexp` Example 319

17 Date and Time......................... 321

    17.1 Processor Time.................................... 321
        17.1.1 Basic CPU Time Inquiry..................... 321
        17.1.2 Detailed Elapsed CPU Time Inquiry 322
    17.2 Calendar Time..................................... 323
        17.2.1 Simple Calendar Time 324
        17.2.2 High-Resolution Calendar 324
        17.2.3 Broken-down Time 327
        17.2.4 Formatting Date and Time................... 329
        17.2.5 Specifying the Time Zone with `TZ` 332
        17.2.6 Functions and Variables for Time Zones 334
        17.2.7 Time Functions Example..................... 335
    17.3 Setting an Alarm.................................. 335
    17.4 Sleeping 338
    17.5 Resource Usage 339
    17.6 Limiting Resource Usage 341
    17.7 Process Priority................................... 343

18 Extended Characters 345

    18.1 Introduction to Extended Characters 345
    18.2 Locales and Extended Characters 346
    18.3 Multibyte Characters............................... 346
    18.4 Wide Character Introduction........................ 349
    18.5 Conversion of Extended Strings 350
    18.6 Multibyte Character Length 351
    18.7 Conversion of Extended Characters One by One 352
    18.8 Character-by-Character Conversion Example.......... 353
    18.9 Multibyte Codes Using Shift Sequences 354

19 Locales and Internationalization 357

    19.1 What Effects a Locale Has.......................... 357
    19.2 Choosing a Locale................................. 358
    19.3 Categories of Activities that Locales Affect............ 358
    19.4 How Programs Set the Locale 359
    19.5 Standard Locales.................................. 361
    19.6 Numeric Formatting............................... 361
        19.6.1 Generic Numeric Formatting Parameters 362
        19.6.2 Printing the Currency Symbol................ 363

19.6.3 Printing the Sign of an Amount of Money 365

20 Non-Local Exits 367
20.1 Introduction to Non-Local Exits 367
20.2 Details of Non-Local Exits 368
20.3 Non-Local Exits and Signals 370

21 Signal Handling 371
21.1 Basic Concepts of Signals 371
    21.1.1 Some Kinds of Signals 371
    21.1.2 Concepts of Signal Generation 372
    21.1.3 How Signals Are Delivered 372
21.2 Standard Signals 373
    21.2.1 Program Error Signals 374
    21.2.2 Termination Signals 377
    21.2.3 Alarm Signals 379
    21.2.4 Asynchronous I/O Signals 379
    21.2.5 Job Control Signals 380
    21.2.6 Operation Error Signals 381
    21.2.7 Miscellaneous Signals 382
    21.2.8 Signal Messages 383
21.3 Specifying Signal Actions 384
    21.3.1 Basic Signal Handling 384
    21.3.2 Advanced Signal Handling 386
    21.3.3 Interaction of `signal` and `sigaction` 388
    21.3.4 `sigaction` Function Example 388
    21.3.5 Flags for `sigaction` 389
    21.3.6 Initial Signal Actions 390
21.4 Defining Signal Handlers 391
    21.4.1 Signal Handlers that Return 391
    21.4.2 Handlers That Terminate the Process 393
    21.4.3 Nonlocal Control Transfer in Handlers 393
    21.4.4 Signals Arriving While a Handler Runs 394
    21.4.5 Signals Close Together Merge into One 395
    21.4.6 Signal Handling and Nonreentrant Functions .. 398
    21.4.7 Atomic Data Access and Signal Handling 400
        21.4.7.1 Problems with Non-Atomic Access ... 400
        21.4.7.2 Atomic Types 401
        21.4.7.3 Atomic Usage Patterns 402
21.5 Primitives Interrupted by Signals 402
21.6 Generating Signals 403
    21.6.1 Signaling Yourself 403
    21.6.2 Signaling Another Process 405
    21.6.3 Permission for using `kill` 406

               21.6.4   Using `kill` for Communication 407
       21.7   Blocking Signals 408
               21.7.1   Why Blocking Signals is Useful 408
               21.7.2   Signal Sets 409
               21.7.3   Process Signal Mask 410
               21.7.4   Blocking to Test for Delivery of a Signal 411
               21.7.5   Blocking Signals for a Handler 412
               21.7.6   Checking for Pending Signals 413
               21.7.7   Remembering a Signal to Act On Later 414
       21.8   Waiting for a Signal 416
               21.8.1   Using `pause` 416
               21.8.2   Problems with `pause` 416
               21.8.3   Using `sigsuspend` 417
       21.9   Using a Separate Signal Stack 418
       21.10   BSD Signal Handling 421
               21.10.1   BSD Function to Establish a Handler 421
               21.10.2   BSD Functions for Blocking Signals 422

22 Process Startup and Termination 425
       22.1   Program Arguments 425
               22.1.1   Program Argument Syntax Conventions 426
               22.1.2   Parsing Program Options 427
               22.1.3   Example of Parsing Arguments with `getopt` ... 428
               22.1.4   Parsing Long Options 430
               22.1.5   Example of Parsing Long Options 431
       22.2   Environment Variables 433
               22.2.1   Environment Access 434
               22.2.2   Standard Environment Variables 435
       22.3   Program Termination 437
               22.3.1   Normal Termination 437
               22.3.2   Exit Status 437
               22.3.3   Cleanups on Exit 439
               22.3.4   Aborting a Program 440
               22.3.5   Termination Internals 440

23 Processes 443
       23.1   Running a Command 443
       23.2   Process Creation Concepts 444
       23.3   Process Identification 444
       23.4   Creating a Process 445
       23.5   Executing a File 446
       23.6   Process Completion 449
       23.7   Process Completion Status 452
       23.8   BSD Process Wait Functions 453

		23.9	Process Creation Example 454

24 Job Control 457
24.1 Concepts of Job Control 457
24.2 Job Control is Optional 458
24.3 Controlling Terminal of a Process 459
24.4 Access to the Controlling Terminal 459
24.5 Orphaned Process Groups 459
24.6 Implementing a Job Control Shell 460
    24.6.1 Data Structures for the Shell 460
    24.6.2 Initializing the Shell 462
    24.6.3 Launching Jobs 464
    24.6.4 Foreground and Background 467
    24.6.5 Stopped and Terminated Jobs 469
    24.6.6 Continuing Stopped Jobs 472
    24.6.7 The Missing Pieces 473
24.7 Functions for Job Control 474
    24.7.1 Identifying the Controlling Terminal 474
    24.7.2 Process Group Functions 475
    24.7.3 Functions for Controlling Terminal Access 476

25 Users and Groups 479
25.1 User and Group IDs 479
25.2 The Persona of a Process 479
25.3 Why Change the Persona of a Process? 480
25.4 How an Application Can Change Persona 481
25.5 Reading the Persona of a Process 481
25.6 Setting the User ID 482
25.7 Setting the Group IDs 483
25.8 Enabling and Disabling Setuid Access 484
25.9 Setuid Program Example 485
25.10 Tips for Writing Setuid Programs 487
25.11 Identifying Who Logged In 488
25.12 User Database 489
    25.12.1 The Data Structure that Describes a User 489
    25.12.2 Looking Up One User 490
    25.12.3 Scanning the List of All Users 490
    25.12.4 Writing a User Entry 491
25.13 Group Database 491
    25.13.1 The Data Structure for a Group 492
    25.13.2 Looking Up One Group 492
    25.13.3 Scanning the List of All Groups 492
25.14 User and Group Database Example 493

26 System Information 495
- 26.1 Host Identification 495
- 26.2 Hardware/Software Type Identification 496

27 System Configuration Parameters 499
- 27.1 General Capacity Limits 499
- 27.2 Overall System Options 500
- 27.3 Which Version of POSIX is Supported 502
- 27.4 Using `sysconf` 503
  - 27.4.1 Definition of `sysconf` 503
  - 27.4.2 Constants for `sysconf` Parameters 503
  - 27.4.3 Examples of `sysconf` 505
- 27.5 Minimum Values for General Capacity Limits 506
- 27.6 Limits on File System Capacity 507
- 27.7 Optional Features in File Support 508
- 27.8 Minimum Values for File System Limits 509
- 27.9 Using `pathconf` 510
- 27.10 Utility Program Capacity Limits 511
- 27.11 Minimum Values for Utility Limits 512
- 27.12 String-Valued Parameters 513

Appendix A C Language Facilities in the Library ... 515
- A.1 Explicitly Checking Internal Consistency 515
- A.2 Variadic Functions 516
  - A.2.1 Why Variadic Functions are Used 516
  - A.2.2 How Variadic Functions are Defined and Used .. 517
    - A.2.2.1 Syntax for Variable Arguments 517
    - A.2.2.2 Receiving the Argument Values 518
    - A.2.2.3 How Many Arguments Were Supplied 519
    - A.2.2.4 Calling Variadic Functions 519
    - A.2.2.5 Argument Access Macros 520
  - A.2.3 Example of a Variadic Function 521
    - A.2.3.1 Old-Style Variadic Functions 522
- A.3 Null Pointer Constant 523
- A.4 Important Data Types 523
- A.5 Data Type Measurements 524
  - A.5.1 Computing the Width of an Integer Data Type 524
  - A.5.2 Range of an Integer Type 525
  - A.5.3 Floating Type Macros 526
    - A.5.3.1 Floating Point Representation Concepts 527

	A.5.3.2	Floating Point Parameters 528
	A.5.3.3	IEEE Floating Point 531
A.5.4	Structure Field Offset Measurement 532

Appendix B   Summary of Library Facilities .. 533

Appendix C   Library Maintenance 621

- C.1 How to Install the GNU C Library 621
  - C.1.1 Recommended Tools to Install the GNU C Library 623
  - C.1.2 Supported Configurations 624
- C.2 Reporting Bugs 625
- C.3 Adding New Functions 626
- C.4 Porting the GNU C Library 627
  - C.4.1 Layout of the 'sysdeps' Directory Hierarchy ... 630
  - C.4.2 Porting the GNU C Library to Unix Systems ... 633
- C.5 Contributors to the GNU C Library 633

Appendix D   GNU LIBRARY GENERAL PUBLIC LICENSE 639

Preamble 639
TERMS AND CONDITIONS FOR COPYING, DISTRIBUTION AND MODIFICATION 641
How to Apply These Terms to Your New Libraries 648

Concept Index 649

Type Index 659

Function and Macro Index 661

Variable and Constant Macro Index 667

Program and File Index 673

1 Introduction

The C language provides no built-in facilities for performing such common operations as input/output, memory management, string manipulation, and the like. Instead, these facilities are defined in a standard *library*, which you compile and link with your programs.

The GNU C library, described in this document, defines all of the library functions that are specified by the ANSI C standard, as well as additional features specific to POSIX and other derivatives of the Unix operating system, and extensions specific to the GNU system.

The purpose of this manual is to tell you how to use the facilities of the GNU library. We have mentioned which features belong to which standards to help you identify things that are potentially nonportable to other systems. But the emphasis in this manual is not on strict portability.

1.1 Getting Started

This manual is written with the assumption that you are at least somewhat familiar with the C programming language and basic programming concepts. Specifically, familiarity with ANSI standard C (see Section 1.2.1 [ANSI C], page 2), rather than "traditional" pre-ANSI C dialects, is assumed.

The GNU C library includes several *header files*, each of which provides definitions and declarations for a group of related facilities; this information is used by the C compiler when processing your program. For example, the header file 'stdio.h' declares facilities for performing input and output, and the header file 'string.h' declares string processing utilities. The organization of this manual generally follows the same division as the header files.

If you are reading this manual for the first time, you should read all of the introductory material and skim the remaining chapters. There are a *lot* of functions in the GNU C library and it's not realistic to expect that you will be able to remember exactly *how* to use each and every one of them. It's more important to become generally familiar with the kinds of facilities that the library provides, so that when you are writing your programs you can recognize *when* to make use of library functions, and *where* in this manual you can find more specific information about them.

1.2 Standards and Portability

This section discusses the various standards and other sources that the GNU C library is based upon. These sources include the ANSI C and POSIX standards, and the System V and Berkeley Unix implementations.

The primary focus of this manual is to tell you how to make effective use of the GNU library facilities. But if you are concerned about making your programs compatible with these standards, or portable to operating systems other than GNU, this can affect how you use the library. This section gives you an overview of these standards, so that you will know what they are when they are mentioned in other parts of the manual.

See Appendix B [Summary of Library Facilities], page 533, for an alphabetical list of the functions and other symbols provided by the library. This list also states which standards each function or symbol comes from.

1.2.1 ANSI C

The GNU C library is compatible with the C standard adopted by the American National Standards Institute (ANSI): *American National Standard X3.159-1989—"ANSI C"*. The header files and library facilities that make up the GNU library are a superset of those specified by the ANSI C standard.

If you are concerned about strict adherence to the ANSI C standard, you should use the '-ansi' option when you compile your programs with the GNU C compiler. This tells the compiler to define *only* ANSI standard features from the library header files, unless you explicitly ask for additional features. See Section 1.3.4 [Feature Test Macros], page 8, for information on how to do this.

Being able to restrict the library to include only ANSI C features is important because ANSI C puts limitations on what names can be defined by the library implementation, and the GNU extensions don't fit these limitations. See Section 1.3.3 [Reserved Names], page 6, for more information about these restrictions.

This manual does not attempt to give you complete details on the differences between ANSI C and older dialects. It gives advice on how to write programs to work portably under multiple C dialects, but does not aim for completeness.

1.2.2 POSIX (The Portable Operating System Interface)

The GNU library is also compatible with the IEEE *POSIX* family of standards, known more formally as the *Portable Operating System Interface for Computer Environments*. POSIX is derived mostly from various versions of the Unix operating system.

The library facilities specified by the POSIX standards are a superset of those required by ANSI C; POSIX specifies additional features for ANSI C functions, as well as specifying new additional functions. In general, the

Chapter 1: Introduction 3

additional requirements and functionality defined by the POSIX standards are aimed at providing lower-level support for a particular kind of operating system environment, rather than general programming language support which can run in many diverse operating system environments.

The GNU C library implements all of the functions specified in *IEEE Std 1003.1-1990, the POSIX System Application Program Interface*, commonly referred to as POSIX.1. The primary extensions to the ANSI C facilities specified by this standard include file system interface primitives (see Chapter 9 [File System Interface], page 169), device-specific terminal control functions (see Chapter 12 [Low-Level Terminal Interface], page 255), and process control functions (see Chapter 23 [Processes], page 443).

Some facilities from *IEEE Std 1003.2-1992, the POSIX Shell and Utilities standard* (POSIX.2) are also implemented in the GNU library. These include utilities for dealing with regular expressions and other pattern matching facilities (see Chapter 16 [Pattern Matching], page 305).

1.2.3 Berkeley Unix

The GNU C library defines facilities from some versions of Unix which are not formally standardized, specifically from the 4.2 BSD, 4.3 BSD, and 4.4 BSD Unix systems (also known as *Berkeley Unix*) and from *SunOS* (a popular 4.2 BSD derivative that includes some Unix System V functionality). These systems support most of the ANSI and POSIX facilities, and 4.4 BSD and newer releases of SunOS in fact support them all.

The BSD facilities include symbolic links (see Section 9.4 [Symbolic Links], page 176), the `select` function (see Section 8.6 [Waiting for Input or Output], page 150), the BSD signal functions (see Section 21.10 [BSD Signal Handling], page 421), and sockets (see Chapter 11 [Sockets], page 207).

1.2.4 SVID (The System V Interface Description)

The *System V Interface Description* (SVID) is a document describing the AT&T Unix System V operating system. It is to some extent a superset of the POSIX standard (see Section 1.2.2 [POSIX (The Portable Operating System Interface)], page 2).

The GNU C library defines some of the facilities required by the SVID that are not also required by the ANSI or POSIX standards, for compatibility with System V Unix and other Unix systems (such as SunOS) which include these facilities. However, many of the more obscure and less generally useful facilities required by the SVID are not included. (In fact, Unix System V itself does not provide them all.)

1.3 Using the Library

This section describes some of the practical issues involved in using the GNU C library.

1.3.1 Header Files

Libraries for use by C programs really consist of two parts: *header files* that define types and macros and declare variables and functions; and the actual library or *archive* that contains the definitions of the variables and functions.

(Recall that in C, a *declaration* merely provides information that a function or variable exists and gives its type. For a function declaration, information about the types of its arguments might be provided as well. The purpose of declarations is to allow the compiler to correctly process references to the declared variables and functions. A *definition*, on the other hand, actually allocates storage for a variable or says what a function does.)

In order to use the facilities in the GNU C library, you should be sure that your program source files include the appropriate header files. This is so that the compiler has declarations of these facilities available and can correctly process references to them. Once your program has been compiled, the linker resolves these references to the actual definitions provided in the archive file.

Header files are included into a program source file by the '`#include`' preprocessor directive. The C language supports two forms of this directive; the first,

```
#include "header"
```

is typically used to include a header file *header* that you write yourself; this would contain definitions and declarations describing the interfaces between the different parts of your particular application. By contrast,

```
#include <file.h>
```

is typically used to include a header file '`file.h`' that contains definitions and declarations for a standard library. This file would normally be installed in a standard place by your system administrator. You should use this second form for the C library header files.

Typically, '`#include`' directives are placed at the top of the C source file, before any other code. If you begin your source files with some comments explaining what the code in the file does (a good idea), put the '`#include`' directives immediately afterwards, following the feature test macro definition (see Section 1.3.4 [Feature Test Macros], page 8).

For more information about the use of header files and '`#include`' directives, see section "Header Files" in *The GNU C Preprocessor Manual*.

Chapter 1: Introduction   5

The GNU C library provides several header files, each of which contains the type and macro definitions and variable and function declarations for a group of related facilities. This means that your programs may need to include several header files, depending on exactly which facilities you are using.

Some library header files include other library header files automatically. However, as a matter of programming style, you should not rely on this; it is better to explicitly include all the header files required for the library facilities you are using. The GNU C library header files have been written in such a way that it doesn't matter if a header file is accidentally included more than once; including a header file a second time has no effect. Likewise, if your program needs to include multiple header files, the order in which they are included doesn't matter.

Compatibility Note: Inclusion of standard header files in any order and any number of times works in any ANSI C implementation. However, this has traditionally not been the case in many older C implementations.

Strictly speaking, you don't *have to* include a header file to use a function it declares; you could declare the function explicitly yourself, according to the specifications in this manual. But it is usually better to include the header file because it may define types and macros that are not otherwise available and because it may define more efficient macro replacements for some functions. It is also a sure way to have the correct declaration.

1.3.2 Macro Definitions of Functions

If we describe something as a function in this manual, it may have a macro definition as well. This normally has no effect on how your program runs—the macro definition does the same thing as the function would. In particular, macro equivalents for library functions evaluate arguments exactly once, in the same way that a function call would. The main reason for these macro definitions is that sometimes they can produce an inline expansion that is considerably faster than an actual function call.

Taking the address of a library function works even if it is also defined as a macro. This is because, in this context, the name of the function isn't followed by the left parenthesis that is syntactically necessary to recognize a macro call.

You might occasionally want to avoid using the macro definition of a function—perhaps to make your program easier to debug. There are two ways you can do this:

- You can avoid a macro definition in a specific use by enclosing the name of the function in parentheses. This works because the name of the function doesn't appear in a syntactic context where it is recognizable as a macro call.

- You can suppress any macro definition for a whole source file by using the '#undef' preprocessor directive, unless otherwise stated explicitly in the description of that facility.

For example, suppose the header file 'stdlib.h' declares a function named **abs** with

```
extern int abs (int);
```

and also provides a macro definition for **abs**. Then, in:

```
#include <stdlib.h>
int f (int *i) { return (abs (++*i)); }
```

the reference to **abs** might refer to either a macro or a function. On the other hand, in each of the following examples the reference is to a function and not a macro.

```
#include <stdlib.h>
int g (int *i) { return ((abs)(++*i)); }
```

```
#undef abs
int h (int *i) { return (abs (++*i)); }
```

Since macro definitions that double for a function behave in exactly the same way as the actual function version, there is usually no need for any of these methods. In fact, removing macro definitions usually just makes your program slower.

1.3.3 Reserved Names

The names of all library types, macros, variables and functions that come from the ANSI C standard are reserved unconditionally; your program **may not** redefine these names. All other library names are reserved if your program explicitly includes the header file that defines or declares them. There are several reasons for these restrictions:

- Other people reading your code could get very confused if you were using a function named **exit** to do something completely different from what the standard **exit** function does, for example. Preventing this situation helps to make your programs easier to understand and contributes to modularity and maintainability.
- It avoids the possibility of a user accidentally redefining a library function that is called by other library functions. If redefinition were allowed, those other functions would not work properly.
- It allows the compiler to do whatever special optimizations it pleases on calls to these functions, without the possibility that they may have been redefined by the user. Some library facilities, such as those for dealing with variadic arguments (see Section A.2 [Variadic Functions], page 516) and non-local exits (see Chapter 20 [Non-Local Exits], page 367), actually require a considerable amount of cooperation on the part of the C

Chapter 1: Introduction 7

compiler, and implementationally it might be easier for the compiler to treat these as built-in parts of the language.

In addition to the names documented in this manual, reserved names include all external identifiers (global functions and variables) that begin with an underscore ('_') and all identifiers regardless of use that begin with either two underscores or an underscore followed by a capital letter are reserved names. This is so that the library and header files can define functions, variables, and macros for internal purposes without risk of conflict with names in user programs.

Some additional classes of identifier names are reserved for future extensions to the C language or the POSIX.1 environment. While using these names for your own purposes right now might not cause a problem, they do raise the possibility of conflict with future versions of the C or POSIX standards, so you should avoid these names.

- Names beginning with a capital 'E' followed a digit or uppercase letter may be used for additional error code names. See Chapter 2 [Error Reporting], page 13.
- Names that begin with either 'is' or 'to' followed by a lowercase letter may be used for additional character testing and conversion functions. See Chapter 4 [Character Handling], page 55.
- Names that begin with 'LC_' followed by an uppercase letter may be used for additional macros specifying locale attributes. See Chapter 19 [Locales and Internationalization], page 357.
- Names of all existing mathematics functions (see Chapter 13 [Mathematics], page 281) suffixed with 'f' or 'l' are reserved for corresponding functions that operate on `float` and `long double` arguments, respectively.
- Names that begin with 'SIG' followed by an uppercase letter are reserved for additional signal names. See Section 21.2 [Standard Signals], page 373.
- Names that begin with 'SIG_' followed by an uppercase letter are reserved for additional signal actions. See Section 21.3.1 [Basic Signal Handling], page 384.
- Names beginning with 'str', 'mem', or 'wcs' followed by a lowercase letter are reserved for additional string and array functions. See Chapter 5 [String and Array Utilities], page 59.
- Names that end with '_t' are reserved for additional type names.

In addition, some individual header files reserve names beyond those that they actually define. You only need to worry about these restrictions if your program includes that particular header file.

- The header file 'dirent.h' reserves names prefixed with 'd_'.

- The header file 'fcntl.h' reserves names prefixed with 'l_', 'F_', 'O_', and 'S_'.
- The header file 'grp.h' reserves names prefixed with 'gr_'.
- The header file 'limits.h' reserves names suffixed with '_MAX'.
- The header file 'pwd.h' reserves names prefixed with 'pw_'.
- The header file 'signal.h' reserves names prefixed with 'sa_' and 'SA_'.
- The header file 'sys/stat.h' reserves names prefixed with 'st_' and 'S_'.
- The header file 'sys/times.h' reserves names prefixed with 'tms_'.
- The header file 'termios.h' reserves names prefixed with 'c_', 'V', 'I', 'O', and 'TC'; and names prefixed with 'B' followed by a digit.

1.3.4 Feature Test Macros

The exact set of features available when you compile a source file is controlled by which *feature test macros* you define.

If you compile your programs using 'gcc -ansi', you get only the ANSI C library features, unless you explicitly request additional features by defining one or more of the feature macros. See section "GNU CC Command Options" in *The GNU CC Manual*, for more information about GCC options.

You should define these macros by using '#define' preprocessor directives at the top of your source code files. These directives *must* come before any #include of a system header file. It is best to make them the very first thing in the file, preceded only by comments. You could also use the '-D' option to GCC, but it's better if you make the source files indicate their own meaning in a self-contained way.

_POSIX_SOURCE   Macro

If you define this macro, then the functionality from the POSIX.1 standard (IEEE Standard 1003.1) is available, as well as all of the ANSI C facilities.

_POSIX_C_SOURCE   Macro

If you define this macro with a value of 1, then the functionality from the POSIX.1 standard (IEEE Standard 1003.1) is made available. If you define this macro with a value of 2, then both the functionality from the POSIX.1 standard and the functionality from the POSIX.2 standard (IEEE Standard 1003.2) are made available. This is in addition to the ANSI C facilities.

_BSD_SOURCE   Macro

If you define this macro, functionality derived from 4.3 BSD Unix is included as well as the ANSI C, POSIX.1, and POSIX.2 material.

Some of the features derived from 4.3 BSD Unix conflict with the corresponding features specified by the POSIX.1 standard. If this macro is defined, the 4.3 BSD definitions take precedence over the POSIX definitions.

Due to the nature of some of the conflicts between 4.3 BSD and POSIX.1, you need to use a special *BSD compatibility library* when linking programs compiled for BSD compatibility. This is because some functions must be defined in two different ways, one of them in the normal C library, and one of them in the compatibility library. If your program defines _BSD_SOURCE, you must give the option '-lbsd-compat' to the compiler or linker when linking the program, to tell it to find functions in this special compatibility library before looking for them in the normal C library.

_SVID_SOURCE   Macro
If you define this macro, functionality derived from SVID is included as well as the ANSI C, POSIX.1, and POSIX.2 material.

_GNU_SOURCE   Macro
If you define this macro, everything is included: ANSI C, POSIX.1, POSIX.2, BSD, SVID, and GNU extensions. In the cases where POSIX.1 conflicts with BSD, the POSIX definitions take precedence.

If you want to get the full effect of _GNU_SOURCE but make the BSD definitions take precedence over the POSIX definitions, use this sequence of definitions:

```
#define _GNU_SOURCE
#define _BSD_SOURCE
#define _SVID_SOURCE
```

Note that if you do this, you must link your program with the BSD compatibility library by passing the '-lbsd-compat' option to the compiler or linker. **Note:** If you forget to do this, you may get very strange errors at run time.

We recommend you use _GNU_SOURCE in new programs. If you don't specify the '-ansi' option to GCC and don't define any of these macros explicitly, the effect is the same as defining _GNU_SOURCE.

When you define a feature test macro to request a larger class of features, it is harmless to define in addition a feature test macro for a subset of those features. For example, if you define _POSIX_C_SOURCE, then defining _POSIX_SOURCE as well has no effect. Likewise, if you define _GNU_SOURCE, then defining either _POSIX_SOURCE or _POSIX_C_SOURCE or _SVID_SOURCE as well has no effect.

Note, however, that the features of _BSD_SOURCE are not a subset of any of the other feature test macros supported. This is because it defines BSD

features that take precedence over the POSIX features that are requested by
the other macros. For this reason, defining `_BSD_SOURCE` in addition to the
other feature test macros does have an effect: it causes the BSD features to
take priority over the conflicting POSIX features.

1.4 Roadmap to the Manual

Here is an overview of the contents of the remaining chapters of this manual.

- Chapter 2 [Error Reporting], page 13, describes how errors detected by the library are reported.
- Appendix A [C Language Facilities in the Library], page 515, contains information about library support for standard parts of the C language, including things like the `sizeof` operator and the symbolic constant `NULL`, how to write functions accepting variable numbers of arguments, and constants describing the ranges and other properties of the numerical types. There is also a simple debugging mechanism which allows you to put assertions in your code, and have diagnostic messages printed if the tests fail.
- Chapter 3 [Memory Allocation], page 27, describes the GNU library's facilities for dynamic allocation of storage. If you do not know in advance how much storage your program needs, you can allocate it dynamically instead, and manipulate it via pointers.
- Chapter 4 [Character Handling], page 55, contains information about character classification functions (such as `isspace`) and functions for performing case conversion.
- Chapter 5 [String and Array Utilities], page 59, has descriptions of functions for manipulating strings (null-terminated character arrays) and general byte arrays, including operations such as copying and comparison.
- Chapter 6 [Input/Output Overview], page 75, gives an overall look at the input and output facilities in the library, and contains information about basic concepts such as file names.
- Chapter 7 [Input/Output on Streams], page 83, describes I/O operations involving streams (or `FILE *` objects). These are the normal C library functions from 'stdio.h'.
- Chapter 8 [Low-Level Input/Output], page 139, contains information about I/O operations on file descriptors. File descriptors are a lower-level mechanism specific to the Unix family of operating systems.
- Chapter 9 [File System Interface], page 169, has descriptions of operations on entire files, such as functions for deleting and renaming them and for creating new directories. This chapter also contains information

Chapter 1: Introduction   11

about how you can access the attributes of a file, such as its owner and file protection modes.

- Chapter 10 [Pipes and FIFOs], page 201, contains information about simple interprocess communication mechanisms. Pipes allow communication between two related processes (such as between a parent and child), while FIFOs allow communication between processes sharing a common file system on the same machine.

- Chapter 11 [Sockets], page 207, describes a more complicated interprocess communication mechanism that allows processes running on different machines to communicate over a network. This chapter also contains information about Internet host addressing and how to use the system network databases.

- Chapter 12 [Low-Level Terminal Interface], page 255, describes how you can change the attributes of a terminal device. If you want to disable echo of characters typed by the user, for example, read this chapter.

- Chapter 13 [Mathematics], page 281, contains information about the math library functions. These include things like random-number generators and remainder functions on integers as well as the usual trigonometric and exponential functions on floating-point numbers.

- Chapter 14 [Low-Level Arithmetic Functions], page 289, describes functions for simple arithmetic, analysis of floating-point values, and reading numbers from strings.

- Chapter 15 [Searching and Sorting], page 299, contains information about functions for searching and sorting arrays. You can use these functions on any kind of array by providing an appropriate comparison function.

- Chapter 16 [Pattern Matching], page 305, presents functions for matching regular expressions and shell file name patterns, and for expanding words as the shell does.

- Chapter 17 [Date and Time], page 321, describes functions for measuring both calendar time and CPU time, as well as functions for setting alarms and timers.

- Chapter 18 [Extended Characters], page 345, contains information about manipulating characters and strings using character sets larger than will fit in the usual `char` data type.

- Chapter 19 [Locales and Internationalization], page 357, describes how selecting a particular country or language affects the behavior of the library. For example, the locale affects collation sequences for strings and how monetary values are formatted.

- Chapter 20 [Non-Local Exits], page 367, contains descriptions of the `setjmp` and `longjmp` functions. These functions provide a facility for `goto`-like jumps which can jump from one function to another.

- Chapter 21 [Signal Handling], page 371, tells you all about signals—what they are, how to establish a handler that is called when a particular kind of signal is delivered, and how to prevent signals from arriving during critical sections of your program.
- Chapter 22 [Process Startup and Termination], page 425, tells how your programs can access their command-line arguments and environment variables.
- Chapter 23 [Processes], page 443, contains information about how to start new processes and run programs.
- Chapter 24 [Job Control], page 457, describes functions for manipulating process groups and the controlling terminal. This material is probably only of interest if you are writing a shell or other program which handles job control specially.
- Section 25.12 [User Database], page 489, and Section 25.13 [Group Database], page 491, tell you how to access the system user and group databases.
- Chapter 26 [System Information], page 495, describes functions for getting information about the hardware and software configuration your program is executing under.
- Chapter 27 [System Configuration Parameters], page 499, tells you how you can get information about various operating system limits. Most of these parameters are provided for compatibility with POSIX.
- Appendix B [Summary of Library Facilities], page 533, gives a summary of all the functions, variables, and macros in the library, with complete data types and function prototypes, and says what standard or system each is derived from.
- Appendix C [Library Maintenance], page 625, explains how to build and install the GNU C library on your system, how to report any bugs you might find, and how to add new functions or port the library to a new system.

If you already know the name of the facility you are interested in, you can look it up in Appendix B [Summary of Library Facilities], page 533. This gives you a summary of its syntax and a pointer to where you can find a more detailed description. This appendix is particularly useful if you just want to verify the order and type of arguments to a function, for example. It also tells you what standard or system each function, variable, or macro is derived from.

2 Error Reporting

Many functions in the GNU C library detect and report error conditions, and sometimes your programs need to check for these error conditions. For example, when you open an input file, you should verify that the file was actually opened correctly, and print an error message or take other appropriate action if the call to the library function failed.

This chapter describes how the error reporting facility works. Your program should include the header file 'errno.h' to use this facility.

2.1 Checking for Errors

Most library functions return a special value to indicate that they have failed. The special value is typically -1, a null pointer, or a constant such as EOF that is defined for that purpose. But this return value tells you only that an error has occurred. To find out what kind of error it was, you need to look at the error code stored in the variable errno. This variable is declared in the header file 'errno.h'.

`volatile int errno`   *Variable*

> The variable errno contains the system error number. You can change the value of errno.
>
> Since errno is declared volatile, it might be changed asynchronously by a signal handler; see Section 21.4 [Defining Signal Handlers], page 391. However, a properly written signal handler saves and restores the value of errno, so you generally do not need to worry about this possibility except when writing signal handlers.
>
> The initial value of errno at program startup is zero. Many library functions are guaranteed to set it to certain nonzero values when they encounter certain kinds of errors. These error conditions are listed for each function. These functions do not change errno when they succeed; thus, the value of errno after a successful call is not necessarily zero, and you should not use errno to determine *whether* a call failed. The proper way to do that is documented for each function. If the call the failed, you can examine errno.
>
> Many library functions can set errno to a nonzero value as a result of calling other library functions which might fail. You should assume that any library function might alter errno when the function returns an error.
>
> **Portability Note:** ANSI C specifies errno as a "modifiable lvalue" rather than as a variable, permitting it to be implemented as a macro. For example, its expansion might involve a function call, like *_errno (). In fact, that is what it is on the GNU system itself. The

GNU library, on non-GNU systems, does whatever is right for the particular system.

There are a few library functions, like `sqrt` and `atan`, that return a perfectly legitimate value in case of an error, but also set `errno`. For these functions, if you want to check to see whether an error occurred, the recommended method is to set `errno` to zero before calling the function, and then check its value afterward.

All the error codes have symbolic names; they are macros defined in 'errno.h'. The names start with 'E' and an upper-case letter or digit; you should consider names of this form to be reserved names. See Section 1.3.3 [Reserved Names], page 6.

The error code values are all positive integers and are all distinct, with one exception: `EWOULDBLOCK` and `EAGAIN` are the same. Since the values are distinct, you can use them as labels in a `switch` statement; just don't use both `EWOULDBLOCK` and `EAGAIN`. Your program should not make any other assumptions about the specific values of these symbolic constants.

The value of `errno` doesn't necessarily have to correspond to any of these macros, since some library functions might return other error codes of their own for other situations. The only values that are guaranteed to be meaningful for a particular library function are the ones that this manual lists for that function.

On non-GNU systems, almost any system call can return `EFAULT` if it is given an invalid pointer as an argument. Since this could only happen as a result of a bug in your program, and since it will not happen on the GNU system, we have saved space by not mentioning `EFAULT` in the descriptions of individual functions.

In some Unix systems, many system calls can also return `EFAULT` if given as an argument a pointer into the stack, and the kernel for some obscure reason fails in its attempt to extend the stack. If this ever happens, you should probably try using statically or dynamically allocated memory instead of stack memory on that system.

2.2 Error Codes

The error code macros are defined in the header file 'errno.h'. All of them expand into integer constant values. Some of these error codes can't occur on the GNU system, but they can occur using the GNU library on other systems.

int EPERM   Macro
Operation not permitted; only the owner of the file (or other resource) or processes with special privileges can perform the operation.

Chapter 2: Error Reporting   15

`int` **ENOENT**   Macro
    No such file or directory. This is a "file doesn't exist" error for ordinary files that are referenced in contexts where they are expected to already exist.

`int` **ESRCH**   Macro
    No process matches the specified process ID.

`int` **EINTR**   Macro
    Interrupted function call; an asynchronous signal occured and prevented completion of the call. When this happens, you should try the call again.

    You can choose to have functions resume after a signal that is handled, rather than failing with `EINTR`; see Section 21.5 [Primitives Interrupted by Signals], page 402.

`int` **EIO**   Macro
    Input/output error; usually used for physical read or write errors.

`int` **ENXIO**   Macro
    No such device or address. The system tried to use the device represented by a file you specified, and it couldn't find the device. This can mean that the device file was installed incorrectly, or that the physical device is missing or not correctly attached to the computer.

`int` **E2BIG**   Macro
    Argument list too long; used when the arguments passed to a new program being executed with one of the `exec` functions (see Section 23.5 [Executing a File], page 446) occupy too much memory space. This condition never arises in the GNU system.

`int` **ENOEXEC**   Macro
    Invalid executable file format. This condition is detected by the `exec` functions; see Section 23.5 [Executing a File], page 446.

`int` **EBADF**   Macro
    Bad file descriptor; for example, I/O on a descriptor that has been closed or reading from a descriptor open only for writing (or vice versa).

`int` **ECHILD**   Macro
    There are no child processes. This error happens on operations that are supposed to manipulate child processes, when there aren't any processes to manipulate.

`int` **EDEADLK**   Macro
    Deadlock avoided; allocating a system resource would have resulted in a deadlock situation. The system does not guarantee that it will

notice all such situations. This error means you got lucky and the system noticed; it might just hang. See Section 8.11 [File Locks], page 164, for an example.

int ENOMEM Macro
No memory available. The system cannot allocate more virtual memory because its capacity is full.

int EACCES Macro
Permission denied; the file permissions do not allow the attempted operation.

int EFAULT Macro
Bad address; an invalid pointer was detected. In the GNU system, this error never happens; you get a signal instead.

int ENOTBLK Macro
A file that isn't a block special file was given in a situation that requires one. For example, trying to mount an ordinary file as a file system in Unix gives this error.

int EBUSY Macro
Resource busy; a system resource that can't be shared is already in use. For example, if you try to delete a file that is the root of a currently mounted filesystem, you get this error.

int EEXIST Macro
File exists; an existing file was specified in a context where it only makes sense to specify a new file.

int EXDEV Macro
An attempt to make an improper link across file systems was detected. This happens not only when you use `link` (see Section 9.3 [Hard Links], page 175) but also when you rename a file with `rename` (see Section 9.6 [Renaming Files], page 179).

int ENODEV Macro
The wrong type of device was given to a function that expects a particular sort of device.

int ENOTDIR Macro
A file that isn't a directory was specified when a directory is required.

int EISDIR Macro
File is a directory; you cannot open a directory for writing, or create or remove hard links to it.

Chapter 2: Error Reporting 17

`int` **EINVAL** Macro
> Invalid argument. This is used to indicate various kinds of problems with passing the wrong argument to a library function.

`int` **EMFILE** Macro
> The current process has too many files open and can't open any more. Duplicate descriptors do count toward this limit.
>
> In BSD and GNU, the number of open files is controlled by a resource limit that can usually be increased. If you get this error, you might want to increase the `RLIMIT_NOFILE` limit or make it unlimited; see Section 17.6 [Limiting Resource Usage], page 341.

`int` **ENFILE** Macro
> There are too many distinct file openings in the entire system. Note that any number of linked channels count as just one file opening; see Section 8.5.1 [Linked Channels], page 148. This error never occurs in the GNU system.

`int` **ENOTTY** Macro
> Inappropriate I/O control operation, such as trying to set terminal modes on an ordinary file.

`int` **ETXTBSY** Macro
> An attempt to execute a file that is currently open for writing, or write to a file that is currently being executed. Often using a debugger to run a program is considered having it open for writing and will cause this error. (The name stands for "text file busy".) This is not an error in the GNU system; the text is copied as necessary.

`int` **EFBIG** Macro
> File too big; the size of a file would be larger than allowed by the system.

`int` **ENOSPC** Macro
> No space left on device; write operation on a file failed because the disk is full.

`int` **ESPIPE** Macro
> Invalid seek operation (such as on a pipe).

`int` **EROFS** Macro
> An attempt was made to modify something on a read-only file system.

`int` **EMLINK** Macro
> Too many links; the link count of a single file would become too large. `rename` can cause this error if the file being renamed already has as many links as it can take (see Section 9.6 [Renaming Files], page 179).

int **EPIPE** Macro
Broken pipe; there is no process reading from the other end of a pipe. Every library function that returns this error code also generates a `SIGPIPE` signal; this signal terminates the program if not handled or blocked. Thus, your program will never actually see `EPIPE` unless it has handled or blocked `SIGPIPE`.

int **EDOM** Macro
Domain error; used by mathematical functions when an argument value does not fall into the domain over which the function is defined.

int **ERANGE** Macro
Range error; used by mathematical functions when the result value is not representable because of overflow or underflow.

int **EAGAIN** Macro
Resource temporarily unavailable; the call might work if you try again later. The macro `EWOULDBLOCK` is another name for `EAGAIN`; they are always the same in the GNU C library.

This error can happen in a few different situations:

- An operation that would block was attempted on an object that has non-blocking mode selected. Trying the same operation again will block until some external condition makes it possible to read, write, or connect (whatever the operation). You can use `select` to find out when the operation will be possible; see Section 8.6 [Waiting for Input or Output], page 150.

  Portability Note: In older Unix many systems, this condition was indicated by `EWOULDBLOCK`, which was a distinct error code different from `EAGAIN`. To make your program portable, you should check for both codes and treat them the same.

- A temporary resource shortage made an operation impossible. `fork` can return this error. It indicates that the shortage is expected to pass, so your program can try the call again later and it may succeed. It is probably a good idea to delay for a few seconds before trying it again, to allow time for other processes to release scarce resources. Such shortages are usually fairly serious and affect the whole system, so usually an interactive program should report the error to the user and return to its command loop.

int **EWOULDBLOCK** Macro
In the GNU C library, this is another name for `EAGAIN` (above). The values are always the same, on every operating system.

C libraries in many older Unix systems have `EWOULDBLOCK` as a separate error code.

Chapter 2: Error Reporting   19

int **EINPROGRESS**   Macro
    An operation that cannot complete immediately was initiated on an object that has non-blocking mode selected. Some functions that must always block (such as `connect`; see Section 11.8.1 [Making a Connection], page 231) never return `EAGAIN`. Instead, they return `EINPROGRESS` to indicate that the operation has begun and will take some time. Attempts to manipulate the object before the call completes return `EALREADY`. You can use the `select` function to find out when the pending operation has completed; see Section 8.6 [Waiting for Input or Output], page 150.

int **EALREADY**   Macro
    An operation is already in progress on an object that has non-blocking mode selected.

int **ENOTSOCK**   Macro
    A file that isn't a socket was specified when a socket is required.

int **EMSGSIZE**   Macro
    The size of a message sent on a socket was larger than the supported maximum size.

int **EPROTOTYPE**   Macro
    The socket type does not support the requested communications protocol.

int **ENOPROTOOPT**   Macro
    You specified a socket option that doesn't make sense for the particular protocol being used by the socket. See Section 11.11 [Socket Options], page 249.

int **EPROTONOSUPPORT**   Macro
    The socket domain does not support the requested communications protocol (perhaps because the requested protocol is completely invalid.) See Section 11.7.1 [Creating a Socket], page 228.

int **ESOCKTNOSUPPORT**   Macro
    The socket type is not supported.

int **EOPNOTSUPP**   Macro
    The operation you requested is not supported. Some socket functions don't make sense for all types of sockets, and others may not be implemented for all communications protocols. In the GNU system, this error can happen for many calls when the object does not support the particular operation; it is a generic indication that the server knows nothing to do for that call.

int EPFNOSUPPORT   Macro
The socket communications protocol family you requested is not supported.

int EAFNOSUPPORT   Macro
The address family specified for a socket is not supported; it is inconsistent with the protocol being used on the socket. See Chapter 11 [Sockets], page 207.

int EADDRINUSE   Macro
The requested socket address is already in use. See Section 11.3 [Socket Addresses], page 209.

int EADDRNOTAVAIL   Macro
The requested socket address is not available; for example, you tried to give a socket a name that doesn't match the local host name. See Section 11.3 [Socket Addresses], page 209.

int ENETDOWN   Macro
A socket operation failed because the network was down.

int ENETUNREACH   Macro
A socket operation failed because the subnet containing the remote host was unreachable.

int ENETRESET   Macro
A network connection was reset because the remote host crashed.

int ECONNABORTED   Macro
A network connection was aborted locally.

int ECONNRESET   Macro
A network connection was closed for reasons outside the control of the local host, such as by the remote machine rebooting or an unrecoverable protocol violation.

int ENOBUFS   Macro
The kernel's buffers for I/O operations are all in use. In GNU, this error is always synonymous with ENOMEM; you may get one or the other from network operations.

int EISCONN   Macro
You tried to connect a socket that is already connected. See Section 11.8.1 [Making a Connection], page 231.

int ENOTCONN   Macro
The socket is not connected to anything. You get this error when you try to transmit data over a socket, without first specifying a destination

Chapter 2: Error Reporting   21

for the data. For a connectionless socket (for datagram protocols, such as UDP), you get `EDESTADDRREQ` instead.

int EDESTADDRREQ   *Macro*
No default destination address was set for the socket. You get this error when you try to transmit data over a connectionless socket, without first specifying a destination for the data with `connect`.

int ESHUTDOWN   *Macro*
The socket has already been shut down.

int ETOOMANYREFS   *Macro*
???

int ETIMEDOUT   *Macro*
A socket operation with a specified timeout received no response during the timeout period.

int ECONNREFUSED   *Macro*
A remote host refused to allow the network connection (typically because it is not running the requested service).

int ELOOP   *Macro*
Too many levels of symbolic links were encountered in looking up a file name. This often indicates a cycle of symbolic links.

int ENAMETOOLONG   *Macro*
Filename too long (longer than `PATH_MAX`; see Section 27.6 [Limits on File System Capacity], page 507) or host name too long (in `gethostname` or `sethostname`; see Section 26.1 [Host Identification], page 495).

int EHOSTDOWN   *Macro*
The remote host for a requested network connection is down.

int EHOSTUNREACH   *Macro*
The remote host for a requested network connection is not reachable.

int ENOTEMPTY   *Macro*
Directory not empty, where an empty directory was expected. Typically, this error occurs when you are trying to delete a directory.

int EPROCLIM   *Macro*
This means that the per-user limit on new process would be exceeded by an attempted `fork`. See Section 17.6 [Limiting Resource Usage], page 341, for details on the `RLIMIT_NPROC` limit.

int EUSERS   *Macro*
The file quota system is confused because there are too many users.

int EDQUOT   Macro
   The user's disk quota was exceeded.

int ESTALE   Macro
   Stale NFS file handle. This indicates an internal confusion in the NFS
   system which is due to file system rearrangements on the server host.
   Repairing this condition usually requires unmounting and remounting
   the NFS file system on the local host.

int EREMOTE   Macro
   An attempt was made to NFS-mount a remote file system with a file
   name that already specifies an NFS-mounted file. (This is an error
   on some operating systems, but we expect it to work properly on the
   GNU system, making this error code impossible.)

int EBADRPC   Macro
   ???

int ERPCMISMATCH   Macro
   ???

int EPROGUNAVAIL   Macro
   ???

int EPROGMISMATCH   Macro
   ???

int EPROCUNAVAIL   Macro
   ???

int ENOLCK   Macro
   No locks available. This is used by the file locking facilities; see Section 8.11 [File Locks], page 164. This error is never generated by the
   GNU system, but it can result from an operation to an NFS server
   running another operating system.

int EFTYPE   Macro
   Inappropriate file type or format. The file was the wrong type for the
   operation, or a data file had the wrong format.

   On some systems `chmod` returns this error if you try to set the sticky bit
   on a non-directory file; see Section 9.8.7 [Assigning File Permissions],
   page 190.

int EAUTH   Macro
   ???

int ENEEDAUTH   Macro
   ???

Chapter 2: Error Reporting   23

int **ENOSYS**   Macro
> Function not implemented. Some functions have commands or options defined that might not be supported in all implementations, and this is the kind of error you get if you request them and they are not supported.

int **EILSEQ**   Macro
> While decoding a multibyte character the function came along an invalid or an incomplete sequence of bytes or the given wide character is invalid.

int **EBACKGROUND**   Macro
> In the GNU system, servers supporting the `term` protocol return this error for certain operations when the caller is not in the foreground process group of the terminal. Users do not usually see this error because functions such as `read` and `write` translate it into a `SIGTTIN` or `SIGTTOU` signal. See Chapter 24 [Job Control], page 457, for information on process groups and these signals.

int **EDIED**   Macro
> In the GNU system, opening a file returns this error when the file is translated by a program and the translator program dies while starting up, before it has connected to the file.

int **ED**   Macro
> The experienced user will know what is wrong.

int **EGREGIOUS**   Macro
> You did **what**?

int **EIEIO**   Macro
> Go home and have a glass of warm, dairy-fresh milk.

int **EGRATUITOUS**   Macro
> This error code has no purpose.

2.3 Error Messages

The library has functions and variables designed to make it easy for your program to report informative error messages in the customary format about the failure of a library call. The functions `strerror` and `perror` give you the standard error message for a given error code; the variable `program_invocation_short_name` gives you convenient access to the name of the program that encountered the error.

char * **strerror** (int *errnum*)   Function
:   The `strerror` function maps the error code (see Section 2.1 [Checking for Errors], page 13) specified by the *errnum* argument to a descriptive error message string. The return value is a pointer to this string.

    The value *errnum* normally comes from the variable `errno`.

    You should not modify the string returned by `strerror`. Also, if you make subsequent calls to `strerror`, the string might be overwritten. (But it's guaranteed that no library function ever calls `strerror` behind your back.)

    The function `strerror` is declared in 'string.h'.

void **perror** (const char *message*)   Function
:   This function prints an error message to the stream `stderr`; see Section 7.2 [Standard Streams], page 83.

    If you call `perror` with a *message* that is either a null pointer or an empty string, `perror` just prints the error message corresponding to `errno`, adding a trailing newline.

    If you supply a non-null *message* argument, then `perror` prefixes its output with this string. It adds a colon and a space character to separate the *message* from the error string corresponding to `errno`.

    The function `perror` is declared in 'stdio.h'.

`strerror` and `perror` produce the exact same message for any given error code; the precise text varies from system to system. On the GNU system, the messages are fairly short; there are no multi-line messages or embedded newlines. Each error message begins with a capital letter and does not include any terminating punctuation.

Compatibility Note: The `strerror` function is a new feature of ANSI C. Many older C systems do not support this function yet.

Many programs that don't read input from the terminal are designed to exit if any system call fails. By convention, the error message from such a program should start with the program's name, sans directories. You can find that name in the variable `program_invocation_short_name`; the full file name is stored the variable `program_invocation_name`:

char * **program_invocation_name**   Variable
:   This variable's value is the name that was used to invoke the program running in the current process. It is the same as `argv[0]`. Note that this is not necessarily a useful file name; often it contains no directory names. See Section 22.1 [Program Arguments], page 425.

char * **program_invocation_short_name**   Variable
:   This variable's value is the name that was used to invoke the program running in the current process, with directory names removed. (That is

to say, it is the same as `program_invocation_name` minus everything up to the last slash, if any.)

The library initialization code sets up both of these variables before calling `main`.

Portability Note: These two variables are GNU extensions. If you want your program to work with non-GNU libraries, you must save the value of `argv[0]` in `main`, and then strip off the directory names yourself. We added these extensions to make it possible to write self-contained error-reporting subroutines that require no explicit cooperation from `main`.

Here is an example showing how to handle failure to open a file correctly. The function `open_sesame` tries to open the named file for reading and returns a stream if successful. The `fopen` library function returns a null pointer if it couldn't open the file for some reason. In that situation, `open_sesame` constructs an appropriate error message using the `strerror` function, and terminates the program. If we were going to make some other library calls before passing the error code to `strerror`, we'd have to save it in a local variable instead, because those other library functions might overwrite `errno` in the meantime.

```
#include <errno.h>
#include <stdio.h>
#include <stdlib.h>
#include <string.h>

FILE *
open_sesame (char *name)
{
  FILE *stream;

  errno = 0;
  stream = fopen (name, "r");
  if (stream == NULL)
    {
      fprintf (stderr, "%s: Couldn't open file %s; %s\n",
               program_invocation_short_name, name, strerror (errno));
      exit (EXIT_FAILURE);
    }
  else
    return stream;
}
```

3 Memory Allocation

The GNU system provides several methods for allocating memory space under explicit program control. They vary in generality and in efficiency.

- The `malloc` facility allows fully general dynamic allocation. See Section 3.3 [Unconstrained Allocation], page 28.
- Obstacks are another facility, less general than `malloc` but more efficient and convenient for stacklike allocation. See Section 3.4 [Obstacks], page 38.
- The function `alloca` lets you allocate storage dynamically that will be freed automatically. See Section 3.5 [Automatic Storage with Variable Size], page 49.

3.1 Dynamic Memory Allocation Concepts

Dynamic memory allocation is a technique in which programs determine as they are running where to store some information. You need dynamic allocation when the number of memory blocks you need, or how long you continue to need them, depends on the data you are working on.

For example, you may need a block to store a line read from an input file; since there is no limit to how long a line can be, you must allocate the storage dynamically and make it dynamically larger as you read more of the line.

Or, you may need a block for each record or each definition in the input data; since you can't know in advance how many there will be, you must allocate a new block for each record or definition as you read it.

When you use dynamic allocation, the allocation of a block of memory is an action that the program requests explicitly. You call a function or macro when you want to allocate space, and specify the size with an argument. If you want to free the space, you do so by calling another function or macro. You can do these things whenever you want, as often as you want.

3.2 Dynamic Allocation and C

The C language supports two kinds of memory allocation through the variables in C programs:

- *Static allocation* is what happens when you declare a static or global variable. Each static or global variable defines one block of space, of a fixed size. The space is allocated once, when your program is started, and is never freed.

- *Automatic allocation* happens when you declare an automatic variable, such as a function argument or a local variable. The space for an automatic variable is allocated when the compound statement containing the declaration is entered, and is freed when that compound statement is exited.

  In GNU C, the length of the automatic storage can be an expression that varies. In other C implementations, it must be a constant.

Dynamic allocation is not supported by C variables; there is no storage class "dynamic", and there can never be a C variable whose value is stored in dynamically allocated space. The only way to refer to dynamically allocated space is through a pointer. Because it is less convenient, and because the actual process of dynamic allocation requires more computation time, programmers generally use dynamic allocation only when neither static nor automatic allocation will serve.

For example, if you want to allocate dynamically some space to hold a `struct foobar`, you cannot declare a variable of type `struct foobar` whose contents are the dynamically allocated space. But you can declare a variable of pointer type `struct foobar *` and assign it the address of the space. Then you can use the operators '`*`' and '`->`' on this pointer variable to refer to the contents of the space:

```
{
  struct foobar *ptr
    = (struct foobar *) malloc (sizeof (struct foobar));
  ptr->name = x;
  ptr->next = current_foobar;
  current_foobar = ptr;
}
```

3.3 Unconstrained Allocation

The most general dynamic allocation facility is `malloc`. It allows you to allocate blocks of memory of any size at any time, make them bigger or smaller at any time, and free the blocks individually at any time (or never).

3.3.1 Basic Storage Allocation

To allocate a block of memory, call `malloc`. The prototype for this function is in '`stdlib.h`'.

void * **malloc** (size_t *size*)   Function

   This function returns a pointer to a newly allocated block *size* bytes long, or a null pointer if the block could not be allocated.

   The contents of the block are undefined; you must initialize it yourself (or use `calloc` instead; see Section 3.3.5 [Allocating Cleared Space], page 32).

Chapter 3: Memory Allocation 29

Normally you would cast the value as a pointer to the kind of object that you want to store in the block. Here we show an example of doing so, and of initializing the space with zeros using the library function `memset` (see Section 5.4 [Copying and Concatenation], page 61):

```
struct foo *ptr;
...
ptr = (struct foo *) malloc (sizeof (struct foo));
if (ptr == 0) abort ();
memset (ptr, 0, sizeof (struct foo));
```

You can store the result of `malloc` into any pointer variable without a cast, because ANSI C automatically converts the type `void *` to another type of pointer when necessary. But the cast is necessary in contexts other than assignment operators or if you might want your code to run in traditional C.

Remember that when allocating space for a string, the argument to `malloc` must be one plus the length of the string. This is because a string is terminated with a null character that doesn't count in the "length" of the string but does need space. For example:

```
char *ptr;
...
ptr = (char *) malloc (length + 1);
```

See Section 5.1 [Representation of Strings], page 59, for more information about this.

3.3.2 Examples of `malloc`

If no more space is available, `malloc` returns a null pointer. You should check the value of *every* call to `malloc`. It is useful to write a subroutine that calls `malloc` and reports an error if the value is a null pointer, returning only if the value is nonzero. This function is conventionally called `xmalloc`. Here it is:

```
void *
xmalloc (size_t size)
{
  register void *value = malloc (size);
  if (value == 0)
    fatal ("virtual memory exhausted");
  return value;
}
```

Here is a real example of using `malloc` (by way of `xmalloc`). The function `savestring` will copy a sequence of characters into a newly allocated null-terminated string:

```
char *
savestring (const char *ptr, size_t len)
{
  register char *value = (char *) xmalloc (len + 1);
  memcpy (value, ptr, len);
  value[len] = '\0';
  return value;
}
```

The block that `malloc` gives you is guaranteed to be aligned so that it can hold any type of data. In the GNU system, the address is always a multiple of eight; if the size of block is 16 or more, then the address is always a multiple of 16. Only rarely is any higher boundary (such as a page boundary) necessary; for those cases, use `memalign` or `valloc` (see Section 3.3.7 [Allocating Aligned Memory Blocks], page 33).

Note that the memory located after the end of the block is likely to be in use for something else; perhaps a block already allocated by another call to `malloc`. If you attempt to treat the block as longer than you asked for it to be, you are liable to destroy the data that `malloc` uses to keep track of its blocks, or you may destroy the contents of another block. If you have already allocated a block and discover you want it to be bigger, use `realloc` (see Section 3.3.4 [Changing the Size of a Block], page 31).

3.3.3 Freeing Memory Allocated with `malloc`

When you no longer need a block that you got with `malloc`, use the function `free` to make the block available to be allocated again. The prototype for this function is in 'stdlib.h'.

void **free** (void *ptr*)   Function
  The `free` function deallocates the block of storage pointed at by *ptr*.

void **cfree** (void *ptr*)   Function
  This function does the same thing as `free`. It's provided for backward compatibility with SunOS; you should use `free` instead.

Freeing a block alters the contents of the block. **Do not expect to find any data (such as a pointer to the next block in a chain of blocks) in the block after freeing it.** Copy whatever you need out of the block before freeing it! Here is an example of the proper way to free all the blocks in a chain, and the strings that they point to:

```
struct chain
  {
    struct chain *next;
    char *name;
  }

void
```

Chapter 3: Memory Allocation 31

```
free_chain (struct chain *chain)
{
  while (chain != 0)
    {
      struct chain *next = chain->next;
      free (chain->name);
      free (chain);
      chain = next;
    }
}
```

Occasionally, `free` can actually return memory to the operating system and make the process smaller. Usually, all it can do is allow a later call to `malloc` to reuse the space. In the meantime, the space remains in your program as part of a free-list used internally by `malloc`.

There is no point in freeing blocks at the end of a program, because all of the program's space is given back to the system when the process terminates.

3.3.4 Changing the Size of a Block

Often you do not know for certain how big a block you will ultimately need at the time you must begin to use the block. For example, the block might be a buffer that you use to hold a line being read from a file; no matter how long you make the buffer initially, you may encounter a line that is longer.

You can make the block longer by calling `realloc`. This function is declared in 'stdlib.h'.

void * **realloc** (void *ptr*, size_t *newsize*) *Function*
> The `realloc` function changes the size of the block whose address is *ptr* to be *newsize*.
>
> Since the space after the end of the block may be in use, `realloc` may find it necessary to copy the block to a new address where more free space is available. The value of `realloc` is the new address of the block. If the block needs to be moved, `realloc` copies the old contents.
>
> If you pass a null pointer for *ptr*, `realloc` behaves just like 'malloc (*newsize*)'. This can be convenient, but beware that older implementations (before ANSI C) may not support this behavior, and will probably crash when `realloc` is passed a null pointer.
>
> Like `malloc`, `realloc` may return a null pointer if no memory space is available to make the block bigger. When this happens, the original block is untouched; it has not been modified or relocated.
>
> In most cases it makes no difference what happens to the original block when `realloc` fails, because the application program cannot continue when

it is out of memory, and the only thing to do is to give a fatal error message. Often it is convenient to write and use a subroutine, conventionally called `xrealloc`, that takes care of the error message as `xmalloc` does for `malloc`:

```
void *
xrealloc (void *ptr, size_t size)
{
  register void *value = realloc (ptr, size);
  if (value == 0)
    fatal ("Virtual memory exhausted");
  return value;
}
```

You can also use `realloc` to make a block smaller. The reason you would do this is to avoid tying up a lot of memory space when only a little is needed. Making a block smaller sometimes necessitates copying it, so it can fail if no other space is available.

If the new size you specify is the same as the old size, `realloc` is guaranteed to change nothing and return the same address that you gave.

3.3.5 Allocating Cleared Space

The function `calloc` allocates memory and clears it to zero. It is declared in 'stdlib.h'.

void * calloc (size_t *count*, **size_t** *eltsize***)** *Function*
This function allocates a block long enough to contain a vector of *count* elements, each of size *eltsize*. Its contents are cleared to zero before `calloc` returns.

You could define `calloc` as follows:

```
void *
calloc (size_t count, size_t eltsize)
{
  size_t size = count * eltsize;
  void *value = malloc (size);
  if (value != 0)
    memset (value, 0, size);
  return value;
}
```

3.3.6 Efficiency Considerations for `malloc`

To make the best use of `malloc`, it helps to know that the GNU version of `malloc` always dispenses small amounts of memory in blocks whose sizes are powers of two. It keeps separate pools for each power of two. This holds for sizes up to a page size. Therefore, if you are free to choose the size of a small block in order to make `malloc` more efficient, make it a power of two.

Chapter 3: Memory Allocation

Once a page is split up for a particular block size, it can't be reused for another size unless all the blocks in it are freed. In many programs, this is unlikely to happen. Thus, you can sometimes make a program use memory more efficiently by using blocks of the same size for many different purposes.

When you ask for memory blocks of a page or larger, `malloc` uses a different strategy; it rounds the size up to a multiple of a page, and it can coalesce and split blocks as needed.

The reason for the two strategies is that it is important to allocate and free small blocks as fast as possible, but speed is less important for a large block since the program normally spends a fair amount of time using it. Also, large blocks are normally fewer in number. Therefore, for large blocks, it makes sense to use a method which takes more time to minimize the wasted space.

3.3.7 Allocating Aligned Memory Blocks

The address of a block returned by `malloc` or `realloc` in the GNU system is always a multiple of eight. If you need a block whose address is a multiple of a higher power of two than that, use `memalign` or `valloc`. These functions are declared in 'stdlib.h'.

With the GNU library, you can use `free` to free the blocks that `memalign` and `valloc` return. That does not work in BSD, however—BSD does not provide any way to free such blocks.

void * **memalign** (size_t *boundary*, size_t *size*) *Function*
:   The `memalign` function allocates a block of *size* bytes whose address is a multiple of *boundary*. The *boundary* must be a power of two! The function `memalign` works by calling `malloc` to allocate a somewhat larger block, and then returning an address within the block that is on the specified boundary.

void * **valloc** (size_t *size*) *Function*
:   Using `valloc` is like using `memalign` and passing the page size as the value of the second argument. It is implemented like this:
    ```
    void *
    valloc (size_t size)
    {
      return memalign (getpagesize (), size);
    }
    ```

3.3.8 Heap Consistency Checking

You can ask `malloc` to check the consistency of dynamic storage by using the `mcheck` function. This function is a GNU extension, declared in 'malloc.h'.

`int` **mcheck** (`void (*`*abortfn*`) (enum mcheck_status` *status*`))* *Function*

Calling `mcheck` tells `malloc` to perform occasional consistency checks. These will catch things such as writing past the end of a block that was allocated with `malloc`.

The *abortfn* argument is the function to call when an inconsistency is found. If you supply a null pointer, then `mcheck` uses a default function which prints a message and calls `abort` (see Section 22.3.4 [Aborting a Program], page 440). The function you supply is called with one argument, which says what sort of inconsistency was detected; its type is described below.

It is too late to begin allocation checking once you have allocated anything with `malloc`. So `mcheck` does nothing in that case. The function returns `-1` if you call it too late, and `0` otherwise (when it is successful).

The easiest way to arrange to call `mcheck` early enough is to use the option '`-lmcheck`' when you link your program; then you don't need to modify your program source at all.

`enum mcheck_status` **mprobe** (`void *`*pointer*`)` *Function*

The `mprobe` function lets you explicitly check for inconsistencies in a particular allocated block. You must have already called `mcheck` at the beginning of the program, to do its occasional checks; calling `mprobe` requests an additional consistency check to be done at the time of the call.

The argument *pointer* must be a pointer returned by `malloc` or `realloc`. `mprobe` returns a value that says what inconsistency, if any, was found. The values are described below.

enum mcheck_status *Data Type*

This enumerated type describes what kind of inconsistency was detected in an allocated block, if any. Here are the possible values:

`MCHECK_DISABLED`
: `mcheck` was not called before the first allocation. No consistency checking can be done.

`MCHECK_OK`
: No inconsistency detected.

`MCHECK_HEAD`
: The data immediately before the block was modified. This commonly happens when an array index or pointer is decremented too far.

Chapter 3: Memory Allocation 35

MCHECK_TAIL
>   The data immediately after the block was modified. This commonly happens when an array index or pointer is incremented too far.

MCHECK_FREE
>   The block was already freed.

3.3.9 Storage Allocation Hooks

The GNU C library lets you modify the behavior of `malloc`, `realloc`, and `free` by specifying appropriate hook functions. You can use these hooks to help you debug programs that use dynamic storage allocation, for example.

The hook variables are declared in 'malloc.h'.

__malloc_hook   Variable
> The value of this variable is a pointer to function that `malloc` uses whenever it is called. You should define this function to look like `malloc`; that is, like:
>
>   void *function (size_t size)

__realloc_hook   Variable
> The value of this variable is a pointer to function that `realloc` uses whenever it is called. You should define this function to look like `realloc`; that is, like:
>
>   void *function (void *ptr, size_t size)

__free_hook   Variable
> The value of this variable is a pointer to function that `free` uses whenever it is called. You should define this function to look like `free`; that is, like:
>
>   void function (void *ptr)

You must make sure that the function you install as a hook for one of these functions does not call that function recursively without restoring the old value of the hook first! Otherwise, your program will get stuck in an infinite recursion.

Here is an example showing how to use `__malloc_hook` properly. It installs a function that prints out information every time `malloc` is called.

```
static void *(*old_malloc_hook) (size_t);
static void *
my_malloc_hook (size_t size)
{
  void *result;
  __malloc_hook = old_malloc_hook;
  result = malloc (size);
```

```
    /* printf might call malloc, so protect it too. */
    printf ("malloc (%u) returns %p\n", (unsigned int) size, result);
    __malloc_hook = my_malloc_hook;
    return result;
}

main ()
{
  ...
  old_malloc_hook = __malloc_hook;
  __malloc_hook = my_malloc_hook;
  ...
}
```

The `mcheck` function (see Section 3.3.8 [Heap Consistency Checking], page 33) works by installing such hooks.

3.3.10 Statistics for Storage Allocation with `malloc`

You can get information about dynamic storage allocation by calling the `mstats` function. This function and its associated data type are declared in 'malloc.h'; they are a GNU extension.

struct mstats Data Type

This structure type is used to return information about the dynamic storage allocator. It contains the following members:

`size_t bytes_total`
: This is the total size of memory managed by `malloc`, in bytes.

`size_t chunks_used`
: This is the number of chunks in use. (The storage allocator internally gets chunks of memory from the operating system, and then carves them up to satisfy individual `malloc` requests; see Section 3.3.6 [Efficiency Considerations for "code malloc], page 32.)

`size_t bytes_used`
: This is the number of bytes in use.

`size_t chunks_free`
: This is the number of chunks which are free – that is, that have been allocated by the operating system to your program, but which are not now being used.

`size_t bytes_free`
: This is the number of bytes which are free.

Chapter 3: Memory Allocation   37

`struct mstats` **mstats** `(void)`   *Function*
:   This function returns information about the current dynamic memory usage in a structure of type `struct mstats`.

3.3.11 Summary of `malloc`-Related Functions

Here is a summary of the functions that work with `malloc`:

`void *malloc (size_t size)`
:   Allocate a block of *size* bytes. See Section 3.3.1 [Basic Storage Allocation], page 28.

`void free (void *addr)`
:   Free a block previously allocated by `malloc`. See Section 3.3.3 [Freeing Memory Allocated with "code malloc], page 30.

`void *realloc (void *addr, size_t size)`
:   Make a block previously allocated by `malloc` larger or smaller, possibly by copying it to a new location. See Section 3.3.4 [Changing the Size of a Block], page 31.

`void *calloc (size_t count, size_t eltsize)`
:   Allocate a block of *count * eltsize* bytes using `malloc`, and set its contents to zero. See Section 3.3.5 [Allocating Cleared Space], page 32.

`void *valloc (size_t size)`
:   Allocate a block of *size* bytes, starting on a page boundary. See Section 3.3.7 [Allocating Aligned Memory Blocks], page 33.

`void *memalign (size_t size, size_t boundary)`
:   Allocate a block of *size* bytes, starting on an address that is a multiple of *boundary*. See Section 3.3.7 [Allocating Aligned Memory Blocks], page 33.

`int mcheck (void (*abortfn) (void))`
:   Tell `malloc` to perform occasional consistency checks on dynamically allocated memory, and to call *abortfn* when an inconsistency is found. See Section 3.3.8 [Heap Consistency Checking], page 33.

`void *(*__malloc_hook) (size_t size)`
:   A pointer to a function that `malloc` uses whenever it is called.

`void *(*__realloc_hook) (void *ptr, size_t size)`
:   A pointer to a function that `realloc` uses whenever it is called.

`void (*__free_hook) (void *ptr)`
:   A pointer to a function that `free` uses whenever it is called.

`struct mstats mstats (void)`
> Return information about the current dynamic memory usage. See Section 3.3.10 [Statistics for Storage Allocation with "code malloc], page 36.

3.4 Obstacks

An *obstack* is a pool of memory containing a stack of objects. You can create any number of separate obstacks, and then allocate objects in specified obstacks. Within each obstack, the last object allocated must always be the first one freed, but distinct obstacks are independent of each other.

Aside from this one constraint of order of freeing, obstacks are totally general: an obstack can contain any number of objects of any size. They are implemented with macros, so allocation is usually very fast as long as the objects are usually small. And the only space overhead per object is the padding needed to start each object on a suitable boundary.

3.4.1 Creating Obstacks

The utilities for manipulating obstacks are declared in the header file 'obstack.h'.

struct obstack Data Type
> An obstack is represented by a data structure of type `struct obstack`. This structure has a small fixed size; it records the status of the obstack and how to find the space in which objects are allocated. It does not contain any of the objects themselves. You should not try to access the contents of the structure directly; use only the functions described in this chapter.

You can declare variables of type `struct obstack` and use them as obstacks, or you can allocate obstacks dynamically like any other kind of object. Dynamic allocation of obstacks allows your program to have a variable number of different stacks. (You can even allocate an obstack structure in another obstack, but this is rarely useful.)

All the functions that work with obstacks require you to specify which obstack to use. You do this with a pointer of type `struct obstack *`. In the following, we often say "an obstack" when strictly speaking the object at hand is such a pointer.

The objects in the obstack are packed into large blocks called *chunks*. The `struct obstack` structure points to a chain of the chunks currently in use.

The obstack library obtains a new chunk whenever you allocate an object that won't fit in the previous chunk. Since the obstack library manages

Chapter 3: Memory Allocation   39

chunks automatically, you don't need to pay much attention to them, but
you do need to supply a function which the obstack library should use to
get a chunk. Usually you supply a function which uses `malloc` directly or
indirectly. You must also supply a function to free a chunk. These matters
are described in the following section.

3.4.2 Preparing for Using Obstacks

Each source file in which you plan to use the obstack functions must
include the header file 'obstack.h', like this:

```
#include <obstack.h>
```

Also, if the source file uses the macro `obstack_init`, it must declare or
define two functions or macros that will be called by the obstack library.
One, `obstack_chunk_alloc`, is used to allocate the chunks of memory into
which objects are packed. The other, `obstack_chunk_free`, is used to return
chunks when the objects in them are freed. These macros should appear
before any use of obstacks in the source file.

Usually these are defined to use `malloc` via the intermediary `xmalloc`
(see Section 3.3 [Unconstrained Allocation], page 28). This is done with the
following pair of macro definitions:

```
#define obstack_chunk_alloc xmalloc
#define obstack_chunk_free free
```

Though the storage you get using obstacks really comes from `malloc`, using
obstacks is faster because `malloc` is called less often, for larger blocks of
memory. See Section 3.4.10 [Obstack Chunks], page 47, for full details.

At run time, before the program can use a `struct obstack` object as an
obstack, it must initialize the obstack by calling `obstack_init`.

int obstack_init (`struct obstack *`*obstack-ptr*)   *Function*
  Initialize obstack *obstack-ptr* for allocation of objects. This function calls the obstack's `obstack_chunk_alloc` function. It returns
  0 if `obstack_chunk_alloc` returns a null pointer, meaning that it is
  out of memory. Otherwise, it returns 1. If you supply an `obstack_chunk_alloc` function that calls `exit` (see Section 22.3 [Program Ter-
  mination], page 437) or `longjmp` (see Chapter 20 [Non-Local Exits],
  page 367) when out of memory, you can safely ignore the value that
  `obstack_init` returns.

Here are two examples of how to allocate the space for an obstack and
initialize it. First, an obstack that is a static variable:

```
static struct obstack myobstack;
...
obstack_init (&myobstack);
```

Second, an obstack that is itself dynamically allocated:

```
struct obstack *myobstack_ptr
  = (struct obstack *) xmalloc (sizeof (struct obstack));

obstack_init (myobstack_ptr);
```

3.4.3 Allocation in an Obstack

The most direct way to allocate an object in an obstack is with `obstack_alloc`, which is invoked almost like `malloc`.

void * obstack_alloc (struct obstack *obstack-ptr, *Function*
       int size)

This allocates an uninitialized block of *size* bytes in an obstack and returns its address. Here *obstack-ptr* specifies which obstack to allocate the block in; it is the address of the `struct obstack` object which represents the obstack. Each obstack function or macro requires you to specify an *obstack-ptr* as the first argument.

This function calls the obstack's `obstack_chunk_alloc` function if it needs to allocate a new chunk of memory; it returns a null pointer if `obstack_chunk_alloc` returns one. In that case, it has not changed the amount of memory allocated in the obstack. If you supply an `obstack_chunk_alloc` function that calls `exit` (see Section 22.3 [Program Termination], page 437) or `longjmp` (see Chapter 20 [Non-Local Exits], page 367) when out of memory, then `obstack_alloc` will never return a null pointer.

For example, here is a function that allocates a copy of a string *str* in a specific obstack, which is in the variable `string_obstack`:

```
struct obstack string_obstack;

char *
copystring (char *string)
{
  char *s = (char *) obstack_alloc (&string_obstack,
                                    strlen (string) + 1);
  memcpy (s, string, strlen (string));
  return s;
}
```

To allocate a block with specified contents, use the function `obstack_copy`, declared like this:

void * obstack_copy (struct obstack *obstack-ptr, *Function*
       void *address, int size)

This allocates a block and initializes it by copying *size* bytes of data starting at *address*. It can return a null pointer under the same conditions as `obstack_alloc`.

Chapter 3: Memory Allocation 41

void * **obstack_copy0** (struct obstack *obstack-ptr,   *Function*
         void *address, int size)

Like obstack_copy, but appends an extra byte containing a null character. This extra byte is not counted in the argument *size*.

The obstack_copy0 function is convenient for copying a sequence of characters into an obstack as a null-terminated string. Here is an example of its use:

```
char *
obstack_savestring (char *addr, int size)
{
  return obstack_copy0 (&myobstack, addr, size);
}
```

Contrast this with the previous example of savestring using malloc (see Section 3.3.1 [Basic Storage Allocation], page 28).

3.4.4 Freeing Objects in an Obstack

To free an object allocated in an obstack, use the function obstack_free. Since the obstack is a stack of objects, freeing one object automatically frees all other objects allocated more recently in the same obstack.

void **obstack_free** (struct obstack *obstack-ptr, void   *Function*
         *object)

If *object* is a null pointer, everything allocated in the obstack is freed. Otherwise, *object* must be the address of an object allocated in the obstack. Then *object* is freed, along with everything allocated in *obstack* since *object*.

Note that if *object* is a null pointer, the result is an uninitialized obstack. To free all storage in an obstack but leave it valid for further allocation, call obstack_free with the address of the first object allocated on the obstack:

```
obstack_free (obstack_ptr, first_object_allocated_ptr);
```

Recall that the objects in an obstack are grouped into chunks. When all the objects in a chunk become free, the obstack library automatically frees the chunk (see Section 3.4.2 [Preparing for Using Obstacks], page 39). Then other obstacks, or non-obstack allocation, can reuse the space of the chunk.

3.4.5 Obstack Functions and Macros

The interfaces for using obstacks may be defined either as functions or as macros, depending on the compiler. The obstack facility works with all C compilers, including both ANSI C and traditional C, but there are precautions you must take if you plan to use compilers other than GNU C.

If you are using an old-fashioned non-ANSI C compiler, all the obstack "functions" are actually defined only as macros. You can call these macros like functions, but you cannot use them in any other way (for example, you cannot take their address).

Calling the macros requires a special precaution: namely, the first operand (the obstack pointer) may not contain any side effects, because it may be computed more than once. For example, if you write this:

```
obstack_alloc (get_obstack (), 4);
```

you will find that `get_obstack` may be called several times. If you use `*obstack_list_ptr++` as the obstack pointer argument, you will get very strange results since the incrementation may occur several times.

In ANSI C, each function has both a macro definition and a function definition. The function definition is used if you take the address of the function without calling it. An ordinary call uses the macro definition by default, but you can request the function definition instead by writing the function name in parentheses, as shown here:

```
char *x;
void *(*funcp) ();
/* Use the macro.  */
x = (char *) obstack_alloc (obptr, size);
/* Call the function.  */
x = (char *) (obstack_alloc) (obptr, size);
/* Take the address of the function.  */
funcp = obstack_alloc;
```

This is the same situation that exists in ANSI C for the standard library functions. See Section 1.3.2 [Macro Definitions of Functions], page 5.

Warning: When you do use the macros, you must observe the precaution of avoiding side effects in the first operand, even in ANSI C.

If you use the GNU C compiler, this precaution is not necessary, because various language extensions in GNU C permit defining the macros so as to compute each argument only once.

3.4.6 Growing Objects

Because storage in obstack chunks is used sequentially, it is possible to build up an object step by step, adding one or more bytes at a time to the end of the object. With this technique, you do not need to know how much data you will put in the object until you come to the end of it. We call this the technique of *growing objects*. The special functions for adding data to the growing object are described in this section.

You don't need to do anything special when you start to grow an object. Using one of the functions to add data to the object automatically starts it. However, it is necessary to say explicitly when the object is finished. This is done with the function `obstack_finish`.

Chapter 3: Memory Allocation

The actual address of the object thus built up is not known until the object is finished. Until then, it always remains possible that you will add so much data that the object must be copied into a new chunk.

While the obstack is in use for a growing object, you cannot use it for ordinary allocation of another object. If you try to do so, the space already added to the growing object will become part of the other object.

void obstack_blank (**struct obstack** *obstack-ptr*, *Function*
 int *size*)

The most basic function for adding to a growing object is `obstack_blank`, which adds space without initializing it.

void obstack_grow (**struct obstack** *obstack-ptr*, *Function*
 void *data*, **int** *size*)

To add a block of initialized space, use `obstack_grow`, which is the growing-object analogue of `obstack_copy`. It adds *size* bytes of data to the growing object, copying the contents from *data*.

void obstack_grow0 (**struct obstack** *obstack-ptr*, *Function*
 void *data*, **int** *size*)

This is the growing-object analogue of `obstack_copy0`. It adds *size* bytes copied from *data*, followed by an additional null character.

void obstack_1grow (**struct obstack** *obstack-ptr*, *Function*
 char *c*)

To add one character at a time, use the function `obstack_1grow`. It adds a single byte containing *c* to the growing object.

void * obstack_finish (**struct obstack** *obstack-ptr*) *Function*

When you are finished growing the object, use the function `obstack_finish` to close it off and return its final address.

Once you have finished the object, the obstack is available for ordinary allocation or for growing another object.

This function can return a null pointer under the same conditions as `obstack_alloc` (see Section 3.4.3 [Allocation in an Obstack], page 40).

When you build an object by growing it, you will probably need to know afterward how long it became. You need not keep track of this as you grow the object, because you can find out the length from the obstack just before finishing the object with the function `obstack_object_size`, declared as follows:

int obstack_object_size (**struct obstack** *Function*
 obstack-ptr)

This function returns the current size of the growing object, in bytes. Remember to call this function *before* finishing the object. After it is finished, `obstack_object_size` will return zero.

If you have started growing an object and wish to cancel it, you should finish it and then free it, like this:

    obstack_free (obstack_ptr, obstack_finish (obstack_ptr));

This has no effect if no object was growing.

You can use `obstack_blank` with a negative size argument to make the current object smaller. Just don't try to shrink it beyond zero length—there's no telling what will happen if you do that.

3.4.7 Extra Fast Growing Objects

The usual functions for growing objects incur overhead for checking whether there is room for the new growth in the current chunk. If you are frequently constructing objects in small steps of growth, this overhead can be significant.

You can reduce the overhead by using special "fast growth" functions that grow the object without checking. In order to have a robust program, you must do the checking yourself. If you do this checking in the simplest way each time you are about to add data to the object, you have not saved anything, because that is what the ordinary growth functions do. But if you can arrange to check less often, or check more efficiently, then you make the program faster.

The function `obstack_room` returns the amount of room available in the current chunk. It is declared as follows:

int obstack_room (`struct obstack *`*obstack-ptr*) *Function*
: This returns the number of bytes that can be added safely to the current growing object (or to an object about to be started) in obstack *obstack* using the fast growth functions.

While you know there is room, you can use these fast growth functions for adding data to a growing object:

void obstack_1grow_fast (`struct obstack` *Function*
`*`*obstack-ptr*, `char` *c*)
: The function `obstack_1grow_fast` adds one byte containing the character *c* to the growing object in obstack *obstack-ptr*.

void obstack_blank_fast (`struct obstack` *Function*
`*`*obstack-ptr*, `int` *size*)
: The function `obstack_blank_fast` adds *size* bytes to the growing object in obstack *obstack-ptr* without initializing them.

When you check for space using `obstack_room` and there is not enough room for what you want to add, the fast growth functions are not safe. In this case, simply use the corresponding ordinary growth function instead.

Chapter 3: Memory Allocation   45

Very soon this will copy the object to a new chunk; then there will be lots of room available again.

So, each time you use an ordinary growth function, check afterward for sufficient space using `obstack_room`. Once the object is copied to a new chunk, there will be plenty of space again, so the program will start using the fast growth functions again.

Here is an example:

```
void
add_string (struct obstack *obstack, const char *ptr, int len)
{
  while (len > 0)
    {
      int room = obstack_room (obstack);
      if (room == 0)
        {
          /* Not enough room. Add one character slowly,
             which may copy to a new chunk and make room.  */
          obstack_1grow (obstack, *ptr++);
          len--;
        }
      else
        {
          if (room > len)
            room = len;
          /* Add fast as much as we have room for. */
          len -= room;
          while (room-- > 0)
            obstack_1grow_fast (obstack, *ptr++);
        }
    }
}
```

3.4.8 Status of an Obstack

Here are functions that provide information on the current status of allocation in an obstack. You can use them to learn about an object while still growing it.

void * obstack_base (**struct obstack** *obstack-ptr*) *Function*
 This function returns the tentative address of the beginning of the currently growing object in *obstack-ptr*. If you finish the object immediately, it will have that address. If you make it larger first, it may outgrow the current chunk—then its address will change!

 If no object is growing, this value says where the next object you allocate will start (once again assuming it fits in the current chunk).

void * obstack_next_free (`struct obstack` *obstack-ptr*) *Function*

This function returns the address of the first free byte in the current chunk of obstack *obstack-ptr*. This is the end of the currently growing object. If no object is growing, `obstack_next_free` returns the same value as `obstack_base`.

int obstack_object_size (`struct obstack` *obstack-ptr*) *Function*

This function returns the size in bytes of the currently growing object. This is equivalent to

```
obstack_next_free (obstack-ptr) - obstack_base (obstack-ptr)
```

3.4.9 Alignment of Data in Obstacks

Each obstack has an *alignment boundary*; each object allocated in the obstack automatically starts on an address that is a multiple of the specified boundary. By default, this boundary is 4 bytes.

To access an obstack's alignment boundary, use the macro `obstack_alignment_mask`, whose function prototype looks like this:

int obstack_alignment_mask (`struct obstack` *obstack-ptr*) *Macro*

The value is a bit mask; a bit that is 1 indicates that the corresponding bit in the address of an object should be 0. The mask value should be one less than a power of 2; the effect is that all object addresses are multiples of that power of 2. The default value of the mask is 3, so that addresses are multiples of 4. A mask value of 0 means an object can start on any multiple of 1 (that is, no alignment is required).

The expansion of the macro `obstack_alignment_mask` is an lvalue, so you can alter the mask by assignment. For example, this statement:

```
obstack_alignment_mask (obstack_ptr) = 0;
```

has the effect of turning off alignment processing in the specified obstack.

Note that a change in alignment mask does not take effect until *after* the next time an object is allocated or finished in the obstack. If you are not growing an object, you can make the new alignment mask take effect immediately by calling `obstack_finish`. This will finish a zero-length object and then do proper alignment for the next object.

3.4.10 Obstack Chunks

Obstacks work by allocating space for themselves in large chunks, and then parceling out space in the chunks to satisfy your requests. Chunks

Chapter 3: Memory Allocation 47

are normally 4096 bytes long unless you specify a different chunk size. The chunk size includes 8 bytes of overhead that are not actually used for storing objects. Regardless of the specified size, longer chunks will be allocated when necessary for long objects.

The obstack library allocates chunks by calling the function `obstack_chunk_alloc`, which you must define. When a chunk is no longer needed because you have freed all the objects in it, the obstack library frees the chunk by calling `obstack_chunk_free`, which you must also define.

These two must be defined (as macros) or declared (as functions) in each source file that uses `obstack_init` (see Section 3.4.1 [Creating Obstacks], page 38). Most often they are defined as macros like this:

```
#define obstack_chunk_alloc xmalloc
#define obstack_chunk_free free
```

Note that these are simple macros (no arguments). Macro definitions with arguments will not work! It is necessary that `obstack_chunk_alloc` or `obstack_chunk_free`, alone, expand into a function name if it is not itself a function name.

If you allocate chunks with `malloc`, the chunk size should be a power of 2. The default chunk size, 4096, was chosen because it is long enough to satisfy many typical requests on the obstack yet short enough not to waste too much memory in the portion of the last chunk not yet used.

`int` **obstack_chunk_size** (`struct obstack *`*obstack-ptr*)   *Macro*
This returns the chunk size of the given obstack.

Since this macro expands to an lvalue, you can specify a new chunk size by assigning it a new value. Doing so does not affect the chunks already allocated, but will change the size of chunks allocated for that particular obstack in the future. It is unlikely to be useful to make the chunk size smaller, but making it larger might improve efficiency if you are allocating many objects whose size is comparable to the chunk size. Here is how to do so cleanly:

```
if (obstack_chunk_size (obstack_ptr) < new-chunk-size)
  obstack_chunk_size (obstack_ptr) = new-chunk-size;
```

3.4.11 Summary of Obstack Functions

Here is a summary of all the functions associated with obstacks. Each takes the address of an obstack (`struct obstack *`) as its first argument.

`void` **obstack_init** (`struct obstack *`*obstack-ptr*)
        Initialize use of an obstack. See Section 3.4.1 [Creating Obstacks], page 38.

`void *obstack_alloc (struct obstack *obstack-ptr, int size)`
: Allocate an object of size uninitialized bytes. See Section 3.4.3 [Allocation in an Obstack], page 40.

`void *obstack_copy (struct obstack *obstack-ptr, void *address, int size)`
: Allocate an object of size bytes, with contents copied from address. See Section 3.4.3 [Allocation in an Obstack], page 40.

`void *obstack_copy0 (struct obstack *obstack-ptr, void *address, int size)`
: Allocate an object of size+1 bytes, with size of them copied from address, followed by a null character at the end. See Section 3.4.3 [Allocation in an Obstack], page 40.

`void obstack_free (struct obstack *obstack-ptr, void *object)`
: Free object (and everything allocated in the specified obstack more recently than object). See Section 3.4.4 [Freeing Objects in an Obstack], page 41.

`void obstack_blank (struct obstack *obstack-ptr, int size)`
: Add size uninitialized bytes to a growing object. See Section 3.4.6 [Growing Objects], page 42.

`void obstack_grow (struct obstack *obstack-ptr, void *address, int size)`
: Add size bytes, copied from address, to a growing object. See Section 3.4.6 [Growing Objects], page 42.

`void obstack_grow0 (struct obstack *obstack-ptr, void *address, int size)`
: Add size bytes, copied from address, to a growing object, and then add another byte containing a null character. See Section 3.4.6 [Growing Objects], page 42.

`void obstack_1grow (struct obstack *obstack-ptr, char data-char)`
: Add one byte containing data-char to a growing object. See Section 3.4.6 [Growing Objects], page 42.

`void *obstack_finish (struct obstack *obstack-ptr)`
: Finalize the object that is growing and return its permanent address. See Section 3.4.6 [Growing Objects], page 42.

`int obstack_object_size (struct obstack *obstack-ptr)`
: Get the current size of the currently growing object. See Section 3.4.6 [Growing Objects], page 42.

`void obstack_blank_fast (struct obstack *obstack-ptr, int size)`
: Add size uninitialized bytes to a growing object without checking that there is enough room. See Section 3.4.7 [Extra Fast Growing Objects], page 44.

Chapter 3: Memory Allocation   49

`void obstack_1grow_fast (struct obstack *`*obstack-ptr*`, char` *data-char*`)`
> Add one byte containing *data-char* to a growing object without checking that there is enough room. See Section 3.4.7 [Extra Fast Growing Objects], page 44.

`int obstack_room (struct obstack *`*obstack-ptr*`)`
> Get the amount of room now available for growing the current object. See Section 3.4.7 [Extra Fast Growing Objects], page 44.

`int obstack_alignment_mask (struct obstack *`*obstack-ptr*`)`
> The mask used for aligning the beginning of an object. This is an lvalue. See Section 3.4.9 [Alignment of Data in Obstacks], page 46.

`int obstack_chunk_size (struct obstack *`*obstack-ptr*`)`
> The size for allocating chunks. This is an lvalue. See Section 3.4.10 [Obstack Chunks], page 47.

`void *obstack_base (struct obstack *`*obstack-ptr*`)`
> Tentative starting address of the currently growing object. See Section 3.4.8 [Status of an Obstack], page 45.

`void *obstack_next_free (struct obstack *`*obstack-ptr*`)`
> Address just after the end of the currently growing object. See Section 3.4.8 [Status of an Obstack], page 45.

3.5 Automatic Storage with Variable Size

The function `alloca` supports a kind of half-dynamic allocation in which blocks are allocated dynamically but freed automatically.

Allocating a block with `alloca` is an explicit action; you can allocate as many blocks as you wish, and compute the size at run time. But all the blocks are freed when you exit the function that `alloca` was called from, just as if they were automatic variables declared in that function. There is no way to free the space explicitly.

The prototype for `alloca` is in 'stdlib.h'. This function is a BSD extension.

`void *` **alloca** `(size_t` *size*`);`   Function
> The return value of `alloca` is the address of a block of *size* bytes of storage, allocated in the stack frame of the calling function.

Do not use `alloca` inside the arguments of a function call—you will get unpredictable results, because the stack space for the `alloca` would appear on the stack in the middle of the space for the function arguments. An example of what to avoid is `foo (x, alloca (4), y)`.

3.5.1 `alloca` Example

As an example of use of `alloca`, here is a function that opens a file name made from concatenating two argument strings, and returns a file descriptor or minus one signifying failure:

```
int
open2 (char *str1, char *str2, int flags, int mode)
{
  char *name = (char *) alloca (strlen (str1) + strlen (str2) + 1);
  strcpy (name, str1);
  strcat (name, str2);
  return open (name, flags, mode);
}
```

Here is how you would get the same results with `malloc` and `free`:

```
int
open2 (char *str1, char *str2, int flags, int mode)
{
  char *name = (char *) malloc (strlen (str1) + strlen (str2) + 1);
  int desc;
  if (name == 0)
    fatal ("virtual memory exceeded");
  strcpy (name, str1);
  strcat (name, str2);
  desc = open (name, flags, mode);
  free (name);
  return desc;
}
```

As you can see, it is simpler with `alloca`. But `alloca` has other, more important advantages, and some disadvantages.

3.5.2 Advantages of `alloca`

Here are the reasons why `alloca` may be preferable to `malloc`:

- Using `alloca` wastes very little space and is very fast. (It is open-coded by the GNU C compiler.)
- Since `alloca` does not have separate pools for different sizes of block, space used for any size block can be reused for any other size. `alloca` does not cause storage fragmentation.
- Nonlocal exits done with `longjmp` (see Chapter 20 [Non-Local Exits], page 367) automatically free the space allocated with `alloca` when they exit through the function that called `alloca`. This is the most important reason to use `alloca`.

  To illustrate this, suppose you have a function `open_or_report_error` which returns a descriptor, like `open`, if it succeeds, but does not return to its caller if it fails. If the file cannot be opened, it prints an error message and jumps out to the command level of your program using

Chapter 3: Memory Allocation   51

`longjmp`. Let's change `open2` (see Section 3.5.1 ["code alloca Example], page 50) to use this subroutine:

```
int
open2 (char *str1, char *str2, int flags, int mode)
{
  char *name = (char *) alloca (strlen (str1) + strlen (str2) + 1);
  strcpy (name, str1);
  strcat (name, str2);
  return open_or_report_error (name, flags, mode);
}
```

Because of the way `alloca` works, the storage it allocates is freed even when an error occurs, with no special effort required.

By contrast, the previous definition of `open2` (which uses `malloc` and `free`) would develop a storage leak if it were changed in this way. Even if you are willing to make more changes to fix it, there is no easy way to do so.

3.5.3 Disadvantages of `alloca`

These are the disadvantages of `alloca` in comparison with `malloc`:

- If you try to allocate more storage than the machine can provide, you don't get a clean error message. Instead you get a fatal signal like the one you would get from an infinite recursion; probably a segmentation violation (see Section 21.2.1 [Program Error Signals], page 374).
- Some non-GNU systems fail to support `alloca`, so it is less portable. However, a slower emulation of `alloca` written in C is available for use on systems with this deficiency.

3.5.4 GNU C Variable-Size Arrays

In GNU C, you can replace most uses of `alloca` with an array of variable size. Here is how `open2` would look then:

```
int open2 (char *str1, char *str2, int flags, int mode)
{
  char name[strlen (str1) + strlen (str2) + 1];
  strcpy (name, str1);
  strcat (name, str2);
  return open (name, flags, mode);
}
```

But `alloca` is not always equivalent to a variable-sized array, for several reasons:

- A variable size array's space is freed at the end of the scope of the name of the array. The space allocated with `alloca` remains until the end of the function.

- It is possible to use `alloca` within a loop, allocating an additional block on each iteration. This is impossible with variable-sized arrays.

Note: If you mix use of `alloca` and variable-sized arrays within one function, exiting a scope in which a variable-sized array was declared frees all blocks allocated with `alloca` during the execution of that scope.

3.6 Relocating Allocator

Any system of dynamic memory allocation has overhead: the amount of space it uses is more than the amount the program asks for. The *relocating memory allocator* achieves very low overhead by moving blocks in memory as necessary, on its own initiative.

3.6.1 Concepts of Relocating Allocation

When you allocate a block with `malloc`, the address of the block never changes unless you use `realloc` to change its size. Thus, you can safely store the address in various places, temporarily or permanently, as you like. This is not safe when you use the relocating memory allocator, because any and all relocatable blocks can move whenever you allocate memory in any fashion. Even calling `malloc` or `realloc` can move the relocatable blocks.

For each relocatable block, you must make a *handle*—a pointer object in memory, designated to store the address of that block. The relocating allocator knows where each block's handle is, and updates the address stored there whenever it moves the block, so that the handle always points to the block. Each time you access the contents of the block, you should fetch its address anew from the handle.

To call any of the relocating allocator functions from a signal handler is almost certainly incorrect, because the signal could happen at any time and relocate all the blocks. The only way to make this safe is to block the signal around any access to the contents of any relocatable block—not a convenient mode of operation. See Section 21.4.6 [Signal Handling and Nonreentrant Functions], page 398.

3.6.2 Allocating and Freeing Relocatable Blocks

In the descriptions below, *handleptr* designates the address of the handle. All the functions are declared in '`malloc.h`'; all are GNU extensions.

void * r_alloc (`void **`*handleptr*, `size_t` *size*) *Function*
  This function allocates a relocatable block of size *size*. It stores the block's address in *handleptr and returns a non-null pointer to indicate success.

Chapter 3: Memory Allocation   53

If `r_alloc` can't get the space needed, it stores a null pointer in *handleptr*, and returns a null pointer.

void **r_alloc_free** (void **handleptr*)   *Function*
This function is the way to free a relocatable block. It frees the block that *handleptr* points to, and stores a null pointer in *handleptr* to show it doesn't point to an allocated block any more.

void * **r_re_alloc** (void **handleptr*, `size_t` *size*)   *Function*
The function `r_re_alloc` adjusts the size of the block that *handleptr* points to, making it *size* bytes long. It stores the address of the resized block in *handleptr* and returns a non-null pointer to indicate success.

If enough memory is not available, this function returns a null pointer and does not modify *handleptr*.

3.7 Memory Usage Warnings

You can ask for warnings as the program approaches running out of memory space, by calling `memory_warnings`. This tells `malloc` to check memory usage every time it asks for more memory from the operating system. This is a GNU extension declared in 'malloc.h'.

void **memory_warnings** (void **start*, void   *Function*
(**warn-func*) (const char *))
Call this function to request warnings for nearing exhaustion of virtual memory.

The argument *start* says where data space begins, in memory. The allocator compares this against the last address used and against the limit of data space, to determine the fraction of available memory in use. If you supply zero for *start*, then a default value is used which is right in most circumstances.

For *warn-func*, supply a function that `malloc` can call to warn you. It is called with a string (a warning message) as argument. Normally it ought to display the string for the user to read.

The warnings come when memory becomes 75% full, when it becomes 85% full, and when it becomes 95% full. Above 95% you get another warning each time memory usage increases.

4 Character Handling

Programs that work with characters and strings often need to classify a character—is it alphabetic, is it a digit, is it whitespace, and so on—and perform case conversion operations on characters. The functions in the header file 'ctype.h' are provided for this purpose.

Since the choice of locale and character set can alter the classifications of particular character codes, all of these functions are affected by the current locale. (More precisely, they are affected by the locale currently selected for character classification—the LC_CTYPE category; see Section 19.3 [Categories of Activities that Locales Affect], page 358.)

4.1 Classification of Characters

This section explains the library functions for classifying characters. For example, isalpha is the function to test for an alphabetic character. It takes one argument, the character to test, and returns a nonzero integer if the character is alphabetic, and zero otherwise. You would use it like this:

```
if (isalpha (c))
    printf ("The character '%c' is alphabetic.\n", c);
```

Each of the functions in this section tests for membership in a particular class of characters; each has a name starting with 'is'. Each of them takes one argument, which is a character to test, and returns an int which is treated as a boolean value. The character argument is passed as an int, and it may be the constant value EOF instead of a real character.

The attributes of any given character can vary between locales. See Chapter 19 [Locales and Internationalization], page 357, for more information on locales.

These functions are declared in the header file 'ctype.h'.

int **islower** (int *c*)   Function
    Returns true if *c* is a lower-case letter.

int **isupper** (int *c*)   Function
    Returns true if *c* is an upper-case letter.

int **isalpha** (int *c*)   Function
    Returns true if *c* is an alphabetic character (a letter). If islower or isupper is true of a character, then isalpha is also true.

    In some locales, there may be additional characters for which isalpha is true–letters which are neither upper case nor lower case. But in the standard "C" locale, there are no such additional characters.

int **isdigit** (int *c*)   Function
Returns true if *c* is a decimal digit ('0' through '9').

int **isalnum** (int *c*)   Function
Returns true if *c* is an alphanumeric character (a letter or number); in other words, if either `isalpha` or `isdigit` is true of a character, then `isalnum` is also true.

int **isxdigit** (int *c*)   Function
Returns true if *c* is a hexadecimal digit. Hexadecimal digits include the normal decimal digits '0' through '9' and the letters 'A' through 'F' and 'a' through 'f'.

int **ispunct** (int *c*)   Function
Returns true if *c* is a punctuation character. This means any printing character that is not alphanumeric or a space character.

int **isspace** (int *c*)   Function
Returns true if *c* is a *whitespace* character. In the standard "C" locale, `isspace` returns true for only the standard whitespace characters:

' '	space
'\f'	formfeed
'\n'	newline
'\r'	carriage return
'\t'	horizontal tab
'\v'	vertical tab

int **isblank** (int *c*)   Function
Returns true if *c* is a blank character; that is, a space or a tab. This function is a GNU extension.

int **isgraph** (int *c*)   Function
Returns true if *c* is a graphic character; that is, a character that has a glyph associated with it. The whitespace characters are not considered graphic.

int **isprint** (int *c*)   Function
Returns true if *c* is a printing character. Printing characters include all the graphic characters, plus the space (' ') character.

Chapter 4: Character Handling   57

`int` **iscntrl** (`int` *c*) Function
> Returns true if *c* is a control character (that is, a character that is not a printing character).

`int` **isascii** (`int` *c*) Function
> Returns true if *c* is a 7-bit `unsigned char` value that fits into the US/UK ASCII character set. This function is a BSD extension and is also an SVID extension.

4.2 Case Conversion

This section explains the library functions for performing conversions such as case mappings on characters. For example, `toupper` converts any character to upper case if possible. If the character can't be converted, `toupper` returns it unchanged.

These functions take one argument of type `int`, which is the character to convert, and return the converted character as an `int`. If the conversion is not applicable to the argument given, the argument is returned unchanged.

Compatibility Note: In pre-ANSI C dialects, instead of returning the argument unchanged, these functions may fail when the argument is not suitable for the conversion. Thus for portability, you may need to write `islower(c) ? toupper(c) : c` rather than just `toupper(c)`.

These functions are declared in the header file 'ctype.h'.

`int` **tolower** (`int` *c*) Function
> If *c* is an upper-case letter, `tolower` returns the corresponding lower-case letter. If *c* is not an upper-case letter, *c* is returned unchanged.

`int` **toupper** (`int` *c*) Function
> If *c* is a lower-case letter, `tolower` returns the corresponding upper-case letter. Otherwise *c* is returned unchanged.

`int` **toascii** (`int` *c*) Function
> This function converts *c* to a 7-bit `unsigned char` value that fits into the US/UK ASCII character set, by clearing the high-order bits. This function is a BSD extension and is also an SVID extension.

`int` **_tolower** (`int` *c*) Function
> This is identical to `tolower`, and is provided for compatibility with the SVID. See Section 1.2.4 [SVID (The System V Interface Description)], page 3.

`int` **_toupper** (`int` *c*) Function
> This is identical to `toupper`, and is provided for compatibility with the SVID.

5 String and Array Utilities

Operations on strings (or arrays of characters) are an important part of many programs. The GNU C library provides an extensive set of string utility functions, including functions for copying, concatenating, comparing, and searching strings. Many of these functions can also operate on arbitrary regions of storage; for example, the `memcpy` function can be used to copy the contents of any kind of array.

It's fairly common for beginning C programmers to "reinvent the wheel" by duplicating this functionality in their own code, but it pays to become familiar with the library functions and to make use of them, since this offers benefits in maintenance, efficiency, and portability.

For instance, you could easily compare one string to another in two lines of C code, but if you use the built-in `strcmp` function, you're less likely to make a mistake. And, since these library functions are typically highly optimized, your program may run faster too.

5.1 Representation of Strings

This section is a quick summary of string concepts for beginning C programmers. It describes how character strings are represented in C and some common pitfalls. If you are already familiar with this material, you can skip this section.

A *string* is an array of `char` objects. But string-valued variables are usually declared to be pointers of type `char *`. Such variables do not include space for the text of a string; that has to be stored somewhere else—in an array variable, a string constant, or dynamically allocated memory (see Chapter 3 [Memory Allocation], page 27). It's up to you to store the address of the chosen memory space into the pointer variable. Alternatively you can store a *null pointer* in the pointer variable. The null pointer does not point anywhere, so attempting to reference the string it points to gets an error.

By convention, a *null character*, '\0', marks the end of a string. For example, in testing to see whether the `char *` variable *p* points to a null character marking the end of a string, you can write !*p* or *p* == '\0'.

A null character is quite different conceptually from a null pointer, although both are represented by the integer 0.

String literals appear in C program source as strings of characters between double-quote characters ('"'). In ANSI C, string literals can also be formed by *string concatenation*: `"a" "b"` is the same as `"ab"`. Modification of string literals is not allowed by the GNU C compiler, because literals are placed in read-only storage.

Character arrays that are declared `const` cannot be modified either. It's generally good style to declare non-modifiable string pointers to be of type `const char *`, since this often allows the C compiler to detect accidental modifications as well as providing some amount of documentation about what your program intends to do with the string.

The amount of memory allocated for the character array may extend past the null character that normally marks the end of the string. In this document, the term *allocation size* is always used to refer to the total amount of memory allocated for the string, while the term *length* refers to the number of characters up to (but not including) the terminating null character.

A notorious source of program bugs is trying to put more characters in a string than fit in its allocated size. When writing code that extends strings or moves characters into a pre-allocated array, you should be very careful to keep track of the length of the text and make explicit checks for overflowing the array. Many of the library functions *do not* do this for you! Remember also that you need to allocate an extra byte to hold the null character that marks the end of the string.

5.2 String and Array Conventions

This chapter describes both functions that work on arbitrary arrays or blocks of memory, and functions that are specific to null-terminated arrays of characters.

Functions that operate on arbitrary blocks of memory have names beginning with 'mem' (such as `memcpy`) and invariably take an argument which specifies the size (in bytes) of the block of memory to operate on. The array arguments and return values for these functions have type `void *`, and as a matter of style, the elements of these arrays are referred to as "bytes". You can pass any kind of pointer to these functions, and the `sizeof` operator is useful in computing the value for the size argument.

In contrast, functions that operate specifically on strings have names beginning with 'str' (such as `strcpy`) and look for a null character to terminate the string instead of requiring an explicit size argument to be passed. (Some of these functions accept a specified maximum length, but they also check for premature termination with a null character.) The array arguments and return values for these functions have type `char *`, and the array elements are referred to as "characters".

In many cases, there are both 'mem' and 'str' versions of a function. The one that is more appropriate to use depends on the exact situation. When your program is manipulating arbitrary arrays or blocks of storage, then you should always use the 'mem' functions. On the other hand, when you are manipulating null-terminated strings it is usually more convenient to use the 'str' functions, unless you already know the length of the string in advance.

5.3 String Length

You can get the length of a string using the `strlen` function. This function is declared in the header file '`string.h`'.

`size_t` **strlen** (`const char *s`) *Function*
> The `strlen` function returns the length of the null-terminated string *s*. (In other words, it returns the offset of the terminating null character within the array.)

For example,
```
strlen ("hello, world")
    ⇒ 12
```

When applied to a character array, the `strlen` function returns the length of the string stored there, not its allocation size. You can get the allocation size of the character array that holds a string using the `sizeof` operator:

```
char string[32] = "hello, world";
sizeof (string)
    ⇒ 32
strlen (string)
    ⇒ 12
```

5.4 Copying and Concatenation

You can use the functions described in this section to copy the contents of strings and arrays, or to append the contents of one string to another. These functions are declared in the header file '`string.h`'.

A helpful way to remember the ordering of the arguments to the functions in this section is that it corresponds to an assignment expression, with the destination array specified to the left of the source array. All of these functions return the address of the destination array.

Most of these functions do not work properly if the source and destination arrays overlap. For example, if the beginning of the destination array overlaps the end of the source array, the original contents of that part of the source array may get overwritten before it is copied. Even worse, in the case of the string functions, the null character marking the end of the string may be lost, and the copy function might get stuck in a loop trashing all the memory allocated to your program.

All functions that have problems copying between overlapping arrays are explicitly identified in this manual. In addition to functions in this section, there are a few others like `sprintf` (see Section 7.10.7 [Formatted Output Functions], page 103) and `scanf` (see Section 7.12.8 [Formatted Input Functions], page 123).

void * **memcpy** (void *to*, const void **from*, size_t *size*)   *Function*

> The memcpy function copies *size* bytes from the object beginning at *from* into the object beginning at *to*. The behavior of this function is undefined if the two arrays *to* and *from* overlap; use memmove instead if overlapping is possible.
>
> The value returned by memcpy is the value of *to*.
>
> Here is an example of how you might use memcpy to copy the contents of an array:
>
> ```
> struct foo *oldarray, *newarray;
> int arraysize;
> ...
> memcpy (new, old, arraysize * sizeof (struct foo));
> ```

void * **memmove** (void *to*, const void **from*, size_t *size*)   *Function*

> memmove copies the *size* bytes at *from* into the *size* bytes at *to*, even if those two blocks of space overlap. In the case of overlap, memmove is careful to copy the original values of the bytes in the block at *from*, including those bytes which also belong to the block at *to*.

void * **memccpy** (void *to*, const void **from*, int *c*, size_t *size*)   *Function*

> This function copies no more than *size* bytes from *from* to *to*, stopping if a byte matching *c* is found. The return value is a pointer into *to* one byte past where *c* was copied, or a null pointer if no byte matching *c* appeared in the first *size* bytes of *from*.

void * **memset** (void **block*, int *c*, size_t *size*)   *Function*

> This function copies the value of *c* (converted to an unsigned char) into each of the first *size* bytes of the object beginning at *block*. It returns the value of *block*.

char * **strcpy** (char **to*, const char **from*)   *Function*

> This copies characters from the string *from* (up to and including the terminating null character) into the string *to*. Like memcpy, this function has undefined results if the strings overlap. The return value is the value of *to*.

char * **strncpy** (char **to*, const char **from*, size_t *size*)   *Function*

> This function is similar to strcpy but always copies exactly *size* characters into *to*.
>
> If the length of *from* is more than *size*, then strncpy copies just the first *size* characters. Note that in this case there is no null terminator written into *to*.

Chapter 5: String and Array Utilities   63

If the length of *from* is less than *size*, then `strncpy` copies all of *from*, followed by enough null characters to add up to *size* characters in all. This behavior is rarely useful, but it is specified by the ANSI C standard.

The behavior of `strncpy` is undefined if the strings overlap.

Using `strncpy` as opposed to `strcpy` is a way to avoid bugs relating to writing past the end of the allocated space for *to*. However, it can also make your program much slower in one common case: copying a string which is probably small into a potentially large buffer. In this case, *size* may be large, and when it is, `strncpy` will waste a considerable amount of time copying null characters.

char * strdup (const char *s)   Function
This function copies the null-terminated string *s* into a newly allocated string. The string is allocated using `malloc`; see Section 3.3 [Unconstrained Allocation], page 28. If `malloc` cannot allocate space for the new string, `strdup` returns a null pointer. Otherwise it returns a pointer to the new string.

char * stpcpy (char *to, const char *from)   Function
This function is like `strcpy`, except that it returns a pointer to the end of the string *to* (that is, the address of the terminating null character) rather than the beginning.

For example, this program uses `stpcpy` to concatenate 'foo' and 'bar' to produce 'foobar', which it then prints.

```
#include <string.h>
#include <stdio.h>

int
main (void)
{
  char buffer[10];
  char *to = buffer;
  to = stpcpy (to, "foo");
  to = stpcpy (to, "bar");
  puts (buffer);
  return 0;
}
```

This function is not part of the ANSI or POSIX standards, and is not customary on Unix systems, but we did not invent it either. Perhaps it comes from MS-DOG.

Its behavior is undefined if the strings overlap.

char * strcat (char *to, const char *from)   Function
The `strcat` function is similar to `strcpy`, except that the characters from *from* are concatenated or appended to the end of *to*, instead of

overwriting it. That is, the first character from *from* overwrites the null character marking the end of *to*.

An equivalent definition for `strcat` would be:

```
char *
strcat (char *to, const char *from)
{
  strcpy (to + strlen (to), from);
  return to;
}
```

This function has undefined results if the strings overlap.

char * strncat (char **to*, const char **from*, size_t *size*)   *Function*

This function is like `strcat` except that not more than *size* characters from *from* are appended to the end of *to*. A single null character is also always appended to *to*, so the total allocated size of *to* must be at least *size* + 1 bytes longer than its initial length.

The `strncat` function could be implemented like this:

```
char *
strncat (char *to, const char *from, size_t size)
{
  strncpy (to + strlen (to), from, size);
  return to;
}
```

The behavior of `strncat` is undefined if the strings overlap.

Here is an example showing the use of `strncpy` and `strncat`. Notice how, in the call to `strncat`, the *size* parameter is computed to avoid overflowing the character array `buffer`.

```
#include <string.h>
#include <stdio.h>

#define SIZE 10

static char buffer[SIZE];

main ()
{
  strncpy (buffer, "hello", SIZE);
  puts (buffer);
  strncat (buffer, ", world", SIZE - strlen (buffer) - 1);
  puts (buffer);
}
```

The output produced by this program looks like:

```
hello
hello, wo
```

Chapter 5: String and Array Utilities   65

void * **bcopy** (void *`from`, const void *`to`, size_t   *Function*
         `size`)
    This is a partially obsolete alternative for `memmove`, derived from BSD.
    Note that it is not quite equivalent to `memmove`, because the arguments
    are not in the same order.

void * **bzero** (void *`block`, size_t `size`)   *Function*
    This is a partially obsolete alternative for `memset`, derived from BSD.
    Note that it is not as general as `memset`, because the only value it can
    store is zero.

5.5 String/Array Comparison

You can use the functions in this section to perform comparisons on
the contents of strings and arrays. As well as checking for equality, these
functions can also be used as the ordering functions for sorting operations.
See Chapter 15 [Searching and Sorting], page 299, for an example of this.

Unlike most comparison operations in C, the string comparison functions
return a nonzero value if the strings are *not* equivalent rather than if they are.
The sign of the value indicates the relative ordering of the first characters in
the strings that are not equivalent: a negative value indicates that the first
string is "less" than the second, while a positive value indicates that the first
string is "greater".

The most common use of these functions is to check only for equality.
This is canonically done with an expression like '! `strcmp (s1, s2)`'.

All of these functions are declared in the header file '`string.h`'.

int **memcmp** (const void *`a1`, const void *`a2`,   *Function*
         size_t `size`)
    The function `memcmp` compares the `size` bytes of memory beginning
    at `a1` against the `size` bytes of memory beginning at `a2`. The value
    returned has the same sign as the difference between the first differing
    pair of bytes (interpreted as `unsigned char` objects, then promoted to
    `int`).

    If the contents of the two blocks are equal, `memcmp` returns 0.

On arbitrary arrays, the `memcmp` function is mostly useful for testing
equality. It usually isn't meaningful to do byte-wise ordering comparisons
on arrays of things other than bytes. For example, a byte-wise comparison
on the bytes that make up floating-point numbers isn't likely to tell you
anything about the relationship between the values of the floating-point
numbers.

You should also be careful about using `memcmp` to compare objects that
can contain "holes", such as the padding inserted into structure objects to

enforce alignment requirements, extra space at the end of unions, and extra characters at the ends of strings whose length is less than their allocated size. The contents of these "holes" are indeterminate and may cause strange behavior when performing byte-wise comparisons. For more predictable results, perform an explicit component-wise comparison.

For example, given a structure type definition like:

```
struct foo
  {
    unsigned char tag;
    union
      {
        double f;
        long i;
        char *p;
      } value;
  };
```

you are better off writing a specialized comparison function to compare `struct foo` objects instead of comparing them with `memcmp`.

int strcmp (const char *s1, const char *s2)   *Function*
The `strcmp` function compares the string *s1* against *s2*, returning a value that has the same sign as the difference between the first differing pair of characters (interpreted as `unsigned char` objects, then promoted to `int`).

If the two strings are equal, `strcmp` returns 0.

A consequence of the ordering used by `strcmp` is that if *s1* is an initial substring of *s2*, then *s1* is considered to be "less than" *s2*.

int strcasecmp (const char *s1, const char *s2)   *Function*
This function is like `strcmp`, except that differences in case are ignored.

`strcasecmp` is derived from BSD.

int strncasecmp (const char *s1, const char *s2, size_t n)   *Function*
This function is like `strncmp`, except that differences in case are ignored.

`strncasecmp` is a GNU extension.

int strncmp (const char *s1, const char *s2, size_t size)   *Function*
This function is the similar to `strcmp`, except that no more than *size* characters are compared. In other words, if the two strings are the same in their first *size* characters, the return value is zero.

Here are some examples showing the use of `strcmp` and `strncmp`. These examples assume the use of the ASCII character set. (If some other character

Chapter 5: String and Array Utilities   67

set—say, EBCDIC—is used instead, then the glyphs are associated with different numeric codes, and the return values and ordering may differ.)

```
strcmp ("hello", "hello")
    ⇒ 0    /* These two strings are the same. */
strcmp ("hello", "Hello")
    ⇒ 32   /* Comparisons are case-sensitive. */
strcmp ("hello", "world")
    ⇒ -15  /* The character 'h' comes before 'w'. */
strcmp ("hello", "hello, world")
    ⇒ -44  /* Comparing a null character against a comma. */
strncmp ("hello", "hello, world"", 5)
    ⇒ 0    /* The initial 5 characters are the same. */
strncmp ("hello, world", "hello, stupid world!!!", 5)
    ⇒ 0    /* The initial 5 characters are the same. */
```

int bcmp (const void *a1, const void *a2, size_t   *Function*
        size)

This is an obsolete alias for **memcmp**, derived from BSD.

5.6 Collation Functions

In some locales, the conventions for lexicographic ordering differ from the strict numeric ordering of character codes. For example, in Spanish most glyphs with diacritical marks such as accents are not considered distinct letters for the purposes of collation. On the other hand, the two-character sequence 'll' is treated as a single letter that is collated immediately after 'l'.

You can use the functions **strcoll** and **strxfrm** (declared in the header file 'string.h') to compare strings using a collation ordering appropriate for the current locale. The locale used by these functions in particular can be specified by setting the locale for the **LC_COLLATE** category; see Chapter 19 [Locales and Internationalization], page 357.

In the standard C locale, the collation sequence for **strcoll** is the same as that for **strcmp**.

Effectively, the way these functions work is by applying a mapping to transform the characters in a string to a byte sequence that represents the string's position in the collating sequence of the current locale. Comparing two such byte sequences in a simple fashion is equivalent to comparing the strings with the locale's collating sequence.

The function **strcoll** performs this translation implicitly, in order to do one comparison. By contrast, **strxfrm** performs the mapping explicitly. If you are making multiple comparisons using the same string or set of strings, it is likely to be more efficient to use **strxfrm** to transform all the strings just once, and subsequently compare the transformed strings with **strcmp**.

int strcoll (`const char *`*s1*`, const char *`*s2*) *Function*
 The `strcoll` function is similar to `strcmp` but uses the collating sequence of the current locale for collation (the `LC_COLLATE` locale).

Here is an example of sorting an array of strings, using `strcoll` to compare them. The actual sort algorithm is not written here; it comes from `qsort` (see Section 15.3 [Array Sort Function], page 300). The job of the code shown here is to say how to compare the strings while sorting them. (Later on in this section, we will show a way to do this more efficiently using `strxfrm`.)

```
/* This is the comparison function used with qsort. */

int
compare_elements (char **p1, char **p2)
{
  return strcoll (*p1, *p2);
}

/* This is the entry point—the function to sort
   strings using the locale's collating sequence. */

void
sort_strings (char **array, int nstrings)
{
  /* Sort temp_array by comparing the strings. */
  qsort (array, sizeof (char *),
         nstrings, compare_elements);
}
```

size_t strxfrm (`char *`*to*`, const char *`*from*`, size_t` *Function*
    size)
 The function `strxfrm` transforms *string* using the collation transformation determined by the locale currently selected for collation, and stores the transformed string in the array *to*. Up to *size* characters (including a terminating null character) are stored.

 The behavior is undefined if the strings *to* and *from* overlap; see Section 5.4 [Copying and Concatenation], page 61.

 The return value is the length of the entire transformed string. This value is not affected by the value of *size*, but if it is greater than *size*, it means that the transformed string did not entirely fit in the array *to*. In this case, only as much of the string as actually fits was stored. To get the whole transformed string, call `strxfrm` again with a bigger output array.

 The transformed string may be longer than the original string, and it may also be shorter.

 If *size* is zero, no characters are stored in *to*. In this case, `strxfrm` simply returns the number of characters that would be the length of

Chapter 5: String and Array Utilities 69

the transformed string. This is useful for determining what size string to allocate. It does not matter what *to* is if *size* is zero; *to* may even be a null pointer.

Here is an example of how you can use **strxfrm** when you plan to do many comparisons. It does the same thing as the previous example, but much faster, because it has to transform each string only once, no matter how many times it is compared with other strings. Even the time needed to allocate and free storage is much less than the time we save, when there are many strings.

```
struct sorter { char *input; char *transformed; };

/* This is the comparison function used with qsort
   to sort an array of struct sorter. */

int
compare_elements (struct sorter *p1, struct sorter *p2)
{
  return strcmp (p1->transformed, p2->transformed);
}

/* This is the entry point—the function to sort
   strings using the locale's collating sequence. */

void
sort_strings_fast (char **array, int nstrings)
{
  struct sorter temp_array[nstrings];
  int i;

  /* Set up temp_array.  Each element contains
     one input string and its transformed string. */
  for (i = 0; i < nstrings; i++)
    {
      size_t length = strlen (array[i]) * 2;

      temp_array[i].input = array[i];

      /* Transform array[i].
         First try a buffer probably big enough. */
      while (1)
        {
          char *transformed = (char *) xmalloc (length);
          if (strxfrm (transformed, array[i], length) < length)
            {
              temp_array[i].transformed = transformed;
              break;
            }
          /* Try again with a bigger buffer. */
          free (transformed);
          length *= 2;
        }
```

```
      }

      /* Sort temp_array by comparing transformed strings. */
      qsort (temp_array, sizeof (struct sorter),
             nstrings, compare_elements);

      /* Put the elements back in the permanent array
         in their sorted order. */
      for (i = 0; i < nstrings; i++)
        array[i] = temp_array[i].input;

      /* Free the strings we allocated. */
      for (i = 0; i < nstrings; i++)
        free (temp_array[i].transformed);
    }
```

Compatibility Note: The string collation functions are a new feature of ANSI C. Older C dialects have no equivalent feature.

5.7 Search Functions

This section describes library functions which perform various kinds of searching operations on strings and arrays. These functions are declared in the header file 'string.h'.

void * **memchr** (const void *block*, int *c*, size_t *size*)   *Function*

This function finds the first occurrence of the byte *c* (converted to an unsigned char) in the initial *size* bytes of the object beginning at *block*. The return value is a pointer to the located byte, or a null pointer if no match was found.

char * **strchr** (const char *string*, int *c*)   *Function*

The strchr function finds the first occurrence of the character *c* (converted to a char) in the null-terminated string beginning at *string*. The return value is a pointer to the located character, or a null pointer if no match was found.

For example,

```
strchr ("hello, world", 'l')
    ⇒ "llo, world"
strchr ("hello, world", '?')
    ⇒ NULL
```

The terminating null character is considered to be part of the string, so you can use this function get a pointer to the end of a string by specifying a null character as the value of the *c* argument.

char * **index** (const char *string*, int *c*)   *Function*

index is another name for strchr; they are exactly the same.

Chapter 5: String and Array Utilities   71

char * **strrchr** (const char *string*, int *c*)   Function

> The function `strrchr` is like `strchr`, except that it searches backwards
> from the end of the string *string* (instead of forwards from the front).
>
> For example,
> ```
> strrchr ("hello, world", 'l')
>     ⇒ "ld"
> ```

char * **rindex** (const char *string*, int *c*)   Function

> `rindex` is another name for `strrchr`; they are exactly the same.

char * **strstr** (const char *haystack*, const char   Function
            **needle*)

> This is like `strchr`, except that it searches *haystack* for a substring
> *needle* rather than just a single character. It returns a pointer into
> the string *haystack* that is the first character of the substring, or a
> null pointer if no match was found. If *needle* is an empty string, the
> function returns *haystack*.
>
> For example,
> ```
> strstr ("hello, world", "l")
>     ⇒ "llo, world"
> strstr ("hello, world", "wo")
>     ⇒ "world"
> ```

void * **memmem** (const void *needle*, size_t   Function
            needle-len,
            const void **haystack*, size_t *haystack-len*)

> This is like `strstr`, but *needle* and *haystack* are byte arrays rather
> than null-terminated strings. *needle-len* is the length of *needle* and
> *haystack-len* is the length of *haystack*.
>
> This function is a GNU extension.

size_t **strspn** (const char *string*, const char   Function
            **skipset*)

> The `strspn` ("string span") function returns the length of the initial
> substring of *string* that consists entirely of characters that are members
> of the set specified by the string *skipset*. The order of the characters
> in *skipset* is not important.
>
> For example,
> ```
> strspn ("hello, world", "abcdefghijklmnopqrstuvwxyz")
>     ⇒ 5
> ```

size_t **strcspn** (const char *string*, const char   Function
            **stopset*)

> The `strcspn` ("string complement span") function returns the length
> of the initial substring of *string* that consists entirely of characters
> that are *not* members of the set specified by the string *stopset*. (In

other words, it returns the offset of the first character in *string* that is a member of the set *stopset*.)

For example,
```
strcspn ("hello, world", " \t\n,.;!?")
    ⇒ 5
```

char * strpbrk (const char *string*, const char   *Function*
        **stopset*)

The `strpbrk` ("string pointer break") function is related to `strcspn`, except that it returns a pointer to the first character in *string* that is a member of the set *stopset* instead of the length of the initial substring. It returns a null pointer if no such character from *stopset* is found.

For example,
```
strpbrk ("hello, world", " \t\n,.;!?")
    ⇒ ", world"
```

5.8 Finding Tokens in a String

It's fairly common for programs to have a need to do some simple kinds of lexical analysis and parsing, such as splitting a command string up into tokens. You can do this with the `strtok` function, declared in the header file 'string.h'.

char * strtok (char *newstring*, const char   *Function*
        **delimiters*)

A string can be split into tokens by making a series of calls to the function `strtok`.

The string to be split up is passed as the *newstring* argument on the first call only. The `strtok` function uses this to set up some internal state information. Subsequent calls to get additional tokens from the same string are indicated by passing a null pointer as the *newstring* argument. Calling `strtok` with another non-null *newstring* argument reinitializes the state information. It is guaranteed that no other library function ever calls `strtok` behind your back (which would mess up this internal state information).

The *delimiters* argument is a string that specifies a set of delimiters that may surround the token being extracted. All the initial characters that are members of this set are discarded. The first character that is *not* a member of this set of delimiters marks the beginning of the next token. The end of the token is found by looking for the next character that is a member of the delimiter set. This character in the original string *newstring* is overwritten by a null character, and the pointer to the beginning of the token in *newstring* is returned.

Chapter 5: String and Array Utilities

On the next call to `strtok`, the searching begins at the next character beyond the one that marked the end of the previous token. Note that the set of delimiters *delimiters* do not have to be the same on every call in a series of calls to `strtok`.

If the end of the string *newstring* is reached, or if the remainder of string consists only of delimiter characters, `strtok` returns a null pointer.

Warning: Since `strtok` alters the string it is parsing, you always copy the string to a temporary buffer before parsing it with `strtok`. If you allow `strtok` to modify a string that came from another part of your program, you are asking for trouble; that string may be part of a data structure that could be used for other purposes during the parsing, when alteration by `strtok` makes the data structure temporarily inaccurate.

The string that you are operating on might even be a constant. Then when `strtok` tries to modify it, your program will get a fatal signal for writing in read-only memory. See Section 21.2.1 [Program Error Signals], page 374.

This is a special case of a general principle: if a part of a program does not have as its purpose the modification of a certain data structure, then it is error-prone to modify the data structure temporarily.

The function `strtok` is not reentrant. See Section 21.4.6 [Signal Handling and Nonreentrant Functions], page 398, for a discussion of where and why reentrancy is important.

Here is a simple example showing the use of `strtok`.

```
#include <string.h>
#include <stddef.h>

...

char string[] = "words separated by spaces -- and, punctuation!";
const char delimiters[] = " .,;:!-";
char *token;

...

token = strtok (string, delimiters);     /* token => "words" */
token = strtok (NULL, delimiters);       /* token => "separated" */
token = strtok (NULL, delimiters);       /* token => "by" */
token = strtok (NULL, delimiters);       /* token => "spaces" */
token = strtok (NULL, delimiters);       /* token => "and" */
token = strtok (NULL, delimiters);       /* token => "punctuation" */
token = strtok (NULL, delimiters);       /* token => NULL */
```

6 Input/Output Overview

Most programs need to do either input (reading data) or output (writing data), or most frequently both, in order to do anything useful. The GNU C library provides such a large selection of input and output functions that the hardest part is often deciding which function is most appropriate!

This chapter introduces concepts and terminology relating to input and output. Other chapters relating to the GNU I/O facilities are:

- Chapter 7 [Input/Output on Streams], page 83, which covers the high-level functions that operate on streams, including formatted input and output.
- Chapter 8 [Low-Level Input/Output], page 139, which covers the basic I/O and control functions on file descriptors.
- Chapter 9 [File System Interface], page 169, which covers functions for operating on directories and for manipulating file attributes such as access modes and ownership.
- Chapter 10 [Pipes and FIFOs], page 201, which includes information on the basic interprocess communication facilities.
- Chapter 11 [Sockets], page 207, which covers a more complicated interprocess communication facility with support for networking.
- Chapter 12 [Low-Level Terminal Interface], page 255, which covers functions for changing how input and output to terminal or other serial devices are processed.

6.1 Input/Output Concepts

Before you can read or write the contents of a file, you must establish a connection or communications channel to the file. This process is called *opening* the file. You can open a file for reading, writing, or both.

The connection to an open file is represented either as a stream or as a file descriptor. You pass this as an argument to the functions that do the actual read or write operations, to tell them which file to operate on. Certain functions expect streams, and others are designed to operate on file descriptors.

When you have finished reading to or writing from the file, you can terminate the connection by *closing* the file. Once you have closed a stream or file descriptor, you cannot do any more input or output operations on it.

6.1.1 Streams and File Descriptors

When you want to do input or output to a file, you have a choice of two basic mechanisms for representing the connection between your program and the file: file descriptors and streams. File descriptors are represented as objects of type `int`, while streams are represented as `FILE *` objects.

File descriptors provide a primitive, low-level interface to input and output operations. Both file descriptors and streams can represent a connection to a device (such as a terminal), or a pipe or socket for communicating with another process, as well as a normal file. But, if you want to do control operations that are specific to a particular kind of device, you must use a file descriptor; there are no facilities to use streams in this way. You must also use file descriptors if your program needs to do input or output in special modes, such as nonblocking (or polled) input (see Section 8.10 [File Status Flags], page 158).

Streams provide a higher-level interface, layered on top of the primitive file descriptor facilities. The stream interface treats all kinds of files pretty much alike—the sole exception being the three styles of buffering that you can choose (see Section 7.17 [Stream Buffering], page 129).

The main advantage of using the stream interface is that the set of functions for performing actual input and output operations (as opposed to control operations) on streams is much richer and more powerful than the corresponding facilities for file descriptors. The file descriptor interface provides only simple functions for transferring blocks of characters, but the stream interface also provides powerful formatted input and output functions (`printf` and `scanf`) as well as functions for character- and line-oriented input and output.

Since streams are implemented in terms of file descriptors, you can extract the file descriptor from a stream and perform low-level operations directly on the file descriptor. You can also initially open a connection as a file descriptor and then make a stream associated with that file descriptor.

In general, you should stick with using streams rather than file descriptors, unless there is some specific operation you want to do that can only be done on a file descriptor. If you are a beginning programmer and aren't sure what functions to use, we suggest that you concentrate on the formatted input functions (see Section 7.12 [Formatted Input], page 115) and formatted output functions (see Section 7.10 [Formatted Output], page 94).

If you are concerned about portability of your programs to systems other than GNU, you should also be aware that file descriptors are not as portable as streams. You can expect any system running ANSI C to support streams, but non-GNU systems may not support file descriptors at all, or may only implement a subset of the GNU functions that operate on file descriptors. Most of the file descriptor functions in the GNU library are included in the POSIX.1 standard, however.

Chapter 6: Input/Output Overview   77

6.1.2 File Position

One of the attributes of an open file is its *file position* that keeps track of where in the file the next character is to be read or written. In the GNU system, and all POSIX.1 systems, the file position is simply an integer representing the number of bytes from the beginning of the file.

The file position is normally set to the beginning of the file when it is opened, and each time a character is read or written, the file position is incremented. In other words, access to the file is normally *sequential*.

Ordinary files permit read or write operations at any position within the file. Some other kinds of files may also permit this. Files which do permit this are sometimes referred to as *random-access* files. You can change the file position using the `fseek` function on a stream (see Section 7.15 [File Positioning], page 126) or the `lseek` function on a file descriptor (see Section 8.2 [Input and Output Primitives], page 141). If you try to change the file position on a file that doesn't support random access, you get the `ESPIPE` error.

Streams and descriptors that are opened for *append access* are treated specially for output: output to such files is *always* appended sequentially to the *end* of the file, regardless of the file position. However, the file position is still used to control where in the file reading is done.

If you think about it, you'll realize that several programs can read a given file at the same time. In order for each program to be able to read the file at its own pace, each program must have its own file pointer, which is not affected by anything the other programs do.

In fact, each opening of a file creates a separate file position. Thus, if you open a file twice even in the same program, you get two streams or descriptors with independent file positions.

By contrast, if you open a descriptor and then duplicate it to get another descriptor, these two descriptors share the same file position: changing the file position of one descriptor will affect the other.

6.2 File Names

In order to open a connection to a file, or to perform other operations such as deleting a file, you need some way to refer to the file. Nearly all files have names that are strings—even files which are actually devices such as tape drives or terminals. These strings are called *file names*. You specify the file name to say which file you want to open or operate on.

This section describes the conventions for file names and how the operating system works with them.

6.2.1 Directories

In order to understand the syntax of file names, you need to understand how the file system is organized into a hierarchy of directories.

A *directory* is a file that contains information to associate other files with names; these associations are called *links* or *directory entries*. Sometimes, people speak of "files in a directory", but in reality, a directory only contains pointers to files, not the files themselves.

The name of a file contained in a directory entry is called a *file name component*. In general, a file name consists of a sequence of one or more such components, separated by the slash character ('/'). A file name which is just one component names a file with respect to its directory. A file name with multiple components names a directory, and then a file in that directory, and so on.

Some other documents, such as the POSIX standard, use the term *pathname* for what we call a file name, and either *filename* or *pathname component* for what this manual calls a file name component. We don't use this terminology because a "path" is something completely different (a list of directories to search), and we think that "pathname" used for something else will confuse users. We always use "file name" and "file name component" (or sometimes just "component", where the context is obvious) in GNU documentation. Some macros use the POSIX terminology in their names, such as `PATH_MAX`. These macros are defined by the POSIX standard, so we cannot change their names.

You can find more detailed information about operations on directories in Chapter 9 [File System Interface], page 169.

6.2.2 File Name Resolution

A file name consists of file name components separated by slash ('/') characters. On the systems that the GNU C library supports, multiple successive '/' characters are equivalent to a single '/' character.

The process of determining what file a file name refers to is called *file name resolution*. This is performed by examining the components that make up a file name in left-to-right order, and locating each successive component in the directory named by the previous component. Of course, each of the files that are referenced as directories must actually exist, be directories instead of regular files, and have the appropriate permissions to be accessible by the process; otherwise the file name resolution fails.

If a file name begins with a '/', the first component in the file name is located in the *root directory* of the process (usually all processes on the system have the same root directory). Such a file name is called an *absolute file name*.

Chapter 6: Input/Output Overview   79

Otherwise, the first component in the file name is located in the current working directory (see Section 9.1 [Working Directory], page 169). This kind of file name is called a *relative file name*.

The file name components '.' ("dot") and '..' ("dot-dot") have special meanings. Every directory has entries for these file name components. The file name component '.' refers to the directory itself, while the file name component '..' refers to its *parent directory* (the directory that contains the link for the directory in question). As a special case, '..' in the root directory refers to the root directory itself, since it has no parent; thus '/..' is the same as '/'.

Here are some examples of file names:

'/a'   The file named 'a', in the root directory.

'/a/b'   The file named 'b', in the directory named 'a' in the root directory.

'a'   The file named 'a', in the current working directory.

'/a/./b'   This is the same as '/a/b'.

'./a'   The file named 'a', in the current working directory.

'../a'   The file named 'a', in the parent directory of the current working directory.

A file name that names a directory may optionally end in a '/'. You can specify a file name of '/' to refer to the root directory, but the empty string is not a meaningful file name. If you want to refer to the current working directory, use a file name of '.' or './'.

Unlike some other operating systems, the GNU system doesn't have any built-in support for file types (or extensions) or file versions as part of its file name syntax. Many programs and utilities use conventions for file names— for example, files containing C source code usually have names suffixed with '.c'—but there is nothing in the file system itself that enforces this kind of convention.

6.2.3 File Name Errors

Functions that accept file name arguments usually detect these `errno` error conditions relating to the file name syntax or trouble finding the named file. These errors are referred to throughout this manual as the *usual file name errors*.

EACCES   The process does not have search permission for a directory component of the file name.

ENAMETOOLONG
> This error is used when either the the total length of a file name is greater than `PATH_MAX`, or when an individual file name component has a length greater than `NAME_MAX`. See Section 27.6 [Limits on File System Capacity], page 507.
>
> In the GNU system, there is no imposed limit on overall file name length, but some file systems may place limits on the length of a component.

ENOENT
> This error is reported when a file referenced as a directory component in the file name doesn't exist, or when a component is a symbolic link whose target file does not exist. See Section 9.4 [Symbolic Links], page 176.

ENOTDIR
> A file that is referenced as a directory component in the file name exists, but it isn't a directory.

ELOOP
> Too many symbolic links were resolved while trying to look up the file name. The system has an arbitrary limit on the number of symbolic links that may be resolved in looking up a single file name, as a primitive way to detect loops. See Section 9.4 [Symbolic Links], page 176.

6.2.4 Portability of File Names

The rules for the syntax of file names discussed in Section 6.2 [File Names], page 77, are the rules normally used by the GNU system and by other POSIX systems. However, other operating systems may use other conventions.

There are two reasons why it can be important for you to be aware of file name portability issues:

- If your program makes assumptions about file name syntax, or contains embedded literal file name strings, it is more difficult to get it to run under other operating systems that use different syntax conventions.

- Even if you are not concerned about running your program on machines that run other operating systems, it may still be possible to access files that use different naming conventions. For example, you may be able to access file systems on another computer running a different operating system over a network, or read and write disks in formats used by other operating systems.

The ANSI C standard says very little about file name syntax, only that file names are strings. In addition to varying restrictions on the length of file names and what characters can validly appear in a file name, different operating systems use different conventions and syntax for concepts such as

Chapter 6: Input/Output Overview

structured directories and file types or extensions. Some concepts such as file versions might be supported in some operating systems and not by others.

The POSIX.1 standard allows implementations to put additional restrictions on file name syntax, concerning what characters are permitted in file names and on the length of file name and file name component strings. However, in the GNU system, you do not need to worry about these restrictions; any character except the null character is permitted in a file name string, and there are no limits on the length of file name strings.

7 Input/Output on Streams

This chapter describes the functions for creating streams and performing input and output operations on them. As discussed in Chapter 6 [Input/Output Overview], page 75, a stream is a fairly abstract, high-level concept representing a communications channel to a file, device, or process.

7.1 Streams

For historical reasons, the type of the C data structure that represents a stream is called `FILE` rather than "stream". Since most of the library functions deal with objects of type `FILE *`, sometimes the term *file pointer* is also used to mean "stream". This leads to unfortunate confusion over terminology in many books on C. This manual, however, is careful to use the terms "file" and "stream" only in the technical sense.

The `FILE` type is declared in the header file 'stdio.h'.

FILE   *Data Type*
> This is the data type used to represent stream objects. A `FILE` object holds all of the internal state information about the connection to the associated file, including such things as the file position indicator and buffering information. Each stream also has error and end-of-file status indicators that can be tested with the `ferror` and `feof` functions; see Section 7.13 [End-Of-File and Errors], page 124.
>
> `FILE` objects are allocated and managed internally by the input/output library functions. Don't try to create your own objects of type `FILE`; let the library do it. Your programs should deal only with pointers to these objects (that is, `FILE *` values) rather than the objects themselves.

7.2 Standard Streams

When the `main` function of your program is invoked, it already has three predefined streams open and available for use. These represent the "standard" input and output channels that have been established for the process.

These streams are declared in the header file 'stdio.h'.

FILE * stdin   *Variable*
> The *standard input* stream, which is the normal source of input for the program.

FILE * stdout   *Variable*
> The *standard output* stream, which is used for normal output from the program.

FILE * stderr   Variable

The *standard error* stream, which is used for error messages and diagnostics issued by the program.

In the GNU system, you can specify what files or processes correspond to these streams using the pipe and redirection facilities provided by the shell. (The primitives shells use to implement these facilities are described in Chapter 9 [File System Interface], page 169.) Most other operating systems provide similar mechanisms, but the details of how to use them can vary.

In the GNU C library, `stdin`, `stdout`, and `stderr` are normal variables which you can set just like any others. For example, to redirect the standard output to a file, you could do:

```
fclose (stdout);
stdout = fopen ("standard-output-file", "w");
```

Note however, that in other systems `stdin`, `stdout`, and `stderr` are macros that you cannot assign to in the normal way. But you can use `freopen` to get the effect of closing one and reopening it. See Section 7.3 [Opening Streams], page 84.

7.3 Opening Streams

Opening a file with the `fopen` function creates a new stream and establishes a connection between the stream and a file. This may involve creating a new file.

Everything described in this section is declared in the header file 'stdio.h'.

FILE * fopen (const char *filename*, const char   Function
    **opentype*)

The `fopen` function opens a stream for I/O to the file *filename*, and returns a pointer to the stream.

The *opentype* argument is a string that controls how the file is opened and specifies attributes of the resulting stream. It must begin with one of the following sequences of characters:

'r'   Open an existing file for reading only.

'w'   Open the file for writing only. If the file already exists, it is truncated to zero length. Otherwise a new file is created.

'a'   Open a file for append access; that is, writing at the end of file only. If the file already exists, its initial contents are unchanged and output to the stream is appended to the end of the file. Otherwise, a new, empty file is created.

Chapter 7: Input/Output on Streams 85

'r+'   Open an existing file for both reading and writing. The initial contents of the file are unchanged and the initial file position is at the beginning of the file.

'w+'   Open a file for both reading and writing. If the file already exists, it is truncated to zero length. Otherwise, a new file is created.

'a+'   Open or create file for both reading and appending. If the file exists, its initial contents are unchanged. Otherwise, a new file is created. The initial file position for reading is at the beginning of the file, but output is always appended to the end of the file.

As you can see, '+' requests a stream that can do both input and output. The ANSI standard says that when using such a stream, you must call `fflush` (see Section 7.17 [Stream Buffering], page 129) or a file positioning function such as `fseek` (see Section 7.15 [File Positioning], page 126) when switching from reading to writing or vice versa. Otherwise, internal buffers might not be emptied properly. The GNU C library does not have this limitation; you can do arbitrary reading and writing operations on a stream in whatever order.

Additional characters may appear after these to specify flags for the call. Always put the mode ('r', 'w+', etc.) first; that is the only part you are guaranteed will be understood by all systems.

The GNU C library defines one additional character for use in *opentype*: the character 'x' insists on creating a new file—if a file *filename* already exists, `fopen` fails rather than opening it. If you use 'x' you can are guaranteed that you will not clobber an existing file. This is equivalent to the `O_EXCL` option to the `open` function (see Section 8.1 [Opening and Closing Files], page 139).

The character 'b' in *opentype* has a standard meaning; it requests a binary stream rather than a text stream. But this makes no difference in POSIX systems (including the GNU system). If both '+' and 'b' are specified, they can appear in either order. See Section 7.14 [Text and Binary Streams], page 125.

Any other characters in *opentype* are simply ignored. They may be meaningful in other systems.

If the open fails, `fopen` returns a null pointer.

You can have multiple streams (or file descriptors) pointing to the same file open at the same time. If you do only input, this works straightforwardly, but you must be careful if any output streams are included. See Section 8.5 [Dangers of Mixing Streams and Descriptors], page 148. This is equally true whether the streams are in one program (not usual) or in several programs (which can easily happen). It may be advantageous to use the file locking facilities to avoid simultaneous access. See Section 8.11 [File Locks], page 164.

int FOPEN_MAX   *Macro*

The value of this macro is an integer constant expression that represents the minimum number of streams that the implementation guarantees can be open simultaneously. You might be able to open more than this many streams, but that is not guaranteed. The value of this constant is at least eight, which includes the three standard streams `stdin`, `stdout`, and `stderr`. In POSIX.1 systems this value is determined by the `OPEN_MAX` parameter; see Section 27.1 [General Capacity Limits], page 499. In BSD and GNU, it is controlled by the `RLIMIT_NOFILE` resource limit; see Section 17.6 [Limiting Resource Usage], page 341.

FILE * freopen (const char *filename, const char   *Function*
          *opentype, FILE *stream)

This function is like a combination of `fclose` and `fopen`. It first closes the stream referred to by *stream*, ignoring any errors that are detected in the process. (Because errors are ignored, you should not use `freopen` on an output stream if you have actually done any output using the stream.) Then the file named by *filename* is opened with mode *opentype* as for `fopen`, and associated with the same stream object *stream*.

If the operation fails, a null pointer is returned; otherwise, `freopen` returns *stream*.

`freopen` has traditionally been used to connect a standard stream such as `stdin` with a file of your own choice. This is useful in programs in which use of a standard stream for certain purposes is hard-coded. In the GNU C library, you can simply close the standard streams and open new ones with `fopen`. But other systems lack this ability, so using `freopen` is more portable.

7.4 Closing Streams

When a stream is closed with `fclose`, the connection between the stream and the file is cancelled. After you have closed a stream, you cannot perform any additional operations on it.

int fclose (FILE *stream)   *Function*

This function causes *stream* to be closed and the connection to the corresponding file to be broken. Any buffered output is written and any buffered input is discarded. The `fclose` function returns a value of 0 if the file was closed successfully, and `EOF` if an error was detected.

Chapter 7: Input/Output on Streams 87

It is important to check for errors when you call `fclose` to close an output stream, because real, everyday errors can be detected at this time. For example, when `fclose` writes the remaining buffered output, it might get an error because the disk is full. Even if you know the buffer is empty, errors can still occur when closing a file if you are using NFS.

The function `fclose` is declared in '`stdio.h`'.

If the `main` function to your program returns, or if you call the `exit` function (see Section 22.3.1 [Normal Termination], page 437), all open streams are automatically closed properly. If your program terminates in any other manner, such as by calling the `abort` function (see Section 22.3.4 [Aborting a Program], page 440) or from a fatal signal (see Chapter 21 [Signal Handling], page 371), open streams might not be closed properly. Buffered output might not be flushed and files may be incomplete. For more information on buffering of streams, see Section 7.17 [Stream Buffering], page 129.

7.5 Simple Output by Characters or Lines

This section describes functions for performing character- and line-oriented output.

These functions are declared in the header file '`stdio.h`'.

`int` **`fputc`** (`int` *c*, `FILE` **stream*) Function
 The `fputc` function converts the character *c* to type `unsigned char`, and writes it to the stream *stream*. `EOF` is returned if a write error occurs; otherwise the character *c* is returned.

`int` **`putc`** (`int` *c*, `FILE` **stream*) Function
 This is just like `fputc`, except that most systems implement it as a macro, making it faster. One consequence is that it may evaluate the *stream* argument more than once, which is an exception to the general rule for macros. `putc` is usually the best function to use for writing a single character.

`int` **`putchar`** (`int` *c*) Function
 The `putchar` function is equivalent to `putc` with `stdout` as the value of the *stream* argument.

`int` **`fputs`** (`const char` **s*, `FILE` **stream*) Function
 The function `fputs` writes the string *s* to the stream *stream*. The terminating null character is not written. This function does *not* add a newline character, either. It outputs only the characters in the string.

 This function returns `EOF` if a write error occurs, and otherwise a non-negative value.

For example:

```
fputs ("Are ", stdout);
fputs ("you ", stdout);
fputs ("hungry?\n", stdout);
```

outputs the text 'Are you hungry?' followed by a newline.

int puts (const char *s)   Function

The puts function writes the string s to the stream stdout followed by a newline. The terminating null character of the string is not written. (Note that fputs does *not* write a newline as this function does.)

puts is the most convenient function for printing simple messages. For example:

```
puts ("This is a message.");
```

int putw (int w, FILE *stream)   Function

This function writes the word w (that is, an int) to stream. It is provided for compatibility with SVID, but we recommend you use fwrite instead (see Section 7.9 [Block Input/Output], page 93).

7.6 Character Input

This section describes functions for performing character-oriented input. These functions are declared in the header file 'stdio.h'.

These functions return an int value that is either a character of input, or the special value EOF (usually -1). It is important to store the result of these functions in a variable of type int instead of char, even when you plan to use it only as a character. Storing EOF in a char variable truncates its value to the size of a character, so that it is no longer distinguishable from the valid character '(char) -1'. So always use an int for the result of getc and friends, and check for EOF after the call; once you've verified that the result is not EOF, you can be sure that it will fit in a 'char' variable without loss of information.

int fgetc (FILE *stream)   Function

This function reads the next character as an unsigned char from the stream *stream* and returns its value, converted to an int. If an end-of-file condition or read error occurs, EOF is returned instead.

int getc (FILE *stream)   Function

This is just like fgetc, except that it is permissible (and typical) for it to be implemented as a macro that evaluates the *stream* argument more than once. getc is often highly optimized, so it is usually the best function to use to read a single character.

Chapter 7: Input/Output on Streams 89

`int getchar (void)` *Function*

The `getchar` function is equivalent to `getc` with `stdin` as the value of the *stream* argument.

Here is an example of a function that does input using `fgetc`. It would work just as well using `getc` instead, or using `getchar ()` instead of `fgetc (stdin)`.

```
int
y_or_n_p (const char *question)
{
  fputs (question, stdout);
  while (1)
    {
      int c, answer;
      /* Write a space to separate answer from question. */
      fputc (' ', stdout);
      /* Read the first character of the line.
         This should be the answer character, but might not be. */
      c = tolower (fgetc (stdin));
      answer = c;
      /* Discard rest of input line. */
      while (c != '\n' && c != EOF)
        c = fgetc (stdin);
      /* Obey the answer if it was valid. */
      if (answer == 'y')
        return 1;
      if (answer == 'n')
        return 0;
      /* Answer was invalid: ask for valid answer. */
      fputs ("Please answer y or n:", stdout);
    }
}
```

`int getw (FILE *stream)` *Function*

This function reads a word (that is, an `int`) from *stream*. It's provided for compatibility with SVID. We recommend you use `fread` instead (see Section 7.9 [Block Input/Output], page 93). Unlike `getc`, any `int` value could be a valid result. `getw` returns `EOF` when it encounters end-of-file or an error, but there is no way to distinguish this from an input word with value -1.

7.7 Line-Oriented Input

Since many programs interpret input on the basis of lines, it's convenient to have functions to read a line of text from a stream.

Standard C has functions to do this, but they aren't very safe: null characters and even (for `gets`) long lines can confuse them. So the GNU library provides the nonstandard `getline` function that makes it easy to read lines reliably.

Another GNU extension, **getdelim**, generalizes **getline**. It reads a delimited record, defined as everything through the next occurrence of a specified delimiter character.

All these functions are declared in '**stdio.h**'.

ssize_t getline (char *******lineptr*, size_t **n*, FILE   *Function*
    *stream)

    This function reads an entire line from *stream*, storing the text (including the newline and a terminating null character) in a buffer and storing the buffer address in **lineptr*.

    Before calling **getline**, you should place in **lineptr* the address of a buffer **n* bytes long, allocated with **malloc**. If this buffer is long enough to hold the line, **getline** stores the line in this buffer. Otherwise, **getline** makes the buffer bigger using **realloc**, storing the new buffer address back in **lineptr* and the increased size back in **n*. See Section 3.3 [Unconstrained Allocation], page 28.

    If you set **lineptr* to a null pointer, and **n* to zero, before the call, then **getline** allocates the initial buffer for you by calling **malloc**.

    In either case, when **getline** returns, **lineptr* is a **char *** which points to the text of the line.

    When **getline** is successful, it returns the number of characters read (including the newline, but not including the terminating null). This value enables you to distinguish null characters that are part of the line from the null character inserted as a terminator.

    This function is a GNU extension, but it is the recommended way to read lines from a stream. The alternative standard functions are unreliable.

    If an error occurs or end of file is reached, **getline** returns -1.

ssize_t getdelim (char *******lineptr*, size_t **n*, int   *Function*
    delimiter, FILE **stream*)

    This function is like **getline** except that the character which tells it to stop reading is not necessarily newline. The argument *delimiter* specifies the delimiter character; **getdelim** keeps reading until it sees that character (or end of file).

    The text is stored in *lineptr*, including the delimiter character and a terminating null. Like **getline**, **getdelim** makes *lineptr* bigger if it isn't big enough.

    getline is in fact implemented in terms of **getdelim**, just like this:

```
ssize_t
getline (char **lineptr, size_t *n, FILE *stream)
{
  return getdelim (lineptr, n, '\n', stream);
}
```

Chapter 7: Input/Output on Streams 91

char * **fgets** (char *s*, int *count*, FILE *stream*) *Function*
> The `fgets` function reads characters from the stream *stream* up to and including a newline character and stores them in the string *s*, adding a null character to mark the end of the string. You must supply *count* characters worth of space in *s*, but the number of characters read is at most *count* − 1. The extra character space is used to hold the null character at the end of the string.
>
> If the system is already at end of file when you call `fgets`, then the contents of the array *s* are unchanged and a null pointer is returned. A null pointer is also returned if a read error occurs. Otherwise, the return value is the pointer *s*.
>
> **Warning:** If the input data has a null character, you can't tell. So don't use `fgets` unless you know the data cannot contain a null. Don't use it to read files edited by the user because, if the user inserts a null character, you should either handle it properly or print a clear error message. We recommend using `getline` instead of `fgets`.

char * **gets** (char *s*) *Deprecated function*
> The function `gets` reads characters from the stream `stdin` up to the next newline character, and stores them in the string *s*. The newline character is discarded (note that this differs from the behavior of `fgets`, which copies the newline character into the string). If `gets` encounters a read error or end-of-file, it returns a null pointer; otherwise it returns *s*.
>
> **Warning:** The `gets` function is **very dangerous** because it provides no protection against overflowing the string *s*. The GNU library includes it for compatibility only. You should **always** use `fgets` or `getline` instead. To remind you of this, the linker (if using GNU `ld`) will issue a warning whenever you use `gets`.

7.8 Unreading

In parser programs it is often useful to examine the next character in the input stream without removing it from the stream. This is called "peeking ahead" at the input because your program gets a glimpse of the input it will read next.

Using stream I/O, you can peek ahead at input by first reading it and then *unreading* it (also called *pushing it back* on the stream). Unreading a character makes it available to be input again from the stream, by the next call to `fgetc` or other input function on that stream.

7.8.1 What Unreading Means

Here is a pictorial explanation of unreading. Suppose you have a stream reading a file that contains just six characters, the letters 'foobar'. Suppose you have read three characters so far. The situation looks like this:

```
f o o b a r
      ^
```

so the next input character will be 'b'.

If instead of reading 'b' you unread the letter 'o', you get a situation like this:

```
f o o b a r
      |
      o--
      ^
```

so that the next input characters will be 'o' and 'b'.

If you unread '9' instead of 'o', you get this situation:

```
f o o b a r
      |
      9--
      ^
```

so that the next input characters will be '9' and 'b'.

7.8.2 Using ungetc To Do Unreading

The function to unread a character is called **ungetc**, because it reverses the action of **getc**.

int ungetc (int *c*, FILE **stream*) *Function*

The **ungetc** function pushes back the character *c* onto the input stream *stream*. So the next input from *stream* will read *c* before anything else.

If *c* is EOF, **ungetc** does nothing and just returns EOF. This lets you call **ungetc** with the return value of **getc** without needing to check for an error from **getc**.

The character that you push back doesn't have to be the same as the last character that was actually read from the stream. In fact, it isn't necessary to actually read any characters from the stream before unreading them with **ungetc**! But that is a strange way to write a program; usually **ungetc** is used only to unread a character that was just read from the same stream.

The GNU C library only supports one character of pushback—in other words, it does not work to call **ungetc** twice without doing input in between. Other systems might let you push back multiple characters; then reading from the stream retrieves the characters in the reverse order that they were pushed.

Pushing back characters doesn't alter the file; only the internal buffering for the stream is affected. If a file positioning function (such as `fseek` or `rewind`; see Section 7.15 [File Positioning], page 126) is called, any pending pushed-back characters are discarded.

Unreading a character on a stream that is at end of file clears the end-of-file indicator for the stream, because it makes the character of input available. After you read that character, trying to read again will encounter end of file.

Here is an example showing the use of `getc` and `ungetc` to skip over whitespace characters. When this function reaches a non-whitespace character, it unreads that character to be seen again on the next read operation on the stream.

```
#include <stdio.h>
#include <ctype.h>

void
skip_whitespace (FILE *stream)
{
  int c;
  do
    /* No need to check for EOF because it is not
       isspace, and ungetc ignores EOF. */
    c = getc (stream);
  while (isspace (c));
  ungetc (c, stream);
}
```

7.9 Block Input/Output

This section describes how to do input and output operations on blocks of data. You can use these functions to read and write binary data, as well as to read and write text in fixed-size blocks instead of by characters or lines.

Binary files are typically used to read and write blocks of data in the same format as is used to represent the data in a running program. In other words, arbitrary blocks of memory—not just character or string objects—can be written to a binary file, and meaningfully read in again by the same program.

Storing data in binary form is often considerably more efficient than using the formatted I/O functions. Also, for floating-point numbers, the binary form avoids possible loss of precision in the conversion process. On the other hand, binary files can't be examined or modified easily using many standard file utilities (such as text editors), and are not portable between different implementations of the language, or different kinds of computers.

These functions are declared in 'stdio.h'.

size_t **fread** (void *`data`, size_t `size`, size_t `count`,   Function
    FILE *`stream`)

> This function reads up to *count* objects of size *size* into the array *data*, from the stream *stream*. It returns the number of objects actually read, which might be less than *count* if a read error occurs or the end of the file is reached. This function returns a value of zero (and doesn't read anything) if either *size* or *count* is zero.
>
> If `fread` encounters end of file in the middle of an object, it returns the number of complete objects read, and discards the partial object. Therefore, the stream remains at the actual end of the file.

size_t **fwrite** (const void *`data`, size_t `size`, size_t   Function
    `count`, FILE *`stream`)

> This function writes up to *count* objects of size *size* from the array *data*, to the stream *stream*. The return value is normally *count*, if the call succeeds. Any other value indicates some sort of error, such as running out of space.

7.10 Formatted Output

The functions described in this section (`printf` and related functions) provide a convenient way to perform formatted output. You call `printf` with a *format string* or *template string* that specifies how to format the values of the remaining arguments.

Unless your program is a filter that specifically performs line- or character-oriented processing, using `printf` or one of the other related functions described in this section is usually the easiest and most concise way to perform output. These functions are especially useful for printing error messages, tables of data, and the like.

7.10.1 Formatted Output Basics

The `printf` function can be used to print any number of arguments. The template string argument you supply in a call provides information not only about the number of additional arguments, but also about their types and what style should be used for printing them.

Ordinary characters in the template string are simply written to the output stream as-is, while *conversion specifications* introduced by a '%' character in the template cause subsequent arguments to be formatted and written to the output stream. For example,

```
int pct = 37;
char filename[] = "foo.txt";
printf ("Processing of '%s' is %d%% finished.\nPlease be patient.\n",
        filename, pct);
```

Chapter 7: Input/Output on Streams   95

produces output like
    Processing of 'foo.txt' is 37% finished.
    Please be patient.

This example shows the use of the '%d' conversion to specify that an `int` argument should be printed in decimal notation, the '%s' conversion to specify printing of a string argument, and the '%%' conversion to print a literal '%' character.

There are also conversions for printing an integer argument as an unsigned value in octal, decimal, or hexadecimal radix ('%o', '%u', or '%x', respectively); or as a character value ('%c').

Floating-point numbers can be printed in normal, fixed-point notation using the '%f' conversion or in exponential notation using the '%e' conversion. The '%g' conversion uses either '%e' or '%f' format, depending on what is more appropriate for the magnitude of the particular number.

You can control formatting more precisely by writing *modifiers* between the '%' and the character that indicates which conversion to apply. These slightly alter the ordinary behavior of the conversion. For example, most conversion specifications permit you to specify a minimum field width and a flag indicating whether you want the result left- or right-justified within the field.

The specific flags and modifiers that are permitted and their interpretation vary depending on the particular conversion. They're all described in more detail in the following sections. Don't worry if this all seems excessively complicated at first; you can almost always get reasonable free-format output without using any of the modifiers at all. The modifiers are mostly used to make the output look "prettier" in tables.

7.10.2 Output Conversion Syntax

This section provides details about the precise syntax of conversion specifications that can appear in a `printf` template string.

Characters in the template string that are not part of a conversion specification are printed as-is to the output stream. Multibyte character sequences (see Chapter 18 [Extended Characters], page 345) are permitted in a template string.

The conversion specifications in a `printf` template string have the general form:

    % flags width [. precision] type conversion

For example, in the conversion specifier '%-10.8ld', the '-' is a flag, '10' specifies the field width, the precision is '8', the letter 'l' is a type modifier, and 'd' specifies the conversion style. (This particular type specifier says to print a `long int` argument in decimal notation, with a minimum of 8 digits left-justified in a field at least 10 characters wide.)

In more detail, output conversion specifications consist of an initial '%' character followed in sequence by:

- Zero or more *flag characters* that modify the normal behavior of the conversion specification.

- An optional decimal integer specifying the *minimum field width*. If the normal conversion produces fewer characters than this, the field is padded with spaces to the specified width. This is a *minimum* value; if the normal conversion produces more characters than this, the field is *not* truncated. Normally, the output is right-justified within the field.

  You can also specify a field width of '*'. This means that the next argument in the argument list (before the actual value to be printed) is used as the field width. The value must be an `int`. If the value is negative, this means to set the '-' flag (see below) and to use the absolute value as the field width.

- An optional *precision* to specify the number of digits to be written for the numeric conversions. If the precision is specified, it consists of a period ('.') followed optionally by a decimal integer (which defaults to zero if omitted).

  You can also specify a precision of '*'. This means that the next argument in the argument list (before the actual value to be printed) is used as the precision. The value must be an `int`, and is ignored if it is negative. If you specify '*' for both the field width and precision, the field width argument precedes the precision argument. Other C library versions may not recognize this syntax.

- An optional *type modifier character*, which is used to specify the data type of the corresponding argument if it differs from the default type. (For example, the integer conversions assume a type of `int`, but you can specify 'h', 'l', or 'L' for other integer types.)

- A character that specifies the conversion to be applied.

The exact options that are permitted and how they are interpreted vary between the different conversion specifiers. See the descriptions of the individual conversions for information about the particular options that they use.

With the '`-Wformat`' option, the GNU C compiler checks calls to `printf` and related functions. It examines the format string and verifies that the correct number and types of arguments are supplied. There is also a GNU C syntax to tell the compiler that a function you write uses a `printf`-style format string. See section "Declaring Attributes of Functions" in *Using GNU CC*, for more information.

Chapter 7: Input/Output on Streams   97

7.10.3 Table of Output Conversions

Here is a table summarizing what all the different conversions do:

'%d', '%i'   Print an integer as a signed decimal number. See Section 7.10.4 [Integer Conversions], page 98, for details. '%d' and '%i' are synonymous for output, but are different when used with scanf for input (see Section 7.12.3 [Table of Input Conversions], page 118).

'%o'   Print an integer as an unsigned octal number. See Section 7.10.4 [Integer Conversions], page 98, for details.

'%u'   Print an integer as an unsigned decimal number. See Section 7.10.4 [Integer Conversions], page 98, for details.

'%x', '%X'   Print an integer as an unsigned hexadecimal number. '%x' uses lower-case letters and '%X' uses upper-case. See Section 7.10.4 [Integer Conversions], page 98, for details.

'%f'   Print a floating-point number in normal (fixed-point) notation. See Section 7.10.5 [Floating-Point Conversions], page 100, for details.

'%e', '%E'   Print a floating-point number in exponential notation. '%e' uses lower-case letters and '%E' uses upper-case. See Section 7.10.5 [Floating-Point Conversions], page 100, for details.

'%g', '%G'   Print a floating-point number in either normal or exponential notation, whichever is more appropriate for its magnitude. '%g' uses lower-case letters and '%G' uses upper-case. See Section 7.10.5 [Floating-Point Conversions], page 100, for details.

'%c'   Print a single character. See Section 7.10.6 [Other Output Conversions], page 101.

'%s'   Print a string. See Section 7.10.6 [Other Output Conversions], page 101.

'%p'   Print the value of a pointer. See Section 7.10.6 [Other Output Conversions], page 101.

'%n'   Get the number of characters printed so far. See Section 7.10.6 [Other Output Conversions], page 101. Note that this conversion specification never produces any output.

'%m'   Print the string corresponding to the value of errno. (This is a GNU extension.) See Section 7.10.6 [Other Output Conversions], page 101.

'%%'   Print a literal '%' character. See Section 7.10.6 [Other Output Conversions], page 101.

If the syntax of a conversion specification is invalid, unpredictable things will happen, so don't do this. If there aren't enough function arguments provided to supply values for all the conversion specifications in the template string, or if the arguments are not of the correct types, the results are unpredictable. If you supply more arguments than conversion specifications, the extra argument values are simply ignored; this is sometimes useful.

7.10.4 Integer Conversions

This section describes the options for the '%d', '%i', '%o', '%u', '%x', and '%X' conversion specifications. These conversions print integers in various formats.

The '%d' and '%i' conversion specifications both print an `int` argument as a signed decimal number; while '%o', '%u', and '%x' print the argument as an unsigned octal, decimal, or hexadecimal number (respectively). The '%X' conversion specification is just like '%x' except that it uses the characters 'ABCDEF' as digits instead of 'abcdef'.

The following flags are meaningful:

'-'   Left-justify the result in the field (instead of the normal right-justification).

'+'   For the signed '%d' and '%i' conversions, print a plus sign if the value is positive.

' '   For the signed '%d' and '%i' conversions, if the result doesn't start with a plus or minus sign, prefix it with a space character instead. Since the '+' flag ensures that the result includes a sign, this flag is ignored if you supply both of them.

'#'   For the '%o' conversion, this forces the leading digit to be '0', as if by increasing the precision. For '%x' or '%X', this prefixes a leading '0x' or '0X' (respectively) to the result. This doesn't do anything useful for the '%d', '%i', or '%u' conversions. Using this flag produces output which can be parsed by the `strtoul` function (see Section 14.7.1 [Parsing of Integers], page 294) and `scanf` with the '%i' conversion (see Section 7.12.4 [Numeric Input Conversions], page 119).

','   Separate the digits into groups as specified by the locale specified for the `LC_NUMERIC` category; see Section 19.6.1 [Generic Numeric Formatting Parameters], page 362. This flag is a GNU extension.

'0'   Pad the field with zeros instead of spaces. The zeros are placed after any indication of sign or base. This flag is ignored if the '-' flag is also specified, or if a precision is specified.

Chapter 7: Input/Output on Streams   99

If a precision is supplied, it specifies the minimum number of digits to appear; leading zeros are produced if necessary. If you don't specify a precision, the number is printed with as many digits as it needs. If you convert a value of zero with an explicit precision of zero, then no characters at all are produced.

Without a type modifier, the corresponding argument is treated as an `int` (for the signed conversions '`%i`' and '`%d`') or `unsigned int` (for the unsigned conversions '`%o`', '`%u`', '`%x`', and '`%X`'). Recall that since `printf` and friends are variadic, any `char` and `short` arguments are automatically converted to `int` by the default argument promotions. For arguments of other integer types, you can use these modifiers:

'h'   Specifies that the argument is a `short int` or `unsigned short int`, as appropriate. A `short` argument is converted to an `int` or `unsigned int` by the default argument promotions anyway, but the 'h' modifier says to convert it back to a `short` again.

'l'   Specifies that the argument is a `long int` or `unsigned long int`, as appropriate. Two 'l' characters is like the 'L' modifier, below.

'L'
'll'
'q'   Specifies that the argument is a `long long int`. (This type is an extension supported by the GNU C compiler. On systems that don't support extra-long integers, this is the same as `long int`.)

The 'q' modifier is another name for the same thing, which comes from 4.4 BSD; a `long long int` is sometimes called a "quad" `int`.

'Z'   Specifies that the argument is a `size_t`. This is a GNU extension.

Here is an example. Using the template string:

```
"|%5d|%-5d|%+5d|%+-5d|% 5d|%05d|%5.0d|%5.2d|%d|\n"
```

to print numbers using the different options for the '`%d`' conversion gives results like:

```
|    0|0    |   +0|+0   |     0|00000|    0|0|
|    1|1    |   +1|+1   |     1|00001|   1|   01|1|
|   -1|-1   |   -1|-1   |    -1|-0001|  -1|  -01|-1|
|100000|100000|+100000|100000|100000|100000|100000|100000|
```

In particular, notice what happens in the last case where the number is too large to fit in the minimum field width specified.

Here are some more examples showing how unsigned integers print under various format options, using the template string:

```
"|%5u|%5o|%5x|%5X|%#5o|%#5x|%#5X|%#10.8x|\n"
|    0|    0|    0|    0|    0|  0x0|  0X0|0x00000000|
|    1|    1|    1|    1|   01|  0x1|  0X1|0x00000001|
|100000|303240|186a0|186A0|0303240|0x186a0|0X186A0|0x000186a0|
```

7.10.5 Floating-Point Conversions

This section discusses the conversion specifications for floating-point numbers: the '%f', '%e', '%E', '%g', and '%G' conversions.

The '%f' conversion prints its argument in fixed-point notation, producing output of the form [-]ddd.ddd, where the number of digits following the decimal point is controlled by the precision you specify.

The '%e' conversion prints its argument in exponential notation, producing output of the form [-]d.ddde[+|-]dd. Again, the number of digits following the decimal point is controlled by the precision. The exponent always contains at least two digits. The '%E' conversion is similar but the exponent is marked with the letter 'E' instead of 'e'.

The '%g' and '%G' conversions print the argument in the style of '%e' or '%E' (respectively) if the exponent would be less than -4 or greater than or equal to the precision; otherwise they use the '%f' style. Trailing zeros are removed from the fractional portion of the result and a decimal-point character appears only if it is followed by a digit.

The following flags can be used to modify the behavior:

'-'   Left-justify the result in the field. Normally the result is right-justified.

'+'   Always include a plus or minus sign in the result.

' '   If the result doesn't start with a plus or minus sign, prefix it with a space instead. Since the '+' flag ensures that the result includes a sign, this flag is ignored if you supply both of them.

'#'   Specifies that the result should always include a decimal point, even if no digits follow it. For the '%g' and '%G' conversions, this also forces trailing zeros after the decimal point to be left in place where they would otherwise be removed.

'''   Separate the digits of the integer part of the result into groups as specified by the locale specified for the LC_NUMERIC category; see Section 19.6.1 [Generic Numeric Formatting Parameters], page 362. This flag is a GNU extension.

'0'   Pad the field with zeros instead of spaces; the zeros are placed after any sign. This flag is ignored if the '-' flag is also specified.

The precision specifies how many digits follow the decimal-point character for the '%f', '%e', and '%E' conversions. For these conversions, the default

Chapter 7: Input/Output on Streams

precision is 6. If the precision is explicitly 0, this suppresses the decimal point character entirely. For the '%g' and '%G' conversions, the precision specifies how many significant digits to print. Significant digits are the first digit before the decimal point, and all the digits after it. If the precision 0 or not specified for '%g' or '%G', it is treated like a value of 1. If the value being printed cannot be expressed accurately in the specified number of digits, the value is rounded to the nearest number that fits.

Without a type modifier, the floating-point conversions use an argument of type **double**. (By the default argument promotions, any **float** arguments are automatically converted to **double**.) The following type modifier is supported:

'L'   An uppercase 'L' specifies that the argument is a **long double**.

Here are some examples showing how numbers print using the various floating-point conversions. All of the numbers were printed using this template string:

```
"|%12.4f|%12.4e|%12.4g|\n"
```

Here is the output:

```
|      0.0000|  0.0000e+00|           0|
|      1.0000|  1.0000e+00|           1|
|     -1.0000| -1.0000e+00|          -1|
|    100.0000|  1.0000e+02|         100|
|   1000.0000|  1.0000e+03|        1000|
|  10000.0000|  1.0000e+04|       1e+04|
|  12345.0000|  1.2345e+04|   1.234e+04|
| 100000.0000|  1.0000e+05|       1e+05|
| 123456.0000|  1.2346e+05|   1.234e+05|
```

Notice how the '%g' conversion drops trailing zeros.

7.10.6 Other Output Conversions

This section describes miscellaneous conversions for **printf**.

The '%c' conversion prints a single character. The **int** argument is first converted to an **unsigned char**. The '-' flag can be used to specify left-justification in the field, but no other flags are defined, and no precision or type modifier can be given. For example:

```
printf ("%c%c%c%c%c", 'h', 'e', 'l', 'l', 'o');
```

prints 'hello'.

The '%s' conversion prints a string. The corresponding argument must be of type **char *** (or **const char ***). A precision can be specified to indicate the maximum number of characters to write; otherwise characters in the string up to but not including the terminating null character are written to the output stream. The '-' flag can be used to specify left-justification in the field, but no other flags or type modifiers are defined for this conversion. For example:

```
printf ("%3s%-6s", "no", "where");
```

prints '`no    where`'.

If you accidentally pass a null pointer as the argument for a '`%s`' conversion, the GNU library prints it as '`(null)`'. We think this is more useful than crashing. But it's not good practice to pass a null argument intentionally.

The '`%m`' conversion prints the string corresponding to the error code in `errno`. See Section 2.3 [Error Messages], page 23. Thus:

```
fprintf (stderr, "can't open '%s': %m\n", filename);
```

is equivalent to:

```
fprintf (stderr, "can't open '%s': %s\n", filename, strerror (errno));
```

The '`%m`' conversion is a GNU C library extension.

The '`%p`' conversion prints a pointer value. The corresponding argument must be of type `void *`. In practice, you can use any type of pointer.

In the GNU system, non-null pointers are printed as unsigned integers, as if a '`%#x`' conversion were used. Null pointers print as '`(nil)`'. (Pointers might print differently in other systems.)

For example:

```
printf ("%p", "testing");
```

prints '`0x`' followed by a hexadecimal number—the address of the string constant `"testing"`. It does not print the word '`testing`'.

You can supply the '`-`' flag with the '`%p`' conversion to specify left-justification, but no other flags, precision, or type modifiers are defined.

The '`%n`' conversion is unlike any of the other output conversions. It uses an argument which must be a pointer to an `int`, but instead of printing anything it stores the number of characters printed so far by this call at that location. The '`h`' and '`l`' type modifiers are permitted to specify that the argument is of type `short int *` or `long int *` instead of `int *`, but no flags, field width, or precision are permitted.

For example,

```
int nchar;
printf ("%d %s%n\n", 3, "bears", &nchar);
```

prints:

```
3 bears
```

and sets `nchar` to 7, because '`3 bears`' is seven characters.

The '`%%`' conversion prints a literal '`%`' character. This conversion doesn't use an argument, and no flags, field width, precision, or type modifiers are permitted.

Chapter 7: Input/Output on Streams

7.10.7 Formatted Output Functions

This section describes how to call `printf` and related functions. Prototypes for these functions are in the header file 'stdio.h'. Because these functions take a variable number of arguments, you *must* declare prototypes for them before using them. Of course, the easiest way to make sure you have all the right prototypes is to just include 'stdio.h'.

`int printf (const char *template, ...)`   Function
: The `printf` function prints the optional arguments under the control of the template string *template* to the stream `stdout`. It returns the number of characters printed, or a negative value if there was an output error.

`int fprintf (FILE *stream, const char *template, ...)`   Function
: This function is just like `printf`, except that the output is written to the stream *stream* instead of `stdout`.

`int sprintf (char *s, const char *template, ...)`   Function
: This is like `printf`, except that the output is stored in the character array *s* instead of written to a stream. A null character is written to mark the end of the string.

  The `sprintf` function returns the number of characters stored in the array *s*, not including the terminating null character.

  The behavior of this function is undefined if copying takes place between objects that overlap—for example, if *s* is also given as an argument to be printed under control of the '`%s`' conversion. See Section 5.4 [Copying and Concatenation], page 61.

  Warning: The `sprintf` function can be **dangerous** because it can potentially output more characters than can fit in the allocation size of the string *s*. Remember that the field width given in a conversion specification is only a *minimum* value.

  To avoid this problem, you can use `snprintf` or `asprintf`, described below.

`int snprintf (char *s, size_t size, const char *template, ...)`   Function
: The `snprintf` function is similar to `sprintf`, except that the *size* argument specifies the maximum number of characters to produce. The trailing null character is counted towards this limit, so you should allocate at least *size* characters for the string *s*.

  The return value is the number of characters stored, not including the terminating null. If this value equals *size* - 1, then there was not enough space in *s* for all the output. You should try again with a bigger output string. Here is an example of doing this:

```
/* Construct a message describing the value of a variable
   whose name is name and whose value is value. */
char *
make_message (char *name, char *value)
{
  /* Guess we need no more than 100 chars of space. */
  int size = 100;
  char *buffer = (char *) xmalloc (size);
  while (1)
    {
      /* Try to print in the allocated space. */
      int nchars = snprintf (buffer, size,
                             "value of %s is %s",
                             name, value);
      /* If that worked, return the string. */
      if (nchars < size)
        return buffer;
      /* Else try again with twice as much space. */
      size *= 2;
      buffer = (char *) xrealloc (size, buffer);
    }
}
```

In practice, it is often easier just to use `asprintf`, below.

7.10.8 Dynamically Allocating Formatted Output

The functions in this section do formatted output and place the results in dynamically allocated memory.

int asprintf (char **ptr*, const char **template*, ...) *Function*
This function is similar to `sprintf`, except that it dynamically allocates a string (as with `malloc`; see Section 3.3 [Unconstrained Allocation], page 28) to hold the output, instead of putting the output in a buffer you allocate in advance. The *ptr* argument should be the address of a `char *` object, and `asprintf` stores a pointer to the newly allocated string at that location.

Here is how to use `asprintf` to get the same result as the `snprintf` example, but more easily:

```
/* Construct a message describing the value of a variable
   whose name is name and whose value is value. */
char *
make_message (char *name, char *value)
{
  char *result;
  asprintf (&result, "value of %s is %s", name, value);
  return result;
}
```

Chapter 7: Input/Output on Streams   105

> **int obstack_printf** (**struct obstack** *obstack*, **const**   *Function*
>   **char** **template*, ...)
> This function is similar to `asprintf`, except that it uses the obstack
> *obstack* to allocate the space. See Section 3.4 [Obstacks], page 38.
>
> The characters are written onto the end of the current object. To
> get at them, you must finish the object with `obstack_finish` (see
> Section 3.4.6 [Growing Objects], page 42).

7.10.9 Variable Arguments Output Functions

The functions `vprintf` and friends are provided so that you can define your own variadic `printf`-like functions that make use of the same internals as the built-in formatted output functions.

The most natural way to define such functions would be to use a language construct to say, "Call `printf` and pass this template plus all of my arguments after the first five." But there is no way to do this in C, and it would be hard to provide a way, since at the C language level there is no way to tell how many arguments your function received.

Since that method is impossible, we provide alternative functions, the `vprintf` series, which lets you pass a `va_list` to describe "all of my arguments after the first five."

When it is sufficient to define a macro rather than a real function, the GNU C compiler provides a way to do this much more easily with macros. For example:

```
#define myprintf(a, b, c, d, e, rest...) printf (mytemplate , ## rest...)
```

See section "Macros with Variable Numbers of Arguments" in *Using GNU CC*, for details. But this is limited to macros, and does not apply to real functions at all.

Before calling `vprintf` or the other functions listed in this section, you *must* call `va_start` (see Section A.2 [Variadic Functions], page 516) to initialize a pointer to the variable arguments. Then you can call `va_arg` to fetch the arguments that you want to handle yourself. This advances the pointer past those arguments.

Once your `va_list` pointer is pointing at the argument of your choice, you are ready to call `vprintf`. That argument and all subsequent arguments that were passed to your function are used by `vprintf` along with the template that you specified separately.

In some other systems, the `va_list` pointer may become invalid after the call to `vprintf`, so you must not use `va_arg` after you call `vprintf`. Instead, you should call `va_end` to retire the pointer from service. However, you can safely call `va_start` on another pointer variable and begin fetching the arguments again through that pointer. Calling `vprintf` does not destroy the argument list of your function, merely the particular pointer that you passed to it.

GNU C does not have such restrictions. You can safely continue to fetch arguments from a `va_list` pointer after passing it to `vprintf`, and `va_end` is a no-op. (Note, however, that subsequent `va_arg` calls will fetch the same arguments which `vprintf` previously used.)

Prototypes for these functions are declared in 'stdio.h'.

int **vprintf** (const char *template, va_list ap) — Function

This function is similar to `printf` except that, instead of taking a variable number of arguments directly, it takes an argument list pointer ap.

int **vfprintf** (FILE *stream, const char *template, va_list ap) — Function

This is the equivalent of `fprintf` with the variable argument list specified directly as for `vprintf`.

int **vsprintf** (char *s, const char *template, va_list ap) — Function

This is the equivalent of `sprintf` with the variable argument list specified directly as for `vprintf`.

int **vsnprintf** (char *s, size_t size, const char *template, va_list ap) — Function

This is the equivalent of `snprintf` with the variable argument list specified directly as for `vprintf`.

int **vasprintf** (char **ptr, const char *template, va_list ap) — Function

The `vasprintf` function is the equivalent of `asprintf` with the variable argument list specified directly as for `vprintf`.

int **obstack_vprintf** (struct obstack *obstack, const char *template, va_list ap) — Function

The `obstack_vprintf` function is the equivalent of `obstack_printf` with the variable argument list specified directly as for `vprintf`.

Here's an example showing how you might use `vfprintf`. This is a function that prints error messages to the stream `stderr`, along with a prefix indicating the name of the program (see Section 2.3 [Error Messages], page 23, for a description of `program_invocation_short_name`).

Chapter 7: Input/Output on Streams   107

```
#include <stdio.h>
#include <stdarg.h>

void
eprintf (const char *template, ...)
{
  va_list ap;
  extern char *program_invocation_short_name;

  fprintf (stderr, "%s: ", program_invocation_short_name);
  va_start (ap, count);
  vfprintf (stderr, template, ap);
  va_end (ap);
}
```

You could call `eprintf` like this:

```
eprintf ("file '%s' does not exist\n", filename);
```

In GNU C, there is a special construct you can use to let the compiler know that a function uses a `printf`-style format string. Then it can check the number and types of arguments in each call to the function, and warn you when they do not match the format string. For example, take this declaration of `eprintf`:

```
void eprintf (const char *template, ...)
     __attribute__ ((format (printf, 1, 2)));
```

This tells the compiler that `eprintf` uses a format string like `printf` (as opposed to `scanf`; see Section 7.12 [Formatted Input], page 115); the format string appears as the first argument; and the arguments to satisfy the format begin with the second. See section "Declaring Attributes of Functions" in *Using GNU CC*, for more information.

7.10.10 Parsing a Template String

You can use the function `parse_printf_format` to obtain information about the number and types of arguments that are expected by a given template string. This function permits interpreters that provide interfaces to `printf` to avoid passing along invalid arguments from the user's program, which could cause a crash.

All the symbols described in this section are declared in the header file 'printf.h'.

size_t parse_printf_format (const char *template,   *Function*
           size_t *n*, int **argtypes*)

This function returns information about the number and types of arguments expected by the `printf` template string *template*. The information is stored in the array *argtypes*; each element of this array describes one argument. This information is encoded using the various 'PA_' macros, listed below.

The *n* argument specifies the number of elements in the array *argtypes*. This is the most elements that `parse_printf_format` will try to write.

`parse_printf_format` returns the total number of arguments required by *template*. If this number is greater than *n*, then the information returned describes only the first *n* arguments. If you want information about more than that many arguments, allocate a bigger array and call `parse_printf_format` again.

The argument types are encoded as a combination of a basic type and modifier flag bits.

int **PA_FLAG_MASK**   Macro
This macro is a bitmask for the type modifier flag bits. You can write the expression (`argtypes[i]` & `PA_FLAG_MASK`) to extract just the flag bits for an argument, or (`argtypes[i]` & `~PA_FLAG_MASK`) to extract just the basic type code.

Here are symbolic constants that represent the basic types; they stand for integer values.

PA_INT   This specifies that the base type is `int`.

PA_CHAR   This specifies that the base type is `int`, cast to `char`.

PA_STRING
:   This specifies that the base type is `char *`, a null-terminated string.

PA_POINTER
:   This specifies that the base type is `void *`, an arbitrary pointer.

PA_FLOAT   This specifies that the base type is `float`.

PA_DOUBLE
:   This specifies that the base type is `double`.

PA_LAST   You can define additional base types for your own programs as offsets from `PA_LAST`. For example, if you have data types 'foo' and 'bar' with their own specialized `printf` conversions, you could define encodings for these types as:

```
#define PA_FOO   PA_LAST
#define PA_BAR   (PA_LAST + 1)
```

Here are the flag bits that modify a basic type. They are combined with the code for the basic type using inclusive-or.

PA_FLAG_PTR
:   If this bit is set, it indicates that the encoded type is a pointer to the base type, rather than an immediate value. For example, '`PA_INT|PA_FLAG_PTR`' represents the type '`int *`'.

Chapter 7: Input/Output on Streams   109

PA_FLAG_SHORT
> If this bit is set, it indicates that the base type is modified with `short`. (This corresponds to the 'h' type modifier.)

PA_FLAG_LONG
> If this bit is set, it indicates that the base type is modified with `long`. (This corresponds to the 'l' type modifier.)

PA_FLAG_LONG_LONG
> If this bit is set, it indicates that the base type is modified with `long long`. (This corresponds to the 'L' type modifier.)

PA_FLAG_LONG_DOUBLE
> This is a synonym for `PA_FLAG_LONG_LONG`, used by convention with a base type of `PA_DOUBLE` to indicate a type of `long double`.

7.10.11 Example of Parsing a Template String

Here is an example of decoding argument types for a format string. We assume this is part of an interpreter which contains arguments of type NUMBER, CHAR, STRING and STRUCTURE (and perhaps others which are not valid here).

```
/* Test whether the nargs specified objects
   in the vector args are valid
   for the format string format:
   if so, return 1.
   If not, return 0 after printing an error message.  */

int
validate_args (char *format, int nargs, OBJECT *args)
{
  int *argtypes;
  int nwanted;

  /* Get the information about the arguments.
     Each conversion specification must be at least two characters
     long, so there cannot be more specifications than half the
     length of the string.  */

  argtypes = (int *) alloca (strlen (format) / 2 * sizeof (int));
  nwanted = parse_printf_format (string, nelts, argtypes);

  /* Check the number of arguments.  */
  if (nwanted > nargs)
    {
      error ("too few arguments (at least %d required)", nwanted);
      return 0;
    }

  /* Check the C type wanted for each argument
     and see if the object given is suitable.  */
  for (i = 0; i < nwanted; i++)
```

```
      {
        int wanted;

        if (argtypes[i] & PA_FLAG_PTR)
          wanted = STRUCTURE;
        else
          switch (argtypes[i] & ~PA_FLAG_MASK)
            {
            case PA_INT:
            case PA_FLOAT:
            case PA_DOUBLE:
              wanted = NUMBER;
              break;
            case PA_CHAR:
              wanted = CHAR;
              break;
            case PA_STRING:
              wanted = STRING;
              break;
            case PA_POINTER:
              wanted = STRUCTURE;
              break;
            }
        if (TYPE (args[i]) != wanted)
          {
            error ("type mismatch for arg number %d", i);
            return 0;
          }
      }
  return 1;
}
```

7.11 Customizing `printf`

The GNU C library lets you define your own custom conversion specifiers for `printf` template strings, to teach `printf` clever ways to print the important data structures of your program.

The way you do this is by registering the conversion with the function `register_printf_function`; see Section 7.11.1 [Registering New Conversions], page 111. One of the arguments you pass to this function is a pointer to a handler function that produces the actual output; see Section 7.11.3 [Defining the Output Handler], page 113, for information on how to write this function.

You can also install a function that just returns information about the number and type of arguments expected by the conversion specifier. See Section 7.10.10 [Parsing a Template String], page 107, for information about this.

The facilities of this section are declared in the header file 'printf.h'.

Chapter 7: Input/Output on Streams   111

Portability Note: The ability to extend the syntax of `printf` template strings is a GNU extension. ANSI standard C has nothing similar.

7.11.1 Registering New Conversions

The function to register a new output conversion is `register_printf_function`, declared in 'printf.h'.

int **register_printf_function** (int *spec*,   *Function*
        printf_function *handler-function*,
        printf_arginfo_function *arginfo-function*)

This function defines the conversion specifier character *spec*. Thus, if *spec* is '`z`', it defines the conversion '`%z`'. You can redefine the built-in conversions like '`%s`', but flag characters like '`#`' and type modifiers like '`l`' can never be used as conversions; calling `register_printf_function` for those characters has no effect.

The *handler-function* is the function called by `printf` and friends when this conversion appears in a template string. See Section 7.11.3 [Defining the Output Handler], page 113, for information about how to define a function to pass as this argument. If you specify a null pointer, any existing handler function for *spec* is removed.

The *arginfo-function* is the function called by `parse_printf_format` when this conversion appears in a template string. See Section 7.10.10 [Parsing a Template String], page 107, for information about this.

Normally, you install both functions for a conversion at the same time, but if you are never going to call `parse_printf_format`, you do not need to define an arginfo function.

The return value is `0` on success, and `-1` on failure (which occurs if *spec* is out of range).

You can redefine the standard output conversions, but this is probably not a good idea because of the potential for confusion. Library routines written by other people could break if you do this.

7.11.2 Conversion Specifier Options

If you define a meaning for '`%A`', what if the template contains '`%+23A`' or '`%-#A`'? To implement a sensible meaning for these, the handler when called needs to be able to get the options specified in the template.

Both the *handler-function* and *arginfo-function* arguments to `register_printf_function` accept an argument that points to a `struct printf_info`, which contains information about the options appearing in an instance of the conversion specifier. This data type is declared in the header file 'printf.h'.

struct printf_info Type

This structure is used to pass information about the options appearing in an instance of a conversion specifier in a `printf` template string to the handler and arginfo functions for that specifier. It contains the following members:

- **int prec** This is the precision specified. The value is `-1` if no precision was specified. If the precision was given as '`*`', the `printf_info` structure passed to the handler function contains the actual value retrieved from the argument list. But the structure passed to the arginfo function contains a value of `INT_MIN`, since the actual value is not known.

- **int width** This is the minimum field width specified. The value is `0` if no width was specified. If the field width was given as '`*`', the `printf_info` structure passed to the handler function contains the actual value retrieved from the argument list. But the structure passed to the arginfo function contains a value of `INT_MIN`, since the actual value is not known.

- **char spec** This is the conversion specifier character specified. It's stored in the structure so that you can register the same handler function for multiple characters, but still have a way to tell them apart when the handler function is called.

- **unsigned int is_long_double**
  This is a boolean that is true if the 'L', 'll', or 'q' type modifier was specified. For integer conversions, this indicates `long long int`, as opposed to `long double` for floating point conversions.

- **unsigned int is_short**
  This is a boolean that is true if the 'h' type modifier was specified.

- **unsigned int is_long**
  This is a boolean that is true if the 'l' type modifier was specified.

- **unsigned int alt**
  This is a boolean that is true if the '#' flag was specified.

- **unsigned int space**
  This is a boolean that is true if the ' ' flag was specified.

- **unsigned int left**
  This is a boolean that is true if the '-' flag was specified.

- **unsigned int showsign**
  This is a boolean that is true if the '+' flag was specified.

Chapter 7: Input/Output on Streams   113

`unsigned int group`
> This is a boolean that is true if the '`'`' flag was specified.

`char pad`   This is the character to use for padding the output to the minimum field width. The value is '`0`' if the '0' flag was specified, and '` `' otherwise.

7.11.3 Defining the Output Handler

Now let's look at how to define the handler and arginfo functions which are passed as arguments to `register_printf_function`.

You should define your handler functions with a prototype like:
```
int function (FILE *stream, const struct printf_info *info,
              va_list *ap_pointer)
```

The `stream` argument passed to the handler function is the stream to which it should write output.

The `info` argument is a pointer to a structure that contains information about the various options that were included with the conversion in the template string. You should not modify this structure inside your handler function. See Section 7.11.2 [Conversion Specifier Options], page 112, for a description of this data structure.

The `ap_pointer` argument is used to pass the tail of the variable argument list containing the values to be printed to your handler. Unlike most other functions that can be passed an explicit variable argument list, this is a *pointer* to a `va_list`, rather than the `va_list` itself. Thus, you should fetch arguments by means of `va_arg (*ap_pointer, `*type*`)`.

(Passing a pointer here allows the function that calls your handler function to update its own `va_list` variable to account for the arguments that your handler processes. See Section A.2 [Variadic Functions], page 516.)

Your handler function should return a value just like `printf` does: it should return the number of characters it has written, or a negative value to indicate an error.

printf_function   Data Type
This is the data type that a handler function should have.

If you are going to use `parse_printf_format` in your application, you should also define a function to pass as the *arginfo-function* argument for each new conversion you install with `register_printf_function`.

You should define these functions with a prototype like:
```
int function (const struct printf_info *info,
              size_t n, int *argtypes)
```

The return value from the function should be the number of arguments the conversion expects. The function should also fill in no more than *n* elements of the *argtypes* array with information about the types of each of these arguments. This information is encoded using the various 'PA_' macros. (You will notice that this is the same calling convention `parse_printf_format` itself uses.)

printf_arginfo_function   Data Type
    This type is used to describe functions that return information about the number and type of arguments used by a conversion specifier.

7.11.4 `printf` Extension Example

Here is an example showing how to define a `printf` handler function. This program defines a data structure called a `Widget` and defines the '%W' conversion to print information about `Widget *` arguments, including the pointer value and the name stored in the data structure. The '%W' conversion supports the minimum field width and left-justification options, but ignores everything else.

```
#include <stdio.h>
#include <printf.h>
#include <stdarg.h>

typedef struct
  {
    char *name;
  } Widget;

int
print_widget (FILE *stream, const struct printf_info *info, va_list *app)
{
  Widget *w;
  char *buffer;
  int len;

  /* Format the output into a string. */
  w = va_arg (*app, Widget *);
  len = asprintf (&buffer, "<Widget %p: %s>", w, w->name);
  if (len == -1)
    return -1;

  /* Pad to the minimum field width and print to the stream. */
  len = fprintf (stream, "%*s",
                 (info->left ? - info->width : info->width),
                 buffer);

  /* Clean up and return. */
  free (buffer);
  return len;
}


int
```

Chapter 7: Input/Output on Streams 115

```
main (void)
{
  /* Make a widget to print. */
  Widget mywidget;
  mywidget.name = "mywidget";

  /* Register the print function for widgets. */
  register_printf_function ('W', print_widget, NULL); /* No arginfo. */

  /* Now print the widget. */
  printf ("|%W|\n", &mywidget);
  printf ("|%35W|\n", &mywidget);
  printf ("|%-35W|\n", &mywidget);

  return 0;
}
```

The output produced by this program looks like:

```
|<Widget 0xffeffb7c: mywidget>|
|     <Widget 0xffeffb7c: mywidget>|
|<Widget 0xffeffb7c: mywidget>     |
```

7.12 Formatted Input

The functions described in this section (**scanf** and related functions) provide facilities for formatted input analogous to the formatted output facilities. These functions provide a mechanism for reading arbitrary values under the control of a *format string* or *template string*.

7.12.1 Formatted Input Basics

Calls to **scanf** are superficially similar to calls to **printf** in that arbitrary arguments are read under the control of a template string. While the syntax of the conversion specifications in the template is very similar to that for **printf**, the interpretation of the template is oriented more towards free-format input and simple pattern matching, rather than fixed-field formatting. For example, most **scanf** conversions skip over any amount of "white space" (including spaces, tabs, and newlines) in the input file, and there is no concept of precision for the numeric input conversions as there is for the corresponding output conversions. Ordinarily, non-whitespace characters in the template are expected to match characters in the input stream exactly, but a matching failure is distinct from an input error on the stream.

Another area of difference between **scanf** and **printf** is that you must remember to supply pointers rather than immediate values as the optional arguments to **scanf**; the values that are read are stored in the objects that the pointers point to. Even experienced programmers tend to forget this occasionally, so if your program is getting strange errors that seem to be related to `scanf`, you might want to double-check this.

When a *matching failure* occurs, `scanf` returns immediately, leaving the first non-matching character as the next character to be read from the stream. The normal return value from `scanf` is the number of values that were assigned, so you can use this to determine if a matching error happened before all the expected values were read.

The `scanf` function is typically used for things like reading in the contents of tables. For example, here is a function that uses `scanf` to initialize an array of `double`:

```
void
readarray (double *array, int n)
{
  int i;
  for (i=0; i<n; i++)
    if (scanf (" %lf", &(array[i])) != 1)
      invalid_input_error ();
}
```

The formatted input functions are not used as frequently as the formatted output functions. Partly, this is because it takes some care to use them properly. Another reason is that it is difficult to recover from a matching error.

If you are trying to read input that doesn't match a single, fixed pattern, you may be better off using a tool such as Flex to generate a lexical scanner, or Bison to generate a parser, rather than using `scanf`. For more information about these tools, see section "" in *Flex: The Lexical Scanner Generator*, and section "" in *The Bison Reference Manual*.

7.12.2 Input Conversion Syntax

A `scanf` template string is a string that contains ordinary multibyte characters interspersed with conversion specifications that start with '%'.

Any whitespace character (as defined by the `isspace` function; see Section 4.1 [Classification of Characters], page 55) in the template causes any number of whitespace characters in the input stream to be read and discarded. The whitespace characters that are matched need not be exactly the same whitespace characters that appear in the template string. For example, write ' , ' in the template to recognize a comma with optional whitespace before and after.

Other characters in the template string that are not part of conversion specifications must match characters in the input stream exactly; if this is not the case, a matching failure occurs.

The conversion specifications in a `scanf` template string have the general form:

Chapter 7: Input/Output on Streams 117

% *flags width type conversion*

In more detail, an input conversion specification consists of an initial '%' character followed in sequence by:

- An optional *flag character* '*', which says to ignore the text read for this specification. When `scanf` finds a conversion specification that uses this flag, it reads input as directed by the rest of the conversion specification, but it discards this input, does not use a pointer argument, and does not increment the count of successful assignments.
- An optional flag character 'a' (valid with string conversions only) which requests allocation of a buffer long enough to store the string in. (This is a GNU extension.) See Section 7.12.6 [Dynamically Allocating String Conversions], page 122.
- An optional decimal integer that specifies the *maximum field width*. Reading of characters from the input stream stops either when this maximum is reached or when a non-matching character is found, whichever happens first. Most conversions discard initial whitespace characters (those that don't are explicitly documented), and these discarded characters don't count towards the maximum field width. String input conversions store a null character to mark the end of the input; the maximum field width does not include this terminator.
- An optional *type modifier character*. For example, you can specify a type modifier of 'l' with integer conversions such as '%d' to specify that the argument is a pointer to a `long int` rather than a pointer to an `int`.
- A character that specifies the conversion to be applied.

The exact options that are permitted and how they are interpreted vary between the different conversion specifiers. See the descriptions of the individual conversions for information about the particular options that they allow.

With the '-Wformat' option, the GNU C compiler checks calls to `scanf` and related functions. It examines the format string and verifies that the correct number and types of arguments are supplied. There is also a GNU C syntax to tell the compiler that a function you write uses a `scanf`-style format string. See section "Declaring Attributes of Functions" in *Using GNU CC*, for more information.

7.12.3 Table of Input Conversions

Here is a table that summarizes the various conversion specifications:

'%d'   Matches an optionally signed integer written in decimal. See Section 7.12.4 [Numeric Input Conversions], page 119.

'%i'   Matches an optionally signed integer in any of the formats that the C language defines for specifying an integer constant. See Section 7.12.4 [Numeric Input Conversions], page 119.

'%o'   Matches an unsigned integer written in octal radix. See Section 7.12.4 [Numeric Input Conversions], page 119.

'%u'   Matches an unsigned integer written in decimal radix. See Section 7.12.4 [Numeric Input Conversions], page 119.

'%x', '%X'
         Matches an unsigned integer written in hexadecimal radix. See Section 7.12.4 [Numeric Input Conversions], page 119.

'%e', '%f', '%g', '%E', '%G'
         Matches an optionally signed floating-point number. See Section 7.12.4 [Numeric Input Conversions], page 119.

'%s'   Matches a string containing only non-whitespace characters. See Section 7.12.5 [String Input Conversions], page 120.

'%['   Matches a string of characters that belong to a specified set. See Section 7.12.5 [String Input Conversions], page 120.

'%c'   Matches a string of one or more characters; the number of characters read is controlled by the maximum field width given for the conversion. See Section 7.12.5 [String Input Conversions], page 120.

'%p'   Matches a pointer value in the same implementation-defined format used by the '%p' output conversion for `printf`. See Section 7.12.7 [Other Input Conversions], page 122.

'%n'   This conversion doesn't read any characters; it records the number of characters read so far by this call. See Section 7.12.7 [Other Input Conversions], page 122.

'%%'   This matches a literal '%' character in the input stream. No corresponding argument is used. See Section 7.12.7 [Other Input Conversions], page 122.

If the syntax of a conversion specification is invalid, the behavior is undefined. If there aren't enough function arguments provided to supply addresses for all the conversion specifications in the template strings that perform assignments, or if the arguments are not of the correct types, the behavior is also undefined. On the other hand, extra arguments are simply ignored.

7.12.4 Numeric Input Conversions

This section describes the `scanf` conversions for reading numeric values.

Chapter 7: Input/Output on Streams   119

The '%d' conversion matches an optionally signed integer in decimal radix. The syntax that is recognized is the same as that for the `strtol` function (see Section 14.7.1 [Parsing of Integers], page 294) with the value 10 for the *base* argument.

The '%i' conversion matches an optionally signed integer in any of the formats that the C language defines for specifying an integer constant. The syntax that is recognized is the same as that for the `strtol` function (see Section 14.7.1 [Parsing of Integers], page 294) with the value 0 for the *base* argument. (You can print integers in this syntax with `printf` by using the '#' flag character with the '%x', '%o', or '%d' conversion. See Section 7.10.4 [Integer Conversions], page 98.)

For example, any of the strings '10', '0xa', or '012' could be read in as integers under the '%i' conversion. Each of these specifies a number with decimal value 10.

The '%o', '%u', and '%x' conversions match unsigned integers in octal, decimal, and hexadecimal radices, respectively. The syntax that is recognized is the same as that for the `strtoul` function (see Section 14.7.1 [Parsing of Integers], page 294) with the appropriate value (8, 10, or 16) for the *base* argument.

The '%X' conversion is identical to the '%x' conversion. They both permit either uppercase or lowercase letters to be used as digits.

The default type of the corresponding argument for the %d and %i conversions is `int *`, and `unsigned int *` for the other integer conversions. You can use the following type modifiers to specify other sizes of integer:

'h'   Specifies that the argument is a `short int *` or `unsigned short int *`.

'l'   Specifies that the argument is a `long int *` or `unsigned long int *`. Two 'l' characters is like the 'L' modifier, below.

'll'
'L'
'q'   Specifies that the argument is a `long long int *` or `unsigned long long int *`. (The `long long` type is an extension supported by the GNU C compiler. For systems that don't provide extra-long integers, this is the same as `long int`.)

            The 'q' modifier is another name for the same thing, which comes from 4.4 BSD; a `long long int` is sometimes called a "quad" `int`.

All of the '%e', '%f', '%g', '%E', and '%G' input conversions are interchangeable. They all match an optionally signed floating point number, in the same syntax as for the `strtod` function (see Section 14.7.2 [Parsing of Floats], page 296).

For the floating-point input conversions, the default argument type is
`float *`. (This is different from the corresponding output conversions, where
the default type is `double`; remember that `float` arguments to `printf` are
converted to `double` by the default argument promotions, but `float *` arguments are not promoted to `double *`.) You can specify other sizes of float
using these type modifiers:

'l'   Specifies that the argument is of type `double *`.

'L'   Specifies that the argument is of type `long double *`.

7.12.5 String Input Conversions

This section describes the `scanf` input conversions for reading string and
character values: '%s', '%[', and '%c'.

You have two options for how to receive the input from these conversions:

- Provide a buffer to store it in. This is the default. You should provide
  an argument of type `char *`.

  Warning: To make a robust program, you must make sure that the
  input (plus its terminating null) cannot possibly exceed the size of the
  buffer you provide. In general, the only way to do this is to specify a
  maximum field width one less than the buffer size. **If you provide the
  buffer, always specify a maximum field width to prevent overflow.**

- Ask `scanf` to allocate a big enough buffer, by specifying the 'a' flag
  character. This is a GNU extension. You should provide an argument
  of type `char **` for the buffer address to be stored in. See Section 7.12.6
  [Dynamically Allocating String Conversions], page 122.

The '%c' conversion is the simplest: it matches a fixed number of characters, always. The maximum field with says how many characters to read;
if you don't specify the maximum, the default is 1. This conversion doesn't
append a null character to the end of the text it reads. It also does not skip
over initial whitespace characters. It reads precisely the next *n* characters,
and fails if it cannot get that many. Since there is always a maximum field
width with '%c' (whether specified, or 1 by default), you can always prevent
overflow by making the buffer long enough.

The '%s' conversion matches a string of non-whitespace characters. It
skips and discards initial whitespace, but stops when it encounters more
whitespace after having read something. It stores a null character at the
end of the text that it reads.

For example, reading the input:

    hello, world

with the conversion '%10c' produces " hello, wo", but reading the same
input with the conversion '%10s' produces "hello,".

Chapter 7: Input/Output on Streams   121

Warning: If you do not specify a field width for '`%s`', then the number of characters read is limited only by where the next whitespace character appears. This almost certainly means that invalid input can make your program crash—which is a bug.

To read in characters that belong to an arbitrary set of your choice, use the '`%[`' conversion. You specify the set between the '`[`' character and a following '`]`' character, using the same syntax used in regular expressions. As special cases:

- A literal '`]`' character can be specified as the first character of the set.
- An embedded '`-`' character (that is, one that is not the first or last character of the set) is used to specify a range of characters.
- If a caret character '`^`' immediately follows the initial '`[`', then the set of allowed input characters is the everything *except* the characters listed.

The '`%[`' conversion does not skip over initial whitespace characters.

Here are some examples of '`%[`' conversions and what they mean:

'`%25[1234567890]`'
: Matches a string of up to 25 digits.

'`%25[][]`' Matches a string of up to 25 square brackets.

'`%25[^ \f\n\r\t\v]`'
: Matches a string up to 25 characters long that doesn't contain any of the standard whitespace characters. This is slightly different from '`%s`', because if the input begins with a whitespace character, '`%[`' reports a matching failure while '`%s`' simply discards the initial whitespace.

'`%25[a-z]`'
: Matches up to 25 lowercase characters.

One more reminder: the '`%s`' and '`%[`' conversions are **dangerous** if you don't specify a maximum width or use the '`a`' flag, because input too long would overflow whatever buffer you have provided for it. No matter how long your buffer is, a user could supply input that is longer. A well-written program reports invalid input with a comprehensible error message, not with a crash.

7.12.6 Dynamically Allocating String Conversions

A GNU extension to formatted input lets you safely read a string with no maximum size. Using this feature, you don't supply a buffer; instead, `scanf` allocates a buffer big enough to hold the data and gives you its address. To use this feature, write '`a`' as a flag character, as in '`%as`' or '`%a[0-9a-z]`'.

The pointer argument you supply for where to store the input should have type `char **`. The `scanf` function allocates a buffer and stores its address in the word that the argument points to. You should free the buffer with `free` when you no longer need it.

Here is an example of using the 'a' flag with the '%[...]' conversion specification to read a "variable assignment" of the form 'variable = value'.

```
{
  char *variable, *value;

  if (2 > scanf ("%a[a-zA-Z0-9] = %a[^\n]\n",
                 &variable, &value))
    {
      invalid_input_error ();
      return 0;
    }

  ...
}
```

7.12.7 Other Input Conversions

This section describes the miscellaneous input conversions.

The '%p' conversion is used to read a pointer value. It recognizes the same syntax as is used by the '%p' output conversion for `printf` (see Section 7.10.6 [Other Output Conversions], page 101); that is, a hexadecimal number just as the '%x' conversion accepts. The corresponding argument should be of type `void **`; that is, the address of a place to store a pointer.

The resulting pointer value is not guaranteed to be valid if it was not originally written during the same program execution that reads it in.

The '%n' conversion produces the number of characters read so far by this call. The corresponding argument should be of type `int *`. This conversion works in the same way as the '%n' conversion for `printf`; see Section 7.10.6 [Other Output Conversions], page 101, for an example.

The '%n' conversion is the only mechanism for determining the success of literal matches or conversions with suppressed assignments. If the '%n' follows the locus of a matching failure, then no value is stored for it since `scanf` returns before processing the '%n'. If you store -1 in that argument slot before calling `scanf`, the presence of -1 after `scanf` indicates an error occurred before the '%n' was reached.

Finally, the '%%' conversion matches a literal '%' character in the input stream, without using an argument. This conversion does not permit any flags, field width, or type modifier to be specified.

7.12.8 Formatted Input Functions

Here are the descriptions of the functions for performing formatted input. Prototypes for these functions are in the header file 'stdio.h'.

`int scanf (const char *template, ...)` *Function*
The `scanf` function reads formatted input from the stream `stdin` under the control of the template string *template*. The optional arguments are pointers to the places which receive the resulting values.

The return value is normally the number of successful assignments. If an end-of-file condition is detected before any matches are performed (including matches against whitespace and literal characters in the template), then `EOF` is returned.

`int fscanf (FILE *stream, const char *template, ...)` *Function*
This function is just like `scanf`, except that the input is read from the stream *stream* instead of `stdin`.

`int sscanf (const char *s, const char *template, ...)` *Function*
This is like `scanf`, except that the characters are taken from the null-terminated string *s* instead of from a stream. Reaching the end of the string is treated as an end-of-file condition.

The behavior of this function is undefined if copying takes place between objects that overlap—for example, if *s* is also given as an argument to receive a string read under control of the '%s' conversion.

7.12.9 Variable Arguments Input Functions

The functions `vscanf` and friends are provided so that you can define your own variadic `scanf`-like functions that make use of the same internals as the built-in formatted output functions. These functions are analogous to the `vprintf` series of output functions. See Section 7.10.9 [Variable Arguments Output Functions], page 105, for important information on how to use them.

Portability Note: The functions listed in this section are GNU extensions.

`int vscanf (const char *template, va_list ap)` *Function*
This function is similar to `scanf` except that, instead of taking a variable number of arguments directly, it takes an argument list pointer *ap* of type `va_list` (see Section A.2 [Variadic Functions], page 516).

`int vfscanf (FILE *stream, const char *template, va_list ap)` *Function*
This is the equivalent of `fscanf` with the variable argument list specified directly as for `vscanf`.

int **vsscanf** (const char *s, const char *template,   Function
    va_list ap)

    This is the equivalent of `sscanf` with the variable argument list specified directly as for `vscanf`.

In GNU C, there is a special construct you can use to let the compiler know that a function uses a `scanf`-style format string. Then it can check the number and types of arguments in each call to the function, and warn you when they do not match the format string. See section "Declaring Attributes of Functions" in *Using GNU CC*, for details.

7.13 End-Of-File and Errors

Many of the functions described in this chapter return the value of the macro `EOF` to indicate unsuccessful completion of the operation. Since `EOF` is used to report both end of file and random errors, it's often better to use the `feof` function to check explicitly for end of file and `ferror` to check for errors. These functions check indicators that are part of the internal state of the stream object, indicators set if the appropriate condition was detected by a previous I/O operation on that stream.

These symbols are declared in the header file 'stdio.h'.

int **EOF**   Macro

    This macro is an integer value that is returned by a number of functions to indicate an end-of-file condition, or some other error situation. With the GNU library, `EOF` is `-1`. In other libraries, its value may be some other negative number.

void **clearerr** (FILE *stream)   Function

    This function clears the end-of-file and error indicators for the stream *stream*.

    The file positioning functions (see Section 7.15 [File Positioning], page 126) also clear the end-of-file indicator for the stream.

int **feof** (FILE *stream)   Function

    The `feof` function returns nonzero if and only if the end-of-file indicator for the stream *stream* is set.

int **ferror** (FILE *stream)   Function

    The `ferror` function returns nonzero if and only if the error indicator for the stream *stream* is set, indicating that an error has occurred on a previous operation on the stream.

In addition to setting the error indicator associated with the stream, the functions that operate on streams also set `errno` in the same way as

Chapter 7: Input/Output on Streams   125

the corresponding low-level functions that operate on file descriptors. For
example, all of the functions that perform output to a stream—such as
`fputc`, `printf`, and `fflush`—are implemented in terms of `write`, and all
of the `errno` error conditions defined for `write` are meaningful for these
functions. For more information about the descriptor-level I/O functions,
see Chapter 8 [Low-Level Input/Output], page 139.

7.14 Text and Binary Streams

The GNU system and other POSIX-compatible operating systems or-
ganize all files as uniform sequences of characters. However, some other
systems make a distinction between files containing text and files containing
binary data, and the input and output facilities of ANSI C provide for this
distinction. This section tells you how to write programs portable to such
systems.

When you open a stream, you can specify either a *text stream* or a
binary stream. You indicate that you want a binary stream by specifying the
'b' modifier in the *opentype* argument to `fopen`; see Section 7.3 [Opening
Streams], page 84. Without this option, `fopen` opens the file as a text
stream.

Text and binary streams differ in several ways:

- The data read from a text stream is divided into *lines* which are terminated by newline ('\n') characters, while a binary stream is simply a
  long series of characters. A text stream might on some systems fail to
  handle lines more than 254 characters long (including the terminating
  newline character).

- On some systems, text files can contain only printing characters, hori-
  zontal tab characters, and newlines, and so text streams may not support other characters. However, binary streams can handle any character value.

- Space characters that are written immediately preceding a newline character in a text stream may disappear when the file is read in again.

- More generally, there need not be a one-to-one mapping between characters that are read from or written to a text stream, and the characters
  in the actual file.

Since a binary stream is always more capable and more predictable than
a text stream, you might wonder what purpose text streams serve. Why not
simply always use binary streams? The answer is that on these operating
systems, text and binary streams use different file formats, and the only
way to read or write "an ordinary file of text" that can work with other
text-oriented programs is through a text stream.

In the GNU library, and on all POSIX systems, there is no difference between text streams and binary streams. When you open a stream, you get the same kind of stream regardless of whether you ask for binary. This stream can handle any file content, and has none of the restrictions that text streams sometimes have.

7.15 File Positioning

The *file position* of a stream describes where in the file the stream is currently reading or writing. I/O on the stream advances the file position through the file. In the GNU system, the file position is represented as an integer, which counts the number of bytes from the beginning of the file. See Section 6.1.2 [File Position], page 77.

During I/O to an ordinary disk file, you can change the file position whenever you wish, so as to read or write any portion of the file. Some other kinds of files may also permit this. Files which support changing the file position are sometimes referred to as *random-access* files.

You can use the functions in this section to examine or modify the file position indicator associated with a stream. The symbols listed below are declared in the header file 'stdio.h'.

long int ftell (FILE *stream*) *Function*

This function returns the current file position of the stream *stream*.

This function can fail if the stream doesn't support file positioning, or if the file position can't be represented in a `long int`, and possibly for other reasons as well. If a failure occurs, a value of -1 is returned.

int fseek (FILE *stream*, long int *offset*, int *whence*) *Function*

The `fseek` function is used to change the file position of the stream *stream*. The value of *whence* must be one of the constants SEEK_SET, SEEK_CUR, or SEEK_END, to indicate whether the *offset* is relative to the beginning of the file, the current file position, or the end of the file, respectively.

This function returns a value of zero if the operation was successful, and a nonzero value to indicate failure. A successful call also clears the end-of-file indicator of *stream* and discards any characters that were "pushed back" by the use of `ungetc`.

`fseek` either flushes any buffered output before setting the file position or else remembers it so it will be written later in its proper place in the file.

Portability Note: In non-POSIX systems, `ftell` and `fseek` might work reliably only on binary streams. See Section 7.14 [Text and Binary Streams], page 125.

Chapter 7: Input/Output on Streams

The following symbolic constants are defined for use as the *whence* argument to `fseek`. They are also used with the `lseek` function (see Section 8.2 [Input and Output Primitives], page 141) and to specify offsets for file locks (see Section 8.7 [Control Operations on Files], page 153).

`int` **SEEK_SET**   *Macro*
> This is an integer constant which, when used as the *whence* argument to the `fseek` function, specifies that the offset provided is relative to the beginning of the file.

`int` **SEEK_CUR**   *Macro*
> This is an integer constant which, when used as the *whence* argument to the `fseek` function, specifies that the offset provided is relative to the current file position.

`int` **SEEK_END**   *Macro*
> This is an integer constant which, when used as the *whence* argument to the `fseek` function, specifies that the offset provided is relative to the end of the file.

`void` **rewind** (`FILE *`*stream*)   *Function*
> The `rewind` function positions the stream *stream* at the begining of the file. It is equivalent to calling `fseek` on the *stream* with an *offset* argument of `0L` and a *whence* argument of `SEEK_SET`, except that the return value is discarded and the error indicator for the stream is reset.

These three aliases for the 'SEEK_...' constants exist for the sake of compatibility with older BSD systems. They are defined in two different header files: 'fcntl.h' and 'sys/file.h'.

`L_SET`   An alias for `SEEK_SET`.

`L_INCR`   An alias for `SEEK_CUR`.

`L_XTND`   An alias for `SEEK_END`.

7.16 Portable File-Position Functions

On the GNU system, the file position is truly a character count. You can specify any character count value as an argument to `fseek` and get reliable results for any random access file. However, some ANSI C systems do not represent file positions in this way.

On some systems where text streams truly differ from binary streams, it is impossible to represent the file position of a text stream as a count of characters from the beginning of the file. For example, the file position on some systems must encode both a record offset within the file, and a character offset within the record.

As a consequence, if you want your programs to be portable to these systems, you must observe certain rules:

- The value returned from `ftell` on a text stream has no predictable relationship to the number of characters you have read so far. The only thing you can rely on is that you can use it subsequently as the *offset* argument to `fseek` to move back to the same file position.

- In a call to `fseek` on a text stream, either the *offset* must either be zero; or *whence* must be `SEEK_SET` and the *offset* must be the result of an earlier call to `ftell` on the same stream.

- The value of the file position indicator of a text stream is undefined while there are characters that have been pushed back with `ungetc` that haven't been read or discarded. See Section 7.8 [Unreading], page 91.

But even if you observe these rules, you may still have trouble for long files, because `ftell` and `fseek` use a `long int` value to represent the file position. This type may not have room to encode all the file positions in a large file.

So if you do want to support systems with peculiar encodings for the file positions, it is better to use the functions `fgetpos` and `fsetpos` instead. These functions represent the file position using the data type `fpos_t`, whose internal representation varies from system to system.

These symbols are declared in the header file 'stdio.h'.

fpos_t *Data Type*

This is the type of an object that can encode information about the file position of a stream, for use by the functions `fgetpos` and `fsetpos`.

In the GNU system, `fpos_t` is equivalent to `off_t` or `long int`. In other systems, it might have a different internal representation.

int fgetpos (FILE **stream*, fpos_t **position*) *Function*

This function stores the value of the file position indicator for the stream *stream* in the `fpos_t` object pointed to by *position*. If successful, `fgetpos` returns zero; otherwise it returns a nonzero value and stores an implementation-defined positive value in `errno`.

int fsetpos (FILE **stream*, const fpos_t *position*) *Function*

This function sets the file position indicator for the stream *stream* to the position *position*, which must have been set by a previous call to `fgetpos` on the same stream. If successful, `fsetpos` clears the end-of-file indicator on the stream, discards any characters that were "pushed back" by the use of `ungetc`, and returns a value of zero. Otherwise, `fsetpos` returns a nonzero value and stores an implementation-defined positive value in `errno`.

7.17 Stream Buffering

Characters that are written to a stream are normally accumulated and transmitted asynchronously to the file in a block, instead of appearing as soon as they are output by the application program. Similarly, streams often retrieve input from the host environment in blocks rather than on a character-by-character basis. This is called *buffering*.

If you are writing programs that do interactive input and output using streams, you need to understand how buffering works when you design the user interface to your program. Otherwise, you might find that output (such as progress or prompt messages) doesn't appear when you intended it to, or other unexpected behavior.

This section deals only with controlling when characters are transmitted between the stream and the file or device, and *not* with how things like echoing, flow control, and the like are handled on specific classes of devices. For information on common control operations on terminal devices, see Chapter 12 [Low-Level Terminal Interface], page 255.

You can bypass the stream buffering facilities altogether by using the low-level input and output functions that operate on file descriptors instead. See Chapter 8 [Low-Level Input/Output], page 139.

7.17.1 Buffering Concepts

There are three different kinds of buffering strategies:
- Characters written to or read from an *unbuffered* stream are transmitted individually to or from the file as soon as possible.
- Characters written to a *line buffered* stream are transmitted to the file in blocks when a newline character is encountered.
- Characters written to or read from a *fully buffered* stream are transmitted to or from the file in blocks of arbitrary size.

Newly opened streams are normally fully buffered, with one exception: a stream connected to an interactive device such as a terminal is initially line buffered. See Section 7.17.3 [Controlling Which Kind of Buffering], page 131, for information on how to select a different kind of buffering. Usually the automatic selection gives you the most convenient kind of buffering for the file or device you open.

The use of line buffering for interactive devices implies that output messages ending in a newline will appear immediately—which is usually what you want. Output that doesn't end in a newline might or might not show up immediately, so if you want them to appear immediately, you should flush buffered output explicitly with `fflush`, as described in Section 7.17.2 [Flushing Buffers], page 130.

7.17.2 Flushing Buffers

Flushing output on a buffered stream means transmitting all accumulated characters to the file. There are many circumstances when buffered output on a stream is flushed automatically:

- When you try to do output and the output buffer is full.
- When the stream is closed. See Section 7.4 [Closing Streams], page 86.
- When the program terminates by calling `exit`. See Section 22.3.1 [Normal Termination], page 437.
- When a newline is written, if the stream is line buffered.
- Whenever an input operation on *any* stream actually reads data from its file.

If you want to flush the buffered output at another time, call `fflush`, which is declared in the header file 'stdio.h'.

int fflush (FILE *stream*) *Function*
    This function causes any buffered output on *stream* to be delivered to the file. If *stream* is a null pointer, then `fflush` causes buffered output on *all* open output streams to be flushed.

    This function returns `EOF` if a write error occurs, or zero otherwise.

    Compatibility Note: Some brain-damaged operating systems have been known to be so thoroughly fixated on line-oriented input and output that flushing a line buffered stream causes a newline to be written! Fortunately, this "feature" seems to be becoming less common. You do not need to worry about this in the GNU system.

7.17.3 Controlling Which Kind of Buffering

After opening a stream (but before any other operations have been performed on it), you can explicitly specify what kind of buffering you want it to have using the `setvbuf` function.

The facilities listed in this section are declared in the header file 'stdio.h'.

int setvbuf (FILE *stream*, char *buf*, int *mode*, size_t *size*) *Function*
    This function is used to specify that the stream *stream* should have the buffering mode *mode*, which can be either `_IOFBF` (for full buffering), `_IOLBF` (for line buffering), or `_IONBF` (for unbuffered input/output).

    If you specify a null pointer as the *buf* argument, then `setvbuf` allocates a buffer itself using `malloc`. This buffer will be freed when you close the stream.

Chapter 7: Input/Output on Streams   131

Otherwise, *buf* should be a character array that can hold at least *size* characters. You should not free the space for this array as long as the stream remains open and this array remains its buffer. You should usually either allocate it statically, or `malloc` (see Section 3.3 [Unconstrained Allocation], page 28) the buffer. Using an automatic array is not a good idea unless you close the file before exiting the block that declares the array.

While the array remains a stream buffer, the stream I/O functions will use the buffer for their internal purposes. You shouldn't try to access the values in the array directly while the stream is using it for buffering.

The `setvbuf` function returns zero on success, or a nonzero value if the value of *mode* is not valid or if the request could not be honored.

int _IOFBF   Macro
The value of this macro is an integer constant expression that can be used as the *mode* argument to the `setvbuf` function to specify that the stream should be fully buffered.

int _IOLBF   Macro
The value of this macro is an integer constant expression that can be used as the *mode* argument to the `setvbuf` function to specify that the stream should be line buffered.

int _IONBF   Macro
The value of this macro is an integer constant expression that can be used as the *mode* argument to the `setvbuf` function to specify that the stream should be unbuffered.

int BUFSIZ   Macro
The value of this macro is an integer constant expression that is good to use for the *size* argument to `setvbuf`. This value is guaranteed to be at least 256.

The value of BUFSIZ is chosen on each system so as to make stream I/O efficient. So it is a good idea to use BUFSIZ as the size for the buffer when you call `setvbuf`.

Actually, you can get an even better value to use for the buffer size by means of the `fstat` system call: it is found in the `st_blksize` field of the file attributes. See Section 9.8.1 [What the File Attribute Values Mean], page 181.

Sometimes people also use BUFSIZ as the allocation size of buffers used for related purposes, such as strings used to receive a line of input with `fgets` (see Section 7.6 [Character Input], page 88). There is no particular reason to use BUFSIZ for this instead of any other integer, except that it might lead to doing I/O in chunks of an efficient size.

`void` **setbuf** (`FILE` *stream*, `char` *buf*)   *Function*
: If *buf* is a null pointer, the effect of this function is equivalent to calling `setvbuf` with a *mode* argument of `_IONBF`. Otherwise, it is equivalent to calling `setvbuf` with *buf*, and a *mode* of `_IOFBF` and a *size* argument of `BUFSIZ`.

  The `setbuf` function is provided for compatibility with old code; use `setvbuf` in all new programs.

`void` **setbuffer** (`FILE` *stream*, `char` *buf*, `size_t` *size*)   *Function*
: If *buf* is a null pointer, this function makes *stream* unbuffered. Otherwise, it makes *stream* fully buffered using *buf* as the buffer. The *size* argument specifies the length of *buf*.

  This function is provided for compatibility with old BSD code. Use `setvbuf` instead.

`void` **setlinebuf** (`FILE` *stream*)   *Function*
: This function makes *stream* be line buffered, and allocates the buffer for you.

  This function is provided for compatibility with old BSD code. Use `setvbuf` instead.

7.18 Other Kinds of Streams

The GNU library provides ways for you to define additional kinds of streams that do not necessarily correspond to an open file.

One such type of stream takes input from or writes output to a string. These kinds of streams are used internally to implement the `sprintf` and `sscanf` functions. You can also create such a stream explicitly, using the functions described in Section 7.18.1 [String Streams], page 133.

More generally, you can define streams that do input/output to arbitrary objects using functions supplied by your program. This protocol is discussed in Section 7.18.3 [Programming Your Own Custom Streams], page 136.

Portability Note: The facilities described in this section are specific to GNU. Other systems or C implementations might or might not provide equivalent functionality.

7.18.1 String Streams

The `fmemopen` and `open_memstream` functions allow you to do I/O to a string or memory buffer. These facilities are declared in '`stdio.h`'.

Chapter 7: Input/Output on Streams   133

FILE * **fmemopen** (void *buf*, size_t *size*, const   Function
         char *opentype*)

This function opens a stream that allows the access specified by the *opentype* argument, that reads from or writes to the buffer specified by the argument *buf*. This array must be at least *size* bytes long.

If you specify a null pointer as the *buf* argument, **fmemopen** dynamically allocates (as with **malloc**; see Section 3.3 [Unconstrained Allocation], page 28) an array *size* bytes long. This is really only useful if you are going to write things to the buffer and then read them back in again, because you have no way of actually getting a pointer to the buffer (for this, try **open_memstream**, below). The buffer is freed when the stream is open.

The argument *opentype* is the same as in **fopen** (See Section 7.3 [Opening Streams], page 84). If the *opentype* specifies append mode, then the initial file position is set to the first null character in the buffer. Otherwise the initial file position is at the beginning of the buffer.

When a stream open for writing is flushed or closed, a null character (zero byte) is written at the end of the buffer if it fits. You should add an extra byte to the *size* argument to account for this. Attempts to write more than *size* bytes to the buffer result in an error.

For a stream open for reading, null characters (zero bytes) in the buffer do not count as "end of file". Read operations indicate end of file only when the file position advances past *size* bytes. So, if you want to read characters from a null-terminated string, you should supply the length of the string as the *size* argument.

Here is an example of using **fmemopen** to create a stream for reading from a string:

```
#include <stdio.h>

static char buffer[] = "foobar";

int
main (void)
{
  int ch;
  FILE *stream;

  stream = fmemopen (buffer, strlen (buffer), "r");
  while ((ch = fgetc (stream)) != EOF)
    printf ("Got %c\n", ch);
  fclose (stream);

  return 0;
}
```

This program produces the following output:

```
Got f
Got o
Got o
Got b
Got a
Got r
```

FILE * open_memstream (char **`*ptr`*, size_t *sizeloc*) *Function*

This function opens a stream for writing to a buffer. The buffer is allocated dynamically (as with `malloc`; see Section 3.3 [Unconstrained Allocation], page 28) and grown as necessary.

When the stream is closed with `fclose` or flushed with `fflush`, the locations *ptr* and *sizeloc* are updated to contain the pointer to the buffer and its size. The values thus stored remain valid only as long as no further output on the stream takes place. If you do more output, you must flush the stream again to store new values before you use them again.

A null character is written at the end of the buffer. This null character is *not* included in the size value stored at *sizeloc*.

You can move the stream's file position with `fseek` (see Section 7.15 [File Positioning], page 126). Moving the file position past the end of the data already written fills the intervening space with zeroes.

Here is an example of using `open_memstream`:

```
#include <stdio.h>

int
main (void)
{
  char *bp;
  size_t size;
  FILE *stream;

  stream = open_memstream (&bp, &size);
  fprintf (stream, "hello");
  fflush (stream);
  printf ("buf = '%s', size = %d\n", bp, size);
  fprintf (stream, ", world");
  fclose (stream);
  printf ("buf = '%s', size = %d\n", bp, size);

  return 0;
}
```

This program produces the following output:

```
buf = 'hello', size = 5
buf = 'hello, world', size = 12
```

Chapter 7: Input/Output on Streams   135

7.18.2 Obstack Streams

You can open an output stream that puts it data in an obstack. See
Section 3.4 [Obstacks], page 38.

FILE * open_obstack_stream (`struct obstack`   *Function*
         obstack)
   This function opens a stream for writing data into the obstack *obstack*.
   This starts an object in the obstack and makes it grow as data is
   written (see Section 3.4.6 [Growing Objects], page 42).

   Calling `fflush` on this stream updates the current size of the object
   to match the amount of data that has been written. After a call to
   `fflush`, you can examine the object temporarily.

   You can move the file position of an obstack stream with `fseek` (see
   Section 7.15 [File Positioning], page 126). Moving the file position past
   the end of the data written fills the intervening space with zeros.

   To make the object permanent, update the obstack with `fflush`, and
   then use `obstack_finish` to finalize the object and get its address.
   The following write to the stream starts a new object in the obstack,
   and later writes add to that object until you do another `fflush` and
   `obstack_finish`.

   But how do you find out how long the object is? You can get the length
   in bytes by calling `obstack_object_size` (see Section 3.4.8 [Status of
   an Obstack], page 45), or you can null-terminate the object like this:

         obstack_1grow (*obstack*, 0);

   Whichever one you do, you must do it *before* calling `obstack_finish`.
   (You can do both if you wish.)

   Here is a sample function that uses `open_obstack_stream`:

```
char *
make_message_string (const char *a, int b)
{
  FILE *stream = open_obstack_stream (&message_obstack);
  output_task (stream);
  fprintf (stream, ": ");
  fprintf (stream, a, b);
  fprintf (stream, "\n");
  fclose (stream);
  obstack_1grow (&message_obstack, 0);
  return obstack_finish (&message_obstack);
}
```

7.18.3 Programming Your Own Custom Streams

This section describes how you can make a stream that gets input from an arbitrary data source or writes output to an arbitrary data sink programmed by you. We call these *custom streams*.

7.18.3.1 Custom Streams and Cookies

Inside every custom stream is a special object called the *cookie*. This is an object supplied by you which records where to fetch or store the data read or written. It is up to you to define a data type to use for the cookie. The stream functions in the library never refer directly to its contents, and they don't even know what the type is; they record its address with type `void *`.

To implement a custom stream, you must specify *how* to fetch or store the data in the specified place. You do this by defining *hook functions* to read, write, change "file position", and close the stream. All four of these functions will be passed the stream's cookie so they can tell where to fetch or store the data. The library functions don't know what's inside the cookie, but your functions will know.

When you create a custom stream, you must specify the cookie pointer, and also the four hook functions stored in a structure of type `cookie_io_functions_t`.

These facilities are declared in 'stdio.h'.

cookie_io_functions_t Data Type

This is a structure type that holds the functions that define the communications protocol between the stream and its cookie. It has the following members:

`cookie_read_function_t *read`
: This is the function that reads data from the cookie. If the value is a null pointer instead of a function, then read operations on ths stream always return `EOF`.

`cookie_write_function_t *write`
: This is the function that writes data to the cookie. If the value is a null pointer instead of a function, then data written to the stream is discarded.

`cookie_seek_function_t *seek`
: This is the function that performs the equivalent of file positioning on the cookie. If the value is a null pointer instead of a function, calls to `fseek` on this stream can only seek to locations within the buffer; any attempt to seek outside the buffer will return an `ESPIPE` error.

Chapter 7: Input/Output on Streams 137

> `cookie_close_function_t *close`
>> This function performs any appropriate cleanup on the cookie when closing the stream. If the value is a null pointer instead of a function, nothing special is done to close the cookie when the stream is closed.

FILE * **fopencookie** (`void` *cookie*, `const char` *Function*
         `*opentype`, `cookie_io_functions_t` io-functions)
This function actually creates the stream for communicating with the *cookie* using the functions in the *io-functions* argument. The *opentype* argument is interpreted as for `fopen`; see Section 7.3 [Opening Streams], page 84. (But note that the "truncate on open" option is ignored.) The new stream is fully buffered.

The `fopencookie` function returns the newly created stream, or a null pointer in case of an error.

7.18.3.2 Custom Stream Hook Functions

Here are more details on how you should define the four hook functions that a custom stream needs.

You should define the function to read data from the cookie as:

> `ssize_t` *reader* (`void` *cookie*, `void` *buffer*, `size_t` *size*)

This is very similar to the `read` function; see Section 8.2 [Input and Output Primitives], page 141. Your function should transfer up to *size* bytes into the *buffer*, and return the number of bytes read, or zero to indicate end-of-file. You can return a value of `-1` to indicate an error.

You should define the function to write data to the cookie as:

> `ssize_t` *writer* (`void` *cookie*, `const void` *buffer*, `size_t` *size*)

This is very similar to the `write` function; see Section 8.2 [Input and Output Primitives], page 141. Your function should transfer up to *size* bytes from the buffer, and return the number of bytes written. You can return a value of `-1` to indicate an error.

You should define the function to perform seek operations on the cookie as:

> `int` *seeker* (`void` *cookie*, `fpos_t` *position*, `int` *whence*)

For this function, the *position* and *whence* arguments are interpreted as for `fgetpos`; see Section 7.16 [Portable File-Position Functions], page 128. In the GNU library, `fpos_t` is equivalent to `off_t` or `long int`, and simply represents the number of bytes from the beginning of the file.

After doing the seek operation, your function should store the resulting file position relative to the beginning of the file in *position*. Your function should return a value of `0` on success and `-1` to indicate an error.

You should define the function to do cleanup operations on the cookie appropriate for closing the stream as:

`int cleaner (void *cookie)`

Your function should return -1 to indicate an error, and 0 otherwise.

cookie_read_function   Data Type
This is the data type that the read function for a custom stream should have. If you declare the function as shown above, this is the type it will have.

cookie_write_function   Data Type
The data type of the write function for a custom stream.

cookie_seek_function   Data Type
The data type of the seek function for a custom stream.

cookie_close_function   Data Type
The data type of the close function for a custom stream.

8 Low-Level Input/Output

This chapter describes functions for performing low-level input/output operations on file descriptors. These functions include the primitives for the higher-level I/O functions described in Chapter 7 [Input/Output on Streams], page 83, as well as functions for performing low-level control operations for which there are no equivalents on streams.

Stream-level I/O is more flexible and usually more convenient; therefore, programmers generally use the descriptor-level functions only when necessary. These are some of the usual reasons:

- For reading binary files in large chunks.
- For reading an entire file into core before parsing it.
- To perform operations other than data transfer, which can only be done with a descriptor. (You can use `fileno` to get the descriptor corresponding to a stream.)
- To pass descriptors to a child process. (The child can create its own stream to use a descriptor that it inherits, but cannot inherit a stream directly.)

8.1 Opening and Closing Files

This section describes the primitives for opening and closing files using file descriptors. The `open` and `creat` functions are declared in the header file 'fcntl.h', while `close` is declared in 'unistd.h'.

`int open (const char *filename, int flags[, mode_t`   Function
    `mode])`

The `open` function creates and returns a new file descriptor for the file named by *filename*. Initially, the file position indicator for the file is at the beginning of the file. The argument *mode* is used only when a file is created, but it doesn't hurt to supply the argument in any case.

The *flags* argument controls how the file is to be opened. This is a bit mask; you create the value by the bitwise OR of the appropriate parameters (using the '|' operator in C). See Section 8.10 [File Status Flags], page 158, for the parameters available.

The normal return value from `open` is a non-negative integer file descriptor. In the case of an error, a value of `-1` is returned instead. In addition to the usual file name errors (see Section 6.2.3 [File Name Errors], page 79), the following `errno` error conditions are defined for this function:

EACCES   The file exists but is not readable/writable as requested by
              the *flags* argument, the file does not exist and the directory
              is unwritable so it cannot be created.

EEXIST   Both `O_CREAT` and `O_EXCL` are set, and the named file
              already exists.

EINTR   The `open` operation was interrupted by a signal. See Section 21.5 [Primitives Interrupted by Signals], page 402.

EISDIR   The *flags* argument specified write access, and the file is a
              directory.

EMFILE   The process has too many files open. The maximum number of file descriptors is controlled by the `RLIMIT_NOFILE` resource limit; see Section 17.6 [Limiting Resource Usage], page 341.

ENFILE   The entire system, or perhaps the file system which contains the directory, cannot support any additional open files at the moment. (This problem cannot happen on the GNU system.)

ENOENT   The named file does not exist, and `O_CREAT` is not specified.

ENOSPC   The directory or file system that would contain the new file cannot be extended, because there is no disk space left.

ENXIO   `O_NONBLOCK` and `O_WRONLY` are both set in the *flags* argument, the file named by *filename* is a FIFO (see Chapter 10 [Pipes and FIFOs], page 201), and no process has the file open for reading.

EROFS   The file resides on a read-only file system and any of `O_WRONLY`, `O_RDWR`, and `O_TRUNC` are set in the *flags* argument, or `O_CREAT` is set and the file does not already exist.

The `open` function is the underlying primitive for the `fopen` and `freopen` functions, that create streams.

int **creat** (const char *filename*, mode_t   Obsolete function
              mode)

This function is obsolete. The call:

    creat (*filename*, *mode*)

is equivalent to:

    open (*filename*, O_WRONLY | O_CREAT | O_TRUNC, *mode*)

Chapter 8: Low-Level Input/Output   141

`int close` (`int` *filedes*)   *Function*
    The function `close` closes the file descriptor *filedes*. Closing a file has
    the following consequences:
    - The file descriptor is deallocated.
    - Any record locks owned by the process on the file are unlocked.
    - When all file descriptors associated with a pipe or FIFO have been
      closed, any unread data is discarded.

    The normal return value from `close` is 0; a value of `-1` is returned in
    case of failure. The following `errno` error conditions are defined for
    this function:

    `EBADF`   The *filedes* argument is not a valid file descriptor.

    `EINTR`   The `close` call was interrupted by a signal. See Section 21.5 [Primitives Interrupted by Signals], page 402.
                Here is an example of how to handle `EINTR` properly:
                    `TEMP_FAILURE_RETRY (close (desc));`

    `ENOSPC`
    `EIO`
    `EDQUOT`   When the file is accessed by NFS, these errors from `write` can sometimes not be detected until `close`. See Section 8.2 [Input and Output Primitives], page 141, for details on their meaning.

To close a stream, call `fclose` (see Section 7.4 [Closing Streams], page 86) instead of trying to close its underlying file descriptor with `close`. This flushes any buffered output and updates the stream object to indicate that it is closed.

8.2 Input and Output Primitives

This section describes the functions for performing primitive input and output operations on file descriptors: `read`, `write`, and `lseek`. These functions are declared in the header file 'unistd.h'.

`ssize_t`   *Data Type*
    This data type is used to represent the sizes of blocks that can be read
    or written in a single operation. It is similar to `size_t`, but must be
    a signed type.

`ssize_t read` (`int` *filedes*, `void` **buffer*, `size_t` *size*)   *Function*
    The `read` function reads up to *size* bytes from the file with descriptor
    filedes, storing the results in the *buffer*. (This is not necessarily a
    character string and there is no terminating null character added.)

The return value is the number of bytes actually read. This might be less than *size*; for example, if there aren't that many bytes left in the file or if there aren't that many bytes immediately available. The exact behavior depends on what kind of file it is. Note that reading less than *size* bytes is not an error.

A value of zero indicates end-of-file (except if the value of the *size* argument is also zero). This is not considered an error. If you keep calling `read` while at end-of-file, it will keep returning zero and doing nothing else.

If `read` returns at least one character, there is no way you can tell whether end-of-file was reached. But if you did reach the end, the next read will return zero.

In case of an error, `read` returns -1. The following `errno` error conditions are defined for this function:

`EAGAIN` Normally, when no input is immediately available, `read` waits for some input. But if the `O_NONBLOCK` flag is set for the file (see Section 8.10 [File Status Flags], page 158), `read` returns immediately without reading any data, and reports this error.

Compatibility Note: Most versions of BSD Unix use a different error code for this: EWOULDBLOCK. In the GNU library, `EWOULDBLOCK` is an alias for `EAGAIN`, so it doesn't matter which name you use.

On some systems, reading a large amount of data from a character special file can also fail with `EAGAIN` if the kernel cannot find enough physical memory to lock down the user's pages. This is limited to devices that transfer with direct memory access into the user's memory, which means it does not include terminals, since they always use separate buffers inside the kernel. This problem never happens in the GNU system.

Any condition that could result in `EAGAIN` can instead result in a successful `read` which returns fewer bytes than requested. Calling `read` again immediately would result in `EAGAIN`.

`EBADF`   The *filedes* argument is not a valid file descriptor, or is not open for reading.

`EINTR`   `read` was interrupted by a signal while it was waiting for input. See Section 21.5 [Primitives Interrupted by Signals], page 402. A signal will not necessary cause `read` to return `EINTR`; it may instead result in a successful `read` which returns fewer bytes than requested.

Chapter 8: Low-Level Input/Output

EIO
: For many devices, and for disk files, this error code indicates a hardware error.

  EIO also occurs when a background process tries to read from the controlling terminal, and the normal action of stopping the process by sending it a SIGTTIN signal isn't working. This might happen if signal is being blocked or ignored, or because the process group is orphaned. See Chapter 24 [Job Control], page 457, for more information about job control, and Chapter 21 [Signal Handling], page 371, for information about signals.

The `read` function is the underlying primitive for all of the functions that read from streams, such as `fgetc`.

ssize_t write (int *filedes*, const void **buffer*, size_t *size*)   *Function*

The `write` function writes up to *size* bytes from *buffer* to the file with descriptor *filedes*. The data in *buffer* is not necessarily a character string and a null character is output like any other character.

The return value is the number of bytes actually written. This may be *size*, but can always be smaller. Your program should always call `write` in a loop, iterating until all the data is written.

Once `write` returns, the data is enqueued to be written and can be read back right away, but it is not necessarily written out to permanent storage immediately. You can use `fsync` when you need to be sure your data has been permanently stored before continuing. (It is more efficient for the system to batch up consecutive writes and do them all at once when convenient. Normally they will always be written to disk within a minute or less.) You can use the O_FSYNC open mode to make `write` always store the data to disk before returning; see Section 8.10.3 [I/O Operating Modes], page 161.

In the case of an error, `write` returns -1. The following `errno` error conditions are defined for this function:

EAGAIN
: Normally, `write` blocks until the write operation is complete. But if the O_NONBLOCK flag is set for the file (see Section 8.7 [Control Operations on Files], page 153), it returns immediately without writing any data, and reports this error. An example of a situation that might cause the process to block on output is writing to a terminal device that supports flow control, where output has been suspended by receipt of a STOP character.

  Compatibility Note: Most versions of BSD Unix use a different error code for this: EWOULDBLOCK. In the GNU library, `EWOULDBLOCK` is an alias for `EAGAIN`, so it doesn't matter which name you use.

On some systems, writing a large amount of data from a character special file can also fail with `EAGAIN` if the kernel cannot find enough physical memory to lock down the user's pages. This is limited to devices that transfer with direct memory access into the user's memory, which means it does not include terminals, since they always use separate buffers inside the kernel. This problem does not arise in the GNU system.

`EBADF` The *filedes* argument is not a valid file descriptor, or is not open for writing.

`EFBIG` The size of the file would become larger than the implementation can support.

`EINTR` The `write` operation was interrupted by a signal while it was blocked waiting for completion. A signal will not necessary cause `write` to return `EINTR`; it may instead result in a successful `write` which writes fewer bytes than requested. See Section 21.5 [Primitives Interrupted by Signals], page 402.

`EIO` For many devices, and for disk files, this error code indicates a hardware error.

`ENOSPC` The device containing the file is full.

`EPIPE` This error is returned when you try to write to a pipe or FIFO that isn't open for reading by any process. When this happens, a `SIGPIPE` signal is also sent to the process; see Chapter 21 [Signal Handling], page 371.

Unless you have arranged to prevent `EINTR` failures, you should check `errno` after each failing call to `write`, and if the error was `EINTR`, you should simply repeat the call. See Section 21.5 [Primitives Interrupted by Signals], page 402. The easy way to do this is with the macro `TEMP_FAILURE_RETRY`, as follows:

```
nbytes = TEMP_FAILURE_RETRY (write (desc, buffer, count));
```

The `write` function is the underlying primitive for all of the functions that write to streams, such as `fputc`.

8.3 Setting the File Position of a Descriptor

Just as you can set the file position of a stream with `fseek`, you can set the file position of a descriptor with `lseek`. This specifies the position in the

Chapter 8: Low-Level Input/Output

file for the next `read` or `write` operation. See Section 7.15 [File Positioning], page 126, for more information on the file position and what it means.

To read the current file position value from a descriptor, use `lseek (desc, 0, SEEK_CUR)`.

`off_t` **lseek** (`int` *filedes*, `off_t` *offset*, `int` *whence*)   *Function*
The `lseek` function is used to change the file position of the file with descriptor *filedes*.

The *whence* argument specifies how the *offset* should be interpreted in the same way as for the `fseek` function, and must be one of the symbolic constants `SEEK_SET`, `SEEK_CUR`, or `SEEK_END`.

`SEEK_SET`   Specifies that *whence* is a count of characters from the beginning of the file.

`SEEK_CUR`   Specifies that *whence* is a count of characters from the current file position. This count may be positive or negative.

`SEEK_END`   Specifies that *whence* is a count of characters from the end of the file. A negative count specifies a position within the current extent of the file; a positive count specifies a position past the current end. If you set the position past the current end, and actually write data, you will extend the file with zeros up to that position.

The return value from `lseek` is normally the resulting file position, measured in bytes from the beginning of the file. You can use this feature together with `SEEK_CUR` to read the current file position.

If you want to append to the file, setting the file position to the current end of file with `SEEK_END` is not sufficient. Another process may write more data after you seek but before you write, extending the file so the position you write onto clobbers their data. Instead, use the `O_APPEND` operating mode; see Section 8.10.3 [I/O Operating Modes], page 161.

You can set the file position past the current end of the file. This does not by itself make the file longer; `lseek` never changes the file. But subsequent output at that position will extend the file. Characters between the previous end of file and the new position are filled with zeros. Extending the file in this way can create a "hole": the blocks of zeros are not actually allocated on disk, so the file takes up less space than it appears so; it is then called a "sparse file".

If the file position cannot be changed, or the operation is in some way invalid, `lseek` returns a value of `-1`. The following `errno` error conditions are defined for this function:

`EBADF`   The *filedes* is not a valid file descriptor.

EINVAL   The *whence* argument value is not valid, or the resulting file offset is not valid. A file offset is invalid.

ESPIPE   The *filedes* corresponds to an object that cannot be positioned, such as a pipe, FIFO or terminal device. (POSIX.1 specifies this error only for pipes and FIFOs, but in the GNU system, you always get **ESPIPE** if the object is not seekable.)

The **lseek** function is the underlying primitive for the **fseek**, **ftell** and **rewind** functions, which operate on streams instead of file descriptors.

You can have multiple descriptors for the same file if you open the file more than once, or if you duplicate a descriptor with **dup**. Descriptors that come from separate calls to **open** have independent file positions; using **lseek** on one descriptor has no effect on the other. For example,

```
{
  int d1, d2;
  char buf[4];
  d1 = open ("foo", O_RDONLY);
  d2 = open ("foo", O_RDONLY);
  lseek (d1, 1024, SEEK_SET);
  read (d2, buf, 4);
}
```

will read the first four characters of the file 'foo'. (The error-checking code necessary for a real program has been omitted here for brevity.)

By contrast, descriptors made by duplication share a common file position with the original descriptor that was duplicated. Anything which alters the file position of one of the duplicates, including reading or writing data, affects all of them alike. Thus, for example,

```
{
  int d1, d2, d3;
  char buf1[4], buf2[4];
  d1 = open ("foo", O_RDONLY);
  d2 = dup (d1);
  d3 = dup (d2);
  lseek (d3, 1024, SEEK_SET);
  read (d1, buf1, 4);
  read (d2, buf2, 4);
}
```

will read four characters starting with the 1024'th character of 'foo', and then four more characters starting with the 1028'th character.

off_t   Data Type

This is an arithmetic data type used to represent file sizes. In the GNU system, this is equivalent to **fpos_t** or **long int**.

Chapter 8: Low-Level Input/Output   147

These aliases for the 'SEEK_...' constants exist for the sake of compatibility with older BSD systems. They are defined in two different header files: 'fcntl.h' and 'sys/file.h'.

L_SET   An alias for SEEK_SET.

L_INCR   An alias for SEEK_CUR.

L_XTND   An alias for SEEK_END.

8.4 Descriptors and Streams

Given an open file descriptor, you can create a stream for it with the `fdopen` function. You can get the underlying file descriptor for an existing stream with the `fileno` function. These functions are declared in the header file 'stdio.h'.

FILE * **fdopen** (int *filedes*, const char **opentype*)   Function
   The `fdopen` function returns a new stream for the file descriptor *filedes*.

   The *opentype* argument is interpreted in the same way as for the `fopen` function (see Section 7.3 [Opening Streams], page 84), except that the 'b' option is not permitted; this is because GNU makes no distinction between text and binary files. Also, "w" and "w+" do not cause truncation of the file; these have affect only when opening a file, and in this case the file has already been opened. You must make sure that the *opentype* argument matches the actual mode of the open file descriptor.

   The return value is the new stream. If the stream cannot be created (for example, if the modes for the file indicated by the file descriptor do not permit the access specified by the *opentype* argument), a null pointer is returned instead.

   In some other systems, `fdopen` may fail to detect that the modes for file descriptor do not permit the access specified by `opentype`. The GNU C library always checks for this.

   For an example showing the use of the `fdopen` function, see Section 10.1 [Creating a Pipe], page 201.

int **fileno** (FILE **stream*)   Function
   This function returns the file descriptor associated with the stream *stream*. If an error is detected (for example, if the *stream* is not valid) or if *stream* does not do I/O to a file, `fileno` returns -1.

   There are also symbolic constants defined in 'unistd.h' for the file descriptors belonging to the standard streams stdin, stdout, and stderr; see Section 7.2 [Standard Streams], page 83.

`STDIN_FILENO`
> This macro has value 0, which is the file descriptor for standard input.

`STDOUT_FILENO`
> This macro has value 1, which is the file descriptor for standard output.

`STDERR_FILENO`
> This macro has value 2, which is the file descriptor for standard error output.

8.5 Dangers of Mixing Streams and Descriptors

You can have multiple file descriptors and streams (let's call both streams and descriptors "channels" for short) connected to the same file, but you must take care to avoid confusion between channels. There are two cases to consider: *linked* channels that share a single file position value, and *independent* channels that have their own file positions.

It's best to use just one channel in your program for actual data transfer to any given file, except when all the access is for input. For example, if you open a pipe (something you can only do at the file descriptor level), either do all I/O with the descriptor, or construct a stream from the descriptor with `fdopen` and then do all I/O with the stream.

8.5.1 Linked Channels

Channels that come from a single opening share the same file position; we call them *linked* channels. Linked channels result when you make a stream from a descriptor using `fdopen`, when you get a descriptor from a stream with `fileno`, when you copy a descriptor with `dup` or `dup2`, and when descriptors are inherited during `fork`. For files that don't support random access, such as terminals and pipes, *all* channels are effectively linked. On random-access files, all append-type output streams are effectively linked to each other.

If you have been using a stream for I/O, and you want to do I/O using another channel (either a stream or a descriptor) that is linked to it, you must first *clean up* the stream that you have been using. See Section 8.5.3 [Cleaning Streams], page 149.

Terminating a process, or executing a new program in the process, destroys all the streams in the process. If descriptors linked to these streams persist in other processes, their file positions become undefined as a result. To prevent this, you must clean up the streams before destroying them.

Chapter 8: Low-Level Input/Output

8.5.2 Independent Channels

When you open channels (streams or descriptors) separately on a seekable file, each channel has its own file position. These are called *independent channels*.

The system handles each channel independently. Most of the time, this is quite predictable and natural (especially for input): each channel can read or write sequentially at its own place in the file. However, if some of the channels are streams, you must take these precautions:

- You should clean an output stream after use, before doing anything else that might read or write from the same part of the file.
- You should clean an input stream before reading data that may have been modified using an independent channel. Otherwise, you might read obsolete data that had been in the stream's buffer.

If you do output to one channel at the end of the file, this will certainly leave the other independent channels positioned somewhere before the new end. You cannot reliably set their file positions to the new end of file before writing, because the file can always be extended by another process between when you set the file position and when you write the data. Instead, use an append-type descriptor or stream; they always output at the current end of the file. In order to make the end-of-file position accurate, you must clean the output channel you were using, if it is a stream.

It's impossible for two channels to have separate file pointers for a file that doesn't support random access. Thus, channels for reading or writing such files are always linked, never independent. Append-type channels are also always linked. For these channels, follow the rules for linked channels; see Section 8.5.1 [Linked Channels], page 148.

8.5.3 Cleaning Streams

On the GNU system, you can clean up any stream with `fclean`:

int fclean (FILE *stream*) *Function*
Clean up the stream *stream* so that its buffer is empty. If *stream* is doing output, force it out. If *stream* is doing input, give the data in the buffer back to the system, arranging to reread it.

On other systems, you can use `fflush` to clean a stream in most cases.

You can skip the `fclean` or `fflush` if you know the stream is already clean. A stream is clean whenever its buffer is empty. For example, an unbuffered stream is always clean. An input stream that is at end-of-file is clean. A line-buffered stream is clean when the last character output was a newline.

There is one case in which cleaning a stream is impossible on most systems. This is when the stream is doing input from a file that is not random-access. Such streams typically read ahead, and when the file is not random access, there is no way to give back the excess data already read. When an input stream reads from a random-access file, `fflush` does clean the stream, but leaves the file pointer at an unpredictable place; you must set the file pointer before doing any further I/O. On the GNU system, using `fclean` avoids both of these problems.

Closing an output-only stream also does `fflush`, so this is a valid way of cleaning an output stream. On the GNU system, closing an input stream does `fclean`.

You need not clean a stream before using its descriptor for control operations such as setting terminal modes; these operations don't affect the file position and are not affected by it. You can use any descriptor for these operations, and all channels are affected simultaneously. However, text already "output" to a stream but still buffered by the stream will be subject to the new terminal modes when subsequently flushed. To make sure "past" output is covered by the terminal settings that were in effect at the time, flush the output streams for that terminal before setting the modes. See Section 12.4 [Terminal Modes], page 257.

8.6 Waiting for Input or Output

Sometimes a program needs to accept input on multiple input channels whenever input arrives. For example, some workstations may have devices such as a digitizing tablet, function button box, or dial box that are connected via normal asynchronous serial interfaces; good user interface style requires responding immediately to input on any device. Another example is a program that acts as a server to several other processes via pipes or sockets.

You cannot normally use `read` for this purpose, because this blocks the program until input is available on one particular file descriptor; input on other channels won't wake it up. You could set nonblocking mode and poll each file descriptor in turn, but this is very inefficient.

A better solution is to use the `select` function. This blocks the program until input or output is ready on a specified set of file descriptors, or until a timer expires, whichever comes first. This facility is declared in the header file 'sys/types.h'.

In the case of a server socket (see Section 11.8.2 [Listening for Connections], page 232), we say that "input" is available when there are pending connections that could be accepted (see Section 11.8.3 [Accepting Connections], page 233). `accept` for server sockets blocks and interacts with `select` just as `read` does for normal input.

Chapter 8: Low-Level Input/Output

The file descriptor sets for the `select` function are specified as `fd_set` objects. Here is the description of the data type and some macros for manipulating these objects.

fd_set — Data Type

The `fd_set` data type represents file descriptor sets for the `select` function. It is actually a bit array.

int FD_SETSIZE — Macro

The value of this macro is the maximum number of file descriptors that a `fd_set` object can hold information about. On systems with a fixed maximum number, `FD_SETSIZE` is at least that number. On some systems, including GNU, there is no absolute limit on the number of descriptors open, but this macro still has a constant value which controls the number of bits in an `fd_set`; if you get a file descriptor with a value as high as `FD_SETSIZE`, you cannot put that descriptor into an `fd_set`.

void FD_ZERO (fd_set *set) — Macro

This macro initializes the file descriptor set *set* to be the empty set.

void FD_SET (int filedes, fd_set *set) — Macro

This macro adds *filedes* to the file descriptor set *set*.

void FD_CLR (int filedes, fd_set *set) — Macro

This macro removes *filedes* from the file descriptor set *set*.

int FD_ISSET (int filedes, fd_set *set) — Macro

This macro returns a nonzero value (true) if *filedes* is a member of the the file descriptor set *set*, and zero (false) otherwise.

Next, here is the description of the `select` function itself.

int select (int nfds, fd_set *read-fds, fd_set *write-fds, fd_set *except-fds, struct timeval *timeout) — Function

The `select` function blocks the calling process until there is activity on any of the specified sets of file descriptors, or until the timeout period has expired.

The file descriptors specified by the *read-fds* argument are checked to see if they are ready for reading; the *write-fds* file descriptors are checked to see if they are ready for writing; and the *except-fds* file descriptors are checked for exceptional conditions. You can pass a null pointer for any of these arguments if you are not interested in checking for that kind of condition.

A file descriptor is considered ready for reading if it is at end of file. A server socket is considered ready for reading if there is a pending connection which can be accepted with `accept`; see Section 11.8.3 [Accepting Connections], page 233. A client socket is ready for writing when its connection is fully established; see Section 11.8.1 [Making a Connection], page 231.

"Exceptional conditions" does not mean errors—errors are reported immediately when an erroneous system call is executed, and do not constitute a state of the descriptor. Rather, they include conditions such as the presence of an urgent message on a socket. (See Chapter 11 [Sockets], page 207, for information on urgent messages.)

The `select` function checks only the first *nfds* file descriptors. The usual thing is to pass `FD_SETSIZE` as the value of this argument.

The *timeout* specifies the maximum time to wait. If you pass a null pointer for this argument, it means to block indefinitely until one of the file descriptors is ready. Otherwise, you should provide the time in `struct timeval` format; see Section 17.2.2 [High-Resolution Calendar], page 324. Specify zero as the time (a `struct timeval` containing all zeros) if you want to find out which descriptors are ready without waiting if none are ready.

The normal return value from `select` is the total number of ready file descriptors in all of the sets. Each of the argument sets is overwritten with information about the descriptors that are ready for the corresponding operation. Thus, to see if a particular descriptor *desc* has input, use `FD_ISSET` (*desc*, *read-fds*) after `select` returns.

If `select` returns because the timeout period expires, it returns a value of zero.

Any signal will cause `select` to return immediately. So if your program uses signals, you can't rely on `select` to keep waiting for the full time specified. If you want to be sure of waiting for a particular amount of time, you must check for `EINTR` and repeat the `select` with a newly calculated timeout based on the current time. See the example below. See also Section 21.5 [Primitives Interrupted by Signals], page 402.

If an error occurs, `select` returns `-1` and does not modify the argument file descriptor sets. The following `errno` error conditions are defined for this function:

`EBADF`   One of the file descriptor sets specified an invalid file descriptor.

`EINTR`   The operation was interrupted by a signal. See Section 21.5 [Primitives Interrupted by Signals], page 402.

`EINVAL` The *timeout* argument is invalid; one of the components is negative or too large.

Chapter 8: Low-Level Input/Output

Portability Note: The `select` function is a BSD Unix feature.

Here is an example showing how you can use `select` to establish a timeout period for reading from a file descriptor. The `input_timeout` function blocks the calling process until input is available on the file descriptor, or until the timeout period expires.

```
#include <stdio.h>
#include <unistd.h>
#include <sys/types.h>
#include <sys/time.h>

int
input_timeout (int filedes, unsigned int seconds)
{
  fd_set set;
  struct timeval timeout;

  /* Initialize the file descriptor set. */
  FD_ZERO (&set);
  FD_SET (filedes, &set);

  /* Initialize the timeout data structure. */
  timeout.tv_sec = seconds;
  timeout.tv_usec = 0;

  /* select returns 0 if timeout, 1 if input available, -1 if error. */
  return TEMP_FAILURE_RETRY (select (FD_SETSIZE,
                                     &set, NULL, NULL,
                                     &timeout));
}

int
main (void)
{
  fprintf (stderr, "select returned %d.\n",
           input_timeout (STDIN_FILENO, 5));
  return 0;
}
```

There is another example showing the use of `select` to multiplex input from multiple sockets in Section 11.8.7 [Byte Stream Connection Server Example], page 238.

8.7 Control Operations on Files

This section describes how you can perform various other operations on file descriptors, such as inquiring about or setting flags describing the status of the file descriptor, manipulating record locks, and the like. All of these operations are performed by the function `fcntl`.

The second argument to the `fcntl` function is a command that specifies which operation to perform. The function and macros that name various flags that are used with it are declared in the header file 'fcntl.h'. Many of these flags are also used by the **open** function; see Section 8.1 [Opening and Closing Files], page 139.

int fcntl (int *filedes*, int *command*, ...) *Function*
The `fcntl` function performs the operation specified by *command* on the file descriptor *filedes*. Some commands require additional arguments to be supplied. These additional arguments and the return value and error conditions are given in the detailed descriptions of the individual commands.

Briefly, here is a list of what the various commands are.

F_DUPFD   Duplicate the file descriptor (return another file descriptor pointing to the same open file). See Section 8.8 [Duplicating Descriptors], page 154.

F_GETFD   Get flags associated with the file descriptor. See Section 8.9 [File Descriptor Flags], page 156.

F_SETFD   Set flags associated with the file descriptor. See Section 8.9 [File Descriptor Flags], page 156.

F_GETFL   Get flags associated with the open file. See Section 8.10 [File Status Flags], page 158.

F_SETFL   Set flags associated with the open file. See Section 8.10 [File Status Flags], page 158.

F_GETLK   Get a file lock. See Section 8.11 [File Locks], page 164.

F_SETLK   Set or clear a file lock. See Section 8.11 [File Locks], page 164.

F_SETLKW Like **F_SETLK**, but wait for completion. See Section 8.11 [File Locks], page 164.

F_GETOWN Get process or process group ID to receive **SIGIO** signals. See Section 8.12 [Interrupt-Driven Input], page 167.

F_SETOWN Set process or process group ID to receive **SIGIO** signals. See Section 8.12 [Interrupt-Driven Input], page 167.

8.8 Duplicating Descriptors

You can *duplicate* a file descriptor, or allocate another file descriptor that refers to the same open file as the original. Duplicate descriptors share one file position and one set of file status flags (see Section 8.10 [File Status Flags], page 158), but each has its own set of file descriptor flags (see Section 8.9 [File Descriptor Flags], page 156).

Chapter 8: Low-Level Input/Output   155

The major use of duplicating a file descriptor is to implement *redirection* of input or output: that is, to change the file or pipe that a particular file descriptor corresponds to.

You can perform this operation using the `fcntl` function with the F_DUPFD command, but there are also convenient functions `dup` and `dup2` for duplicating descriptors.

The `fcntl` function and flags are declared in 'fcntl.h', while prototypes for `dup` and `dup2` are in the header file 'unistd.h'.

int **dup** (int *old*)   Function
  This function copies descriptor *old* to the first available descriptor number (the first number not currently open). It is equivalent to `fcntl (old, F_DUPFD, 0)`.

int **dup2** (int *old*, int *new*)   Function
  This function copies the descriptor *old* to descriptor number *new*.

  If *old* is an invalid descriptor, then `dup2` does nothing; it does not close *new*. Otherwise, the new duplicate of *old* replaces any previous meaning of descriptor *new*, as if *new* were closed first.

  If *old* and *new* are different numbers, and *old* is a valid descriptor number, then `dup2` is equivalent to:
      close (*new*);
      fcntl (*old*, F_DUPFD, *new*)

  However, `dup2` does this atomically; there is no instant in the middle of calling `dup2` at which *new* is closed and not yet a duplicate of *old*.

int **F_DUPFD**   Macro
  This macro is used as the *command* argument to `fcntl`, to copy the file descriptor given as the first argument.

  The form of the call in this case is:
      fcntl (*old*, F_DUPFD, *next-filedes*)

  The *next-filedes* argument is of type `int` and specifies that the file descriptor returned should be the next available one greater than or equal to this value.

  The return value from `fcntl` with this command is normally the value of the new file descriptor. A return value of -1 indicates an error. The following `errno` error conditions are defined for this command:

  EBADF   The *old* argument is invalid.

  EINVAL   The *next-filedes* argument is invalid.

  EMFILE   There are no more file descriptors available—your program is already using the maximum. In BSD and GNU, the maximum is controlled by a resource limit that can be changed; see Section 17.6 [Limiting Resource Usage], page 341, for more information about the `RLIMIT_NOFILE` limit.

`ENFILE` is not a possible error code for `dup2` because `dup2` does not create a new opening of a file; duplicate descriptors do not count toward the limit which `ENFILE` indicates. `EMFILE` is possible because it refers to the limit on distinct descriptor numbers in use in one process.

Here is an example showing how to use `dup2` to do redirection. Typically, redirection of the standard streams (like `stdin`) is done by a shell or shell-like program before calling one of the `exec` functions (see Section 23.5 [Executing a File], page 446) to execute a new program in a child process. When the new program is executed, it creates and initializes the standard streams to point to the corresponding file descriptors, before its `main` function is invoked.

So, to redirect standard input to a file, the shell could do something like:

```
pid = fork ();
if (pid == 0)
  {
    char *filename;
    char *program;
    int file;
    ...
    file = TEMP_FAILURE_RETRY (open (filename, O_RDONLY));
    dup2 (file, STDIN_FILENO);
    TEMP_FAILURE_RETRY (close (file));
    execv (program, NULL);
  }
```

There is also a more detailed example showing how to implement redirection in the context of a pipeline of processes in Section 24.6.3 [Launching Jobs], page 464.

8.9 File Descriptor Flags

File descriptor flags are miscellaneous attributes of a file descriptor. These flags are associated with particular file descriptors, so that if you have created duplicate file descriptors from a single opening of a file, each descriptor has its own set of flags.

Currently there is just one file descriptor flag: `FD_CLOEXEC`, which causes the descriptor to be closed if you use any of the `exec...` functions (see Section 23.5 [Executing a File], page 446).

The symbols in this section are defined in the header file 'fcntl.h'.

Chapter 8: Low-Level Input/Output 157

int **F_GETFD** — Macro

This macro is used as the *command* argument to `fcntl`, to specify that it should return the file descriptor flags associated with the *filedes* argument.

The normal return value from `fcntl` with this command is a non-negative number which can be interpreted as the bitwise OR of the individual flags (except that currently there is only one flag to use).

In case of an error, `fcntl` returns -1. The following `errno` error conditions are defined for this command:

EBADF   The *filedes* argument is invalid.

int **F_SETFD** — Macro

This macro is used as the *command* argument to `fcntl`, to specify that it should set the file descriptor flags associated with the *filedes* argument. This requires a third `int` argument to specify the new flags, so the form of the call is:

> `fcntl (`*filedes*`, F_SETFD, `*new-flags*`)`

The normal return value from `fcntl` with this command is an unspecified value other than -1, which indicates an error. The flags and error conditions are the same as for the `F_GETFD` command.

The following macro is defined for use as a file descriptor flag with the `fcntl` function. The value is an integer constant usable as a bit mask value.

int **FD_CLOEXEC** — Macro

This flag specifies that the file descriptor should be closed when an `exec` function is invoked; see Section 23.5 [Executing a File], page 446. When a file descriptor is allocated (as with `open` or `dup`), this bit is initially cleared on the new file descriptor, meaning that descriptor will survive into the new program after `exec`.

If you want to modify the file descriptor flags, you should get the current flags with `F_GETFD` and modify the value. Don't assume that the flags listed here are the only ones that are implemented; your program may be run years from now and more flags may exist then. For example, here is a function to set or clear the flag `FD_CLOEXEC` without altering any other flags:

```
/* Set the FD_CLOEXEC flag of desc if value is nonzero,
   or clear the flag if value is 0.
   Return 0 on success, or -1 on error with errno set. */

int
set_cloexec_flag (int desc, int value)
{
  int oldflags = fcntl (desc, F_GETFD, 0);
  /* If reading the flags failed, return error indication now. */
  if (oldflags < 0)
```

```
      return oldflags;
   /* Set just the flag we want to set. */
   if (value != 0)
     oldflags |= FD_CLOEXEC;
   else
     oldflags &= ~FD_CLOEXEC;
   /* Store modified flag word in the descriptor. */
   return fcntl (desc, F_SETFD, oldflags);
}
```

8.10 File Status Flags

File status flags are used to specify attributes of the opening of a file. Unlike the file descriptor flags discussed in Section 8.9 [File Descriptor Flags], page 156, the file status flags are shared by duplicated file descriptors resulting from a single opening of the file. The file status flags are specified with the *flags* argument to **open**; see Section 8.1 [Opening and Closing Files], page 139.

File status flags fall into three categories, which are described in the following sections.

- Section 8.10.1 [File Access Modes], page 158, specify what type of access is allowed to the file: reading, writing, or both. They are set by **open** and are returned by **fcntl**, but cannot be changed.
- Section 8.10.2 [Open-time Flags], page 159, control details of what **open** will do. These flags are not preserved after the **open** call.
- Section 8.10.3 [I/O Operating Modes], page 161, affect how operations such as **read** and **write** are done. They are set by **open**, and can be fetched or changed with **fcntl**.

The symbols in this section are defined in the header file 'fcntl.h'.

8.10.1 File Access Modes

The file access modes allow a file descriptor to be used for reading, writing, or both. (In the GNU system, they can also allow none of these, and allow execution of the file as a program.) The access modes are chosen when the file is opened, and never change.

int O_RDONLY   Macro
    Open the file for read access.

int O_WRONLY   Macro
    Open the file for write access.

int O_RDWR   Macro
    Open the file for both reading and writing.

Chapter 8: Low-Level Input/Output

In the GNU system (and not in other systems), `O_RDONLY` and `O_WRONLY` are independent bits that can be bitwise-ORed together, and it is valid for either bit to be set or clear. This means that `O_RDWR` is the same as `O_RDONLY|O_WRONLY`. A file access mode of zero is permissible; it allows no operations that do input or output to the file, but does allow other operations such as `fchmod`. On the GNU system, since "read-only" or "write-only" is a misnomer, 'fcntl.h' defines additional names for the file access modes. These names are preferred when writing GNU-specific code. But most programs will want to be portable to other POSIX.1 systems and should use the POSIX.1 names above instead.

int O_READ   Macro
Open the file for reading. Same as `O_RDWR`; only defined on GNU.

int O_WRITE   Macro
Open the file for reading. Same as `O_WRONLY`; only defined on GNU.

int O_EXEC   Macro
Open the file for executing. Only defined on GNU.

To determine the file access mode with `fcntl`, you must extract the access mode bits from the retrieved file status flags. In the GNU system, you can just test the `O_READ` and `O_WRITE` bits in the flags word. But in other POSIX.1 systems, reading and writing access modes are not stored as distinct bit flags. The portable way to extract the file access mode bits is with `O_ACCMODE`.

int O_ACCMODE   Macro
This macro stands for a mask that can be bitwise-ANDed with the file status flag value to produce a value representing the file access mode. The mode will be `O_RDONLY`, `O_WRONLY`, or `O_RDWR`. (In the GNU system it could also be zero, and it never includes the `O_EXEC` bit.)

8.10.2 Open-time Flags

The open-time flags specify options affecting how **open** will behave. These options are not preserved once the file is open. The exception to this is `O_NONBLOCK`, which is also an I/O operating mode and so it *is* saved. See Section 8.1 [Opening and Closing Files], page 139, for how to call **open**.

There are two sorts of options specified by open-time flags.

- *File name translation flags* affect how **open** looks up the file name to locate the file, and whether the file can be created.
- *Open-time action flags* specify extra operations that **open** will perform on the file once it is open.

Here are the file name translation flags.

int O_CREAT   Macro
If set, the file will be created if it doesn't already exist.

int O_EXCL   Macro
If both `O_CREAT` and `O_EXCL` are set, then `open` fails if the specified file already exists. This is guaranteed to never clobber an existing file.

int O_NONBLOCK   Macro
This prevents `open` from blocking for a "long time" to open the file. This is only meaningful for some kinds of files, usually devices such as serial ports; when it is not meaningful, it is harmless and ignored. Often opening a port to a modem blocks until the modem reports carrier detection; if `O_NONBLOCK` is specified, `open` will return immediately without a carrier.

Note that the `O_NONBLOCK` flag is overloaded as both an I/O operating mode and a file name translation flag. This means that specifying O_NONBLOCK in `open` also sets nonblocking I/O mode; see Section 8.10.3 [I/O Operating Modes], page 161. To open the file without blocking but do normal I/O that blocks, you must call `open` with `O_NONBLOCK` set and then call `fcntl` to turn the bit off.

int O_NOCTTY   Macro
If the named file is a terminal device, don't make it the controlling terminal for the process. See Chapter 24 [Job Control], page 457, for information about what it means to be the controlling terminal.

In the GNU system and 4.4 BSD, opening a file never makes it the controlling terminal and `O_NOCTTY` is zero. However, other systems may use a nonzero value for `O_NOCTTY` and set the controlling terminal when you open a file that is a terminal device; so to be portable, use `O_NOCTTY` when it is important to avoid this.

The following three file name translation flags exist only in the GNU system.

int O_IGNORE_CTTY   Macro
Do not recognize the named file as the controlling terminal, even if it refers to the process's existing controlling terminal device. Operations on the new file descriptor will never induce job control signals. See Chapter 24 [Job Control], page 457.

int O_NOLINK   Macro
If the named file is a symbolic link, open the link itself instead of the file it refers to. (`fstat` on the new file descriptor will return the information returned by `lstat` on the link's name.)

Chapter 8: Low-Level Input/Output 161

int O_NOTRANS   Macro
If the named file is specially translated, do not invoke the translator. Open the bare file the translator itself sees.

The open-time action flags tell `open` to do additional operations which are not really related to opening the file. The reason to do them as part of `open` instead of in separate calls is that `open` can do them *atomically*.

int O_TRUNC   Macro
Truncate the file to zero length. This option is only useful for regular files, not special files such as directories or FIFOs. POSIX.1 requires that you open the file for writing to use `O_TRUNC`. In BSD and GNU you must have permission to write the file to truncate it, but you need not open for write access.

This is the only open-time action flag specified by POSIX.1. There is no good reason for truncation to be done by `open`, instead of by calling `ftruncate` afterwards. The `O_TRUNC` flag existed in Unix before `ftruncate` was invented, and is retained for backward compatibility.

int O_SHLOCK   Macro
Acquire a shared lock on the file, as with `flock`. See Section 8.11 [File Locks], page 164.

If `O_CREAT` is specified, the locking is done atomically when creating the file. You are guaranteed that no other process will get the lock on the new file first.

int O_EXLOCK   Macro
Acquire an exclusive lock on the file, as with `flock`. See Section 8.11 [File Locks], page 164. This is atomic like `O_SHLOCK`.

8.10.3 I/O Operating Modes

The operating modes affect how input and output operations using a file descriptor work. These flags are set by `open` and can be fetched and changed with `fcntl`.

int O_APPEND   Macro
The bit that enables append mode for the file. If set, then all `write` operations write the data at the end of the file, extending it, regardless of the current file position. This is the only reliable way to append to a file. In append mode, you are guaranteed that the data you write will always go to the current end of the file, regardless of other processes writing to the file. Conversely, if you simply set the file position to the end of file and write, then another process can extend the file after you set the file position but before you write, resulting in your data appearing someplace before the real end of file.

The bit that enables nonblocking mode for   O_NONBLOCK
the file. If this bit is set,
`read` requests on the file can return immediately with a failure status if there is no input immediately available, instead of blocking. Likewise, `write` requests can also return immediately with a failure status if the output can't be written immediately.

Note that the `O_NONBLOCK` flag is overloaded as both an I/O operating mode and a file name translation flag; see Section 8.10.2 [Open-time Flags], page 159.

int O_NDELAY   *Macro*
This is an obsolete name for `O_NONBLOCK`, provided for compatibility with BSD. It is not defined by the POSIX.1 standard.

The remaining operating modes are BSD and GNU extensions. They exist only on some systems. On other systems, these macros are not defined.

int O_ASYNC   *Macro*
The bit that enables asynchronous input mode. If set, then `SIGIO` signals will be generated when input is available. See Section 8.12 [Interrupt-Driven Input], page 167.

Asynchronous input mode is a BSD feature.

int O_FSYNC   *Macro*
The bit that enables synchronous writing for the file. If set, each `write` call will make sure the data is reliably stored on disk before returning.

Synchronous writing is a BSD feature.

int O_SYNC   *Macro*
This is another name for `O_FSYNC`. They have the same value.

int O_NOATIME   *Macro*
If this bit is set, `read` will not update the access time of the file. See Section 9.8.9 [File Times], page 194. This is used by programs that do backups, so that backing a file up does not count as reading it. Only the owner of the file or the superuser may use this bit.

This is a GNU extension.

8.10.4 Getting and Setting File Status Flags

The `fcntl` function can fetch or change file status flags.

int F_GETFL   *Macro*
This macro is used as the *command* argument to `fcntl`, to read the file status flags for the open file with descriptor *filedes*.

Chapter 8: Low-Level Input/Output

The normal return value from `fcntl` with this command is a non-negative number which can be interpreted as the bitwise OR of the individual flags. Since the file access modes are not single-bit values, you can mask off other bits in the returned flags with `O_ACCMODE` to compare them.

In case of an error, `fcntl` returns -1. The following `errno` error conditions are defined for this command:

EBADF   The *filedes* argument is invalid.

int **F_SETFL** *Macro*

This macro is used as the *command* argument to `fcntl`, to set the file status flags for the open file corresponding to the *filedes* argument. This command requires a third `int` argument to specify the new flags, so the call looks like this:

    fcntl (*filedes*, F_SETFL, *new-flags*)

You can't change the access mode for the file in this way; that is, whether the file descriptor was opened for reading or writing.

The normal return value from `fcntl` with this command is an unspecified value other than -1, which indicates an error. The error conditions are the same as for the `F_GETFL` command.

If you want to modify the file status flags, you should get the current flags with `F_GETFL` and modify the value. Don't assume that the flags listed here are the only ones that are implemented; your program may be run years from now and more flags may exist then. For example, here is a function to set or clear the flag `O_NONBLOCK` without altering any other flags:

```
/* Set the O_NONBLOCK flag of desc if value is nonzero,
   or clear the flag if value is 0.
   Return 0 on success, or -1 on error with errno set. */

int
set_nonblock_flag (int desc, int value)
{
  int oldflags = fcntl (desc, F_GETFL, 0);
  /* If reading the flags failed, return error indication now. */
  if (oldflags == -1)
    return -1;
  /* Set just the flag we want to set. */
  if (value != 0)
    oldflags |= O_NONBLOCK;
  else
    oldflags &= ~O_NONBLOCK;
  /* Store modified flag word in the descriptor. */
  return fcntl (desc, F_SETFL, oldflags);
}
```

8.11 File Locks

The remaining `fcntl` commands are used to support *record locking*, which permits multiple cooperating programs to prevent each other from simultaneously accessing parts of a file in error-prone ways.

An *exclusive* or *write* lock gives a process exclusive access for writing to the specified part of the file. While a write lock is in place, no other process can lock that part of the file.

A *shared* or *read* lock prohibits any other process from requesting a write lock on the specified part of the file. However, other processes can request read locks.

The `read` and `write` functions do not actually check to see whether there are any locks in place. If you want to implement a locking protocol for a file shared by multiple processes, your application must do explicit `fcntl` calls to request and clear locks at the appropriate points.

Locks are associated with processes. A process can only have one kind of lock set for each byte of a given file. When any file descriptor for that file is closed by the process, all of the locks that process holds on that file are released, even if the locks were made using other descriptors that remain open. Likewise, locks are released when a process exits, and are not inherited by child processes created using `fork` (see Section 23.4 [Creating a Process], page 445).

When making a lock, use a `struct flock` to specify what kind of lock and where. This data type and the associated macros for the `fcntl` function are declared in the header file 'fcntl.h'.

struct flock   Data Type
   This structure is used with the `fcntl` function to describe a file lock. It has these members:

   short int l_type
   : Specifies the type of the lock; one of `F_RDLCK`, `F_WRLCK`, or `F_UNLCK`.

   short int l_whence
   : This corresponds to the *whence* argument to `fseek` or `lseek`, and specifies what the offset is relative to. Its value can be one of `SEEK_SET`, `SEEK_CUR`, or `SEEK_END`.

   off_t l_start
   : This specifies the offset of the start of the region to which the lock applies, and is given in bytes relative to the point specified by `l_whence` member.

Chapter 8: Low-Level Input/Output 165

`off_t l_len`
: This specifies the length of the region to be locked. A value of 0 is treated specially; it means the region extends to the end of the file.

`pid_t l_pid`
: This field is the process ID (see Section 23.2 [Process Creation Concepts], page 444) of the process holding the lock. It is filled in by calling `fcntl` with the `F_GETLK` command, but is ignored when making a lock.

int F_GETLK   Macro

This macro is used as the *command* argument to `fcntl`, to specify that it should get information about a lock. This command requires a third argument of type `struct flock *` to be passed to `fcntl`, so that the form of the call is:

    fcntl (filedes, F_GETLK, lockp)

If there is a lock already in place that would block the lock described by the *lockp* argument, information about that lock overwrites *lockp*. Existing locks are not reported if they are compatible with making a new lock as specified. Thus, you should specify a lock type of `F_WRLCK` if you want to find out about both read and write locks, or `F_RDLCK` if you want to find out about write locks only.

There might be more than one lock affecting the region specified by the *lockp* argument, but `fcntl` only returns information about one of them. The `l_whence` member of the *lockp* structure is set to `SEEK_SET` and the `l_start` and `l_len` fields set to identify the locked region.

If no lock applies, the only change to the *lockp* structure is to update the `l_type` to a value of `F_UNLCK`.

The normal return value from `fcntl` with this command is an unspecified value other than `-1`, which is reserved to indicate an error. The following `errno` error conditions are defined for this command:

`EBADF`
: The *filedes* argument is invalid.

`EINVAL`
: Either the *lockp* argument doesn't specify valid lock information, or the file associated with *filedes* doesn't support locks.

int F_SETLK   Macro

This macro is used as the *command* argument to `fcntl`, to specify that it should set or clear a lock. This command requires a third argument of type `struct flock *` to be passed to `fcntl`, so that the form of the call is:

    fcntl (filedes, F_SETLK, lockp)

If the process already has a lock on any part of the region, the old lock on that part is replaced with the new lock. You can remove a lock by specifying a lock type of `F_UNLCK`.

If the lock cannot be set, `fcntl` returns immediately with a value of -1. This function does not block waiting for other processes to release locks. If `fcntl` succeeds, it return a value other than -1.

The following `errno` error conditions are defined for this function:

EAGAIN
EACCES   The lock cannot be set because it is blocked by an existing lock on the file. Some systems use `EAGAIN` in this case, and other systems use `EACCES`; your program should treat them alike, after `F_SETLK`. (The GNU system always uses `EAGAIN`.)

EBADF   Either: the *filedes* argument is invalid; you requested a read lock but the *filedes* is not open for read access; or, you requested a write lock but the *filedes* is not open for write access.

EINVAL   Either the *lockp* argument doesn't specify valid lock information, or the file associated with *filedes* doesn't support locks.

ENOLCK   The system has run out of file lock resources; there are already too many file locks in place.

Well-designed file systems never report this error, because they have no limitation on the number of locks. However, you must still take account of the possibility of this error, as it could result from network access to a file system on another machine.

int F_SETLKW   Macro

This macro is used as the *command* argument to `fcntl`, to specify that it should set or clear a lock. It is just like the `F_SETLK` command, but causes the process to block (or wait) until the request can be specified.

This command requires a third argument of type `struct flock *`, as for the `F_SETLK` command.

The `fcntl` return values and errors are the same as for the `F_SETLK` command, but these additional `errno` error conditions are defined for this command:

EINTR   The function was interrupted by a signal while it was waiting. See Section 21.5 [Primitives Interrupted by Signals], page 402.

Chapter 8: Low-Level Input/Output   167

> `EDEADLK`   The specified region is being locked by another process. But that process is waiting to lock a region which the current process has locked, so waiting for the lock would result in deadlock. The system does not guarantee that it will detect all such conditions, but it lets you know if it notices one.

The following macros are defined for use as values for the `l_type` member of the `flock` structure. The values are integer constants.

`F_RDLCK`   This macro is used to specify a read (or shared) lock.

`F_WRLCK`   This macro is used to specify a write (or exclusive) lock.

`F_UNLCK`   This macro is used to specify that the region is unlocked.

As an example of a situation where file locking is useful, consider a program that can be run simultaneously by several different users, that logs status information to a common file. One example of such a program might be a game that uses a file to keep track of high scores. Another example might be a program that records usage or accounting information for billing purposes.

Having multiple copies of the program simultaneously writing to the file could cause the contents of the file to become mixed up. But you can prevent this kind of problem by setting a write lock on the file before actually writing to the file.

If the program also needs to read the file and wants to make sure that the contents of the file are in a consistent state, then it can also use a read lock. While the read lock is set, no other process can lock that part of the file for writing.

Remember that file locks are only a *voluntary* protocol for controlling access to a file. There is still potential for access to the file by programs that don't use the lock protocol.

8.12 Interrupt-Driven Input

If you set the `O_ASYNC` status flag on a file descriptor (see Section 8.10 [File Status Flags], page 158), a `SIGIO` signal is sent whenever input or output becomes possible on that file descriptor. The process or process group to receive the signal can be selected by using the `F_SETOWN` command to the `fcntl` function. If the file descriptor is a socket, this also selects the recipient of `SIGURG` signals that are delivered when out-of-band data arrives on that socket; see Section 11.8.8 [Out-of-Band Data], page 241. (`SIGURG` is sent in any situation where `select` would report the socket as having an "exceptional condition". See Section 8.6 [Waiting for Input or Output], page 150.)

If the file descriptor corresponds to a terminal device, then `SIGIO` signals are sent to the foreground process group of the terminal. See Chapter 24 [Job Control], page 457.

The symbols in this section are defined in the header file 'fcntl.h'.

int F_GETOWN *Macro*

This macro is used as the *command* argument to `fcntl`, to specify that it should get information about the process or process group to which `SIGIO` signals are sent. (For a terminal, this is actually the foreground process group ID, which you can get using `tcgetpgrp`; see Section 24.7.3 [Functions for Controlling Terminal Access], page 476.)

The return value is interpreted as a process ID; if negative, its absolute value is the process group ID.

The following `errno` error condition is defined for this command:

EBADF   The *filedes* argument is invalid.

int F_SETOWN *Macro*

This macro is used as the *command* argument to `fcntl`, to specify that it should set the process or process group to which `SIGIO` signals are sent. This command requires a third argument of type `pid_t` to be passed to `fcntl`, so that the form of the call is:

```
fcntl (filedes, F_SETOWN, pid)
```

The *pid* argument should be a process ID. You can also pass a negative number whose absolute value is a process group ID.

The return value from `fcntl` with this command is -1 in case of error and some other value if successful. The following `errno` error conditions are defined for this command:

EBADF   The *filedes* argument is invalid.

ESRCH   There is no process or process group corresponding to *pid*.

9 File System Interface

This chapter describes the GNU C library's functions for manipulating files. Unlike the input and output functions described in Chapter 7 [Input/Output on Streams], page 83 and Chapter 8 [Low-Level Input/Output], page 139, these functions are concerned with operating on the files themselves, rather than on their contents.

Among the facilities described in this chapter are functions for examining or modifying directories, functions for renaming and deleting files, and functions for examining and setting file attributes such as access permissions and modification times.

9.1 Working Directory

Each process has associated with it a directory, called its *current working directory* or simply *working directory*, that is used in the resolution of relative file names (see Section 6.2.2 [File Name Resolution], page 78).

When you log in and begin a new session, your working directory is initially set to the home directory associated with your login account in the system user database. You can find any user's home directory using the `getpwuid` or `getpwnam` functions; see Section 25.12 [User Database], page 489.

Users can change the working directory using shell commands like `cd`. The functions described in this section are the primitives used by those commands and by other programs for examining and changing the working directory.

Prototypes for these functions are declared in the header file 'unistd.h'.

char * getcwd (char *buffer*, size_t *size*)   *Function*
 The `getcwd` function returns an absolute file name representing the current working directory, storing it in the character array *buffer* that you provide. The *size* argument is how you tell the system the allocation size of *buffer*.

 The GNU library version of this function also permits you to specify a null pointer for the *buffer* argument. Then `getcwd` allocates a buffer automatically, as with `malloc` (see Section 3.3 [Unconstrained Allocation], page 28). If the *size* is greater than zero, then the buffer is that large; otherwise, the buffer is as large as necessary to hold the result.

 The return value is *buffer* on success and a null pointer on failure. The following `errno` error conditions are defined for this function:

 EINVAL   The *size* argument is zero and *buffer* is not a null pointer.

ERANGE   The *size* argument is less than the length of the working directory name. You need to allocate a bigger array and try again.

EACCES   Permission to read or search a component of the file name was denied.

Here is an example showing how you could implement the behavior of GNU's `getcwd (NULL, 0)` using only the standard behavior of `getcwd`:

```
char *
gnu_getcwd ()
{
  int size = 100;
  char *buffer = (char *) xmalloc (size);

  while (1)
    {
      char *value = getcwd (buffer, size);
      if (value != 0)
        return buffer;
      size *= 2;
      free (buffer);
      buffer = (char *) xmalloc (size);
    }
}
```

See Section 3.3.2 [Examples of "code malloc], page 29, for information about `xmalloc`, which is not a library function but is a customary name used in most GNU software.

char * getwd (`char *buffer`)   *Function*
   This is similar to `getcwd`, but has no way to specify the size of the buffer. The GNU library provides `getwd` only for backwards compatibility with BSD.

   The *buffer* argument should be a pointer to an array at least `PATH_MAX` bytes long (see Section 27.6 [Limits on File System Capacity], page 507). In the GNU system there is no limit to the size of a file name, so this is not necessarily enough space to contain the directory name. That is why this function is deprecated.

int chdir (`const char *filename`)   *Function*
   This function is used to set the process's working directory to *filename*.

   The normal, successful return value from `chdir` is 0. A value of -1 is returned to indicate an error. The `errno` error conditions defined for this function are the usual file name syntax errors (see Section 6.2.3 [File Name Errors], page 79), plus `ENOTDIR` if the file *filename* is not a directory.

Chapter 9: File System Interface   171

9.2 Accessing Directories

The facilities described in this section let you read the contents of a directory file. This is useful if you want your program to list all the files in a directory, perhaps as part of a menu.

The `opendir` function opens a *directory stream* whose elements are directory entries. You use the `readdir` function on the directory stream to retrieve these entries, represented as `struct dirent` objects. The name of the file for each entry is stored in the `d_name` member of this structure. There are obvious parallels here to the stream facilities for ordinary files, described in Chapter 7 [Input/Output on Streams], page 83.

9.2.1 Format of a Directory Entry

This section describes what you find in a single directory entry, as you might obtain it from a directory stream. All the symbols are declared in the header file 'dirent.h'.

struct dirent   Data Type

This is a structure type used to return information about directory entries. It contains the following fields:

- `char d_name[]`

    This is the null-terminated file name component. This is the only field you can count on in all POSIX systems.

- `ino_t d_fileno`

    This is the file serial number. For BSD compatibility, you can also refer to this member as `d_ino`. In the GNU system and most POSIX systems, for most files this the same as the `st_ino` member that `stat` will return for the file. See Section 9.8 [File Attributes], page 181.

- `unsigned char d_namlen`

    This is the length of the file name, not including the terminating null character. Its type is `unsigned char` because that is the integer type of the appropriate size

- `unsigned char d_type`

    This is the type of the file, possibly unknown. The following constants are defined for its value:

    - `DT_UNKNOWN`

        The type is unknown. On some systems this is the only value returned.

    - `DT_REG`   A regular file.

DT_DIR   A directory.

DT_FIFO   A named pipe, or FIFO. See Section 10.3 [FIFO Special Files], page 204.

DT_SOCK   A local-domain socket.

DT_CHR   A character device.

DT_BLK   A block device.

This member is a BSD extension. Each value except DT_UNKNOWN corresponds to the file type bits in the st_mode member of struct statbuf. These two macros convert between d_type values and st_mode values:

int **IFTODT** (mode_t *mode*)   *Function*
    This returns the d_type value corresponding to *mode*.

mode_t **DTTOIF** (int *dirtype*)   *Function*
    This returns the st_mode value corresponding to *dirtype*.

This structure may contain additional members in the future.

When a file has multiple names, each name has its own directory entry. The only way you can tell that the directory entries belong to a single file is that they have the same value for the d_fileno field.

File attributes such as size, modification times, and the like are part of the file itself, not any particular directory entry. See Section 9.8 [File Attributes], page 181.

9.2.2 Opening a Directory Stream

This section describes how to open a directory stream. All the symbols are declared in the header file 'dirent.h'.

DIR   *Data Type*
The DIR data type represents a directory stream.

You shouldn't ever allocate objects of the struct dirent or DIR data types, since the directory access functions do that for you. Instead, you refer to these objects using the pointers returned by the following functions.

DIR * **opendir** (const char *dirname*)   *Function*
    The opendir function opens and returns a directory stream for reading the directory whose file name is *dirname*. The stream has type DIR *.

Chapter 9: File System Interface   173

If unsuccessful, `opendir` returns a null pointer. In addition to the usual file name errors (see Section 6.2.3 [File Name Errors], page 79), the following `errno` error conditions are defined for this function:

`EACCES`   Read permission is denied for the directory named by `dirname`.

`EMFILE`   The process has too many files open.

`ENFILE`   The entire system, or perhaps the file system which contains the directory, cannot support any additional open files at the moment. (This problem cannot happen on the GNU system.)

The `DIR` type is typically implemented using a file descriptor, and the `opendir` function in terms of the `open` function. See Chapter 8 [Low-Level Input/Output], page 139. Directory streams and the underlying file descriptors are closed on `exec` (see Section 23.5 [Executing a File], page 446).

9.2.3 Reading and Closing a Directory Stream

This section describes how to read directory entries from a directory stream, and how to close the stream when you are done with it. All the symbols are declared in the header file 'dirent.h'.

struct dirent * readdir (DIR *dirstream*)   *Function*
   This function reads the next entry from the directory. It normally returns a pointer to a structure containing information about the file. This structure is statically allocated and can be rewritten by a subsequent call.

   Portability Note: On some systems, `readdir` may not return entries for '.' and '..', even though these are always valid file names in any directory. See Section 6.2.2 [File Name Resolution], page 78.

   If there are no more entries in the directory or an error is detected, `readdir` returns a null pointer. The following `errno` error conditions are defined for this function:

   `EBADF`   The *dirstream* argument is not valid.

int closedir (DIR *dirstream*)   *Function*
   This function closes the directory stream *dirstream*. It returns 0 on success and -1 on failure.

   The following `errno` error conditions are defined for this function:

   `EBADF`   The *dirstream* argument is not valid.

9.2.4 Simple Program to List a Directory

Here's a simple program that prints the names of the files in the current working directory:

```
#include <stddef.h>
#include <stdio.h>
#include <sys/types.h>
#include <dirent.h>

int
main (void)
{
  DIR *dp;
  struct dirent *ep;

  dp = opendir ("./");
  if (dp != NULL)
    {
      while (ep = readdir (dp))
        puts (ep->d_name);
      (void) closedir (dp);
    }
  else
    puts ("Couldn't open the directory.");

  return 0;
}
```

The order in which files appear in a directory tends to be fairly random. A more useful program would sort the entries (perhaps by alphabetizing them) before printing them; see Section 15.3 [Array Sort Function], page 300.

9.2.5 Random Access in a Directory Stream

This section describes how to reread parts of a directory that you have already read from an open directory stream. All the symbols are declared in the header file 'dirent.h'.

void rewinddir (DIR *dirstream*)   *Function*

The `rewinddir` function is used to reinitialize the directory stream *dirstream*, so that if you call `readdir` it returns information about the first entry in the directory again. This function also notices if files have been added or removed to the directory since it was opened with `opendir`. (Entries for these files might or might not be returned by `readdir` if they were added or removed since you last called `opendir` or `rewinddir`.)

Chapter 9: File System Interface   175

`off_t` **telldir** (`DIR` *dirstream*)   Function
> The `telldir` function returns the file position of the directory stream *dirstream*. You can use this value with `seekdir` to restore the directory stream to that position.

`void` **seekdir** (`DIR` *dirstream*, `off_t` *pos*)   Function
> The `seekdir` function sets the file position of the directory stream *dirstream* to *pos*. The value *pos* must be the result of a previous call to `telldir` on this particular stream; closing and reopening the directory can invalidate values returned by `telldir`.

9.3 Hard Links

In POSIX systems, one file can have many names at the same time. All of the names are equally real, and no one of them is preferred to the others.

To add a name to a file, use the `link` function. (The new name is also called a *hard link* to the file.) Creating a new link to a file does not copy the contents of the file; it simply makes a new name by which the file can be known, in addition to the file's existing name or names.

One file can have names in several directories, so the the organization of the file system is not a strict hierarchy or tree.

In most implementations, it is not possible to have hard links to the same file in multiple file systems. `link` reports an error if you try to make a hard link to the file from another file system when this cannot be done.

The prototype for the `link` function is declared in the header file 'unistd.h'.

`int` **link** (`const char` *oldname*, `const char` *newname*)   Function

> The `link` function makes a new link to the existing file named by *oldname*, under the new name *newname*.
>
> This function returns a value of `0` if it is successful and `-1` on failure. In addition to the usual file name errors (see Section 6.2.3 [File Name Errors], page 79) for both *oldname* and *newname*, the following `errno` error conditions are defined for this function:
>
> `EACCES`   You are not allowed to write the directory in which the new link is to be written.
>
> `EEXIST`   There is already a file named *newname*. If you want to replace this link with a new link, you must remove the old link explicitly first.
>
> `EMLINK`   There are already too many links to the file named by *oldname*. (The maximum number of links to a file is

	`LINK_MAX`; see Section 27.6 [Limits on File System Capacity], page 507.)
`ENOENT`	The file named by *oldname* doesn't exist. You can't make a link to a file that doesn't exist.
`ENOSPC`	The directory or file system that would contain the new link is full and cannot be extended.
`EPERM`	In the GNU system and some others, you cannot make links to directories. Many systems allow only privileged users to do so. This error is used to report the problem.
`EROFS`	The directory containing the new link can't be modified because it's on a read-only file system.
`EXDEV`	The directory specified in *newname* is on a different file system than the existing file.
`EIO`	A hardware error occurred while trying to read or write the to filesystem.

9.4 Symbolic Links

The GNU system supports *soft links* or *symbolic links*. This is a kind of "file" that is essentially a pointer to another file name. Unlike hard links, symbolic links can be made to directories or across file systems with no restrictions. You can also make a symbolic link to a name which is not the name of any file. (Opening this link will fail until a file by that name is created.) Likewise, if the symbolic link points to an existing file which is later deleted, the symbolic link continues to point to the same file name even though the name no longer names any file.

The reason symbolic links work the way they do is that special things happen when you try to open the link. The `open` function realizes you have specified the name of a link, reads the file name contained in the link, and opens that file name instead. The `stat` function likewise operates on the file that the symbolic link points to, instead of on the link itself.

By contrast, other operations such as deleting or renaming the file operate on the link itself. The functions `readlink` and `lstat` also refrain from following symbolic links, because their purpose is to obtain information about the link. So does `link`, the function that makes a hard link—it makes a hard link to the symbolic link, which one rarely wants.

Prototypes for the functions listed in this section are in '`unistd.h`'.

int symlink (const char **oldname*, const char **newname*)   Function

The `symlink` function makes a symbolic link to *oldname* named *newname*.

Chapter 9: File System Interface   177

The normal return value from `symlink` is 0. A return value of -1 indicates an error. In addition to the usual file name syntax errors (see Section 6.2.3 [File Name Errors], page 79), the following `errno` error conditions are defined for this function:

EEXIST   There is already an existing file named *newname*.

EROFS   The file *newname* would exist on a read-only file system.

ENOSPC   The directory or file system cannot be extended to make the new link.

EIO   A hardware error occurred while reading or writing data on the disk.

int `readlink` (const char *filename*, char *buffer*,   *Function*
         size_t *size*)

The `readlink` function gets the value of the symbolic link *filename*. The file name that the link points to is copied into *buffer*. This file name string is *not* null-terminated; `readlink` normally returns the number of characters copied. The *size* argument specifies the maximum number of characters to copy, usually the allocation size of *buffer*.

If the return value equals *size*, you cannot tell whether or not there was room to return the entire name. So make a bigger buffer and call `readlink` again. Here is an example:

```
char *
readlink_malloc (char *filename)
{
  int size = 100;

  while (1)
    {
      char *buffer = (char *) xmalloc (size);
      int nchars = readlink (filename, buffer, size);
      if (nchars < size)
        return buffer;
      free (buffer);
      size *= 2;
    }
}
```

A value of -1 is returned in case of error. In addition to the usual file name errors (see Section 6.2.3 [File Name Errors], page 79), the following `errno` error conditions are defined for this function:

EINVAL   The named file is not a symbolic link.

EIO   A hardware error occurred while reading or writing data on the disk.

9.5 Deleting Files

You can delete a file with the functions `unlink` or `remove`.

Deletion actually deletes a file name. If this is the file's only name, then the file is deleted as well. If the file has other names as well (see Section 9.3 [Hard Links], page 175), it remains accessible under its other names.

`int unlink (const char *filename)`   *Function*

The `unlink` function deletes the file name *filename*. If this is a file's sole name, the file itself is also deleted. (Actually, if any process has the file open when this happens, deletion is postponed until all processes have closed the file.)

The function `unlink` is declared in the header file 'unistd.h'.

This function returns 0 on successful completion, and -1 on error. In addition to the usual file name errors (see Section 6.2.3 [File Name Errors], page 79), the following `errno` error conditions are defined for this function:

EACCES
: Write permission is denied for the directory from which the file is to be removed, or the directory has the sticky bit set and you do not own the file.

EBUSY
: This error indicates that the file is being used by the system in such a way that it can't be unlinked. For example, you might see this error if the file name specifies the root directory or a mount point for a file system.

ENOENT
: The file name to be deleted doesn't exist.

EPERM
: On some systems, `unlink` cannot be used to delete the name of a directory, or can only be used this way by a privileged user. To avoid such problems, use `rmdir` to delete directories. (In the GNU system `unlink` can never delete the name of a directory.)

EROFS
: The directory in which the file name is to be deleted is on a read-only file system, and can't be modified.

`int rmdir (const char *filename)`   *Function*

The `rmdir` function deletes a directory. The directory must be empty before it can be removed; in other words, it can only contain entries for '.' and '..'.

In most other respects, `rmdir` behaves like `unlink`. There are two additional `errno` error conditions defined for `rmdir`:

ENOTEMPTY
EEXIST
: The directory to be deleted is not empty.

Chapter 9: File System Interface   179

These two error codes are synonymous; some systems use one, and some use the other. The GNU system always uses `ENOTEMPTY`.

The prototype for this function is declared in the header file '`unistd.h`'.

`int remove` (`const char *`*filename*)   *Function*
This is the ANSI C function to remove a file. It works like `unlink` for files and like `rmdir` for directories. `remove` is declared in '`stdio.h`'.

9.6 Renaming Files

The `rename` function is used to change a file's name.

`int rename` (`const char *`*oldname*`, const char`   *Function*
        `*`*newname*)
The `rename` function renames the file name *oldname* with *newname*. The file formerly accessible under the name *oldname* is afterward accessible as *newname* instead. (If the file had any other names aside from *oldname*, it continues to have those names.)

The directory containing the name *newname* must be on the same file system as the file (as indicated by the name *oldname*).

One special case for `rename` is when *oldname* and *newname* are two names for the same file. The consistent way to handle this case is to delete *oldname*. However, POSIX requires that in this case `rename` do nothing and report success—which is inconsistent. We don't know what your operating system will do.

If the *oldname* is not a directory, then any existing file named *newname* is removed during the renaming operation. However, if *newname* is the name of a directory, `rename` fails in this case.

If the *oldname* is a directory, then either *newname* must not exist or it must name a directory that is empty. In the latter case, the existing directory named *newname* is deleted first. The name *newname* must not specify a subdirectory of the directory *oldname* which is being renamed.

One useful feature of `rename` is that the meaning of the name *newname* changes "atomically" from any previously existing file by that name to its new meaning (the file that was called *oldname*). There is no instant at which *newname* is nonexistent "in between" the old meaning and the new meaning. If there is a system crash during the operation, it is possible for both names to still exist; but *newname* will always be intact if it exists at all.

If `rename` fails, it returns `-1`. In addition to the usual file name errors (see Section 6.2.3 [File Name Errors], page 79), the following `errno` error conditions are defined for this function:

`EACCES`   One of the directories containing *newname* or *oldname* refuses write permission; or *newname* and *oldname* are directories and write permission is refused for one of them.

`EBUSY`   A directory named by *oldname* or *newname* is being used by the system in a way that prevents the renaming from working. This includes directories that are mount points for filesystems, and directories that are the current working directories of processes.

`ENOTEMPTY`
`EEXIST`   The directory *newname* isn't empty. The GNU system always returns `ENOTEMPTY` for this, but some other systems return `EEXIST`.

`EINVAL`   The *oldname* is a directory that contains *newname*.

`EISDIR`   The *newname* names a directory, but the *oldname* doesn't.

`EMLINK`   The parent directory of *newname* would have too many links.

`ENOENT`   The file named by *oldname* doesn't exist.

`ENOSPC`   The directory that would contain *newname* has no room for another entry, and there is no space left in the file system to expand it.

`EROFS`   The operation would involve writing to a directory on a read-only file system.

`EXDEV`   The two file names *newname* and *oldnames* are on different file systems.

9.7 Creating Directories

Directories are created with the `mkdir` function. (There is also a shell command `mkdir` which does the same thing.)

`int `**`mkdir`**` (const char *`*filename*`, mode_t `*mode*`)`   *Function*
The `mkdir` function creates a new, empty directory whose name is *filename*.

The argument *mode* specifies the file permissions for the new directory file. See Section 9.8.5 [The Mode Bits for Access Permission], page 188, for more information about this.

Chapter 9: File System Interface   181

A return value of 0 indicates successful completion, and -1 indicates failure. In addition to the usual file name syntax errors (see Section 6.2.3 [File Name Errors], page 79), the following `errno` error conditions are defined for this function:

EACCES   Write permission is denied for the parent directory in which the new directory is to be added.

EEXIST   A file named *filename* already exists.

EMLINK   The parent directory has too many links.

            Well-designed file systems never report this error, because they permit more links than your disk could possibly hold. However, you must still take account of the possibility of this error, as it could result from network access to a file system on another machine.

ENOSPC   The file system doesn't have enough room to create the new directory.

EROFS   The parent directory of the directory being created is on a read-only file system, and cannot be modified.

To use this function, your program should include the header file 'sys/stat.h'.

9.8 File Attributes

When you issue an 'ls -l' shell command on a file, it gives you information about the size of the file, who owns it, when it was last modified, and the like. This kind of information is called the *file attributes*; it is associated with the file itself and not a particular one of its names.

This section contains information about how you can inquire about and modify these attributes of files.

9.8.1 What the File Attribute Values Mean

When you read the attributes of a file, they come back in a structure called `struct stat`. This section describes the names of the attributes, their data types, and what they mean. For the functions to read the attributes of a file, see Section 9.8.2 [Reading the Attributes of a File], page 184.

The header file 'sys/stat.h' declares all the symbols defined in this section.

struct stat   Data Type
    The `stat` structure type is used to return information about the attributes of a file. It contains at least the following members:

`mode_t st_mode`
> Specifies the mode of the file. This includes file type information (see Section 9.8.3 [Testing the Type of a File], page 185) and the file permission bits (see Section 9.8.5 [The Mode Bits for Access Permission], page 188).

`ino_t st_ino`
> The file serial number, which distinguishes this file from all other files on the same device.

`dev_t st_dev`
> Identifies the device containing the file. The `st_ino` and `st_dev`, taken together, uniquely identify the file. The `st_dev` value is not necessarily consistent across reboots or system crashes, however.

`nlink_t st_nlink`
> The number of hard links to the file. This count keeps track of how many directories have entries for this file. If the count is ever decremented to zero, then the file itself is discarded as soon as no process still holds it open. Symbolic links are not counted in the total.

`uid_t st_uid`
> The user ID of the file's owner. See Section 9.8.4 [File Owner], page 186.

`gid_t st_gid`
> The group ID of the file. See Section 9.8.4 [File Owner], page 186.

`off_t st_size`
> This specifies the size of a regular file in bytes. For files that are really devices and the like, this field isn't usually meaningful. For symbolic links, this specifies the length of the file name the link refers to.

`time_t st_atime`
> This is the last access time for the file. See Section 9.8.9 [File Times], page 194.

`unsigned long int st_atime_usec`
> This is the fractional part of the last access time for the file. See Section 9.8.9 [File Times], page 194.

`time_t st_mtime`
> This is the time of the last modification to the contents of the file. See Section 9.8.9 [File Times], page 194.

Chapter 9: File System Interface   183

`unsigned long int st_mtime_usec`
:   This is the fractional part of the time of last modification to the contents of the file. See Section 9.8.9 [File Times], page 194.

`time_t st_ctime`
:   This is the time of the last modification to the attributes of the file. See Section 9.8.9 [File Times], page 194.

`unsigned long int st_ctime_usec`
:   This is the fractional part of the time of last modification to the attributes of the file. See Section 9.8.9 [File Times], page 194.

`unsigned int st_blocks`
:   This is the amount of disk space that the file occupies, measured in units of 512-byte blocks.

    The number of disk blocks is not strictly proportional to the size of the file, for two reasons: the file system may use some blocks for internal record keeping; and the file may be sparse—it may have "holes" which contain zeros but do not actually take up space on the disk.

    You can tell (approximately) whether a file is sparse by comparing this value with `st_size`, like this:

    `(st.st_blocks * 512 < st.st_size)`

    This test is not perfect because a file that is just slightly sparse might not be detected as sparse at all. For practical applications, this is not a problem.

`unsigned int st_blksize`
:   The optimal block size for reading of writing this file, in bytes. You might use this size for allocating the buffer space for reading of writing the file. (This is unrelated to `st_blocks`.)

Some of the file attributes have special data type names which exist specifically for those attributes. (They are all aliases for well-known integer types that you know and love.) These typedef names are defined in the header file 'sys/types.h' as well as in 'sys/stat.h'. Here is a list of them.

mode_t   Data Type

This is an integer data type used to represent file modes. In the GNU system, this is equivalent to `unsigned int`.

ino_t   Data Type

This is an arithmetic data type used to represent file serial numbers. (In Unix jargon, these are sometimes called *inode numbers*.) In the GNU system, this type is equivalent to `unsigned long int`.

dev_t   Data Type

This is an arithmetic data type used to represent file device numbers. In the GNU system, this is equivalent to `int`.

nlink_t   Data Type

This is an arithmetic data type used to represent file link counts. In the GNU system, this is equivalent to `unsigned short int`.

9.8.2 Reading the Attributes of a File

To examine the attributes of files, use the functions `stat`, `fstat` and `lstat`. They return the attribute information in a `struct stat` object. All three functions are declared in the header file 'sys/stat.h'.

int stat (`const char *`*filename*, `struct stat *`*buf*)   Function

The `stat` function returns information about the attributes of the file named by *filename* in the structure pointed at by *buf*.

If *filename* is the name of a symbolic link, the attributes you get describe the file that the link points to. If the link points to a nonexistent file name, then `stat` fails, reporting a nonexistent file.

The return value is `0` if the operation is successful, and `-1` on failure. In addition to the usual file name errors (see Section 6.2.3 [File Name Errors], page 79, the following `errno` error conditions are defined for this function:

`ENOENT`   The file named by *filename* doesn't exist.

int fstat (`int` *filedes*, `struct stat *`*buf*)   Function

The `fstat` function is like `stat`, except that it takes an open file descriptor as an argument instead of a file name. See Chapter 8 [Low-Level Input/Output], page 139.

Like `stat`, `fstat` returns `0` on success and `-1` on failure. The following `errno` error conditions are defined for `fstat`:

`EBADF`   The *filedes* argument is not a valid file descriptor.

int lstat (`const char *`*filename*, `struct stat *`*buf*)   Function

The `lstat` function is like `stat`, except that it does not follow symbolic links. If *filename* is the name of a symbolic link, `lstat` returns information about the link itself; otherwise, `lstat` works like `stat`. See Section 9.4 [Symbolic Links], page 176.

Chapter 9: File System Interface

9.8.3 Testing the Type of a File

The *file mode*, stored in the `st_mode` field of the file attributes, contains two kinds of information: the file type code, and the access permission bits. This section discusses only the type code, which you can use to tell whether the file is a directory, whether it is a socket, and so on. For information about the access permission, Section 9.8.5 [The Mode Bits for Access Permission], page 188.

There are two predefined ways you can access the file type portion of the file mode. First of all, for each type of file, there is a *predicate macro* which examines a file mode value and returns true or false—is the file of that type, or not. Secondly, you can mask out the rest of the file mode to get just a file type code. You can compare this against various constants for the supported file types.

All of the symbols listed in this section are defined in the header file 'sys/stat.h'.

The following predicate macros test the type of a file, given the value *m* which is the `st_mode` field returned by `stat` on that file:

int **S_ISDIR** (mode_t *m*)   Macro
    This macro returns nonzero if the file is a directory.

int **S_ISCHR** (mode_t *m*)   Macro
    This macro returns nonzero if the file is a character special file (a device like a terminal).

int **S_ISBLK** (mode_t *m*)   Macro
    This macro returns nonzero if the file is a block special file (a device like a disk).

int **S_ISREG** (mode_t *m*)   Macro
    This macro returns nonzero if the file is a regular file.

int **S_ISFIFO** (mode_t *m*)   Macro
    This macro returns nonzero if the file is a FIFO special file, or a pipe. See Chapter 10 [Pipes and FIFOs], page 201.

int **S_ISLNK** (mode_t *m*)   Macro
    This macro returns nonzero if the file is a symbolic link. See Section 9.4 [Symbolic Links], page 176.

int **S_ISSOCK** (mode_t *m*)   Macro
    This macro returns nonzero if the file is a socket. See Chapter 11 [Sockets], page 207.

An alterate non-POSIX method of testing the file type is supported for compatibility with BSD. The mode can be bitwise ANDed with `S_IFMT` to extract the file type code, and compared to the appropriate type code constant. For example,

> `S_ISCHR (`*mode*`)`

is equivalent to:

> `((`*mode* `& S_IFMT) == S_IFCHR)`

int S_IFMT   Macro
This is a bit mask used to extract the file type code portion of a mode value.

These are the symbolic names for the different file type codes:

`S_IFDIR`   This macro represents the value of the file type code for a directory file.

`S_IFCHR`   This macro represents the value of the file type code for a character-oriented device file.

`S_IFBLK`   This macro represents the value of the file type code for a block-oriented device file.

`S_IFREG`   This macro represents the value of the file type code for a regular file.

`S_IFLNK`   This macro represents the value of the file type code for a symbolic link.

`S_IFSOCK` This macro represents the value of the file type code for a socket.

`S_IFIFO`   This macro represents the value of the file type code for a FIFO or pipe.

9.8.4 File Owner

Every file has an *owner* which is one of the registered user names defined on the system. Each file also has a *group*, which is one of the defined groups. The file owner can often be useful for showing you who edited the file (especially when you edit with GNU Emacs), but its main purpose is for access control.

The file owner and group play a role in determining access because the file has one set of access permission bits for the user that is the owner, another set that apply to users who belong to the file's group, and a third set of bits that apply to everyone else. See Section 9.8.6 [How Your Access to a File is Decided], page 190, for the details of how access is decided based on this data.

Chapter 9: File System Interface 187

When a file is created, its owner is set from the effective user ID of the process that creates it (see Section 25.2 [The Persona of a Process], page 479). The file's group ID may be set from either effective group ID of the process, or the group ID of the directory that contains the file, depending on the system where the file is stored. When you access a remote file system, it behaves according to its own rule, not according to the system your program is running on. Thus, your program must be prepared to encounter either kind of behavior, no matter what kind of system you run it on.

You can change the owner and/or group owner of an existing file using the `chown` function. This is the primitive for the `chown` and `chgrp` shell commands.

The prototype for this function is declared in 'unistd.h'.

`int chown` (const char *filename, uid_t owner, gid_t group) *Function*

The `chown` function changes the owner of the file filename to owner, and its group owner to group.

Changing the owner of the file on certain systems clears the set-user-ID and set-group-ID bits of the file's permissions. (This is because those bits may not be appropriate for the new owner.) The other file permission bits are not changed.

The return value is 0 on success and -1 on failure. In addition to the usual file name errors (see Section 6.2.3 [File Name Errors], page 79), the following `errno` error conditions are defined for this function:

EPERM   This process lacks permission to make the requested change.

Only privileged users or the file's owner can change the file's group. On most file systems, only privileged users can change the file owner; some file systems allow you to change the owner if you are currently the owner. When you access a remote file system, the behavior you encounter is determined by the system that actually holds the file, not by the system your program is running on.

See Section 27.7 [Optional Features in File Support], page 508, for information about the `_POSIX_CHOWN_RESTRICTED` macro.

EROFS   The file is on a read-only file system.

`int fchown` (int filedes, int owner, int group) *Function*

This is like `chown`, except that it changes the owner of the file with open file descriptor filedes.

The return value from `fchown` is 0 on success and -1 on failure. The following `errno` error codes are defined for this function:

EBADF   The *filedes* argument is not a valid file descriptor.

EINVAL   The *filedes* argument corresponds to a pipe or socket, not an ordinary file.

EPERM   This process lacks permission to make the requested change. For details, see `chmod`, above.

EROFS   The file resides on a read-only file system.

9.8.5 The Mode Bits for Access Permission

The *file mode*, stored in the `st_mode` field of the file attributes, contains two kinds of information: the file type code, and the access permission bits. This section discusses only the access permission bits, which control who can read or write the file. See Section 9.8.3 [Testing the Type of a File], page 185, for information about the file type code.

All of the symbols listed in this section are defined in the header file 'sys/stat.h'.

These symbolic constants are defined for the file mode bits that control access permission for the file:

`S_IRUSR`
`S_IREAD`   Read permission bit for the owner of the file. On many systems, this bit is 0400. `S_IREAD` is an obsolete synonym provided for BSD compatibility.

`S_IWUSR`
`S_IWRITE` Write permission bit for the owner of the file. Usually 0200. `S_IWRITE` is an obsolete synonym provided for BSD compatibility.

`S_IXUSR`
`S_IEXEC`   Execute (for ordinary files) or search (for directories) permission bit for the owner of the file. Usually 0100. `S_IEXEC` is an obsolete synonym provided for BSD compatibility.

`S_IRWXU`   This is equivalent to '(S_IRUSR | S_IWUSR | S_IXUSR)'.

`S_IRGRP`   Read permission bit for the group owner of the file. Usually 040.

`S_IWGRP`   Write permission bit for the group owner of the file. Usually 020.

`S_IXGRP`   Execute or search permission bit for the group owner of the file. Usually 010.

`S_IRWXG`   This is equivalent to '(S_IRGRP | S_IWGRP | S_IXGRP)'.

`S_IROTH`   Read permission bit for other users. Usually 04.

Chapter 9: File System Interface 189

`S_IWOTH` Write permission bit for other users. Usually 02.

`S_IXOTH` Execute or search permission bit for other users. Usually 01.

`S_IRWXO` This is equivalent to '`(S_IROTH | S_IWOTH | S_IXOTH)`'.

`S_ISUID` This is the set-user-ID on execute bit, usually 04000. See Section 25.4 [How an Application Can Change Persona], page 481.

`S_ISGID` This is the set-group-ID on execute bit, usually 02000. See Section 25.4 [How an Application Can Change Persona], page 481.

`S_ISVTX` This is the *sticky* bit, usually 01000.

On a directory, it gives permission to delete a file in the directory only if you own that file. Ordinarily, a user either can delete all the files in the directory or cannot delete any of them (based on whether the user has write permission for the directory). The same restriction applies—you must both have write permission for the directory and own the file you want to delete. The one exception is that the owner of the directory can delete any file in the directory, no matter who owns it (provided the owner has given himself write permission for the directory). This is commonly used for the '`/tmp`' directory, where anyone may create files, but not delete files created by other users.

Originally the sticky bit on an executable file modified the swapping policies of the system. Normally, when a program terminated, its pages in core were immediately freed and reused. If the sticky bit was set on the executable file, the system kept the pages in core for a while as if the program were still running. This was advantageous for a program likely to be run many times in succession. This usage is obsolete in modern systems. When a program terminates, its pages always remain in core as long as there is no shortage of memory in the system. When the program is next run, its pages will still be in core if no shortage arose since the last run.

On some modern systems where the sticky bit has no useful meaning for an executable file, you cannot set the bit at all for a non-directory. If you try, `chmod` fails with `EFTYPE`; see Section 9.8.7 [Assigning File Permissions], page 190.

Some systems (particularly SunOS) have yet another use for the sticky bit. If the sticky bit is set on a file that is *not* executable, it means the opposite: never cache the pages of this file at all. The main use of this is for the files on an NFS server machine which are used as the swap area of diskless client machines. The idea is that the pages of the file will be cached in the client's memory, so it is a waste of the server's memory to cache them a second time. In this use the sticky bit also says that the filesystem may fail to record the file's modification time onto disk reliably (the idea being that noone cares for a swap file).

The actual bit values of the symbols are listed in the table above so you can decode file mode values when debugging your programs. These bit values are correct for most systems, but they are not guaranteed.

Warning: Writing explicit numbers for file permissions is bad practice. It is not only nonportable, it also requires everyone who reads your program to remember what the bits mean. To make your program clean, use the symbolic names.

9.8.6 How Your Access to a File is Decided

Recall that the operating system normally decides access permission for a file based on the effective user and group IDs of the process, and its supplementary group IDs, together with the file's owner, group and permission bits. These concepts are discussed in detail in Section 25.2 [The Persona of a Process], page 479.

If the effective user ID of the process matches the owner user ID of the file, then permissions for read, write, and execute/search are controlled by the corresponding "user" (or "owner") bits. Likewise, if any of the effective group ID or supplementary group IDs of the process matches the group owner ID of the file, then permissions are controlled by the "group" bits. Otherwise, permissions are controlled by the "other" bits.

Privileged users, like 'root', can access any file, regardless of its file permission bits. As a special case, for a file to be executable even for a privileged user, at least one of its execute bits must be set.

9.8.7 Assigning File Permissions

The primitive functions for creating files (for example, `open` or `mkdir`) take a *mode* argument, which specifies the file permissions for the newly created file. But the specified mode is modified by the process's *file creation mask*, or *umask*, before it is used.

The bits that are set in the file creation mask identify permissions that are always to be disabled for newly created files. For example, if you set all the "other" access bits in the mask, then newly created files are not accessible at all to processes in the "other" category, even if the *mode* argument specified to the creation function would permit such access. In other words, the file creation mask is the complement of the ordinary access permissions you want to grant.

Programs that create files typically specify a *mode* argument that includes all the permissions that make sense for the particular file. For an

Chapter 9: File System Interface   191

ordinary file, this is typically read and write permission for all classes of users. These permissions are then restricted as specified by the individual user's own file creation mask.

To change the permission of an existing file given its name, call **chmod**. This function ignores the file creation mask; it uses exactly the specified permission bits.

In normal use, the file creation mask is initialized in the user's login shell (using the **umask** shell command), and inherited by all subprocesses. Application programs normally don't need to worry about the file creation mask. It will do automatically what it is supposed to do.

When your program should create a file and bypass the umask for its access permissions, the easiest way to do this is to use **fchmod** after opening the file, rather than changing the umask.

In fact, changing the umask is usually done only by shells. They use the **umask** function.

The functions in this section are declared in 'sys/stat.h'.

mode_t umask (mode_t *mask*)   Function

The **umask** function sets the file creation mask of the current process to *mask*, and returns the previous value of the file creation mask.

Here is an example showing how to read the mask with **umask** without changing it permanently:

```
mode_t
read_umask (void)
{
  mask = umask (0);
  umask (mask);
}
```

However, it is better to use **getumask** if you just want to read the mask value, because that is reentrant (at least if you use the GNU operating system).

mode_t getumask (void)   Function

Return the current value of the file creation mask for the current process. This function is a GNU extension.

int chmod (const char **filename*, mode_t *mode*)   Function

The **chmod** function sets the access permission bits for the file named by *filename* to *mode*.

If the *filename* names a symbolic link, **chmod** changes the permission of the file pointed to by the link, not those of the link itself.

This function returns 0 if successful and -1 if not. In addition to the usual file name errors (see Section 6.2.3 [File Name Errors], page 79), the following **errno** error conditions are defined for this function:

ENOENT   The named file doesn't exist.

EPERM   This process does not have permission to change the access permission of this file. Only the file's owner (as judged by the effective user ID of the process) or a privileged user can change them.

EROFS   The file resides on a read-only file system.

EFTYPE   *mode* has the `S_ISVTX` bit (the "sticky bit") set, and the named file is not a directory. Some systems do not allow setting the sticky bit on non-directory files, and some do (and only some of those assign a useful meaning to the bit for non-directory files).

You only get `EFTYPE` on systems where the sticky bit has no useful meaning for non-directory files, so it is always safe to just clear the bit in *mode* and call `chmod` again. See Section 9.8.5 [The Mode Bits for Access Permission], page 188, for full details on the sticky bit.

int fchmod (int *filedes*, int *mode*)   Function

This is like `chmod`, except that it changes the permissions of the file currently open via descriptor *filedes*.

The return value from `fchmod` is 0 on success and -1 on failure. The following `errno` error codes are defined for this function:

EBADF   The *filedes* argument is not a valid file descriptor.

EINVAL   The *filedes* argument corresponds to a pipe or socket, or something else that doesn't really have access permissions.

EPERM   This process does not have permission to change the access permission of this file. Only the file's owner (as judged by the effective user ID of the process) or a privileged user can change them.

EROFS   The file resides on a read-only file system.

9.8.8 Testing Permission to Access a File

When a program runs as a privileged user, this permits it to access files off-limits to ordinary users—for example, to modify '/etc/passwd'. Programs designed to be run by ordinary users but access such files use the setuid bit feature so that they always run with `root` as the effective user ID.

Such a program may also access files specified by the user, files which conceptually are being accessed explicitly by the user. Since the program

Chapter 9: File System Interface   193

runs as `root`, it has permission to access whatever file the user specifies—but usually the desired behavior is to permit only those files which the user could ordinarily access.

The program therefore must explicitly check whether *the user* would have the necessary access to a file, before it reads or writes the file.

To do this, use the function `access`, which checks for access permission based on the process's *real* user ID rather than the effective user ID. (The setuid feature does not alter the real user ID, so it reflects the user who actually ran the program.)

There is another way you could check this access, which is easy to describe, but very hard to use. This is to examine the file mode bits and mimic the system's own access computation. This method is undesirable because many systems have additional access control features; your program cannot portably mimic them, and you would not want to try to keep track of the diverse features that different systems have. Using `access` is simple and automatically does whatever is appropriate for the system you are using.

`access` is *only* only appropriate to use in setuid programs. A non-setuid program will always use the effective ID rather than the real ID.

The symbols in this section are declared in '`unistd.h`'.

`int` **`access`** `(const char *`*filename*`, int` *how*`)`   Function

The `access` function checks to see whether the file named by *filename* can be accessed in the way specified by the *how* argument. The *how* argument either can be the bitwise OR of the flags `R_OK`, `W_OK`, `X_OK`, or the existence test `F_OK`.

This function uses the *real* user and group ID's of the calling process, rather than the *effective* ID's, to check for access permission. As a result, if you use the function from a `setuid` or `setgid` program (see Section 25.4 [How an Application Can Change Persona], page 481), it gives information relative to the user who actually ran the program.

The return value is `0` if the access is permitted, and `-1` otherwise. (In other words, treated as a predicate function, `access` returns true if the requested access is *denied*.)

In addition to the usual file name errors (see Section 6.2.3 [File Name Errors], page 79), the following `errno` error conditions are defined for this function:

`EACCES`   The access specified by *how* is denied.

`ENOENT`   The file doesn't exist.

`EROFS`   Write permission was requested for a file on a read-only file system.

These macros are defined in the header file 'unistd.h' for use as the *how* argument to the `access` function. The values are integer constants.

int R_OK   Macro
Argument that means, test for read permission.

int W_OK   Macro
Argument that means, test for write permission.

int X_OK   Macro
Argument that means, test for execute/search permission.

int F_OK   Macro
Argument that means, test for existence of the file.

9.8.9 File Times

Each file has three timestamps associated with it: its access time, its modification time, and its attribute modification time. These correspond to the `st_atime`, `st_mtime`, and `st_ctime` members of the `stat` structure; see Section 9.8 [File Attributes], page 181.

All of these times are represented in calendar time format, as `time_t` objects. This data type is defined in 'time.h'. For more information about representation and manipulation of time values, see Section 17.2 [Calendar Time], page 323.

Reading from a file updates its access time attribute, and writing updates its modification time. When a file is created, all three timestamps for that file are set to the current time. In addition, the attribute change time and modification time fields of the directory that contains the new entry are updated.

Adding a new name for a file with the `link` function updates the attribute change time field of the file being linked, and both the attribute change time and modification time fields of the directory containing the new name. These same fields are affected if a file name is deleted with `unlink`, `remove`, or `rmdir`. Renaming a file with `rename` affects only the attribute change time and modification time fields of the two parent directories involved, and not the times for the file being renamed.

Changing attributes of a file (for example, with `chmod`) updates its attribute change time field.

You can also change some of the timestamps of a file explicitly using the `utime` function—all except the attribute change time. You need to include the header file 'utime.h' to use this facility.

Chapter 9: File System Interface   195

struct utimbuf   Data Type
   The `utimbuf` structure is used with the `utime` function to specify new
   access and modification times for a file. It contains the following members:

   `time_t actime`
            This is the access time for the file.

   `time_t modtime`
            This is the modification time for the file.

int utime (`const char *`*filename*`, const struct`   Function
         `utimbuf *`*times*)
   This function is used to modify the file times associated with the file
   named *filename*.

   If *times* is a null pointer, then the access and modification times of the
   file are set to the current time. Otherwise, they are set to the values
   from the `actime` and `modtime` members (respectively) of the `utimbuf`
   structure pointed at by *times*.

   The attribute modification time for the file is set to the current time
   in either case (since changing the timestamps is itself a modification
   of the file attributes).

   The `utime` function returns `0` if successful and `-1` on failure. In addition to the usual file name errors (see Section 6.2.3 [File Name Errors],
   page 79), the following `errno` error conditions are defined for this function:

   `EACCES`   There is a permission problem in the case where a null
               pointer was passed as the *times* argument. In order to
               update the timestamp on the file, you must either be the
               owner of the file, have write permission on the file, or be
               a privileged user.

   `ENOENT`   The file doesn't exist.

   `EPERM`   If the *times* argument is not a null pointer, you must either
               be the owner of the file or be a privileged user. This error
               is used to report the problem.

   `EROFS`   The file lives on a read-only file system.

   Each of the three time stamps has a corresponding microsecond part,
which extends its resolution. These fields are called `st_atime_usec`, `st_mtime_usec`, and `st_ctime_usec`; each has a value between 0 and 999,999,
which indicates the time in microseconds. They correspond to the `tv_usec`
field of a `timeval` structure; see Section 17.2.2 [High-Resolution Calendar],
page 324.

The `utimes` function is like `utime`, but also lets you specify the fractional part of the file times. The prototype for this function is in the header file 'sys/time.h'.

int utimes (const char *filename*, struct timeval *tvp*[2]) *Function*

This function sets the file access and modification times for the file named by *filename*. The new file access time is specified by *tvp*[0], and the new modification time by *tvp*[1]. This function comes from BSD.

The return values and error conditions are the same as for the `utime` function.

9.9 Making Special Files

The `mknod` function is the primitive for making special files, such as files that correspond to devices. The GNU library includes this function for compatibility with BSD.

The prototype for `mknod` is declared in 'sys/stat.h'.

int mknod (const char *filename*, int *mode*, int *dev*) *Function*

The `mknod` function makes a special file with name *filename*. The *mode* specifies the mode of the file, and may include the various special file bits, such as `S_IFCHR` (for a character special file) or `S_IFBLK` (for a block special file). See Section 9.8.3 [Testing the Type of a File], page 185.

The *dev* argument specifies which device the special file refers to. Its exact interpretation depends on the kind of special file being created.

The return value is 0 on success and -1 on error. In addition to the usual file name errors (see Section 6.2.3 [File Name Errors], page 79), the following `errno` error conditions are defined for this function:

EPERM   The calling process is not privileged. Only the superuser can create special files.

ENOSPC   The directory or file system that would contain the new file is full and cannot be extended.

EROFS   The directory containing the new file can't be modified because it's on a read-only file system.

EEXIST   There is already a file named *filename*. If you want to replace this file, you must remove the old file explicitly first.

Chapter 9: File System Interface   197

9.10 Temporary Files

If you need to use a temporary file in your program, you can use the `tmpfile` function to open it. Or you can use the `tmpnam` function make a name for a temporary file and then open it in the usual way with `fopen`.

The `tempnam` function is like `tmpnam` but lets you choose what directory temporary files will go in, and something about what their file names will look like.

These facilities are declared in the header file 'stdio.h'.

FILE * **tmpfile** (void)   Function
: This function creates a temporary binary file for update mode, as if by calling `fopen` with mode `"wb+"`. The file is deleted automatically when it is closed or when the program terminates. (On some other ANSI C systems the file may fail to be deleted if the program terminates abnormally).

char * **tmpnam** (char *result*)   Function
: This function constructs and returns a file name that is a valid file name and that does not name any existing file. If the *result* argument is a null pointer, the return value is a pointer to an internal static string, which might be modified by subsequent calls. Otherwise, the *result* argument should be a pointer to an array of at least `L_tmpnam` characters, and the result is written into that array.

: It is possible for `tmpnam` to fail if you call it too many times. This is because the fixed length of a temporary file name gives room for only a finite number of different names. If `tmpnam` fails, it returns a null pointer.

int **L_tmpnam**   Macro
: The value of this macro is an integer constant expression that represents the minimum allocation size of a string large enough to hold the file name generated by the `tmpnam` function.

int **TMP_MAX**   Macro
: The macro `TMP_MAX` is a lower bound for how many temporary names you can create with `tmpnam`. You can rely on being able to call `tmpnam` at least this many times before it might fail saying you have made too many temporary file names.

: With the GNU library, you can create a very large number of temporary file names—if you actually create the files, you will probably run out of disk space before you run out of names. Some other systems have a fixed, small limit on the number of temporary files. The limit is never less than 25.

char * **tempnam** (const char *dir, const char   Function
         *prefix)
  This function generates a unique temporary filename. If prefix is not
  a null pointer, up to five characters of this string are used as a prefix
  for the file name. The return value is a string newly allocated with
  `malloc`; you should release its storage with `free` when it is no longer
  needed.

  The directory prefix for the temporary file name is determined by
  testing each of the following, in sequence. The directory must exist
  and be writable.

  - The environment variable `TMPDIR`, if it is defined.
  - The dir argument, if it is not a null pointer.
  - The value of the `P_tmpdir` macro.
  - The directory '/tmp'.

  This function is defined for SVID compatibility.

char * **P_tmpdir**   SVID Macro
  This macro is the name of the default directory for temporary files.

Older Unix systems did not have the functions just described. Instead they used `mktemp` and `mkstemp`. Both of these functions work by modifying a file name template string you pass. The last six characters of this string must be 'XXXXXX'. These six 'X's are replaced with six characters which make the whole string a unique file name. Usually the template string is something like '/tmp/prefixXXXXXX', and each program uses a unique prefix.

Note: Because `mktemp` and `mkstemp` modify the template string, you *must not* pass string constants to them. String constants are normally in read-only storage, so your program would crash when `mktemp` or `mkstemp` tried to modify the string.

char * **mktemp** (char *template)   Function
  The `mktemp` function generates a unique file name by modifying *template* as described above. If successful, it returns *template* as modified. If `mktemp` cannot find a unique file name, it makes *template* an empty string and returns that. If *template* does not end with 'XXXXXX', `mktemp` returns a null pointer.

int **mkstemp** (char *template)   Function
  The `mkstemp` function generates a unique file name just as `mktemp` does, but it also opens the file for you with `open` (see Section 8.1 [Opening and Closing Files], page 139). If successful, it modifies *template* in place and returns a file descriptor open on that file for reading and writing. If `mkstemp` cannot create a uniquely-named file, it makes

Chapter 9: File System Interface   199

template an empty string and returns `-1`. If *template* does not end with 'XXXXXX', `mkstemp` returns `-1` and does not modify *template*.

Unlike `mktemp`, `mkstemp` is actually guaranteed to create a unique file that cannot possibly clash with any other program trying to create a temporary file. This is because it works by calling `open` with the `O_EXCL` flag bit, which says you want to always create a new file, and get an error if the file already exists.

10 Pipes and FIFOs

A *pipe* is a mechanism for interprocess communication; data written to the pipe by one process can be read by another process. The data is handled in a first-in, first-out (FIFO) order. The pipe has no name; it is created for one use and both ends must be inherited from the single process which created the pipe.

A *FIFO special file* is similar to a pipe, but instead of being an anonymous, temporary connection, a FIFO has a name or names like any other file. Processes open the FIFO by name in order to communicate through it.

A pipe or FIFO has to be open at both ends simultaneously. If you read from a pipe or FIFO file that doesn't have any processes writing to it (perhaps because they have all closed the file, or exited), the read returns end-of-file. Writing to a pipe or FIFO that doesn't have a reading process is treated as an error condition; it generates a `SIGPIPE` signal, and fails with error code `EPIPE` if the signal is handled or blocked.

Neither pipes nor FIFO special files allow file positioning. Both reading and writing operations happen sequentially; reading from the beginning of the file and writing at the end.

10.1 Creating a Pipe

The primitive for creating a pipe is the `pipe` function. This creates both the reading and writing ends of the pipe. It is not very useful for a single process to use a pipe to talk to itself. In typical use, a process creates a pipe just before it forks one or more child processes (see Section 23.4 [Creating a Process], page 445). The pipe is then used for communication either between the parent or child processes, or between two sibling processes.

The `pipe` function is declared in the header file 'unistd.h'.

`int` **pipe** (`int` *filedes*[2])   Function

> The `pipe` function creates a pipe and puts the file descriptors for the reading and writing ends of the pipe (respectively) into *filedes*[0] and *filedes*[1].
>
> An easy way to remember that the input end comes first is that file descriptor 0 is standard input, and file descriptor 1 is standard output.
>
> If successful, `pipe` returns a value of 0. On failure, -1 is returned. The following `errno` error conditions are defined for this function:
>
> EMFILE
> : The process has too many files open.
>
> ENFILE
> : There are too many open files in the entire system. See Section 2.2 [Error Codes], page 14, for more information about `ENFILE`. This error never occurs in the GNU system.

Here is an example of a simple program that creates a pipe. This program uses the `fork` function (see Section 23.4 [Creating a Process], page 445) to create a child process. The parent process writes data to the pipe, which is read by the child process.

```
#include <sys/types.h>
#include <unistd.h>
#include <stdio.h>
#include <stdlib.h>

/* Read characters from the pipe and echo them to stdout. */

void
read_from_pipe (int file)
{
  FILE *stream;
  int c;
  stream = fdopen (file, "r");
  while ((c = fgetc (stream)) != EOF)
    putchar (c);
  fclose (stream);
}

/* Write some random text to the pipe. */

void
write_to_pipe (int file)
{
  FILE *stream;
  stream = fdopen (file, "w");
  fprintf (stream, "hello, world!\n");
  fprintf (stream, "goodbye, world!\n");
  fclose (stream);
}

int
main (void)
{
  pid_t pid;
  int mypipe[2];

  /* Create the pipe. */
  if (pipe (mypipe))
    {
      fprintf (stderr, "Pipe failed.\n");
      return EXIT_FAILURE;
    }

  /* Create the child process. */
  pid = fork ();
  if (pid == (pid_t) 0)
    {
      /* This is the child process. */
      read_from_pipe (mypipe[0]);
```

```
      return EXIT_SUCCESS;
    }
  else if (pid < (pid_t) 0)
    {
      /* The fork failed. */
      fprintf (stderr, "Fork failed.\n");
      return EXIT_FAILURE;
    }
  else
    {
      /* This is the parent process. */
      write_to_pipe (mypipe[1]);
      return EXIT_SUCCESS;
    }
}
```

10.2 Pipe to a Subprocess

A common use of pipes is to send data to or receive data from a program being run as subprocess. One way of doing this is by using a combination of `pipe` (to create the pipe), `fork` (to create the subprocess), `dup2` (to force the subprocess to use the pipe as its standard input or output channel), and `exec` (to execute the new program). Or, you can use `popen` and `pclose`.

The advantage of using `popen` and `pclose` is that the interface is much simpler and easier to use. But it doesn't offer as much flexibility as using the low-level functions directly.

FILE * popen (`const char *command, const char *mode`) *Function*

The `popen` function is closely related to the `system` function; see Section 23.1 [Running a Command], page 443. It executes the shell command *command* as a subprocess. However, instead of waiting for the command to complete, it creates a pipe to the subprocess and returns a stream that corresponds to that pipe.

If you specify a *mode* argument of `"r"`, you can read from the stream to retrieve data from the standard output channel of the subprocess. The subprocess inherits its standard input channel from the parent process.

Similarly, if you specify a *mode* argument of `"w"`, you can write to the stream to send data to the standard input channel of the subprocess. The subprocess inherits its standard output channel from the parent process.

In the event of an error, `popen` returns a null pointer. This might happen if the pipe or stream cannot be created, if the subprocess cannot be forked, or if the program cannot be executed.

int pclose (FILE *stream*)   *Function*

The `pclose` function is used to close a stream created by `popen`. It waits for the child process to terminate and returns its status value, as for the `system` function.

Here is an example showing how to use `popen` and `pclose` to filter output through another program, in this case the paging program `more`.

```
#include <stdio.h>
#include <stdlib.h>

void
write_data (FILE * stream)
{
  int i;
  for (i = 0; i < 100; i++)
    fprintf (stream, "%d\n", i);
  if (ferror (stream))
    {
      fprintf (stderr, "Output to stream failed.\n");
      exit (EXIT_FAILURE);
    }
}

int
main (void)
{
  FILE *output;

  output = popen ("more", "w");
  if (!output)
    {
      fprintf (stderr, "Could not run more.\n");
      return EXIT_FAILURE;
    }
  write_data (output);
  pclose (output);
  return EXIT_SUCCESS;
}
```

10.3 FIFO Special Files

A FIFO special file is similar to a pipe, except that it is created in a different way. Instead of being an anonymous communications channel, a FIFO special file is entered into the file system by calling `mkfifo`.

Once you have created a FIFO special file in this way, any process can open it for reading or writing, in the same way as an ordinary file. However, it has to be open at both ends simultaneously before you can proceed to do any input or output operations on it. Opening a FIFO for reading normally

Chapter 10: Pipes and FIFOs 205

blocks until some other process opens the same FIFO for writing, and vice versa.

The `mkfifo` function is declared in the header file 'sys/stat.h'.

int mkfifo (**const char** *filename*, **mode_t** *mode*) *Function*
The `mkfifo` function makes a FIFO special file with name *filename*. The *mode* argument is used to set the file's permissions; see Section 9.8.7 [Assigning File Permissions], page 190.

The normal, successful return value from `mkfifo` is 0. In the case of an error, `-1` is returned. In addition to the usual file name errors (see Section 6.2.3 [File Name Errors], page 79), the following `errno` error conditions are defined for this function:

EEXIST   The named file already exists.

ENOSPC   The directory or file system cannot be extended.

EROFS   The directory that would contain the file resides on a read-only file system.

10.4 Atomicity of Pipe I/O

Reading or writing pipe data is *atomic* if the size of data written is not greater than `PIPE_BUF`. This means that the data transfer seems to be an instantaneous unit, in that nothing else in the system can observe a state in which it is partially complete. Atomic I/O may not begin right away (it may need to wait for buffer space or for data), but once it does begin, it finishes immediately.

Reading or writing a larger amount of data may not be atomic; for example, output data from other processes sharing the descriptor may be interspersed. Also, once `PIPE_BUF` characters have been written, further writes will block until some characters are read.

See Section 27.6 [Limits on File System Capacity], page 507, for information about the `PIPE_BUF` parameter.

11 Sockets

This chapter describes the GNU facilities for interprocess communication using sockets.

A *socket* is a generalized interprocess communication channel. Like a pipe, a socket is represented as a file descriptor. But, unlike pipes, sockets support communication between unrelated processes, and even between processes running on different machines that communicate over a network. Sockets are the primary means of communicating with other machines; `telnet`, `rlogin`, `ftp`, `talk`, and the other familiar network programs use sockets.

Not all operating systems support sockets. In the GNU library, the header file '`sys/socket.h`' exists regardless of the operating system, and the socket functions always exist, but if the system does not really support sockets, these functions always fail.

Incomplete: We do not currently document the facilities for broadcast messages or for configuring Internet interfaces.

11.1 Socket Concepts

When you create a socket, you must specify the style of communication you want to use and the type of protocol that should implement it. The *communication style* of a socket defines the user-level semantics of sending and receiving data on the socket. Choosing a communication style specifies the answers to questions such as these:

- **What are the units of data transmission?** Some communication styles regard the data as a sequence of bytes, with no larger structure; others group the bytes into records (which are known in this context as *packets*).

- **Can data be lost during normal operation?** Some communication styles guarantee that all the data sent arrives in the order it was sent (barring system or network crashes); other styles occasionally lose data as a normal part of operation, and may sometimes deliver packets more than once or in the wrong order.

  Designing a program to use unreliable communication styles usually involves taking precautions to detect lost or misordered packets and to retransmit data as needed.

- **Is communication entirely with one partner?** Some communication styles are like a telephone call—you make a *connection* with one remote socket, and then exchange data freely. Other styles are like mailing letters—you specify a destination address for each message you send.

You must also choose a *namespace* for naming the socket. A socket name ("address") is meaningful only in the context of a particular namespace.

In fact, even the data type to use for a socket name may depend on the namespace. Namespaces are also called "domains", but we avoid that word as it can be confused with other usage of the same term. Each namespace has a symbolic name that starts with 'PF_'. A corresponding symbolic name starting with 'AF_' designates the address format for that namespace.

Finally you must choose the *protocol* to carry out the communication. The protocol determines what low-level mechanism is used to transmit and receive data. Each protocol is valid for a particular namespace and communication style; a namespace is sometimes called a *protocol family* because of this, which is why the namespace names start with 'PF_'.

The rules of a protocol apply to the data passing between two programs, perhaps on different computers; most of these rules are handled by the operating system, and you need not know about them. What you do need to know about protocols is this:

- In order to have communication between two sockets, they must specify the *same* protocol.
- Each protocol is meaningful with particular style/namespace combinations and cannot be used with inappropriate combinations. For example, the TCP protocol fits only the byte stream style of communication and the Internet namespace.
- For each combination of style and namespace, there is a *default protocol* which you can request by specifying 0 as the protocol number. And that's what you should normally do—use the default.

11.2 Communication Styles

The GNU library includes support for several different kinds of sockets, each with different characteristics. This section describes the supported socket types. The symbolic constants listed here are defined in 'sys/socket.h'.

int **SOCK_STREAM**   Macro

    The SOCK_STREAM style is like a pipe (see Chapter 10 [Pipes and FIFOs], page 201); it operates over a connection with a particular remote socket, and transmits data reliably as a stream of bytes.

    Use of this style is covered in detail in Section 11.8 [Using Sockets with Connections], page 230.

int **SOCK_DGRAM**   Macro

    The SOCK_DGRAM style is used for sending individually-addressed packets, unreliably. It is the diametrical opposite of SOCK_STREAM.

Chapter 11: Sockets   209

Each time you write data to a socket of this kind, that data becomes one packet. Since `SOCK_DGRAM` sockets do not have connections, you must specify the recipient address with each packet.

The only guarantee that the system makes about your requests to transmit data is that it will try its best to deliver each packet you send. It may succeed with the sixth packet after failing with the fourth and fifth packets; the seventh packet may arrive before the sixth, and may arrive a second time after the sixth.

The typical use for `SOCK_DGRAM` is in situations where it is acceptable to simply resend a packet if no response is seen in a reasonable amount of time.

See Section 11.9 [Datagram Socket Operations], page 243, for detailed information about how to use datagram sockets.

int `SOCK_RAW`   Macro
This style provides access to low-level network protocols and interfaces. Ordinary user programs usually have no need to use this style.

11.3 Socket Addresses

The name of a socket is normally called an *address*. The functions and symbols for dealing with socket addresses were named inconsistently, sometimes using the term "name" and sometimes using "address". You can regard these terms as synonymous where sockets are concerned.

A socket newly created with the `socket` function has no address. Other processes can find it for communication only if you give it an address. We call this *binding* the address to the socket, and the way to do it is with the `bind` function.

You need be concerned with the address of a socket if other processes are to find it and start communicating with it. You can specify an address for other sockets, but this is usually pointless; the first time you send data from a socket, or use it to initiate a connection, the system assigns an address automatically if you have not specified one.

Occasionally a client needs to specify an address because the server discriminates based on addresses; for example, the rsh and rlogin protocols look at the client's socket address and don't bypass password checking unless it is less than `IPPORT_RESERVED` (see Section 11.5.3 [Internet Ports], page 221).

The details of socket addresses vary depending on what namespace you are using. See Section 11.4 [The File Namespace], page 212, or Section 11.5 [The Internet Namespace], page 215, for specific information.

Regardless of the namespace, you use the same functions `bind` and `getsockname` to set and examine a socket's address. These functions use a phony data type, `struct sockaddr *`, to accept the address. In practice, the address lives in a structure of some other data type appropriate to the address format you are using, but you cast its address to `struct sockaddr *` when you pass it to `bind`.

11.3.1 Address Formats

The functions `bind` and `getsockname` use the generic data type `struct sockaddr *` to represent a pointer to a socket address. You can't use this data type effectively to interpret an address or construct one; for that, you must use the proper data type for the socket's namespace.

Thus, the usual practice is to construct an address in the proper namespace-specific type, then cast a pointer to `struct sockaddr *` when you call `bind` or `getsockname`.

The one piece of information that you can get from the `struct sockaddr` data type is the *address format* designator which tells you which data type to use to understand the address fully.

The symbols in this section are defined in the header file 'sys/socket.h'.

struct sockaddr   Date Type

The `struct sockaddr` type itself has the following members:

short int sa_family
: This is the code for the address format of this address. It identifies the format of the data which follows.

char sa_data[14]
: This is the actual socket address data, which is format-dependent. Its length also depends on the format, and may well be more than 14. The length 14 of `sa_data` is essentially arbitrary.

Each address format has a symbolic name which starts with 'AF_'. Each of them corresponds to a 'PF_' symbol which designates the corresponding namespace. Here is a list of address format names:

AF_FILE
: This designates the address format that goes with the file namespace. (PF_FILE is the name of that namespace.) See Section 11.4.2 [Details of File Namespace], page 213, for information about this address format.

AF_UNIX
: This is a synonym for AF_FILE, for compatibility. (PF_UNIX is likewise a synonym for PF_FILE.)

AF_INET
: This designates the address format that goes with the Internet namespace. (PF_INET is the name of that namespace.) See Section 11.5.1 [Internet Socket Address Format], page 215.

Chapter 11: Sockets

AF_UNSPEC
> This designates no particular address format. It is used only in rare cases, such as to clear out the default destination address of a "connected" datagram socket. See Section 11.9.1 [Sending Datagrams], page 244.
>
> The corresponding namespace designator symbol `PF_UNSPEC` exists for completeness, but there is no reason to use it in a program.

'`sys/socket.h`' defines symbols starting with '`AF_`' for many different kinds of networks, all or most of which are not actually implemented. We will document those that really work, as we receive information about how to use them.

11.3.2 Setting the Address of a Socket

Use the `bind` function to assign an address to a socket. The prototype for `bind` is in the header file '`sys/socket.h`'. For examples of use, see Section 11.4 [The File Namespace], page 212, or see Section 11.5.7 [Internet Socket Example], page 226.

int bind (int *socket*, struct sockaddr **addr*, size_t *length*) *Function*
> The `bind` function assigns an address to the socket *socket*. The *addr* and *length* arguments specify the address; the detailed format of the address depends on the namespace. The first part of the address is always the format designator, which specifies a namespace, and says that the address is in the format for that namespace.
>
> The return value is 0 on success and -1 on failure. The following `errno` error conditions are defined for this function:
>
> **EBADF**   The *socket* argument is not a valid file descriptor.
>
> **ENOTSOCK**   The descriptor *socket* is not a socket.
>
> **EADDRNOTAVAIL**
> > The specified address is not available on this machine.
>
> **EADDRINUSE**
> > Some other socket is already using the specified address.
>
> **EINVAL**   The socket *socket* already has an address.
>
> **EACCES**   You do not have permission to access the requested address. (In the Internet domain, only the super-user is allowed to specify a port number in the range 0 through `IPPORT_RESERVED` minus one; see Section 11.5.3 [Internet Ports], page 221.)

Additional conditions may be possible depending on the particular namespace of the socket.

11.3.3 Reading the Address of a Socket

Use the function `getsockname` to examine the address of an Internet socket. The prototype for this function is in the header file 'sys/socket.h'.

int getsockname (int *socket*, struct sockaddr *addr*, size_t *length-ptr*) *Function*

The `getsockname` function returns information about the address of the socket *socket* in the locations specified by the *addr* and *length-ptr* arguments. Note that the *length-ptr* is a pointer; you should initialize it to be the allocation size of *addr*, and on return it contains the actual size of the address data.

The format of the address data depends on the socket namespace. The length of the information is usually fixed for a given namespace, so normally you can know exactly how much space is needed and can provide that much. The usual practice is to allocate a place for the value using the proper data type for the socket's namespace, then cast its address to `struct sockaddr *` to pass it to `getsockname`.

The return value is `0` on success and `-1` on error. The following `errno` error conditions are defined for this function:

`EBADF`   The *socket* argument is not a valid file descriptor.

`ENOTSOCK` The descriptor *socket* is not a socket.

`ENOBUFS` There are not enough internal buffers available for the operation.

You can't read the address of a socket in the file namespace. This is consistent with the rest of the system; in general, there's no way to find a file's name from a descriptor for that file.

11.4 The File Namespace

This section describes the details of the file namespace, whose symbolic name (required when you create a socket) is `PF_FILE`.

11.4.1 File Namespace Concepts

In the file namespace, socket addresses are file names. You can specify any file name you want as the address of the socket, but you must have write permission on the directory containing it. In order to connect to a socket,

Chapter 11: Sockets   213

you must have read permission for it. It's common to put these files in the '/tmp' directory.

One peculiarity of the file namespace is that the name is only used when opening the connection; once that is over with, the address is not meaningful and may not exist.

Another peculiarity is that you cannot connect to such a socket from another machine–not even if the other machine shares the file system which contains the name of the socket. You can see the socket in a directory listing, but connecting to it never succeeds. Some programs take advantage of this, such as by asking the client to send its own process ID, and using the process IDs to distinguish between clients. However, we recommend you not use this method in protocols you design, as we might someday permit connections from other machines that mount the same file systems. Instead, send each new client an identifying number if you want it to have one.

After you close a socket in the file namespace, you should delete the file name from the file system. Use **unlink** or **remove** to do this; see Section 9.5 [Deleting Files], page 178.

The file namespace supports just one protocol for any communication style; it is protocol number 0.

11.4.2 Details of File Namespace

To create a socket in the file namespace, use the constant **PF_FILE** as the *namespace* argument to **socket** or **socketpair**. This constant is defined in 'sys/socket.h'.

int **PF_FILE**   Macro
This designates the file namespace, in which socket addresses are file names, and its associated family of protocols.

int **PF_UNIX**   Macro
This is a synonym for **PF_FILE**, for compatibility's sake.

The structure for specifying socket names in the file namespace is defined in the header file 'sys/un.h':

struct sockaddr_un   Data Type
This structure is used to specify file namespace socket addresses. It has the following members:

short int sun_family
This identifies the address family or format of the socket address. You should store the value **AF_FILE** to designate the file namespace. See Section 11.3 [Socket Addresses], page 209.

`char sun_path[108]`
> This is the file name to use.
>
> **Incomplete:** Why is 108 a magic number? RMS suggests making this a zero-length array and tweaking the example following to use `alloca` to allocate an appropriate amount of storage based on the length of the filename.

You should compute the *length* parameter for a socket address in the file namespace as the sum of the size of the `sun_family` component and the string length (*not* the allocation size!) of the file name string.

11.4.3 Example of File-Namespace Sockets

Here is an example showing how to create and name a socket in the file namespace.

```
#include <stddef.h>
#include <stdio.h>
#include <errno.h>
#include <stdlib.h>
#include <sys/socket.h>
#include <sys/un.h>

int
make_named_socket (const char *filename)
{
  struct sockaddr_un name;
  int sock;
  size_t size;

  /* Create the socket. */

  sock = socket (PF_UNIX, SOCK_DGRAM, 0);
  if (sock < 0)
    {
      perror ("socket");
      exit (EXIT_FAILURE);
    }

  /* Bind a name to the socket. */

  name.sun_family = AF_FILE;
  strcpy (name.sun_path, filename);

  /* The size of the address is
     the offset of the start of the filename,
     plus its length,
     plus one for the terminating null byte. */
  size = (offsetof (struct sockaddr_un, sun_path)
          + strlen (name.sun_path) + 1);
```

Chapter 11: Sockets   215

```
    if (bind (sock, (struct sockaddr *) &name, size) < 0)
      {
        perror ("bind");
        exit (EXIT_FAILURE);
      }

    return sock;
  }
```

11.5 The Internet Namespace

This section describes the details the protocols and socket naming conventions used in the Internet namespace.

To create a socket in the Internet namespace, use the symbolic name `PF_INET` of this namespace as the *namespace* argument to `socket` or `socketpair`. This macro is defined in 'sys/socket.h'.

int PF_INET   Macro
This designates the Internet namespace and associated family of protocols.

A socket address for the Internet namespace includes the following components:

- The address of the machine you want to connect to. Internet addresses can be specified in several ways; these are discussed in Section 11.5.1 [Internet Socket Address Format], page 215, Section 11.5.2 [Host Addresses], page 216, and Section 11.5.2.4 [Host Names], page 219.
- A port number for that machine. See Section 11.5.3 [Internet Ports], page 221.

You must ensure that the address and port number are represented in a canonical format called *network byte order*. See Section 11.5.5 [Byte Order Conversion], page 224, for information about this.

11.5.1 Internet Socket Address Format

In the Internet namespace, a socket address consists of a host address and a port on that host. In addition, the protocol you choose serves effectively as a part of the address because local port numbers are meaningful only within a particular protocol.

The data type for representing socket addresses in the Internet namespace is defined in the header file 'netinet/in.h'.

struct sockaddr_in   Data Type
This is the data type used to represent socket addresses in the Internet namespace. It has the following members:

`short int sin_family`
>This identifies the address family or format of the socket address. You should store the value of `AF_INET` in this member. See Section 11.3 [Socket Addresses], page 209.

`struct in_addr sin_addr`
>This is the Internet address of the host machine. See Section 11.5.2 [Host Addresses], page 216, and Section 11.5.2.4 [Host Names], page 219, for how to get a value to store here.

`unsigned short int sin_port`
>This is the port number. See Section 11.5.3 [Internet Ports], page 221.

When you call `bind` or `getsockname`, you should specify `sizeof (struct sockaddr_in)` as the *length* parameter if you are using an Internet namespace socket address.

11.5.2 Host Addresses

Each computer on the Internet has one or more *Internet addresses*, numbers which identify that computer among all those on the Internet. Users typically write numeric host addresses as sequences of four numbers, separated by periods, as in '`128.52.46.32`'.

Each computer also has one or more *host names*, which are strings of words separated by periods, as in '`churchy.gnu.ai.mit.edu`'.

Programs that let the user specify a host typically accept both numeric addresses and host names. But the program needs a numeric address to open a connection; to use a host name, you must convert it to the numeric address it stands for.

11.5.2.1 Internet Host Addresses

An Internet host address is a number containing four bytes of data. These are divided into two parts, a *network number* and a *local network address number* within that network. The network number consists of the first one, two or three bytes; the rest of the bytes are the local address.

Network numbers are registered with the Network Information Center (NIC), and are divided into three classes—A, B, and C. The local network address numbers of individual machines are registered with the administrator of the particular network.

Class A networks have single-byte numbers in the range 0 to 127. There are only a small number of Class A networks, but they can each support

Chapter 11: Sockets

a very large number of hosts. Medium-sized Class B networks have two-byte network numbers, with the first byte in the range 128 to 191. Class C networks are the smallest; they have three-byte network numbers, with the first byte in the range 192-255. Thus, the first 1, 2, or 3 bytes of an Internet address specifies a network. The remaining bytes of the Internet address specify the address within that network.

The Class A network 0 is reserved for broadcast to all networks. In addition, the host number 0 within each network is reserved for broadcast to all hosts in that network.

The Class A network 127 is reserved for loopback; you can always use the Internet address '127.0.0.1' to refer to the host machine.

Since a single machine can be a member of multiple networks, it can have multiple Internet host addresses. However, there is never supposed to be more than one machine with the same host address.

There are four forms of the *standard numbers-and-dots notation* for Internet addresses:

a.b.c.d   This specifies all four bytes of the address individually.

a.b.c   The last part of the address, *c*, is interpreted as a 2-byte quantity. This is useful for specifying host addresses in a Class B network with network address number *a.b*.

a.b   The last part of the address, *c*, is interpreted as a 3-byte quantity. This is useful for specifying host addresses in a Class A network with network address number *a*.

a   If only one part is given, this corresponds directly to the host address number.

Within each part of the address, the usual C conventions for specifying the radix apply. In other words, a leading '0x' or '0X' implies hexadecimal radix; a leading '0' implies octal; and otherwise decimal radix is assumed.

11.5.2.2 Host Address Data Type

Internet host addresses are represented in some contexts as integers (type `unsigned long int`). In other contexts, the integer is packaged inside a structure of type `struct in_addr`. It would be better if the usage were made consistent, but it is not hard to extract the integer from the structure or put the integer into a structure.

The following basic definitions for Internet addresses appear in the header file '`netinet/in.h`':

218   The GNU C Library

struct in_addr   Data Type
> This data type is used in certain contexts to contain an Internet host address. It has just one field, named `s_addr`, which records the host address number as an `unsigned long int`.

unsigned long int INADDR_LOOPBACK   Macro
> You can use this constant to stand for "the address of this machine," instead of finding its actual address. It is the Internet address '127.0.0.1', which is usually called '`localhost`'. This special constant saves you the trouble of looking up the address of your own machine. Also, the system usually implements `INADDR_LOOPBACK` specially, avoiding any network traffic for the case of one machine talking to itself.

unsigned long int INADDR_ANY   Macro
> You can use this constant to stand for "any incoming address," when binding to an address. See Section 11.3.2 [Setting the Address of a Socket], page 211. This is the usual address to give in the `sin_addr` member of `struct sockaddr_in` when you want to accept Internet connections.

unsigned long int INADDR_BROADCAST   Macro
> This constant is the address you use to send a broadcast message.

unsigned long int INADDR_NONE   Macro
> This constant is returned by some functions to indicate an error.

11.5.2.3 Host Address Functions

These additional functions for manipulating Internet addresses are declared in '`arpa/inet.h`'. They represent Internet addresses in network byte order; they represent network numbers and local-address-within-network numbers in host byte order. See Section 11.5.5 [Byte Order Conversion], page 224, for an explanation of network and host byte order.

int inet_aton (const char *name*, struct in_addr *addr*)   Function
> This function converts the Internet host address *name* from the standard numbers-and-dots notation into binary data and stores it in the `struct in_addr` that *addr* points to. `inet_aton` returns nonzero if the address is valid, zero if not.

unsigned long int inet_addr (const char *name*)   Function
> This function converts the Internet host address *name* from the standard numbers-and-dots notation into binary data. If the input is not valid, `inet_addr` returns `INADDR_NONE`. This is an obsolete interface

Chapter 11: Sockets 219

to `inet_aton`, described immediately above; it is obsolete because `INADDR_NONE` is a valid address (255.255.255.255), and `inet_aton` provides a cleaner way to indicate error return.

`unsigned long int` **inet_network** (`const char *name`) *Function*
This function extracts the network number from the address *name*, given in the standard numbers-and-dots notation. If the input is not valid, `inet_network` returns -1.

`char *` **inet_ntoa** (`struct in_addr` *addr*) *Function*
This function converts the Internet host address *addr* to a string in the standard numbers-and-dots notation. The return value is a pointer into a statically-allocated buffer. Subsequent calls will overwrite the same buffer, so you should copy the string if you need to save it.

`struct in_addr` **inet_makeaddr** (`int` *net*, `int` *local*) *Function*
This function makes an Internet host address by combining the network number *net* with the local-address-within-network number *local*.

`int` **inet_lnaof** (`struct in_addr` *addr*) *Function*
This function returns the local-address-within-network part of the Internet host address *addr*.

`int` **inet_netof** (`struct in_addr` *addr*) *Function*
This function returns the network number part of the Internet host address *addr*.

11.5.2.4 Host Names

Besides the standard numbers-and-dots notation for Internet addresses, you can also refer to a host by a symbolic name. The advantage of a symbolic name is that it is usually easier to remember. For example, the machine with Internet address '`128.52.46.32`' is also known as '`churchy.gnu.ai.mit.edu`'; and other machines in the '`gnu.ai.mit.edu`' domain can refer to it simply as '`churchy`'.

Internally, the system uses a database to keep track of the mapping between host names and host numbers. This database is usually either the file '`/etc/hosts`' or an equivalent provided by a name server. The functions and other symbols for accessing this database are declared in '`netdb.h`'. They are BSD features, defined unconditionally if you include '`netdb.h`'.

struct hostent *Data Type*
This data type is used to represent an entry in the hosts database. It has the following members:

`char *h_name`
: This is the "official" name of the host.

`char **h_aliases`
: These are alternative names for the host, represented as a null-terminated vector of strings.

`int h_addrtype`
: This is the host address type; in practice, its value is always `AF_INET`. In principle other kinds of addresses could be represented in the data base as well as Internet addresses; if this were done, you might find a value in this field other than `AF_INET`. See Section 11.3 [Socket Addresses], page 209.

`int h_length`
: This is the length, in bytes, of each address.

`char **h_addr_list`
: This is the vector of addresses for the host. (Recall that the host might be connected to multiple networks and have different addresses on each one.) The vector is terminated by a null pointer.

`char *h_addr`
: This is a synonym for `h_addr_list[0]`; in other words, it is the first host address.

As far as the host database is concerned, each address is just a block of memory `h_length` bytes long. But in other contexts there is an implicit assumption that you can convert this to a `struct in_addr` or an `unsigned long int`. Host addresses in a `struct hostent` structure are always given in network byte order; see Section 11.5.5 [Byte Order Conversion], page 224.

You can use `gethostbyname` or `gethostbyaddr` to search the hosts database for information about a particular host. The information is returned in a statically-allocated structure; you must copy the information if you need to save it across calls.

struct hostent * gethostbyname (`const char *name`) *Function*

The `gethostbyname` function returns information about the host named *name*. If the lookup fails, it returns a null pointer.

struct hostent * gethostbyaddr (`const char *addr, int length, int format`) *Function*

The `gethostbyaddr` function returns information about the host with Internet address *addr*. The *length* argument is the size (in bytes) of the

Chapter 11: Sockets   221

address at *addr*. *format* specifies the address format; for an Internet address, specify a value of `AF_INET`.

If the lookup fails, `gethostbyaddr` returns a null pointer.

If the name lookup by `gethostbyname` or `gethostbyaddr` fails, you can find out the reason by looking at the value of the variable `h_errno`. (It would be cleaner design for these functions to set `errno`, but use of `h_errno` is compatible with other systems.) Before using `h_errno`, you must declare it like this:

```
extern int h_errno;
```

Here are the error codes that you may find in `h_errno`:

HOST_NOT_FOUND
> No such host is known in the data base.

TRY_AGAIN
> This condition happens when the name server could not be contacted. If you try again later, you may succeed then.

NO_RECOVERY
> A non-recoverable error occurred.

NO_ADDRESS
> The host database contains an entry for the name, but it doesn't have an associated Internet address.

You can also scan the entire hosts database one entry at a time using `sethostent`, `gethostent`, and `endhostent`. Be careful in using these functions, because they are not reentrant.

void sethostent (int *stayopen*)   *Function*
This function opens the hosts database to begin scanning it. You can then call `gethostent` to read the entries.

If the *stayopen* argument is nonzero, this sets a flag so that subsequent calls to `gethostbyname` or `gethostbyaddr` will not close the database (as they usually would). This makes for more efficiency if you call those functions several times, by avoiding reopening the database for each call.

struct hostent * gethostent ()   *Function*
This function returns the next entry in the hosts database. It returns a null pointer if there are no more entries.

void endhostent ()   *Function*
This function closes the hosts database.

11.5.3 Internet Ports

A socket address in the Internet namespace consists of a machine's Internet address plus a *port number* which distinguishes the sockets on a given machine (for a given protocol). Port numbers range from 0 to 65,535.

Port numbers less than `IPPORT_RESERVED` are reserved for standard servers, such as `finger` and `telnet`. There is a database that keeps track of these, and you can use the `getservbyname` function to map a service name onto a port number; see Section 11.5.4 [The Services Database], page 222.

If you write a server that is not one of the standard ones defined in the database, you must choose a port number for it. Use a number greater than `IPPORT_USERRESERVED`; such numbers are reserved for servers and won't ever be generated automatically by the system. Avoiding conflicts with servers being run by other users is up to you.

When you use a socket without specifying its address, the system generates a port number for it. This number is between `IPPORT_RESERVED` and `IPPORT_USERRESERVED`.

On the Internet, it is actually legitimate to have two different sockets with the same port number, as long as they never both try to communicate with the same socket address (host address plus port number). You shouldn't duplicate a port number except in special circumstances where a higher-level protocol requires it. Normally, the system won't let you do it; `bind` normally insists on distinct port numbers. To reuse a port number, you must set the socket option `SO_REUSEADDR`. See Section 11.11.2 [Socket-Level Options], page 250.

These macros are defined in the header file 'netinet/in.h'.

int IPPORT_RESERVED   Macro
Port numbers less than `IPPORT_RESERVED` are reserved for superuser use.

int IPPORT_USERRESERVED   Macro
Port numbers greater than or equal to `IPPORT_USERRESERVED` are reserved for explicit use; they will never be allocated automatically.

11.5.4 The Services Database

The database that keeps track of "well-known" services is usually either the file '/etc/services' or an equivalent from a name server. You can use these utilities, declared in 'netdb.h', to access the services database.

struct servent   Data Type
This data type holds information about entries from the services database. It has the following members:

Chapter 11: Sockets

`char *s_name`
: This is the "official" name of the service.

`char **s_aliases`
: These are alternate names for the service, represented as an array of strings. A null pointer terminates the array.

`int s_port`
: This is the port number for the service. Port numbers are given in network byte order; see Section 11.5.5 [Byte Order Conversion], page 224.

`char *s_proto`
: This is the name of the protocol to use with this service. See Section 11.5.6 [Protocols Database], page 225.

To get information about a particular service, use the `getservbyname` or `getservbyport` functions. The information is returned in a statically-allocated structure; you must copy the information if you need to save it across calls.

`struct servent * `**`getservbyname`**` (const char *name, const char *proto)` *Function*

The `getservbyname` function returns information about the service named *name* using protocol *proto*. If it can't find such a service, it returns a null pointer.

This function is useful for servers as well as for clients; servers use it to determine which port they should listen on (see Section 11.8.2 [Listening for Connections], page 232).

`struct servent * `**`getservbyport`**` (int port, const char *proto)` *Function*

The `getservbyport` function returns information about the service at port *port* using protocol *proto*. If it can't find such a service, it returns a null pointer.

You can also scan the services database using `setservent`, `getservent`, and `endservent`. Be careful in using these functions, because they are not reentrant.

`void `**`setservent`**` (int stayopen)` *Function*

This function opens the services database to begin scanning it.

If the *stayopen* argument is nonzero, this sets a flag so that subsequent calls to `getservbyname` or `getservbyport` will not close the database (as they usually would). This makes for more efficiency if you call those functions several times, by avoiding reopening the database for each call.

`struct servent * `**`getservent`**` (void)` *Function*
: This function returns the next entry in the services database. If there are no more entries, it returns a null pointer.

`void `**`endservent`**` (void)` *Function*
: This function closes the services database.

11.5.5 Byte Order Conversion

Different kinds of computers use different conventions for the ordering of bytes within a word. Some computers put the most significant byte within a word first (this is called "big-endian" order), and others put it last ("little-endian" order).

So that machines with different byte order conventions can communicate, the Internet protocols specify a canonical byte order convention for data transmitted over the network. This is known as the *network byte order*.

When establishing an Internet socket connection, you must make sure that the data in the `sin_port` and `sin_addr` members of the `sockaddr_in` structure are represented in the network byte order. If you are encoding integer data in the messages sent through the socket, you should convert this to network byte order too. If you don't do this, your program may fail when running on or talking to other kinds of machines.

If you use `getservbyname` and `gethostbyname` or `inet_addr` to get the port number and host address, the values are already in the network byte order, and you can copy them directly into the `sockaddr_in` structure.

Otherwise, you have to convert the values explicitly. Use `htons` and `ntohs` to convert values for the `sin_port` member. Use `htonl` and `ntohl` to convert values for the `sin_addr` member. (Remember, `struct in_addr` is equivalent to `unsigned long int`.) These functions are declared in 'netinet/in.h'.

`unsigned short int `**`htons`**` (unsigned short int ` *Function*
   hostshort`)`
: This function converts the `short` integer *hostshort* from host byte order to network byte order.

`unsigned short int `**`ntohs`**` (unsigned short int ` *Function*
   netshort`)`
: This function converts the `short` integer *netshort* from network byte order to host byte order.

`unsigned long int `**`htonl`**` (unsigned long int ` *Function*
   hostlong`)`
: This function converts the `long` integer *hostlong* from host byte order to network byte order.

Chapter 11: Sockets   225

unsigned long int ntohl (unsigned long int *netlong*)   *Function*

   This function converts the `long` integer *netlong* from network byte order to host byte order.

11.5.6 Protocols Database

   The communications protocol used with a socket controls low-level details of how data is exchanged. For example, the protocol implements things like checksums to detect errors in transmissions, and routing instructions for messages. Normal user programs have little reason to mess with these details directly.

   The default communications protocol for the Internet namespace depends on the communication style. For stream communication, the default is TCP ("transmission control protocol"). For datagram communication, the default is UDP ("user datagram protocol"). For reliable datagram communication, the default is RDP ("reliable datagram protocol"). You should nearly always use the default.

   Internet protocols are generally specified by a name instead of a number. The network protocols that a host knows about are stored in a database. This is usually either derived from the file '/etc/protocols', or it may be an equivalent provided by a name server. You look up the protocol number associated with a named protocol in the database using the `getprotobyname` function.

   Here are detailed descriptions of the utilities for accessing the protocols database. These are declared in '`netdb.h`'.

struct protoent   *Data Type*
   This data type is used to represent entries in the network protocols database. It has the following members:

   `char *p_name`
           This is the official name of the protocol.

   `char **p_aliases`
           These are alternate names for the protocol, specified as an array of strings. The last element of the array is a null pointer.

   `int p_proto`
           This is the protocol number (in host byte order); use this member as the *protocol* argument to `socket`.

   You can use `getprotobyname` and `getprotobynumber` to search the protocols database for a specific protocol. The information is returned in a statically-allocated structure; you must copy the information if you need to save it across calls.

struct protoent * getprotobyname (const char *name*) *Function*

The `getprotobyname` function returns information about the network protocol named *name*. If there is no such protocol, it returns a null pointer.

struct protoent * getprotobynumber (int *protocol*) *Function*

The `getprotobynumber` function returns information about the network protocol with number *protocol*. If there is no such protocol, it returns a null pointer.

You can also scan the whole protocols database one protocol at a time by using `setprotoent`, `getprotoent`, and `endprotoent`. Be careful in using these functions, because they are not reentrant.

void setprotoent (int *stayopen*) *Function*

This function opens the protocols database to begin scanning it.

If the *stayopen* argument is nonzero, this sets a flag so that subsequent calls to `getprotobyname` or `getprotobynumber` will not close the database (as they usually would). This makes for more efficiency if you call those functions several times, by avoiding reopening the database for each call.

struct protoent * getprotoent (void) *Function*

This function returns the next entry in the protocols database. It returns a null pointer if there are no more entries.

void endprotoent (void) *Function*

This function closes the protocols database.

11.5.7 Internet Socket Example

Here is an example showing how to create and name a socket in the Internet namespace. The newly created socket exists on the machine that the program is running on. Rather than finding and using the machine's Internet address, this example specifies `INADDR_ANY` as the host address; the system replaces that with the machine's actual address.

```
#include <stdio.h>
#include <stdlib.h>
#include <sys/socket.h>
#include <netinet/in.h>
```

Chapter 11: Sockets   227

```
int
make_socket (unsigned short int port)
{
  int sock;
  struct sockaddr_in name;

  /* Create the socket. */
  sock = socket (PF_INET, SOCK_STREAM, 0);
  if (sock < 0)
    {
      perror ("socket");
      exit (EXIT_FAILURE);
    }

  /* Give the socket a name. */
  name.sin_family = AF_INET;
  name.sin_port = htons (port);
  name.sin_addr.s_addr = htonl (INADDR_ANY);
  if (bind (sock, (struct sockaddr *) &name, sizeof (name)) < 0)
    {
      perror ("bind");
      exit (EXIT_FAILURE);
    }

  return sock;
}
```

Here is another example, showing how you can fill in a `sockaddr_in` structure, given a host name string and a port number:

```
#include <stdio.h>
#include <stdlib.h>
#include <sys/socket.h>
#include <netinet/in.h>
#include <netdb.h>

void
init_sockaddr (struct sockaddr_in *name,
               const char *hostname,
               unsigned short int port)
{
  struct hostent *hostinfo;

  name->sin_family = AF_INET;
  name->sin_port = htons (port);
  hostinfo = gethostbyname (hostname);
  if (hostinfo == NULL)
    {
      fprintf (stderr, "Unknown host %s.\n", hostname);
      exit (EXIT_FAILURE);
    }
  name->sin_addr = *(struct in_addr *) hostinfo->h_addr;
}
```

11.6 Other Namespaces

Certain other namespaces and associated protocol families are supported but not documented yet because they are not often used. `PF_NS` refers to the Xerox Network Software protocols. `PF_ISO` stands for Open Systems Interconnect. `PF_CCITT` refers to protocols from CCITT. 'socket.h' defines these symbols and others naming protocols not actually implemented.

`PF_IMPLINK` is used for communicating between hosts and Internet Message Processors. For information on this, and on `PF_ROUTE`, an occasionally-used local area routing protocol, see the GNU Hurd Manual (to appear in the future).

11.7 Opening and Closing Sockets

This section describes the actual library functions for opening and closing sockets. The same functions work for all namespaces and connection styles.

11.7.1 Creating a Socket

The primitive for creating a socket is the `socket` function, declared in 'sys/socket.h'.

int socket (int *namespace*, int *style*, int *protocol*) *Function*
: This function creates a socket and specifies communication style *style*, which should be one of the socket styles listed in Section 11.2 [Communication Styles], page 208. The *namespace* argument specifies the namespace; it must be `PF_FILE` (see Section 11.4 [The File Namespace], page 212) or `PF_INET` (see Section 11.5 [The Internet Namespace], page 215). *protocol* designates the specific protocol (see Section 11.1 [Socket Concepts], page 207); zero is usually right for *protocol*.

    The return value from `socket` is the file descriptor for the new socket, or `-1` in case of error. The following `errno` error conditions are defined for this function:

    EPROTONOSUPPORT
    : The *protocol* or *style* is not supported by the *namespace* specified.

    EMFILE
    : The process already has too many file descriptors open.

    ENFILE
    : The system already has too many file descriptors open.

    EACCESS
    : The process does not have privilege to create a socket of the specified *style* or *protocol*.

Chapter 11: Sockets

ENOBUFS   The system ran out of internal buffer space.

The file descriptor returned by the `socket` function supports both read and write operations. But, like pipes, sockets do not support file positioning operations.

For examples of how to call the `socket` function, see Section 11.4 [The File Namespace], page 212, or Section 11.5.7 [Internet Socket Example], page 226.

11.7.2 Closing a Socket

When you are finished using a socket, you can simply close its file descriptor with `close`; see Section 8.1 [Opening and Closing Files], page 139. If there is still data waiting to be transmitted over the connection, normally `close` tries to complete this transmission. You can control this behavior using the `SO_LINGER` socket option to specify a timeout period; see Section 11.11 [Socket Options], page 249.

You can also shut down only reception or only transmission on a connection by calling `shutdown`, which is declared in 'sys/socket.h'.

int shutdown (int *socket*, int *how*)   *Function*
    The `shutdown` function shuts down the connection of socket *socket*.
    The argument *how* specifies what action to perform:

0   Stop receiving data for this socket. If further data arrives, reject it.

1   Stop trying to transmit data from this socket. Discard any data waiting to be sent. Stop looking for acknowledgement of data already sent; don't retransmit it if it is lost.

2   Stop both reception and transmission.

The return value is 0 on success and -1 on failure. The following `errno` error conditions are defined for this function:

EBADF   *socket* is not a valid file descriptor.

ENOTSOCK   *socket* is not a socket.

ENOTCONN   *socket* is not connected.

11.7.3 Socket Pairs

A *socket pair* consists of a pair of connected (but unnamed) sockets. It is very similar to a pipe and is used in much the same way. Socket pairs are created with the `socketpair` function, declared in 'sys/socket.h'. A socket pair is much like a pipe; the main difference is that the socket pair is bidirectional, whereas the pipe has one input-only end and one output-only end (see Chapter 10 [Pipes and FIFOs], page 201).

`int` **socketpair** (`int` *namespace*, `int` *style*, `int` *protocol*, `int` *filedes*[2]) *Function*

This function creates a socket pair, returning the file descriptors in *filedes*[0] and *filedes*[1]. The socket pair is a full-duplex communications channel, so that both reading and writing may be performed at either end.

The *namespace*, *style*, and *protocol* arguments are interpreted as for the `socket` function. *style* should be one of the communication styles listed in Section 11.2 [Communication Styles], page 208. The *namespace* argument specifies the namespace, which must be `AF_FILE` (see Section 11.4 [The File Namespace], page 212); *protocol* specifies the communications protocol, but zero is the only meaningful value.

If *style* specifies a connectionless communication style, then the two sockets you get are not *connected*, strictly speaking, but each of them knows the other as the default destination address, so they can send packets to each other.

The `socketpair` function returns `0` on success and `-1` on failure. The following `errno` error conditions are defined for this function:

`EMFILE`   The process has too many file descriptors open.

`EAFNOSUPPORT`
: The specified namespace is not supported.

`EPROTONOSUPPORT`
: The specified protocol is not supported.

`EOPNOTSUPP`
: The specified protocol does not support the creation of socket pairs.

11.8 Using Sockets with Connections

The most common communication styles involve making a connection to a particular other socket, and then exchanging data with that socket over and over. Making a connection is asymmetric; one side (the *client*) acts to request a connection, while the other side (the *server*) makes a socket and waits for the connection request.

- Section 11.8.1 [Making a Connection], page 231, describes what the client program must do to initiate a connection with a server.
- Section 11.8.2 [Listening for Connections], page 232, and Section 11.8.3 [Accepting Connections], page 233, describe what the server program must do to wait for and act upon connection requests from clients.

- Section 11.8.5 [Transferring Data], page 235, describes how data is transferred through the connected socket.

11.8.1 Making a Connection

In making a connection, the client makes a connection while the server waits for and accepts the connection. Here we discuss what the client program must do, using the `connect` function, which is declared in 'sys/socket.h'.

`int` **`connect`** (`int` *socket*, `struct sockaddr` **addr*, *Function*
        `size_t` *length*)

The `connect` function initiates a connection from the socket with file descriptor *socket* to the socket whose address is specified by the *addr* and *length* arguments. (This socket is typically on another machine, and it must be already set up as a server.) See Section 11.3 [Socket Addresses], page 209, for information about how these arguments are interpreted.

Normally, `connect` waits until the server responds to the request before it returns. You can set nonblocking mode on the socket *socket* to make `connect` return immediately without waiting for the response. See Section 8.10 [File Status Flags], page 158, for information about nonblocking mode.

The normal return value from `connect` is 0. If an error occurs, `connect` returns -1. The following `errno` error conditions are defined for this function:

`EBADF`   The socket *socket* is not a valid file descriptor.

`ENOTSOCK` The socket *socket* is not a socket.

`EADDRNOTAVAIL`
        The specified address is not available on the remote machine.

`EAFNOSUPPORT`
        The namespace of the *addr* is not supported by this socket.

`EISCONN`   The socket *socket* is already connected.

`ETIMEDOUT`
        The attempt to establish the connection timed out.

`ECONNREFUSED`
        The server has actively refused to establish the connection.

`ENETUNREACH`
        The network of the given *addr* isn't reachable from this host.

`EADDRINUSE`
: The socket address of the given *addr* is already in use.

`EINPROGRESS`
: The socket *socket* is non-blocking and the connection could not be established immediately. You can determine when the connection is completely established with `select`; see Section 8.6 [Waiting for Input or Output], page 150. Another `connect` call on the same socket, before the connection is completely established, will fail with `EALREADY`.

`EALREADY`
: The socket *socket* is non-blocking and already has a pending connection in progress (see `EINPROGRESS` above).

11.8.2 Listening for Connections

Now let us consider what the server process must do to accept connections on a socket. First it must use the `listen` function to enable connection requests on the socket, and then accept each incoming connection with a call to `accept` (see Section 11.8.3 [Accepting Connections], page 233). Once connection requests are enabled on a server socket, the `select` function reports when the socket has a connection ready to be accepted (see Section 8.6 [Waiting for Input or Output], page 150).

The `listen` function is not allowed for sockets using connectionless communication styles.

You can write a network server that does not even start running until a connection to it is requested. See Section 11.10.1 ["code inetd Servers], page 248.

In the Internet namespace, there are no special protection mechanisms for controlling access to connect to a port; any process on any machine can make a connection to your server. If you want to restrict access to your server, make it examine the addresses associated with connection requests or implement some other handshaking or identification protocol.

In the File namespace, the ordinary file protection bits control who has access to connect to the socket.

int listen (int *socket*, unsigned int *n*)   *Function*
: The `listen` function enables the socket *socket* to accept connections, thus making it a server socket.

  The argument *n* specifies the length of the queue for pending connections. When the queue fills, new clients attempting to connect fail with `ECONNREFUSED` until the server calls `accept` to accept a connection from the queue.

Chapter 11: Sockets

The `listen` function returns 0 on success and -1 on failure. The following `errno` error conditions are defined for this function:

`EBADF`   The argument *socket* is not a valid file descriptor.

`ENOTSOCK`   The argument *socket* is not a socket.

`EOPNOTSUPP`
           The socket *socket* does not support this operation.

11.8.3 Accepting Connections

When a server receives a connection request, it can complete the connection by accepting the request. Use the function `accept` to do this.

A socket that has been established as a server can accept connection requests from multiple clients. The server's original socket *does not become part* of the connection; instead, `accept` makes a new socket which participates in the connection. `accept` returns the descriptor for this socket. The server's original socket remains available for listening for further connection requests.

The number of pending connection requests on a server socket is finite. If connection requests arrive from clients faster than the server can act upon them, the queue can fill up and additional requests are refused with a `ECONNREFUSED` error. You can specify the maximum length of this queue as an argument to the `listen` function, although the system may also impose its own internal limit on the length of this queue.

int **accept** (int *socket*, struct sockaddr **addr*,   Function
        size_t **length-ptr*)

This function is used to accept a connection request on the server socket *socket*.

The `accept` function waits if there are no connections pending, unless the socket *socket* has nonblocking mode set. (You can use `select` to wait for a pending connection, with a nonblocking socket.) See Section 8.10 [File Status Flags], page 158, for information about non-blocking mode.

The *addr* and *length-ptr* arguments are used to return information about the name of the client socket that initiated the connection. See Section 11.3 [Socket Addresses], page 209, for information about the format of the information.

Accepting a connection does not make *socket* part of the connection. Instead, it creates a new socket which becomes connected. The normal return value of `accept` is the file descriptor for the new socket.

After `accept`, the original socket *socket* remains open and unconnected, and continues listening until you close it. You can accept further connections with *socket* by calling `accept` again.

If an error occurs, `accept` returns `-1`. The following `errno` error conditions are defined for this function:

EBADF
: The *socket* argument is not a valid file descriptor.

ENOTSOCK
: The descriptor *socket* argument is not a socket.

EOPNOTSUPP
: The descriptor *socket* does not support this operation.

EWOULDBLOCK
: *socket* has nonblocking mode set, and there are no pending connections immediately available.

The `accept` function is not allowed for sockets using connectionless communication styles.

11.8.4 Who is Connected to Me?

int getpeername (int *socket*, struct sockaddr **addr*, size_t **length-ptr*) *Function*

The `getpeername` function returns the address of the socket that *socket* is connected to; it stores the address in the memory space specified by *addr* and *length-ptr*. It stores the length of the address in **length-ptr*.

See Section 11.3 [Socket Addresses], page 209, for information about the format of the address. In some operating systems, `getpeername` works only for sockets in the Internet domain.

The return value is `0` on success and `-1` on error. The following `errno` error conditions are defined for this function:

EBADF
: The argument *socket* is not a valid file descriptor.

ENOTSOCK
: The descriptor *socket* is not a socket.

ENOTCONN
: The socket *socket* is not connected.

ENOBUFS
: There are not enough internal buffers available.

11.8.5 Transferring Data

Once a socket has been connected to a peer, you can use the ordinary `read` and `write` operations (see Section 8.2 [Input and Output Primitives], page 141) to transfer data. A socket is a two-way communications channel, so read and write operations can be performed at either end.

Chapter 11: Sockets   235

There are also some I/O modes that are specific to socket operations. In order to specify these modes, you must use the `recv` and `send` functions instead of the more generic `read` and `write` functions. The `recv` and `send` functions take an additional argument which you can use to specify various flags to control the special I/O modes. For example, you can specify the `MSG_OOB` flag to read or write out-of-band data, the `MSG_PEEK` flag to peek at input, or the `MSG_DONTROUTE` flag to control inclusion of routing information on output.

11.8.5.1 Sending Data

The `send` function is declared in the header file 'sys/socket.h'. If your *flags* argument is zero, you can just as well use `write` instead of `send`; see Section 8.2 [Input and Output Primitives], page 141. If the socket was connected but the connection has broken, you get a `SIGPIPE` signal for any use of `send` or `write` (see Section 21.2.7 [Miscellaneous Signals], page 382).

`int send` (`int` *socket*, `void` **buffer*, `size_t` *size*, `int`   Function
         flags)

> The `send` function is like `write`, but with the additional flags *flags*. The possible values of *flags* are described in Section 11.8.5.3 [Socket Data Options], page 237.
>
> This function returns the number of bytes transmitted, or `-1` on failure. If the socket is nonblocking, then `send` (like `write`) can return after sending just part of the data. See Section 8.10 [File Status Flags], page 158, for information about nonblocking mode.
>
> Note, however, that a successful return value merely indicates that the message has been sent without error, not necessarily that it has been received without error.
>
> The following `errno` error conditions are defined for this function:
>
> `EBADF`   The *socket* argument is not a valid file descriptor.
>
> `EINTR`   The operation was interrupted by a signal before any data was sent. See Section 21.5 [Primitives Interrupted by Signals], page 402.
>
> `ENOTSOCK` The descriptor *socket* is not a socket.
>
> `EMSGSIZE` The socket type requires that the message be sent atomically, but the message is too large for this to be possible.
>
> `EWOULDBLOCK`
>   Nonblocking mode has been set on the socket, and the write operation would block. (Normally `send` blocks until the operation can be completed.)

ENOBUFS   There is not enough internal buffer space available.

ENOTCONN   You never connected this socket.

EPIPE   This socket was connected but the connection is now broken. In this case, **send** generates a `SIGPIPE` signal first; if that signal is ignored or blocked, or if its handler returns, then **send** fails with `EPIPE`.

11.8.5.2 Receiving Data

The **recv** function is declared in the header file 'sys/socket.h'. If your *flags* argument is zero, you can just as well use **read** instead of **recv**; see Section 8.2 [Input and Output Primitives], page 141.

int recv (int *socket*, void **buffer*, size_t *size*, int *flags*)   Function

The **recv** function is like **read**, but with the additional flags *flags*. The possible values of *flags* are described In Section 11.8.5.3 [Socket Data Options], page 237.

If nonblocking mode is set for *socket*, and no data is available to be read, **recv** fails immediately rather than waiting. See Section 8.10 [File Status Flags], page 158, for information about nonblocking mode.

This function returns the number of bytes received, or `-1` on failure. The following **errno** error conditions are defined for this function:

EBADF   The *socket* argument is not a valid file descriptor.

ENOTSOCK   The descriptor *socket* is not a socket.

EWOULDBLOCK
           Nonblocking mode has been set on the socket, and the read operation would block. (Normally, **recv** blocks until there is input available to be read.)

EINTR   The operation was interrupted by a signal before any data was read. See Section 21.5 [Primitives Interrupted by Signals], page 402.

ENOTCONN   You never connected this socket.

11.8.5.3 Socket Data Options

The *flags* argument to **send** and **recv** is a bit mask. You can bitwise-OR the values of the following macros together to obtain a value for this argument. All are defined in the header file 'sys/socket.h'.

Chapter 11: Sockets

int **MSG_OOB** — Macro
Send or receive out-of-band data. See Section 11.8.8 [Out-of-Band Data], page 241.

int **MSG_PEEK** — Macro
Look at the data but don't remove it from the input queue. This is only meaningful with input functions such as `recv`, not with `send`.

int **MSG_DONTROUTE** — Macro
Don't include routing information in the message. This is only meaningful with output operations, and is usually only of interest for diagnostic or routing programs. We don't try to explain it here.

11.8.6 Byte Stream Socket Example

Here is an example client program that makes a connection for a byte stream socket in the Internet namespace. It doesn't do anything particularly interesting once it has connected to the server; it just sends a text string to the server and exits.

```
#include <stdio.h>
#include <errno.h>
#include <stdlib.h>
#include <unistd.h>
#include <sys/types.h>
#include <sys/socket.h>
#include <netinet/in.h>
#include <netdb.h>

#define PORT            5555
#define MESSAGE         "Yow!!! Are we having fun yet?!?"
#define SERVERHOST      "churchy.gnu.ai.mit.edu"

void
write_to_server (int filedes)
{
  int nbytes;

  nbytes = write (filedes, MESSAGE, strlen (MESSAGE) + 1);
  if (nbytes < 0)
    {
      perror ("write");
      exit (EXIT_FAILURE);
    }
}


int
main (void)
{
  extern void init_sockaddr (struct sockaddr_in *name,
```

```
                              const char *hostname,
                              unsigned short int port);
  int sock;
  struct sockaddr_in servername;

  /* Create the socket. */
  sock = socket (PF_INET, SOCK_STREAM, 0);
  if (sock < 0)
    {
      perror ("socket (client)");
      exit (EXIT_FAILURE);
    }

  /* Connect to the server. */
  init_sockaddr (&servername, SERVERHOST, PORT);
  if (0 > connect (sock,
                   (struct sockaddr *) &servername,
                   sizeof (servername)))
    {
      perror ("connect (client)");
      exit (EXIT_FAILURE);
    }

  /* Send data to the server. */
  write_to_server (sock);
  close (sock);
  exit (EXIT_SUCCESS);
}
```

11.8.7 Byte Stream Connection Server Example

The server end is much more complicated. Since we want to allow multiple clients to be connected to the server at the same time, it would be incorrect to wait for input from a single client by simply calling **read** or **recv**. Instead, the right thing to do is to use **select** (see Section 8.6 [Waiting for Input or Output], page 150) to wait for input on all of the open sockets. This also allows the server to deal with additional connection requests.

This particular server doesn't do anything interesting once it has gotten a message from a client. It does close the socket for that client when it detects an end-of-file condition (resulting from the client shutting down its end of the connection).

This program uses **make_socket** and **init_sockaddr** to set up the socket address; see Section 11.5.7 [Internet Socket Example], page 226.

```
#include <stdio.h>
#include <errno.h>
#include <stdlib.h>
#include <unistd.h>
#include <sys/types.h>
#include <sys/socket.h>
```

Chapter 11: Sockets

```c
#include <netinet/in.h>
#include <netdb.h>

#define PORT    5555
#define MAXMSG  512

int
read_from_client (int filedes)
{
  char buffer[MAXMSG];
  int nbytes;

  nbytes = read (filedes, buffer, MAXMSG);
  if (nbytes < 0)
    {
      /* Read error. */
      perror ("read");
      exit (EXIT_FAILURE);
    }
  else if (nbytes == 0)
    /* End-of-file. */
    return -1;
  else
    {
      /* Data read. */
      fprintf (stderr, "Server: got message: '%s'\n", buffer);
      return 0;
    }
}

int
main (void)
{
  extern int make_socket (unsigned short int port);
  int sock;
  fd_set active_fd_set, read_fd_set;
  int i;
  struct sockaddr_in clientname;
  size_t size;

  /* Create the socket and set it up to accept connections. */
  sock = make_socket (PORT);
  if (listen (sock, 1) < 0)
    {
      perror ("listen");
      exit (EXIT_FAILURE);
    }

  /* Initialize the set of active sockets. */
  FD_ZERO (&active_fd_set);
  FD_SET (sock, &active_fd_set);

  while (1)
```

```
    {
      /* Block until input arrives on one or more active sockets. */
      read_fd_set = active_fd_set;
      if (select (FD_SETSIZE, &read_fd_set, NULL, NULL, NULL) < 0)
        {
          perror ("select");
          exit (EXIT_FAILURE);
        }

      /* Service all the sockets with input pending. */
      for (i = 0; i < FD_SETSIZE; ++i)
        if (FD_ISSET (i, &read_fd_set))
          {
            if (i == sock)
              {
                /* Connection request on original socket. */
                int new;
                size = sizeof (clientname);
                new = accept (sock,
                              (struct sockaddr *) &clientname,
                              &size);
                if (new < 0)
                  {
                    perror ("accept");
                    exit (EXIT_FAILURE);
                  }
                fprintf (stderr,
                         "Server: connect from host %s, port %hd.\n",
                         inet_ntoa (clientname.sin_addr),
                         ntohs (clientname.sin_port));
                FD_SET (new, &active_fd_set);
              }
            else
              {
                /* Data arriving on an already-connected socket. */
                if (read_from_client (i) < 0)
                  {
                    close (i);
                    FD_CLR (i, &active_fd_set);
                  }
              }
          }
    }
}
```

11.8.8 Out-of-Band Data

Streams with connections permit *out-of-band* data that is delivered with higher priority than ordinary data. Typically the reason for sending out-of-band data is to send notice of an exceptional condition. The way to send out-of-band data is using **send**, specifying the flag MSG_OOB (see Section 11.8.5.1 [Sending Data], page 235).

Out-of-band data is received with higher priority because the receiving process need not read it in sequence; to read the next available out-of-band data, use `recv` with the `MSG_OOB` flag (see Section 11.8.5.2 [Receiving Data], page 236). Ordinary read operations do not read out-of-band data; they read only the ordinary data.

When a socket finds that out-of-band data is on its way, it sends a `SIGURG` signal to the owner process or process group of the socket. You can specify the owner using the `F_SETOWN` command to the `fcntl` function; see Section 8.12 [Interrupt-Driven Input], page 167. You must also establish a handler for this signal, as described in Chapter 21 [Signal Handling], page 371, in order to take appropriate action such as reading the out-of-band data.

Alternatively, you can test for pending out-of-band data, or wait until there is out-of-band data, using the `select` function; it can wait for an exceptional condition on the socket. See Section 8.6 [Waiting for Input or Output], page 150, for more information about `select`.

Notification of out-of-band data (whether with `SIGURG` or with `select`) indicates that out-of-band data is on the way; the data may not actually arrive until later. If you try to read the out-of-band data before it arrives, `recv` fails with an `EWOULDBLOCK` error.

Sending out-of-band data automatically places a "mark" in the stream of ordinary data, showing where in the sequence the out-of-band data "would have been". This is useful when the meaning of out-of-band data is "cancel everything sent so far". Here is how you can test, in the receiving process, whether any ordinary data was sent before the mark:

```
success = ioctl (socket, SIOCATMARK, &result);
```

Here's a function to discard any ordinary data preceding the out-of-band mark:

```
int
discard_until_mark (int socket)
{
  while (1)
    {
      /* This is not an arbitrary limit; any size will do.  */
      char buffer[1024];
      int result, success;

      /* If we have reached the mark, return.  */
      success = ioctl (socket, SIOCATMARK, &result);
      if (success < 0)
        perror ("ioctl");
      if (result)
        return;

      /* Otherwise, read a bunch of ordinary data and discard it.
         This is guaranteed not to read past the mark
         if it starts before the mark.  */
```

```
      success = read (socket, buffer, sizeof buffer);
      if (success < 0)
        perror ("read");
    }
}
```

If you don't want to discard the ordinary data preceding the mark, you may need to read some of it anyway, to make room in internal system buffers for the out-of-band data. If you try to read out-of-band data and get an **EWOULDBLOCK** error, try reading some ordinary data (saving it so that you can use it when you want it) and see if that makes room. Here is an example:

```
struct buffer
{
  char *buffer;
  int size;
  struct buffer *next;
};

/* Read the out-of-band data from SOCKET and return it
   as a 'struct buffer', which records the address of the data
   and its size.

   It may be necessary to read some ordinary data
   in order to make room for the out-of-band data.
   If so, the ordinary data is saved as a chain of buffers
   found in the 'next' field of the value.   */

struct buffer *
read_oob (int socket)
{
  struct buffer *tail = 0;
  struct buffer *list = 0;

  while (1)
    {
      /* This is an arbitrary limit.
         Does anyone know how to do this without a limit?   */
      char *buffer = (char *) xmalloc (1024);
      struct buffer *link;
      int success;
      int result;

      /* Try again to read the out-of-band data.  */
      success = recv (socket, buffer, sizeof buffer, MSG_OOB);
      if (success >= 0)
        {
          /* We got it, so return it.  */
          struct buffer *link
            = (struct buffer *) xmalloc (sizeof (struct buffer));
          link->buffer = buffer;
          link->size = success;
          link->next = list;
          return link;
```

Chapter 11: Sockets

```
      }

    /* If we fail, see if we are at the mark.  */
    success = ioctl (socket, SIOCATMARK, &result);
    if (success < 0)
      perror ("ioctl");
    if (result)
      {
        /* At the mark; skipping past more ordinary data cannot help.
           So just wait a while.  */
        sleep (1);
        continue;
      }

    /* Otherwise, read a bunch of ordinary data and save it.
       This is guaranteed not to read past the mark
       if it starts before the mark.  */
    success = read (socket, buffer, sizeof buffer);
    if (success < 0)
      perror ("read");

    /* Save this data in the buffer list.  */
    {
      struct buffer *link
        = (struct buffer *) xmalloc (sizeof (struct buffer));
      link->buffer = buffer;
      link->size = success;

      /* Add the new link to the end of the list.  */
      if (tail)
        tail->next = link;
      else
        list = link;
      tail = link;
    }
  }
}
```

11.9 Datagram Socket Operations

This section describes how to use communication styles that don't use connections (styles `SOCK_DGRAM` and `SOCK_RDM`). Using these styles, you group data into packets and each packet is an independent communication. You specify the destination for each packet individually.

Datagram packets are like letters: you send each one independently, with its own destination address, and they may arrive in the wrong order or not at all.

The `listen` and `accept` functions are not allowed for sockets using connectionless communication styles.

11.9.1 Sending Datagrams

The normal way of sending data on a datagram socket is by using the `sendto` function, declared in 'sys/socket.h'.

You can call `connect` on a datagram socket, but this only specifies a default destination for further data transmission on the socket. When a socket has a default destination, then you can use `send` (see Section 11.8.5.1 [Sending Data], page 235) or even `write` (see Section 8.2 [Input and Output Primitives], page 141) to send a packet there. You can cancel the default destination by calling `connect` using an address format of `AF_UNSPEC` in the *addr* argument. See Section 11.8.1 [Making a Connection], page 231, for more information about the `connect` function.

int **sendto** (int *socket*, void **buffer*. size_t *size*, int *flags*, struct sockaddr **addr*, size_t *length*)   Function

The `sendto` function transmits the data in the *buffer* through the socket *socket* to the destination address specified by the *addr* and *length* arguments. The *size* argument specifies the number of bytes to be transmitted.

The *flags* are interpreted the same way as for `send`; see Section 11.8.5.3 [Socket Data Options], page 237.

The return value and error conditions are also the same as for `send`, but you cannot rely on the system to detect errors and report them; the most common error is that the packet is lost or there is no one at the specified address to receive it, and the operating system on your machine usually does not know this.

It is also possible for one call to `sendto` to report an error due to a problem related to a previous call.

11.9.2 Receiving Datagrams

The `recvfrom` function reads a packet from a datagram socket and also tells you where it was sent from. This function is declared in 'sys/socket.h'.

int **recvfrom** (int *socket*, void **buffer*, size_t *size*, int *flags*, struct sockaddr **addr*, size_t **length-ptr*)   Function

The `recvfrom` function reads one packet from the socket *socket* into the buffer *buffer*. The *size* argument specifies the maximum number of bytes to be read.

If the packet is longer than *size* bytes, then you get the first *size* bytes of the packet, and the rest of the packet is lost. There's no way to read the rest of the packet. Thus, when you use a packet protocol, you must always know how long a packet to expect.

Chapter 11: Sockets   245

The *addr* and *length-ptr* arguments are used to return the address where the packet came from. See Section 11.3 [Socket Addresses], page 209. For a socket in the file domain, the address information won't be meaningful, since you can't read the address of such a socket (see Section 11.4 [The File Namespace], page 212). You can specify a null pointer as the *addr* argument if you are not interested in this information.

The *flags* are interpreted the same way as for `recv` (see Section 11.8.5.3 [Socket Data Options], page 237). The return value and error conditions are also the same as for `recv`.

You can use plain `recv` (see Section 11.8.5.2 [Receiving Data], page 236) instead of `recvfrom` if you know don't need to find out who sent the packet (either because you know where it should come from or because you treat all possible senders alike). Even `read` can be used if you don't want to specify *flags* (see Section 8.2 [Input and Output Primitives], page 141).

11.9.3 Datagram Socket Example

Here is a set of example programs that send messages over a datagram stream in the file namespace. Both the client and server programs use the `make_named_socket` function that was presented in Section 11.4 [The File Namespace], page 212, to create and name their sockets.

First, here is the server program. It sits in a loop waiting for messages to arrive, bouncing each message back to the sender. Obviously, this isn't a particularly useful program, but it does show the general ideas involved.

```
#include <stdio.h>
#include <errno.h>
#include <stdlib.h>
#include <sys/socket.h>
#include <sys/un.h>

#define SERVER   "/tmp/serversocket"
#define MAXMSG   512

int
main (void)
{
  int sock;
  char message[MAXMSG];
  struct sockaddr_un name;
  size_t size;
  int nbytes;

  /* Make the socket, then loop endlessly. */

  sock = make_named_socket (SERVER);
```

```
      while (1)
        {
          /* Wait for a datagram. */
          size = sizeof (name);
          nbytes = recvfrom (sock, message, MAXMSG, 0,
                             (struct sockaddr *) & name, &size);
          if (nbytes < 0)
            {
              perror ("recfrom (server)");
              exit (EXIT_FAILURE);
            }

          /* Give a diagnostic message. */
          fprintf (stderr, "Server: got message: %s\n", message);

          /* Bounce the message back to the sender. */
          nbytes = sendto (sock, message, nbytes, 0,
                           (struct sockaddr *) & name, size);
          if (nbytes < 0)
            {
              perror ("sendto (server)");
              exit (EXIT_FAILURE);
            }
        }
    }
```

11.9.4 Example of Reading Datagrams

Here is the client program corresponding to the server above.

It sends a datagram to the server and then waits for a reply. Notice that the socket for the client (as well as for the server) in this example has to be given a name. This is so that the server can direct a message back to the client. Since the socket has no associated connection state, the only way the server can do this is by referencing the name of the client.

```
#include <stdio.h>
#include <errno.h>
#include <unistd.h>
#include <stdlib.h>
#include <sys/socket.h>
#include <sys/un.h>

#define SERVER  "/tmp/serversocket"
#define CLIENT  "/tmp/mysocket"
#define MAXMSG  512
#define MESSAGE "Yow!!! Are we having fun yet?!?"

int
main (void)
{
  extern int make_named_socket (const char *name);
  int sock;
```

Chapter 11: Sockets

```
      char message[MAXMSG];
      struct sockaddr_un name;
      size_t size;
      int nbytes;

      /* Make the socket. */
      sock = make_named_socket (CLIENT);

      /* Initialize the server socket address. */
      name.sun_family = AF_UNIX;
      strcpy (name.sun_path, SERVER);
      size = strlen (name.sun_path) + sizeof (name.sun_family);

      /* Send the datagram. */
      nbytes = sendto (sock, MESSAGE, strlen (MESSAGE) + 1, 0,
                       (struct sockaddr *) & name, size);
      if (nbytes < 0)
        {
          perror ("sendto (client)");
          exit (EXIT_FAILURE);
        }

      /* Wait for a reply. */
      nbytes = recvfrom (sock, message, MAXMSG, 0, NULL, 0);
      if (nbytes < 0)
        {
          perror ("recfrom (client)");
          exit (EXIT_FAILURE);
        }

      /* Print a diagnostic message. */
      fprintf (stderr, "Client: got message: %s\n", message);

      /* Clean up. */
      remove (CLIENT);
      close (sock);
    }
```

Keep in mind that datagram socket communications are unreliable. In this example, the client program waits indefinitely if the message never reaches the server or if the server's response never comes back. It's up to the user running the program to kill it and restart it, if desired. A more automatic solution could be to use `select` (see Section 8.6 [Waiting for Input or Output], page 150) to establish a timeout period for the reply, and in case of timeout either resend the message or shut down the socket and exit.

11.10 The `inetd` Daemon

We've explained above how to write a server program that does its own listening. Such a server must already be running in order for anyone to connect to it.

Another way to provide service for an Internet port is to let the daemon program `inetd` do the listening. `inetd` is a program that runs all the time and waits (using `select`) for messages on a specified set of ports. When it receives a message, it accepts the connection (if the socket style calls for connections) and then forks a child process to run the corresponding server program. You specify the ports and their programs in the file '/etc/inetd.conf'.

11.10.1 `inetd` Servers

Writing a server program to be run by `inetd` is very simple. Each time someone requests a connection to the appropriate port, a new server process starts. The connection already exists at this time; the socket is available as the standard input descriptor and as the standard output descriptor (descriptors 0 and 1) in the server process. So the server program can begin reading and writing data right away. Often the program needs only the ordinary I/O facilities; in fact, a general-purpose filter program that knows nothing about sockets can work as a byte stream server run by `inetd`.

You can also use `inetd` for servers that use connectionless communication styles. For these servers, `inetd` does not try to accept a connection, since no connection is possible. It just starts the server program, which can read the incoming datagram packet from descriptor 0. The server program can handle one request and then exit, or you can choose to write it to keep reading more requests until no more arrive, and then exit. You must specify which of these two techniques the server uses, when you configure `inetd`.

11.10.2 Configuring `inetd`

The file '/etc/inetd.conf' tells `inetd` which ports to listen to and what server programs to run for them. Normally each entry in the file is one line, but you can split it onto multiple lines provided all but the first line of the entry start with whitespace. Lines that start with '#' are comments.

Here are two standard entries in '/etc/inetd.conf':

```
ftp stream tcp nowait root /libexec/ftpd ftpd
talk dgram udp wait root /libexec/talkd talkd
```

An entry has this format:

service style protocol wait username program arguments

The *service* field says which service this program provides. It should be the name of a service defined in '/etc/services'. `inetd` uses *service* to decide which port to listen on for this entry.

The fields *style* and *protocol* specify the communication style and the protocol to use for the listening socket. The style should be the name of a communication style, converted to lower case and with 'SOCK_' deleted—for

Chapter 11: Sockets   249

example, 'stream' or 'dgram'. *protocol* should be one of the protocols listed in '/etc/protocols'. The typical protocol names are 'tcp' for byte stream connections and 'udp' for unreliable datagrams.

The *wait* field should be either 'wait' or 'nowait'. Use 'wait' if *style* is a connectionless style and the server, once started, handles multiple requests, as many as come in. Use 'nowait' if inetd should start a new process for each message or request that comes in. If *style* uses connections, then *wait* **must** be 'nowait'.

user is the user name that the server should run as. inetd runs as root, so it can set the user ID of its children arbitrarily. It's best to avoid using 'root' for *user* if you can; but some servers, such as Telnet and FTP, read a username and password themselves. These servers need to be root initially so they can log in as commanded by the data coming over the network.

program together with *arguments* specifies the command to run to start the server. *program* should be an absolute file name specifying the executable file to run. *arguments* consists of any number of whitespace-separated words, which become the command-line arguments of *program*. The first word in *arguments* is argument zero, which should by convention be the program name itself (sans directories).

If you edit '/etc/inetd.conf', you can tell inetd to reread the file and obey its new contents by sending the inetd process the SIGHUP signal. You'll have to use ps to determine the process ID of the inetd process, as it is not fixed.

11.11 Socket Options

This section describes how to read or set various options that modify the behavior of sockets and their underlying communications protocols.

When you are manipulating a socket option, you must specify which *level* the option pertains to. This describes whether the option applies to the socket interface, or to a lower-level communications protocol interface.

11.11.1 Socket Option Functions

Here are the functions for examining and modifying socket options. They are declared in 'sys/socket.h'.

int **getsockopt** (int *socket*, int *level*, int *optname*,   Function
         void *optval*, size_t **optlen-ptr*)

The getsockopt function gets information about the value of option *optname* at level *level* for socket *socket*.

The option value is stored in a buffer that *optval* points to. Before the call, you should supply in **optlen-ptr* the size of this buffer; on return, it contains the number of bytes of information actually stored in the buffer.

Most options interpret the *optval* buffer as a single `int` value.

The actual return value of `getsockopt` is 0 on success and -1 on failure. The following `errno` error conditions are defined:

EBADF
: The *socket* argument is not a valid file descriptor.

ENOTSOCK
: The descriptor *socket* is not a socket.

ENOPROTOOPT
: The *optname* doesn't make sense for the given *level*.

`int setsockopt (int` *socket*`, int` *level*`, int` *optname*`,`   *Function*
    `void *`*optval*`, size_t` *optlen*`)`

This function is used to set the socket option *optname* at level *level* for socket *socket*. The value of the option is passed in the buffer *optval*, which has size *optlen*.

The return value and error codes for `setsockopt` are the same as for `getsockopt`.

11.11.2 Socket-Level Options

`int SOL_SOCKET`   *Constant*

Use this constant as the *level* argument to `getsockopt` or `setsockopt` to manipulate the socket-level options described in this section.

Here is a table of socket-level option names; all are defined in the header file 'sys/socket.h'.

SO_DEBUG
: This option toggles recording of debugging information in the underlying protocol modules. The value has type `int`; a nonzero value means "yes".

SO_REUSEADDR
: This option controls whether `bind` (see Section 11.3.2 [Setting the Address of a Socket], page 211) should permit reuse of local addresses for this socket. If you enable this option, you can actually have two sockets with the same Internet port number; but the system won't allow you to use the two identically-named sockets in a way that would confuse the Internet. The reason for this option is that some higher-level Internet protocols, including FTP, require you to keep reusing the same socket number.

: The value has type `int`; a nonzero value means "yes".

Chapter 11: Sockets   251

`SO_KEEPALIVE`
> This option controls whether the underlying protocol should periodically transmit messages on a connected socket. If the peer fails to respond to these messages, the connection is considered broken. The value has type `int`; a nonzero value means "yes".

`SO_DONTROUTE`
> This option controls whether outgoing messages bypass the normal message routing facilities. If set, messages are sent directly to the network interface instead. The value has type `int`; a nonzero value means "yes".

`SO_LINGER`
> This option specifies what should happen when the socket of a type that promises reliable delivery still has untransmitted messages when it is closed; see Section 11.7.2 [Closing a Socket], page 229. The value has type `struct linger`.
>
> **struct linger**   Data Type
> This structure type has the following members:
>
> > `int l_onoff`
> > > This field is interpreted as a boolean. If nonzero, `close` blocks until the data is transmitted or the timeout period has expired.
> >
> > `int l_linger`
> > > This specifies the timeout period, in seconds.

`SO_BROADCAST`
> This option controls whether datagrams may be broadcast from the socket. The value has type `int`; a nonzero value means "yes".

`SO_OOBINLINE`
> If this option is set, out-of-band data received on the socket is placed in the normal input queue. This permits it to be read using `read` or `recv` without specifying the `MSG_OOB` flag. See Section 11.8.8 [Out-of-Band Data], page 241. The value has type `int`; a nonzero value means "yes".

`SO_SNDBUF`
> This option gets or sets the size of the output buffer. The value is a `size_t`, which is the size in bytes.

`SO_RCVBUF`
> This option gets or sets the size of the input buffer. The value is a `size_t`, which is the size in bytes.

SO_STYLE
SO_TYPE   This option can be used with `getsockopt` only. It is used to get the socket's communication style. `SO_TYPE` is the historical name, and `SO_STYLE` is the preferred name in GNU. The value has type `int` and its value designates a communication style; see Section 11.2 [Communication Styles], page 208.

SO_ERROR
             This option can be used with `getsockopt` only. It is used to reset the error status of the socket. The value is an `int`, which represents the previous error status.

11.12 Networks Database

Many systems come with a database that records a list of networks known to the system developer. This is usually kept either in the file '/etc/networks' or in an equivalent from a name server. This data base is useful for routing programs such as `route`, but it is not useful for programs that simply communicate over the network. We provide functions to access this data base, which are declared in 'netdb.h'.

struct netent   Data Type
   This data type is used to represent information about entries in the networks database. It has the following members:

   char *n_name
            This is the "official" name of the network.

   char **n_aliases
            These are alternative names for the network, represented as a vector of strings. A null pointer terminates the array.

   int n_addrtype
            This is the type of the network number; this is always equal to `AF_INET` for Internet networks.

   unsigned long int n_net
            This is the network number. Network numbers are returned in host byte order; see Section 11.5.5 [Byte Order Conversion], page 224.

Use the `getnetbyname` or `getnetbyaddr` functions to search the networks database for information about a specific network. The information is returned in a statically-allocated structure; you must copy the information if you need to save it.

Chapter 11: Sockets

struct netent * getnetbyname (const char *name*) *Function*

The `getnetbyname` function returns information about the network named *name*. It returns a null pointer if there is no such network.

struct netent * getnetbyaddr (long *net*, int *type*) *Function*
The `getnetbyaddr` function returns information about the network of type *type* with number *net*. You should specify a value of `AF_INET` for the *type* argument for Internet networks.

`getnetbyaddr` returns a null pointer if there is no such network.

You can also scan the networks database using `setnetent`, `getnetent`, and `endnetent`. Be careful in using these functions, because they are not reentrant.

void setnetent (int *stayopen*) *Function*
This function opens and rewinds the networks database.

If the *stayopen* argument is nonzero, this sets a flag so that subsequent calls to `getnetbyname` or `getnetbyaddr` will not close the database (as they usually would). This makes for more efficiency if you call those functions several times, by avoiding reopening the database for each call.

struct netent * getnetent (void) *Function*
This function returns the next entry in the networks database. It returns a null pointer if there are no more entries.

void endnetent (void) *Function*
This function closes the networks database.

12 Low-Level Terminal Interface

This chapter describes functions that are specific to terminal devices. You can use these functions to do things like turn off input echoing; set serial line characteristics such as line speed and flow control; and change which characters are used for end-of-file, command-line editing, sending signals, and similar control functions.

Most of the functions in this chapter operate on file descriptors. See Chapter 8 [Low-Level Input/Output], page 139, for more information about what a file descriptor is and how to open a file descriptor for a terminal device.

12.1 Identifying Terminals

The functions described in this chapter only work on files that correspond to terminal devices. You can find out whether a file descriptor is associated with a terminal by using the `isatty` function.

Prototypes for both `isatty` and `ttyname` are declared in the header file 'unistd.h'.

int **isatty** (int *filedes*) .... Function
  This function returns 1 if *filedes* is a file descriptor associated with an open terminal device, and 0 otherwise.

If a file descriptor is associated with a terminal, you can get its associated file name using the `ttyname` function. See also the `ctermid` function, described in Section 24.7.1 [Identifying the Controlling Terminal], page 474.

char * **ttyname** (int *filedes*) .... Function
  If the file descriptor *filedes* is associated with a terminal device, the `ttyname` function returns a pointer to a statically-allocated, null-terminated string containing the file name of the terminal file. The value is a null pointer if the file descriptor isn't associated with a terminal, or the file name cannot be determined.

12.2 I/O Queues

Many of the remaining functions in this section refer to the input and output queues of a terminal device. These queues implement a form of buffering *within the kernel* independent of the buffering implemented by I/O streams (see Chapter 7 [Input/Output on Streams], page 83).

The *terminal input queue* is also sometimes referred to as its *typeahead buffer*. It holds the characters that have been received from the terminal but not yet read by any process.

The size of the terminal's input queue is described by the `MAX_INPUT` and `_POSIX_MAX_INPUT` parameters; see Section 27.6 [Limits on File System Capacity], page 507. You are guaranteed a queue size of at least `MAX_INPUT`, but the queue might be larger, and might even dynamically change size. If input flow control is enabled by setting the `IXOFF` input mode bit (see Section 12.4.4 [Input Modes], page 261), the terminal driver transmits STOP and START characters to the terminal when necessary to prevent the queue from overflowing. Otherwise, input may be lost if it comes in too fast from the terminal. In canonical mode, all input stays in the queue until a newline character is received, so the terminal input queue can fill up when you type a very long line. See Section 12.3 [Two Styles of Input: Canonical or Not], page 256.

The *terminal output queue* is like the input queue, but for output; it contains characters that have been written by processes, but not yet transmitted to the terminal. If output flow control is enabled by setting the `IXON` input mode bit (see Section 12.4.4 [Input Modes], page 261), the terminal driver obeys STOP and STOP characters sent by the terminal to stop and restart transmission of output.

Clearing the terminal input queue means discarding any characters that have been received but not yet read. Similarly, clearing the terminal output queue means discarding any characters that have been written but not yet transmitted.

12.3 Two Styles of Input: Canonical or Not

POSIX systems support two basic modes of input: canonical and non-canonical.

In *canonical input processing* mode, terminal input is processed in lines terminated by newline ('\n'), EOF, or EOL characters. No input can be read until an entire line has been typed by the user, and the `read` function (see Section 8.2 [Input and Output Primitives], page 141) returns at most a single line of input, no matter how many bytes are requested.

In canonical input mode, the operating system provides input editing facilities: some characters are interpreted specially to perform editing operations within the current line of text, such as ERASE and KILL. See Section 12.4.9.1 [Characters for Input Editing], page 271.

The constants `_POSIX_MAX_CANON` and `MAX_CANON` parameterize the maximum number of bytes which may appear in a single line of canonical input. See Section 27.6 [Limits on File System Capacity], page 507. You are guaranteed a maximum line length of at least `MAX_CANON` bytes, but the maximum might be larger, and might even dynamically change size.

In *noncanonical input processing* mode, characters are not grouped into lines, and ERASE and KILL processing is not performed. The granularity

Chapter 12: Low-Level Terminal Interface   257

with which bytes are read in noncanonical input mode is controlled by the MIN and TIME settings. See Section 12.4.10 [Noncanonical Input], page 275.

Most programs use canonical input mode, because this gives the user a way to edit input line by line. The usual reason to use noncanonical mode is when the program accepts single-character commands or provides its own editing facilities.

The choice of canonical or noncanonical input is controlled by the `ICANON` flag in the `c_lflag` member of `struct termios`. See Section 12.4.7 [Local Modes], page 266.

12.4 Terminal Modes

This section describes the various terminal attributes that control how input and output are done. The functions, data structures, and symbolic constants are all declared in the header file 'termios.h'.

12.4.1 Terminal Mode Data Types

The entire collection of attributes of a terminal is stored in a structure of type `struct termios`. This structure is used with the functions `tcgetattr` and `tcsetattr` to read and set the attributes.

struct termios   Data Type

Structure that records all the I/O attributes of a terminal. The structure includes at least the following members:

`tcflag_t c_iflag`
: A bit mask specifying flags for input modes; see Section 12.4.4 [Input Modes], page 261.

`tcflag_t c_oflag`
: A bit mask specifying flags for output modes; see Section 12.4.5 [Output Modes], page 263.

`tcflag_t c_cflag`
: A bit mask specifying flags for control modes; see Section 12.4.6 [Control Modes], page 264.

`tcflag_t c_lflag`
: A bit mask specifying flags for local modes; see Section 12.4.7 [Local Modes], page 266.

`cc_t c_cc[NCCS]`
: An array specifying which characters are associated with various control functions; see Section 12.4.9 [Special Characters], page 270.

The `struct termios` structure also contains members which encode input and output transmission speeds, but the representation is not specified. See Section 12.4.8 [Line Speed], page 268, for how to examine and store the speed values.

The following sections describe the details of the members of the `struct termios` structure.

tcflag_t *Data Type*
This is an unsigned integer type used to represent the various bit masks for terminal flags.

cc_t *Data Type*
This is an unsigned integer type used to represent characters associated with various terminal control functions.

int NCCS *Macro*
The value of this macro is the number of elements in the `c_cc` array.

12.4.2 Terminal Mode Functions

int tcgetattr (int *filedes*, struct termios *termios-p*) *Function*
This function is used to examine the attributes of the terminal device with file descriptor *filedes*. The attributes are returned in the structure that *termios-p* points to.

If successful, `tcgetattr` returns 0. A return value of -1 indicates an error. The following `errno` error conditions are defined for this function:

EBADF   The *filedes* argument is not a valid file descriptor.

ENOTTY The *filedes* is not associated with a terminal.

int tcsetattr (int *filedes*, int *when*, const struct *Function*
        termios *termios-p*)
This function sets the attributes of the terminal device with file descriptor *filedes*. The new attributes are taken from the structure that *termios-p* points to.

The *when* argument specifies how to deal with input and output already queued. It can be one of the following values:

TCSANOW Make the change immediately.

TCSADRAIN
          Make the change after waiting until all queued output has been written. You should usually use this option when changing parameters that affect output.

Chapter 12: Low-Level Terminal Interface

TCSAFLUSH
: This is like `TCSADRAIN`, but also discards any queued input.

TCSASOFT
: This is a flag bit that you can add to any of the above alternatives. Its meaning is to inhibit alteration of the state of the terminal hardware. It is a BSD extension; it is only supported on BSD systems and the GNU system.

  Using `TCSASOFT` is exactly the same as setting the `CIGNORE` bit in the `c_cflag` member of the structure *termios-p* points to. See Section 12.4.6 [Control Modes], page 264, for a description of `CIGNORE`.

If this function is called from a background process on its controlling terminal, normally all processes in the process group are sent a `SIGTTOU` signal, in the same way as if the process were trying to write to the terminal. The exception is if the calling process itself is ignoring or blocking `SIGTTOU` signals, in which case the operation is performed and no signal is sent. See Chapter 24 [Job Control], page 457.

If successful, `tcsetattr` returns 0. A return value of -1 indicates an error. The following `errno` error conditions are defined for this function:

EBADF
: The *filedes* argument is not a valid file descriptor.

ENOTTY
: The *filedes* is not associated with a terminal.

EINVAL
: Either the value of the **when** argument is not valid, or there is something wrong with the data in the *termios-p* argument.

Although `tcgetattr` and `tcsetattr` specify the terminal device with a file descriptor, the attributes are those of the terminal device itself and not of the file descriptor. This means that the effects of changing terminal attributes are persistent; if another process opens the terminal file later on, it will see the changed attributes even though it doesn't have anything to do with the open file descriptor you originally specified in changing the attributes.

Similarly, if a single process has multiple or duplicated file descriptors for the same terminal device, changing the terminal attributes affects input and output to all of these file descriptors. This means, for example, that you can't open one file descriptor or stream to read from a terminal in the normal line-buffered, echoed mode; and simultaneously have another file descriptor for the same terminal that you use to read from it in single-character, non-echoed mode. Instead, you have to explicitly switch the terminal back and forth between the two modes.

12.4.3 Setting Terminal Modes Properly

When you set terminal modes, you should call `tcgetattr` first to get the current modes of the particular terminal device, modify only those modes that you are really interested in, and store the result with `tcsetattr`.

It's a bad idea to simply initialize a `struct termios` structure to a chosen set of attributes and pass it directly to `tcsetattr`. Your program may be run years from now, on systems that support members not documented in this manual. The way to avoid setting these members to unreasonable values is to avoid changing them.

What's more, different terminal devices may require different mode settings in order to function properly. So you should avoid blindly copying attributes from one terminal device to another.

When a member contains a collection of independent flags, as the `c_iflag`, `c_oflag` and `c_cflag` members do, even setting the entire member is a bad idea, because particular operating systems have their own flags. Instead, you should start with the current value of the member and alter only the flags whose values matter in your program, leaving any other flags unchanged.

Here is an example of how to set one flag (`ISTRIP`) in the `struct termios` structure while properly preserving all the other data in the structure:

```
int
set_istrip (int desc, int value)
{
  struct termios settings;
  int result;

  result = tcgetattr (desc, &settings);
  if (result < 0)
    {
      perror ("error in tcgetattr");
      return 0;
    }
  settings.c_iflag &= ~ISTRIP;
  if (value)
    settings.c_iflag |= ISTRIP;
  result = tcsetattr (desc, TCSANOW, &settings);
  if (result < 0)
    {
      perror ("error in tcgetattr");
      return;
    }
  return 1;
}
```

Chapter 12: Low-Level Terminal Interface 261

12.4.4 Input Modes

This section describes the terminal attribute flags that control fairly low-level aspects of input processing: handling of parity errors, break signals, flow control, and *RET* and *LFD* characters.

All of these flags are bits in the `c_iflag` member of the **struct termios** structure. The member is an integer, and you change flags using the operators &, | and ^. Don't try to specify the entire value for `c_iflag`—instead, change only specific flags and leave the rest untouched (see Section 12.4.3 [Setting Terminal Modes Properly], page 260).

tcflag_t INPCK   *Macro*
> If this bit is set, input parity checking is enabled. If it is not set, no checking at all is done for parity errors on input; the characters are simply passed through to the application.
>
> Parity checking on input processing is independent of whether parity detection and generation on the underlying terminal hardware is enabled; see Section 12.4.6 [Control Modes], page 264. For example, you could clear the `INPCK` input mode flag and set the `PARENB` control mode flag to ignore parity errors on input, but still generate parity on output.
>
> If this bit is set, what happens when a parity error is detected depends on whether the `IGNPAR` or `PARMRK` bits are set. If neither of these bits are set, a byte with a parity error is passed to the application as a '\0' character.

tcflag_t IGNPAR   *Macro*
> If this bit is set, any byte with a framing or parity error is ignored. This is only useful if `INPCK` is also set.

tcflag_t PARMRK   *Macro*
> If this bit is set, input bytes with parity or framing errors are marked when passed to the program. This bit is meaningful only when `INPCK` is set and `IGNPAR` is not set.
>
> The way erroneous bytes are marked is with two preceding bytes, 377 and 0. Thus, the program actually reads three bytes for one erroneous byte received from the terminal.
>
> If a valid byte has the value 0377, and `ISTRIP` (see below) is not set, the program might confuse it with the prefix that marks a parity error. So a valid byte 0377 is passed to the program as two bytes, 0377 0377, in this case.

tcflag_t ISTRIP   *Macro*
> If this bit is set, valid input bytes are stripped to seven bits; otherwise, all eight bits are available for programs to read.

tcflag_t **IGNBRK**   Macro
If this bit is set, break conditions are ignored.

A *break condition* is defined in the context of asynchronous serial data transmission as a series of zero-value bits longer than a single byte.

tcflag_t **BRKINT**   Macro
If this bit is set and `IGNBRK` is not set, a break condition clears the terminal input and output queues and raises a `SIGINT` signal for the foreground process group associated with the terminal.

If neither `BRKINT` nor `IGNBRK` are set, a break condition is passed to the application as a single '\0' character if `PARMRK` is not set, or otherwise as a three-character sequence '\377', '\0', '\0'.

tcflag_t **IGNCR**   Macro
If this bit is set, carriage return characters ('\r') are discarded on input. Discarding carriage return may be useful on terminals that send both carriage return and linefeed when you type the *RET* key.

tcflag_t **ICRNL**   Macro
If this bit is set and `IGNCR` is not set, carriage return characters ('\r') received as input are passed to the application as newline characters ('\n').

tcflag_t **INLCR**   Macro
If this bit is set, newline characters ('\n') received as input are passed to the application as carriage return characters ('\r').

tcflag_t **IXOFF**   Macro
If this bit is set, start/stop control on input is enabled. In other words, the computer sends STOP and START characters as necessary to prevent input from coming in faster than programs are reading it. The idea is that the actual terminal hardware that is generating the input data responds to a STOP character by suspending transmission, and to a START character by resuming transmission. See Section 12.4.9.3 [Special Characters for Flow Control], page 274.

tcflag_t **IXON**   Macro
If this bit is set, start/stop control on output is enabled. In other words, if the computer receives a STOP character, it suspends output until a START character is received. In this case, the STOP and START characters are never passed to the application program. If this bit is not set, then START and STOP can be read as ordinary characters. See Section 12.4.9.3 [Special Characters for Flow Control], page 274.

Chapter 12: Low-Level Terminal Interface   263

tcflag_t IXANY   Macro
  If this bit is set, any input character restarts output when output has been suspended with the STOP character. Otherwise, only the START character restarts output.

  This is a BSD extension; it exists only on BSD systems and the GNU system.

tcflag_t IMAXBEL   Macro
  If this bit is set, then filling up the terminal input buffer sends a BEL character (code 007) to the terminal to ring the bell.

  This is a BSD extension.

12.4.5 Output Modes

This section describes the terminal flags and fields that control how output characters are translated and padded for display. All of these are contained in the `c_oflag` member of the **struct termios** structure.

The `c_oflag` member itself is an integer, and you change the flags and fields using the operators &, |, and ^. Don't try to specify the entire value for `c_oflag`—instead, change only specific flags and leave the rest untouched (see Section 12.4.3 [Setting Terminal Modes Properly], page 260).

tcflag_t OPOST   Macro
  If this bit is set, output data is processed in some unspecified way so that it is displayed appropriately on the terminal device. This typically includes mapping newline characters ('\n') onto carriage return and linefeed pairs.

  If this bit isn't set, the characters are transmitted as-is.

The following three bits are BSD features, and they exist only BSD systems and the GNU system. They are effective only if OPOST is set.

tcflag_t ONLCR   Macro
  If this bit is set, convert the newline character on output into a pair of characters, carriage return followed by linefeed.

tcflag_t OXTABS   Macro
  If this bit is set, convert tab characters on output into the appropriate number of spaces to emulate a tab stop every eight columns.

tcflag_t ONOEOT   Macro
  If this bit is set, discard C-d characters (code 004) on output. These characters cause many dial-up terminals to disconnect.

12.4.6 Control Modes

This section describes the terminal flags and fields that control parameters usually associated with asynchronous serial data transmission. These flags may not make sense for other kinds of terminal ports (such as a network connection pseudo-terminal). All of these are contained in the `c_cflag` member of the `struct termios` structure.

The `c_cflag` member itself is an integer, and you change the flags and fields using the operators &, |, and ^. Don't try to specify the entire value for `c_cflag`—instead, change only specific flags and leave the rest untouched (see Section 12.4.3 [Setting Terminal Modes Properly], page 260).

tcflag_t CLOCAL *Macro*

If this bit is set, it indicates that the terminal is connected "locally" and that the modem status lines (such as carrier detect) should be ignored.

On many systems if this bit is not set and you call `open` without the `O_NONBLOCK` flag set, `open` blocks until a modem connection is established.

If this bit is not set and a modem disconnect is detected, a `SIGHUP` signal is sent to the controlling process group for the terminal (if it has one). Normally, this causes the process to exit; see Chapter 21 [Signal Handling], page 371. Reading from the terminal after a disconnect causes an end-of-file condition, and writing causes an `EIO` error to be returned. The terminal device must be closed and reopened to clear the condition.

tcflag_t HUPCL *Macro*

If this bit is set, a modem disconnect is generated when all processes that have the terminal device open have either closed the file or exited.

tcflag_t CREAD *Macro*

If this bit is set, input can be read from the terminal. Otherwise, input is discarded when it arrives.

tcflag_t CSTOPB *Macro*

If this bit is set, two stop bits are used. Otherwise, only one stop bit is used.

tcflag_t PARENB *Macro*

If this bit is set, generation and detection of a parity bit are enabled. See Section 12.4.4 [Input Modes], page 261, for information on how input parity errors are handled.

If this bit is not set, no parity bit is added to output characters, and input characters are not checked for correct parity.

Chapter 12: Low-Level Terminal Interface   265

`tcflag_t` **PARODD**   Macro
> This bit is only useful if `PARENB` is set. If `PARODD` is set, odd parity is used, otherwise even parity is used.

The control mode flags also includes a field for the number of bits per character. You can use the `CSIZE` macro as a mask to extract the value, like this: `settings.c_cflag & CSIZE`.

`tcflag_t` **CSIZE**   Macro
> This is a mask for the number of bits per character.

`tcflag_t` **CS5**   Macro
> This specifies five bits per byte.

`tcflag_t` **CS6**   Macro
> This specifies six bits per byte.

`tcflag_t` **CS7**   Macro
> This specifies seven bits per byte.

`tcflag_t` **CS8**   Macro
> This specifies eight bits per byte.

The following four bits are BSD extensions; this exist only on BSD systems and the GNU system.

`tcflag_t` **CCTS_OFLOW**   Macro
> If this bit is set, enable flow control of output based on the CTS wire (RS232 protocol).

`tcflag_t` **CRTS_IFLOW**   Macro
> If this bit is set, enable flow control of input based on the RTS wire (RS232 protocol).

`tcflag_t` **MDMBUF**   Macro
> If this bit is set, enable carrier-based flow control of output.

`tcflag_t` **CIGNORE**   Macro
> If this bit is set, it says to ignore the control modes and line speed values entirely. This is only meaningful in a call to `tcsetattr`.
>
> The `c_cflag` member and the line speed values returned by `cfgetispeed` and `cfgetospeed` will be unaffected by the call. `CIGNORE` is useful if you want to set all the software modes in the other members, but leave the hardware details in `c_cflag` unchanged. (This is how the `TCSASOFT` flag to `tcsettattr` works.)
>
> This bit is never set in the structure filled in by `tcgetattr`.

12.4.7 Local Modes

This section describes the flags for the `c_lflag` member of the **struct termios** structure. These flags generally control higher-level aspects of input processing than the input modes flags described in Section 12.4.4 [Input Modes], page 261, such as echoing, signals, and the choice of canonical or noncanonical input.

The `c_lflag` member itself is an integer, and you change the flags and fields using the operators &, |, and ^. Don't try to specify the entire value for `c_lflag`—instead, change only specific flags and leave the rest untouched (see Section 12.4.3 [Setting Terminal Modes Properly], page 260).

tcflag_t ICANON   *Macro*
  This bit, if set, enables canonical input processing mode. Otherwise, input is processed in noncanonical mode. See Section 12.3 [Two Styles of Input: Canonical or Not], page 256.

tcflag_t ECHO   *Macro*
  If this bit is set, echoing of input characters back to the terminal is enabled.

tcflag_t ECHOE   *Macro*
  If this bit is set, echoing indicates erasure of input with the ERASE character by erasing the last character in the current line from the screen. Otherwise, the character erased is re-echoed to show what has happened (suitable for a printing terminal).

  This bit only controls the display behavior; the `ICANON` bit by itself controls actual recognition of the ERASE character and erasure of input, without which `ECHOE` is simply irrelevant.

tcflag_t ECHOPRT   *Macro*
  This bit is like `ECHOE`, enables display of the ERASE character in a way that is geared to a hardcopy terminal. When you type the ERASE character, a '\' character is printed followed by the first character erased. Typing the ERASE character again just prints the next character erased. Then, the next time you type a normal character, a '/' character is printed before the character echoes.

  This is a BSD extension, and exists only in BSD systems and the GNU system.

tcflag_t ECHOK   *Macro*
  This bit enables special display of the KILL character by moving to a new line after echoing the KILL character normally. The behavior of `ECHOKE` (below) is nicer to look at.

  If this bit is not set, the KILL character echoes just as it would if it were not the KILL character. Then it is up to the user to remember that the KILL character has erased the preceding input; there is no indication of this on the screen.

This bit only controls the display behavior; the `ICANON` bit by itself controls actual recognition of the KILL character and erasure of input, without which `ECHOK` is simply irrelevant.

`tcflag_t` **ECHOKE** *Macro*
This bit is similar to `ECHOK`. It enables special display of the KILL character by erasing on the screen the entire line that has been killed. This is a BSD extension, and exists only in BSD systems and the GNU system.

`tcflag_t` **ECHONL** *Macro*
If this bit is set and the `ICANON` bit is also set, then the newline (`'\n'`) character is echoed even if the `ECHO` bit is not set.

`tcflag_t` **ECHOCTL** *Macro*
If this bit is set and the `ECHO` bit is also set, echo control characters with '^' followed by the corresponding text character. Thus, control-A echoes as '^A'. This is usually the preferred mode for interactive input, because echoing a control character back to the terminal could have some undesired effect on the terminal.

This is a BSD extension, and exists only in BSD systems and the GNU system.

`tcflag_t` **ISIG** *Macro*
This bit controls whether the INTR, QUIT, and SUSP characters are recognized. The functions associated with these characters are performed if and only if this bit is set. Being in canonical or noncanonical input mode has no affect on the interpretation of these characters.

You should use caution when disabling recognition of these characters. Programs that cannot be interrupted interactively are very user-unfriendly. If you clear this bit, your program should provide some alternate interface that allows the user to interactively send the signals associated with these characters, or to escape from the program.

See Section 12.4.9.2 [Characters that Cause Signals], page 272.

`tcflag_t` **IEXTEN** *Macro*
POSIX.1 gives `IEXTEN` implementation-defined meaning, so you cannot rely on this interpretation on all systems.

On BSD systems and the GNU system, it enables the LNEXT and DISCARD characters. See Section 12.4.9.4 [Other Special Characters], page 274.

`tcflag_t` **NOFLSH** Macro

Normally, the INTR, QUIT, and SUSP characters cause input and output queues for the terminal to be cleared. If this bit is set, the queues are not cleared.

`tcflag_t` **TOSTOP** Macro

If this bit is set and the system supports job control, then `SIGTTOU` signals are generated by background processes that attempt to write to the terminal. See Section 24.4 [Access to the Controlling Terminal], page 459.

The following bits are BSD extensions; they exist only in BSD systems and the GNU system.

`tcflag_t` **ALTWERASE** Macro

This bit determines how far the WERASE character should erase. The WERASE character erases back to the beginning of a word; the question is, where do words begin?

If this bit is clear, then the beginning of a word is a nonwhitespace character following a whitespace character. If the bit is set, then the beginning of a word is an alphanumeric character or underscore following a character which is none of those.

See Section 12.4.9.1 [Characters for Input Editing], page 271, for more information about the WERASE character.

`tcflag_t` **FLUSHO** Macro

This is the bit that toggles when the user types the DISCARD character. While this bit is set, all output is discarded. See Section 12.4.9.4 [Other Special Characters], page 274.

`tcflag_t` **NOKERNINFO** Macro

Setting this bit disables handling of the STATUS character. See Section 12.4.9.4 [Other Special Characters], page 274.

`tcflag_t` **PENDIN** Macro

If this bit is set, it indicates that there is a line of input that needs to be reprinted. Typing the REPRINT character sets this bit; the bit remains set until reprinting is finished. See Section 12.4.9.1 [Characters for Input Editing], page 271.

12.4.8 Line Speed

The terminal line speed tells the computer how fast to read and write data on the terminal.

If the terminal is connected to a real serial line, the terminal speed you specify actually controls the line—if it doesn't match the terminal's own

Chapter 12: Low-Level Terminal Interface   269

idea of the speed, communication does not work. Real serial ports accept only certain standard speeds. Also, particular hardware may not support even all the standard speeds. Specifying a speed of zero hangs up a dialup connection and turns off modem control signals.

If the terminal is not a real serial line (for example, if it is a network connection), then the line speed won't really affect data transmission speed, but some programs will use it to determine the amount of padding needed. It's best to specify a line speed value that matches the actual speed of the actual terminal, but you can safely experiment with different values to vary the amount of padding.

There are actually two line speeds for each terminal, one for input and one for output. You can set them independently, but most often terminals use the same speed for both directions.

The speed values are stored in the `struct termios` structure, but don't try to access them in the `struct termios` structure directly. Instead, you should use the following functions to read and store them:

speed_t cfgetospeed (`const struct termios *termios-p`)   *Function*

This function returns the output line speed stored in the structure *termios-p*.

speed_t cfgetispeed (`const struct termios *termios-p`)   *Function*

This function returns the input line speed stored in the structure *termios-p*.

int cfsetospeed (`struct termios *termios-p, speed_t speed`)   *Function*

This function stores *speed* in *termios-p* as the output speed. The normal return value is 0; a value of -1 indicates an error. If *speed* is not a speed, `cfsetospeed` returns -1.

int cfsetispeed (`struct termios *termios-p, speed_t speed`)   *Function*

This function stores *speed* in *termios-p* as the input speed. The normal return value is 0; a value of -1 indicates an error. If *speed* is not a speed, `cfsetospeed` returns -1.

int cfsetspeed (`struct termios *termios-p, speed_t speed`)   *Function*

This function stores *speed* in *termios-p* as both the input and output speeds. The normal return value is 0; a value of -1 indicates an error. If *speed* is not a speed, `cfsetspeed` returns -1. This function is an extension in 4.4 BSD.

speed_t   *Data Type*

The `speed_t` type is an unsigned integer data type used to represent line speeds.

The functions `cfsetospeed` and `cfsetispeed` report errors only for speed values that the system simply cannot handle. If you specify a speed value that is basically acceptable, then those functions will succeed. But they do not check that a particular hardware device can actually support the specified speeds—in fact, they don't know which device you plan to set the speed for. If you use `tcsetattr` to set the speed of a particular device to a value that it cannot handle, `tcsetattr` returns -1.

Portability note: In the GNU library, the functions above accept speeds measured in bits per second as input, and return speed values measured in bits per second. Other libraries require speeds to be indicated by special codes. For POSIX.1 portability, you must use one of the following symbols to represent the speed; their precise numeric values are system-dependent, but each name has a fixed meaning: `B110` stands for 110 bps, `B300` for 300 bps, and so on. There is no portable way to represent any speed but these, but these are the only speeds that typical serial lines can support.

```
B0    B50    B75    B110   B134   B150   B200
B300  B600   B1200  B1800  B2400  B4800
B9600 B19200 B38400
```

BSD defines two additional speed symbols as aliases: `EXTA` is an alias for `B19200` and `EXTB` is an alias for `B38400`. These aliases are obsolete.

12.4.9 Special Characters

In canonical input, the terminal driver recognizes a number of special characters which perform various control functions. These include the ERASE character (usually *DEL*) for editing input, and other editing characters. The INTR character (normally *C-c*) for sending a SIGINT signal, and other signal-raising characters, may be available in either canonical or noncanonical input mode. All these characters are described in this section.

The particular characters used are specified in the `c_cc` member of the `struct termios` structure. This member is an array; each element specifies the character for a particular role. Each element has a symbolic constant that stands for the index of that element—for example, `INTR` is the index of the element that specifies the INTR character, so storing '=' in *termios.c_cc[INTR]* specifies '=' as the INTR character.

On some systems, you can disable a particular special character function by specifying the value `_POSIX_VDISABLE` for that role. This value is unequal to any possible character code. See Section 27.7 [Optional Features in File Support], page 508, for more information about how to tell whether the operating system you are using supports `_POSIX_VDISABLE`.

Chapter 12: Low-Level Terminal Interface

12.4.9.1 Characters for Input Editing

These special characters are active only in canonical input mode. See Section 12.3 [Two Styles of Input: Canonical or Not], page 256.

`int` **VEOF** *Macro*

This is the subscript for the EOF character in the special control character array. *termios.*`c_cc[VEOF]` holds the character itself.

The EOF character is recognized only in canonical input mode. It acts as a line terminator in the same way as a newline character, but if the EOF character is typed at the beginning of a line it causes `read` to return a byte count of zero, indicating end-of-file. The EOF character itself is discarded.

Usually, the EOF character is *C-d*.

`int` **VEOL** *Macro*

This is the subscript for the EOL character in the special control character array. *termios.*`c_cc[VEOL]` holds the character itself.

The EOL character is recognized only in canonical input mode. It acts as a line terminator, just like a newline character. The EOL character is not discarded; it is read as the last character in the input line.

You don't need to use the EOL character to make *RET* end a line. Just set the ICRNL flag. In fact, this is the default state of affairs.

`int` **VEOL2** *Macro*

This is the subscript for the EOL2 character in the special control character array. *termios.*`c_cc[VEOL2]` holds the character itself.

The EOL2 character works just like the EOL character (see above), but it can be a different character. Thus, you can specify two characters to terminate an input line, by setting EOL to one of them and EOL2 to the other.

The EOL2 character is a BSD extension; it exists only on BSD systems and the GNU system.

`int` **VERASE** *Macro*

This is the subscript for the ERASE character in the special control character array. *termios.*`c_cc[VERASE]` holds the character itself.

The ERASE character is recognized only in canonical input mode. When the user types the erase character, the previous character typed is discarded. (If the terminal generates multibyte character sequences, this may cause more than one byte of input to be discarded.) This cannot be used to erase past the beginning of the current line of text. The ERASE character itself is discarded.

Usually, the ERASE character is *DEL*.

int **VWERASE** Macro

This is the subscript for the WERASE character in the special control character array. *termios.*c_cc[VWERASE] holds the character itself.

The WERASE character is recognized only in canonical mode. It erases an entire word of prior input, and any whitespace after it; whitespace characters before the word are not erased.

The definition of a "word" depends on the setting of the ALTWERASE mode; see Section 12.4.7 [Local Modes], page 266.

If the ALTWERASE mode is not set, a word is defined as a sequence of any characters except space or tab.

If the ALTWERASE mode is set, a word is defined as a sequence of characters containing only letters, numbers, and underscores, optionally followed by one character that is not a letter, number, or underscore.

The WERASE character is usually *C-w*.

This is a BSD extension.

int **VKILL** Macro

This is the subscript for the KILL character in the special control character array. *termios.*c_cc[VKILL] holds the character itself.

The KILL character is recognized only in canonical input mode. When the user types the kill character, the entire contents of the current line of input are discarded. The kill character itself is discarded too.

The KILL character is usually *C-u*.

int **VREPRINT** Macro

This is the subscript for the REPRINT character in the special control character array. *termios.*c_cc[VREPRINT] holds the character itself.

The REPRINT character is recognized only in canonical mode. It reprints the current input line. If some asynchronous output has come while you are typing, this lets you see the line you are typing clearly again.

The REPRINT character is usually *C-r*.

This is a BSD extension.

12.4.9.2 Characters that Cause Signals

These special characters may be active in either canonical or noncanonical input mode, but only when the ISIG flag is set (see Section 12.4.7 [Local Modes], page 266).

int **VINTR** Macro

This is the subscript for the INTR character in the special control character array. *termios.*c_cc[VINTR] holds the character itself.

Chapter 12: Low-Level Terminal Interface   273

The INTR (interrupt) character raises a `SIGINT` signal for all processes in the foreground job associated with the terminal. The INTR character itself is then discarded. See Chapter 21 [Signal Handling], page 371, for more information about signals.

Typically, the INTR character is `C-c`.

int **VQUIT**   Macro

This is the subscript for the QUIT character in the special control character array. `termios.c_cc[VQUIT]` holds the character itself.

The QUIT character raises a `SIGQUIT` signal for all processes in the foreground job associated with the terminal. The QUIT character itself is then discarded. See Chapter 21 [Signal Handling], page 371, for more information about signals.

Typically, the QUIT character is `C-\`.

int **VSUSP**   Macro

This is the subscript for the SUSP character in the special control character array. `termios.c_cc[VSUSP]` holds the character itself.

The SUSP (suspend) character is recognized only if the implementation supports job control (see Chapter 24 [Job Control], page 457). It causes a `SIGTSTP` signal to be sent to all processes in the foreground job associated with the terminal. The SUSP character itself is then discarded. See Chapter 21 [Signal Handling], page 371, for more information about signals.

Typically, the SUSP character is `C-z`.

Few applications disable the normal interpretation of the SUSP character. If your program does this, it should provide some other mechanism for the user to stop the job. When the user invokes this mechanism, the program should send a `SIGTSTP` signal to the process group of the process, not just to the process itself. See Section 21.6.2 [Signaling Another Process], page 405.

int **VDSUSP**   Macro

This is the subscript for the DSUSP character in the special control character array. `termios.c_cc[VDSUSP]` holds the character itself.

The DSUSP (suspend) character is recognized only if the implementation supports job control (see Chapter 24 [Job Control], page 457). It sends a `SIGTSTP` signal, like the SUSP character, but not right away—only when the program tries to read it as input. Not all systems with job control support DSUSP; only BSD-compatible systems (including the GNU system).

See Chapter 21 [Signal Handling], page 371, for more information about signals.

Typically, the DSUSP character is `C-y`.

12.4.9.3 Special Characters for Flow Control

These special characters may be active in either canonical or noncanonical input mode, but their use is controlled by the flags `IXON` and `IXOFF` (see Section 12.4.4 [Input Modes], page 261).

int VSTART   *Macro*

This is the subscript for the START character in the special control character array. *termios*.`c_cc[VSTART]` holds the character itself.

The START character is used to support the `IXON` and `IXOFF` input modes. If `IXON` is set, receiving a START character resumes suspended output; the START character itself is discarded. If `IXANY` is set, receiving any character at all resumes suspended output; the resuming character is not discarded unless it is the START character. `IXOFF` is set, the system may also transmit START characters to the terminal.

The usual value for the START character is *C-q*. You may not be able to change this value—the hardware may insist on using *C-q* regardless of what you specify.

int VSTOP   *Macro*

This is the subscript for the STOP character in the special control character array. *termios*.`c_cc[VSTOP]` holds the character itself.

The STOP character is used to support the `IXON` and `IXOFF` input modes. If `IXON` is set, receiving a STOP character causes output to be suspended; the STOP character itself is discarded. If `IXOFF` is set, the system may also transmit STOP characters to the terminal, to prevent the input queue from overflowing.

The usual value for the STOP character is *C-s*. You may not be able to change this value—the hardware may insist on using *C-s* regardless of what you specify.

12.4.9.4 Other Special Characters

These special characters exist only in BSD systems and the GNU system.

int VLNEXT   *Macro*

This is the subscript for the LNEXT character in the special control character array. *termios*.`c_cc[VLNEXT]` holds the character itself.

The LNEXT character is recognized only when `IEXTEN` is set, but in both canonical and noncanonical mode. It disables any special significance of the next character the user types. Even if the character would normally perform some editing function or generate a signal, it is read as a plain character. This is the analogue of the *C-q* command in Emacs. "LNEXT" stands for "literal next."

Chapter 12: Low-Level Terminal Interface   275

The LNEXT character is usually *C-v*.

int **VDISCARD**   Macro
This is the subscript for the DISCARD character in the special control character array. *termios.*`c_cc[VDISCARD]` holds the character itself.

The DISCARD character is recognized only when `IEXTEN` is set, but in both canonical and noncanonical mode. Its effect is to toggle the discard-output flag. When this flag is set, all program output is discarded. Setting the flag also discards all output currently in the output buffer. Typing any other character resets the flag.

int **VSTATUS**   Macro
This is the subscript for the STATUS character in the special control character array. *termios.*`c_cc[VSTATUS]` holds the character itself.

The STATUS character's effect is to print out a status message about how the current process is running.

The STATUS character is recognized only in canonical mode, and only if `NOKERNINFO` is not set.

12.4.10 Noncanonical Input

In noncanonical input mode, the special editing characters such as ERASE and KILL are ignored. The system facilities for the user to edit input are disabled in noncanonical mode, so that all input characters (unless they are special for signal or flow-control purposes) are passed to the application program exactly as typed. It is up to the application program to give the user ways to edit the input, if appropriate.

Noncanonical mode offers special parameters called MIN and TIME for controlling whether and how long to wait for input to be available. You can even use them to avoid ever waiting—to return immediately with whatever input is available, or with no input.

The MIN and TIME are stored in elements of the `c_cc` array, which is a member of the **struct termios** structure. Each element of this array has a particular role, and each element has a symbolic constant that stands for the index of that element. `VMIN` and `VMAX` are the names for the indices in the array of the MIN and TIME slots.

int **VMIN**   Macro
This is the subscript for the MIN slot in the `c_cc` array. Thus, *termios.*`c_cc[VMIN]` is the value itself.

The MIN slot is only meaningful in noncanonical input mode; it specifies the minimum number of bytes that must be available in the input queue in order for **read** to return.

int VTIME   Macro

This is the subscript for the TIME slot in the `c_cc` array. Thus, *termios*.`c_cc[VTIME]` is the value itself.

The TIME slot is only meaningful in noncanonical input mode; it specifies how long to wait for input before returning, in units of 0.1 seconds.

The MIN and TIME values interact to determine the criterion for when `read` should return; their precise meanings depend on which of them are nonzero. There are four possible cases:

- Both TIME and MIN are nonzero.

  In this case, TIME specifies how long to wait after each input character to see if more input arrives. After the first character received, `read` keeps waiting until either MIN bytes have arrived in all, or TIME elapses with no further input.

  `read` always blocks until the first character arrives, even if TIME elapses first. `read` can return more than MIN characters if more than MIN happen to be in the queue.

- Both MIN and TIME are zero.

  In this case, `read` always returns immediately with as many characters as are available in the queue, up to the number requested. If no input is immediately available, `read` returns a value of zero.

- MIN is zero but TIME has a nonzero value.

  In this case, `read` waits for time TIME for input to become available; the availability of a single byte is enough to satisfy the read request and cause `read` to return. When it returns, it returns as many characters as are available, up to the number requested. If no input is available before the timer expires, `read` returns a value of zero.

- TIME is zero but MIN has a nonzero value.

  In this case, `read` waits until at least MIN bytes are available in the queue. At that time, `read` returns as many characters as are available, up to the number requested. `read` can return more than MIN characters if more than MIN happen to be in the queue.

What happens if MIN is 50 and you ask to read just 10 bytes? Normally, `read` waits until there are 50 bytes in the buffer (or, more generally, the wait condition described above is satisfied), and then reads 10 of them, leaving the other 40 buffered in the operating system for a subsequent call to `read`.

Portability note: On some systems, the MIN and TIME slots are actually the same as the EOF and EOL slots. This causes no serious problem because the MIN and TIME slots are used only in noncanonical input and the EOF and EOL slots are used only in canonical input, but it isn't very clean. The GNU library allocates separate slots for these uses.

Chapter 12: Low-Level Terminal Interface   277

`int **cfmakeraw** (struct termios *termios-p)`   *Function*
    This function provides an easy way to set up *termios-p* for what has
    traditionally been called "raw mode" in BSD. This uses noncanonical
    input, and turns off most processing to give an unmodified channel to
    the terminal.

    It does exactly this:
```
termios-p->c_iflag &= ~(IGNBRK|BRKINT|PARMRK|ISTRIP
                                |INLCR|IGNCR|ICRNL|IXON);
termios-p->c_oflag &= ~OPOST;
termios-p->c_lflag &= ~(ECHO|ECHONL|ICANON|ISIG|IEXTEN);
termios-p->c_cflag &= ~(CSIZE|PARENB);
termios-p->c_cflag |= CS8;
```

12.5 Line Control Functions

These functions perform miscellaneous control actions on terminal devices. As regards terminal access, they are treated like doing output: if any of these functions is used by a background process on its controlling terminal, normally all processes in the process group are sent a `SIGTTOU` signal. The exception is if the calling process itself is ignoring or blocking `SIGTTOU` signals, in which case the operation is performed and no signal is sent. See Chapter 24 [Job Control], page 457.

`int **tcsendbreak** (int filedes, int duration)`   *Function*
    This function generates a break condition by transmitting a stream
    of zero bits on the terminal associated with the file descriptor *filedes*.
    The duration of the break is controlled by the *duration* argument. If
    zero, the duration is between 0.25 and 0.5 seconds. The meaning of a
    nonzero value depends on the operating system.

    This function does nothing if the terminal is not an asynchronous serial
    data port.

    The return value is normally zero. In the event of an error, a value of
    -1 is returned. The following `errno` error conditions are defined for
    this function:

    `EBADF`   The *filedes* is not a valid file descriptor.

    `ENOTTY`   The *filedes* is not associated with a terminal device.

`int **tcdrain** (int filedes)`   *Function*
    The `tcdrain` function waits until all queued output to the terminal
    filedes has been transmitted.

    The return value is normally zero. In the event of an error, a value of
    -1 is returned. The following `errno` error conditions are defined for
    this function:

EBADF   The *filedes* is not a valid file descriptor.

ENOTTY   The *filedes* is not associated with a terminal device.

EINTR   The operation was interrupted by delivery of a signal. See Section 21.5 [Primitives Interrupted by Signals], page 402.

int tcflush (int *filedes*, int *queue*)   *Function*
The `tcflush` function is used to clear the input and/or output queues associated with the terminal file *filedes*. The *queue* argument specifies which queue(s) to clear, and can be one of the following values:

TCIFLUSH
:   Clear any input data received, but not yet read.

TCOFLUSH
:   Clear any output data written, but not yet transmitted.

TCIOFLUSH
:   Clear both queued input and output.

The return value is normally zero. In the event of an error, a value of `-1` is returned. The following `errno` error conditions are defined for this function:

EBADF   The *filedes* is not a valid file descriptor.

ENOTTY   The *filedes* is not associated with a terminal device.

EINVAL   A bad value was supplied as the *queue* argument.

It is unfortunate that this function is named `tcflush`, because the term "flush" is normally used for quite another operation—waiting until all output is transmitted—and using it for discarding input or output would be confusing. Unfortunately, the name `tcflush` comes from POSIX and we cannot change it.

int tcflow (int *filedes*, int *action*)   *Function*
The `tcflow` function is used to perform operations relating to XON/XOFF flow control on the terminal file specified by *filedes*.

The *action* argument specifies what operation to perform, and can be one of the following values:

TCOOFF   Suspend transmission of output.

TCOON   Restart transmission of output.

TCIOFF   Transmit a STOP character.

TCION   Transmit a START character.

Chapter 12: Low-Level Terminal Interface

For more information about the STOP and START characters, see Section 12.4.9 [Special Characters], page 270.

The return value is normally zero. In the event of an error, a value of -1 is returned. The following `errno` error conditions are defined for this function:

`EBADF`   The *filedes* is not a valid file descriptor.

`ENOTTY` The *filedes* is not associated with a terminal device.

`EINVAL` A bad value was supplied as the *action* argument.

12.6 Noncanonical Mode Example

Here is an example program that shows how you can set up a terminal device to read single characters in noncanonical input mode, without echo.

```
#include <unistd.h>
#include <stdio.h>
#include <stdlib.h>
#include <termios.h>

/* Use this variable to remember original terminal attributes. */

struct termios saved_attributes;

void
reset_input_mode (void)
{
  tcsetattr (STDIN_FILENO, TCSANOW, &saved_attributes);
}

void
set_input_mode (void)
{
  struct termios tattr;
  char *name;

  /* Make sure stdin is a terminal. */
  if (!isatty (STDIN_FILENO))
    {
      fprintf (stderr, "Not a terminal.\n");
      exit (EXIT_FAILURE);
    }

  /* Save the terminal attributes so we can restore them later. */
  tcgetattr (STDIN_FILENO, &saved_attributes);
  atexit (reset_input_mode);
```

```c
  /* Set the funny terminal modes. */
  tcgetattr (STDIN_FILENO, &tattr);
  tattr.c_lflag &= ~(ICANON|ECHO); /* Clear ICANON and ECHO. */
  tattr.c_cc[VMIN] = 1;
  tattr.c_cc[VTIME] = 0;
  tcsetattr (STDIN_FILENO, TCSAFLUSH, &tattr);
}

int
main (void)
{
  char c;

  set_input_mode ();

  while (1)
    {
      read (STDIN_FILENO, &c, 1);
      if (c == '\004')          /* C-d */
        break;
      else
        putchar (c);
    }

  return EXIT_SUCCESS;
}
```

This program is careful to restore the original terminal modes before exiting or terminating with a signal. It uses the **atexit** function (see Section 22.3.3 [Cleanups on Exit], page 439) to make sure this is done by **exit**.

The shell is supposed to take care of resetting the terminal modes when a process is stopped or continued; see Chapter 24 [Job Control], page 457. But some existing shells do not actually do this, so you may wish to establish handlers for job control signals that reset terminal modes. The above example does so.

13 Mathematics

This chapter contains information about functions for performing mathematical computations, such as trigonometric functions. Most of these functions have prototypes declared in the header file 'math.h'.

All of the functions that operate on floating-point numbers accept arguments and return results of type `double`. In the future, there may be additional functions that operate on `float` and `long double` values. For example, `cosf` and `cosl` would be versions of the `cos` function that operate on `float` and `long double` arguments, respectively. In the meantime, you should avoid using these names yourself. See Section 1.3.3 [Reserved Names], page 6.

13.1 Domain and Range Errors

Many of the functions listed in this chapter are defined mathematically over a domain that is only a subset of real numbers. For example, the `acos` function is defined over the domain between -1 and 1. If you pass an argument to one of these functions that is outside the domain over which it is defined, the function sets `errno` to `EDOM` to indicate a *domain error*. On machines that support IEEE floating point, functions reporting error `EDOM` also return a NaN.

Some of these functions are defined mathematically to result in a complex value over parts of their domains. The most familiar example of this is taking the square root of a negative number. The functions in this chapter take only real arguments and return only real values; therefore, if the value ought to be nonreal, this is treated as a domain error.

A related problem is that the mathematical result of a function may not be representable as a floating point number. If magnitude of the correct result is too large to be represented, the function sets `errno` to `ERANGE` to indicate a *range error*, and returns a particular very large value (named by the macro `HUGE_VAL`) or its negation (- `HUGE_VAL`).

If the magnitude of the result is too small, a value of zero is returned instead. In this case, `errno` might or might not be set to `ERANGE`.

The only completely reliable way to check for domain and range errors is to set `errno` to 0 before you call the mathematical function and test `errno` afterward. As a consequence of this use of `errno`, use of the mathematical functions is not reentrant if you check for errors.

None of the mathematical functions ever generates signals as a result of domain or range errors. In particular, this means that you won't see `SIGFPE` signals generated within these functions. (See Chapter 21 [Signal Handling], page 371, for more information about signals.)

double HUGE_VAL   *Macro*
> An expression representing a particular very large number. On machines that use IEEE floating point format, the value is "infinity". On other machines, it's typically the largest positive number that can be represented.
>
> The value of this macro is used as the return value from various mathematical functions in overflow situations.

For more information about floating-point representations and limits, see Section A.5.3.2 [Floating Point Parameters], page 528. In particular, the macro `DBL_MAX` might be more appropriate than `HUGE_VAL` for many uses other than testing for an error in a mathematical function.

13.2 Trigonometric Functions

These are the familiar `sin`, `cos`, and `tan` functions. The arguments to all of these functions are in units of radians; recall that pi radians equals 180 degrees.

The math library doesn't define a symbolic constant for pi, but you can define your own if you need one:

```
#define PI 3.14159265358979323846264338327
```

You can also compute the value of pi with the expression `acos (-1.0)`.

double sin (double *x*)   *Function*
> This function returns the sine of *x*, where *x* is given in radians. The return value is in the range -1 to 1.

double cos (double *x*)   *Function*
> This function returns the cosine of *x*, where *x* is given in radians. The return value is in the range -1 to 1.

double tan (double *x*)   *Function*
> This function returns the tangent of *x*, where *x* is given in radians.
>
> The following `errno` error conditions are defined for this function:
>
> `ERANGE`   Mathematically, the tangent function has singularities at odd multiples of pi/2. If the argument *x* is too close to one of these singularities, `tan` sets `errno` to `ERANGE` and returns either positive or negative `HUGE_VAL`.

13.3 Inverse Trigonometric Functions

These are the usual arc sine, arc cosine and arc tangent functions, which are the inverses of the sine, cosine and tangent functions, respectively.

Chapter 13: Mathematics

double asin (double x) *Function*

This function computes the arc sine of x—that is, the value whose sine is x. The value is in units of radians. Mathematically, there are infinitely many such values; the one actually returned is the one between `-pi/2` and `pi/2` (inclusive).

`asin` fails, and sets `errno` to `EDOM`, if x is out of range. The arc sine function is defined mathematically only over the domain -1 to 1.

double acos (double x) *Function*

This function computes the arc cosine of x—that is, the value whose cosine is x. The value is in units of radians. Mathematically, there are infinitely many such values; the one actually returned is the one between `0` and `pi` (inclusive).

`acos` fails, and sets `errno` to `EDOM`, if x is out of range. The arc cosine function is defined mathematically only over the domain -1 to 1.

double atan (double x) *Function*

This function computes the arc tangent of x—that is, the value whose tangent is x. The value is in units of radians. Mathematically, there are infinitely many such values; the one actually returned is the one between `-pi/2` and `pi/2` (inclusive).

double atan2 (double y, double x) *Function*

This is the two argument arc tangent function. It is similar to computing the arc tangent of y/x, except that the signs of both arguments are used to determine the quadrant of the result, and x is permitted to be zero. The return value is given in radians and is in the range `-pi` to `pi`, inclusive.

If x and y are coordinates of a point in the plane, `atan2` returns the signed angle between the line from the origin to that point and the x-axis. Thus, `atan2` is useful for converting Cartesian coordinates to polar coordinates. (To compute the radial coordinate, use `hypot`; see Section 13.4 [Exponentiation and Logarithms], page 283.)

The function `atan2` sets `errno` to `EDOM` if both x and y are zero; the return value is not defined in this case.

13.4 Exponentiation and Logarithms

double exp (double x) *Function*

The `exp` function returns the value of e (the base of natural logarithms) raised to power x.

The function fails, and sets `errno` to `ERANGE`, if the magnitude of the result is too large to be representable.

double **log** (double *x*)   Function
:   This function returns the natural logarithm of *x*. `exp (log (x))` equals *x*, exactly in mathematics and approximately in C.

    The following `errno` error conditions are defined for this function:

    EDOM
    :   The argument *x* is negative. The log function is defined mathematically to return a real result only on positive arguments.

    ERANGE
    :   The argument is zero. The log of zero is not defined.

double **log10** (double *x*)   Function
:   This function returns the base-10 logarithm of *x*. Except for the different base, it is similar to the `log` function. In fact, `log10 (x)` equals `log (x) / log (10)`.

double **pow** (double *base*, double *power*)   Function
:   This is a general exponentiation function, returning *base* raised to *power*.

    The following `errno` error conditions are defined for this function:

    EDOM
    :   The argument *base* is negative and *power* is not an integral value. Mathematically, the result would be a complex number in this case.

    ERANGE
    :   An underflow or overflow condition was detected in the result.

double **sqrt** (double *x*)   Function
:   This function returns the nonnegative square root of *x*.

    The `sqrt` function fails, and sets `errno` to EDOM, if *x* is negative. Mathematically, the square root would be a complex number.

double **cbrt** (double *x*)   Function
:   This function returns the cube root of *x*. This function cannot fail; every representable real value has a representable real cube root.

double **hypot** (double *x*, double *y*)   Function
:   The `hypot` function returns `sqrt (x*x + y*y)`. (This is the length of the hypotenuse of a right triangle with sides of length *x* and *y*, or the distance of the point (*x*, *y*) from the origin.) See also the function `cabs` in Section 14.3 [Absolute Value], page 290.

double **expm1** (double *x*)   Function
:   This function returns a value equivalent to `exp (x) - 1`. It is computed in a way that is accurate even if the value of *x* is near zero—a case where `exp (x) - 1` would be inaccurate due to subtraction of two numbers that are nearly equal.

Chapter 13: Mathematics 285

`double` **`log1p`** `(double x)` *Function*
> This function returns a value equivalent to `log (1 + x)`. It is computed in a way that is accurate even if the value of x is near zero.

13.5 Hyperbolic Functions

The functions in this section are related to the exponential functions; see Section 13.4 [Exponentiation and Logarithms], page 283.

`double` **`sinh`** `(double x)` *Function*
> The `sinh` function returns the hyperbolic sine of x, defined mathematically as `exp (x) - exp (-x) / 2`. The function fails, and sets `errno` to `ERANGE`, if the value of x is too large; that is, if overflow occurs.

`double` **`cosh`** `(double x)` *Function*
> The `cosh` function returns the hyperbolic cosine of x, defined mathematically as `exp (x) + exp (-x) / 2`. The function fails, and sets `errno` to `ERANGE`, if the value of x is too large; that is, if overflow occurs.

`double` **`tanh`** `(double x)` *Function*
> This function returns the hyperbolic tangent of x, whose mathematical definition is `sinh (x) / cosh (x)`.

`double` **`asinh`** `(double x)` *Function*
> This function returns the inverse hyperbolic sine of x—the value whose hyperbolic sine is x.

`double` **`acosh`** `(double x)` *Function*
> This function returns the inverse hyperbolic cosine of x—the value whose hyperbolic cosine is x. If x is less than 1, `acosh` returns `HUGE_VAL`.

`double` **`atanh`** `(double x)` *Function*
> This function returns the inverse hyperbolic tangent of x—the value whose hyperbolic tangent is x. If the absolute value of x is greater than or equal to 1, `atanh` returns `HUGE_VAL`.

13.6 Pseudo-Random Numbers

This section describes the GNU facilities for generating a series of pseudo-random numbers. The numbers generated are not truly random; typically, they form a sequence that repeats periodically, with a period so large that you can ignore it for ordinary purposes. The random number generator works by remembering at all times a *seed* value which it uses to compute the next random number and also to compute a new seed.

Although the generated numbers look unpredictable within one run of a program, the sequence of numbers is *exactly the same* from one run to the next. This is because the initial seed is always the same. This is convenient when you are debugging a program, but it is unhelpful if you want the program to behave unpredictably. If you want truly random numbers, not just pseudo-random, specify a seed based on the current time.

You can get repeatable sequences of numbers on a particular machine type by specifying the same initial seed value for the random number generator. There is no standard meaning for a particular seed value; the same seed, used in different C libraries or on different CPU types, will give you different random numbers.

The GNU library supports the standard ANSI C random number functions plus another set derived from BSD. We recommend you use the standard ones, **rand** and **srand**.

13.6.1 ANSI C Random Number Functions

This section describes the random number functions that are part of the ANSI C standard.

To use these facilities, you should include the header file 'stdlib.h' in your program.

int **RAND_MAX**   Macro

The value of this macro is an integer constant expression that represents the maximum possible value returned by the **rand** function. In the GNU library, it is 037777777, which is the largest signed integer representable in 32 bits. In other libraries, it may be as low as 32767.

int **rand** ()   Function

The **rand** function returns the next pseudo-random number in the series. The value is in the range from 0 to **RAND_MAX**.

void **srand** (unsigned int *seed*)   Function

This function establishes *seed* as the seed for a new series of pseudo-random numbers. If you call **rand** before a seed has been established with **srand**, it uses the value 1 as a default seed.

To produce truly random numbers (not just pseudo-random), do **srand (time (0))**.

13.6.2 BSD Random Number Functions

This section describes a set of random number generation functions that are derived from BSD. There is no advantage to using these functions with the GNU C library; we support them for BSD compatibility only.

The prototypes for these functions are in 'stdlib.h'.

long int **random** ()   *Function*
This function returns the next pseudo-random number in the sequence. The range of values returned is from 0 to RAND_MAX.

void **srandom** (unsigned int *seed*)   *Function*
The srandom function sets the seed for the current random number state based on the integer *seed*. If you supply a *seed* value of 1, this will cause random to reproduce the default set of random numbers.

To produce truly random numbers (not just pseudo-random), do srandom (time (0)).

void * **initstate** (unsigned int *seed*, void *state*,   *Function*
    size_t *size*)
The initstate function is used to initialize the random number generator state. The argument *state* is an array of *size* bytes, used to hold the state information. The size must be at least 8 bytes, and optimal sizes are 8, 16, 32, 64, 128, and 256. The bigger the *state* array, the better.

The return value is the previous value of the state information array. You can use this value later as an argument to setstate to restore that state.

void * **setstate** (void *state*)   *Function*
The setstate function restores the random number state information *state*. The argument must have been the result of a previous call to *initstate* or *setstate*.

The return value is the previous value of the state information array. You can use thise value later as an argument to setstate to restore that state.

14 Low-Level Arithmetic Functions

This chapter contains information about functions for doing basic arithmetic operations, such as splitting a float into its integer and fractional parts. These functions are declared in the header file 'math.h'.

14.1 "Not a Number" Values

The IEEE floating point format used by most modern computers supports values that are "not a number". These values are called *NaNs*. "Not a number" values result from certain operations which have no meaningful numeric result, such as zero divided by zero or infinity divided by infinity.

One noteworthy property of NaNs is that they are not equal to themselves. Thus, x == x can be 0 if the value of x is a NaN. You can use this to test whether a value is a NaN or not: if it is not equal to itself, then it is a NaN. But the recommended way to test for a NaN is with the `isnan` function (see Section 14.2 [Predicates on Floats], page 289).

Almost any arithmetic operation in which one argument is a NaN returns a NaN.

double NAN *Macro*
An expression representing a value which is "not a number". This macro is a GNU extension, available only on machines that support "not a number" values—that is to say, on all machines that support IEEE floating point.

You can use '#ifdef NAN' to test whether the machine supports NaNs. (Of course, you must arrange for GNU extensions to be visible, such as by defining _GNU_SOURCE, and then you must include 'math.h'.)

14.2 Predicates on Floats

This section describes some miscellaneous test functions on doubles. Prototypes for these functions appear in 'math.h'. These are BSD functions, and thus are available if you define _BSD_SOURCE or _GNU_SOURCE.

int isinf (double *x*) *Function*
This function returns -1 if *x* represents negative infinity, 1 if *x* represents positive infinity, and 0 otherwise.

int isnan (double *x*) *Function*
This function returns a nonzero value if *x* is a "not a number" value, and zero otherwise. (You can just as well use *x* != *x* to get the same result).

int **finite** (double *x*)   Function
    This function returns a nonzero value if *x* is finite or a "not a number" value, and zero otherwise.

double **infnan** (int *error*)   Function
    This function is provided for compatibility with BSD. The other mathematical functions use `infnan` to decide what to return on occasion of an error. Its argument is an error code, `EDOM` or `ERANGE`; `infnan` returns a suitable value to indicate this with. `-ERANGE` is also acceptable as an argument, and corresponds to `-HUGE_VAL` as a value.

    In the BSD library, on certain machines, `infnan` raises a fatal signal in all cases. The GNU library does not do likewise, because that does not fit the ANSI C specification.

    Portability Note: The functions listed in this section are BSD extensions.

14.3 Absolute Value

    These functions are provided for obtaining the *absolute value* (or *magnitude*) of a number. The absolute value of a real number *x* is *x* is *x* is positive, $-x$ if *x* is negative. For a complex number *z*, whose real part is *x* and whose imaginary part is *y*, the absolute value is `sqrt (x*x + y*y)`.

    Prototypes for `abs` and `labs` are in 'stdlib.h'; `fabs` and `cabs` are declared in 'math.h'.

int **abs** (int *number*)   Function
    This function returns the absolute value of *number*.

    Most computers use a two's complement integer representation, in which the absolute value of `INT_MIN` (the smallest possible `int`) cannot be represented; thus, `abs (INT_MIN)` is not defined.

long int **labs** (long int *number*)   Function
    This is similar to `abs`, except that both the argument and result are of type `long int` rather than `int`.

double **fabs** (double *number*)   Function
    This function returns the absolute value of the floating-point number *number*.

double **cabs** (struct { double *real*, *imag*; } *z*)   Function
    The `cabs` function returns the absolute value of the complex number *z*, whose real part is `z.real` and whose imaginary part is `z.imag`. (See also the function `hypot` in Section 13.4 [Exponentiation and Logarithms], page 283.) The value is:

        `sqrt (z.real*z.real + z.imag*z.imag)`

14.4 Normalization Functions

The functions described in this section are primarily provided as a way to efficiently perform certain low-level manipulations on floating point numbers that are represented internally using a binary radix; see Section A.5.3.1 [Floating Point Representation Concepts], page 527. These functions are required to have equivalent behavior even if the representation does not use a radix of 2, but of course they are unlikely to be particularly efficient in those cases.

All these functions are declared in 'math.h'.

double frexp (double *value*, int **exponent*) *Function*
The `frexp` function is used to split the number *value* into a normalized fraction and an exponent.

If the argument *value* is not zero, the return value is *value* times a power of two, and is always in the range 1/2 (inclusive) to 1 (exclusive). The corresponding exponent is stored in **exponent*; the return value multiplied by 2 raised to this exponent equals the original number *value*.

For example, `frexp (12.8, &exponent)` returns 0.8 and stores 4 in *exponent*.

If *value* is zero, then the return value is zero and zero is stored in **exponent*.

double ldexp (double *value*, int *exponent*) *Function*
This function returns the result of multiplying the floating-point number *value* by 2 raised to the power *exponent*. (It can be used to reassemble floating-point numbers that were taken apart by `frexp`.)

For example, `ldexp (0.8, 4)` returns 12.8.

The following functions which come from BSD provide facilities equivalent to those of `ldexp` and `frexp`:

double scalb (double *value*, int *exponent*) *Function*
The `scalb` function is the BSD name for `ldexp`.

double logb (double *x*) *Function*
This BSD function returns the integer part of the base-2 logarithm of *x*, an integer value represented in type **double**. This is the highest integer power of 2 contained in *x*. The sign of *x* is ignored. For example, `logb (3.5)` is 1.0 and `logb (4.0)` is 2.0.

When 2 raised to this power is divided into *x*, it gives a quotient between 1 (inclusive) and 2 (exclusive).

If *x* is zero, the value is minus infinity (if the machine supports such a value), or else a very small number. If *x* is infinity, the value is infinity.

The value returned by `logb` is one less than the value that `frexp` would store into *exponent*.

double copysign (double *value*, double *sign*) *Function*
The `copysign` function returns a value whose absolute value is the same as that of *value*, and whose sign matches that of *sign*. This is a BSD function.

14.5 Rounding and Remainder Functions

The functions listed here perform operations such as rounding, truncation, and remainder in division of floating point numbers. Some of these functions convert floating point numbers to integer values. They are all declared in 'math.h'.

You can also convert floating-point numbers to integers simply by casting them to `int`. This discards the fractional part, effectively rounding towards zero. However, this only works if the result can actually be represented as an `int`—for very large numbers, this is impossible. The functions listed here return the result as a `double` instead to get around this problem.

double ceil (double *x*) *Function*
The `ceil` function rounds *x* upwards to the nearest integer, returning that value as a `double`. Thus, `ceil (1.5)` is `2.0`.

double floor (double *x*) *Function*
The `ceil` function rounds *x* downwards to the nearest integer, returning that value as a `double`. Thus, `floor (1.5)` is `1.0` and `floor (-1.5)` is `-2.0`.

double rint (double *x*) *Function*
This function rounds *x* to an integer value according to the current rounding mode. See Section A.5.3.2 [Floating Point Parameters], page 528, for information about the various rounding modes. The default rounding mode is to round to the nearest integer; some machines support other modes, but round-to-nearest is always used unless you explicit select another.

double modf (double *value*, double **integer-part*) *Function*
This function breaks the argument *value* into an integer part and a fractional part (between -1 and 1, exclusive). Their sum equals *value*. Each of the parts has the same sign as *value*, so the rounding of the integer part is towards zero.

`modf` stores the integer part in **integer-part*, and returns the fractional part. For example, `modf (2.5, &intpart)` returns `0.5` and stores `2.0` into `intpart`.

Chapter 14: Low-Level Arithmetic Functions   293

double fmod (`double` *numerator*, `double` *denominator*)   *Function*
This function computes the remainder from the division of *numerator* by *denominator*. Specifically, the return value is *numerator* - n * *denominator*, where n is the quotient of *numerator* divided by *denominator*, rounded towards zero to an integer. Thus, `fmod (6.5, 2.3)` returns `1.9`, which is `6.5` minus `4.6`.

The result has the same sign as the *numerator* and has magnitude less than the magnitude of the *denominator*.

If *denominator* is zero, `fmod` fails and sets `errno` to `EDOM`.

double drem (`double` *numerator*, `double` *denominator*)   *Function*

The function `drem` is like `fmod` except that it rounds the internal quotient n to the nearest integer instead of towards zero to an integer. For example, `drem (6.5, 2.3)` returns `-0.4`, which is `6.5` minus `6.9`.

The absolute value of the result is less than or equal to half the absolute value of the *denominator*. The difference between `fmod` (*numerator*, *denominator*) and `drem` (*numerator*, *denominator*) is always either *denominator*, minus *denominator*, or zero.

If *denominator* is zero, `drem` fails and sets `errno` to `EDOM`.

14.6 Integer Division

This section describes functions for performing integer division. These functions are redundant in the GNU C library, since in GNU C the '/' operator always rounds towards zero. But in other C implementations, '/' may round differently with negative arguments. `div` and `ldiv` are useful because they specify how to round the quotient: towards zero. The remainder has the same sign as the numerator.

These functions are specified to return a result *r* such that the value *r*.`quot`**denominator + *r*.`rem` equals *numerator*.

To use these facilities, you should include the header file 'stdlib.h' in your program.

div_t   *Data Type*
This is a structure type used to hold the result returned by the `div` function. It has the following members:

    `int quot`   The quotient from the division.

    `int rem`   The remainder from the division.

div_t div (int *numerator*, int *denominator*)   *Function*
: This function `div` computes the quotient and remainder from the division of *numerator* by *denominator*, returning the result in a structure of type `div_t`.

    If the result cannot be represented (as in a division by zero), the behavior is undefined.

    Here is an example, albeit not a very useful one.
    ```
    div_t result;
    result = div (20, -6);
    ```
    Now `result.quot` is -3 and `result.rem` is 2.

ldiv_t   *Data Type*
: This is a structure type used to hold the result returned by the `ldiv` function. It has the following members:

    long int quot
    : The quotient from the division.

    long int rem
    : The remainder from the division.

    (This is identical to `div_t` except that the components are of type `long int` rather than `int`.)

ldiv_t ldiv (long int *numerator*, long int *denominator*)   *Function*
: The `ldiv` function is similar to `div`, except that the arguments are of type `long int` and the result is returned as a structure of type `ldiv`.

14.7 Parsing of Numbers

This section describes functions for "reading" integer and floating-point numbers from a string. It may be more convenient in some cases to use `sscanf` or one of the related functions; see Section 7.12 [Formatted Input], page 115. But often you can make a program more robust by finding the tokens in the string by hand, then converting the numbers one by one.

14.7.1 Parsing of Integers

These functions are declared in 'stdlib.h'.

long int strtol (const char **string*, char ***tailptr*, int *base*)   *Function*
: The `strtol` ("string-to-long") function converts the initial part of *string* to a signed integer, which is returned as a value of type `long int`.

Chapter 14: Low-Level Arithmetic Functions

This function attempts to decompose *string* as follows:

- A (possibly empty) sequence of whitespace characters. Which characters are whitespace is determined by the `isspace` function (see Section 4.1 [Classification of Characters], page 55). These are discarded.
- An optional plus or minus sign ('+' or '-').
- A nonempty sequence of digits in the radix specified by *base*.

    If *base* is zero, decimal radix is assumed unless the series of digits begins with '0' (specifying octal radix), or '0x' or '0X' (specifying hexadecimal radix); in other words, the same syntax used for integer constants in C.

    Otherwise *base* must have a value between 2 and 35. If *base* is 16, the digits may optionally be preceded by '0x' or '0X'.

- Any remaining characters in the string. If *tailptr* is not a null pointer, `strtol` stores a pointer to this tail in *tailptr*.

If the string is empty, contains only whitespace, or does not contain an initial substring that has the expected syntax for an integer in the specified *base*, no conversion is performed. In this case, `strtol` returns a value of zero and the value stored in *tailptr* is the value of *string*.

In a locale other than the standard `"C"` locale, this function may recognize additional implementation-dependent syntax.

If the string has valid syntax for an integer but the value is not representable because of overflow, `strtol` returns either `LONG_MAX` or `LONG_MIN` (see Section A.5.2 [Range of an Integer Type], page 525), as appropriate for the sign of the value. It also sets `errno` to `ERANGE` to indicate there was overflow.

There is an example at the end of this section.

unsigned long int strtoul (const char *string*, char **tailptr*, int *base*) *Function*

The `strtoul` ("string-to-unsigned-long") function is like `strtol` except it deals with unsigned numbers, and returns its value with type **unsigned long int**. No '+' or '-' sign may appear before the number, but the syntax is otherwise the same as described above for `strtol`. The value returned in case of overflow is `ULONG_MAX` (see Section A.5.2 [Range of an Integer Type], page 525).

long int atol (const char *string*) *Function*

This function is similar to the `strtol` function with a *base* argument of 10, except that it need not detect overflow errors. The `atol` function is provided mostly for compatibility with existing code; using `strtol` is more robust.

int atoi (**const char** *string*)   *Function*
> This function is like `atol`, except that it returns an `int` value rather than `long int`. The `atoi` function is also considered obsolete; use `strtol` instead.
>
> Here is a function which parses a string as a sequence of integers and returns the sum of them:
>
> ```
> int
> sum_ints_from_string (char *string)
> {
>   int sum = 0;
>
>   while (1) {
>     char *tail;
>     int next;
>
>     /* Skip whitespace by hand, to detect the end.  */
>     while (isspace (*string)) string++;
>     if (*string == 0)
>       break;
>
>     /* There is more nonwhitespace,  */
>     /* so it ought to be another number.  */
>     errno = 0;
>     /* Parse it.  */
>     next = strtol (string, &tail, 0);
>     /* Add it in, if not overflow.  */
>     if (errno)
>       printf ("Overflow\n");
>     else
>       sum += next;
>     /* Advance past it.  */
>     string = tail;
>   }
>
>   return sum;
> }
> ```

14.7.2 Parsing of Floats

These functions are declared in 'stdlib.h'.

double strtod (**const char** *string*, **char** **tailptr*)   *Function*
> The `strtod` ("string-to-double") function converts the initial part of *string* to a floating-point number, which is returned as a value of type `double`.
>
> This function attempts to decompose *string* as follows:
> - A (possibly empty) sequence of whitespace characters. Which characters are whitespace is determined by the `isspace` function

Chapter 14: Low-Level Arithmetic Functions

(see Section 4.1 [Classification of Characters], page 55). These are discarded.

- An optional plus or minus sign ('+' or '-').
- A nonempty sequence of digits optionally containing a decimal-point character—normally '.', but it depends on the locale (see Section 19.6 [Numeric Formatting], page 361).
- An optional exponent part, consisting of a character 'e' or 'E', an optional sign, and a sequence of digits.
- Any remaining characters in the string. If *tailptr* is not a null pointer, a pointer to this tail of the string is stored in *tailptr*.

If the string is empty, contains only whitespace, or does not contain an initial substring that has the expected syntax for a floating-point number, no conversion is performed. In this case, `strtod` returns a value of zero and the value returned in *tailptr* is the value of *string*.

In a locale other than the standard "C" locale, this function may recognize additional locale-dependent syntax.

If the string has valid syntax for a floating-point number but the value is not representable because of overflow, `strtod` returns either positive or negative `HUGE_VAL` (see Chapter 13 [Mathematics], page 281), depending on the sign of the value. Similarly, if the value is not representable because of underflow, `strtod` returns zero. It also sets `errno` to `ERANGE` if there was overflow or underflow.

double atof (`const char *`*string*) *Function*
This function is similar to the `strtod` function, except that it need not detect overflow and underflow errors. The `atof` function is provided mostly for compatibility with existing code; using `strtod` is more robust.

15 Searching and Sorting

This chapter describes functions for searching and sorting arrays of arbitrary objects. You pass the appropriate comparison function to be applied as an argument, along with the size of the objects in the array and the total number of elements.

15.1 Defining the Comparison Function

In order to use the sorted array library functions, you have to describe how to compare the elements of the array.

To do this, you supply a comparison function to compare two elements of the array. The library will call this function, passing as arguments pointers to two array elements to be compared. Your comparison function should return a value the way `strcmp` (see Section 5.5 [String/Array Comparison], page 65) does: negative if the first argument is "less" than the second, zero if they are "equal", and positive if the first argument is "greater".

Here is an example of a comparison function which works with an array of numbers of type `double`:

```
int
compare_doubles (const double *a, const double *b)
{
  return (int) (*a - *b);
}
```

The header file 'stdlib.h' defines a name for the data type of comparison functions. This type is a GNU extension.

```
int comparison_fn_t (const void *, const void *);
```

15.2 Array Search Function

To search a sorted array for an element matching the key, use the `bsearch` function. The prototype for this function is in the header file 'stdlib.h'.

void * bsearch (`const void *key, const void *array,`   *Function*
       `size_t count, size_t size, comparison_fn_t compare`)

The `bsearch` function searches the sorted array *array* for an object that is equivalent to *key*. The array contains *count* elements, each of which is of size *size* bytes.

The *compare* function is used to perform the comparison. This function is called with two pointer arguments and should return an integer less than, equal to, or greater than zero corresponding to whether its first argument is considered less than, equal to, or greater than its second argument. The elements of the *array* must already be sorted in ascending order according to this comparison function.

The return value is a pointer to the matching array element, or a null pointer if no match is found. If the array contains more than one element that matches, the one that is returned is unspecified.

This function derives its name from the fact that it is implemented using the binary search algorithm.

15.3 Array Sort Function

To sort an array using an arbitrary comparison function, use the `qsort` function. The prototype for this function is in 'stdlib.h'.

void **qsort** (void *array*, size_t *count*, size_t *size*,   *Function*
        comparison_fn_t *compare*)

The *qsort* function sorts the array *array*. The array contains *count* elements, each of which is of size *size*.

The *compare* function is used to perform the comparison on the array elements. This function is called with two pointer arguments and should return an integer less than, equal to, or greater than zero corresponding to whether its first argument is considered less than, equal to, or greater than its second argument.

Warning: If two objects compare as equal, their order after sorting is unpredictable. That is to say, the sorting is not stable. This can make a difference when the comparison considers only part of the elements. Two elements with the same sort key may differ in other respects.

If you want the effect of a stable sort, you can get this result by writing the comparison function so that, lacking other reason distinguish between two elements, it compares them by their addresses. Note that doing this may make the sorting algorithm less efficient, so do it only if necessary.

Here is a simple example of sorting an array of doubles in numerical order, using the comparison function defined above (see Section 15.1 [Defining the Comparison Function], page 299):

```
{
  double *array;
  int size;
  ...
  qsort (array, size, sizeof (double), compare_doubles);
}
```

The `qsort` function derives its name from the fact that it was originally implemented using the "quick sort" algorithm.

Chapter 15: Searching and Sorting

15.4 Searching and Sorting Example

Here is an example showing the use of `qsort` and `bsearch` with an array of structures. The objects in the array are sorted by comparing their `name` fields with the `strcmp` function. Then, we can look up individual objects based on their names.

```
#include <stdlib.h>
#include <stdio.h>
#include <string.h>

/* Define an array of critters to sort. */

struct critter
  {
    const char *name;
    const char *species;
  };

struct critter muppets[] =
  {
    {"Kermit", "frog"},
    {"Piggy", "pig"},
    {"Gonzo", "whatever"},
    {"Fozzie", "bear"},
    {"Sam", "eagle"},
    {"Robin", "frog"},
    {"Animal", "animal"},
    {"Camilla", "chicken"},
    {"Sweetums", "monster"},
    {"Dr. Strangepork", "pig"},
    {"Link Hogthrob", "pig"},
    {"Zoot", "human"},
    {"Dr. Bunsen Honeydew", "human"},
    {"Beaker", "human"},
    {"Swedish Chef", "human"}
  };

int count = sizeof (muppets) / sizeof (struct critter);


/* This is the comparison function used for sorting and searching. */

int
critter_cmp (const struct critter *c1, const struct critter *c2)
{
  return strcmp (c1->name, c2->name);
}


/* Print information about a critter. */
```

```
void
print_critter (const struct critter *c)
{
  printf ("%s, the %s\n", c->name, c->species);
}


/* Do the lookup into the sorted array. */

void
find_critter (const char *name)
{
  struct critter target, *result;
  target.name = name;
  result = bsearch (&target, muppets, count, sizeof (struct critter),
                    critter_cmp);
  if (result)
    print_critter (result);
  else
    printf ("Couldn't find %s.\n", name);
}
/* Main program. */

int
main (void)
{
  int i;

  for (i = 0; i < count; i++)
    print_critter (&muppets[i]);
  printf ("\n");

  qsort (muppets, count, sizeof (struct critter), critter_cmp);

  for (i = 0; i < count; i++)
    print_critter (&muppets[i]);
  printf ("\n");

  find_critter ("Kermit");
  find_critter ("Gonzo");
  find_critter ("Janice");

  return 0;
}
```

The output from this program looks like:

```
Kermit, the frog
Piggy, the pig
Gonzo, the whatever
Fozzie, the bear
Sam, the eagle
Robin, the frog
Animal, the animal
```

Chapter 15: Searching and Sorting

```
Camilla, the chicken
Sweetums, the monster
Dr. Strangepork, the pig
Link Hogthrob, the pig
Zoot, the human
Dr. Bunsen Honeydew, the human
Beaker, the human
Swedish Chef, the human

Animal, the animal
Beaker, the human
Camilla, the chicken
Dr. Bunsen Honeydew, the human
Dr. Strangepork, the pig
Fozzie, the bear
Gonzo, the whatever
Kermit, the frog
Link Hogthrob, the pig
Piggy, the pig
Robin, the frog
Sam, the eagle
Swedish Chef, the human
Sweetums, the monster
Zoot, the human

Kermit, the frog
Gonzo, the whatever
Couldn't find Janice.
```

16 Pattern Matching

The GNU C Library provides pattern matching facilities for two kinds of patterns: regular expressions and file-name wildcards. The library also provides a facility for expanding variable and command references and parsing text into words in the way the shell does.

16.1 Wildcard Matching

This section describes how to match a wildcard pattern against a particular string. The result is a yes or no answer: does the string fit the pattern or not. The symbols described here are all declared in 'fnmatch.h'.

`int fnmatch (const char *pattern, const char *string, int flags)` *Function*

    This function tests whether the string *string* matches the pattern *pattern*. It returns 0 if they do match; otherwise, it returns the nonzero value `FNM_NOMATCH`. The arguments *pattern* and *string* are both strings.

    The argument *flags* is a combination of flag bits that alter the details of matching. See below for a list of the defined flags.

    In the GNU C Library, `fnmatch` cannot experience an "error"—it always returns an answer for whether the match succeeds. However, other implementations of `fnmatch` might sometimes report "errors". They would do so by returning nonzero values that are not equal to `FNM_NOMATCH`.

    These are the available flags for the *flags* argument:

`FNM_FILE_NAME`
    Treat the '/' character specially, for matching file names. If this flag is set, wildcard constructs in *pattern* cannot match '/' in *string*. Thus, the only way to match '/' is with an explicit '/' in *pattern*.

`FNM_PATHNAME`
    This is an alias for `FNM_FILE_NAME`; it comes from POSIX.2. We don't recommend this name because we don't use the term "pathname" for file names.

`FNM_PERIOD`
    Treat the '.' character specially if it appears at the beginning of *string*. If this flag is set, wildcard constructs in *pattern* cannot match '.' as the first character of *string*.

    If you set both `FNM_PERIOD` and `FNM_FILE_NAME`, then the special treatment applies to '.' following '/' as well as to '.' at the beginning of *string*. (The shell uses the `FNM_PERIOD` and `FNM_FILE_NAME` falgs together for matching file names.)

`FNM_NOESCAPE`
Don't treat the '\' character specially in patterns. Normally, '\' quotes the following character, turning off its special meaning (if any) so that it matches only itself. When quoting is enabled, the pattern '\?' matches only the string '?', because the question mark in the pattern acts like an ordinary character.

If you use `FNM_NOESCAPE`, then '\' is an ordinary character.

`FNM_LEADING_DIR`
Ignore a trailing sequence of characters starting with a '/' in *string*; that is to say, test whether *string* starts with a directory name that *pattern* matches.

If this flag is set, either 'foo*' or 'foobar' as a pattern would match the string 'foobar/frobozz'.

`FNM_CASEFOLD`
Ignore case in comparing *string* to *pattern*.

16.2 Globbing

The archetypal use of wildcards is for matching against the files in a directory, and making a list of all the matches. This is called *globbing*.

You could do this using `fnmatch`, by reading the directory entries one by one and testing each one with `fnmatch`. But that would be slow (and complex, since you would have to handle subdirectories by hand).

The library provides a function `glob` to make this particular use of wildcards convenient. `glob` and the other symbols in this section are declared in 'glob.h'.

16.2.1 Calling `glob`

The result of globbing is a vector of file names (strings). To return this vector, `glob` uses a special data type, `glob_t`, which is a structure. You pass `glob` the address of the structure, and it fills in the structure's fields to tell you about the results.

glob_t   Data Type
This data type holds a pointer to a word vector. More precisely, it records both the address of the word vector and its size.

   `gl_pathc`   The number of elements in the vector.

   `gl_pathv`   The address of the vector. This field has type `char **`.

Chapter 16: Pattern Matching

gl_offs
: The offset of the first real element of the vector, from its nominal address in the `gl_pathv` field. Unlike the other fields, this is always an input to `glob`, rather than an output from it.

    If you use a nonzero offset, then that many elements at the beginning of the vector are left empty. (The `glob` function fills them with null pointers.)

    The `gl_offs` field is meaningful only if you use the `GLOB_DOOFFS` flag. Otherwise, the offset is always zero regardless of what is in this field, and the first real element comes at the beginning of the vector.

int glob (**const char** *pattern*, **int** *flags*, **int** (*errfunc*) (**const char** *filename*, **int** *error-code*), **glob_t** *vector-ptr*) *Function*

The function `glob` does globbing using the pattern *pattern* in the current directory. It puts the result in a newly allocated vector, and stores the size and address of this vector into *vector-ptr*. The argument *flags* is a combination of bit flags; see Section 16.2.2 [Flags for Globbing], page 308, for details of the flags.

The result of globbing is a sequence of file names. The function `glob` allocates a string for each resulting word, then allocates a vector of type `char **` to store the addresses of these strings. The last element of the vector is a null pointer. This vector is called the *word vector*.

To return this vector, `glob` stores both its address and its length (number of elements, not counting the terminating null pointer) into *vector-ptr*.

Normally, `glob` sorts the file names alphabetically before returning them. You can turn this off with the flag `GLOB_NOSORT` if you want to get the information as fast as possible. Usually it's a good idea to let `glob` sort them—if you process the files in alphabetical order, the users will have a feel for the rate of progress that your application is making.

If `glob` succeeds, it returns 0. Otherwise, it returns one of these error codes:

GLOB_ABORTED
: There was an error opening a directory, and you used the flag `GLOB_ERR` or your specified *errfunc* returned a nonzero value. See below for an explanation of the `GLOB_ERR` flag and *errfunc*.

GLOB_NOMATCH
: The pattern didn't match any existing files. If you use the `GLOB_NOCHECK` flag, then you never get this error code,

because that flag tells `glob` to *pretend* that the pattern matched at least one file.

GLOB_NOSPACE
It was impossible to allocate memory to hold the result.

In the event of an error, `glob` stores information in *vector-ptr* about all the matches it has found so far.

16.2.2 Flags for Globbing

This section describes the flags that you can specify in the *flags* argument to `glob`. Choose the flags you want, and combine them with the C bitwise OR operator |.

GLOB_APPEND
Append the words from this expansion to the vector of words produced by previous calls to `glob`. This way you can effectively expand several words as if they were concatenated with spaces between them.

In order for appending to work, you must not modify the contents of the word vector structure between calls to `glob`. And, if you set `GLOB_DOOFFS` in the first call to `glob`, you must also set it when you append to the results.

Note that the pointer stored in `gl_pathv` may no longer be valid after you call `glob` the second time, because `glob` might have relocated the vector. So always fetch `gl_pathv` from the `glob_t` structure after each `glob` call; **never** save the pointer across calls.

GLOB_DOOFFS
Leave blank slots at the beginning of the vector of words. The `gl_offs` field says how many slots to leave. The blank slots contain null pointers.

GLOB_ERR Give up right away and report an error if there is any difficulty reading the directories that must be read in order to expand *pattern* fully. Such difficulties might include a directory in which you don't have the requisite access. Normally, `glob` tries its best to keep on going despite any errors, reading whatever directories it can.

You can exercise even more control than this by specifying an error-handler function *errfunc* when you call `glob`. If *errfunc* is not a null pointer, then `glob` doesn't give up right away when it can't read a directory; instead, it calls *errfunc* with two arguments, like this:

Chapter 16: Pattern Matching 309

>   (*errfunc) (filename, error-code)
> The argument *filename* is the name of the directory that `glob` couldn't open or couldn't read, and *error-code* is the `errno` value that was reported to `glob`.
>
> If the error handler function returns nonzero, then `glob` gives up right away. Otherwise, it continues.

`GLOB_MARK`
> If the pattern matches the name of a directory, append '/' to the directory's name when returning it.

`GLOB_NOCHECK`
> If the pattern doesn't match any file names, return the pattern itself as if it were a file name that had been matched. (Normally, when the pattern doesn't match anything, `glob` returns that there were no matches.)

`GLOB_NOSORT`
> Don't sort the file names; return them in no particular order. (In practice, the order will depend on the order of the entries in the directory.) The only reason *not* to sort is to save time.

`GLOB_NOESCAPE`
> Don't treat the '\' character specially in patterns. Normally, '\' quotes the following character, turning off its special meaning (if any) so that it matches only itself. When quoting is enabled, the pattern '\?' matches only the string '?', because the question mark in the pattern acts like an ordinary character.
>
> If you use `GLOB_NOESCAPE`, then '\' is an ordinary character.
>
> `glob` does its work by calling the function `fnmatch` repeatedly. It handles the flag `GLOB_NOESCAPE` by turning on the `FNM_NOESCAPE` flag in calls to `fnmatch`.

16.3 Regular Expression Matching

The GNU C library supports two interfaces for matching regular expressions. One is the standard POSIX.2 interface, and the other is what the GNU system has had for many years.

Both interfaces are declared in the header file 'regex.h'. If you define `_POSIX_C_SOURCE`, then only the POSIX.2 functions, structures, and constants are declared.

16.3.1 POSIX Regular Expression Compilation

Before you can actually match a regular expression, you must *compile* it. This is not true compilation—it produces a special data structure, not machine instructions. But it is like ordinary compilation in that its purpose is to enable you to "execute" the pattern fast. (See Section 16.3.3 [Matching a Compiled POSIX Regular Expression], page 312, for how to use the compiled regular expression for matching.)

There is a special data type for compiled regular expressions:

regex_t   Data Type

This type of object holds a compiled regular expression. It is actually a structure. It has just one field that your programs should look at:

> re_nsub   This field holds the number of parenthetical subexpressions in the regular expression that was compiled.

There are several other fields, but we don't describe them here, because only the functions in the library should use them.

After you create a `regex_t` object, you can compile a regular expression into it by calling `regcomp`.

int regcomp (`regex_t *compiled`, `const char *pattern`, `int cflags`)   Function

The function `regcomp` "compiles" a regular expression into a data structure that you can use with `regexec` to match against a string. The compiled regular expression format is designed for efficient matching. `regcomp` stores it into *compiled*.

It's up to you to allocate an object of type `regex_t` and pass its address to `regcomp`.

The argument *cflags* lets you specify various options that control the syntax and semantics of regular expressions. See Section 16.3.2 [Flags for POSIX Regular Expressions], page 311.

If you use the flag `REG_NOSUB`, then `regcomp` omits from the compiled regular expression the information necessary to record how subexpressions actually match. In this case, you might as well pass 0 for the *matchptr* and *nmatch* arguments when you call `regexec`.

If you don't use `REG_NOSUB`, then the compiled regular expression does have the capacity to record how subexpressions match. Also, `regcomp` tells you how many subexpressions *pattern* has, by storing the number in *compiled->re_nsub*. You can use that value to decide how long an array to allocate to hold information about subexpression matches.

`regcomp` returns 0 if it succeeds in compiling the regular expression; otherwise, it returns a nonzero error code (see the table below). You can use `regerror` to produce an error message string describing the reason for a nonzero value; see Section 16.3.6 [POSIX Regexp Matching Cleanup], page 314.

Chapter 16: Pattern Matching   311

Here are the possible nonzero values that `regcomp` can return:

`REG_BADBR`
: There was an invalid '\{...\}' construct in the regular expression. A valid '\{...\}' construct must contain either a single number, or two numbers in increasing order separated by a comma.

`REG_BADPAT`
: There was a syntax error in the regular expression.

`REG_BADRPT`
: A repetition operator such as '?' or '*' appeared in a bad position (with no preceding subexpression to act on).

`REG_ECOLLATE`
: The regular expression referred to an invalid collating element (one not defined in the current locale for string collation). See Section 19.3 [Categories of Activities that Locales Affect], page 358.

`REG_ECTYPE`
: The regular expression referred to an invalid character class name.

`REG_EESCAPE`
: The regular expression ended with '\'.

`REG_ESUBREG`
: There was an invalid number in the '\digit' construct.

`REG_EBRACK`
: There were unbalanced square brackets in the regular expression.

`REG_EPAREN`
: An extended regular expression had unbalanced parentheses, or a basic regular expression had unbalanced '\(' and '\)'.

`REG_EBRACE`
: The regular expression had unbalanced '\{' and '\}'.

`REG_ERANGE`
: One of the endpoints in a range expression was invalid.

`REG_ESPACE`
: `regcomp` ran out of memory.

16.3.2 Flags for POSIX Regular Expressions

These are the bit flags that you can use in the *cflags* operand when compiling a regular expression with `regcomp`.

`REG_EXTENDED`
: Treat the pattern as an extended regular expression, rather than as a basic regular expression.

`REG_ICASE`
: Ignore case when matching letters.

`REG_NOSUB`
: Don't bother storing the contents of the *matches-ptr* array.

`REG_NEWLINE`
: Treat a newline in *string* as dividing *string* into multiple lines, so that '$' can match before the newline and '^' can match after. Also, don't permit '.' to match a newline, and don't permit '[^...]' to match a newline.

   Otherwise, newline acts like any other ordinary character.

16.3.3 Matching a Compiled POSIX Regular Expression

Once you have compiled a regular expression, as described in Section 16.3.1 [POSIX Regular Expression Compilation], page 309, you can match it against strings using `regexec`. A match anywhere inside the string counts as success, unless the regular expression contains anchor characters ('^' or '$').

`int regexec (regex_t *compiled, char *string, size_t`   *Function*
    `nmatch, regmatch_t matchptr [], int eflags)`
: This function tries to match the compiled regular expression *compiled against *string*.

   `regexec` returns 0 if the regular expression matches; otherwise, it returns a nonzero value. See the table below for what nonzero values mean. You can use `regerror` to produce an error message string describing the reason for a nonzero value; see Section 16.3.6 [POSIX Regexp Matching Cleanup], page 314.

   The argument *eflags* is a word of bit flags that enable various options.

   If you want to get information about what part of *string* actually matched the regular expression or its subexpressions, use the arguments *matchptr* and *nmatch*. Otherwise, pass 0 for *nmatch*, and `NULL` for *matchptr*. See Section 16.3.4 [Match Results with Subexpressions], page 313.

   You must match the regular expression with the same set of current locales that were in effect when you compiled the regular expression.

   The function `regexec` accepts the following flags in the *eflags* argument:

Chapter 16: Pattern Matching   313

`REG_NOTBOL`
>   Do not regard the beginning of the specified string as the beginning of a line; more generally, don't make any assumptions about what text might precede it.

`REG_NOTEOL`
>   Do not regard the end of the specified string as the end of a line; more generally, don't make any assumptions about what text might follow it.

Here are the possible nonzero values that `regexec` can return:

`REG_NOMATCH`
>   The pattern didn't match the string. This isn't really an error.

`REG_ESPACE`
>   `regexec` ran out of memory.

16.3.4 Match Results with Subexpressions

When `regexec` matches parenthetical subexpressions of *pattern*, it records which parts of *string* they match. It returns that information by storing the offsets into an array whose elements are structures of type `regmatch_t`. The first element of the array (index 0) records the part of the string that matched the entire regular expression. Each other element of the array records the beginning and end of the part that matched a single parenthetical subexpression.

regmatch_t   Data Type
>   This is the data type of the *matcharray* array that you pass to `regexec`. It contains two structure fields, as follows:
>
>   `rm_so`   The offset in *string* of the beginning of a substring. Add this value to *string* to get the address of that part.
>
>   `rm_eo`   The offset in *string* of the end of the substring.

regoff_t   Data Type
>   `regoff_t` is an alias for another signed integer type. The fields of `regmatch_t` have type `regoff_t`.

The `regmatch_t` elements correspond to subexpressions positionally; the first element (index 1) records where the first subexpression matched, the second element records the second subexpression, and so on. The order of the subexpressions is the order in which they begin.

When you call `regexec`, you specify how long the *matchptr* array is, with the *nmatch* argument. This tells `regexec` how many elements to store. If the actual regular expression has more than *nmatch* subexpressions, then you won't get offset information about the rest of them. But this doesn't alter whether the pattern matches a particular string or not.

If you don't want `regexec` to return any information about where the subexpressions matched, you can either supply 0 for *nmatch*, or use the flag `REG_NOSUB` when you compile the pattern with `regcomp`.

16.3.5 Complications in Subexpression Matching

Sometimes a subexpression matches a substring of no characters. This happens when 'f\(o*\)' matches the string 'fum'. (It really matches just the 'f'.) In this case, both of the offsets identify the point in the string where the null substring was found. In this example, the offsets are both 1.

Sometimes the entire regular expression can match without using some of its subexpressions at all—for example, when 'ba\(na\)*' matches the string 'ba', the parenthetical subexpression is not used. When this happens, `regexec` stores -1 in both fields of the element for that subexpression.

Sometimes matching the entire regular expression can match a particular subexpression more than once—for example, when 'ba\(na\)*' matches the string 'bananana', the parenthetical subexpression matches three times. When this happens, `regexec` usually stores the offsets of the last part of the string that matched the subexpression. In the case of 'bananana', these offsets are 6 and 8.

But the last match is not always the one that is chosen. It's more accurate to say that the last *opportunity* to match is the one that takes precedence. What this means is that when one subexpression appears within another, then the results reported for the inner subexpression reflect whatever happened on the last match of the outer subexpression. For an example, consider '\(ba\(na\)*s \)*' matching the string 'bananas bas '. The last time the inner expression actually matches is near the end of the first word. But it is *considered* again in the second word, and fails to match there. `regexec` reports nonuse of the "na" subexpression.

Another place where this rule applies is when the regular expression '\(ba\(na\)*s \|nefer\(ti\)* \)*' matches 'bananas nefertiti'. The "na" subexpression does match in the first word, but it doesn't match in the second word because the other alternative is used there. Once again, the second repetition of the outer subexpression overrides the first, and within that second repetition, the "na" subexpression is not used. So `regexec` reports nonuse of the "na" subexpression.

16.3.6 POSIX Regexp Matching Cleanup

When you are finished using a compiled regular expression, you can free the storage it uses by calling `regfree`.

Chapter 16: Pattern Matching   315

void **regfree** (regex_t *compiled)   Function
> Calling **regfree** frees all the storage that *compiled* points to. This
> includes various internal fields of the **regex_t** structure that aren't
> documented in this manual.
>
> **regfree** does not free the object *compiled* itself.

You should always free the space in a **regex_t** structure with **regfree** before using the structure to compile another regular expression.

When **regcomp** or **regexec** reports an error, you can use the function **regerror** to turn it into an error message string.

size_t **regerror** (int *errcode*, regex_t *compiled,   Function
        char *buffer, size_t *length*)
> This function produces an error message string for the error code *errcode*, and stores the string in *length* bytes of memory starting at *buffer*. For the *compiled* argument, supply the same compiled regular expression structure that **regcomp** or **regexec** was working with when it got the error. Alternatively, you can supply NULL for *compiled*; you will still get a meaningful error message, but it might not be as detailed.
>
> If the error message can't fit in *length* bytes (including a terminating null character), then **regerror** truncates it. The string that **regerror** stores is always null-terminated even if it has been truncated.
>
> The return value of **regerror** is the minimum length needed to store the entire error message. If this is less than *length*, then the error message was not truncated, and you can use it. Otherwise, you should call **regerror** again with a larger buffer.
>
> Here is a function which uses **regerror**, but always dynamically allocates a buffer for the error message:
>
> ```
> char *get_regerror (int errcode, regex_t *compiled)
> {
>   size_t length = regerror (errcode, compiled, NULL, 0);
>   char *buffer = xmalloc (length);
>   (void) regerror (errcode, compiled, buffer, length);
>   return buffer;
> }
> ```

16.4 Shell-Style Word Expansion

Word expansion means the process of splitting a string into *words* and substituting for variables, commands, and wildcards just as the shell does.

For example, when you write 'ls -l foo.c', this string is split into three separate words—'ls', '-l' and 'foo.c'. This is the most basic function of word expansion.

When you write 'ls *.c', this can become many words, because the word '*.c' can be replaced with any number of file names. This is called *wildcard expansion*, and it is also a part of word expansion.

When you use 'echo $PATH' to print your path, you are taking advantage of *variable substitution*, which is also part of word expansion.

Ordinary programs can perform word expansion just like the shell by calling the library function `wordexp`.

16.4.1 The Stages of Word Expansion

When word expansion is applied to a sequence of words, it performs the following transformations in the order shown here:

1. *Tilde expansion*: Replacement of '~foo' with the name of the home directory of 'foo'.
2. Next, three different transformations are applied in the same step, from left to right:
    - *Variable substitution*: Environment variables are substituted for references such as '$foo'.
    - *Command substitution*: Constructs such as '`cat foo`' and the equivalent '$(cat foo)' are replaced with the output from the inner command.
    - *Arithmetic expansion*: Constructs such as '$(($x-1))' are replaced with the result of the arithmetic computation.
3. *Field splitting*: subdivision of the text into *words*.
4. *Wildcard expansion*: The replacement of a construct such as '*.c' with a list of '.c' file names. Wildcard expansion applies to an entire word at a time, and replaces that word with 0 or more file names that are themselves words.
5. *Quote removal*: The deletion of string-quotes, now that they have done their job by inhibiting the above transformations when appropriate.

For the details of these transformations, and how to write the constructs that use them, see *The BASH Manual* (to appear).

16.4.2 Calling `wordexp`

All the functions, constants and data types for word expansion are declared in the header file 'wordexp.h'.

Word expansion produces a vector of words (strings). To return this vector, `wordexp` uses a special data type, `wordexp_t`, which is a structure. You pass `wordexp` the address of the structure, and it fills in the structure's fields to tell you about the results.

Chapter 16: Pattern Matching 317

wordexp_t   Data Type

This data type holds a pointer to a word vector. More precisely, it records both the address of the word vector and its size.

`we_wordc`   The number of elements in the vector.

`we_wordv`   The address of the vector. This field has type `char **`.

`we_offs`   The offset of the first real element of the vector, from its nominal address in the `we_wordv` field. Unlike the other fields, this is always an input to `wordexp`, rather than an output from it.

If you use a nonzero offset, then that many elements at the beginning of the vector are left empty. (The `wordexp` function fills them with null pointers.)

The `we_offs` field is meaningful only if you use the `WRDE_DOOFFS` flag. Otherwise, the offset is always zero regardless of what is in this field, and the first real element comes at the beginning of the vector.

int wordexp (const char *words*, wordexp_t *word-vector-ptr*, int *flags*)   Function

Perform word expansion on the string *words*, putting the result in a newly allocated vector, and store the size and address of this vector into **word-vector-ptr*. The argument *flags* is a combination of bit flags; see Section 16.4.3 [Flags for Word Expansion], page 318, for details of the flags.

You shouldn't use any of the characters '`|&;<>`' in the string *words* unless they are quoted; likewise for newline. If you use these characters unquoted, you will get the `WRDE_BADCHAR` error code. Don't use parentheses or braces unless they are quoted or part of a word expansion construct. If you use quotation characters '`'"\``', they should come in pairs that balance.

The results of word expansion are a sequence of words. The function `wordexp` allocates a string for each resulting word, then allocates a vector of type `char **` to store the addresses of these strings. The last element of the vector is a null pointer. This vector is called the *word vector*.

To return this vector, `wordexp` stores both its address and its length (number of elements, not counting the terminating null pointer) into **word-vector-ptr*.

If `wordexp` succeeds, it returns 0. Otherwise, it returns one of these error codes:

WRDE_BADCHAR
> The input string *words* contains an unquoted invalid character such as '|'.

WRDE_BADVAL
> The input string refers to an undefined shell variable, and you used the flag `WRDE_UNDEF` to forbid such references.

WRDE_CMDSUB
> The input string uses command substitution, and you used the flag `WRDE_NOCMD` to forbid command substitution.

WRDE_NOSPACE
> It was impossible to allocate memory to hold the result. In this case, `wordexp` can store part of the results—as much as it could allocate room for.

WRDE_SYNTAX
> There was a syntax error in the input string. For example, an unmatched quoting character is a syntax error.

void **wordfree** (`wordexp_t` **word-vector-ptr*)   *Function*
> Free the storage used for the word-strings and vector that **word-vector-ptr* points to. This does not free the structure **word-vector-ptr* itself—only the other data it points to.

16.4.3 Flags for Word Expansion

This section describes the flags that you can specify in the *flags* argument to `wordexp`. Choose the flags you want, and combine them with the C operator |.

WRDE_APPEND
> Append the words from this expansion to the vector of words produced by previous calls to `wordexp`. This way you can effectively expand several words as if they were concatenated with spaces between them.
>
> In order for appending to work, you must not modify the contents of the word vector structure between calls to `wordexp`. And, if you set `WRDE_DOOFFS` in the first call to `wordexp`, you must also set it when you append to the results.

WRDE_DOOFFS
> Leave blank slots at the beginning of the vector of words. The `we_offs` field says how many slots to leave. The blank slots contain null pointers.

Chapter 16: Pattern Matching

WRDE_NOCMD
: Don't do command substitution; if the input requests command substitution, report an error.

WRDE_REUSE
: Reuse a word vector made by a previous call to **wordexp**. Instead of allocating a new vector of words, this call to **wordexp** will use the vector that already exists (making it larger if necessary).

    Note that the vector may move, so it is not safe to save an old pointer and use it again after calling **wordexp**. You must fetch **we_pathv** anew after each call.

WRDE_SHOWERR
: Do show any error messages printed by commands run by command substitution. More precisely, allow these commands to inherit the standard error output stream of the current process. By default, **wordexp** gives these commands a standard error stream that discards all output.

WRDE_UNDEF
: If the input refers to a shell variable that is not defined, report an error.

16.4.4 wordexp Example

Here is an example of using **wordexp** to expand several strings and use the results to run a shell command. It also shows the use of **WRDE_APPEND** to concatenate the expansions and of **wordfree** to free the space allocated by **wordexp**.

```
int
expand_and_execute (const char *program, const char *options)
{
  wordexp_t result;
  pid_t pid
  int status, i;

  /* Expand the string for the program to run.  */
  switch (wordexp (program, &result, 0))
    {
    case 0: /* Successful.  */
      break;
    case WRDE_NOSPACE:
      /* If the error was WRDE_NOSPACE,
         then perhaps part of the result was allocated.  */
      wordfree (&result);
    default:                     /* Some other error.  */
      return -1;
    }
```

```
            /* Expand the strings specified for the arguments.  */
            for (i = 0; args[i]; i++)
              {
                if (wordexp (options, &result, WRDE_APPEND))
                  {
                    wordfree (&result);
                    return -1;
                  }
              }

            pid = fork ();
            if (pid == 0)
              {
                /* This is the child process.  Execute the command.  */
                execv (result.we_wordv[0], result.we_wordv);
                exit (EXIT_FAILURE);
              }
            else if (pid < 0)
              /* The fork failed.  Report failure.  */
              status = -1;
            else
              /* This is the parent process.  Wait for the child to complete.  */
              if (waitpid (pid, &status, 0) != pid)
                status = -1;

            wordfree (&result);
            return status;
          }
```

In practice, since **wordexp** is executed by running a subshell, it would be faster to do this by concatenating the strings with spaces between them and running that as a shell command using 'sh -c'.

17 Date and Time

This chapter describes functions for manipulating dates and times, including functions for determining what the current time is and conversion between different time representations.

The time functions fall into three main categories:

- Functions for measuring elapsed CPU time are discussed in Section 17.1 [Processor Time], page 321.
- Functions for measuring absolute clock or calendar time are discussed in Section 17.2 [Calendar Time], page 323.
- Functions for setting alarms and timers are discussed in Section 17.3 [Setting an Alarm], page 335.

17.1 Processor Time

If you're trying to optimize your program or measure its efficiency, it's very useful to be able to know how much *processor time* or *CPU time* it has used at any given point. Processor time is different from actual wall clock time because it doesn't include any time spent waiting for I/O or when some other process is running. Processor time is represented by the data type `clock_t`, and is given as a number of *clock ticks* relative to an arbitrary base time marking the beginning of a single program invocation.

17.1.1 Basic CPU Time Inquiry

To get the elapsed CPU time used by a process, you can use the `clock` function. This facility is declared in the header file 'time.h'.

In typical usage, you call the `clock` function at the beginning and end of the interval you want to time, subtract the values, and then divide by `CLOCKS_PER_SEC` (the number of clock ticks per second), like this:

```
#include <time.h>

clock_t start, end;
double elapsed;

start = clock();
... /* Do the work. */
end = clock();
elapsed = ((double) (end - start)) / CLOCKS_PER_SEC;
```

Different computers and operating systems vary wildly in how they keep track of processor time. It's common for the internal processor clock to have a resolution somewhere between hundredths and millionths of a second.

In the GNU system, `clock_t` is equivalent to `long int` and `CLOCKS_PER_SEC` is an integer value. But in other systems, both `clock_t` and the type of the macro `CLOCKS_PER_SEC` can be either integer or floating-point types. Casting processor time values to `double`, as in the example above, makes sure that operations such as arithmetic and printing work properly and consistently no matter what the underlying representation is.

int CLOCKS_PER_SEC   *Macro*
> The value of this macro is the number of clock ticks per second measured by the `clock` function.

int CLK_TCK   *Macro*
> This is an obsolete name for `CLOCKS_PER_SEC`.

clock_t   *Data Type*
> This is the type of the value returned by the `clock` function. Values of type `clock_t` are in units of clock ticks.

clock_t clock (void)   *Function*
> This function returns the elapsed processor time. The base time is arbitrary but doesn't change within a single process. If the processor time is not available or cannot be represented, `clock` returns the value `(clock_t)(-1)`.

17.1.2 Detailed Elapsed CPU Time Inquiry

The `times` function returns more detailed information about elapsed processor time in a `struct tms` object. You should include the header file 'sys/times.h' to use this facility.

struct tms   *Data Type*
> The `tms` structure is used to return information about process times. It contains at least the following members:
>
> `clock_t tms_utime`
> > This is the CPU time used in executing the instructions of the calling process.
>
> `clock_t tms_stime`
> > This is the CPU time used by the system on behalf of the calling process.
>
> `clock_t tms_cutime`
> > This is the sum of the `tms_utime` values and the `tms_cutime` values of all terminated child processes of the calling process, whose status has been reported to the parent process by `wait` or `waitpid`; see Section 23.6 [Process

Chapter 17: Date and Time   323

Completion], page 449. In other words, it represents the total CPU time used in executing the instructions of all the terminated child processes of the calling process, excluding child processes which have not yet been reported by `wait` or `waitpid`.

`clock_t tms_cstime`
: This is similar to `tms_cutime`, but represents the total CPU time used by the system on behalf of all the terminated child processes of the calling process.

All of the times are given in clock ticks. These are absolute values; in a newly created process, they are all zero. See Section 23.4 [Creating a Process], page 445.

`clock_t` **times** (`struct tms` *buffer*)   *Function*
The `times` function stores the processor time information for the calling process in *buffer*.

The return value is the same as the value of `clock()`: the elapsed real time relative to an arbitrary base. The base is a constant within a particular process, and typically represents the time since system start-up. A value of `(clock_t)(-1)` is returned to indicate failure.

Portability Note: The `clock` function described in Section 17.1.1 [Basic CPU Time Inquiry], page 321, is specified by the ANSI C standard. The `times` function is a feature of POSIX.1. In the GNU system, the value returned by the `clock` function is equivalent to the sum of the `tms_utime` and `tms_stime` fields returned by `times`.

17.2 Calendar Time

This section describes facilities for keeping track of dates and times according to the Gregorian calendar.

There are three representations for date and time information:

- *Calendar time* (the `time_t` data type) is a compact representation, typically giving the number of seconds elapsed since some implementation-specific base time.

- There is also a *high-resolution time* representation (the `struct timeval` data type) that includes fractions of a second. Use this time representation instead of ordinary calendar time when you need greater precision.

- *Local time* or *broken-down time* (the `struct tm` data type) represents the date and time as a set of components specifying the year, month, and so on, for a specific time zone. This time representation is usually used in conjunction with formatting date and time values.

17.2.1 Simple Calendar Time

This section describes the `time_t` data type for representing calendar time, and the functions which operate on calendar time objects. These facilities are declared in the header file 'time.h'.

time_t   Data Type

This is the data type used to represent calendar time. When interpreted as an absolute time value, it represents the number of seconds elapsed since 00:00:00 on January 1, 1970, Coordinated Universal Time. (This date is sometimes referred to as the *epoch*.) POSIX requires that this count ignore leap seconds, but on some hosts this count includes leap seconds if you set `TZ` to certain values (see Section 17.2.5 [Specifying the Time Zone with "code TZ], page 332).

In the GNU C library, `time_t` is equivalent to `long int`. In other systems, `time_t` might be either an integer or floating-point type.

double difftime (time_t *time1*, time_t *time0*)   Function

The `difftime` function returns the number of seconds elapsed between time *time1* and time *time0*, as a value of type `double`. The difference ignores leap seconds unless leap second support is enabled.

In the GNU system, you can simply subtract `time_t` values. But on other systems, the `time_t` data type might use some other encoding where subtraction doesn't work directly.

time_t time (time_t **result*)   Function

The `time` function returns the current time as a value of type `time_t`. If the argument *result* is not a null pointer, the time value is also stored in **result*. If the calendar time is not available, the value `(time_t)(-1)` is returned.

17.2.2 High-Resolution Calendar

The `time_t` data type used to represent calendar times has a resolution of only one second. Some applications need more precision.

So, the GNU C library also contains functions which are capable of representing calendar times to a higher resolution than one second. The functions and the associated data types described in this section are declared in 'sys/time.h'.

struct timeval   Data Type

The `struct timeval` structure represents a calendar time. It has the following members:

Chapter 17: Date and Time

`long int tv_sec`
> This represents the number of seconds since the epoch. It is equivalent to a normal `time_t` value.

`long int tv_usec`
> This is the fractional second value, represented as the number of microseconds.
>
> Some times struct timeval values are used for time intervals. Then the `tv_sec` member is the number of seconds in the interval, and `tv_usec` is the number of additional microseconds.

struct timezone   Data Type

The `struct timezone` structure is used to hold minimal information about the local time zone. It has the following members:

`int tz_minuteswest`
> This is the number of minutes west of GMT.

`int tz_dsttime`
> If nonzero, daylight savings time applies during some part of the year.

The `struct timezone` type is obsolete and should never be used. Instead, use the facilities described in Section 17.2.6 [Functions and Variables for Time Zones], page 334.

It is often necessary to subtract two values of type `struct timeval`. Here is the best way to do this. It works even on some peculiar operating systems where the `tv_sec` member has an unsigned type.

```
/* Subtract the 'struct timeval' values X and Y,
   storing the result in RESULT.
   Return 1 if the difference is negative, otherwise 0.  */

int
timeval_subtract (result, x, y)
     struct timeval *result, *x, *y;
{
  /* Perform the carry for the later subtraction by updating y. */
  if (x->tv_usec < y->tv_usec) {
    int nsec = (y->tv_usec - x->tv_usec) / 1000000 + 1;
    y->tv_usec -= 1000000 * nsec;
    y->tv_sec += nsec;
  }
  if (x->tv_usec - y->tv_usec > 1000000) {
    int nsec = (y->tv_usec - x->tv_usec) / 1000000;
    y->tv_usec += 1000000 * nsec;
    y->tv_sec -= nsec;
  }
```

```
          /* Compute the time remaining to wait.
             tv_usec is certainly positive. */
          result->tv_sec = x->tv_sec - y->tv_sec;
          result->tv_usec = x->tv_usec - y->tv_usec;

          /* Return 1 if result is negative. */
          return x->tv_sec < y->tv_sec;
        }
```

int gettimeofday (`struct timeval *`*tp*`, struct` *Function*
          `timezone *`*tzp*`)`

The `gettimeofday` function returns the current date and time in the `struct timeval` structure indicated by *tp*. Information about the time zone is returned in the structure pointed at *tzp*. If the *tzp* argument is a null pointer, time zone information is ignored.

The return value is 0 on success and -1 on failure. The following `errno` error condition is defined for this function:

`ENOSYS`   The operating system does not support getting time zone information, and *tzp* is not a null pointer. The GNU operating system does not support using `struct timezone` to represent time zone information; that is an obsolete feature of 4.3 BSD. Instead, use the facilities described in Section 17.2.6 [Functions and Variables for Time Zones], page 334.

int settimeofday (`const struct timeval *`*tp*`, const` *Function*
          `struct timezone *`*tzp*`)`

The `settimeofday` function sets the current date and time according to the arguments. As for `gettimeofday`, time zone information is ignored if *tzp* is a null pointer.

You must be a privileged user in order to use `settimeofday`.

The return value is 0 on success and -1 on failure. The following `errno` error conditions are defined for this function:

`EPERM`   This process cannot set the time because it is not privileged.

`ENOSYS`   The operating system does not support setting time zone information, and *tzp* is not a null pointer.

int adjtime (`const struct timeval *`*delta*`, struct` *Function*
          `timeval *`*olddelta*`)`

This function speeds up or slows down the system clock in order to make gradual adjustments in the current time. This ensures that the time reported by the system clock is always monotonically increasing, which might not happen if you simply set the current time.

The *delta* argument specifies a relative adjustment to be made to the current time. If negative, the system clock is slowed down for a while until it has lost this much time. If positive, the system clock is speeded up for a while.

If the *olddelta* argument is not a null pointer, the `adjtime` function returns information about any previous time adjustment that has not yet completed.

This function is typically used to synchronize the clocks of computers in a local network. You must be a privileged user to use it. The return value is 0 on success and -1 on failure. The following `errno` error condition is defined for this function:

`EPERM`   You do not have privilege to set the time.

Portability Note: The `gettimeofday`, `settimeofday`, and `adjtime` functions are derived from BSD.

17.2.3 Broken-down Time

Calendar time is represented as a number of seconds. This is convenient for calculation, but has no resemblance to the way people normally represent dates and times. By contrast, *broken-down time* is a binary representation separated into year, month, day, and so on. Broken down time values are not useful for calculations, but they are useful for printing human readable time.

A broken-down time value is always relative to a choice of local time zone, and it also indicates which time zone was used.

The symbols in this section are declared in the header file 'time.h'.

struct tm   Data Type

This is the data type used to represent a broken-down time. The structure contains at least the following members, which can appear in any order:

`int tm_sec`

>   This is the number of seconds after the minute, normally in the range 0 to 59. (The actual upper limit is 60, to allow for leap seconds if leap second support is available.)

`int tm_min`

>   This is the number of minutes after the hour, in the range 0 to 59.

`int tm_hour`

>   This is the number of hours past midnight, in the range 0 to 23.

`int tm_mday`
> This is the day of the month, in the range 1 to 31.

`int tm_mon`
> This is the number of months since January, in the range 0 to 11.

`int tm_year`
> This is the number of years since 1900.

`int tm_wday`
> This is the number of days since Sunday, in the range 0 to 6.

`int tm_yday`
> This is the number of days since January 1, in the range 0 to 365.

`int tm_isdst`
> This is a flag that indicates whether Daylight Saving Time is (or was, or will be) in effect at the time described. The value is positive if Daylight Saving Time is in effect, zero if it is not, and negative if the information is not available.

`long int tm_gmtoff`
> This field describes the time zone that was used to compute this broken-down time value; it is the amount you must add to the local time in that zone to get GMT, in units of seconds. The value is like that of the variable `timezone` (see Section 17.2.6 [Functions and Variables for Time Zones], page 334). You can also think of this as the "number of seconds west" of GMT. The `tm_gmtoff` field is a GNU library extension.

`const char *tm_zone`
> This field is the name for the time zone that was used to compute this broken-down time value. It is a GNU library extension.

`struct tm * ` **`localtime`** ` (const time_t *time)`   *Function*
The `localtime` function converts the calendar time pointed to by *time* to broken-down time representation, expressed relative to the user's specified time zone.

The return value is a pointer to a static broken-down time structure, which might be overwritten by subsequent calls to `ctime`, `gmtime`, or `localtime`. (But no other library function overwrites the contents of this object.)

Chapter 17: Date and Time

Calling `localtime` has one other effect: it sets the variable `tzname` with information about the current time zone. See Section 17.2.6 [Functions and Variables for Time Zones], page 334.

struct tm * gmtime (const time_t *_time_) *Function*

This function is similar to `localtime`, except that the broken-down time is expressed as Coordinated Universal Time (UTC)—that is, as Greenwich Mean Time (GMT) rather than relative to the local time zone.

Recall that calendar times are *always* expressed in coordinated universal time.

time_t mktime (struct tm *_brokentime_) *Function*

The `mktime` function is used to convert a broken-down time structure to a calendar time representation. It also "normalizes" the contents of the broken-down time structure, by filling in the day of week and day of year based on the other date and time components.

The `mktime` function ignores the specified contents of the `tm_wday` and `tm_yday` members of the broken-down time structure. It uses the values of the other components to compute the calendar time; it's permissible for these components to have unnormalized values outside of their normal ranges. The last thing that `mktime` does is adjust the components of the *brokentime* structure (including the `tm_wday` and `tm_yday`).

If the specified broken-down time cannot be represented as a calendar time, `mktime` returns a value of `(time_t)(-1)` and does not modify the contents of *brokentime*.

Calling `mktime` also sets the variable `tzname` with information about the current time zone. See Section 17.2.6 [Functions and Variables for Time Zones], page 334.

17.2.4 Formatting Date and Time

The functions described in this section format time values as strings. These functions are declared in the header file 'time.h'.

char * asctime (const struct tm *_brokentime_) *Function*

The `asctime` function converts the broken-down time value that *brokentime* points to into a string in a standard format:

    "Tue May 21 13:46:22 1991\n"

The abbreviations for the days of week are: 'Sun', 'Mon', 'Tue', 'Wed', 'Thu', 'Fri', and 'Sat'.

The abbreviations for the months are: 'Jan', 'Feb', 'Mar', 'Apr', 'May', 'Jun', 'Jul', 'Aug', 'Sep', 'Oct', 'Nov', and 'Dec'.

The return value points to a statically allocated string, which might be overwritten by subsequent calls to `asctime` or `ctime`. (But no other library function overwrites the contents of this string.)

char * ctime (const time_t *time)   *Function*
The `ctime` function is similar to `asctime`, except that the time value is specified as a `time_t` calendar time value rather than in broken-down local time format. It is equivalent to

```
asctime (localtime (time))
```

`ctime` sets the variable `tzname`, because `localtime` does so. See Section 17.2.6 [Functions and Variables for Time Zones], page 334.

size_t strftime (char *s, size_t *size*, const char *template, const struct tm *brokentime)   *Function*
This function is similar to the `sprintf` function (see Section 7.12 [Formatted Input], page 115), but the conversion specifications that can appear in the format template *template* are specialized for printing components of the date and time *brokentime* according to the locale currently specified for time conversion (see Chapter 19 [Locales and Internationalization], page 357).

Ordinary characters appearing in the *template* are copied to the output string *s*; this can include multibyte character sequences. Conversion specifiers are introduced by a '%' character, and are replaced in the output string as follows:

%a   The abbreviated weekday name according to the current locale.

%A   The full weekday name according to the current locale.

%b   The abbreviated month name according to the current locale.

%B   The full month name according to the current locale.

%c   The preferred date and time representation for the current locale.

%d   The day of the month as a decimal number (range 01 to 31).

%H   The hour as a decimal number, using a 24-hour clock (range 00 to 23).

%I   The hour as a decimal number, using a 12-hour clock (range 01 to 12).

%j   The day of the year as a decimal number (range 001 to 366).

Chapter 17: Date and Time 331

%m
: The month as a decimal number (range 01 to 12).

%M
: The minute as a decimal number.

%p
: Either 'am' or 'pm', according to the given time value; or the corresponding strings for the current locale.

%S
: The second as a decimal number.

%U
: The week number of the current year as a decimal number, starting with the first Sunday as the first day of the first week. All days preceding the first Sunday in the year are considered to be in week 0.

%V
: The week number of the current year as a decimal number, starting with the first Monday as the first day of the first week. If the week containing January 1 has four or more days in the new year it is considered to be week 1. Otherwise it is week 53 of the previous year. This is standardized in ISO 8601:1988.

%W
: The week number of the current year as a decimal number, starting with the first Monday as the first day of the first week. All days preceding the first Monday in the year are considered to be in week 0.

%w
: The day of the week as a decimal number, Sunday being 0.

%x
: The preferred date representation for the current locale, but without the time.

%X
: The preferred time representation for the current locale, but with no date.

%y
: The year as a decimal number, but without a century (range 00 to 99).

%Y
: The year as a decimal number, including the century.

%Z
: The time zone or name or abbreviation (empty if the time zone can't be determined).

%%
: A literal '%' character.

The *size* parameter can be used to specify the maximum number of characters to be stored in the array *s*, including the terminating null character. If the formatted time requires more than *size* characters, the excess characters are discarded. The return value from `strftime` is the number of characters placed in the array *s*, not including the terminating null character. If the value equals *size*, it means that the array *s* was too small; you should repeat the call, providing a bigger array.

If *s* is a null pointer, `strftime` does not actually write anything, but instead returns the number of characters it would have written.

For an example of `strftime`, see Section 17.2.7 [Time Functions Example], page 335.

17.2.5 Specifying the Time Zone with TZ

In POSIX systems, a user can specify the time zone by means of the `TZ` environment variable. For information about how to set environment variables, see Section 22.2 [Environment Variables], page 433. The functions for accessing the time zone are declared in 'time.h'.

You should not normally need to set `TZ`. If the system is configured properly, the default timezone will be correct. You might set `TZ` if you are using a computer over the network from a different timezone, and would like times reported to you in the timezone that local for you, rather than what is local for the computer.

In POSIX.1 systems the value of the `TZ` variable can be of one of three formats. With the GNU C library, the most common format is the last one, which can specify a selection from a large database of time zone information for many regions of the world. The first two formats are used to describe the time zone information directly, which is both more cumbersome and less precise. But the POSIX.1 standard only specifies the details of the first two formats, so it is good to be familiar with them in case you come across a POSIX.1 system that doesn't support a time zone information database.

The first format is used when there is no Daylight Saving Time (or summer time) in the local time zone:

std offset

The *std* string specifies the name of the time zone. It must be three or more characters long and must not contain a leading colon or embedded digits, commas, or plus or minus signs. There is no space character separating the time zone name from the *offset*, so these restrictions are necessary to parse the specification correctly.

The *offset* specifies the time value one must add to the local time to get a Coordinated Universal Time value. It has syntax like [+|-]*hh*[:*mm*[:*ss*]]. This is positive if the local time zone is west of the Prime Meridian and negative if it is east. The hour must be between 0 and 23, and the minute and seconds between 0 and 59.

For example, here is how we would specify Eastern Standard Time, but without any daylight savings time alternative:

   EST+5

Chapter 17: Date and Time

The second format is used when there is Daylight Saving Time:

std offset dst [*offset*],*start*[/*time*],*end*[/*time*]

The initial *std* and *offset* specify the standard time zone, as described above. The *dst* string and *offset* specify the name and offset for the corresponding daylight savings time time zone; if the *offset* is omitted, it defaults to one hour ahead of standard time.

The remainder of the specification describes when daylight savings time is in effect. The *start* field is when daylight savings time goes into effect and the *end* field is when the change is made back to standard time. The following formats are recognized for these fields:

J*n* This specifies the Julian day, with *n* between 1 and 365. February 29 is never counted, even in leap years.

n This specifies the Julian day, with *n* between 0 and 365. February 29 is counted in leap years.

M*m.w.d* This specifies day *d* of week *w* of month *m*. The day *d* must be between 0 (Sunday) and 6. The week *w* must be between 1 and 5; week 1 is the first week in which day *d* occurs, and week 5 specifies the *last* *d* day in the month. The month *m* should be between 1 and 12.

The *time* fields specify when, in the local time currently in effect, the change to the other time occurs. If omitted, the default is 02:00:00.

For example, here is how one would specify the Eastern time zone in the United States, including the appropriate daylight saving time and its dates of applicability. The normal offset from GMT is 5 hours; since this is west of the prime meridian, the sign is positive. Summer time begins on the first Sunday in April at 2:00am, and ends on the last Sunday in October at 2:00am.

`EST+5EDT,M4.1.0/M10.5.0`

The schedule of daylight savings time in any particular jurisdiction has changed over the years. To be strictly correct, the conversion of dates and times in the past should be based on the schedule that was in effect then. However, this format has no facilities to let you specify how the schedule has changed from year to year. The most you can do is specify one particular schedule—usually the present day schedule—and this is used to convert any date, no matter when. For precise time zone specifications, it is best to use the time zone information database (see below).

The third format looks like this:

:*characters*

Each operating system interprets this format differently; in the GNU C library, *characters* is the name of a file which describes the time zone.

If the `TZ` environment variable does not have a value, the operation chooses a time zone by default. In the GNU C library, the default time zone is like the specification 'TZ=:/etc/localtime' (or 'TZ=:/usr/local/etc/localtime', depending on how GNU C library was configured; see Section C.1 [How to Install the GNU C Library], page 625). Other C libraries use their own rule for choosing the default time zone, so there is little we can say about them.

If *characters* begins with a slash, it is an absolute file name; otherwise the library looks for the file '/share/lib/zoneinfo/*characters*'. The 'zoneinfo' directory contains data files describing local time zones in many different parts of the world. The names represent major cities, with subdirectories for geographical areas; for example, 'America/New_York', 'Europe/London', 'Asia/Hong_Kong'. These data files are installed by the system administrator, who also sets '/etc/localtime' to point to the data file for the local time zone. The GNU C library comes with a large database of time zone information for most regions of the world, which is maintained by a community of volunteers and put in the public domain.

17.2.6 Functions and Variables for Time Zones

char * **tzname** [2]   *Variable*
   The array `tzname` contains two strings, which are the standard names of the pair of time zones (standard and daylight savings) that the user has selected. `tzname[0]` is the name of the standard time zone (for example, "EST"), and `tzname[1]` is the name for the time zone when daylight savings time is in use (for example, "EDT"). These correspond to the *std* and *dst* strings (respectively) from the `TZ` environment variable.

   The `tzname` array is initialized from the `TZ` environment variable whenever `tzset`, `ctime`, `strftime`, `mktime`, or `localtime` is called.

void **tzset** (void)   *Function*
   The `tzset` function initializes the `tzname` variable from the value of the `TZ` environment variable. It is not usually necessary for your program to call this function, because it is called automatically when you use the other time conversion functions that depend on the time zone.

The following variables are defined for compatibility with System V Unix. These variables are set by calling `tzset`.

long int **timezone**   *Variable*
   This contains the difference between GMT and local standard time, in seconds. For example, in the U.S. Eastern time zone, the value is 5*60*60.

Chapter 17: Date and Time

int daylight   *Variable*
This variable has a nonzero value if daylight savings time rules apply.
A nonzero value does not necessarily mean that daylight savings time
is now in effect; it means only that daylight savings time is sometimes
in effect.

17.2.7 Time Functions Example

Here is an example program showing the use of some of the local time
and calendar time functions.

```
#include <time.h>
#include <stdio.h>

#define SIZE 256

int
main (void)
{
  char buffer[SIZE];
  time_t curtime;
  struct tm *loctime;

  /* Get the current time. */
  curtime = time (NULL);

  /* Convert it to local time representation. */
  loctime = localtime (&curtime);

  /* Print out the date and time in the standard format. */
  fputs (asctime (loctime), stdout);

  /* Print it out in a nice format. */
  strftime (buffer, SIZE, "Today is %A, %B %d.\n", loctime);
  fputs (buffer, stdout);
  strftime (buffer, SIZE, "The time is %I:%M %p.\n", loctime);
  fputs (buffer, stdout);

  return 0;
}
```

It produces output like this:

```
Wed Jul 31 13:02:36 1991
Today is Wednesday, July 31.
The time is 01:02 PM.
```

17.3 Setting an Alarm

The `alarm` and `setitimer` functions provide a mechanism for a process
to interrupt itself at some future time. They do this by setting a timer; when
the timer expires, the process receives a signal.

Each process has three independent interval timers available:
- A real-time timer that counts clock time. This timer sends a `SIGALRM` signal to the process when it expires.
- A virtual timer that counts CPU time used by the process. This timer sends a `SIGVTALRM` signal to the process when it expires.
- A profiling timer that counts both CPU time used by the process, and CPU time spent in system calls on behalf of the process. This timer sends a `SIGPROF` signal to the process when it expires.

  This timer is useful for profiling in interpreters. The interval timer mechanism does not have the fine granularity necessary for profiling native code.

You can only have one timer of each kind set at any given time. If you set a timer that has not yet expired, that timer is simply reset to the new value.

You should establish a handler for the appropriate alarm signal using `signal` or `sigaction` before issuing a call to `setitimer` or `alarm`. Otherwise, an unusual chain of events could cause the timer to expire before your program establishes the handler, and in that case it would be terminated, since that is the default action for the alarm signals. See Chapter 21 [Signal Handling], page 371.

The `setitimer` function is the primary means for setting an alarm. This facility is declared in the header file 'sys/time.h'. The `alarm` function, declared in 'unistd.h', provides a somewhat simpler interface for setting the real-time timer.

struct itimerval   Data Type

This structure is used to specify when a timer should expire. It contains the following members:

struct timeval it_interval
: This is the interval between successive timer interrupts. If zero, the alarm will only be sent once.

struct timeval it_value
: This is the interval to the first timer interrupt. If zero, the alarm is disabled.

The `struct timeval` data type is described in Section 17.2.2 [High-Resolution Calendar], page 324.

int setitimer (int *which*, struct itimerval **new*,   Function
       struct itimerval **old*)

The `setitimer` function sets the timer specified by *which* according to *new*. The *which* argument can have a value of `ITIMER_REAL`, `ITIMER_VIRTUAL`, or `ITIMER_PROF`.

Chapter 17: Date and Time

If *old* is not a null pointer, `setitimer` returns information about any previous unexpired timer of the same kind in the structure it points to.

The return value is 0 on success and -1 on failure. The following `errno` error conditions are defined for this function:

`EINVAL`   The timer interval was too large.

int getitimer (int *which*, struct itimerval *old*)   Function
The `getitimer` function stores information about the timer specified by *which* in the structure pointed at by *old*.

The return value and error conditions are the same as for `setitimer`.

`ITIMER_REAL`
> This constant can be used as the *which* argument to the `setitimer` and `getitimer` functions to specify the real-time timer.

`ITIMER_VIRTUAL`
> This constant can be used as the *which* argument to the `setitimer` and `getitimer` functions to specify the virtual timer.

`ITIMER_PROF`
> This constant can be used as the *which* argument to the `setitimer` and `getitimer` functions to specify the profiling timer.

unsigned int alarm (unsigned int *seconds*)   Function
The `alarm` function sets the real-time timer to expire in *seconds* seconds. If you want to cancel any existing alarm, you can do this by calling `alarm` with a *seconds* argument of zero.

The return value indicates how many seconds remain before the previous alarm would have been sent. If there is no previous alarm, `alarm` returns zero.

The `alarm` function could be defined in terms of `setitimer` like this:

```
unsigned int
alarm (unsigned int seconds)
{
  struct itimerval old, new;
  new.it_interval.tv_usec = 0;
  new.it_interval.tv_sec = 0;
  new.it_value.tv_usec = 0;
  new.it_value.tv_sec = (long int) seconds;
  if (setitimer (ITIMER_REAL, &new, &old) < 0)
    return 0;
  else
    return old.it_value.tv_sec;
```

}

There is an example showing the use of the `alarm` function in Section 21.4.1 [Signal Handlers that Return], page 391.

If you simply want your process to wait for a given number of seconds, you should use the `sleep` function. See Section 17.4 [Sleeping], page 338.

You shouldn't count on the signal arriving precisely when the timer expires. In a multiprocessing environment there is typically some amount of delay involved.

Portability Note: The `setitimer` and `getitimer` functions are derived from BSD Unix, while the `alarm` function is specified by the POSIX.1 standard. `setitimer` is more powerful than `alarm`, but `alarm` is more widely used.

17.4 Sleeping

The function `sleep` gives a simple way to make the program wait for short periods of time. If your program doesn't use signals (except to terminate), then you can expect `sleep` to wait reliably for the specified amount of time. Otherwise, `sleep` can return sooner if a signal arrives; if you want to wait for a given period regardless of signals, use `select` (see Section 8.6 [Waiting for Input or Output], page 150) and don't specify any descriptors to wait for.

unsigned int sleep (unsigned int *seconds*)   *Function*
The `sleep` function waits for *seconds* or until a signal is delivered, whichever happens first.

If `sleep` function returns because the requested time has elapsed, it returns a value of zero. If it returns because of delivery of a signal, its return value is the remaining time in the sleep period.

The `sleep` function is declared in 'unistd.h'.

Resist the temptation to implement a sleep for a fixed amount of time by using the return value of `sleep`, when nonzero, to call `sleep` again. This will work with a certain amount of accuracy as long as signals arrive infrequently. But each signal can cause the eventual wakeup time to be off by an additional second or so. Suppose a few signals happen to arrive in rapid succession by bad luck—there is no limit on how much this could shorten or lengthen the wait.

Instead, compute the time at which the program should stop waiting, and keep trying to wait until that time. This won't be off by more than a second. With just a little more work, you can use `select` and make the waiting period quite accurate. (Of course, heavy system load can cause unavoidable

Chapter 17: Date and Time   339

additional delays—unless the machine is dedicated to one application, there is no way you can avoid this.)

On some systems, `sleep` can do strange things if your program uses SIGALRM explicitly. Even if SIGALRM signals are being ignored or blocked when `sleep` is called, `sleep` might return prematurely on delivery of a SIGALRM signal. If you have established a handler for SIGALRM signals and a SIGALRM signal is delivered while the process is sleeping, the action taken might be just to cause `sleep` to return instead of invoking your handler. And, if `sleep` is interrupted by delivery of a signal whose handler requests an alarm or alters the handling of SIGALRM, this handler and `sleep` will interfere.

On the GNU system, it is safe to use `sleep` and SIGALRM in the same program, because `sleep` does not work by means of SIGALRM.

17.5 Resource Usage

The function `getrusage` and the data type `struct rusage` are used for examining the usage figures of a process. They are declared in 'sys/resource.h'.

int getrusage (int *processes*, struct rusage **rusage*)   *Function*
This function reports the usage totals for processes specified by *processes*, storing the information in **rusage*.

In most systems, *processes* has only two valid values:

RUSAGE_SELF
       Just the current process.

RUSAGE_CHILDREN
       All child processes (direct and indirect) that have terminated already.

In the GNU system, you can also inquire about a particular child process by specifying its process ID.

The return value of `getrusage` is zero for success, and -1 for failure.

EINVAL   The argument *processes* is not valid.

One way of getting usage figures for a particular child process is with the function `wait4`, which returns totals for a child when it terminates. See Section 23.8 [BSD Process Wait Functions], page 453.

struct rusage   *Data Type*
This data type records a collection usage amounts for various sorts of resources. It has the following members, and possibly others:

`struct timeval ru_utime`
: Time spent executing user instructions.

`struct timeval ru_stime`
: Time spent in operating system code on behalf of *processes*.

`long int ru_maxrss`
: The maximum resident set size used, in kilobytes. That is, the maximum number of kilobytes that *processes* used in real memory simultaneously.

`long int ru_ixrss`
: An integral value expressed in kilobytes times ticks of execution, which indicates the amount of memory used by text that was shared with other processes.

`long int ru_idrss`
: An integral value expressed the same way, which is the amount of unshared memory used in data.

`long int ru_isrss`
: An integral value expressed the same way, which is the amount of unshared memory used in stack space.

`long int ru_minflt`
: The number of page faults which were serviced without requiring any I/O.

`long int ru_majflt`
: The number of page faults which were serviced by doing I/O.

`long int ru_nswap`
: The number of times *processes* was swapped entirely out of main memory.

`long int ru_inblock`
: The number of times the file system had to read from the disk on behalf of *processes*.

`long int ru_oublock`
: The number of times the file system had to write to the disk on behalf of *processes*.

`long int ru_msgsnd`
: Number of IPC messages sent.

`long ru_msgrcv`
: Number of IPC messages received.

Chapter 17: Date and Time 341

long int ru_nsignals
>Number of signals received.

long int ru_nvcsw
>The number of times *processes* voluntarily invoked a context switch (usually to wait for some service).

long int ru_nivcsw
>The number of times an involuntary context switch took place (because the time slice expired, or another process of higher priority became runnable).

An additional historical function for examining usage figures, `vtimes`, is supported but not documented here. It is declared in 'sys/vtimes.h'.

17.6 Limiting Resource Usage

You can specify limits for the resource usage of a process. When the process tries to exceed a limit, it may get a signal, or the system call by which it tried to do so may fail, depending on the limit. Each process initially inherits its limit values from its parent, but it can subsequently change them.

The symbols in this section are defined in 'sys/resource.h'.

int getrlimit (int *resource*, struct rlimit **rlp*)   Function
>Read the current value and the maximum value of resource *resource* and store them in **rlp*.
>
>The return value is 0 on success and -1 on failure. The only possible `errno` error condition is `EFAULT`.

int setrlimit (int *resource*, struct rlimit **rlp*)   Function
>Store the current value and the maximum value of resource *resource* in **rlp*.
>
>The return value is 0 on success and -1 on failure. The following `errno` error condition is possible:
>
>>EPERM   You tried to change the maximum permissible limit value, but you don't have privileges to do so.

struct rlimit   Data Type
>This structure is used with `getrlimit` to receive limit values, and with `setrlimit` to specify limit values. It has two fields:
>
>>rlim_cur   The current value of the limit in question. This is also called the "soft limit".

`rlim_max` The maximum permissible value of the limit in question. You cannot set the current value of the limit to a larger number than this maximum. Only the super user can change the maximum permissible value. This is also called the "hard limit".

In `getrlimit`, the structure is an output; it receives the current values. In `setrlimit`, it specifies the new values.

Here is a list of resources that you can specify a limit for. Those that are sizes are measured in bytes.

`RLIMIT_CPU`
> The maximum amount of cpu time the process can use. If it runs for longer than this, it gets a signal: `SIGXCPU`. The value is measured in seconds. See Section 21.2.6 [Operation Error Signals], page 382.

`RLIMIT_FSIZE`
> The maximum size of file the process can create. Trying to write a larger file causes a signal: `SIGXFSZ`. See Section 21.2.6 [Operation Error Signals], page 382.

`RLIMIT_DATA`
> The maximum size of data memory for the process. If the process tries to allocate data memory beyond this amount, the allocation function fails.

`RLIMIT_STACK`
> The maximum stack size for the process. If the process tries to extend its stack past this size, it gets a `SIGSEGV` signal. See Section 21.2.1 [Program Error Signals], page 374.

`RLIMIT_CORE`
> The maximum size core file that this process can create. If the process terminates and would dump a core file larger than this maximum size, then no core file is created. So setting this limit to zero prevents core files from ever being created.

`RLIMIT_RSS`
> The maximum amount of physical memory that this process should get. This parameter is a guide for the system's scheduler and memory allocator; the system may give the process more memory when there is a surplus.

`RLIMIT_MEMLOCK`
> The maximum amount of memory that can be locked into physical memory (so it will never be paged out).

Chapter 17: Date and Time   343

RLIMIT_NPROC
> The maximum number of processes that can be created with the same user ID. If you have reached the limit for your user ID, `fork` will fail with `EAGAIN`. See Section 23.4 [Creating a Process], page 445.

RLIMIT_NOFILE
RLIMIT_OFILE
> The maximum number of files that the process can open. If it tries to open more files than this, it gets error code `EMFILE`. See Section 2.2 [Error Codes], page 14. Not all systems support this limit; GNU does, and 4.4 BSD does.

RLIM_NLIMITS
> The number of different resource limits. Any valid *resource* operand must be less than `RLIM_NLIMITS`.

int RLIM_INFINITY   Constant
This constant stands for a value of "infinity" when supplied as the limit value in `setrlimit`.

Two historical functions for setting resource limits, `ulimit` and `vlimit`, are not documented here. The latter is declared in 'sys/vlimit.h' and comes from BSD.

17.7 Process Priority

When several processes try to run, their respective priorities determine what share of the CPU each process gets. This section describes how you can read and set the priority of a process. All these functions and macros are declared in 'sys/resource.h'.

The range of valid priority values depends on the operating system, but typically it runs from -20 to 20. A lower priority value means the process runs more often. These constants describe the range of priority values:

PRIO_MIN   The smallest valid priority value.

PRIO_MAX   The smallest valid priority value.

int getpriority (**int** *class*, **int** *id*)   Function
> Read the priority of a class of processes; *class* and *id* specify which ones (see below). If the processes specified do not all have the same priority, this returns the smallest value that any of them has.
>
> The return value is the priority value on success, and -1 on failure. The following `errno` error condition are possible for this function:
>
> ESRCH   The combination of *class* and *id* does not match any existing process.

EINVAL   The value of *class* is not valid.

When the return value is -1, it could indicate failure, or it could be the priority value. The only way to make certain is to set `errno = 0` before calling `getpriority`, then use `errno != 0` afterward as the criterion for failure.

int setpriority (int *class*, int *id*, int *priority*)   *Function*
Set the priority of a class of processes to *priority*; *class* and *id* specify which ones (see below).

The return value is 0 on success and -1 on failure. The following `errno` error condition are defined for this function:

ESRCH   The combination of *class* and *id* does not match any existing process.

EINVAL   The value of *class* is not valid.

EPERM   You tried to set the priority of some other user's process, and you don't have privileges for that.

EACCES   You tried to lower the priority of a process, and you don't have privileges for that.

The arguments *class* and *id* together specify a set of processes you are interested in. These are the possible values for *class*:

PRIO_PROCESS
Read or set the priority of one process. The argument *id* is a process ID.

PRIO_PGRP
Read or set the priority of one process group. The argument *id* is a process group ID.

PRIO_USER
Read or set the priority of one user's processes. The argument *id* is a user ID.

If the argument *id* is 0, it stands for the current process, current process group, or the current user, according to *class*.

int nice (int *increment*)   *Function*
Increment the priority of the current process by *increment*. The return value is the same as for `setpriority`.

Here is an equivalent definition for `nice`:
```
int
nice (int increment)
{
  int old = getpriority (PRIO_PROCESS, 0);
  return setpriority (PRIO_PROCESS, 0, old + increment);
}
```

18 Extended Characters

A number of languages use character sets that are larger than the range of values of type `char`. Japanese and Chinese are probably the most familiar examples.

The GNU C library includes support for two mechanisms for dealing with extended character sets: multibyte characters and wide characters. This chapter describes how to use these mechanisms, and the functions for converting between them.

The behavior of the functions in this chapter is affected by the current locale for character classification—the `LC_CTYPE` category; see Section 19.3 [Categories of Activities that Locales Affect], page 358. This choice of locale selects which multibyte code is used, and also controls the meanings and characteristics of wide character codes.

18.1 Introduction to Extended Characters

You can represent extended characters in either of two ways:

- As *multibyte characters* which can be embedded in an ordinary string, an array of `char` objects. Their advantage is that many programs and operating systems can handle occasional multibyte characters scattered among ordinary ASCII characters, without any change.

- As *wide characters*, which are like ordinary characters except that they occupy more bits. The wide character data type, `wchar_t`, has a range large enough to hold extended character codes as well as old-fashioned ASCII codes.

An advantage of wide characters is that each character is a single data object, just like ordinary ASCII characters. There are a few disadvantages:

  - Each existing program must be modified and recompiled to make it use wide characters.

  - Files of wide characters cannot be read by programs that expect ordinary characters.

Typically, you use the multibyte character representation as part of the external program interface, such as reading or writing text to files. However, it's usually easier to perform internal manipulations on strings containing extended characters on arrays of `wchar_t` objects, since the uniform representation makes most editing operations easier. If you do use multibyte characters for files and wide characters for internal operations, you need to convert between them when you read and write data.

If your system supports extended characters, then it supports them both as multibyte characters and as wide characters. The library includes functions you can use to convert between the two representations. These functions are described in this chapter.

18.2 Locales and Extended Characters

A computer system can support more than one multibyte character code, and more than one wide character code. The user controls the choice of codes through the current locale for character classification (see Chapter 19 [Locales and Internationalization], page 357). Each locale specifies a particular multibyte character code and a particular wide character code. The choice of locale influences the behavior of the conversion functions in the library.

Some locales support neither wide characters nor nontrivial multibyte characters. In these locales, the library conversion functions still work, even though what they do is basically trivial.

If you select a new locale for character classification, the internal shift state maintained by these functions can become confused, so it's not a good idea to change the locale while you are in the middle of processing a string.

18.3 Multibyte Characters

In the ordinary ASCII code, a sequence of characters is a sequence of bytes, and each character is one byte. This is very simple, but allows for only 256 distinct characters.

In a *multibyte character code*, a sequence of characters is a sequence of bytes, but each character may occupy one or more consecutive bytes of the sequence.

There are many different ways of designing a multibyte character code; different systems use different codes. To specify a particular code means designating the *basic* byte sequences—those which represent a single character—and what characters they stand for. A code that a computer can actually use must have a finite number of these basic sequences, and typically none of them is more than a few characters long.

These sequences need not all have the same length. In fact, many of them are just one byte long. Because the basic ASCII characters in the range from 0 to 0177 are so important, they stand for themselves in all multibyte character codes. That is to say, a byte whose value is 0 through 0177 is always a character in itself. The characters which are more than one byte must always start with a byte in the range from 0200 through 0377.

The byte value 0 can be used to terminate a string, just as it is often used in a string of ASCII characters.

Chapter 18: Extended Characters 347

Specifying the basic byte sequences that represent single characters automatically gives meanings to many longer byte sequences, as more than one character. For example, if the two byte sequence 0205 049 stands for the Greek letter alpha, then 0205 049 065 must stand for an alpha followed by an 'A' (ASCII code 065), and 0205 049 0205 049 must stand for two alphas in a row.

If any byte sequence can have more than one meaning as a sequence of characters, then the multibyte code is ambiguous—and no good. The codes that systems actually use are all unambiguous.

In most codes, there are certain sequences of bytes that have no meaning as a character or characters. These are called *invalid*.

The simplest possible multibyte code is a trivial one:

The basic sequences consist of single bytes.

This particular code is equivalent to not using multibyte characters at all. It has no invalid sequences. But it can handle only 256 different characters.

Here is another possible code which can handle 9376 different characters:

The basic sequences consist of

- single bytes with values in the range 0 through 0237.
- two-byte sequences, in which both of the bytes have values in the range from 0240 through 0377.

This code or a similar one is used on some systems to represent Japanese characters. The invalid sequences are those which consist of an odd number of consecutive bytes in the range from 0240 through 0377.

Here is another multibyte code which can handle more distinct extended characters—in fact, almost thirty million:

The basic sequences consist of

- single bytes with values in the range 0 through 0177.
- sequences of up to four bytes in which the first byte is in the range from 0200 through 0237, and the remaining bytes are in the range from 0240 through 0377.

In this code, any sequence that starts with a byte in the range from 0240 through 0377 is invalid.

And here is another variant which has the advantage that removing the last byte or bytes from a valid character can never produce another valid character. (This property is convenient when you want to search strings for particular characters.)

The basic sequences consist of

- single bytes with values in the range 0 through 0177.

- two-byte sequences in which the first byte is in the range from 0200 through 0207, and the second byte is in the range from 0240 through 0377.

- three-byte sequences in which the first byte is in the range from 0210 through 0217, and the other bytes are in the range from 0240 through 0377.

- four-byte sequences in which the first byte is in the range from 0220 through 0227, and the other bytes are in the range from 0240 through 0377.

The list of invalid sequences for this code is long and not worth stating in full; examples of invalid sequences include 0240 and 0220 0300 065.

The number of *possible* multibyte codes is astronomical. But a given computer system will support at most a few different codes. (One of these codes may allow for thousands of different characters.) Another computer system may support a completely different code. The library facilities described in this chapter are helpful because they package up the knowledge of the details of a particular computer system's multibyte code, so your programs need not know them.

You can use special standard macros to find out the maximum possible number of bytes in a character in the currently selected multibyte code with MB_CUR_MAX, and the maximum for *any* multibyte code supported on your computer with MB_LEN_MAX.

int MB_LEN_MAX   Macro
This is the maximum length of a multibyte character for any supported locale. It is defined in 'limits.h'.

int MB_CUR_MAX   Macro
This macro expands into a (possibly non-constant) positive integer expression that is the maximum number of bytes in a multibyte character in the current locale. The value is never greater than MB_LEN_MAX.

MB_CUR_MAX is defined in 'stdlib.h'.

Normally, each basic sequence in a particular character code stands for one character, the same character regardless of context. Some multibyte character codes have a concept of *shift state*; certain codes, called *shift sequences*, change to a different shift state, and the meaning of some or all basic sequences varies according to the current shift state. In fact, the set of basic sequences might even be different depending on the current shift state. See Section 18.9 [Multibyte Codes Using Shift Sequences], page 354, for more information on handling this sort of code.

What happens if you try to pass a string containing multibyte characters to a function that doesn't know about them? Normally, such a function treats a string as a sequence of bytes, and interprets certain byte values specially; all other byte values are "ordinary". As long as a multibyte character doesn't contain any of the special byte values, the function should pass it through as if it were several ordinary characters.

For example, let's figure out what happens if you use multibyte characters in a file name. The functions such as `open` and `unlink` that operate on file names treat the name as a sequence of byte values, with '/' as the only special value. Any other byte values are copied, or compared, in sequence, and all byte values are treated alike. Thus, you may think of the file name as a sequence of bytes or as a string containing multibyte characters; the same behavior makes sense equally either way, provided no multibyte character contains a '/'.

18.4 Wide Character Introduction

Wide characters are much simpler than multibyte characters. They are simply characters with more than eight bits, so that they have room for more than 256 distinct codes. The wide character data type, `wchar_t`, has a range large enough to hold extended character codes as well as old-fashioned ASCII codes.

An advantage of wide characters is that each character is a single data object, just like ordinary ASCII characters. Wide characters also have some disadvantages:

- A program must be modified and recompiled in order to use wide characters at all.
- Files of wide characters cannot be read by programs that expect ordinary characters.

Wide character values 0 through 0177 are always identical in meaning to the ASCII character codes. The wide character value zero is often used to terminate a string of wide characters, just as a single byte with value zero often terminates a string of ordinary characters.

wchar_t   Data Type

> This is the "wide character" type, an integer type whose range is large enough to represent all distinct values in any extended character set in the supported locales. See Chapter 19 [Locales and Internationalization], page 357, for more information about locales. This type is defined in the header file '`stddef.h`'.

If your system supports extended characters, then each extended character has both a wide character code and a corresponding multibyte basic sequence.

In this chapter, the term *code* is used to refer to a single extended character object to emphasize the distinction from the `char` data type.

18.5 Conversion of Extended Strings

The `mbstowcs` function converts a string of multibyte characters to a wide character array. The `wcstombs` function does the reverse. These functions are declared in the header file 'stdlib.h'.

In most programs, these functions are the only ones you need for conversion between wide strings and multibyte character strings. But they have limitations. If your data is not null-terminated or is not all in core at once, you probably need to use the low-level conversion functions to convert one character at a time. See Section 18.7 [Conversion of Extended Characters One by One], page 352.

size_t mbstowcs (wchar_t *wstring*, const char *string*, size_t *size*) *Function*

The `mbstowcs` ("multibyte string to wide character string") function converts the null-terminated string of multibyte characters *string* to an array of wide character codes, storing not more than *size* wide characters into the array beginning at *wstring*. The terminating null character counts towards the size, so if *size* is less than the actual number of wide characters resulting from *string*, no terminating null character is stored.

The conversion of characters from *string* begins in the initial shift state.

If an invalid multibyte character sequence is found, this function returns a value of -1. Otherwise, it returns the number of wide characters stored in the array *wstring*. This number does not include the terminating null character, which is present if the number is less than *size*.

Here is an example showing how to convert a string of multibyte characters, allocating enough space for the result.

```
wchar_t *
mbstowcs_alloc (const char *string)
{
  size_t size = strlen (string) + 1;
  wchar_t *buf = xmalloc (size * sizeof (wchar_t));

  size = mbstowcs (buf, string, size);
  if (size == (size_t) -1)
    return NULL;
  buf = xrealloc (buf, (size + 1) * sizeof (wchar_t));
  return buf;
}
```

Chapter 18: Extended Characters   351

`size_t` **wcstombs** (`char *`*string*, `const wchar_t`   Function
         wstring, `size_t` *size*)

The `wcstombs` ("wide character string to multibyte string") function converts the null-terminated wide character array *wstring* into a string containing multibyte characters, storing not more than *size* bytes starting at *string*, followed by a terminating null character if there is room. The conversion of characters begins in the initial shift state.

The terminating null character counts towards the size, so if *size* is less than or equal to the number of bytes needed in *wstring*, no terminating null character is stored.

If a code that does not correspond to a valid multibyte character is found, this function returns a value of `-1`. Otherwise, the return value is the number of bytes stored in the array *string*. This number does not include the terminating null character, which is present if the number is less than *size*.

18.6 Multibyte Character Length

This section describes how to scan a string containing multibyte characters, one character at a time. The difficulty in doing this is to know how many bytes each character contains. Your program can use `mblen` to find this out.

`int` **mblen** (`const char *`*string*, `size_t` *size*)   Function

The `mblen` function with a non-null *string* argument returns the number of bytes that make up the multibyte character beginning at *string*, never examining more than *size* bytes. (The idea is to supply for *size* the number of bytes of data you have in hand.)

The return value of `mblen` distinguishes three possibilities: the first *size* bytes at *string* start with valid multibyte character, they start with an invalid byte sequence or just part of a character, or *string* points to an empty string (a null character).

For a valid multibyte character, `mblen` returns the number of bytes in that character (always at least `1`, and never more than *size*). For an invalid byte sequence, `mblen` returns `-1`. For an empty string, it returns `0`.

If the multibyte character code uses shift characters, then `mblen` maintains and updates a shift state as it scans. If you call `mblen` with a null pointer for *string*, that initializes the shift state to its standard initial value. It also returns nonzero if the multibyte character code in use actually has a shift state. See Section 18.9 [Multibyte Codes Using Shift Sequences], page 354.

The function `mblen` is declared in '`stdlib.h`'.

18.7 Conversion of Extended Characters One by One

You can convert multibyte characters one at a time to wide characters with the `mbtowc` function. The `wctomb` function does the reverse. These functions are declared in 'stdlib.h'.

int mbtowc (wchar_t *result*, const char *string*, size_t *size*) *Function*

The `mbtowc` ("multibyte to wide character") function when called with non-null *string* converts the first multibyte character beginning at *string* to its corresponding wide character code. It stores the result in *result*.

`mbtowc` never examines more than *size* bytes. (The idea is to supply for *size* the number of bytes of data you have in hand.)

`mbtowc` with non-null *string* distinguishes three possibilities: the first *size* bytes at *string* start with valid multibyte character, they start with an invalid byte sequence or just part of a character, or *string* points to an empty string (a null character).

For a valid multibyte character, `mbtowc` converts it to a wide character and stores that in *result*, and returns the number of bytes in that character (always at least 1, and never more than *size*).

For an invalid byte sequence, `mbtowc` returns -1. For an empty string, it returns 0, also storing 0 in *result*.

If the multibyte character code uses shift characters, then `mbtowc` maintains and updates a shift state as it scans. If you call `mbtowc` with a null pointer for *string*, that initializes the shift state to its standard initial value. It also returns nonzero if the multibyte character code in use actually has a shift state. See Section 18.9 [Multibyte Codes Using Shift Sequences], page 354.

int wctomb (char *string*, wchar_t *wchar*) *Function*

The `wctomb` ("wide character to multibyte") function converts the wide character code *wchar* to its corresponding multibyte character sequence, and stores the result in bytes starting at *string*. At most `MB_CUR_MAX` characters are stored.

`wctomb` with non-null *string* distinguishes three possibilities for *wchar*: a valid wide character code (one that can be translated to a multibyte character), an invalid code, and 0.

Given a valid code, `wctomb` converts it to a multibyte character, storing the bytes starting at *string*. Then it returns the number of bytes in that character (always at least 1, and never more than `MB_CUR_MAX`).

If *wchar* is an invalid wide character code, `wctomb` returns -1. If *wchar* is 0, it returns 0, also storing 0 in *string*.

Chapter 18: Extended Characters 353

If the multibyte character code uses shift characters, then `wctomb` maintains and updates a shift state as it scans. If you call `wctomb` with a null pointer for *string*, that initializes the shift state to its standard initial value. It also returns nonzero if the multibyte character code in use actually has a shift state. See Section 18.9 [Multibyte Codes Using Shift Sequences], page 354.

Calling this function with a *wchar* argument of zero when *string* is not null has the side-effect of reinitializing the stored shift state *as well as* storing the multibyte character 0 and returning 0.

18.8 Character-by-Character Conversion Example

Here is an example that reads multibyte character text from descriptor `input` and writes the corresponding wide characters to descriptor `output`. We need to convert characters one by one for this example because `mbstowcs` is unable to continue past a null character, and cannot cope with an apparently invalid partial character by reading more input.

```
int
file_mbstowcs (int input, int output)
{
  char buffer[BUFSIZ + MB_LEN_MAX];
  int filled = 0;
  int eof = 0;

  while (!eof)
    {
      int nread;
      int nwrite;
      char *inp = buffer;
      wchar_t outbuf[BUFSIZ];
      wchar_t *outp = outbuf;

      /* Fill up the buffer from the input file.  */
      nread = read (input, buffer + filled, BUFSIZ);
      if (nread < 0)
        {
          perror ("read");
          return 0;
        }
      /* If we reach end of file, make a note to read no more.  */
      if (nread == 0)
        eof = 1;

      /* filled is now the number of bytes in buffer.  */
      filled += nread;

      /* Convert those bytes to wide characters–as many as we can.  */
      while (1)
        {
```

```
          int thislen = mbtowc (outp, inp, filled);
          /* Stop converting at invalid character;
             this can mean we have read just the first part
             of a valid character.  */
          if (thislen == -1)
            break;
          /* Treat null character like any other,
             but also reset shift state.  */
          if (thislen == 0) {
            thislen = 1;
            mbtowc (NULL, NULL, 0);
          }
          /* Advance past this character.  */
          inp += thislen;
          filled -= thislen;
          outp++;
        }

        /* Write the wide characters we just made.  */
        nwrite = write (output, outbuf,
                       (outp - outbuf) * sizeof (wchar_t));
        if (nwrite < 0)
          {
            perror ("write");
            return 0;
          }

        /* See if we have a real invalid character.  */
        if ((eof && filled > 0) || filled >= MB_CUR_MAX)
          {
            error ("invalid multibyte character");
            return 0;
          }

        /* If any characters must be carried forward,
           put them at the beginning of buffer.  */
        if (filled > 0)
          memcpy (inp, buffer, filled);
      }

    return 1;
  }
```

18.9 Multibyte Codes Using Shift Sequences

In some multibyte character codes, the *meaning* of any particular byte sequence is not fixed; it depends on what other sequences have come earlier in the same string. Typically there are just a few sequences that can change the meaning of other sequences; these few are called *shift sequences* and we say that they set the *shift state* for other sequences that follow.

Chapter 18: Extended Characters

To illustrate shift state and shift sequences, suppose we decide that the sequence 0200 (just one byte) enters Japanese mode, in which pairs of bytes in the range from 0240 to 0377 are single characters, while 0201 enters Latin-1 mode, in which single bytes in the range from 0240 to 0377 are characters, and interpreted according to the ISO Latin-1 character set. This is a multibyte code which has two alternative shift states ("Japanese mode" and "Latin-1 mode"), and two shift sequences that specify particular shift states.

When the multibyte character code in use has shift states, then `mblen`, `mbtowc` and `wctomb` must maintain and update the current shift state as they scan the string. To make this work properly, you must follow these rules:

- Before starting to scan a string, call the function with a null pointer for the multibyte character address—for example, `mblen (NULL, 0)`. This initializes the shift state to its standard initial value.
- Scan the string one character at a time, in order. Do not "back up" and rescan characters already scanned, and do not intersperse the processing of different strings.

Here is an example of using `mblen` following these rules:
```
void
scan_string (char *s)
{
  int length = strlen (s);

  /* Initialize shift state. */
  mblen (NULL, 0);

  while (1)
    {
      int thischar = mblen (s, length);
      /* Deal with end of string and invalid characters. */
      if (thischar == 0)
        break;
      if (thischar == -1)
        {
          error ("invalid multibyte character");
          break;
        }
      /* Advance past this character. */
      s += thischar;
      length -= thischar;
    }
}
```

The functions `mblen`, `mbtowc` and `wctomb` are not reentrant when using a multibyte code that uses a shift state. However, no other library functions call these functions, so you don't have to worry that the shift state will be changed mysteriously.

19 Locales and Internationalization

Different countries and cultures have varying conventions for how to communicate. These conventions range from very simple ones, such as the format for representing dates and times, to very complex ones, such as the language spoken.

Internationalization of software means programming it to be able to adapt to the user's favorite conventions. In ANSI C, internationalization works by means of *locales*. Each locale specifies a collection of conventions, one convention for each purpose. The user chooses a set of conventions by specifying a locale (via environment variables).

All programs inherit the chosen locale as part of their environment. Provided the programs are written to obey the choice of locale, they will follow the conventions preferred by the user.

19.1 What Effects a Locale Has

Each locale specifies conventions for several purposes, including the following:

- What multibyte character sequences are valid, and how they are interpreted (see Chapter 18 [Extended Characters], page 345).
- Classification of which characters in the local character set are considered alphabetic, and upper- and lower-case conversion conventions (see Chapter 4 [Character Handling], page 55).
- The collating sequence for the local language and character set (see Section 5.6 [Collation Functions], page 67).
- Formatting of numbers and currency amounts (see Section 19.6 [Numeric Formatting], page 361).
- Formatting of dates and times (see Section 17.2.4 [Formatting Date and Time], page 329).
- What language to use for output, including error messages. (The C library doesn't yet help you implement this.)
- What language to use for user answers to yes-or-no questions.
- What language to use for more complex user input. (The C library doesn't yet help you implement this.)

Some aspects of adapting to the specified locale are handled automatically by the library subroutines. For example, all your program needs to do in order to use the collating sequence of the chosen locale is to use `strcoll` or `strxfrm` to compare strings.

Other aspects of locales are beyond the comprehension of the library. For example, the library can't automatically translate your program's output

messages into other languages. The only way you can support output in the
user's favorite language is to program this more or less by hand. (Eventually,
we hope to provide facilities to make this easier.)

This chapter discusses the mechanism by which you can modify the current locale. The effects of the current locale on specific library functions are
discussed in more detail in the descriptions of those functions.

19.2 Choosing a Locale

The simplest way for the user to choose a locale is to set the environment
variable `LANG`. This specifies a single locale to use for all purposes. For example, a user could specify a hypothetical locale named 'espana-castellano'
to use the standard conventions of most of Spain.

The set of locales supported depends on the operating system you are
using, and so do their names. We can't make any promises about what
locales will exist, except for one standard locale called 'C' or 'POSIX'.

A user also has the option of specifying different locales for different
purposes—in effect, choosing a mixture of multiple locales.

For example, the user might specify the locale 'espana-castellano' for
most purposes, but specify the locale 'usa-english' for currency formatting.
This might make sense if the user is a Spanish-speaking American, working
in Spanish, but representing monetary amounts in US dollars.

Note that both locales 'espana-castellano' and 'usa-english', like all
locales, would include conventions for all of the purposes to which locales
apply. However, the user can choose to use each locale for a particular subset
of those purposes.

19.3 Categories of Activities that Locales Affect

The purposes that locales serve are grouped into *categories*, so that a user
or a program can choose the locale for each category independently. Here is
a table of categories; each name is both an environment variable that a user
can set, and a macro name that you can use as an argument to `setlocale`.

LC_COLLATE
This category applies to collation of strings (functions `strcoll`
and `strxfrm`); see Section 5.6 [Collation Functions], page 67.

LC_CTYPE This category applies to classification and conversion of characters, and to multibyte and wide characters; see Chapter 4 [Character Handling], page 55 and Chapter 18 [Extended Characters],
page 345.

Chapter 19: Locales and Internationalization   359

LC_MONETARY
             This category applies to formatting monetary values; see Section 19.6 [Numeric Formatting], page 361.

LC_NUMERIC
             This category applies to formatting numeric values that are not monetary; see Section 19.6 [Numeric Formatting], page 361.

LC_TIME   This category applies to formatting date and time values; see Section 17.2.4 [Formatting Date and Time], page 329.

LC_ALL   This is not an environment variable; it is only a macro that you can use with `setlocale` to set a single locale for all purposes.

LANG   If this environment variable is defined, its value specifies the locale to use for all purposes except as overridden by the variables above.

19.4 How Programs Set the Locale

A C program inherits its locale environment variables when it starts up. This happens automatically. However, these variables do not automatically control the locale used by the library functions, because ANSI C says that all programs start by default in the standard 'C' locale. To use the locales specified by the environment, you must call `setlocale`. Call it as follows:

     setlocale (LC_ALL, "");

to select a locale based on the appropriate environment variables.

You can also use `setlocale` to specify a particular locale, for general use or for a specific category.

The symbols in this section are defined in the header file '`locale.h`'.

char * setlocale (int *category*, const char *locale*)   *Function*
    The function `setlocale` sets the current locale for category *category* to *locale*.

    If *category* is `LC_ALL`, this specifies the locale for all purposes. The other possible values of *category* specify an individual purpose (see Section 19.3 [Categories of Activities that Locales Affect], page 358).

    You can also use this function to find out the current locale by passing a null pointer as the *locale* argument. In this case, `setlocale` returns a string that is the name of the locale currently selected for category *category*.

    The string returned by `setlocale` can be overwritten by subsequent calls, so you should make a copy of the string (see Section 5.4 [Copying and Concatenation], page 61) if you want to save it past any further calls to `setlocale`. (The standard library is guaranteed never to call `setlocale` itself.)

You should not modify the string returned by `setlocale`. It might be the same string that was passed as an argument in a previous call to `setlocale`.

When you read the current locale for category `LC_ALL`, the value encodes the entire combination of selected locales for all categories. In this case, the value is not just a single locale name. In fact, we don't make any promises about what it looks like. But if you specify the same "locale name" with `LC_ALL` in a subsequent call to `setlocale`, it restores the same combination of locale selections.

When the *locale* argument is not a null pointer, the string returned by `setlocale` reflects the newly modified locale.

If you specify an empty string for *locale*, this means to read the appropriate environment variable and use its value to select the locale for *category*.

If you specify an invalid locale name, `setlocale` returns a null pointer and leaves the current locale unchanged.

Here is an example showing how you might use `setlocale` to temporarily switch to a new locale.

```
#include <stddef.h>
#include <locale.h>
#include <stdlib.h>
#include <string.h>

void
with_other_locale (char *new_locale,
                   void (*subroutine) (int),
                   int argument)
{
  char *old_locale, *saved_locale;

  /* Get the name of the current locale.  */
  old_locale = setlocale (LC_ALL, NULL);

  /* Copy the name so it won't be clobbered by setlocale. */
  saved_locale = strdup (old_locale);
  if (old_locale == NULL)
    fatal ("Out of memory");

  /* Now change the locale and do some stuff with it. */
  setlocale (LC_ALL, new_locale);
  (*subroutine) (argument);

  /* Restore the original locale. */
  setlocale (LC_ALL, saved_locale);
  free (saved_locale);
```

}

Portability Note: Some ANSI C systems may define additional locale categories. For portability, assume that any symbol beginning with 'LC_' might be defined in 'locale.h'.

19.5 Standard Locales

The only locale names you can count on finding on all operating systems are these three standard ones:

"C"   This is the standard C locale. The attributes and behavior it provides are specified in the ANSI C standard. When your program starts up, it initially uses this locale by default.

"POSIX"   This is the standard POSIX locale. Currently, it is an alias for the standard C locale.

""   The empty name says to select a locale based on environment variables. See Section 19.3 [Categories of Activities that Locales Affect], page 358.

Defining and installing named locales is normally a responsibility of the system administrator at your site (or the person who installed the GNU C library). Some systems may allow users to create locales, but we don't discuss that here.

If your program needs to use something other than the 'C' locale, it will be more portable if you use whatever locale the user specifies with the environment, rather than trying to specify some non-standard locale explicitly by name. Remember, different machines might have different sets of locales installed.

19.6 Numeric Formatting

When you want to format a number or a currency amount using the conventions of the current locale, you can use the function `localeconv` to get the data on how to do it. The function `localeconv` is declared in the header file 'locale.h'.

struct lconv * localeconv (void)   *Function*

The `localeconv` function returns a pointer to a structure whose components contain information about how numeric and monetary values should be formatted in the current locale.

You shouldn't modify the structure or its contents. The structure might be overwritten by subsequent calls to `localeconv`, or by calls to `setlocale`, but no other function in the library overwrites this value.

struct lconv   Data Type
   This is the data type of the value returned by `localeconv`.

   If a member of the structure `struct lconv` has type `char`, and the value is `CHAR_MAX`, it means that the current locale has no value for that parameter.

19.6.1 Generic Numeric Formatting Parameters

   These are the standard members of `struct lconv`; there may be others.

`char *decimal_point`
`char *mon_decimal_point`
   These are the decimal-point separators used in formatting non-monetary and monetary quantities, respectively. In the 'C' locale, the value of `decimal_point` is ".", and the value of `mon_decimal_point` is "".

`char *thousands_sep`
`char *mon_thousands_sep`
   These are the separators used to delimit groups of digits to the left of the decimal point in formatting non-monetary and monetary quantities, respectively. In the 'C' locale, both members have a value of "" (the empty string).

`char *grouping`
`char *mon_grouping`
   These are strings that specify how to group the digits to the left of the decimal point. `grouping` applies to non-monetary quantities and `mon_grouping` applies to monetary quantities. Use either `thousands_sep` or `mon_thousands_sep` to separate the digit groups.

   Each string is made up of decimal numbers separated by semicolons. Successive numbers (from left to right) give the sizes of successive groups (from right to left, starting at the decimal point). The last number in the string is used over and over for all the remaining groups.

   If the last integer is `-1`, it means that there is no more grouping—or, put another way, any remaining digits form one large group without separators.

   For example, if `grouping` is "4;3;2", the correct grouping for the number `123456787654321` is '12', '34', '56', '78', '765', '4321'. This uses a group of 4 digits at the end, preceded by a group of 3 digits, preceded by groups of 2 digits (as many as needed). With a separator of ',', the number would be printed as '12,34,56,78,765,4321'.

A value of "3" indicates repeated groups of three digits, as normally used in the U.S.

In the standard 'C' locale, both `grouping` and `mon_grouping` have a value of "". This value specifies no grouping at all.

`char int_frac_digits`
`char frac_digits`
    These are small integers indicating how many fractional digits (to the right of the decimal point) should be displayed in a monetary value in international and local formats, respectively. (Most often, both members have the same value.)

    In the standard 'C' locale, both of these members have the value `CHAR_MAX`, meaning "unspecified". The ANSI standard doesn't say what to do when you find this the value; we recommend printing no fractional digits. (This locale also specifies the empty string for `mon_decimal_point`, so printing any fractional digits would be confusing!)

19.6.2 Printing the Currency Symbol

These members of the `struct lconv` structure specify how to print the symbol to identify a monetary value—the international analog of '$' for US dollars.

Each country has two standard currency symbols. The *local currency symbol* is used commonly within the country, while the *international currency symbol* is used internationally to refer to that country's currency when it is necessary to indicate the country unambiguously.

For example, many countries use the dollar as their monetary unit, and when dealing with international currencies it's important to specify that one is dealing with (say) Canadian dollars instead of U.S. dollars or Australian dollars. But when the context is known to be Canada, there is no need to make this explicit—dollar amounts are implicitly assumed to be in Canadian dollars.

`char *currency_symbol`
    The local currency symbol for the selected locale.

    In the standard 'C' locale, this member has a value of "" (the empty string), meaning "unspecified". The ANSI standard doesn't say what to do when you find this value; we recommend you simply print the empty string as you would print any other string found in the appropriate member.

`char *int_curr_symbol`
    The international currency symbol for the selected locale.

The value of `int_curr_symbol` should normally consist of a three-letter abbreviation determined by the international standard *ISO 4217 Codes for the Representation of Currency and Funds*, followed by a one-character separator (often a space).

In the standard 'C' locale, this member has a value of `""` (the empty string), meaning "unspecified". We recommend you simply print the empty string as you would print any other string found in the appropriate member.

`char p_cs_precedes`
`char n_cs_precedes`

These members are 1 if the `currency_symbol` string should precede the value of a monetary amount, or 0 if the string should follow the value. The `p_cs_precedes` member applies to positive amounts (or zero), and the `n_cs_precedes` member applies to negative amounts.

In the standard 'C' locale, both of these members have a value of `CHAR_MAX`, meaning "unspecified". The ANSI standard doesn't say what to do when you find this value, but we recommend printing the currency symbol before the amount. That's right for most countries. In other words, treat all nonzero values alike in these members.

The POSIX standard says that these two members apply to the `int_curr_symbol` as well as the `currency_symbol`. The ANSI C standard seems to imply that they should apply only to the `currency_symbol`—so the `int_curr_symbol` should always precede the amount.

We can only guess which of these (if either) matches the usual conventions for printing international currency symbols. Our guess is that they should always preceed the amount. If we find out a reliable answer, we will put it here.

`char p_sep_by_space`
`char n_sep_by_space`

These members are 1 if a space should appear between the `currency_symbol` string and the amount, or 0 if no space should appear. The `p_sep_by_space` member applies to positive amounts (or zero), and the `n_sep_by_space` member applies to negative amounts.

In the standard 'C' locale, both of these members have a value of `CHAR_MAX`, meaning "unspecified". The ANSI standard doesn't say what you should do when you find this value; we suggest you treat it as one (print a space). In other words, treat all nonzero values alike in these members.

Chapter 19: Locales and Internationalization

These members apply only to `currency_symbol`. When you use `int_curr_symbol`, you never print an additional space, because `int_curr_symbol` itself contains the appropriate separator.

The POSIX standard says that these two members apply to the `int_curr_symbol` as well as the `currency_symbol`. But an example in the ANSI C standard clearly implies that they should apply only to the `currency_symbol`—that the `int_curr_symbol` contains any appropriate separator, so you should never print an additional space.

Based on what we know now, we recommend you ignore these members when printing international currency symbols, and print no extra space.

19.6.3 Printing the Sign of an Amount of Money

These members of the `struct lconv` structure specify how to print the sign (if any) in a monetary value.

`char *positive_sign`
`char *negative_sign`

> These are strings used to indicate positive (or zero) and negative (respectively) monetary quantities.
>
> In the standard 'C' locale, both of these members have a value of "" (the empty string), meaning "unspecified".
>
> The ANSI standard doesn't say what to do when you find this value; we recommend printing `positive_sign` as you find it, even if it is empty. For a negative value, print `negative_sign` as you find it unless both it and `positive_sign` are empty, in which case print '-' instead. (Failing to indicate the sign at all seems rather unreasonable.)

`char p_sign_posn`
`char n_sign_posn`

> These members have values that are small integers indicating how to position the sign for nonnegative and negative monetary quantities, respectively. (The string used by the sign is what was specified with `positive_sign` or `negative_sign`.) The possible values are as follows:
>
> 0   The currency symbol and quantity should be surrounded by parentheses.
>
> 1   Print the sign string before the quantity and currency symbol.
>
> 2   Print the sign string after the quantity and currency symbol.

3 Print the sign string right before the currency symbol.

4 Print the sign string right after the currency symbol.

CHAR_MAX "Unspecified". Both members have this value in the standard 'C' locale.

The ANSI standard doesn't say what you should do when the value is **CHAR_MAX**. We recommend you print the sign after the currency symbol.

It is not clear whether you should let these members apply to the international currency format or not. POSIX says you should, but intuition plus the examples in the ANSI C standard suggest you should not. We hope that someone who knows well the conventions for formatting monetary quantities will tell us what we should recommend.

20 Non-Local Exits

Sometimes when your program detects an unusual situation inside a deeply nested set of function calls, you would like to be able to immediately return to an outer level of control. This section describes how you can do such *non-local exits* using the `setjmp` and `longjmp` functions.

20.1 Introduction to Non-Local Exits

As an example of a situation where a non-local exit can be useful, suppose you have an interactive program that has a "main loop" that prompts for and executes commands. Suppose the "read" command reads input from a file, doing some lexical analysis and parsing of the input while processing it. If a low-level input error is detected, it would be useful to be able to return immediately to the "main loop" instead of having to make each of the lexical analysis, parsing, and processing phases all have to explicitly deal with error situations initially detected by nested calls.

(On the other hand, if each of these phases has to do a substantial amount of cleanup when it exits—such as closing files, deallocating buffers or other data structures, and the like—then it can be more appropriate to do a normal return and have each phase do its own cleanup, because a non-local exit would bypass the intervening phases and their associated cleanup code entirely. Alternatively, you could use a non-local exit but do the cleanup explicitly either before or after returning to the "main loop".)

In some ways, a non-local exit is similar to using the '`return`' statement to return from a function. But while '`return`' abandons only a single function call, transferring control back to the point at which it was called, a non-local exit can potentially abandon many levels of nested function calls.

You identify return points for non-local exits calling the function `setjmp`. This function saves information about the execution environment in which the call to `setjmp` appears in an object of type `jmp_buf`. Execution of the program continues normally after the call to `setjmp`, but if a exit is later made to this return point by calling `longjmp` with the corresponding `jmp_buf` object, control is transferred back to the point where `setjmp` was called. The return value from `setjmp` is used to distinguish between an ordinary return and a return made by a call to `longjmp`, so calls to `setjmp` usually appear in an '`if`' statement.

Here is how the example program described above might be set up:

```
#include <setjmp.h>
#include <stdlib.h>
#include <stdio.h>

jmp_buf main_loop;
```

```
void
abort_to_main_loop (int status)
{
  longjmp (main_loop, status);
}

int
main (void)
{
  while (1)
    if (setjmp (main_loop))
      puts ("Back at main loop....");
    else
      do_command ();
}

void
do_command (void)
{
  char buffer[128];
  if (fgets (buffer, 128, stdin) == NULL)
    abort_to_main_loop (-1);
  else
    exit (EXIT_SUCCESS);
}
```

The function `abort_to_main_loop` causes an immediate transfer of control back to the main loop of the program, no matter where it is called from.

The flow of control inside the `main` function may appear a little mysterious at first, but it is actually a common idiom with `setjmp`. A normal call to `setjmp` returns zero, so the "else" clause of the conditional is executed. If `abort_to_main_loop` is called somewhere within the execution of `do_command`, then it actually appears as if the *same* call to `setjmp` in `main` were returning a second time with a value of -1.

So, the general pattern for using `setjmp` looks something like:

```
if (setjmp (buffer))
  /* Code to clean up after premature return. */
  ...
else
  /* Code to be executed normally after setting up the return point. */
  ...
```

20.2 Details of Non-Local Exits

Here are the details on the functions and data structures used for performing non-local exits. These facilities are declared in 'setjmp.h'.

Chapter 20: Non-Local Exits   369

jmp_buf   Data Type
Objects of type `jmp_buf` hold the state information to be restored by a non-local exit. The contents of a `jmp_buf` identify a specific place to return to.

int setjmp (jmp_buf *state*)   Macro
When called normally, `setjmp` stores information about the execution state of the program in *state* and returns zero. If `longjmp` is later used to perform a non-local exit to this *state*, `setjmp` returns a nonzero value.

void **longjmp** (jmp_buf *state*, int *value*)   Function
This function restores current execution to the state saved in *state*, and continues execution from the call to `setjmp` that established that return point. Returning from `setjmp` by means of `longjmp` returns the *value* argument that was passed to `longjmp`, rather than 0. (But if *value* is given as 0, `setjmp` returns 1).

There are a lot of obscure but important restrictions on the use of `setjmp` and `longjmp`. Most of these restrictions are present because non-local exits require a fair amount of magic on the part of the C compiler and can interact with other parts of the language in strange ways.

The `setjmp` function is actually a macro without an actual function definition, so you shouldn't try to '#undef' it or take its address. In addition, calls to `setjmp` are safe in only the following contexts:

- As the test expression of a selection or iteration statement (such as 'if', 'switch', or 'while').
- As one operand of a equality or comparison operator that appears as the test expression of a selection or iteration statement. The other operand must be an integer constant expression.
- As the operand of a unary '!' operator, that appears as the test expression of a selection or iteration statement.
- By itself as an expression statement.

Return points are valid only during the dynamic extent of the function that called `setjmp` to establish them. If you `longjmp` to a return point that was established in a function that has already returned, unpredictable and disastrous things are likely to happen.

You should use a nonzero *value* argument to `longjmp`. While `longjmp` refuses to pass back a zero argument as the return value from `setjmp`, this is intended as a safety net against accidental misuse and is not really good programming style.

When you perform a non-local exit, accessible objects generally retain whatever values they had at the time `longjmp` was called. The exception is

that the values of automatic variables local to the function containing the
`setjmp` call that have been changed since the call to `setjmp` are indeterminate, unless you have declared them `volatile`.

20.3 Non-Local Exits and Signals

In BSD Unix systems, `setjmp` and `longjmp` also save and restore the set
of blocked signals; see Section 21.7 [Blocking Signals], page 408. However,
the POSIX.1 standard requires `setjmp` and `longjmp` not to change the set
of blocked signals, and provides an additional pair of functions (`sigsetjmp`
and `sigsetjmp`) to get the BSD behavior.

The behavior of `setjmp` and `longjmp` in the GNU library is controlled
by feature test macros; see Section 1.3.4 [Feature Test Macros], page 8. The
default in the GNU system is the POSIX.1 behavior rather than the BSD
behavior.

The facilities in this section are declared in the header file 'setjmp.h'.

sigjmp_buf   Data Type
   This is similar to `jmp_buf`, except that it can also store state information about the set of blocked signals.

int sigsetjmp (`sigjmp_buf` *state*, `int` *savesigs*)   Function
   This is similar to `setjmp`. If *savesigs* is nonzero, the set of blocked
   signals is saved in *state* and will be restored if a `siglongjmp` is later
   performed with this *state*.

void siglongjmp (`sigjmp_buf` *state*, `int` *value*)   Function
   This is similar to `longjmp` except for the type of its *state* argument.
   If the `sigsetjmp` call that set this *state* used a nonzero *savesigs* flag,
   `siglongjmp` also restores the set of blocked signals.

21 Signal Handling

A *signal* is a software interrupt delivered to a process. The operating system uses signals to report exceptional situations to an executing program. Some signals report errors such as references to invalid memory addresses; others report asynchronous events, such as disconnection of a phone line.

The GNU C library defines a variety of signal types, each for a particular kind of event. Some kinds of events make it inadvisable or impossible for the program to proceed as usual, and the corresponding signals normally abort the program. Other kinds of signals that report harmless events are ignored by default.

If you anticipate an event that causes signals, you can define a handler function and tell the operating system to run it when that particular type of signal arrives.

Finally, one process can send a signal to another process; this allows a parent process to abort a child, or two related processes to communicate and synchronize.

21.1 Basic Concepts of Signals

This section explains basic concepts of how signals are generated, what happens after a signal is delivered, and how programs can handle signals.

21.1.1 Some Kinds of Signals

A signal reports the occurrence of an exceptional event. These are some of the events that can cause (or *generate*, or *raise*) a signal:

- A program error such as dividing by zero or issuing an address outside the valid range.
- A user request to interrupt or terminate the program. Most environments are set up to let a user suspend the program by typing `C-z`, or terminate it with `C-c`. Whatever key sequence is used, the operating system sends the proper signal to interrupt the process.
- The termination of a child process.
- Expiration of a timer or alarm.
- A call to `kill` or `raise` by the same process.
- A call to `kill` from another process. Signals are a limited but useful form of interprocess communication.
- An attempt to perform an I/O operation that cannot be done. Examples are reading from a pipe that has no writer (see Chapter 10 [Pipes and FIFOs], page 201), and reading or writing to a terminal in certain situations (see Chapter 24 [Job Control], page 457).

Each of these kinds of events (excepting explicit calls to `kill` and `raise`) generates its own particular kind of signal. The various kinds of signals are listed and described in detail in Section 21.2 [Standard Signals], page 373.

21.1.2 Concepts of Signal Generation

In general, the events that generate signals fall into three major categories: errors, external events, and explicit requests.

An error means that a program has done something invalid and cannot continue execution. But not all kinds of errors generate signals—in fact, most do not. For example, opening a nonexistent file is an error, but it does not raise a signal; instead, `open` returns -1. In general, errors that are necessarily associated with certain library functions are reported by returning a value that indicates an error. The errors which raise signals are those which can happen anywhere in the program, not just in library calls. These include division by zero and invalid memory addresses.

An external event generally has to do with I/O or other processes. These include the arrival of input, the expiration of a timer, and the termination of a child process.

An explicit request means the use of a library function such as `kill` whose purpose is specifically to generate a signal.

Signals may be generated *synchronously* or *asynchronously*. A synchronous signal pertains to a specific action in the program, and is delivered (unless blocked) during that action. Most errors generate signals synchronously, and so do explicit requests by a process to generate a signal for that same process. On some machines, certain kinds of hardware errors (usually floating-point exceptions) are not reported completely synchronously, but may arrive a few instructions later.

Asynchronous signals are generated by events outside the control of the process that receives them. These signals arrive at unpredictable times during execution. External events generate signals asynchronously, and so do explicit requests that apply to some other process.

A given type of signal is either typically synchrous or typically asynchronous. For example, signals for errors are typically synchronous because errors generate signals synchronously. But any type of signal can be generated synchronously or asynchronously with an explicit request.

21.1.3 How Signals Are Delivered

When a signal is generated, it becomes *pending*. Normally it remains pending for just a short period of time and then is *delivered* to the process that was signaled. However, if that kind of signal is currently *blocked*, it may remain pending indefinitely—until signals of that kind are *unblocked*.

Chapter 21: Signal Handling

Once unblocked, it will be delivered immediately. See Section 21.7 [Blocking Signals], page 408.

When the signal is delivered, whether right away or after a long delay, the *specified action* for that signal is taken. For certain signals, such as `SIGKILL` and `SIGSTOP`, the action is fixed, but for most signals, the program has a choice: ignore the signal, specify a *handler function*, or accept the *default action* for that kind of signal. The program specifies its choice using functions such as `signal` or `sigaction` (see Section 21.3 [Specifying Signal Actions], page 384). We sometimes say that a handler *catches* the signal. While the handler is running, that particular signal is normally blocked.

If the specified action for a kind of signal is to ignore it, then any such signal which is generated is discarded immediately. This happens even if the signal is also blocked at the time. A signal discarded in this way will never be delivered, not even if the program subsequently specifies a different action for that kind of signal and then unblocks it.

If a signal arrives which the program has neither handled nor ignored, its *default action* takes place. Each kind of signal has its own default action, documented below (see Section 21.2 [Standard Signals], page 373). For most kinds of signals, the default action is to terminate the process. For certain kinds of signals that represent "harmless" events, the default action is to do nothing.

When a signal terminates a process, its parent process can determine the cause of termination by examining the termination status code reported by the `wait` or `waitpid` functions. (This is discussed in more detail in Section 23.6 [Process Completion], page 449.) The information it can get includes the fact that termination was due to a signal, and the kind of signal involved. If a program you run from a shell is terminated by a signal, the shell typically prints some kind of error message.

The signals that normally represent program errors have a special property: when one of these signals terminates the process, it also writes a *core dump file* which records the state of the process at the time of termination. You can examine the core dump with a debugger to investigate what caused the error.

If you raise a "program error" signal by explicit request, and this terminates the process, it makes a core dump file just as if the signal had been due directly to an error.

21.2 Standard Signals

This section lists the names for various standard kinds of signals and describes what kind of event they mean. Each signal name is a macro which stands for a positive integer—the *signal number* for that kind of signal.

Your programs should never make assumptions about the numeric code for a particular kind of signal, but rather refer to them always by the names defined here. This is because the number for a given kind of signal can vary from system to system, but the meanings of the names are standardized and fairly uniform.

The signal names are defined in the header file 'signal.h'.

int NSIG Macro

The value of this symbolic constant is the total number of signals defined. Since the signal numbers are allocated consecutively, NSIG is also one greater than the largest defined signal number.

21.2.1 Program Error Signals

The following signals are generated when a serious program error is detected by the operating system or the computer itself. In general, all of these signals are indications that your program is seriously broken in some way, and there's usually no way to continue the computation which encountered the error.

Some programs handle program error signals in order to tidy up before terminating; for example, programs that turn off echoing of terminal input should handle program error signals in order to turn echoing back on. The handler should end by specifying the default action for the signal that happened and then reraising it; this will cause the program to terminate with that signal, as if it had not had a handler. (See Section 21.4.2 [Handlers That Terminate the Process], page 393.)

Termination is the sensible ultimate outcome from a program error in most programs. However, programming systems such as Lisp that can load compiled user programs might need to keep executing even if a user program incurs an error. These programs have handlers which use `longjmp` to return control to the command level.

The default action for all of these signals is to cause the process to terminate. If you block or ignore these signals or establish handlers for them that return normally, your program will probably break horribly when such signals happen, unless they are generated by `raise` or `kill` instead of a real error.

When one of these program error signals terminates a process, it also writes a *core dump file* which records the state of the process at the time of termination. The core dump file is named 'core' and is written in whichever directory is current in the process at the time. (On the GNU system, you can specify the file name for core dumps with the environment variable **COREFILE**.) The purpose of core dump files is so that you can examine them with a debugger to investigate what caused the error.

int **SIGFPE** *Macro*

The `SIGFPE` signal reports a fatal arithmetic error. Although the name is derived from "floating-point exception", this signal actually covers all arithmetic errors, including division by zero and overflow. If a program stores integer data in a location which is then used in a floating-point operation, this often causes an "invalid operation" exception, because the processor cannot recognize the data as a floating-point number.

Actual floating-point exceptions are a complicated subject because there are many types of exceptions with subtly different meanings, and the `SIGFPE` signal doesn't distinguish between them. The *IEEE Standard for Binary Floating-Point Arithmetic (ANSI/IEEE Std 754-1985)* defines various floating-point exceptions and requires conforming computer systems to report their occurrences. However, this standard does not specify how the exceptions are reported, or what kinds of handling and control the operating system can offer to the programmer.

BSD systems provide the `SIGFPE` handler with an extra argument that distinguishes various causes of the exception. In order to access this argument, you must define the handler to accept two arguments, which means you must cast it to a one-argument function type in order to establish the handler. The GNU library does provide this extra argument, but the value is meaningful only on operating systems that provide the information (BSD systems and GNU systems).

`FPE_INTOVF_TRAP`
: Integer overflow (impossible in a C program unless you enable overflow trapping in a hardware-specific fashion).

`FPE_INTDIV_TRAP`
: Integer division by zero.

`FPE_SUBRNG_TRAP`
: Subscript-range (something that C programs never check for).

`FPE_FLTOVF_TRAP`
: Floating overflow trap.

`FPE_FLTDIV_TRAP`
: Floating/decimal division by zero.

`FPE_FLTUND_TRAP`
: Floating underflow trap. (Trapping on floating underflow is not normally enabled.)

`FPE_DECOVF_TRAP`
: Decimal overflow trap. (Only a few machines have decimal arithmetic and C never uses it.)

int SIGILL   Macro

The name of this signal is derived from "illegal instruction"; it usually means your program is trying to execute garbage or a privileged instruction. Since the C compiler generates only valid instructions, `SIGILL` typically indicates that the executable file is corrupted, or that you are trying to execute data. Some common ways of getting into the latter situation are by passing an invalid object where a pointer to a function was expected, or by writing past the end of an automatic array (or similar problems with pointers to automatic variables) and corrupting other data on the stack such as the return address of a stack frame.

`SIGILL` can also be generated when the stack overflows, or when the system has trouble running the handler for a signal.

int SIGSEGV   Macro

This signal is generated when a program tries to read or write outside the memory that is allocated for it, or to write memory that can only be read. (Actually, the signals only occur when the program goes far enough outside to be detected by the system's memory protection mechanism.) The name is an abbreviation for "segmentation violation".

Common ways of getting a `SIGSEGV` condition include dereferencing a null or uninitialized pointer, or when you use a pointer to step through an array, but fail to check for the end of the array. It varies among systems whether dereferencing a null pointer generates `SIGSEGV` or `SIGBUS`.

int SIGBUS   Macro

This signal is generated when an invalid pointer is dereferenced. Like `SIGSEGV`, this signal is typically the result of dereferencing an uninitialized pointer. The difference between the two is that `SIGSEGV` indicates an invalid access to valid memory, while `SIGBUS` indicates an access to an invalid address. In particular, `SIGBUS` signals often result from dereferencing a misaligned pointer, such as referring to a four-word integer at an address not divisible by four. (Each kind of computer has its own requirements for address alignment.)

The name of this signal is an abbreviation for "bus error".

int SIGABRT   Macro

This signal indicates an error detected by the program itself and reported by calling `abort`. See Section 22.3.4 [Aborting a Program], page 440.

Chapter 21: Signal Handling							377

int SIGIOT						Macro

Generated by the PDP-11 "iot" instruction. On most machines, this is just another name for `SIGABRT`.

int SIGTRAP						Macro

Generated by the machine's breakpoint instruction, and possibly other trap instructions. This signal is used by debuggers. Your program will probably only see `SIGTRAP` if it is somehow executing bad instructions.

int SIGEMT						Macro

Emulator trap; this results from certain unimplemented instructions which might be emulated in software, or the operating system's failure to properly emulate them.

int SIGSYS						Macro

Bad system call; that is to say, the instruction to trap to the operating system was executed, but the code number for the system call to perform was invalid.

21.2.2 Termination Signals

These signals are all used to tell a process to terminate, in one way or another. They have different names because they're used for slightly different purposes, and programs might want to handle them differently.

The reason for handling these signals is usually so your program can tidy up as appropriate before actually terminating. For example, you might want to save state information, delete temporary files, or restore the previous terminal modes. Such a handler should end by specifying the default action for the signal that happened and then reraising it; this will cause the program to terminate with that signal, as if it had not had a handler. (See Section 21.4.2 [Handlers That Terminate the Process], page 393.)

The (obvious) default action for all of these signals is to cause the process to terminate.

int SIGTERM						Macro

The `SIGTERM` signal is a generic signal used to cause program termination. Unlike `SIGKILL`, this signal can be blocked, handled, and ignored. It is the normal way to politely ask a program to terminate.

The shell command `kill` generates `SIGTERM` by default.

int SIGINT						Macro

The `SIGINT` ("program interrupt") signal is sent when the user types the INTR character (normally `C-c`). See Section 12.4.9 [Special Characters], page 270, for information about terminal driver support for `C-c`.

int **SIGQUIT**   *Macro*

The `SIGQUIT` signal is similar to `SIGINT`, except that it's controlled by a different key—the QUIT character, usually `C-\`—and produces a core dump when it terminates the process, just like a program error signal. You can think of this as a program error condition "detected" by the user.

See Section 21.2.1 [Program Error Signals], page 374, for information about core dumps. See Section 12.4.9 [Special Characters], page 270, for information about terminal driver support.

Certain kinds of cleanups are best omitted in handling `SIGQUIT`. For example, if the program creates temporary files, it should handle the other termination requests by deleting the temporary files. But it is better for `SIGQUIT` not to delete them, so that the user can examine them in conjunction with the core dump.

int **SIGKILL**   *Macro*

The `SIGKILL` signal is used to cause immediate program termination. It cannot be handled or ignored, and is therefore always fatal. It is also not possible to block this signal.

This signal is usually generated only by explicit request. Since it cannot be handled, you should generate it only as a last resort, after first trying a less drastic method such as `C-c` or `SIGTERM`. If a process does not respond to any other termination signals, sending it a `SIGKILL` signal will almost always cause it to go away.

In fact, if `SIGKILL` fails to terminate a process, that by itself constitutes an operating system bug which you should report.

The system will generate `SIGKILL` for a process itself under some unusual conditions where the program cannot possible continue to run (even to run a signal handler).

int **SIGHUP**   *Macro*

The `SIGHUP` ("hang-up") signal is used to report that the user's terminal is disconnected, perhaps because a network or telephone connection was broken. For more information about this, see Section 12.4.6 [Control Modes], page 264.

This signal is also used to report the termination of the controlling process on a terminal to jobs associated with that session; this termination effectively disconnects all processes in the session from the controlling terminal. For more information, see Section 22.3.5 [Termination Internals], page 440.

Chapter 21: Signal Handling   379

21.2.3 Alarm Signals

These signals are used to indicate the expiration of timers. See Section 17.3 [Setting an Alarm], page 335, for information about functions that cause these signals to be sent.

The default behavior for these signals is to cause program termination. This default is rarely useful, but no other default would be useful; most of the ways of using these signals would require handler functions in any case.

int SIGALRM   Macro

This signal typically indicates expiration of a timer that measures real or clock time. It is used by the `alarm` function, for example.

int SIGVTALRM   Macro

This signal typically indicates expiration of a timer that measures CPU time used by the current process. The name is an abbreviation for "virtual time alarm".

int SIGPROF   Macro

This signal is typically indicates expiration of a timer that measures both CPU time used by the current process, and CPU time expended on behalf of the process by the system. Such a timer is used to implement code profiling facilities, hence the name of this signal.

21.2.4 Asynchronous I/O Signals

The signals listed in this section are used in conjunction with asynchronous I/O facilities. You have to take explicit action by calling `fcntl` to enable a particular file descriptior to generate these signals (see Section 8.12 [Interrupt-Driven Input], page 167). The default action for these signals is to ignore them.

int SIGIO   Macro

This signal is sent when a file descriptor is ready to perform input or output.

On most operating systems, terminals and sockets are the only kinds of files that can generate `SIGIO`; other kinds, including ordinary files, never generate `SIGIO` even if you ask them to.

In the GNU system `SIGIO` will always be generated properly if you successfully set asynchronous mode with `fcntl`.

int SIGURG   Macro

This signal is sent when "urgent" or out-of-band data arrives on a socket. See Section 11.8.8 [Out-of-Band Data], page 241.

int SIGPOLL   Macro
    This is a System V signal name, more or less similar to `SIGIO`. It is
    defined only for compatibility.

21.2.5 Job Control Signals

These signals are used to support job control. If your system doesn't
support job control, then these macros are defined but the signals themselves
can't be raised or handled.

You should generally leave these signals alone unless you really understand how job control works. See Chapter 24 [Job Control], page 457.

int SIGCHLD   Macro
    This signal is sent to a parent process whenever one of its child processes terminates or stops.

    The default action for this signal is to ignore it. If you establish a handler for this signal while there are child processes that have terminated but not reported their status via `wait` or `waitpid` (see Section 23.6 [Process Completion], page 449), whether your new handler applies to those processes or not depends on the particular operating system.

int SIGCLD   Macro
    This is an obsolete name for `SIGCHLD`.

int SIGCONT   Macro
    You can send a `SIGCONT` signal to a process to make it continue. This signal is special—it always makes the process continue if it is stopped, before the signal is delivered. The default behavior is to do nothing else. You cannot block this signal. You can set a handler, but `SIGCONT` always makes the process continue regardless.

    Most programs have no reason to handle `SIGCONT`; they simply resume execution without realizing they were ever stopped. You can use a handler for `SIGCONT` to make a program do something special when it is stopped and continued—for example, to reprint a prompt when it is suspended while waiting for input.

int SIGSTOP   Macro
    The `SIGSTOP` signal stops the process. It cannot be handled, ignored, or blocked.

int SIGTSTP   Macro
    The `SIGTSTP` signal is an interactive stop signal. Unlike `SIGSTOP`, this signal can be handled and ignored.

    Your program should handle this signal if you have a special need to leave files or system tables in a secure state when a process is stopped.

Chapter 21: Signal Handling

For example, programs that turn off echoing should handle `SIGTSTP` so they can turn echoing back on before stopping.

This signal is generated when the user types the SUSP character (normally `C-z`). For more information about terminal driver support, see Section 12.4.9 [Special Characters], page 270.

`int` **SIGTTIN** *Macro*

A process cannot read from the the user's terminal while it is running as a background job. When any process in a background job tries to read from the terminal, all of the processes in the job are sent a `SIGTTIN` signal. The default action for this signal is to stop the process. For more information about how this interacts with the terminal driver, see Section 24.4 [Access to the Controlling Terminal], page 459.

`int` **SIGTTOU** *Macro*

This is similar to `SIGTTIN`, but is generated when a process in a background job attempts to write to the terminal or set its modes. Again, the default action is to stop the process. `SIGTTOU` is only generated for an attempt to write to the terminal if the `TOSTOP` output mode is set; see Section 12.4.5 [Output Modes], page 263.

While a process is stopped, no more signals can be delivered to it until it is continued, except `SIGKILL` signals and (obviously) `SIGCONT` signals. The signals are marked as pending, but not delivered until the process is continued. The `SIGKILL` signal always causes termination of the process and can't be blocked, handled or ignored. You can ignore `SIGCONT`, but it always causes the process to be continued anyway if it is stopped. Sending a `SIGCONT` signal to a process causes any pending stop signals for that process to be discarded. Likewise, any pending `SIGCONT` signals for a process are discarded when it receives a stop signal.

When a process in an orphaned process group (see Section 24.5 [Orphaned Process Groups], page 459) receives a `SIGTSTP`, `SIGTTIN`, or `SIGTTOU` signal and does not handle it, the process does not stop. Stopping the process would probably not be very useful, since there is no shell program that will notice it stop and allow the user to continue it. What happens instead depends on the operating system you are using. Some systems may do nothing; others may deliver another signal instead, such as `SIGKILL` or `SIGHUP`. In the GNU system, the process dies with `SIGKILL`; this avoids the problem of many stopped, orphaned processes lying around the system.

21.2.6 Operation Error Signals

These signals are used to report various errors generated by an operation done by the program. They do not necessarily indicate a programming error in the program, but an error that prevents an operating system call from completing. The default action for all of them is to cause the process to terminate.

int SIGPIPE   Macro

Broken pipe. If you use pipes or FIFOs, you have to design your application so that one process opens the pipe for reading before another starts writing. If the reading process never starts, or terminates unexpectedly, writing to the pipe or FIFO raises a `SIGPIPE` signal. If `SIGPIPE` is blocked, handled or ignored, the offending call fails with `EPIPE` instead.

Pipes and FIFO special files are discussed in more detail in Chapter 10 [Pipes and FIFOs], page 201.

Another cause of `SIGPIPE` is when you try to output to a socket that isn't connected. See Section 11.8.5.1 [Sending Data], page 235.

int SIGLOST   Macro

Resource lost. This signal is generated when you have an advisory lock on an NFS file, and the NFS server reboots and forgets about your lock.

In the GNU system, `SIGLOST` is generated when any server program dies unexpectedly. It is usually fine to ignore the signal; whatever call was made to the server that died just returns an error.

int SIGXCPU   Macro

CPU time limit exceeded. This signal is generated when the process exceeds its soft resource limit on CPU time. See Section 17.6 [Limiting Resource Usage], page 341.

int SIGXFSZ   Macro

File size limit exceeded. This signal is generated when the process attempts to extend a file so it exceeds the process's soft resource limit on file size. See Section 17.6 [Limiting Resource Usage], page 341.

21.2.7 Miscellaneous Signals

These signals are used for various other purposes. In general, they will not affect your program unless it explicitly uses them for something.

int SIGUSR1   Macro

int SIGUSR2   Macro

The `SIGUSR1` and `SIGUSR2` signals are set aside for you to use any way you want. They're useful for simple interprocess communication, if you write a signal handler for them in the program that receives the signal.

Chapter 21: Signal Handling   383

There is an example showing the use of `SIGUSR1` and `SIGUSR2` in Section 21.6.2 [Signaling Another Process], page 405.

The default action is to terminate the process.

int SIGWINCH   Macro

Window size change. This is generated on some systems (including GNU) when the terminal driver's record of the number of rows and columns on the screen is changed. The default action is to ignore it.

If a program does full-screen display, it should handle `SIGWINCH`. When the signal arrives, it should fetch the new screen size and reformat its display accordingly.

int SIGINFO   Macro

Information request. In 4.4 BSD and the GNU system, this signal is sent to all the processes in the foreground process group of the controlling terminal when the user types the STATUS character in canonical mode; see Section 12.4.9.2 [Characters that Cause Signals], page 272.

If the process is the leader of the process group, the default action is to print some status information about the system and what the process is doing. Otherwise the default is to do nothing.

21.2.8 Signal Messages

We mentioned above that the shell prints a message describing the signal that terminated a child process. The clean way to print a message describing a signal is to use the functions `strsignal` and `psignal`. These functions use a signal number to specify which kind of signal to describe. The signal number may come from the termination status of a child process (see Section 23.6 [Process Completion], page 449) or it may come from a signal handler in the same process.

char * strsignal (int *signum*)   Function

This function returns a pointer to a statically-allocated string containing a message describing the signal *signum*. You should not modify the contents of this string; and, since it can be rewritten on subsequent calls, you should save a copy of it if you need to reference it later.

This function is a GNU extension, declared in the header file 'string.h'.

void psignal (int *signum*, const char *message*)   Function

This function prints a message describing the signal *signum* to the standard error output stream `stderr`; see Section 7.2 [Standard Streams], page 83.

If you call `psignal` with a *message* that is either a null pointer or an empty string, `psignal` just prints the message corresponding to *signum*, adding a trailing newline.

If you supply a non-null *message* argument, then `psignal` prefixes its output with this string. It adds a colon and a space character to separate the *message* from the string corresponding to *signum*.

This function is a BSD feature, declared in the header file '`signal.h`'.

There is also an array `sys_siglist` which contains the messages for the various signal codes. This array exists on BSD systems, unlike `strsignal`.

21.3 Specifying Signal Actions

The simplest way to change the action for a signal is to use the `signal` function. You can specify a built-in action (such as to ignore the signal), or you can *establish a handler*.

The GNU library also implements the more versatile `sigaction` facility. This section describes both facilities and gives suggestions on which to use when.

21.3.1 Basic Signal Handling

The `signal` function provides a simple interface for establishing an action for a particular signal. The function and associated macros are declared in the header file '`signal.h`'.

sighandler_t   Data Type

This is the type of signal handler functions. Signal handlers take one integer argument specifying the signal number, and have return type `void`. So, you should define handler functions like this:

        `void handler (int signum) { ... }`

The name `sighandler_t` for this data type is a GNU extension.

sighandler_t signal (int *signum*, sighandler_t   Function
        action)

The `signal` function establishes *action* as the action for the signal *signum*.

The first argument, *signum*, identifies the signal whose behavior you want to control, and should be a signal number. The proper way to specify a signal number is with one of the symbolic signal names described in Section 21.2 [Standard Signals], page 373—don't use an explicit number, because the numerical code for a given kind of signal may vary from operating system to operating system.

Chapter 21: Signal Handling 385

The second argument, *action*, specifies the action to use for the signal *signum*. This can be one of the following:

SIG_DFL SIG_DFL specifies the default action for the particular signal. The default actions for various kinds of signals are stated in Section 21.2 [Standard Signals], page 373.

SIG_IGN SIG_IGN specifies that the signal should be ignored.

Your program generally should not ignore signals that represent serious events or that are normally used to request termination. You cannot ignore the SIGKILL or SIGSTOP signals at all. You can ignore program error signals like SIGSEGV, but ignoring the error won't enable the program to continue executing meaningfully. Ignoring user requests such as SIGINT, SIGQUIT, and SIGTSTP is unfriendly.

When you do not wish signals to be delivered during a certain part of the program, the thing to do is to block them, not ignore them. See Section 21.7 [Blocking Signals], page 408.

handler Supply the address of a handler function in your program, to specify running this handler as the way to deliver the signal.

For more information about defining signal handler functions, see Section 21.4 [Defining Signal Handlers], page 391.

If you set the action for a signal to SIG_IGN, or if you set it to SIG_DFL and the default action is to ignore that signal, then any pending signals of that type are discarded (even if they are blocked). Discarding the pending signals means that they will never be delivered, not even if you subsequently specify another action and unblock this kind of signal.

The **signal** function returns the action that was previously in effect for the specified *signum*. You can save this value and restore it later by calling **signal** again.

If **signal** can't honor the request, it returns SIG_ERR instead. The following **errno** error conditions are defined for this function:

EINVAL You specified an invalid *signum*; or you tried to ignore or provide a handler for SIGKILL or SIGSTOP.

Here is a simple example of setting up a handler to delete temporary files when certain fatal signals happen:

```
#include <signal.h>

void
termination_handler (int signum)
```

```
{
  struct temp_file *p;

  for (p = temp_file_list; p; p = p->next)
    unlink (p->name);
}

int
main (void)
{
  ...
  if (signal (SIGINT, termination_handler) == SIG_IGN)
    signal (SIGINT, SIG_IGN);
  if (signal (SIGHUP, termination_handler) == SIG_IGN)
    signal (SIGHUP, SIG_IGN);
  if (signal (SIGTERM, termination_handler) == SIG_IGN)
    signal (SIGTERM, SIG_IGN);
  ...
}
```

Note how if a given signal was previously set to be ignored, this code avoids altering that setting. This is because non-job-control shells often ignore certain signals when starting children, and it is important for the children to respect this.

We do not handle `SIGQUIT` or the program error signals in this example because these are designed to provide information for debugging (a core dump), and the temporary files may give useful information.

sighandler_t ssignal (int *signum*, sighandler_t *action*) *Function*

The `ssignal` function does the same thing as `signal`; it is provided only for compatibility with SVID.

sighandler_t SIG_ERR *Macro*

The value of this macro is used as the return value from `signal` to indicate an error.

21.3.2 Advanced Signal Handling

The `sigaction` function has the same basic effect as `signal`: to specify how a signal should be handled by the process. However, `sigaction` offers more control, at the expense of more complexity. In particular, `sigaction` allows you to specify additional flags to control when the signal is generated and how the handler is invoked.

The `sigaction` function is declared in 'signal.h'.

struct sigaction   Data Type

Structures of type `struct sigaction` are used in the `sigaction` function to specify all the information about how to handle a particular signal. This structure contains at least the following members:

`sighandler_t sa_handler`
: This is used in the same way as the *action* argument to the `signal` function. The value can be `SIG_DFL`, `SIG_IGN`, or a function pointer. See Section 21.3.1 [Basic Signal Handling], page 384.

`sigset_t sa_mask`
: This specifies a set of signals to be blocked while the handler runs. Blocking is explained in Section 21.7.5 [Blocking Signals for a Handler], page 412. Note that the signal that was delivered is automatically blocked by default before its handler is started; this is true regardless of the value in `sa_mask`. If you want that signal not to be blocked within its handler, you must write code in the handler to unblock it.

`int sa_flags`
: This specifies various flags which can affect the behavior of the signal. These are described in more detail in Section 21.3.5 [Flags for "code sigaction], page 389.

int sigaction (int *signum*, const struct sigaction *action*, struct sigaction *old-action*)   Function

The *action* argument is used to set up a new action for the signal *signum*, while the *old-action* argument is used to return information about the action previously associated with this symbol. (In other words, *old-action* has the same purpose as the `signal` function's return value—you can check to see what the old action in effect for the signal was, and restore it later if you want.)

Either *action* or *old-action* can be a null pointer. If *old-action* is a null pointer, this simply suppresses the return of information about the old action. If *action* is a null pointer, the action associated with the signal *signum* is unchanged; this allows you to inquire about how a signal is being handled without changing that handling.

The return value from `sigaction` is zero if it succeeds, and -1 on failure. The following `errno` error conditions are defined for this function:

`EINVAL`
: The *signum* argument is not valid, or you are trying to trap or ignore `SIGKILL` or `SIGSTOP`.

21.3.3 Interaction of `signal` and `sigaction`

It's possible to use both the `signal` and `sigaction` functions within a single program, but you have to be careful because they can interact in slightly strange ways.

The `sigaction` function specifies more information than the `signal` function, so the return value from `signal` cannot express the full range of `sigaction` possibilities. Therefore, if you use `signal` to save and later reestablish an action, it may not be able to reestablish properly a handler that was established with `sigaction`.

To avoid having problems as a result, always use `sigaction` to save and restore a handler if your program uses `sigaction` at all. Since `sigaction` is more general, it can properly save and reestablish any action, regardless of whether it was established originally with `signal` or `sigaction`.

On some systems if you establish an action with `signal` and then examine it with `sigaction`, the handler address that you get may not be the same as what you specified with `signal`. It may not even be suitable for use as an action argument with `signal`. But you can rely on using it as an argument to `sigaction`. This problem never happens on the GNU system.

So, you're better off using one or the other of the mechanisms consistently within a single program.

Portability Note: The basic `signal` function is a feature of ANSI C, while `sigaction` is part of the POSIX.1 standard. If you are concerned about portability to non-POSIX systems, then you should use the `signal` function instead.

21.3.4 `sigaction` Function Example

In Section 21.3.1 [Basic Signal Handling], page 384, we gave an example of establishing a simple handler for termination signals using `signal`. Here is an equivalent example using `sigaction`:

```
#include <signal.h>

void
termination_handler (int signum)
{
  struct temp_file *p;

  for (p = temp_file_list; p; p = p->next)
    unlink (p->name);
}

int
main (void)
{
```

Chapter 21: Signal Handling

```
    ...
    struct sigaction new_action, old_action;

    /* Set up the structure to specify the new action. */
    new_action.sa_handler = termination_handler;
    sigemptyset (&new_action.sa_mask);
    new_action.sa_flags = 0;

    sigaction (SIGINT, NULL, &old_action);
    if (old_action.sa_handler != SIG_IGN)
      sigaction (SIGINT, &new_action, NULL);
    sigaction (SIGHUP, NULL, &old_action);
    if (old_action.sa_handler != SIG_IGN)
      sigaction (SIGHUP, &new_action, NULL);
    sigaction (SIGTERM, NULL, &old_action);
    if (old_action.sa_handler != SIG_IGN)
      sigaction (SIGTERM, &new_action, NULL);
    ...
}
```

The program just loads the `new_action` structure with the desired parameters and passes it in the `sigaction` call. The usage of `sigemptyset` is described later; see Section 21.7 [Blocking Signals], page 408.

As in the example using `signal`, we avoid handling signals previously set to be ignored. Here we can avoid altering the signal handler even momentarily, by using the feature of `sigaction` that lets us examine the current action without specifying a new one.

Here is another example. It retrieves information about the current action for `SIGINT` without changing that action.

```
    struct sigaction query_action;

    if (sigaction (SIGINT, NULL, &query_action) < 0)
      /* sigaction returns -1 in case of error. */
    else if (query_action.sa_handler == SIG_DFL)
      /* SIGINT is handled in the default, fatal manner. */
    else if (query_action.sa_handler == SIG_IGN)
      /* SIGINT is ignored. */
    else
      /* A programmer-defined signal handler is in effect. */
```

21.3.5 Flags for `sigaction`

The `sa_flags` member of the `sigaction` structure is a catch-all for special features. Most of the time, `SA_RESTART` is a good value to use for this field.

The value of `sa_flags` is interpreted as a bit mask. Thus, you should choose the flags you want to set, OR those flags together, and store the result in the `sa_flags` member of your `sigaction` structure.

Each signal number has its own set of flags. Each call to `sigaction` affects one particular signal number, and the flags that you specify apply only to that particular signal.

In the GNU C library, establishing a handler with `signal` sets all the flags to zero except for `SA_RESTART`, whose value depends on the settings you have made with `siginterrupt`. See Section 21.5 [Primitives Interrupted by Signals], page 402, to see what this is about.

These macros are defined in the header file 'signal.h'.

int SA_NOCLDSTOP *Macro*
This flag is meaningful only for the `SIGCHLD` signal. When the flag is set, the system delivers the signal for a terminated child process but not for one that is stopped. By default, `SIGCHLD` is delivered for both terminated children and stopped children.

Setting this flag for a signal other than `SIGCHLD` has no effect.

int SA_ONSTACK *Macro*
If this flag is set for a particular signal number, the system uses the signal stack when delivering that kind of signal. See Section 21.9 [Using a Separate Signal Stack], page 418. If a signal with this flag arrives and you have not set a signal stack, the system terminates the program with `SIGILL`.

int SA_RESTART *Macro*
This flag controls what happens when a signal is delivered during certain primitives (such as `open`, `read` or `write`), and the signal handler returns normally. There are two alternatives: the library function can resume, or it can return failure with error code `EINTR`.

The choice is controlled by the `SA_RESTART` flag for the particular kind of signal that was delivered. If the flag is set, returning from a handler resumes the library function. If the flag is clear, returning from a handler makes the function fail. See Section 21.5 [Primitives Interrupted by Signals], page 402.

21.3.6 Initial Signal Actions

When a new process is created (see Section 23.4 [Creating a Process], page 445), it inherits handling of signals from its parent process. However, when you load a new process image using the `exec` function (see Section 23.5 [Executing a File], page 446), any signals that you've defined your own handlers for revert to their `SIG_DFL` handling. (If you think about it a little, this makes sense; the handler functions from the old program are specific to that program, and aren't even present in the address space of the new program image.) Of course, the new program can establish its own handlers.

Chapter 21: Signal Handling

When a program is run by a shell, the shell normally sets the initial actions for the child process to `SIG_DFL` or `SIG_IGN`, as appropriate. It's a good idea to check to make sure that the shell has not set up an initial action of `SIG_IGN` before you establish your own signal handlers.

Here is an example of how to establish a handler for `SIGHUP`, but not if `SIGHUP` is currently ignored:

```
...
struct sigaction temp;

sigaction (SIGHUP, NULL, &temp);

if (temp.sa_handler != SIG_IGN)
  {
    temp.sa_handler = handle_sighup;
    sigemptyset (&temp.sa_mask);
    sigaction (SIGHUP, &temp, NULL);
  }
```

21.4 Defining Signal Handlers

This section describes how to write a signal handler function that can be established with the `signal` or `sigaction` functions.

A signal handler is just a function that you compile together with the rest of the program. Instead of directly invoking the function, you use `signal` or `sigaction` to tell the operating system to call it when a signal arrives. This is known as *establishing* the handler. See Section 21.3 [Specifying Signal Actions], page 384.

There are two basic strategies you can use in signal handler functions:

- You can have the handler function note that the signal arrived by tweaking some global data structures, and then return normally.
- You can have the handler function terminate the program or transfer control to a point where it can recover from the situation that caused the signal.

You need to take special care in writing handler functions because they can be called asynchronously. That is, a handler might be called at any point in the program, unpredictably. If two signals arrive during a very short interval, one handler can run within another. This section describes what your handler should do, and what you should avoid.

21.4.1 Signal Handlers that Return

Handlers which return normally are usually used for signals such as `SIGALRM` and the I/O and interprocess communication signals. But a handler for `SIGINT` might also return normally after setting a flag that tells the program to exit at a convenient time.

It is not safe to return normally from the handler for a program error signal, because the behavior of the program when the handler function returns is not defined after a program error. See Section 21.2.1 [Program Error Signals], page 374.

Handlers that return normally must modify some global variable in order to have any effect. Typically, the variable is one that is examined periodically by the program during normal operation. Its data type should be `sig_atomic_t` for reasons described in Section 21.4.7 [Atomic Data Access and Signal Handling], page 400.

Here is a simple example of such a program. It executes the body of the loop until it has noticed that a `SIGALRM` signal has arrived. This technique is useful because it allows the iteration in progress when the signal arrives to complete before the loop exits.

```
#include <signal.h>
#include <stdio.h>
#include <stdlib.h>

/* This flag controls termination of the main loop. */
volatile sig_atomic_t keep_going = 1;

/* The signal handler just clears the flag and re-enables itself. */
void
catch_alarm (int sig)
{
  keep_going = 0;
  signal (sig, catch_alarm);
}

void
do_stuff (void)
{
  puts ("Doing stuff while waiting for alarm....");
}

int
main (void)
{
  /* Establish a handler for SIGALRM signals. */
  signal (SIGALRM, catch_alarm);

  /* Set an alarm to go off in a little while. */
  alarm (2);

  /* Check the flag once in a while to see when to quit. */
  while (keep_going)
    do_stuff ();
```

```
    return EXIT_SUCCESS;
}
```

21.4.2 Handlers That Terminate the Process

Handler functions that terminate the program are typically used to cause orderly cleanup or recovery from program error signals and interactive interrupts.

The cleanest way for a handler to terminate the process is to raise the same signal that ran the handler in the first place. Here is how to do this:

```
volatile sig_atomic_t fatal_error_in_progress = 0;

void
fatal_error_signal (int sig)
{
  /* Since this handler is established for more than one kind of signal,
     it might still get invoked recursively by delivery of some other kind
     of signal. Use a static variable to keep track of that. */
  if (fatal_error_in_progress)
    raise (sig);
  fatal_error_in_progress = 1;

  /* Now do the clean up actions:
     - reset terminal modes
     - kill child processes
     - remove lock files */
  ...

  /* Now reraise the signal. Since the signal is blocked,
     it will receive its default handling, which is
     to terminate the process. We could just call
     exit or abort, but reraising the signal
     sets the return status from the process correctly. */
  raise (sig);
}
```

21.4.3 Nonlocal Control Transfer in Handlers

You can do a nonlocal transfer of control out of a signal handler using the setjmp and longjmp facilities (see Chapter 20 [Non-Local Exits], page 367).

When the handler does a nonlocal control transfer, the part of the program that was running will not continue. If this part of the program was in the middle of updating an important data structure, the data structure will remain inconsistent. Since the program does not terminate, the inconsistency is likely to be noticed later on.

There are two ways to avoid this problem. One is to block the signal for the parts of the program that update important data structures. Blocking the signal delays its delivery until it is unblocked, once the critical updating is finished. See Section 21.7 [Blocking Signals], page 408.

The other way to re-initialize the crucial data structures in the signal handler, or make their values consistent.

Here is a rather schematic example showing the reinitialization of one global variable.

```
#include <signal.h>
#include <setjmp.h>

jmp_buf return_to_top_level;

volatile sig_atomic_t waiting_for_input;

void
handle_sigint (int signum)
{
  /* We may have been waiting for input when the signal arrived,
     but we are no longer waiting once we transfer control. */
  waiting_for_input = 0;
  longjmp (return_to_top_level, 1);
}

int
main (void)
{
  ...
  signal (SIGINT, sigint_handler);
  ...
  while (1) {
    prepare_for_command ();
    if (setjmp (return_to_top_level) == 0)
      read_and_execute_command ();
  }
}

/* Imagine this is a subroutine used by various commands. */
char *
read_data ()
{
  if (input_from_terminal) {
    waiting_for_input = 1;
    ...
    waiting_for_input = 0;
  } else {
    ...
  }
}
```

21.4.4 Signals Arriving While a Handler Runs

What happens if another signal arrives while your signal handler function is running?

Chapter 21: Signal Handling

When the handler for a particular signal is invoked, that signal is automatically blocked until the handler returns. That means that if two signals of the same kind arrive close together, the second one will be held until the first has been handled. (The handler can explicitly unblock the signal using `sigprocmask`, if you want to allow more signals of this type to arrive; see Section 21.7.3 [Process Signal Mask], page 410.)

However, your handler can still be interrupted by delivery of another kind of signal. To avoid this, you can use the `sa_mask` member of the action structure passed to `sigaction` to explicitly specify which signals should be blocked while the signal handler runs. These signals are in addition to the signal for which the handler was invoked, and any other signals that are normally blocked by the process. See Section 21.7.5 [Blocking Signals for a Handler], page 412.

When the handler returns, the set of blocked signals is restored to the value it had before the handler ran. So using `sigprocmask` inside the handler only affects what signals can arrive during the execution of the handler itself, not what signals can arrive once the handler returns.

Portability Note: Always use `sigaction` to establish a handler for a signal that you expect to receive asynchronously, if you want your program to work properly on System V Unix. On this system, the handling of a signal whose handler was established with `signal` automatically sets the signal's action back to `SIG_DFL`, and the handler must re-establish itself each time it runs. This practice, while inconvenient, does work when signals cannot arrive in succession. However, if another signal can arrive right away, it may arrive before the handler can re-establish itself. Then the second signal would receive the default handling, which could terminate the process.

21.4.5 Signals Close Together Merge into One

If multiple signals of the same type are delivered to your process before your signal handler has a chance to be invoked at all, the handler may only be invoked once, as if only a single signal had arrived. In effect, the signals merge into one. This situation can arise when the signal is blocked, or in a multiprocessing environment where the system is busy running some other processes while the signals are delivered. This means, for example, that you cannot reliably use a signal handler to count signals. The only distinction you can reliably make is whether at least one signal has arrived since a given time in the past.

Here is an example of a handler for `SIGCHLD` that compensates for the fact that the number of signals recieved may not equal the number of child processes generate them. It assumes that the program keeps track of all the child processes with a chain of structures as follows:

```
struct process
```

```
{
  struct process *next;
  /* The process ID of this child.  */
  int pid;
  /* The descriptor of the pipe or pseudo terminal
     on which output comes from this child.  */
  int input_descriptor;
  /* Nonzero if this process has stopped or terminated.  */
  sig_atomic_t have_status;
  /* The status of this child; 0 if running,
     otherwise a status value from waitpid.  */
  int status;
};

struct process *process_list;
```

This example also uses a flag to indicate whether signals have arrived since some time in the past—whenever the program last cleared it to zero.

```
/* Nonzero means some child's status has changed
   so look at process_list for the details.  */
int process_status_change;
```

Here is the handler itself:

```
void
sigchld_handler (int signo)
{
  int old_errno = errno;

  while (1) {
    register int pid;
    int w;
    struct process *p;

    /* Keep asking for a status until we get a definitive result.  */
    do
      {
        errno = 0;
        pid = waitpid (WAIT_ANY, &w, WNOHANG | WUNTRACED);
      }
    while (pid <= 0 && errno == EINTR);

    if (pid <= 0) {
      /* A real failure means there are no more
         stopped or terminated child processes, so return.  */
      errno = old_errno;
      return;
    }

    /* Find the process that signaled us, and record its status.  */

    for (p = process_list; p; p = p->next)
      if (p->pid == pid) {
        p->status = w;
```

Chapter 21: Signal Handling

```
            /* Indicate that the status field
                  has data to look at.  We do this only after storing it.  */
            p->have_status = 1;

            /* If process has terminated, stop waiting for its output.  */
            if (WIFSIGNALED (w) || WIFEXITED (w))
              if (p->input_descriptor)
                FD_CLR (p->input_descriptor, &input_wait_mask);

            /* The program should check this flag from time to time
                  to see if there is any news in process_list.  */
            ++process_status_change;
          }

        /* Loop around to handle all the processes
              that have something to tell us.  */
      }
    }
```

Here is the proper way to check the flag `process_status_change`:

```
if (process_status_change) {
  struct process *p;
  process_status_change = 0;
  for (p = process_list; p; p = p->next)
    if (p->have_status) {
      ... Examine p->status ...
    }
}
```

It is vital to clear the flag before examining the list; otherwise, if a signal were delivered just before the clearing of the flag, and after the appropriate element of the process list had been checked, the status change would go unnoticed until the next signal arrived to set the flag again. You could, of course, avoid this problem by blocking the signal while scanning the list, but it is much more elegant to guarantee correctness by doing things in the right order.

The loop which checks process status avoids examining `p->status` until it sees that status has been validly stored. This is to make sure that the status cannot change in the middle of accessing it. Once `p->have_status` is set, it means that the child process is stopped or terminated, and in either case, it cannot stop or terminate again until the program has taken notice. See Section 21.4.7.3 [Atomic Usage Patterns], page 402, for more information about coping with interruptions during accessings of a variable.

Here is another way you can test whether the handler has run since the last time you checked. This technique uses a counter which is never changed outside the handler. Instead of clearing the count, the program remembers the previous value and sees whether it has changed since the previous check. The advantage of this method is that different parts of the program can

check independently, each part checking whether there has been a signal
since that part last checked.

```
sig_atomic_t process_status_change;

sig_atomic_t last_process_status_change;

...
{
  sig_atomic_t prev = last_process_status_change;
  last_process_status_change = process_status_change;
  if (last_process_status_change != prev) {
    struct process *p;
    for (p = process_list; p; p = p->next)
      if (p->have_status) {
        ... Examine p->status ...
      }
  }
}
```

21.4.6 Signal Handling and Nonreentrant Functions

Handler functions usually don't do very much. The best practice is to write a handler that does nothing but set an external variable that the program checks regularly, and leave all serious work to the program. This is best because the handler can be called at asynchronously, at unpredictable times—perhaps in the middle of a primitive function, or even between the beginning and the end of a C operator that requires multiple instructions. The data structures being manipulated might therefore be in an inconsistent state when the handler function is invoked. Even copying one `int` variable into another can take two instructions on most machines.

This means you have to be very careful about what you do in a signal handler.

- If your handler needs to access any global variables from your program, declare those variables `volatile`. This tells the compiler that the value of the variable might change asynchronously, and inhibits certain optimizations that would be invalidated by such modifications.

- If you call a function in the handler, make sure it is *reentrant* with respect to signals, or else make sure that the signal cannot interrupt a call to a related function.

A function can be non-reentrant if it uses memory that is not on the stack.

- If a function uses a static variable or a global variable, or a dynamically-allocated object that it finds for itself, then it is non-reentrant and any two calls to the function can interfere.

Chapter 21: Signal Handling

For example, suppose that the signal handler uses `gethostbyname`. This function returns its value in a static object, reusing the same object each time. If the signal happens to arrive during a call to `gethostbyname`, or even after one (while the program is still using the value), it will clobber the value that the program asked for.

However, if the program does not use `gethostbyname` or any other function that returns information in the same object, or if it always blocks signals around each use, then you are safe.

There are a large number of library functions that return values in a fixed object, always reusing the same object in this fashion, and all of them cause the same problem. The description of a function in this manual always mentions this behavior.

- If a function uses and modifies an object that you supply, then it is potentially non-reentrant; two calls can interfere if they use the same object.

  This case arises when you do I/O using streams. Suppose that the signal handler prints a message with `fprintf`. Suppose that the program was in the middle of an `fprintf` call using the same stream when the signal was delivered. Both the signal handler's message and the program's data could be corrupted, because both calls operate on the same data structure—the stream itself.

  However, if you know that the stream that the handler uses cannot possibly be used by the program at a time when signals can arrive, then you are safe. It is no problem if the program uses some other stream.

- On most systems, `malloc` and `free` are not reentrant, because they use a static data structure which records what memory blocks are free. As a result, no library functions that allocate or free memory are reentrant. This includes functions that allocate space to store a result.

  The best way to avoid the need to allocate memory in a handler is to allocate in advance space for signal handlers to use.

  The best way to avoid freeing memory in a handler is to flag or record the objects to be freed, and have the program check from time to time whether anything is waiting to be freed. But this must be done with care, because placing an object on a chain is not atomic, and if it is interrupted by another signal handler that does the same thing, you could "lose" one of the objects.

  The relocating allocation functions (see Section 3.6 [Relocating Allocator], page 52) are certainly not safe to use in a signal handler.

- Any function that modifies `errno` is non-reentrant, but you can correct for this: in the handler, save the original value of `errno` and restore it before returning normally. This prevents errors that occur within the signal handler from being confused with errors from system calls at the point the program is interrupted to run the handler.

This technique is generally applicable; if you want to call in a handler a function that modifies a particular object in memory, you can make this safe by saving and restoring that object.

- Merely reading from a memory object is safe provided that you can deal with any of the values that might appear in the object at a time when the signal can be delivered. Keep in mind that assignment to some data types requires more than one instruction, which means that the handler could run "in the middle of" an assignment to the variable if its type is not atomic. See Section 21.4.7 [Atomic Data Access and Signal Handling], page 400.

- Merely writing into a memory object is safe as long as a sudden change in the value, at any time when the handler might run, will not disturb anything.

21.4.7 Atomic Data Access and Signal Handling

Whether the data in your application concerns atoms, or mere text, you have to be careful about the fact that access to a single datum is not necessarily *atomic*. This means that it can take more than one instruction to read or write a single object. In such cases, a signal handler might in the middle of reading or writing the object.

There are three ways you can cope with this problem. You can use data types that are always accessed atomically; you can carefully arrange that nothing untoward happens if an access is interrupted, or you can block all signals around any access that had better not be interrupted (see Section 21.7 [Blocking Signals], page 408).

21.4.7.1 Problems with Non-Atomic Access

Here is an example which shows what can happen if a signal handler runs in the middle of modifying a variable. (Interrupting the reading of a variable can also lead to paradoxical results, but here we only show writing.)

```
#include <signal.h>
#include <stdio.h>

struct two_words { int a, b; } memory;

void
handler(int signum)
{
   printf ("%d,%d\n", memory.a, memory.b);
   alarm (1);
}
```

Chapter 21: Signal Handling   401

```
int
main (void)
{
   static struct two_words zeros = { 0, 0 }, ones = { 1, 1 };
   signal (SIGALRM, handler);
   memory = zeros;
   alarm (1);
   while (1)
     {
       memory = zeros;
       memory = ones;
     }
}
```

This program fills `memory` with zeros, ones, zeros, ones, alternating forever; meanwhile, once per second, the alarm signal handler prints the current contents. (Calling `printf` in the handler is safe in this program because it is certainly not being called outside the handler when the signal happens.)

Clearly, this program can print a pair of zeros or a pair of ones. But that's not all it can do! On most machines, it takes several instructions to store a new value in `memory`, and the value is stored one word at a time. If the signal is delivered in between these instructions, the handler might find that `memory.a` is zero and `memory.b` is one (or vice versa).

On some machines it may be possible to store a new value in `memory` with just one instruction that cannot be interrupted. On these machines, the handler will always print two zeros or two ones.

21.4.7.2 Atomic Types

To avoid uncertainty about interrupting access to a variable, you can use a particular data type for which access is always atomic: `sig_atomic_t`. Reading and writing this data type is guaranteed to happen in a single instruction, so there's no way for a handler to run "in the middle" of an access.

The type `sig_atomic_t` is always an integer data type, but which one it is, and how many bits it contains, may vary from machine to machine.

sig_atomic_t   Data Type
This is an integer data type. Objects of this type are always accessed atomically.

In practice, you can assume that `int` and other integer types no longer than `int` are atomic. You can also assume that pointer types are atomic; that is very convenient. Both of these are true on all of the machines that the GNU C library supports, and on all POSIX systems we know of.

21.4.7.3 Atomic Usage Patterns

Certain patterns of access avoid any problem even if an access is interrupted. For example, a flag which is set by the handler, and tested and cleared by the main program from time to time, is always safe even if access actually requires two instructions. To show that this is so, we must consider each access that could be interrupted, and show that there is no problem if it is interrupted.

An interrupt in the middle of testing the flag is safe because either it's recognized to be nonzero, in which case the precise value doesn't matter, or it will be seen to be nonzero the next time it's tested.

An interrupt in the middle of clearing the flag is no problem because either the value ends up zero, which is what happens if a signal comes in just before the flag is cleared, or the value ends up nonzero, and subsequent events occur as if the signal had come in just after the flag was cleared. As long as the code handles both of these cases properly, it can also handle a signal in the middle of clearing the flag. (This is an example of the sort of reasoning you need to do to figure out whether non-atomic usage is safe.)

Sometimes you can insure uninterrupted access to one object by protecting its use with another object, perhaps one whose type guarantees atomicity. See Section 21.4.5 [Signals Close Together Merge into One], page 395, for an example.

21.5 Primitives Interrupted by Signals

A signal can arrive and be handled while an I/O primitive such as `open` or `read` is waiting for an I/O device. If the signal handler returns, the system faces the question: what should happen next?

POSIX specifies one approach: make the primitive fail right away. The error code for this kind of failure is `EINTR`. This is flexible, but usually inconvenient. Typically, POSIX applications that use signal handlers must check for `EINTR` after each library function that can return it, in order to try the call again. Often programmers forget to check, which is a common source of error.

The GNU library provides a convenient way to retry a call after a temporary failure, with the macro `TEMP_FAILURE_RETRY`:

TEMP_FAILURE_RETRY (*expression*) *Macro*

    This macro evaluates *expression* once. If it fails and reports error code `EINTR`, `TEMP_FAILURE_RETRY` evaluates it again, and over and over until the result is not a temporary failure.

    The value returned by `TEMP_FAILURE_RETRY` is whatever value *expression* produced.

BSD avoids `EINTR` entirely and provides a more convenient approach: to restart the interrupted primitive, instead of making it fail. If you choose this approach, you need not be concerned with `EINTR`.

You can choose either approach with the GNU library. If you use `sigaction` to establish a signal handler, you can specify how that handler should behave. If you specify the `SA_RESTART` flag, return from that handler will resume a primitive; otherwise, return from that handler will cause `EINTR`. See Section 21.3.5 [Flags for "code sigaction], page 389.

Another way to specify the choice is with the `siginterrupt` function. See Section 21.10.1 [BSD Function to Establish a Handler], page 421.

When you don't specify with `sigaction` or `siginterrupt` what a particular handler should do, it uses a default choice. The default choice in the GNU library depends on the feature test macros you have defined. If you define `_BSD_SOURCE` or `_GNU_SOURCE` before calling `signal`, the default is to resume primitives; otherwise, the default is to make them fail with `EINTR`. (The library contains alternate versions of the `signal` function, and the feature test macros determine which one you really call.) See Section 1.3.4 [Feature Test Macros], page 8.

The description of each primitive affected by this issue lists `EINTR` among the error codes it can return.

There is one situation where resumption never happens no matter which choice you make: when a data-transfer function such as `read` or `write` is interrupted by a signal after transferring part of the data. In this case, the function returns the number of bytes already transferred, indicating partial success.

This might at first appear to cause unreliable behavior on record-oriented devices (including datagram sockets; see Section 11.9 [Datagram Socket Operations], page 243), where splitting one `read` or `write` into two would read or write two records. Actually, there is no problem, because interruption after a partial transfer cannot happen on such devices; they always transfer an entire record in one burst, with no waiting once data transfer has started.

21.6 Generating Signals

Besides signals that are generated as a result of a hardware trap or interrupt, your program can explicitly send signals to itself or to another process.

21.6.1 Signaling Yourself

A process can send itself a signal with the `raise` function. This function is declared in 'signal.h'.

int raise (int *signum*)   *Function*
   The `raise` function sends the signal *signum* to the calling process. It
   returns zero if successful and a nonzero value if it fails. About the only
   reason for failure would be if the value of *signum* is invalid.

int gsignal (int *signum*)   *Function*
   The `gsignal` function does the same thing as `raise`; it is provided
   only for compatibility with SVID.

One convenient use for `raise` is to reproduce the default behavior of a
signal that you have trapped. For instance, suppose a user of your program
types the SUSP character (usually *C-z*; see Section 12.4.9 [Special Characters], page 270) to send it an interactive stop stop signal (`SIGTSTP`), and you
want to clean up some internal data buffers before stopping. You might set
this up like this:

```
#include <signal.h>

/* When a stop signal arrives, set the action back to the default
   and then resend the signal after doing cleanup actions. */

void
tstp_handler (int sig)
{
  signal (SIGTSTP, SIG_DFL);
  /* Do cleanup actions here. */
  ...
  raise (SIGTSTP);
}

/* When the process is continued again, restore the signal handler. */

void
cont_handler (int sig)
{
  signal (SIGCONT, cont_handler);
  signal (SIGTSTP, tstp_handler);
}

/* Enable both handlers during program initialization. */

int
main (void)
{
  signal (SIGCONT, cont_handler);
  signal (SIGTSTP, tstp_handler);
  ...
}
```

Portability note: `raise` was invented by the ANSI C committee. Older
systems may not support it, so using `kill` may be more portable. See
Section 21.6.2 [Signaling Another Process], page 405.

21.6.2 Signaling Another Process

The `kill` function can be used to send a signal to another process. In spite of its name, it can be used for a lot of things other than causing a process to terminate. Some examples of situations where you might want to send signals between processes are:

- A parent process starts a child to perform a task—perhaps having the child running an infinite loop—and then terminates the child when the task is no longer needed.
- A process executes as part of a group, and needs to terminate or notify the other processes in the group when an error or other event occurs.
- Two processes need to synchronize while working together.

This section assumes that you know a little bit about how processes work. For more information on this subject, see Chapter 23 [Processes], page 443.

The `kill` function is declared in 'signal.h'.

int kill (pid_t *pid*, int *signum*) *Function*
   The `kill` function sends the signal *signum* to the process or process group specified by *pid*. Besides the signals listed in Section 21.2 [Standard Signals], page 373, *signum* can also have a value of zero to check the validity of the *pid*.

   The *pid* specifies the process or process group to receive the signal:

   pid > 0   The process whose identifier is *pid*.

   pid == 0   All processes in the same process group as the sender.

   pid < -1   The process group whose identifier is −*pid*.

   pid == -1 If the process is privileged, send the signal to all processes except for some special system processes. Otherwise, send the signal to all processes with the same effective user ID.

   A process can send a signal *signum* to itself with a call like `kill (getpid(), signum)`. If `kill` is used by a process to send a signal to itself, and the signal is not blocked, then `kill` delivers at least one signal (which might be some other pending unblocked signal instead of the signal *signum*) to that process before it returns.

   The return value from `kill` is zero if the signal can be sent successfully. Otherwise, no signal is sent, and a value of -1 is returned. If *pid* specifies sending a signal to several processes, `kill` succeeds if it can send the signal to at least one of them. There's no way you can tell which of the processes got the signal or whether all of them did.

   The following `errno` error conditions are defined for this function:

EINVAL   The *signum* argument is an invalid or unsupported number.

EPERM   You do not have the privilege to send a signal to the process or any of the processes in the process group named by *pid*.

ESCRH   The *pid* argument does not refer to an existing process or group.

int **killpg** (int *pgid*, int *signum*)   Function
This is similar to `kill`, but sends signal *signum* to the process group *pgid*. This function is provided for compatibility with BSD; using `kill` to do this is more portable.

As a simple example of `kill`, the call `kill (getpid (), sig)` has the same effect as `raise (sig)`.

21.6.3 Permission for using `kill`

There are restrictions that prevent you from using `kill` to send signals to any random process. These are intended to prevent antisocial behavior such as arbitrarily killing off processes belonging to another user. In typical use, `kill` is used to pass signals between parent, child, and sibling processes, and in these situations you normally do have permission to send signals. The only common execption is when you run a setuid program in a child process; if the program changes its real UID as well as its effective UID, you may not have permission to send a signal. The `su` program does this.

Whether a process has permission to send a signal to another process is determined by the user IDs of the two processes. This concept is discussed in detail in Section 25.2 [The Persona of a Process], page 479.

Generally, for a process to be able to send a signal to another process, either the sending process must belong to a privileged user (like '`root`'), or the real or effective user ID of the sending process must match the real or effective user ID of the receiving process. If the receiving process has changed its effective user ID from the set-user-ID mode bit on its process image file, then the owner of the process image file is used in place of its current effective user ID. In some implementations, a parent process might be able to send signals to a child process even if the user ID's don't match, and other implementations might enforce other restrictions.

The `SIGCONT` signal is a special case. It can be sent if the sender is part of the same session as the receiver, regardless of user IDs.

Chapter 21: Signal Handling

21.6.4 Using `kill` for Communication

Here is a longer example showing how signals can be used for interprocess communication. This is what the SIGUSR1 and SIGUSR2 signals are provided for. Since these signals are fatal by default, the process that is supposed to receive them must trap them through `signal` or `sigaction`.

In this example, a parent process forks a child process and then waits for the child to complete its initialization. The child process tells the parent when it is ready by sending it a SIGUSR1 signal, using the `kill` function.

```c
#include <signal.h>
#include <stdio.h>
#include <sys/types.h>
#include <unistd.h>

/* When a SIGUSR1 signal arrives, set this variable. */
volatile sig_atomic_t usr_interrupt = 0;

void
synch_signal (int sig)
{
  usr_interrupt = 1;
}

/* The child process executes this function. */
void
child_function (void)
{
  /* Perform initialization. */
  printf ("I'm here!!!  My pid is %d.\n", (int) getpid ());

  /* Let parent know you're done. */
  kill (getppid (), SIGUSR1);

  /* Continue with execution. */
  puts ("Bye, now....");
  exit (0);
}

int
main (void)
{
  struct sigaction usr_action;
  sigset_t block_mask;
  pid_t child_id;

  /* Establish the signal handler. */
  sigfillset (&block_mask);
  usr_action.sa_handler = synch_signal;
  usr_action.sa_mask = block_mask;
  usr_action.sa_flags = 0;
  sigaction (SIGUSR1, &usr_action, NULL);
```

```
  /* Create the child process. */
  child_id = fork ();
  if (child_id == 0)
    child_function ();          /* Does not return. */

  /* Busy wait for the child to send a signal. */
  while (!usr_interrupt)
    ;
  /* Now continue execution. */
  puts ("That's all, folks!");

  return 0;
}
```

This example uses a busy wait, which is bad, because it wastes CPU cycles that other programs could otherwise use. It is better to ask the system to wait until the signal arrives. See the example in Section 21.8 [Waiting for a Signal], page 416.

21.7 Blocking Signals

Blocking a signal means telling the operating system to hold it and deliver it later. Generally, a program does not block signals indefinitely—it might as well ignore them by setting their actions to `SIG_IGN`. But it is useful to block signals briefly, to prevent them from interrupting sensitive operations. For instance:

- You can use the `sigprocmask` function to block signals while you modify global variables that are also modified by the handlers for these signals.
- You can set `sa_mask` in your `sigaction` call to block certain signals while a particular signal handler runs. This way, the signal handler can run without being interrupted itself by signals.

21.7.1 Why Blocking Signals is Useful

Temporary blocking of signals with `sigprocmask` gives you a way to prevent interrupts during critical parts of your code. If signals arrive in that part of the program, they are delivered later, after you unblock them.

One example where this is useful is for sharing data between a signal handler and the rest of the program. If the type of the data is not `sig_atomic_t` (see Section 21.4.7 [Atomic Data Access and Signal Handling], page 400), then the signal handler could run when the rest of the program has only half finished reading or writing the data. This would lead to confusing consequences.

To make the program reliable, you can prevent the signal handler from running while the rest of the program is examining or modifying that data—

Chapter 21: Signal Handling

by blocking the appropriate signal around the parts of the program that touch the data.

Blocking signals is also necessary when you want to perform a certain action only if a signal has not arrived. Suppose that the handler for the signal sets a flag of type `sig_atomic_t`; you would like to test the flag and perform the action if the flag is not set. This is unreliable. Suppose the signal is delivered immediately after you test the flag, but before the consequent action: then the program will perform the action even though the signal has arrived.

The only way to test reliably for whether a signal has yet arrived is to test while the signal is blocked.

21.7.2 Signal Sets

All of the signal blocking functions use a data structure called a *signal set* to specify what signals are affected. Thus, every activity involves two stages: creating the signal set, and then passing it as an argument to a library function.

These facilities are declared in the header file '`signal.h`'.

sigset_t   Data Type

The `sigset_t` data type is used to represent a signal set. Internally, it may be implemented as either an integer or structure type.

For portability, use only the functions described in this section to initialize, change, and retrieve information from `sigset_t` objects— don't try to manipulate them directly.

There are two ways to initialize a signal set. You can initially specify it to be empty with `sigemptyset` and then add specified signals individually. Or you can specify it to be full with `sigfillset` and then delete specified signals individually.

You must always initialize the signal set with one of these two functions before using it in any other way. Don't try to set all the signals explicitly because the `sigset_t` object might include some other information (like a version field) that needs to be initialized as well. (In addition, it's not wise to put into your program an assumption that the system has no signals aside from the ones you know about.)

int sigemptyset (`sigset_t *set`)   Function

This function initializes the signal set *set* to exclude all of the defined signals. It always returns 0.

int sigfillset (`sigset_t *set`)   Function

This function initializes the signal set *set* to include all of the defined signals. Again, the return value is 0.

int sigaddset (`sigset_t *set`, `int` *signum*) *Function*
This function adds the signal *signum* to the signal set *set*. All `sigaddset` does is modify *set*; it does not block or unblock any signals.

The return value is 0 on success and -1 on failure. The following `errno` error condition is defined for this function:

EINVAL   The *signum* argument doesn't specify a valid signal.

int sigdelset (`sigset_t *set`, `int` *signum*) *Function*
This function removes the signal *signum* from the signal set *set*. All `sigdelset` does is modify *set*; it does not block or unblock any signals. The return value and error conditions are the same as for `sigaddset`.

Finally, there is a function to test what signals are in a signal set:

int sigismember (`const sigset_t *set`, `int` *signum*) *Function*
The `sigismember` function tests whether the signal *signum* is a member of the signal set *set*. It returns 1 if the signal is in the set, 0 if not, and -1 if there is an error.

The following `errno` error condition is defined for this function:

EINVAL   The *signum* argument doesn't specify a valid signal.

21.7.3 Process Signal Mask

The collection of signals that are currently blocked is called the *signal mask*. Each process has its own signal mask. When you create a new process (see Section 23.4 [Creating a Process], page 445), it inherits its parent's mask. You can block or unblock signals with total flexibility by modifying the signal mask.

The prototype for the `sigprocmask` function is in 'signal.h'.

int sigprocmask (`int` *how*, `const sigset_t *set`, *Function*
        `sigset_t *`*oldset*)
The `sigprocmask` function is used to examine or change the calling process's signal mask. The *how* argument determines how the signal mask is changed, and must be one of the following values:

SIG_BLOCK
        Block the signals in `set`—add them to the existing mask. In other words, the new mask is the union of the existing mask and *set*.

SIG_UNBLOCK
        Unblock the signals in *set*—remove them from the existing mask.

Chapter 21: Signal Handling 411

SIG_SETMASK
> Use *set* for the mask; ignore the previous value of the mask.

The last argument, *oldset*, is used to return information about the old process signal mask. If you just want to change the mask without looking at it, pass a null pointer as the *oldset* argument. Similarly, if you want to know what's in the mask without changing it, pass a null pointer for *set* (in this case the *how* argument is not significant). The *oldset* argument is often used to remember the previous signal mask in order to restore it later. (Since the signal mask is inherited over **fork** and **exec** calls, you can't predict what its contents are when your program starts running.)

If invoking **sigprocmask** causes any pending signals to be unblocked, at least one of those signals is delivered to the process before **sigprocmask** returns. The order in which pending signals are delivered is not specified, but you can control the order explicitly by making multiple **sigprocmask** calls to unblock various signals one at a time.

The **sigprocmask** function returns 0 if successful, and -1 to indicate an error. The following **errno** error conditions are defined for this function:

EINVAL   The *how* argument is invalid.

You can't block the **SIGKILL** and **SIGSTOP** signals, but if the signal set includes these, **sigprocmask** just ignores them instead of returning an error status.

Remember, too, that blocking program error signals such as **SIGFPE** leads to undesirable results for signals generated by an actual program error (as opposed to signals sent with **raise** or **kill**). This is because your program may be too broken to be able to continue executing to a point where the signal is unblocked again. See Section 21.2.1 [Program Error Signals], page 374.

21.7.4 Blocking to Test for Delivery of a Signal

Now for a simple example. Suppose you establish a handler for **SIGALRM** signals that sets a flag whenever a signal arrives, and your main program checks this flag from time to time and then resets it. You can prevent additional **SIGALRM** signals from arriving in the meantime by wrapping the critical part of the code with calls to **sigprocmask**, like this:

```
/* This variable is set by the SIGALRM signal handler. */
volatile sig_atomic_t flag = 0;
```

```
int
main (void)
{
  sigset_t block_alarm;

  ...

  /* Initialize the signal mask. */
  sigemptyset (&block_alarm);
  sigaddset (&block_alarm, SIGALRM);

  while (1)
    {
      /* Check if a signal has arrived; if so, reset the flag. */
      sigprocmask (SIG_BLOCK, &block_alarm, NULL);
      if (flag)
        {
          actions-if-not-arrived
          flag = 0;
        }
      sigprocmask (SIG_UNBLOCK, &block_alarm, NULL);

      ...
    }
}
```

21.7.5 Blocking Signals for a Handler

When a signal handler is invoked, you usually want it to be able to finish without being interrupted by another signal. From the moment the handler starts until the moment it finishes, you must block signals that might confuse it or corrupt its data.

When a handler function is invoked on a signal, that signal is automatically blocked (in addition to any other signals that are already in the process's signal mask) during the time the handler is running. If you set up a handler for SIGTSTP, for instance, then the arrival of that signal forces further SIGTSTP signals to wait during the execution of the handler.

However, by default, other kinds of signals are not blocked; they can arrive during handler execution.

The reliable way to block other kinds of signals during the execution of the handler is to use the `sa_mask` member of the `sigaction` structure.

Here is an example:

```
#include <signal.h>
#include <stddef.h>

void catch_stop ();

void
```

Chapter 21: Signal Handling

```
install_handler (void)
{
  struct sigaction setup_action;
  sigset_t block_mask;

  sigemptyset (&block_mask);
  /* Block other terminal-generated signals while handler runs. */
  sigaddset (&block_mask, SIGINT);
  sigaddset (&block_mask, SIGQUIT);
  setup_action.sa_handler = catch_stop;
  setup_action.sa_mask = block_mask;
  setup_action.sa_flags = 0;
  sigaction (SIGTSTP, &setup_action, NULL);
}
```

This is more reliable than blocking the other signals explicitly in the code for the handler. If you block signals explicity in the handler, you can't avoid at least a short interval at the beginning of the handler where they are not yet blocked.

You cannot remove signals from the process's current mask using this mechanism. However, you can make calls to `sigprocmask` within your handler to block or unblock signals as you wish.

In any case, when the handler returns, the system restores the mask that was in place before the handler was entered. If any signals that become unblocked by this restoration are pending, the process will receive those signals immediately, before returning to the code that was interrupted.

21.7.6 Checking for Pending Signals

You can find out which signals are pending at any time by calling `sigpending`. This function is declared in 'signal.h'.

int sigpending (sigset_t *set*)   *Function*
The `sigpending` function stores information about pending signals in *set*. If there is a pending signal that is blocked from delivery, then that signal is a member of the returned set. (You can test whether a particular signal is a member of this set using `sigismember`; see Section 21.7.2 [Signal Sets], page 409.)

The return value is 0 if successful, and -1 on failure.

Testing whether a signal is pending is not often useful. Testing when that signal is not blocked is almost certainly bad design.

Here is an example.

```
#include <signal.h>
#include <stddef.h>

sigset_t base_mask, waiting_mask;
```

```
sigemptyset (&base_mask);
sigaddset (&base_mask, SIGINT);
sigaddset (&base_mask, SIGTSTP);

/* Block user interrupts while doing other processing. */
sigprocmask (SIG_SETMASK, &base_mask, NULL);
...

/* After a while, check to see whether any signals are pending. */
sigpending (&waiting_mask);
if (sigismember (&waiting_mask, SIGINT)) {
  /* User has tried to kill the process. */
}
else if (sigismember (&waiting_mask, SIGTSTP)) {
  /* User has tried to stop the process. */
}
```

Remember that if there is a particular signal pending for your process, additional signals of that same type that arrive in the meantime might be discarded. For example, if a SIGINT signal is pending when another SIGINT signal arrives, your program will probably only see one of them when you unblock this signal.

Portability Note: The sigpending function is new in POSIX.1. Older systems have no equivalent facility.

21.7.7 Remembering a Signal to Act On Later

Instead of blocking a signal using the library facilities, you can get almost the same results by making the handler set a flag to be tested later, when you "unblock". Here is an example:

```
/* If this flag is nonzero, don't handle the signal right away. */
volatile sig_atomic_t signal_pending;

/* This is nonzero if a signal arrived and was not handled. */
volatile sig_atomic_t defer_signal;

void
handler (int signum)
{
  if (defer_signal)
    signal_pending = signum;
  else
    ... /* "Really" handle the signal. */
}

...

void
update_mumble (int frob)
{
```

```
    /* Prevent signals from having immediate effect. */
    defer_signal++;
    /* Now update mumble, without worrying about interruption. */
    mumble.a = 1;
    mumble.b = hack ();
    mumble.c = frob;
    /* We have updated mumble.  Handle any signal that came in. */
    defer_signal--;
    if (defer_signal == 0 && signal_pending != 0)
      raise (signal_pending);
}
```

Note how the particular signal that arrives is stored in `signal_pending`. That way, we can handle several types of inconvenient signals with the same mechanism.

We increment and decrement `defer_signal` so that nested critical sections will work properly; thus, if `update_mumble` were called with `signal_pending` already nonzero, signals would be deferred not only within `update_mumble`, but also within the caller. This is also why we do not check `signal_pending` if `defer_signal` is still nonzero.

The incrementing and decrementing of `defer_signal` require more than one instruction; it is possible for a signal to happen in the middle. But that does not cause any problem. If the signal happens early enough to see the value from before the increment or decrement, that is equivalent to a signal which came before the beginning of the increment or decrement, which is a case that works properly.

It is absolutely vital to decrement `defer_signal` before testing `signal_pending`, because this avoids a subtle bug. If we did these things in the other order, like this,

```
    if (defer_signal == 1 && signal_pending != 0)
      raise (signal_pending);
    defer_signal--;
```

then a signal arriving in between the `if` statement and the decrement would be effetively "lost" for an indefinite amount of time. The handler would merely set `defer_signal`, but the program having already tested this variable, it would not test the variable again.

Bugs like these are called *timing errors*. They are especially bad because they happen only rarely and are nearly impossible to reproduce. You can't expect to find them with a debugger as you would find a reproducible bug. So it is worth being especially careful to avoid them.

(You would not be tempted to write the code in this order, given the use of `defer_signal` as a counter which must be tested along with `signal_pending`. After all, testing for zero is cleaner than testing for one. But if you did not use `defer_signal` as a counter, and gave it values of zero and one only, then either order might seem equally simple. This is a further advantage of using a counter for `defer_signal`: it will reduce the chance you will write the code in the wrong order and create a subtle bug.)

21.8 Waiting for a Signal

If your program is driven by external events, or uses signals for synchronization, then when it has nothing to do it should probably wait until a signal arrives.

21.8.1 Using pause

The simple way to wait until a signal arrives is to call **pause**. Please read about its disadvantages, in the following section, before you use it.

int pause () *Function*

The **pause** function suspends program execution until a signal arrives whose action is either to execute a handler function, or to terminate the process.

If the signal causes a handler function to be executed, then **pause** returns. This is considered an unsuccessful return (since "successful" behavior would be to suspend the program forever), so the return value is **-1**. Even if you specify that other primitives should resume when a system handler returns (see Section 21.5 [Primitives Interrupted by Signals], page 402), this has no effect on **pause**; it always fails when a signal is handled.

The following **errno** error conditions are defined for this function:

EINTR   The function was interrupted by delivery of a signal.

If the signal causes program termination, **pause** doesn't return (obviously).

The **pause** function is declared in 'unistd.h'.

21.8.2 Problems with pause

The simplicity of **pause** can conceal serious timing errors that can make a program hang mysteriously.

It is safe to use **pause** if the real work of your program is done by the signal handlers themselves, and the "main program" does nothing but call **pause**. Each time a signal is delivered, the handler will do the next batch of work that is to be done, and then return, so that the main loop of the program can call **pause** again.

You can't safely use **pause** to wait until one more signal arrives, and then resume real work. Even if you arrange for the signal handler to cooperate

Chapter 21: Signal Handling

by setting a flag, you still can't use **pause** reliably. Here is an example of this problem:

```
/* usr_interrupt is set by the signal handler.  */
if (!usr_interrupt)
  pause ();

/* Do work once the signal arrives.  */
...
```

This has a bug: the signal could arrive after the variable `usr_interrupt` is checked, but before the call to **pause**. If no further signals arrive, the process would never wake up again.

You can put an upper limit on the excess waiting by using **sleep** in a loop, instead of using **pause**. (See Section 17.4 [Sleeping], page 338, for more about **sleep**.) Here is what this looks like:

```
/* usr_interrupt is set by the signal handler.
while (!usr_interrupt)
  sleep (1);

/* Do work once the signal arrives.  */
...
```

For some purposes, that is good enough. But with a little more complexity, you can wait reliably until a particular signal handler is run, using sigsuspend.

21.8.3 Using sigsuspend

The clean and reliable way to wait for a signal to arrive is to block it and then use **sigsuspend**. By using **sigsuspend** in a loop, you can wait for certain kinds of signals, while letting other kinds of signals be handled by their handlers.

int sigsuspend (`const sigset_t *set`) *Function*
    This function replaces the process's signal mask with *set* and then suspends the process until a signal is delivered whose action is either to terminate the process or invoke a signal handling function. In other words, the program is effectively suspended until one of the signals that is not a member of *set* arrives.

    If the process is woken up by deliver of a signal that invokes a handler function, and the handler function returns, then **sigsuspend** also returns.

    The mask remains *set* only as long as **sigsuspend** is waiting. The function **sigsuspend** always restores the previous signal mask when it returns.

    The return value and error conditions are the same as for **pause**.

With `sigsuspend`, you can replace the `pause` or `sleep` loop in the previous section with something completely reliable:

```
sigset_t mask, oldmask;

...

/* Set up the mask of signals to temporarily block. */
sigemptyset (&mask);
sigaddset (&mask, SIGUSR1);

...

/* Wait for a signal to arrive. */
sigprocmask (SIG_BLOCK, &mask, &oldmask);
while (!usr_interrupt)
  sigsuspend (&oldmask);
sigprocmask (SIG_UNBLOCK, &mask, NULL);
```

This last piece of code is a little tricky. The key point to remember here is that when `sigsuspend` returns, it resets the process's signal mask to the original value, the value from before the call to `sigsuspend`—in this case, the `SIGUSR1` signal is once again blocked. The second call to `sigprocmask` is necessary to explicitly unblock this signal.

One other point: you may be wondering why the `while` loop is necessary at all, since the program is apparently only waiting for one `SIGUSR1` signal. The answer is that the mask passed to `sigsuspend` permits the process to be woken up by the delivery of other kinds of signals, as well—for example, job control signals. If the process is woken up by a signal that doesn't set `usr_interrupt`, it just suspends itself again until the "right" kind of signal eventually arrives.

This technique takes a few more lines of preparation, but that is needed just once for each kind of wait criterion you want to use. The code that actually waits is just four lines.

21.9 Using a Separate Signal Stack

A signal stack is a special area of memory to be used as the execution stack during signal handlers. It should be fairly large, to avoid any danger that it will overflow in turn; the macro `SIGSTKSZ` is defined to a canonical size for signal stacks. You can use `malloc` to allocate the space for the stack. Then call `sigaltstack` or `sigstack` to tell the system to use that space for the signal stack.

You don't need to write signal handlers differently in order to use a signal stack. Switching from one stack to the other happens automatically. (Some non-GNU debuggers on some machines may get confused if you examine a stack trace while a handler that uses the signal stack is running.)

Chapter 21: Signal Handling

There are two interfaces for telling the system to use a separate signal stack. `sigstack` is the older interface, which comes from 4.2 BSD. `sigaltstack` is the newer interface, and comes from 4.4 BSD. The `sigaltstack` interface has the advantage that it does not require your program to know which direction the stack grows, which depends on the specific machine and operating system.

struct sigaltstack   Data Type

This structure describes a signal stack. It contains the following members:

`void *ss_sp`

This points to the base of the signal stack.

`size_t ss_size`

This is the size (in bytes) of the signal stack which 'ss_sp' points to. You should set this to however much space you allocated for the stack.

There are two macros defined in 'signal.h' that you should use in calculating this size:

SIGSTKSZ   This is the canonical size for a signal stack. It is judged to be sufficient for normal uses.

MINSIGSTKSZ

This is the amount of signal stack space the operating system needs just to implement signal delivery. The size of a signal stack **must** be greater than this.

For most cases, just using `SIGSTKSZ` for `ss_size` is sufficient. But if you know how much stack space your program's signal handlers will need, you may want to use a different size. In this case, you should allocate `MINSIGSTKSZ` additional bytes for the signal stack and increase `ss_size` accordingly.

`int ss_flags`

This field contains the bitwise OR of these flags:

SA_DISABLE

This tells the system that it should not use the signal stack.

SA_ONSTACK

This is set by the system, and indicates that the signal stack is currently in use. If this bit is not set, then signals will be delivered on the normal user stack.

int sigaltstack (const struct sigaltstack *stack,   Function
      struct sigaltstack *oldstack)

The sigaltstack function specifies an alternate stack for use during signal handling. When a signal is received by the process and its action indicates that the signal stack is used, the system arranges a switch to the currently installed signal stack while the handler for that signal is executed.

If *oldstack* is not a null pointer, information about the currently installed signal stack is returned in the location it points to. If *stack* is not a null pointer, then this is installed as the new stack for use by signal handlers.

The return value is 0 on success and -1 on failure. If sigaltstack fails, it sets errno to one of these values:

> EINVAL   You tried to disable a stack that was in fact currently in use.
>
> ENOMEM   The size of the alternate stack was too small. It must be greater than MINSIGSTKSZ.

Here is the older sigstack interface. You should use sigaltstack instead on systems that have it.

struct sigstack   Data Type

This structure describes a signal stack. It contains the following members:

> void *ss_sp
>   This is the stack pointer. If the stack grows downwards on your machine, this should point to the top of the area you allocated. If the stack grows upwards, it should point to the bottom.
>
> int ss_onstack
>   This field is true if the process is currently using this stack.

int sigstack (const struct sigstack *stack, struct   Function
      sigstack *oldstack)

The sigstack function specifies an alternate stack for use during signal handling. When a signal is received by the process and its action indicates that the signal stack is used, the system arranges a switch to the currently installed signal stack while the handler for that signal is executed.

If *oldstack* is not a null pointer, information about the currently installed signal stack is returned in the location it points to. If *stack* is

not a null pointer, then this is installed as the new stack for use by
signal handlers.

The return value is 0 on success and -1 on failure.

21.10 BSD Signal Handling

This section describes alternative signal handling functions derived from
BSD Unix. These facilities were an advance, in their time; today, they are
mostly obsolete, and supported mainly for compatibility with BSD Unix.

There are many similarities between the BSD and POSIX signal handling
facilities, because the POSIX facilities were inspired by the BSD facilities.
Besides having different names for all the functions to avoid conflicts, the
main differences between the two are:

- BSD Unix represents signal masks as an `int` bit mask, rather than as a
  `sigset_t` object.
- The BSD facilities use a different default for whether an interrupted
  primitive should fail or resume. The POSIX facilities make system calls
  fail unless you specify that they should resume. With the BSD facility,
  the default is to make system calls resume unless you say they should
  fail. See Section 21.5 [Primitives Interrupted by Signals], page 402.

The BSD facilities are declared in 'signal.h'.

21.10.1 BSD Function to Establish a Handler

struct sigvec Data Type

This data type is the BSD equivalent of `struct sigaction` (see Section 21.3.2 [Advanced Signal Handling], page 386); it is used to specify signal actions to the `sigvec` function. It contains the following members:

sighandler_t sv_handler
This is the handler function.

int sv_mask
This is the mask of additional signals to be blocked while
the handler function is being called.

int sv_flags
This is a bit mask used to specify various flags which affect
the behavior of the signal. You can also refer to this field
as `sv_onstack`.

These symbolic constants can be used to provide values for the `sv_flags`
field of a `sigvec` structure. This field is a bit mask value, so you bitwise-OR
the flags of interest to you together.

int SV_ONSTACK   Macro
If this bit is set in the `sv_flags` field of a `sigvec` structure, it means to use the signal stack when delivering the signal.

int SV_INTERRUPT   Macro
If this bit is set in the `sv_flags` field of a `sigvec` structure, it means that system calls interrupted by this kind of signal should not be restarted if the handler returns; instead, the system calls should return with a EINTR error status. See Section 21.5 [Primitives Interrupted by Signals], page 402.

int SV_RESETHAND   Macro
If this bit is set in the `sv_flags` field of a `sigvec` structure, it means to reset the action for the signal back to `SIG_DFL` when the signal is received.

int sigvec (int *signum*, const struct sigvec *action*, struct sigvec *old-action*)   Function
This function is the equivalent of `sigaction` (see Section 21.3.2 [Advanced Signal Handling], page 386); it installs the action *action* for the signal *signum*, returning information about the previous action in effect for that signal in *old-action*.

int siginterrupt (int *signum*, int *failflag*)   Function
This function specifies which approach to use when certain primitives are interrupted by handling signal *signum*. If *failflag* is false, signal *signum* restarts primitives. If *failflag* is true, handling *signum* causes these primitives to fail with error code EINTR. See Section 21.5 [Primitives Interrupted by Signals], page 402.

21.10.2 BSD Functions for Blocking Signals

int sigmask (int *signum*)   Macro
This macro returns a signal mask that has the bit for signal *signum* set. You can bitwise-OR the results of several calls to `sigmask` together to specify more than one signal. For example,

```
(sigmask (SIGTSTP) | sigmask (SIGSTOP)
 | sigmask (SIGTTIN) | sigmask (SIGTTOU))
```

specifies a mask that includes all the job-control stop signals.

int sigblock (int *mask*)   Function
This function is equivalent to `sigprocmask` (see Section 21.7.3 [Process Signal Mask], page 410) with a *how* argument of `SIG_BLOCK`: it adds the signals specified by *mask* to the calling process's set of blocked signals. The return value is the previous set of blocked signals.

Chapter 21: Signal Handling 423

`int` **sigsetmask** (`int` *mask*) Function
    This function equivalent to `sigprocmask` (see Section 21.7.3 [Process Signal Mask], page 410) with a *how* argument of `SIG_SETMASK`: it sets the calling process's signal mask to *mask*. The return value is the previous set of blocked signals.

`int` **sigpause** (`int` *mask*) Function
    This function is the equivalent of `sigsuspend` (see Section 21.8 [Waiting for a Signal], page 416): it sets the calling process's signal mask to *mask*, and waits for a signal to arrive. On return the previous set of blocked signals is restored.

22 Process Startup and Termination

Processes are the primitive units for allocation of system resources. Each process has its own address space and (usually) one thread of control. A process executes a program; you can have multiple processes executing the same program, but each process has its own copy of the program within its own address space and executes it independently of the other copies.

This chapter explains what your program should do to handle the startup of a process, to terminate its process, and to receive information (arguments and the environment) from the parent process.

22.1 Program Arguments

The system starts a C program by calling the function `main`. It is up to you to write a function named `main`—otherwise, you won't even be able to link your program without errors.

In ANSI C you can define `main` either to take no arguments, or to take two arguments that represent the command line arguments to the program, like this:

```
int main (int argc, char *argv[])
```

The command line arguments are the whitespace-separated tokens given in the shell command used to invoke the program; thus, in 'cat foo bar', the arguments are 'foo' and 'bar'. The only way a program can look at its command line arguments is via the arguments of `main`. If `main` doesn't take arguments, then you cannot get at the command line.

The value of the *argc* argument is the number of command line arguments. The *argv* argument is a vector of C strings; its elements are the individual command line argument strings. The file name of the program being run is also included in the vector as the first element; the value of *argc* counts this element. A null pointer always follows the last element: *argv*[*argc*] is this null pointer.

For the command 'cat foo bar', *argc* is 3 and *argv* has three elements, "cat", "foo" and "bar".

If the syntax for the command line arguments to your program is simple enough, you can simply pick the arguments off from *argv* by hand. But unless your program takes a fixed number of arguments, or all of the arguments are interpreted in the same way (as file names, for example), you are usually better off using `getopt` to do the parsing.

In Unix systems you can define `main` a third way, using three arguments:

```
int main (int argc, char *argv[], char *envp)
```

The first two arguments are just the same. The third argument *envp* gives the process's environment; it is the same as the value of `environ`. See

Section 22.2 [Environment Variables], page 433. POSIX.1 does not allow this three-argument form, so to be portable it is best to write `main` to take two arguments, and use the value of `environ`.

22.1.1 Program Argument Syntax Conventions

POSIX recommends these conventions for command line arguments. `getopt` (see Section 22.1.2 [Parsing Program Options], page 427) makes it easy to implement them.

- Arguments are options if they begin with a hyphen delimiter ('-').
- Multiple options may follow a hyphen delimiter in a single token if the options do not take arguments. Thus, '`-abc`' is equivalent to '`-a -b -c`'.
- Option names are single alphanumeric characters (as for `isalnum`; see Section 4.1 [Classification of Characters], page 55).
- Certain options require an argument. For example, the '`-o`' command of the `ld` command requires an argument—an output file name.
- An option and its argument may or may not appear as separate tokens. (In other words, the whitespace separating them is optional.) Thus, '`-o foo`' and '`-ofoo`' are equivalent.
- Options typically precede other non-option arguments.

  The implementation of `getopt` in the GNU C library normally makes it appear as if all the option arguments were specified before all the non-option arguments for the purposes of parsing, even if the user of your program intermixed option and non-option arguments. It does this by reordering the elements of the *argv* array. This behavior is nonstandard; if you want to suppress it, define the `_POSIX_OPTION_ORDER` environment variable. See Section 22.2.2 [Standard Environment Variables], page 435.

- The argument '`--`' terminates all options; any following arguments are treated as non-option arguments, even if they begin with a hyphen.
- A token consisting of a single hyphen character is interpreted as an ordinary non-option argument. By convention, it is used to specify input from or output to the standard input and output streams.
- Options may be supplied in any order, or appear multiple times. The interpretation is left up to the particular application program.

GNU adds *long options* to these conventions. Long options consist of '`--`' followed by a name made of alphanumeric characters and dashes. Option names are typically one to three words long, with hyphens to separate words. Users can abbreviate the option names as long as the abbreviations are unique.

To specify an argument for a long option, write '`--name=value`'. This syntax enables a long option to accept an argument that is itself optional.

Chapter 22: Process Startup and Termination   427

Eventually, the GNU system will provide completion for long option names in the shell.

22.1.2 Parsing Program Options

Here are the details about how to call the `getopt` function. To use this facility, your program must include the header file 'unistd.h'.

int opterr   Variable
    If the value of this variable is nonzero, then `getopt` prints an error message to the standard error stream if it encounters an unknown option character or an option with a missing required argument. This is the default behavior. If you set this variable to zero, `getopt` does not print any messages, but it still returns the character ? to indicate an error.

int optopt   Variable
    When `getopt` encounters an unknown option character or an option with a missing required argument, it stores that option character in this variable. You can use this for providing your own diagnostic messages.

int optind   Variable
    This variable is set by `getopt` to the index of the next element of the *argv* array to be processed. Once `getopt` has found all of the option arguments, you can use this variable to determine where the remaining non-option arguments begin. The initial value of this variable is 1.

char * optarg   Variable
    This variable is set by `getopt` to point at the value of the option argument, for those options that accept arguments.

int getopt (int *argc*, char **argv*, const char   Function
         **options*)
    The `getopt` function gets the next option argument from the argument list specified by the *argv* and *argc* arguments. Normally these values come directly from the arguments received by `main`.

    The *options* argument is a string that specifies the option characters that are valid for this program. An option character in this string can be followed by a colon (':') to indicate that it takes a required argument.

    If the *options* argument string begins with a hyphen ('-'), this is treated specially. It permits arguments that are not options to be returned as if they were associated with option character '\0'.

The `getopt` function returns the option character for the next command line option. When no more option arguments are available, it returns -1. There may still be more non-option arguments; you must compare the external variable `optind` against the *argc* parameter to check this.

If the option has an argument, `getopt` returns the argument by storing it in the varables *optarg*. You don't ordinarily need to copy the `optarg` string, since it is a pointer into the original *argv* array, not into a static area that might be overwritten.

If `getopt` finds an option character in *argv* that was not included in *options*, or a missing option argument, it returns '?' and sets the external variable `optopt` to the actual option character. If the first character of *options* is a colon (':'), then `getopt` returns ':' instead of '?' to indicate a missing option argument. In addition, if the external variable `opterr` is nonzero (which is the default), `getopt` prints an error message.

22.1.3 Example of Parsing Arguments with `getopt`

Here is an example showing how `getopt` is typically used. The key points to notice are:

- Normally, `getopt` is called in a loop. When `getopt` returns -1, indicating no more options are present, the loop terminates.

- A `switch` statement is used to dispatch on the return value from `getopt`. In typical use, each case just sets a variable that is used later in the program.

- A second loop is used to process the remaining non-option arguments.

```
#include <unistd.h>
#include <stdio.h>

int
main (int argc, char **argv)
{
  int aflag = 0;
  int bflag = 0;
  char *cvalue = NULL;
  int index;
  int c;

  opterr = 0;
```

Chapter 22: Process Startup and Termination

```
      while ((c = getopt (argc, argv, "abc:")) != -1)
        switch (c)
          {
          case 'a':
            aflag = 1;
            break;
          case 'b':
            bflag = 1;
            break;
          case 'c':
            cvalue = optarg;
            break;
          case '?':
            if (isprint (optopt))
              fprintf (stderr, "Unknown option '-%c'.\n", optopt);
            else
              fprintf (stderr,
                       "Unknown option character '\\x%x'.\n",
                       optopt);
            return 1;
          default:
            abort ();
          }
      printf ("aflag = %d, bflag = %d, cvalue = %s\n", aflag, bflag, cvalue);

      for (index = optind; index < argc; index++)
        printf ("Non-option argument %s\n", argv[index]);
      return 0;
    }
```

Here are some examples showing what this program prints with different combinations of arguments:

```
% testopt
aflag = 0, bflag = 0, cvalue = (null)

% testopt -a -b
aflag = 1, bflag = 1, cvalue = (null)

% testopt -ab
aflag = 1, bflag = 1, cvalue = (null)

% testopt -c foo
aflag = 0, bflag = 0, cvalue = foo

% testopt -cfoo
aflag = 0, bflag = 0, cvalue = foo

% testopt arg1
aflag = 0, bflag = 0, cvalue = (null)
Non-option argument arg1

% testopt -a arg1
aflag = 1, bflag = 0, cvalue = (null)
```

```
Non-option argument arg1

% testopt -c foo arg1
aflag = 0, bflag = 0, cvalue = foo
Non-option argument arg1

% testopt -a -- -b
aflag = 1, bflag = 0, cvalue = (null)
Non-option argument -b

% testopt -a -
aflag = 1, bflag = 0, cvalue = (null)
Non-option argument -
```

22.1.4 Parsing Long Options

To accept GNU-style long options as well as single-character options, use `getopt_long` instead of `getopt`. This function is declared in 'getopt.h', not 'unistd.h'. You should make every program accept long options if it uses any options, for this takes little extra work and helps beginners remember how to use the program.

struct option *Data Type*

This structure describes a single long option name for the sake of `getopt_long`. The argument *longopts* must be an array of these structures, one for each long option. Terminate the array with an element containing all zeros.

The `struct option` structure has these fields:

`const char *name`
> This field is the name of the option. It is a string.

`int has_arg`
> This field says whether the option takes an argument. It is an integer, and there are three legitimate values: `no_argument`, `required_argument` and `optional_argument`.

`int *flag`
`int val`
> These fields control how to report or act on the option when it occurs.
>
> If `flag` is a null pointer, then the `val` is a value which identifies this option. Often these values are chosen to uniquely identify particular long options.
>
> If `flag` is not a null pointer, it should be the address of an `int` variable which is the flag for this option. The value in `val` is the value to store in the flag to indicate that the option was seen.

Chapter 22: Process Startup and Termination 431

int getopt_long (int *argc*, char **argv, const char   Function
         *shortopts, struct option *longopts, int *indexptr)

Decode options from the vector *argv* (whose length is *argc*). The argument *shortopts* describes the short options to accept, just as it does in getopt. The argument *longopts* describes the long options to accept (see above).

When getopt_long encounters a short option, it does the same thing that getopt would do: it returns the character code for the option, and stores the options argument (if it has one) in optarg.

When getopt_long encounters a long option, it takes actions based on the flag and val fields of the definition of that option.

If flag is a null pointer, then getopt_long returns the contents of val to indicate which option it found. You should arrange distinct values in the val field for options with different meanings, so you can decode these values after getopt_long returns. If the long option is equivalent to a short option, you can use the short option's character code in val.

If flag is not a null pointer, that means this option should just set a flag in the program. The flag is a variable of type int that you define. Put the address of the flag in the flag field. Put in the val field the value you would like this option to store in the flag. In this case, getopt_long returns 0.

For any long option, getopt_long tells you the index in the array *longopts* of the options definition, by storing it into *indexptr*. You can get the name of the option with *longopts*[*indexptr*].name. So you can distinguish among long options either by the values in their val fields or by their indices. You can also distinguish in this way among long options that set flags.

When a long option has an argument, getopt_long puts the argument value in the variable optarg before returning. When the option has no argument, the value in optarg is a null pointer. This is how you can tell whether an optional argument was supplied.

When getopt_long has no more options to handle, it returns -1, and leaves in the variable optind the index in *argv* of the next remaining argument.

22.1.5 Example of Parsing Long Options

```
#include <stdio.h>
#include <stdlib.h>
#include <getopt.h>

/* Flag set by '--verbose'. */
static int verbose_flag;
```

```c
int
main (argc, argv)
     int argc;
     char **argv;
{
  int c;

  while (1)
    {
      static struct option long_options[] =
        {
          /* These options set a flag. */
          {"verbose", 0, &verbose_flag, 1},
          {"brief", 0, &verbose_flag, 0},
          /* These options don't set a flag.
             We distinguish them by their indices. */
          {"add", 1, 0, 0},
          {"append", 0, 0, 0},
          {"delete", 1, 0, 0},
          {"create", 0, 0, 0},
          {"file", 1, 0, 0},
          {0, 0, 0, 0}
        };
      /* getopt_long stores the option index here. */
      int option_index = 0;

      c = getopt_long (argc, argv, "abc:d:",
                       long_options, &option_index);

      /* Detect the end of the options. */
      if (c == -1)
        break;

      switch (c)
        {
        case 0:
          /* If this option set a flag, do nothing else now. */
          if (long_options[option_index].flag != 0)
            break;
          printf ("option %s", long_options[option_index].name);
          if (optarg)
            printf (" with arg %s", optarg);
          printf ("\n");
          break;

        case 'a':
          puts ("option -a\n");
          break;

        case 'b':
          puts ("option -b\n");
          break;
```

```
          case 'c':
            printf ("option -c with value '%s'\n", optarg);
            break;

          case 'd':
            printf ("option -d with value '%s'\n", optarg);
            break;

          case '?':
            /* getopt_long already printed an error message. */
            break;

          default:
            abort ();
          }
      }

     /* Instead of reporting '--verbose'
        and '--brief' as they are encountered,
        we report the final status resulting from them. */
     if (verbose_flag)
       puts ("verbose flag is set");

     /* Print any remaining command line arguments (not options). */
     if (optind < argc)
       {
         printf ("non-option ARGV-elements: ");
         while (optind < argc)
           printf ("%s ", argv[optind++]);
         putchar ('\n');
       }

     exit (0);
   }
```

22.2 Environment Variables

When a program is executed, it receives information about the context in which it was invoked in two ways. The first mechanism uses the *argv* and *argc* arguments to its `main` function, and is discussed in Section 22.1 [Program Arguments], page 425. The second mechanism uses *environment variables* and is discussed in this section.

The *argv* mechanism is typically used to pass command-line arguments specific to the particular program being invoked. The environment, on the other hand, keeps track of information that is shared by many programs, changes infrequently, and that is less frequently used.

The environment variables discussed in this section are the same environment variables that you set using assignments and the **export** command in the shell. Programs executed from the shell inherit all of the environment variables from the shell.

Standard environment variables are used for information about the user's home directory, terminal type, current locale, and so on; you can define additional variables for other purposes. The set of all environment variables that have values is collectively known as the *environment*.

Names of environment variables are case-sensitive and must not contain the character '='. System-defined environment variables are invariably uppercase.

The values of environment variables can be anything that can be represented as a string. A value must not contain an embedded null character, since this is assumed to terminate the string.

22.2.1 Environment Access

The value of an environment variable can be accessed with the `getenv` function. This is declared in the header file 'stdlib.h'.

char * getenv (const char *name) *Function*
This function returns a string that is the value of the environment variable *name*. You must not modify this string. In some non-Unix systems not using the GNU library, it might be overwritten by subsequent calls to `getenv` (but not by any other library function). If the environment variable *name* is not defined, the value is a null pointer.

int putenv (const char *string) *Function*
The `putenv` function adds or removes definitions from the environment. If the *string* is of the form '*name=value*', the definition is added to the environment. Otherwise, the *string* is interpreted as the name of an environment variable, and any definition for this variable in the environment is removed.

The GNU library provides this function for compatibility with SVID; it may not be available in other systems.

You can deal directly with the underlying representation of environment objects to add more variables to the environment (for example, to communicate with another program you are about to execute; see Section 23.5 [Executing a File], page 446).

char ** environ *Variable*
The environment is represented as an array of strings. Each string is of the format '*name=value*'. The order in which strings appear in the environment is not significant, but the same *name* must not appear more than once. The last element of the array is a null pointer.

Chapter 22: Process Startup and Termination

This variable is declared in the header file 'unistd.h'.

If you just want to get the value of an environment variable, use `getenv`.

Unix systems, and the GNU system, pass the initial value of `environ` as the third argument to `main`. See Section 22.1 [Program Arguments], page 425.

22.2.2 Standard Environment Variables

These environment variables have standard meanings. This doesn't mean that they are always present in the environment; but if these variables *are* present, they have these meanings. You shouldn't try to use these environment variable names for some other purpose.

HOME
: This is a string representing the user's *home directory*, or initial default working directory.

    The user can set `HOME` to any value. If you need to make sure to obtain the proper home directory for a particular user, you should not use `HOME`; instead, look up the user's name in the user database (see Section 25.12 [User Database], page 489).

    For most purposes, it is better to use `HOME`, precisely because this lets the user specify the value.

LOGNAME
: This is the name that the user used to log in. Since the value in the environment can be tweaked arbitrarily, this is not a reliable way to identify the user who is running a process; a function like `getlogin` (see Section 25.11 [Identifying Who Logged In], page 488) is better for that purpose.

    For most purposes, it is better to use `LOGNAME`, precisely because this lets the user specify the value.

PATH
: A *path* is a sequence of directory names which is used for searching for a file. The variable `PATH` holds a path used for searching for programs to be run.

    The `execlp` and `execvp` functions (see Section 23.5 [Executing a File], page 446) use this environment variable, as do many shells and other utilities which are implemented in terms of those functions.

    The syntax of a path is a sequence of directory names separated by colons. An empty string instead of a directory name stands for the current directory (see Section 9.1 [Working Directory], page 169).

A typical value for this environment variable might be a string like:

```
:/bin:/etc:/usr/bin:/usr/new/X11:/usr/new:/usr/local/bin
```

This means that if the user tries to execute a program named foo, the system will look for files named 'foo', '/bin/foo', '/etc/foo', and so on. The first of these files that exists is the one that is executed.

TERM

This specifies the kind of terminal that is receiving program output. Some programs can make use of this information to take advantage of special escape sequences or terminal modes supported by particular kinds of terminals. Many programs which use the termcap library (see section "Finding a Terminal Description" in *The Termcap Library Manual*) use the TERM environment variable, for example.

TZ

This specifies the time zone. See Section 17.2.5 [Specifying the Time Zone with "code TZ], page 332, for information about the format of this string and how it is used.

LANG

This specifies the default locale to use for attribute categories where neither LC_ALL nor the specific environment variable for that category is set. See Chapter 19 [Locales and Internationalization], page 357, for more information about locales.

LC_COLLATE

This specifies what locale to use for string sorting.

LC_CTYPE

This specifies what locale to use for character sets and character classification.

LC_MONETARY

This specifies what locale to use for formatting monetary values.

LC_NUMERIC

This specifies what locale to use for formatting numbers.

LC_TIME

This specifies what locale to use for formatting date/time values.

Chapter 22: Process Startup and Termination

`_POSIX_OPTION_ORDER`
> If this environment variable is defined, it suppresses the usual reordering of command line arguments by `getopt`. See Section 22.1.1 [Program Argument Syntax Conventions], page 426.

22.3 Program Termination

The usual way for a program to terminate is simply for its `main` function to return. The *exit status value* returned from the `main` function is used to report information back to the process's parent process or shell.

A program can also terminate normally by calling the `exit` function.

In addition, programs can be terminated by signals; this is discussed in more detail in Chapter 21 [Signal Handling], page 371. The `abort` function causes a signal that kills the program.

22.3.1 Normal Termination

A process terminates normally when the program calls `exit`. Returning from `main` is equivalent to calling `exit`, and the value that `main` returns is used as the argument to `exit`.

`void` **`exit`** (`int` *status*) Function
> The `exit` function terminates the process with status *status*. This function does not return.

Normal termination causes the following actions:

1. Functions that were registered with the `atexit` or `on_exit` functions are called in the reverse order of their registration. This mechanism allows your application to specify its own "cleanup" actions to be performed at program termination. Typically, this is used to do things like saving program state information in a file, or unlocking locks in shared data bases.
2. All open streams are closed, writing out any buffered output data. See Section 7.4 [Closing Streams], page 86. In addition, temporary files opened with the `tmpfile` function are removed; see Section 9.10 [Temporary Files], page 196.
3. `_exit` is called, terminating the program. See Section 22.3.5 [Termination Internals], page 440.

22.3.2 Exit Status

When a program exits, it can return to the parent process a small amount of information about the cause of termination, using the *exit status*. This is a value between 0 and 255 that the exiting process passes as an argument to `exit`.

Normally you should use the exit status to report very broad information about success or failure. You can't provide a lot of detail about the reasons for the failure, and most parent processes would not want much detail anyway.

There are conventions for what sorts of status values certain programs should return. The most common convention is simply 0 for success and 1 for failure. Programs that perform comparison use a different convention: they use status 1 to indicate a mismatch, and status 2 to indicate an inability to compare. Your program should follow an existing convention if an existing convention makes sense for it.

A general convention reserves status values 128 and up for special purposes. In particular, the value 128 is used to indicate failure to execute another program in a subprocess. This convention is not universally obeyed, but it is a good idea to follow it in your programs.

Warning: Don't try to use the number of errors as the exit status. This is actually not very useful; a parent process would generally not care how many errors occurred. Worse than that, it does not work, because the status value is truncated to eight bits. Thus, if the program tried to report 256 errors, the parent would receive a report of 0 errors—that is, success.

For the same reason, it does not work to use the value of `errno` as the exit status—these can exceed 255.

Portability note: Some non-POSIX systems use different conventions for exit status values. For greater portability, you can use the macros `EXIT_SUCCESS` and `EXIT_FAILURE` for the conventional status value for success and failure, respectively. They are declared in the file '`stdlib.h`'.

int **EXIT_SUCCESS** *Macro*

This macro can be used with the `exit` function to indicate successful program completion.

On POSIX systems, the value of this macro is 0. On other systems, the value might be some other (possibly non-constant) integer expression.

int **EXIT_FAILURE** *Macro*

This macro can be used with the `exit` function to indicate unsuccessful program completion in a general sense.

On POSIX systems, the value of this macro is 1. On other systems, the value might be some other (possibly non-constant) integer expression. Other nonzero status values also indicate future. Certain programs use different nonzero status values to indicate particular kinds of "non-success". For example, `diff` uses status value 1 to mean that the

Chapter 22: Process Startup and Termination

files are different, and 2 or more to mean that there was difficulty in opening the files.

22.3.3 Cleanups on Exit

Your program can arrange to run its own cleanup functions if normal termination happens. If you are writing a library for use in various application programs, then it is unreliable to insist that all applications call the library's cleanup functions explicitly before exiting. It is much more robust to make the cleanup invisible to the application, by setting up a cleanup function in the library itself using `atexit` or `on_exit`.

int atexit (void (*function) (void))   Function
   The `atexit` function registers the function <i>function</i> to be called at normal program termination. The <i>function</i> is called with no arguments.

   The return value from `atexit` is zero on success and nonzero if the function cannot be registered.

int on_exit (void (*function)(int status, void *arg),   Function
         void *<i>arg</i>)
   This function is a somewhat more powerful variant of `atexit`. It accepts two arguments, a function <i>function</i> and an arbitrary pointer <i>arg</i>. At normal program termination, the <i>function</i> is called with two arguments: the <i>status</i> value passed to `exit`, and the <i>arg</i>.

   This function is included in the GNU C library only for compatibility for SunOS, and may not be supported by other implementations.

Here's a trivial program that illustrates the use of `exit` and `atexit`:

```
#include <stdio.h>
#include <stdlib.h>

void
bye (void)
{
  puts ("Goodbye, cruel world....");
}

int
main (void)
{
  atexit (bye);
  exit (EXIT_SUCCESS);
}
```

When this program is executed, it just prints the message and exits.

22.3.4 Aborting a Program

You can abort your program using the `abort` function. The prototype for this function is in 'stdlib.h'.

void abort (void)   *Function*
The `abort` function causes abnormal program termination. This does not execute cleanup functions registered with `atexit` or `on_exit`.

This function actually terminates the process by raising a `SIGABRT` signal, and your program can include a handler to intercept this signal; see Chapter 21 [Signal Handling], page 371.

> **Future Change Warning:** Proposed Federal censorship regulations may prohibit us from giving you information about the possibility of calling this function. We would be required to say that this is not an acceptable way of terminating a program.

22.3.5 Termination Internals

The `_exit` function is the primitive used for process termination by `exit`. It is declared in the header file 'unistd.h'.

void _exit (int *status*)   *Function*
The `_exit` function is the primitive for causing a process to terminate with status *status*. Calling this function does not execute cleanup functions registered with `atexit` or `on_exit`.

When a process terminates for any reason—either by an explicit termination call, or termination as a result of a signal—the following things happen:

- All open file descriptors in the process are closed. See Chapter 8 [Low-Level Input/Output], page 139. Note that streams are not flushed automatically when the process terminates; See Chapter 7 [Input/Output on Streams], page 83.
- The low-order 8 bits of the return status code are saved to be reported back to the parent process via `wait` or `waitpid`; see Section 23.6 [Process Completion], page 449.
- Any child processes of the process being terminated are assigned a new parent process. (On most systems, including GNU, this is the `init` process, with process ID 1.)
- A `SIGCHLD` signal is sent to the parent process.
- If the process is a session leader that has a controlling terminal, then a `SIGHUP` signal is sent to each process in the foreground job, and the

Chapter 22: Process Startup and Termination

controlling terminal is disassociated from that session. See Chapter 24 [Job Control], page 457.

- If termination of a process causes a process group to become orphaned, and any member of that process group is stopped, then a `SIGHUP` signal and a `SIGCONT` signal are sent to each process in the group. See Chapter 24 [Job Control], page 457.

23 Processes

Processes are the primitive units for allocation of system resources. Each process has its own address space and (usually) one thread of control. A process executes a program; you can have multiple processes executing the same program, but each process has its own copy of the program within its own address space and executes it independently of the other copies.

Processes are organized hierarchically. Each process has a *parent process* which explicitly arranged to create it. The processes created by a given parent are called its *child processes*. A child inherits many of its attributes from the parent process.

This chapter describes how a program can create, terminate, and control child processes. Actually, there are three distinct operations involved: creating a new child process, causing the new process to execute a program, and coordinating the completion of the child process with the original program.

The `system` function provides a simple, portable mechanism for running another program; it does all three steps automatically. If you need more control over the details of how this is done, you can use the primitive functions to do each step individually instead.

23.1 Running a Command

The easy way to run another program is to use the `system` function. This function does all the work of running a subprogram, but it doesn't give you much control over the details: you have to wait until the subprogram terminates before you can do anything else.

`int system` (`const char *command`) Function
> This function executes *command* as a shell command. In the GNU C library, it always uses the default shell `sh` to run the command. In particular, it searches the directories in `PATH` to find programs to execute. The return value is `-1` if it wasn't possible to create the shell process, and otherwise is the status of the shell process. See Section 23.6 [Process Completion], page 449, for details on how this status code can be interpreted.
>
> The `system` function is declared in the header file '`stdlib.h`'.

Portability Note: Some C implementations may not have any notion of a command processor that can execute other programs. You can determine whether a command processor exists by executing `system (NULL)`; if the return value is nonzero, a command processor is available.

The `popen` and `pclose` functions (see Section 10.2 [Pipe to a Subprocess], page 203) are closely related to the `system` function. They allow the parent process to communicate with the standard input and output channels of the command being executed.

23.2 Process Creation Concepts

This section gives an overview of processes and of the steps involved in creating a process and making it run another program.

Each process is named by a *process ID* number. A unique process ID is allocated to each process when it is created. The *lifetime* of a process ends when its termination is reported to its parent process; at that time, all of the process resources, including its process ID, are freed.

Processes are created with the `fork` system call (so the operation of creating a new process is sometimes called *forking* a process). The *child process* created by `fork` is a copy of the original *parent process*, except that it has its own process ID.

After forking a child process, both the parent and child processes continue to execute normally. If you want your program to wait for a child process to finish executing before continuing, you must do this explicitly after the fork operation, by calling `wait` or `waitpid` (see Section 23.6 [Process Completion], page 449). These functions give you limited information about why the child terminated—for example, its exit status code.

A newly forked child process continues to execute the same program as its parent process, at the point where the `fork` call returns. You can use the return value from `fork` to tell whether the program is running in the parent process or the child.

Having several processes run the same program is only occasionally useful. But the child can execute another program using one of the `exec` functions; see Section 23.5 [Executing a File], page 446. The program that the process is executing is called its *process image*. Starting execution of a new program causes the process to forget all about its previous process image; when the new program exits, the process exits too, instead of returning to the previous process image.

23.3 Process Identification

The `pid_t` data type represents process IDs. You can get the process ID of a process by calling `getpid`. The function `getppid` returns the process ID of the parent of the current process (this is also known as the *parent process ID*). Your program should include the header files 'unistd.h' and 'sys/types.h' to use these functions.

Chapter 23: Processes 445

pid_t   Data Type

The `pid_t` data type is a signed integer type which is capable of representing a process ID. In the GNU library, this is an `int`.

pid_t getpid (`void`)   Function

The `getpid` function returns the process ID of the current process.

pid_t getppid (`void`)   Function

The `getppid` function returns the process ID of the parent of the current process.

23.4 Creating a Process

The `fork` function is the primitive for creating a process. It is declared in the header file 'unistd.h'.

pid_t fork (`void`)   Function

The `fork` function creates a new process.

If the operation is successful, there are then both parent and child processes and both see `fork` return, but with different values: it returns a value of 0 in the child process and returns the child's process ID in the parent process.

If process creation failed, `fork` returns a value of -1 in the parent process. The following `errno` error conditions are defined for `fork`:

EAGAIN   There aren't enough system resources to create another process, or the user already has too many processes running. This means exceeding the `RLIMIT_NPROC` resource limit, which can usually be increased; see Section 17.6 [Limiting Resource Usage], page 341.

ENOMEM   The process requires more space than the system can supply.

The specific attributes of the child process that differ from the parent process are:

- The child process has its own unique process ID.
- The parent process ID of the child process is the process ID of its parent process.
- The child process gets its own copies of the parent process's open file descriptors. Subsequently changing attributes of the file descriptors in the parent process won't affect the file descriptors in the child, and vice versa. See Section 8.7 [Control Operations on Files], page 153. However, the file position associated with each descriptor is shared by both processes; see Section 6.1.2 [File Position], page 77.

- The elapsed processor times for the child process are set to zero; see Section 17.1 [Processor Time], page 321.
- The child doesn't inherit file locks set by the parent process. See Section 8.7 [Control Operations on Files], page 153.
- The child doesn't inherit alarms set by the parent process. See Section 17.3 [Setting an Alarm], page 335.
- The set of pending signals (see Section 21.1.3 [How Signals Are Delivered], page 372) for the child process is cleared. (The child process inherits its mask of blocked signals and signal actions from the parent process.)

pid_t **vfork** (void)   Function

   The `vfork` function is similar to `fork` but on systems it is more efficient; however, there are restrictions you must follow to use it safely.

   While `fork` makes a complete copy of the calling process's address space and allows both the parent and child to execute independently, `vfork` does not make this copy. Instead, the child process created with `vfork` shares its parent's address space until it calls exits or one of the `exec` functions. In the meantime, the parent process suspends execution.

   You must be very careful not to allow the child process created with `vfork` to modify any global data or even local variables shared with the parent. Furthermore, the child process cannot return from (or do a long jump out of) the function that called `vfork`! This would leave the parent process's control information very confused. If in doubt, use `fork` instead.

   Some operating systems don't really implement `vfork`. The GNU C library permits you to use `vfork` on all systems, but actually executes `fork` if `vfork` isn't available. If you follow the proper precautions for using `vfork`, your program will still work even if the system uses `fork` instead.

23.5 Executing a File

   This section describes the `exec` family of functions, for executing a file as a process image. You can use these functions to make a child process execute a new program after it has been forked.

   The functions in this family differ in how you specify the arguments, but otherwise they all do the same thing. They are declared in the header file 'unistd.h'.

Chapter 23: Processes

`int execv (const char *`*filename*`, char *const `*argv*`[])` Function

The `execv` function executes the file named by *filename* as a new process image.

The *argv* argument is an array of null-terminated strings that is used to provide a value for the `argv` argument to the `main` function of the program to be executed. The last element of this array must be a null pointer. By convention, the first element of this array is the file name of the program sans directory names. See Section 22.1 [Program Arguments], page 425, for full details on how programs can access these arguments.

The environment for the new process image is taken from the `environ` variable of the current process image; see Section 22.2 [Environment Variables], page 433, for information about environments.

`int execl (const char *`*filename*`, const char *`*arg0*`, ...)` Function

This is similar to `execv`, but the *argv* strings are specified individually instead of as an array. A null pointer must be passed as the last such argument.

`int execve (const char *`*filename*`, char *const `*argv*`[], char *const `*env*`[])` Function

This is similar to `execv`, but permits you to specify the environment for the new program explicitly as the *env* argument. This should be an array of strings in the same format as for the `environ` variable; see Section 22.2.1 [Environment Access], page 434.

`int execle (const char *`*filename*`, const char *`*arg0*`, char *const `*env*`[], ...)` Function

This is similar to `execl`, but permits you to specify the environment for the new program explicitly. The environment argument is passed following the null pointer that marks the last *argv* argument, and should be an array of strings in the same format as for the `environ` variable.

`int execvp (const char *`*filename*`, char *const `*argv*`[])` Function

The `execvp` function is similar to `execv`, except that it searches the directories listed in the `PATH` environment variable (see Section 22.2.2 [Standard Environment Variables], page 435) to find the full file name of a file from *filename* if *filename* does not contain a slash.

This function is useful for executing system utility programs, because it looks for them in the places that the user has chosen. Shells use it to run the commands that users type.

int execlp (`const char *`*filename*`, const char *`*arg0*`,`   *Function*
    `...)`

This function is like `execl`, except that it performs the same file name searching as the `execvp` function.

The size of the argument list and environment list taken together must not be greater than `ARG_MAX` bytes. See Section 27.1 [General Capacity Limits], page 499. In the GNU system, the size (which compares against `ARG_MAX`) includes, for each string, the number of characters in the string, plus the size of a `char *`, plus one, rounded up to a multiple of the size of a `char *`. Other systems may have somewhat different rules for counting.

These functions normally don't return, since execution of a new program causes the currently executing program to go away completely. A value of `-1` is returned in the event of a failure. In addition to the usual file name errors (see Section 6.2.3 [File Name Errors], page 79), the following `errno` error conditions are defined for these functions:

`E2BIG`   The combined size of the new program's argument list and environment list is larger than `ARG_MAX` bytes. The GNU system has no specific limit on the argument list size, so this error code cannot result, but you may get `ENOMEM` instead if the arguments are too big for available memory.

`ENOEXEC`   The specified file can't be executed because it isn't in the right format.

`ENOMEM`   Executing the specified file requires more storage than is available.

If execution of the new file succeeds, it updates the access time field of the file as if the file had been read. See Section 9.8.9 [File Times], page 194, for more details about access times of files.

The point at which the file is closed again is not specified, but is at some point before the process exits or before another process image is executed.

Executing a new process image completely changes the contents of memory, copying only the argument and environment strings to new locations. But many other attributes of the process are unchanged:

- The process ID and the parent process ID. See Section 23.2 [Process Creation Concepts], page 444.
- Session and process group membership. See Section 24.1 [Concepts of Job Control], page 457.
- Real user ID and group ID, and supplementary group IDs. See Section 25.2 [The Persona of a Process], page 479.
- Pending alarms. See Section 17.3 [Setting an Alarm], page 335.

Chapter 23: Processes   449

- Current working directory and root directory. See Section 9.1 [Working Directory], page 169. In the GNU system, the root directory is not copied when executing a setuid program; instead the system default root directory is used for the new program.
- File mode creation mask. See Section 9.8.7 [Assigning File Permissions], page 190.
- Process signal mask; see Section 21.7.3 [Process Signal Mask], page 410.
- Pending signals; see Section 21.7 [Blocking Signals], page 408.
- Elapsed processor time associated with the process; see Section 17.1 [Processor Time], page 321.

If the set-user-ID and set-group-ID mode bits of the process image file are set, this affects the effective user ID and effective group ID (respectively) of the process. These concepts are discussed in detail in Section 25.2 [The Persona of a Process], page 479.

Signals that are set to be ignored in the existing process image are also set to be ignored in the new process image. All other signals are set to the default action in the new process image. For more information about signals, see Chapter 21 [Signal Handling], page 371.

File descriptors open in the existing process image remain open in the new process image, unless they have the **FD_CLOEXEC** (close-on-exec) flag set. The files that remain open inherit all attributes of the open file description from the existing process image, including file locks. File descriptors are discussed in Chapter 8 [Low-Level Input/Output], page 139.

Streams, by contrast, cannot survive through **exec** functions, because they are located in the memory of the process itself. The new process image has no streams except those it creates afresh. Each of the streams in the pre-**exec** process image has a descriptor inside it, and these descriptors do survive through **exec** (provided that they do not have **FD_CLOEXEC** set). The new process image can reconnect these to new streams using **fdopen** (see Section 8.4 [Descriptors and Streams], page 147).

23.6 Process Completion

The functions described in this section are used to wait for a child process to terminate or stop, and determine its status. These functions are declared in the header file 'sys/wait.h'.

pid_t waitpid (pid_t *pid*, int **status-ptr*, int   *Function*
     options)
     The **waitpid** function is used to request status information from a child process whose process ID is *pid*. Normally, the calling process is

suspended until the child process makes status information available by terminating.

Other values for the *pid* argument have special interpretations. A value of `-1` or `WAIT_ANY` requests status information for any child process; a value of `0` or `WAIT_MYPGRP` requests information for any child process in the same process group as the calling process; and any other negative value − *pgid* requests information for any child process whose process group ID is *pgid*.

If status information for a child process is available immediately, this function returns immediately without waiting. If more than one eligible child process has status information available, one of them is chosen randomly, and its status is returned immediately. To get the status from the other eligible child processes, you need to call `waitpid` again.

The *options* argument is a bit mask. Its value should be the bitwise OR (that is, the '|' operator) of zero or more of the `WNOHANG` and `WUNTRACED` flags. You can use the `WNOHANG` flag to indicate that the parent process shouldn't wait; and the `WUNTRACED` flag to request status information from stopped processes as well as processes that have terminated.

The status information from the child process is stored in the object that *status-ptr* points to, unless *status-ptr* is a null pointer.

The return value is normally the process ID of the child process whose status is reported. If the `WNOHANG` option was specified and no child process is waiting to be noticed, the value is zero. A value of `-1` is returned in case of error. The following `errno` error conditions are defined for this function:

`EINTR`   The function was interrupted by delivery of a signal to the calling process. See Section 21.5 [Primitives Interrupted by Signals], page 402.

`ECHILD` There are no child processes to wait for, or the specified *pid* is not a child of the calling process.

`EINVAL` An invalid value was provided for the *options* argument.

These symbolic constants are defined as values for the *pid* argument to the `waitpid` function.

`WAIT_ANY`

This constant macro (whose value is `-1`) specifies that `waitpid` should return status information about any child process.

Chapter 23: Processes

WAIT_MYPGRP
> This constant (with value 0) specifies that `waitpid` should return status information about any child process in the same process group as the calling process.

These symbolic constants are defined as flags for the *options* argument to the `waitpid` function. You can bitwise-OR the flags together to obtain a value to use as the argument.

WNOHANG
> This flag specifies that `waitpid` should return immediately instead of waiting, if there is no child process ready to be noticed.

WUNTRACED
> This flag specifies that `waitpid` should report the status of any child processes that have been stopped as well as those that have terminated.

pid_t wait (int *status-ptr*)   *Function*
This is a simplified version of `waitpid`, and is used to wait until any one child process terminates. The call:

```
wait (&status)
```

is exactly equivalent to:

```
waitpid (-1, &status, 0)
```

pid_t wait4 (pid_t *pid*, int *status-ptr*, int *options*,   *Function*
        struct rusage *usage*)
If *usage* is a null pointer, `wait4` is equivalent to `waitpid (pid, status-ptr, options)`.

If *usage* is not null, `wait4` stores usage figures for the child process in *rusage* (but only if the child has terminated, not if it has stopped). See Section 17.5 [Resource Usage], page 339.

This function is a BSD extension.

Here's an example of how to use `waitpid` to get the status from all child processes that have terminated, without ever waiting. This function is designed to be a handler for `SIGCHLD`, the signal that indicates that at least one child process has terminated.

```
void
sigchld_handler (int signum)
{
  int pid;
  int status;
  while (1)
    {
      pid = waitpid (WAIT_ANY, &status, WNOHANG);
      if (pid < 0)
        {
          perror ("waitpid");
          break;
        }
      if (pid == 0)
        break;
      notice_termination (pid, status);
    }
}
```

23.7 Process Completion Status

If the exit status value (see Section 22.3 [Program Termination], page 437) of the child process is zero, then the status value reported by `waitpid` or `wait` is also zero. You can test for other kinds of information encoded in the returned status value using the following macros. These macros are defined in the header file 'sys/wait.h'.

int **WIFEXITED** (int *status*)   Macro
This macro returns a nonzero value if the child process terminated normally with `exit` or `_exit`.

int **WEXITSTATUS** (int *status*)   Macro
If `WIFEXITED` is true of *status*, this macro returns the low-order 8 bits of the exit status value from the child process. See Section 22.3.2 [Exit Status], page 437.

int **WIFSIGNALED** (int *status*)   Macro
This macro returns a nonzero value if the child process terminated because it received a signal that was not handled. See Chapter 21 [Signal Handling], page 371.

int **WTERMSIG** (int *status*)   Macro
If `WIFSIGNALED` is true of *status*, this macro returns the signal number of the signal that terminated the child process.

int **WCOREDUMP** (int *status*)   Macro
This macro returns a nonzero value if the child process terminated and produced a core dump.

int **WIFSTOPPED** (int *status*) Macro
This macro returns a nonzero value if the child process is stopped.

int **WSTOPSIG** (int *status*) Macro
If `WIFSTOPPED` is true of *status*, this macro returns the signal number of the signal that caused the child process to stop.

23.8 BSD Process Wait Functions

The GNU library also provides these related facilities for compatibility with BSD Unix. BSD uses the `union wait` data type to represent status values rather than an `int`. The two representations are actually interchangeable; they describe the same bit patterns. The GNU C Library defines macros such as `WEXITSTATUS` so that they will work on either kind of object, and the `wait` function is defined to accept either type of pointer as its *status-ptr* argument.

These functions are declared in 'sys/wait.h'.

union wait Data Type
This data type represents program termination status values. It has the following members:

int w_termsig
: The value of this member is the same as the result of the `WTERMSIG` macro.

int w_coredump
: The value of this member is the same as the result of the `WCOREDUMP` macro.

int w_retcode
: The value of this member is the same as the result of the `WEXITSTATUS` macro.

int w_stopsig
: The value of this member is the same as the result of the `WSTOPSIG` macro.

Instead of accessing these members directly, you should use the equivalent macros.

The `wait3` function is the predecessor to `wait4`, which is more flexible. `wait3` is now obsolete.

pid_t **wait3** (union wait *status-ptr*, int *options*, struct rusage *usage*) Function
If *usage* is a null pointer, `wait3` is equivalent to `waitpid (-1, status-ptr, options)`.

If *usage* is not null, `wait3` stores usage figures for the child process in
rusage (but only if the child has terminated, not if it has stopped).
See Section 17.5 [Resource Usage], page 339.

23.9 Process Creation Example

Here is an example program showing how you might write a function
similar to the built-in `system`. It executes its *command* argument using the
equivalent of 'sh -c *command*'.

```
#include <stddef.h>
#include <stdlib.h>
#include <unistd.h>
#include <sys/types.h>
#include <sys/wait.h>

/* Execute the command using this shell program.  */
#define SHELL "/bin/sh"

int
my_system (const char *command)
{
  int status;
  pid_t pid;

  pid = fork ();
  if (pid == 0)
    {
      /* This is the child process.  Execute the shell command. */
      execl (SHELL, SHELL, "-c", command, NULL);
      _exit (EXIT_FAILURE);
    }
  else if (pid < 0)
    /* The fork failed.  Report failure.  */
    status = -1;
  else
    /* This is the parent process.  Wait for the child to complete.  */
    if (waitpid (pid, &status, 0) != pid)
      status = -1;
  return status;
}
```

There are a couple of things you should pay attention to in this example.

Remember that the first `argv` argument supplied to the program represents the name of the program being executed. That is why, in the call to `execl`, SHELL is supplied once to name the program to execute and a second time to supply a value for `argv[0]`.

The `execl` call in the child process doesn't return if it is successful. If it fails, you must do something to make the child process terminate. Just returning a bad status code with `return` would leave two processes running

Chapter 23: Processes   455

the original program. Instead, the right behavior is for the child process to
report failure to its parent process.

Call `_exit` to accomplish this. The reason for using `_exit` instead of `exit`
is to avoid flushing fully buffered streams such as `stdout`. The buffers of
these streams probably contain data that was copied from the parent process
by the `fork`, data that will be output eventually by the parent process.
Calling `exit` in the child would output the data twice. See Section 22.3.5
[Termination Internals], page 440.

24 Job Control

Job control refers to the protocol for allowing a user to move between multiple *process groups* (or *jobs*) within a single *login session*. The job control facilities are set up so that appropriate behavior for most programs happens automatically and they need not do anything special about job control. So you can probably ignore the material in this chapter unless you are writing a shell or login program.

You need to be familiar with concepts relating to process creation (see Section 23.2 [Process Creation Concepts], page 444) and signal handling (see Chapter 21 [Signal Handling], page 371) in order to understand this material presented in this chapter.

24.1 Concepts of Job Control

The fundamental purpose of an interactive shell is to read commands from the user's terminal and create processes to execute the programs specified by those commands. It can do this using the `fork` (see Section 23.4 [Creating a Process], page 445) and `exec` (see Section 23.5 [Executing a File], page 446) functions.

A single command may run just one process—but often one command uses several processes. If you use the '|' operator in a shell command, you explicitly request several programs in their own processes. But even if you run just one program, it can use multiple processes internally. For example, a single compilation command such as 'cc -c foo.c' typically uses four processes (though normally only two at any given time). If you run `make`, its job is to run other programs in separate processes.

The processes belonging to a single command are called a *process group* or *job*. This is so that you can operate on all of them at once. For example, typing `C-c` sends the signal `SIGINT` to terminate all the processes in the foreground process group.

A *session* is a larger group of processes. Normally all the proccesses that stem from a single login belong to the same session.

Every process belongs to a process group. When a process is created, it becomes a member of the same process group and session as its parent process. You can put it in another process group using the `setpgid` function, provided the process group belongs to the same session.

The only way to put a process in a different session is to make it the initial process of a new session, or a *session leader*, using the `setsid` function. This also puts the session leader into a new process group, and you can't move it out of that process group again.

Usually, new sessions are created by the system login program, and the session leader is the process running the user's login shell.

A shell that supports job control must arrange to control which job can use the terminal at any time. Otherwise there might be multiple jobs trying to read from the terminal at once, and confusion about which process should receive the input typed by the user. To prevent this, the shell must cooperate with the terminal driver using the protocol described in this chapter.

The shell can give unlimited access to the controlling terminal to only one process group at a time. This is called the *foreground job* on that controlling terminal. Other process groups managed by the shell that are executing without such access to the terminal are called *background jobs*.

If a background job needs to read from its controlling terminal, it is *stopped* by the terminal driver; if the `TOSTOP` mode is set, likewise for writing. The user can stop a foreground job by typing the SUSP character (see Section 12.4.9 [Special Characters], page 270) and a program can stop any job by sending it a `SIGSTOP` signal. It's the responsibility of the shell to notice when jobs stop, to notify the user about them, and to provide mechanisms for allowing the user to interactively continue stopped jobs and switch jobs between foreground and background.

See Section 24.4 [Access to the Controlling Terminal], page 459, for more information about I/O to the controlling terminal,

24.2 Job Control is Optional

Not all operating systems support job control. The GNU system does support job control, but if you are using the GNU library on some other system, that system may not support job control itself.

You can use the `_POSIX_JOB_CONTROL` macro to test at compile-time whether the system supports job control. See Section 27.2 [Overall System Options], page 500.

If job control is not supported, then there can be only one process group per session, which behaves as if it were always in the foreground. The functions for creating additional process groups simply fail with the error code `ENOSYS`.

The macros naming the various job control signals (see Section 21.2.5 [Job Control Signals], page 380) are defined even if job control is not supported. However, the system never generates these signals, and attempts to send a job control signal or examine or specify their actions report errors or do nothing.

24.3 Controlling Terminal of a Process

One of the attributes of a process is its controlling terminal. Child processes created with `fork` inherit the controlling terminal from their parent process. In this way, all the processes in a session inherit the controlling terminal from the session leader. A session leader that has control of a terminal is called the *controlling process* of that terminal.

You generally do not need to worry about the exact mechanism used to allocate a controlling terminal to a session, since it is done for you by the system when you log in.

An individual process disconnects from its controlling terminal when it calls `setsid` to become the leader of a new session. See Section 24.7.2 [Process Group Functions], page 475.

24.4 Access to the Controlling Terminal

Processes in the foreground job of a controlling terminal have unrestricted access to that terminal; background proesses do not. This section describes in more detail what happens when a process in a background job tries to access its controlling terminal.

When a process in a background job tries to read from its controlling terminal, the process group is usually sent a `SIGTTIN` signal. This normally causes all of the processes in that group to stop (unless they handle the signal and don't stop themselves). However, if the reading process is ignoring or blocking this signal, then `read` fails with an `EIO` error instead.

Similarly, when a process in a background job tries to write to its controlling terminal, the default behavior is to send a `SIGTTOU` signal to the process group. However, the behavior is modified by the `TOSTOP` bit of the local modes flags (see Section 12.4.7 [Local Modes], page 266). If this bit is not set (which is the default), then writing to the controlling terminal is always permitted without sending a signal. Writing is also permitted if the `SIGTTOU` signal is being ignored or blocked by the writing process.

Most other terminal operations that a program can do are treated as reading or as writing. (The description of each operation should say which.)

For more information about the primitive `read` and `write` functions, see Section 8.2 [Input and Output Primitives], page 141.

24.5 Orphaned Process Groups

When a controlling process terminates, its terminal becomes free and a new session can be established on it. (In fact, another user could log in on the terminal.) This could cause a problem if any processes from the old session are still trying to use that terminal.

To prevent problems, process groups that continue running even after the session leader has terminated are marked as *orphaned process groups*.

When a process group becomes an orphan, its processes are sent a `SIGHUP` signal. Ordinarily, this causes the processes to terminate. However, if a program ignores this signal or establishes a handler for it (see Chapter 21 [Signal Handling], page 371), it can continue running as in the orphan process group even after its controlling process terminates; but it still cannot access the terminal any more.

24.6 Implementing a Job Control Shell

This section describes what a shell must do to implement job control, by presenting an extensive sample program to illustrate the concepts involved.

- Section 24.6.1 [Data Structures for the Shell], page 460, introduces the example and presents its primary data structures.
- Section 24.6.2 [Initializing the Shell], page 462, discusses actions which the shell must perform to prepare for job control.
- Section 24.6.3 [Launching Jobs], page 464, includes information about how to create jobs to execute commands.
- Section 24.6.4 [Foreground and Background], page 467, discusses what the shell should do differently when launching a job in the foreground as opposed to a background job.
- Section 24.6.5 [Stopped and Terminated Jobs], page 469, discusses reporting of job status back to the shell.
- Section 24.6.6 [Continuing Stopped Jobs], page 472, tells you how to continue jobs that have been stopped.
- Section 24.6.7 [The Missing Pieces], page 473, discusses other parts of the shell.

24.6.1 Data Structures for the Shell

All of the program examples included in this chapter are part of a simple shell program. This section presents data structures and utility functions which are used throughout the example.

The sample shell deals mainly with two data structures. The `job` type contains information about a job, which is a set of subprocesses linked together with pipes. The `process` type holds information about a single subprocess. Here are the relevant data structure declarations:

Chapter 24: Job Control

```
/* A process is a single process.  */
typedef struct process
{
  struct process *next;       /* next process in pipeline */
  char **argv;                /* for exec */
  pid_t pid;                  /* process ID */
  char completed;             /* true if process has completed */
  char stopped;               /* true if process has stopped */
  int status;                 /* reported status value */
} process;

/* A job is a pipeline of processes.  */
typedef struct job
{
  struct job *next;           /* next active job */
  char *command;              /* command line, used for messages */
  process *first_process;     /* list of processes in this job */
  pid_t pgid;                 /* process group ID */
  char notified;              /* true if user told about stopped job */
  struct termios tmodes;      /* saved terminal modes */
  int stdin, stdout, stderr;  /* standard i/o channels */
} job;

/* The active jobs are linked into a list.  This is its head.  */
job *first_job = NULL;
```

Here are some utility functions that are used for operating on `job` objects.

```
/* Find the active job with the indicated pgid.  */
job *
find_job (pid_t pgid)
{
  job *j;

  for (j = first_job; j; j = j->next)
    if (j->pgid == pgid)
      return j;
  return NULL;
}

/* Return true if all processes in the job have stopped or completed.  */
int
job_is_stopped (job *j)
{
  process *p;

  for (p = j->first_process; p; p = p->next)
    if (!p->completed && !p->stopped)
      return 0;
  return 1;
}
```

```
/* Return true if all processes in the job have completed.  */
int
job_is_completed (job *j)
{
  process *p;

  for (p = j->first_process; p; p = p->next)
    if (!p->completed)
      return 0;
  return 1;
}
```

24.6.2 Initializing the Shell

When a shell program that normally performs job control is started, it has to be careful in case it has been invoked from another shell that is already doing its own job control.

A subshell that runs interactively has to ensure that it has been placed in the foreground by its parent shell before it can enable job control itself. It does this by getting its initial process group ID with the `getpgrp` function, and comparing it to the process group ID of the current foreground job associated with its controlling terminal (which can be retrieved using the `tcgetpgrp` function).

If the subshell is not running as a foreground job, it must stop itself by sending a `SIGTTIN` signal to its own process group. It may not arbitrarily put itself into the foreground; it must wait for the user to tell the parent shell to do this. If the subshell is continued again, it should repeat the check and stop itself again if it is still not in the foreground.

Once the subshell has been placed into the foreground by its parent shell, it can enable its own job control. It does this by calling `setpgid` to put itself into its own process group, and then calling `tcsetpgrp` to place this process group into the foreground.

When a shell enables job control, it should set itself to ignore all the job control stop signals so that it doesn't accidentally stop itself. You can do this by setting the action for all the stop signals to `SIG_IGN`.

A subshell that runs non-interactively cannot and should not support job control. It must leave all processes it creates in the same process group as the shell itself; this allows the non-interactive shell and its child processes to be treated as a single job by the parent shell. This is easy to do—just don't use any of the job control primitives—but you must remember to make the shell do it.

Here is the initialization code for the sample shell that shows how to do all of this.

```
/* Keep track of attributes of the shell.  */
```

Chapter 24: Job Control

```
#include <sys/types.h>
#include <termios.h>
#include <unistd.h>

pid_t shell_pgid;
struct termios shell_tmodes;
int shell_terminal;
int shell_is_interactive;


/* Make sure the shell is running interactively as the foreground job
   before proceeding. */

void
init_shell ()
{

  /* See if we are running interactively.  */
  shell_terminal = STDIN_FILENO;
  shell_is_interactive = isatty (shell_terminal);

  if (shell_is_interactive)
    {
      /* Loop until we are in the foreground.  */
      while (tcgetpgrp (shell_terminal) != (shell_pgid = getpgrp ()))
        kill (- shell_pgid, SIGTTIN);

      /* Ignore interactive and job-control signals.  */
      signal (SIGINT, SIG_IGN);
      signal (SIGQUIT, SIG_IGN);
      signal (SIGTSTP, SIG_IGN);
      signal (SIGTTIN, SIG_IGN);
      signal (SIGTTOU, SIG_IGN);
      signal (SIGCHLD, SIG_IGN);

      /* Put ourselves in our own process group.  */
      shell_pgid = getpid ();
      if (setpgid (shell_pgid, shell_pgid) < 0)
        {
          perror ("Couldn't put the shell in its own process group");
          exit (1);
        }

      /* Grab control of the terminal.  */
      tcsetpgrp (shell_terminal, shell_pgid);

      /* Save default terminal attributes for shell.  */
      tcgetattr (shell_terminal, &shell_tmodes);
    }
}
```

24.6.3 Launching Jobs

Once the shell has taken responsibility for performing job control on its controlling terminal, it can launch jobs in response to commands typed by the user.

To create the processes in a process group, you use the same `fork` and `exec` functions described in Section 23.2 [Process Creation Concepts], page 444. Since there are multiple child processes involved, though, things are a little more complicated and you must be careful to do things in the right order. Otherwise, nasty race conditions can result.

You have two choices for how to structure the tree of parent-child relationships among the processes. You can either make all the processes in the process group be children of the shell process, or you can make one process in group be the ancestor of all the other processes in that group. The sample shell program presented in this chapter uses the first approach because it makes bookkeeping somewhat simpler.

As each process is forked, it should put itself in the new process group by calling `setpgid`; see Section 24.7.2 [Process Group Functions], page 475. The first process in the new group becomes its *process group leader*, and its process ID becomes the *process group ID* for the group.

The shell should also call `setpgid` to put each of its child processes into the new process group. This is because there is a potential timing problem: each child process must be put in the process group before it begins executing a new program, and the shell depends on having all the child processes in the group before it continues executing. If both the child processes and the shell call `setpgid`, this ensures that the right things happen no matter which process gets to it first.

If the job is being launched as a foreground job, the new process group also needs to be put into the foreground on the controlling terminal using `tcsetpgrp`. Again, this should be done by the shell as well as by each of its child processes, to avoid race conditions.

The next thing each child process should do is to reset its signal actions.

During initialization, the shell process set itself to ignore job control signals; see Section 24.6.2 [Initializing the Shell], page 462. As a result, any child processes it creates also ignore these signals by inheritance. This is definitely undesirable, so each child process should explicitly set the actions for these signals back to `SIG_DFL` just after it is forked.

Since shells follow this convention, applications can assume that they inherit the correct handling of these signals from the parent process. But every application has a responsibility not to mess up the handling of stop signals. Applications that disable the normal interpretation of the SUSP character should provide some other mechanism for the user to stop the job. When the user invokes this mechanism, the program should send a `SIGTSTP`

Chapter 24: Job Control

signal to the process group of the process, not just to the process itself. See Section 21.6.2 [Signaling Another Process], page 405.

Finally, each child process should call **exec** in the normal way. This is also the point at which redirection of the standard input and output channels should be handled. See Section 8.8 [Duplicating Descriptors], page 154, for an explanation of how to do this.

Here is the function from the sample shell program that is responsible for launching a program. The function is executed by each child process immediately after it has been forked by the shell, and never returns.

```
void
launch_process (process *p, pid_t pgid,
                int infile, int outfile, int errfile,
                int foreground)
{
  pid_t pid;

  if (shell_is_interactive)
    {
      /* Put the process into the process group and give the process group
         the terminal, if appropriate.
         This has to be done both by the shell and in the individual
         child processes because of potential race conditions.  */
      pid = getpid ();
      if (pgid == 0) pgid = pid;
      setpgid (pid, pgid);
      if (foreground)
        tcsetpgrp (shell_terminal, pgid);

      /* Set the handling for job control signals back to the default.  */
      signal (SIGINT, SIG_DFL);
      signal (SIGQUIT, SIG_DFL);
      signal (SIGTSTP, SIG_DFL);
      signal (SIGTTIN, SIG_DFL);
      signal (SIGTTOU, SIG_DFL);
      signal (SIGCHLD, SIG_DFL);
    }

  /* Set the standard input/output channels of the new process.  */
  if (infile != STDIN_FILENO)
    {
      dup2 (infile, STDIN_FILENO);
      close (infile);
    }
  if (outfile != STDOUT_FILENO)
    {
      dup2 (outfile, STDOUT_FILENO);
      close (outfile);
    }
  if (errfile != STDERR_FILENO)
    {
      dup2 (errfile, STDERR_FILENO);
```

```
      close (errfile);
    }

  /* Exec the new process.  Make sure we exit.  */
  execvp (p->argv[0], p->argv);
  perror ("execvp");
  exit (1);
}
```

If the shell is not running interactively, this function does not do anything with process groups or signals. Remember that a shell not performing job control must keep all of its subprocesses in the same process group as the shell itself.

Next, here is the function that actually launches a complete job. After creating the child processes, this function calls some other functions to put the newly created job into the foreground or background; these are discussed in Section 24.6.4 [Foreground and Background], page 467.

```
void
launch_job (job *j, int foreground)
{
  process *p;
  pid_t pid;
  int mypipe[2], infile, outfile;

  infile = j->stdin;
  for (p = j->first_process; p; p = p->next)
    {
      /* Set up pipes, if necessary.  */
      if (p->next)
        {
          if (pipe (mypipe) < 0)
            {
              perror ("pipe");
              exit (1);
            }
          outfile = mypipe[1];
        }
      else
        outfile = j->stdout;

      /* Fork the child processes.  */
      pid = fork ();
      if (pid == 0)
        /* This is the child process.  */
        launch_process (p, j->pgid, infile,
                        outfile, j->stderr, foreground);
      else if (pid < 0)
        {
          /* The fork failed.  */
          perror ("fork");
          exit (1);
        }
```

Chapter 24: Job Control

```
          else
            {
              /* This is the parent process.  */
              p->pid = pid;
              if (shell_is_interactive)
                {
                  if (!j->pgid)
                    j->pgid = pid;
                  setpgid (pid, j->pgid);
                }
            }

          /* Clean up after pipes.  */
          if (infile != j->stdin)
            close (infile);
          if (outfile != j->stdout)
            close (outfile);
          infile = mypipe[0];
        }

      format_job_info (j, "launched");

      if (!shell_is_interactive)
        wait_for_job (j);
      else if (foreground)
        put_job_in_foreground (j, 0);
      else
        put_job_in_background (j, 0);
    }
```

24.6.4 Foreground and Background

Now let's consider what actions must be taken by the shell when it launches a job into the foreground, and how this differs from what must be done when a background job is launched.

When a foreground job is launched, the shell must first give it access to the controlling terminal by calling `tcsetpgrp`. Then, the shell should wait for processes in that process group to terminate or stop. This is discussed in more detail in Section 24.6.5 [Stopped and Terminated Jobs], page 469.

When all of the processes in the group have either completed or stopped, the shell should regain control of the terminal for its own process group by calling `tcsetpgrp` again. Since stop signals caused by I/O from a background process or a SUSP character typed by the user are sent to the process group, normally all the processes in the job stop together.

The foreground job may have left the terminal in a strange state, so the shell should restore its own saved terminal modes before continuing. In case the job is merely been stopped, the shell should first save the current terminal modes so that it can restore them later if the job is continued. The functions for dealing with terminal modes are `tcgetattr` and `tcsetattr`; these are described in Section 12.4 [Terminal Modes], page 257.

Here is the sample shell's function for doing all of this.

```
/* Put job j in the foreground.  If cont is nonzero,
   restore the saved terminal modes and send the process group a
   SIGCONT signal to wake it up before we block.  */

void
put_job_in_foreground (job *j, int cont)
{
  /* Put the job into the foreground.  */
  tcsetpgrp (shell_terminal, j->pgid);

  /* Send the job a continue signal, if necessary.  */
  if (cont)
    {
      tcsetattr (shell_terminal, TCSADRAIN, &j->tmodes);
      if (kill (- j->pgid, SIGCONT) < 0)
        perror ("kill (SIGCONT)");
    }

  /* Wait for it to report.  */
  wait_for_job (j);

  /* Put the shell back in the foreground.  */
  tcsetpgrp (shell_terminal, shell_pgid);

  /* Restore the shell's terminal modes.  */
  tcgetattr (shell_terminal, &j->tmodes);
  tcsetattr (shell_terminal, TCSADRAIN, &shell_tmodes);
}
```

If the process group is launched as a background job, the shell should remain in the foreground itself and continue to read commands from the terminal.

In the sample shell, there is not much that needs to be done to put a job into the background. Here is the function it uses:

```
/* Put a job in the background.  If the cont argument is true, send
   the process group a SIGCONT signal to wake it up.  */

void
put_job_in_background (job *j, int cont)
{
  /* Send the job a continue signal, if necessary.  */
  if (cont)
    if (kill (-j->pgid, SIGCONT) < 0)
      perror ("kill (SIGCONT)");
}
```

Chapter 24: Job Control

24.6.5 Stopped and Terminated Jobs

When a foreground process is launched, the shell must block until all of the processes in that job have either terminated or stopped. It can do this by calling the `waitpid` function; see Section 23.6 [Process Completion], page 449. Use the WUNTRACED option so that status is reported for processes that stop as well as processes that terminate.

The shell must also check on the status of background jobs so that it can report terminated and stopped jobs to the user; this can be done by calling `waitpid` with the WNOHANG option. A good place to put a such a check for terminated and stopped jobs is just before prompting for a new command.

The shell can also receive asynchronous notification that there is status information available for a child process by establishing a handler for SIGCHLD signals. See Chapter 21 [Signal Handling], page 371.

In the sample shell program, the SIGCHLD signal is normally ignored. This is to avoid reentrancy problems involving the global data structures the shell manipulates. But at specific times when the shell is not using these data structures—such as when it is waiting for input on the terminal—it makes sense to enable a handler for SIGCHLD. The same function that is used to do the synchronous status checks (`do_job_notification`, in this case) can also be called from within this handler.

Here are the parts of the sample shell program that deal with checking the status of jobs and reporting the information to the user.

```
/* Store the status of the process pid that was returned by waitpid.
   Return 0 if all went well, nonzero otherwise.  */

int
mark_process_status (pid_t pid, int status)
{
  job *j;
  process *p;
```

```
          if (pid > 0)
            {
              /* Update the record for the process.  */
              for (j = first_job; j; j = j->next)
                for (p = j->first_process; p; p = p->next)
                  if (p->pid == pid)
                    {
                      p->status = status;
                      if (WIFSTOPPED (status))
                        p->stopped = 1;
                      else
                        {
                          p->completed = 1;
                          if (WIFSIGNALED (status))
                            fprintf (stderr, "%d: Terminated by signal %d.\n",
                                     (int) pid, WTERMSIG (p->status));
                        }
                      return 0;
                     }
              fprintf (stderr, "No child process %d.\n", pid);
              return -1;
            }
          else if (pid == 0 || errno == ECHILD)
            /* No processes ready to report.  */
            return -1;
          else {
            /* Other weird errors.  */
            perror ("waitpid");
            return -1;
          }
        }

        /* Check for processes that have status information available,
           without blocking.  */

        void
        update_status (void)
        {
          int status;
          pid_t pid;

          do
            pid = waitpid (WAIT_ANY, &status, WUNTRACED|WNOHANG);
          while (!mark_process_status (pid, status));
        }
```

Chapter 24: Job Control

```
/* Check for processes that have status information available,
   blocking until all processes in the given job have reported.  */

void
wait_for_job (job *j)
{
  int status;
  pid_t pid;

  do
    pid = waitpid (WAIT_ANY, &status, WUNTRACED);
  while (!mark_process_status (pid, status)
         && !job_is_stopped (j)
         && !job_is_completed (j));
}

/* Format information about job status for the user to look at.  */

void
format_job_info (job *j, const char *status)
{
  fprintf (stderr, "%ld (%s): %s\n", (long)j->pgid, status, j->command);
}
```

```
/* Notify the user about stopped or terminated jobs.
   Delete terminated jobs from the active job list.  */

void
do_job_notification (void)
{
  job *j, *jlast, *jnext;
  process *p;

  /* Update status information for child processes.  */
  update_status ();

  jlast = NULL;
  for (j = first_job; j; j = jnext)
    {
      jnext = j->next;

      /* If all processes have completed, tell the user the job has
         completed and delete it from the list of active jobs.  */
      if (job_is_completed (j)) {
        format_job_info (j, "completed");
        if (jlast)
          jlast->next = jnext;
        else
          first_job = jnext;
        free_job (j);
      }

      /* Notify the user about stopped jobs,
         marking them so that we won't do this more than once.  */
      else if (job_is_stopped (j) && !j->notified) {
        format_job_info (j, "stopped");
        j->notified = 1;
        jlast = j;
      }

      /* Don't say anything about jobs that are still running.  */
      else
        jlast = j;
    }
}
```

24.6.6 Continuing Stopped Jobs

The shell can continue a stopped job by sending a SIGCONT signal to its process group. If the job is being continued in the foreground, the shell should first invoke tcsetpgrp to give the job access to the terminal, and restore the saved terminal settings. After continuing a job in the foreground, the shell should wait for the job to stop or complete, as if the job had just been launched in the foreground.

Chapter 24: Job Control

The sample shell program handles both newly created and continued jobs with the same pair of functions, `put_job_in_foreground` and `put_job_in_background`. The definitions of these functions were given in Section 24.6.4 [Foreground and Background], page 467. When continuing a stopped job, a nonzero value is passed as the *cont* argument to ensure that the `SIGCONT` signal is sent and the terminal modes reset, as appropriate.

This leaves only a function for updating the shell's internal bookkeeping about the job being continued:

```
/* Mark a stopped job J as being running again.  */

void
mark_job_as_running (job *j)
{
  Process *p;

  for (p = j->first_process; p; p = p->next)
    p->stopped = 0;
  j->notified = 0;
}

/* Continue the job J.  */

void
continue_job (job *j, int foreground)
{
  mark_job_as_running (j);
  if (foreground)
    put_job_in_foreground (j, 1);
  else
    put_job_in_background (j, 1);
}
```

24.6.7 The Missing Pieces

The code extracts for the sample shell included in this chapter are only a part of the entire shell program. In particular, nothing at all has been said about how **job** and **program** data structures are allocated and initialized.

Most real shells provide a complex user interface that has support for a command language; variables; abbreviations, substitutions, and pattern matching on file names; and the like. All of this is far too complicated to explain here! Instead, we have concentrated on showing how to implement the core process creation and job control functions that can be called from such a shell.

Here is a table summarizing the major entry points we have presented:

`void init_shell (void)`
>   Initialize the shell's internal state. See Section 24.6.2 [Initializing the Shell], page 462.

`void launch_job (job *j, int `*foreground*`)`
> Launch the job *j* as either a foreground or background job. See Section 24.6.3 [Launching Jobs], page 464.

`void do_job_notification (void)`
> Check for and report any jobs that have terminated or stopped. Can be called synchronously or within a handler for `SIGCHLD` signals. See Section 24.6.5 [Stopped and Terminated Jobs], page 469.

`void continue_job (job *j, int `*foreground*`)`
> Continue the job *j*. See Section 24.6.6 [Continuing Stopped Jobs], page 472.

Of course, a real shell would also want to provide other functions for managing jobs. For example, it would be useful to have commands to list all active jobs or to send a signal (such as `SIGKILL`) to a job.

24.7 Functions for Job Control

This section contains detailed descriptions of the functions relating to job control.

24.7.1 Identifying the Controlling Terminal

You can use the `ctermid` function to get a file name that you can use to open the controlling terminal. In the GNU library, it returns the same string all the time: `"/dev/tty"`. That is a special "magic" file name that refers to the controlling terminal of the current process (if it has one). To find the name of the specific terminal device, use `ttyname`; see Section 12.1 [Identifying Terminals], page 255.

The function `ctermid` is declared in the header file '`stdio.h`'.

`char * `**`ctermid`**` (char *`*string*`)`   *Function*
> The `ctermid` function returns a string containing the file name of the controlling terminal for the current process. If *string* is not a null pointer, it should be an array that can hold at least `L_ctermid` characters; the string is returned in this array. Otherwise, a pointer to a string in a static area is returned, which might get overwritten on subsequent calls to this function.
>
> An empty string is returned if the file name cannot be determined for any reason. Even if a file name is returned, access to the file it represents is not guaranteed.

Chapter 24: Job Control

`int L_ctermid`   Macro
   The value of this macro is an integer constant expression that represents the size of a string large enough to hold the file name returned by `ctermid`.

   See also the `isatty` and `ttyname` functions, in Section 12.1 [Identifying Terminals], page 255.

24.7.2 Process Group Functions

Here are descriptions of the functions for manipulating process groups. Your program should include the header files '`sys/types.h`' and '`unistd.h`' to use these functions.

`pid_t setsid (void)`   Function
   The `setsid` function creates a new session. The calling process becomes the session leader, and is put in a new process group whose process group ID is the same as the process ID of that process. There are initially no other processes in the new process group, and no other process groups in the new session.

   This function also makes the calling process have no controlling terminal.

   The `setsid` function returns the new process group ID of the calling process if successful. A return value of `-1` indicates an error. The following `errno` error conditions are defined for this function:

   EPERM   The calling process is already a process group leader, or there is already another process group around that has the same process group ID.

   The `getpgrp` function has two definitions: one derived from BSD Unix, and one from the POSIX.1 standard. The feature test macros you have selected (see Section 1.3.4 [Feature Test Macros], page 8) determine which definition you get. Specifically, you get the BSD version if you define `_BSD_SOURCE`; otherwise, you get the POSIX version if you define `_POSIX_SOURCE` or `_GNU_SOURCE`. Programs written for old BSD systems will not include '`unistd.h`', which defines `getpgrp` specially under `_BSD_SOURCE`. You must link such programs with the `-lbsd-compat` option to get the BSD definition.

`pid_t getpgrp (void)`   POSIX.1 Function
   The POSIX.1 definition of `getpgrp` returns the process group ID of the calling process.

`pid_t getpgrp (pid_t pid)`   BSD Function
   The BSD definition of `getpgrp` returns the process group ID of the process *pid*. You can supply a value of `0` for the *pid* argument to get information about the calling process.

int setpgid (pid_t *pid*, pid_t *pgid*)   *Function*

The `setpgid` function puts the process *pid* into the process group *pgid*. As a special case, either *pid* or *pgid* can be zero to indicate the process ID of the calling process.

This function fails on a system that does not support job control. See Section 24.2 [Job Control is Optional], page 458, for more information.

If the operation is successful, `setpgid` returns zero. Otherwise it returns -1. The following `errno` error conditions are defined for this function:

`EACCES`   The child process named by *pid* has executed an `exec` function since it was forked.

`EINVAL`   The value of the *pgid* is not valid.

`ENOSYS`   The system doesn't support job control.

`EPERM`   The process indicated by the *pid* argument is a session leader, or is not in the same session as the calling process, or the value of the *pgid* argument doesn't match a process group ID in the same session as the calling process.

`ESRCH`   The process indicated by the *pid* argument is not the calling process or a child of the calling process.

int setpgrp (pid_t *pid*, pid_t *pgid*)   *Function*

This is the BSD Unix name for `setpgid`. Both functions do exactly the same thing.

24.7.3 Functions for Controlling Terminal Access

These are the functions for reading or setting the foreground process group of a terminal. You should include the header files 'sys/types.h' and 'unistd.h' in your application to use these functions.

Although these functions take a file descriptor argument to specify the terminal device, the foreground job is associated with the terminal file itself and not a particular open file descriptor.

pid_t tcgetpgrp (int *filedes*)   *Function*

This function returns the process group ID of the foreground process group associated with the terminal open on descriptor *filedes*.

If there is no foreground process group, the return value is a number greater than 1 that does not match the process group ID of any existing process group. This can happen if all of the processes in the job that was formerly the foreground job have terminated, and no other job has yet been moved into the foreground.

Chapter 24: Job Control

In case of an error, a value of -1 is returned. The following **errno** error conditions are defined for this function:

EBADF   The *filedes* argument is not a valid file descriptor.

ENOSYS   The system doesn't support job control.

ENOTTY   The terminal file associated with the *filedes* argument isn't the controlling terminal of the calling process.

int tcsetpgrp (int *filedes*, pid_t *pgid*)   *Function*

This function is used to set a terminal's foreground process group ID. The argument *filedes* is a descriptor which specifies the terminal; *pgid* specifies the process group. The calling process must be a member of the same session as *pgid* and must have the same controlling terminal.

For terminal access purposes, this function is treated as output. If it is called from a background process on its controlling terminal, normally all processes in the process group are sent a **SIGTTOU** signal. The exception is if the calling process itself is ignoring or blocking **SIGTTOU** signals, in which case the operation is performed and no signal is sent.

If successful, **tcsetpgrp** returns 0. A return value of -1 indicates an error. The following **errno** error conditions are defined for this function:

EBADF   The *filedes* argument is not a valid file descriptor.

EINVAL   The *pgid* argument is not valid.

ENOSYS   The system doesn't support job control.

ENOTTY   The *filedes* isn't the controlling terminal of the calling process.

EPERM   The *pgid* isn't a process group in the same session as the calling process.

25 Users and Groups

Every user who can log in on the system is identified by a unique number called the *user ID*. Each process has an effective user ID which says which user's access permissions it has.

Users are classified into *groups* for access control purposes. Each process has one or more *group ID values* which say which groups the process can use for access to files.

The effective user and group IDs of a process collectively form its *persona*. This determines which files the process can access. Normally, a process inherits its persona from the parent process, but under special circumstances a process can change its persona and thus change its access permissions.

Each file in the system also has a user ID and a group ID. Access control works by comparing the user and group IDs of the file with those of the running process.

The system keeps a database of all the registered users, and another database of all the defined groups. There are library functions you can use to examine these databases.

25.1 User and Group IDs

Each user account on a computer system is identified by a *user name* (or *login name*) and *user ID*. Normally, each user name has a unique user ID, but it is possible for several login names to have the same user ID. The user names and corresponding user IDs are stored in a data base which you can access as described in Section 25.12 [User Database], page 489.

Users are classified in *groups*. Each user name also belongs to one or more groups, and has one *default group*. Users who are members of the same group can share resources (such as files) that are not accessible to users who are not a member of that group. Each group has a *group name* and *group ID*. See Section 25.13 [Group Database], page 491, for how to find information about a group ID or group name.

25.2 The Persona of a Process

At any time, each process has a single user ID and a group ID which determine the privileges of the process. These are collectively called the *persona* of the process, because they determine "who it is" for purposes of access control. These IDs are also called the *effective user ID* and *effective group ID* of the process.

Your login shell starts out with a persona which consists of your user ID and your default group ID. In normal circumstances, all your other processes inherit these values.

A process also has a *real user ID* which identifies the user who created the process, and a *real group ID* which identifies that user's default group. These values do not play a role in access control, so we do not consider them part of the persona. But they are also important.

Both the real and effective user ID can be changed during the lifetime of a process. See Section 25.3 [Why Change the Persona of a Process?], page 480.

In addition, a user can belong to multiple groups, so the persona includes *supplementary group IDs* that also contribute to access permission.

For details on how a process's effective user IDs and group IDs affect its permission to access files, see Section 9.8.6 [How Your Access to a File is Decided], page 190.

The user ID of a process also controls permissions for sending signals using the `kill` function. See Section 21.6.2 [Signaling Another Process], page 405.

25.3 Why Change the Persona of a Process?

The most obvious situation where it is necessary for a process to change its user and/or group IDs is the `login` program. When `login` starts running, its user ID is `root`. Its job is to start a shell whose user and group IDs are those of the user who is logging in. (To accomplish this fully, `login` must set the real user and group IDs as well as its persona. But this is a special case.)

The more common case of changing persona is when an ordinary user program needs access to a resource that wouldn't ordinarily be accessible to the user actually running it.

For example, you may have a file that is controlled by your program but that shouldn't be read or modified directly by other users, either because it implements some kind of locking protocol, or because you want to preserve the integrity or privacy of the information it contains. This kind of restricted access can be implemented by having the program change its effective user or group ID to match that of the resource.

Thus, imagine a game program that saves scores in a file. The game program itself needs to be able to update this file no matter who is running it, but if users can write the file without going through the game, they can give themselves any scores they like. Some people consider this undesirable, or even reprehensible. It can be prevented by creating a new user ID and login name (say, **games**) to own the scores file, and make the file writable

Chapter 25: Users and Groups   481

only by this user. Then, when the game program wants to update this file, it
can change its effective user ID to be that for `games`. In effect, the program
must adopt the persona of `games` so it can write the scores file.

25.4 How an Application Can Change Persona

The ability to change the persona of a process can be a source of uninten-
tional privacy violations, or even intentional abuse. Because of the potential
for problems, changing persona is restricted to special circumstances.

You can't arbitrarily set your user ID or group ID to anything you want;
only privileged processes can do that. Instead, the normal way for a program
to change its persona is that it has been set up in advance to change to a
particular user or group. This is the function of the setuid and setgid bits of
a file's access mode. See Section 9.8.5 [The Mode Bits for Access Permission],
page 188.

When the setuid bit of an executable file is set, executing that file au-
tomatically changes the effective user ID to the user that owns the file.
Likewise, executing a file whose setgid bit is set changes the effective group
ID to the group of the file. See Section 23.5 [Executing a File], page 446.
Creating a file that changes to a particular user or group ID thus requires
full access to that user or group ID.

See Section 9.8 [File Attributes], page 181, for a more general discussion
of file modes and accessibility.

A process can always change its effective user (or group) ID back to its
real ID. Programs do this so as to turn off their special privileges when they
are not needed, which makes for more robustness.

25.5 Reading the Persona of a Process

Here are detailed descriptions of the functions for reading the user and
group IDs of a process, both real and effective. To use these facilities, you
must include the header files '`sys/types.h`' and '`unistd.h`'.

uid_t   Data Type
  This is an integer data type used to represent user IDs. In the GNU
  library, this is an alias for `unsigned int`.

gid_t   Data Type
  This is an integer data type used to represent group IDs. In the GNU
  library, this is an alias for `unsigned int`.

uid_t getuid (`void`)   Function
  The `getuid` function returns the real user ID of the process.

gid_t getgid (void)   *Function*
   The `getgid` function returns the real group ID of the process.

uid_t geteuid (void)   *Function*
   The `geteuid` function returns the effective user ID of the process.

gid_t getegid (void)   *Function*
   The `getegid` function returns the effective group ID of the process.

int getgroups (int *count*, gid_t **groups*)   *Function*
   The `getgroups` function is used to inquire about the supplementary group IDs of the process. Up to *count* of these group IDs are stored in the array *groups*; the return value from the function is the number of group IDs actually stored. If *count* is smaller than the total number of supplementary group IDs, then `getgroups` returns a value of -1 and `errno` is set to `EINVAL`.

   If *count* is zero, then `getgroups` just returns the total number of supplementary group IDs. On systems that do not support supplementary groups, this will always be zero.

   Here's how to use `getgroups` to read all the supplementary group IDs:

```
gid_t *
read_all_groups (void)
{
  int ngroups = getgroups (0, NULL);
  gid_t *groups
    = (gid_t *) xmalloc (ngroups * sizeof (gid_t));
  int val = getgroups (ngroups, groups);
  if (val < 0)
    {
      free (groups);
      return NULL;
    }
  return groups;
}
```

25.6 Setting the User ID

This section describes the functions for altering the user ID (real and/or effective) of a process. To use these facilities, you must include the header files 'sys/types.h' and 'unistd.h'.

int setuid (uid_t *newuid*)   *Function*
   This function sets both the real and effective user ID of the process to *newuid*, provided that the process has appropriate privileges.

   If the process is not privileged, then *newuid* must either be equal to the real user ID or the saved user ID (if the system supports the _

Chapter 25: Users and Groups

POSIX_SAVED_IDS feature). In this case, `setuid` sets only the effective user ID and not the real user ID.

The `setuid` function returns a value of 0 to indicate successful completion, and a value of -1 to indicate an error. The following `errno` error conditions are defined for this function:

EINVAL   The value of the *newuid* argument is invalid.

EPERM   The process does not have the appropriate privileges; you do not have permission to change to the specified ID.

int setreuid (uid_t *ruid*, uid_t *euid*)   *Function*
This function sets the real user ID of the process to *ruid* and the effective user ID to *euid*. If *ruid* is -1, it means not to change the real user ID; likewise if *euid* is -1, it means not to change the effective user ID.

The `setreuid` function exists for compatibility with 4.3 BSD Unix, which does not support saved IDs. You can use this function to swap the effective and real user IDs of the process. (Privileged processes are not limited to this particular usage.) If saved IDs are supported, you should use that feature instead of this function. See Section 25.8 [Enabling and Disabling Setuid Access], page 484.

The return value is 0 on success and -1 on failure. The following `errno` error conditions are defined for this function:

EPERM   The process does not have the appropriate privileges; you do not have permission to change to the specified ID.

25.7 Setting the Group IDs

This section describes the functions for altering the group IDs (real and effective) of a process. To use these facilities, you must include the header files 'sys/types.h' and 'unistd.h'.

int setgid (gid_t *newgid*)   *Function*
This function sets both the real and effective group ID of the process to *newgid*, provided that the process has appropriate privileges.

If the process is not privileged, then *newgid* must either be equal to the real group ID or the saved group ID. In this case, `setgid` sets only the effective group ID and not the real group ID.

The return values and error conditions for `setgid` are the same as those for `setuid`.

int setregid (gid_t *rgid*, fid_t *egid*)   *Function*
This function sets the real group ID of the process to *rgid* and the effective group ID to *egid*. If *rgid* is -1, it means not to change the

real group ID; likewise if *egid* is -1, it means not to change the effective group ID.

The `setregid` function is provided for compatibility with 4.3 BSD Unix, which does not support saved IDs. You can use this function to swap the effective and real group IDs of the process. (Privileged processes are not limited to this usage.) If saved IDs are supported, you should use that feature instead of using this function. See Section 25.8 [Enabling and Disabling Setuid Access], page 484.

The return values and error conditions for `setregid` are the same as those for `setreuid`.

The GNU system also lets privileged processes change their supplementary group IDs. To use `setgroups` or `initgroups`, your programs should include the header file 'grp.h'.

int **setgroups** (`size_t` *count*, `gid_t` *groups*)   Function
This function sets the process's supplementary group IDs. It can only be called from privileged processes. The *count* argument specifies the number of group IDs in the array *groups*.

This function returns 0 if successful and -1 on error. The following `errno` error conditions are defined for this function:

EPERM   The calling process is not privileged.

int **initgroups** (`const char` *user*, `gid_t` *gid*)   Function
The `initgroups` function effectively calls `setgroups` to set the process's supplementary group IDs to be the normal default for the user name *user*. The group ID *gid* is also included.

25.8 Enabling and Disabling Setuid Access

A typical setuid program does not need its special access all of the time. It's a good idea to turn off this access when it isn't needed, so it can't possibly give unintended access.

If the system supports the saved user ID feature, you can accomplish this with `setuid`. When the game program starts, its real user ID is `jdoe`, its effective user ID is `games`, and its saved user ID is also `games`. The program should record both user ID values once at the beginning, like this:

```
user_user_id = getuid ();
game_user_id = geteuid ();
```

Then it can turn off game file access with

```
setuid (user_user_id);
```

and turn it on with

Chapter 25: Users and Groups

```
setuid (game_user_id);
```

Throughout this process, the real user ID remains **jdoe** and the saved user ID remains **games**, so the program can always set its effective user ID to either one.

On other systems that don't support the saved user ID feature, you can turn setuid access on and off by using **setreuid** to swap the real and effective user IDs of the process, as follows:

```
setreuid (geteuid (), getuid ());
```

This special case is always allowed—it cannot fail.

Why does this have the effect of toggling the setuid access? Suppose a game program has just started, and its real user ID is **jdoe** while its effective user ID is **games**. In this state, the game can write the scores file. If it swaps the two uids, the real becomes **games** and the effective becomes **jdoe**; now the program has only **jdoe** access. Another swap brings **games** back to the effective user ID and restores access to the scores file.

In order to handle both kinds of systems, test for the saved user ID feature with a preprocessor conditional, like this:

```
#ifdef _POSIX_SAVED_IDS
  setuid (user_user_id);
#else
  setreuid (geteuid (), getuid ());
#endif
```

25.9 Setuid Program Example

Here's an example showing how to set up a program that changes its effective user ID.

This is part of a game program called **caber-toss** that manipulates a file 'scores' that should be writable only by the game program itself. The program assumes that its executable file will be installed with the set-user-ID bit set and owned by the same user as the 'scores' file. Typically, a system administrator will set up an account like **games** for this purpose.

The executable file is given mode **4755**, so that doing an 'ls -l' on it produces output like:

```
-rwsr-xr-x   1 games      184422 Jul 30 15:17 caber-toss
```

The set-user-ID bit shows up in the file modes as the 's'.

The scores file is given mode **644**, and doing an 'ls -l' on it shows:

```
-rw-r--r--   1 games           0 Jul 31 15:33 scores
```

Here are the parts of the program that show how to set up the changed user ID. This program is conditionalized so that it makes use of the saved IDs feature if it is supported, and otherwise uses **setreuid** to swap the effective and real user IDs.

```
#include <stdio.h>
#include <sys/types.h>
#include <unistd.h>
#include <stdlib.h>


/* Save the effective and real UIDs. */

static uid_t euid, ruid;


/* Restore the effective UID to its original value. */

void
do_setuid (void)
{
  int status;

#ifdef _POSIX_SAVED_IDS
  status = setuid (euid);
#else
  status = setreuid (ruid, euid);
#endif
  if (status < 0) {
    fprintf (stderr, "Couldn't set uid.\n");
    exit (status);
    }
}


/* Set the effective UID to the real UID. */

void
undo_setuid (void)
{
  int status;

#ifdef _POSIX_SAVED_IDS
  status = setuid (ruid);
#else
  status = setreuid (euid, ruid);
#endif
  if (status < 0) {
    fprintf (stderr, "Couldn't set uid.\n");
    exit (status);
    }
}
/* Main program. */

int
main (void)
{
  /* Save the real and effective user IDs.  */
```

Chapter 25: Users and Groups

```
    ruid = getuid ();
    euid = geteuid ();
    undo_setuid ();

    /* Do the game and record the score.  */
    ...
}
```

Notice how the first thing the `main` function does is to set the effective user ID back to the real user ID. This is so that any other file accesses that are performed while the user is playing the game use the real user ID for determining permissions. Only when the program needs to open the scores file does it switch back to the original effective user ID, like this:

```
/* Record the score.  */

int
record_score (int score)
{
  FILE *stream;
  char *myname;

  /* Open the scores file.  */
  do_setuid ();
  stream = fopen (SCORES_FILE, "a");
  undo_setuid ();

  /* Write the score to the file.  */
  if (stream)
    {
      myname = cuserid (NULL);
      if (score < 0)
        fprintf (stream, "%10s: Couldn't lift the caber.\n", myname);
      else
        fprintf (stream, "%10s: %d feet.\n", myname, score);
      fclose (stream);
      return 0;
    }
  else
    return -1;
}
```

25.10 Tips for Writing Setuid Programs

It is easy for setuid programs to give the user access that isn't intended—in fact, if you want to avoid this, you need to be careful. Here are some guidelines for preventing unintended access and minimizing its consequences when it does occur:

- Don't have `setuid` programs with privileged user IDs such as `root` unless it is absolutely necessary. If the resource is specific to your particular program, it's better to define a new, nonprivileged user ID or group ID just to manage that resource.

- Be cautious about using the `system` and `exec` functions in combination with changing the effective user ID. Don't let users of your program execute arbitrary programs under a changed user ID. Executing a shell is especially bad news. Less obviously, the `execlp` and `execvp` functions are a potential risk (since the program they execute depends on the user's `PATH` environment variable).

  If you must `exec` another program under a changed ID, specify an absolute file name (see Section 6.2.2 [File Name Resolution], page 78) for the executable, and make sure that the protections on that executable and *all* containing directories are such that ordinary users cannot replace it with some other program.

- Only use the user ID controlling the resource in the part of the program that actually uses that resource. When you're finished with it, restore the effective user ID back to the actual user's user ID. See Section 25.8 [Enabling and Disabling Setuid Access], page 484.

- If the `setuid` part of your program needs to access other files besides the controlled resource, it should verify that the real user would ordinarily have permission to access those files. You can use the `access` function (see Section 9.8.6 [How Your Access to a File is Decided], page 190) to check this; it uses the real user and group IDs, rather than the effective IDs.

25.11 Identifying Who Logged In

You can use the functions listed in this section to determine the login name of the user who is running a process, and the name of the user who logged in the current session. See also the function `getuid` and friends (see Section 25.5 [Reading the Persona of a Process], page 481).

The `getlogin` function is declared in 'unistd.h', while `cuserid` and `L_cuserid` are declared in 'stdio.h'.

char * getlogin (void)   *Function*
  The `getlogin` function returns a pointer to a string containing the name of the user logged in on the controlling terminal of the process, or a null pointer if this information cannot be determined. The string is statically allocated and might be overwritten on subsequent calls to this function or to `cuserid`.

char * cuserid (char *string)   *Function*
  The `cuserid` function returns a pointer to a string containing a user name associated with the effective ID of the process. If *string* is not

Chapter 25: Users and Groups   489

a null pointer, it should be an array that can hold at least `L_cuserid` characters; the string is returned in this array. Otherwise, a pointer to a string in a static area is returned. This string is statically allocated and might be overwritten on subsequent calls to this function or to `getlogin`.

int L_cuserid   Macro
An integer constant that indicates how long an array you might need to store a user name.

These functions let your program identify positively the user who is running or the user who logged in this session. (These can differ when setuid programs are involved; See Section 25.2 [The Persona of a Process], page 479.) The user cannot do anything to fool these functions.

For most purposes, it is more useful to use the environment variable `LOGNAME` to find out who the user is. This is more flexible precisely because the user can set `LOGNAME` arbitrarily. See Section 22.2.2 [Standard Environment Variables], page 435.

25.12 User Database

This section describes all about how to search and scan the database of registered users. The database itself is kept in the file '/etc/passwd' on most systems, but on some systems a special network server gives access to it.

25.12.1 The Data Structure that Describes a User

The functions and data structures for accessing the system user database are declared in the header file 'pwd.h'.

struct passwd   Data Type
The `passwd` data structure is used to hold information about entries in the system user data base. It has at least the following members:

`char *pw_name`
   The user's login name.

`char *pw_passwd.`
   The encrypted password string.

`uid_t pw_uid`
   The user ID number.

`gid_t pw_gid`
   The user's default group ID number.

`char *pw_gecos`
: A string typically containing the user's real name, and possibly other information such as a phone number.

`char *pw_dir`
: The user's home directory, or initial working directory. This might be a null pointer, in which case the interpretation is system-dependent.

`char *pw_shell`
: The user's default shell, or the initial program run when the user logs in. This might be a null pointer, indicating that the system default should be used.

25.12.2 Looking Up One User

You can search the system user database for information about a specific user using `getpwuid` or `getpwnam`. These functions are declared in 'pwd.h'.

struct passwd * getpwuid (`uid_t` *uid*) *Function*
This function returns a pointer to a statically-allocated structure containing information about the user whose user ID is *uid*. This structure may be overwritten on subsequent calls to `getpwuid`.

A null pointer value indicates there is no user in the data base with user ID *uid*.

struct passwd * getpwnam (`const char *`*name*) *Function*
This function returns a pointer to a statically-allocated structure containing information about the user whose user name is *name*. This structure may be overwritten on subsequent calls to `getpwnam`.

A null pointer value indicates there is no user named *name*.

25.12.3 Scanning the List of All Users

This section explains how a program can read the list of all users in the system, one user at a time. The functions described here are declared in 'pwd.h'.

You can use the `fgetpwent` function to read user entries from a particular file.

struct passwd * fgetpwent (`FILE *`*stream*) *Function*
This function reads the next user entry from *stream* and returns a pointer to the entry. The structure is statically allocated and is rewritten on subsequent calls to `fgetpwent`. You must copy the contents of the structure if you wish to save the information.

Chapter 25: Users and Groups   491

This stream must correspond to a file in the same format as the standard password database file. This function comes from System V.

The way to scan all the entries in the user database is with `setpwent`, `getpwent`, and `endpwent`.

`void` **`setpwent`** `(void)`   *Function*
This function initializes a stream which `getpwent` uses to read the user database.

`struct passwd *` **`getpwent`** `(void)`   *Function*
The `getpwent` function reads the next entry from the stream initialized by `setpwent`. It returns a pointer to the entry. The structure is statically allocated and is rewritten on subsequent calls to `getpwent`. You must copy the contents of the structure if you wish to save the information.

`void` **`endpwent`** `(void)`   *Function*
This function closes the internal stream used by `getpwent`.

25.12.4 Writing a User Entry

`int` **`putpwent`** `(const struct passwd *p, FILE`   *Function*
     `*stream)`
This function writes the user entry *p to the stream *stream*, in the format used for the standard user database file. The return value is zero on success and nonzero on failure.

This function exists for compatibility with SVID. We recommend that you avoid using it, because it makes sense only on the assumption that the `struct passwd` structure has no members except the standard ones; on a system which merges the traditional Unix data base with other extended information about users, adding an entry using this function would inevitably leave out much of the important information.

The function `putpwent` is declared in 'pwd.h'.

25.13 Group Database

This section describes all about how to search and scan the database of registered groups. The database itself is kept in the file '/etc/group' on most systems, but on some systems a special network service provides access to it.

25.13.1 The Data Structure for a Group

The functions and data structures for accessing the system group database are declared in the header file 'grp.h'.

struct group   Data Type

The group structure is used to hold information about an entry in the system group database. It has at least the following members:

char *gr_name
: The name of the group.

gid_t gr_gid
: The group ID of the group.

char **gr_mem
: A vector of pointers to the names of users in the group. Each user name is a null-terminated string, and the vector itself is terminated by a null pointer.

25.13.2 Looking Up One Group

You can search the group database for information about a specific group using getgrgid or getgrnam. These functions are declared in 'grp.h'.

struct group * getgrgid (gid_t *gid*)   Function

This function returns a pointer to a statically-allocated structure containing information about the group whose group ID is *gid*. This structure may be overwritten by subsequent calls to getgrgid.

A null pointer indicates there is no group with ID *gid*.

struct group * getgrnam (const char **name*)   Function

This function returns a pointer to a statically-allocated structure containing information about the group whose group name is *name*. This structure may be overwritten by subsequent calls to getgrnam.

A null pointer indicates there is no group named *name*.

25.13.3 Scanning the List of All Groups

This section explains how a program can read the list of all groups in the system, one group at a time. The functions described here are declared in 'grp.h'.

You can use the fgetgrent function to read group entries from a particular file.

Chapter 25: Users and Groups 493

struct group * fgetgrent (FILE *stream*)   *Function*
  The `fgetgrent` function reads the next entry from *stream*. It returns a pointer to the entry. The structure is statically allocated and is rewritten on subsequent calls to `fgetgrent`. You must copy the contents of the structure if you wish to save the information.

  The stream must correspond to a file in the same format as the standard group database file.

  The way to scan all the entries in the group database is with `setgrent`, `getgrent`, and `endgrent`.

void setgrent (void)   *Function*
  This function initializes a stream for reading from the group data base. You use this stream by calling `getgrent`.

struct group * getgrent (void)   *Function*
  The `getgrent` function reads the next entry from the stream initialized by `setgrent`. It returns a pointer to the entry. The structure is statically allocated and is rewritten on subsequent calls to `getgrent`. You must copy the contents of the structure if you wish to save the information.

void endgrent (void)   *Function*
  This function closes the internal stream used by `getgrent`.

25.14 User and Group Database Example

Here is an example program showing the use of the system database inquiry functions. The program prints some information about the user running the program.

```
#include <grp.h>
#include <pwd.h>
#include <sys/types.h>
#include <unistd.h>
#include <stdlib.h>

int
main (void)
{
  uid_t me;
  struct passwd *my_passwd;
  struct group *my_group;
  char **members;

  /* Get information about the user ID. */
  me = getuid ();
  my_passwd = getpwuid (me);
  if (!my_passwd)
```

```
    {
      printf ("Couldn't find out about user %d.\n", (int) me);
      exit (EXIT_FAILURE);
    }

  /* Print the information. */
  printf ("I am %s.\n", my_passwd->pw_gecos);
  printf ("My login name is %s.\n", my_passwd->pw_name);
  printf ("My uid is %d.\n", (int) (my_passwd->pw_uid));
  printf ("My home directory is %s.\n", my_passwd->pw_dir);
  printf ("My default shell is %s.\n", my_passwd->pw_shell);

  /* Get information about the default group ID. */
  my_group = getgrgid (my_passwd->pw_gid);
  if (!my_group)
    {
      printf ("Couldn't find out about group %d.\n",
              (int) my_passwd->pw_gid);
      exit (EXIT_FAILURE);
    }

  /* Print the information. */
  printf ("My default group is %s (%d).\n",
          my_group->gr_name, (int) (my_passwd->pw_gid));
  printf ("The members of this group are:\n");
  members = my_group->gr_mem;
  while (*members)
    {
      printf ("  %s\n", *(members));
      members++;
    }

  return EXIT_SUCCESS;
}
```

Here is some output from this program:

```
I am Throckmorton Snurd.
My login name is snurd.
My uid is 31093.
My home directory is /home/fsg/snurd.
My default shell is /bin/sh.
My default group is guest (12).
The members of this group are:
  friedman
  tami
```

26 System Information

This chapter describes functions that return information about the particular machine that is in use—the type of hardware, the type of software, and the individual machine's name.

26.1 Host Identification

This section explains how to identify the particular machine that your program is running on. The identification of a machine consists of its Internet host name and Internet address; see Section 11.5 [The Internet Namespace], page 215. The host name should always be a fully qualified domain name, like 'crispy-wheats-n-chicken.ai.mit.edu', not a simple name like just 'crispy-wheats-n-chicken'.

Prototypes for these functions appear in 'unistd.h'. The shell commands `hostname` and `hostid` work by calling them.

int gethostname (char *name*, size_t *size*) *Function*

This function returns the name of the host machine in the array *name*. The *size* argument specifies the size of this array, in bytes.

The return value is 0 on success and -1 on failure. In the GNU C library, `gethostname` fails if *size* is not large enough; then you can try again with a larger array. The following `errno` error condition is defined for this function:

ENAMETOOLONG
    The *size* argument is less than the size of the host name plus one.

On some systems, there is a symbol for the maximum possible host name length: **MAXHOSTNAMELEN**. It is defined in 'sys/param.h'. But you can't count on this to exist, so it is cleaner to handle failure and try again.

`gethostname` stores the beginning of the host name in *name* even if the host name won't entirely fit. For some purposes, a truncated host name is good enough. If it is, you can ignore the error code.

int sethostname (const char *name*, size_t *length*) *Function*

The `sethostname` function sets the name of the host machine to *name*, a string with length *length*. Only privileged processes are allowed to do this. Usually it happens just once, at system boot time.

The return value is 0 on success and -1 on failure. The following `errno` error condition is defined for this function:

EPERM   This process cannot set the host name because it is not privileged.

`long int` **gethostid** (`void`)   *Function*
:   This function returns the "host ID" of the machine the program is running on. By convention, this is usually the primary Internet address of that machine, converted to a `long int`. However, on some systems it is a meaningless but unique number which is hard-coded for each machine.

`int` **sethostid** (`long int` *id*)   *Function*
:   The `sethostid` function sets the "host ID" of the host machine to *id*. Only privileged processes are allowed to do this. Usually it happens just once, at system boot time.

    The return value is `0` on success and `-1` on failure. The following `errno` error condition is defined for this function:

    `EPERM`
    :   This process cannot set the host name because it is not privileged.

    `ENOSYS`
    :   The operating system does not support setting the host ID. On some systems, the host ID is a meaningless but unique number hard-coded for each machine.

26.2 Hardware/Software Type Identification

You can use the `uname` function to find out some information about the type of computer your program is running on. This function and the associated data type are declared in the header file 'sys/utsname.h'.

struct utsname   *Data Type*
:   The `utsname` structure is used to hold information returned by the `uname` function. It has the following members:

    `char sysname[]`
    :   This is the name of the operating system in use.

    `char nodename[]`
    :   This is the network name of this particular computer. In the GNU library, the value is the same as that returned by `gethostname`; see Section 26.1 [Host Identification], page 495.

    `char release[]`
    :   This is the current release level of the operating system implementation.

    `char version[]`
    :   This is the current version level within the release of the operating system.

char machine[]

This is a description of the type of hardware that is in use.

Some systems provide a mechanism to interrogate the kernel directly for this information. On systems without such a mechanism, the GNU C library fills in this field based on the configuration name that was specified when building and installing the library.

GNU uses a three-part name to describe a system configuration; the three parts are *cpu*, *manufacturer* and *system-type*, and they are separated with dashes. Any possible combination of three names is potentially meaningful, but most such combinations are meaningless in practice and even the meaningful ones are not necessarily supported by any particular GNU program.

Since the value in `machine` is supposed to describe just the hardware, it consists of the first two parts of the configuration name: '*cpu-manufacturer*'. For example, it might be one of these:

"sparc-sun", "i386-*anything*", "m68k-hp", "m68k-sony", "m68k-sun", "mips-dec"

int **uname** (struct utsname *info*) *Function*

The **uname** function fills in the structure pointed to by *info* with information about the operating system and host machine. A non-negative value indicates that the data was successfully stored.

-1 as the value indicates an error. The only error possible is **EFAULT**, which we normally don't mention as it is always a possibility.

27 System Configuration Parameters

The functions and macros listed in this chapter give information about configuration parameters of the operating system—for example, capacity limits, presence of optional POSIX features, and the default path for executable files (see Section 27.12 [String-Valued Parameters], page 513).

27.1 General Capacity Limits

The POSIX.1 and POSIX.2 standards specify a number of parameters that describe capacity limitations of the system. These limits can be fixed constants for a given operating system, or they can vary from machine to machine. For example, some limit values may be configurable by the system administrator, either at run time or by rebuilding the kernel, and this should not require recompiling application programs.

Each of the following limit parameters has a macro that is defined in 'limits.h' only if the system has a fixed, uniform limit for the parameter in question. If the system allows different file systems or files to have different limits, then the macro is undefined; use `sysconf` to find out the limit that applies at a particular time on a particular machine. See Section 27.4 [Using "code sysconf], page 502.

Each of these parameters also has another macro, with a name starting with '_POSIX', which gives the lowest value that the limit is allowed to have on *any* POSIX system. See Section 27.5 [Minimum Values for General Capacity Limits], page 506.

int **ARG_MAX** Macro
    If defined, the unvarying maximum combined length of the *argv* and *environ* arguments that can be passed to the `exec` functions.

int **CHILD_MAX** Macro
    If defined, the unvarying maximum number of processes that can exist with the same real user ID at any one time. In BSD and GNU, this is controlled by the `RLIMIT_NPROC` resource limit; see Section 17.6 [Limiting Resource Usage], page 341.

int **OPEN_MAX** Macro
    If defined, the unvarying maximum number of files that a single process can have open simultaneously. In BSD and GNU, this is controlled by the `RLIMIT_NOFILE` resource limit; see Section 17.6 [Limiting Resource Usage], page 341.

int STREAM_MAX   Macro
If defined, the unvarying maximum number of streams that a single process can have open simultaneously. See Section 7.3 [Opening Streams], page 84.

int TZNAME_MAX   Macro
If defined, the unvarying maximum length of a time zone name. See Section 17.2.6 [Functions and Variables for Time Zones], page 334.

These limit macros are always defined in 'limits.h'.

int NGROUPS_MAX   Macro
The maximum number of supplementary group IDs that one process can have.

The value of this macro is actually a lower bound for the maximum. That is, you can count on being able to have that many supplementary group IDs, but a particular machine might let you have even more. You can use sysconf to see whether a particular machine will let you have more (see Section 27.4 [Using "code sysconf], page 502).

int SSIZE_MAX   Macro
The largest value that can fit in an object of type ssize_t. Effectively, this is the limit on the number of bytes that can be read or written in a single operation.

This macro is defined in all POSIX systems because this limit is never configurable.

int RE_DUP_MAX   Macro
The largest number of repetitions you are guaranteed is allowed in the construct '\{min,max\}' in a regular expression.

The value of this macro is actually a lower bound for the maximum. That is, you can count on being able to have that many repetitions, but a particular machine might let you have even more. You can use sysconf to see whether a particular machine will let you have more (see Section 27.4 [Using "code sysconf], page 502). And even the value that sysconf tells you is just a lower bound—larger values might work.

This macro is defined in all POSIX.2 systems, because POSIX.2 says it should always be defined even if there is no specific imposed limit.

27.2 Overall System Options

POSIX defines certain system-specific options that not all POSIX systems support. Since these options are provided in the kernel, not in the library,

Chapter 27: System Configuration Parameters

simply using the GNU C library does not guarantee any of these features is supported; it depends on the system you are using.

You can test for the availability of a given option using the macros in this section, together with the function `sysconf`. The macros are defined only if you include 'unistd.h'.

For the following macros, if the macro is defined in 'unistd.h', then the option is supported. Otherwise, the option may or may not be supported; use `sysconf` to find out. See Section 27.4 [Using "code sysconf], page 502.

int _POSIX_JOB_CONTROL   Macro
If this symbol is defined, it indicates that the system supports job control. Otherwise, the implementation behaves as if all processes within a session belong to a single process group. See Chapter 24 [Job Control], page 457.

int _POSIX_SAVED_IDS   Macro
If this symbol is defined, it indicates that the system remembers the effective user and group IDs of a process before it executes an executable file with the set-user-ID or set-group-ID bits set, and that explicitly changing the effective user or group IDs back to these values is permitted. If this option is not defined, then if a nonprivileged process changes its effective user or group ID to the real user or group ID of the process, it can't change it back again. See Section 25.8 [Enabling and Disabling Setuid Access], page 484.

For the following macros, if the macro is defined in 'unistd.h', then its value indicates whether the option is supported. A value of `-1` means no, and any other value means yes. If the macro is not defined, then the option may or may not be supported; use `sysconf` to find out. See Section 27.4 [Using "code sysconf], page 502.

int _POSIX2_C_DEV   Macro
If this symbol is defined, it indicates that the system has the POSIX.2 C compiler command, `c89`. The GNU C library always defines this as `1`, on the assumption that you would not have installed it if you didn't have a C compiler.

int _POSIX2_FORT_DEV   Macro
If this symbol is defined, it indicates that the system has the POSIX.2 Fortran compiler command, `fort77`. The GNU C library never defines this, because we don't know what the system has.

int _POSIX2_FORT_RUN   Macro
If this symbol is defined, it indicates that the system has the POSIX.2 `asa` command to interpret Fortran carriage control. The GNU C library never defines this, because we don't know what the system has.

int _POSIX2_LOCALEDEF   Macro
If this symbol is defined, it indicates that the system has the POSIX.2 `localedef` command. The GNU C library never defines this, because we don't know what the system has.

int _POSIX2_SW_DEV   Macro
If this symbol is defined, it indicates that the system has the POSIX.2 commands `ar`, `make`, and `strip`. The GNU C library always defines this as 1, on the assumption that you had to have `ar` and `make` to install the library, and it's unlikely that `strip` would be absent when those are present.

27.3 Which Version of POSIX is Supported

long int _POSIX_VERSION   Macro
This constant represents the version of the POSIX.1 standard to which the implementation conforms. For an implementation conforming to the 1990 POSIX.1 standard, the value is the integer 199009L.

_POSIX_VERSION is always defined (in 'unistd.h') in any POSIX system.

Usage Note: Don't try to test whether the system supports POSIX by including 'unistd.h' and then checking whether _POSIX_VERSION is defined. On a non-POSIX system, this will probably fail because there is no 'unistd.h'. We do not know of *any* way you can reliably test at compilation time whether your target system supports POSIX or whether 'unistd.h' exists.

The GNU C compiler predefines the symbol __POSIX__ if the target system is a POSIX system. Provided you do not use any other compilers on POSIX systems, testing `defined (__POSIX__)` will reliably detect such systems.

long int _POSIX2_C_VERSION   Macro
This constant represents the version of the POSIX.2 standard which the library and system kernel support. We don't know what value this will be for the first version of the POSIX.2 standard, because the value is based on the year and month in which the standard is officially adopted.

The value of this symbol says nothing about the utilities installed on the system.

Usage Note: You can use this macro to tell whether a POSIX.1 system library supports POSIX.2 as well. Any POSIX.1 system contains 'unistd.h', so include that file and then test `defined (_POSIX2_C_VERSION)`.

Chapter 27: System Configuration Parameters 503

27.4 Using `sysconf`

When your system has configurable system limits, you can use the `sysconf` function to find out the value that applies to any particular machine. The function and the associated *parameter* constants are declared in the header file 'unistd.h'.

27.4.1 Definition of `sysconf`

`long int` **sysconf** (`int` *parameter*) Function

This function is used to inquire about runtime system parameters. The *parameter* argument should be one of the '_SC_' symbols listed below.

The normal return value from `sysconf` is the value you requested. A value of `-1` is returned both if the implementation does not impose a limit, and in case of an error.

The following `errno` error conditions are defined for this function:

EINVAL   The value of the *parameter* is invalid.

27.4.2 Constants for `sysconf` Parameters

Here are the symbolic constants for use as the *parameter* argument to `sysconf`. The values are all integer constants (more specifically, enumeration type values).

_SC_ARG_MAX
: Inquire about the parameter corresponding to `ARG_MAX`.

_SC_CHILD_MAX
: Inquire about the parameter corresponding to `CHILD_MAX`.

_SC_OPEN_MAX
: Inquire about the parameter corresponding to `OPEN_MAX`.

_SC_STREAM_MAX
: Inquire about the parameter corresponding to `STREAM_MAX`.

_SC_TZNAME_MAX
: Inquire about the parameter corresponding to `TZNAME_MAX`.

_SC_NGROUPS_MAX
: Inquire about the parameter corresponding to `NGROUPS_MAX`.

_SC_JOB_CONTROL
: Inquire about the parameter corresponding to `_POSIX_JOB_CONTROL`.

`_SC_SAVED_IDS`
: Inquire about the parameter corresponding to `_POSIX_SAVED_IDS`.

`_SC_VERSION`
: Inquire about the parameter corresponding to `_POSIX_VERSION`.

`_SC_CLK_TCK`
: Inquire about the parameter corresponding to `CLOCKS_PER_SEC`; see Section 17.1.1 [Basic CPU Time Inquiry], page 321.

`_SC_2_C_DEV`
: Inquire about whether the system has the POSIX.2 C compiler command, `c89`.

`_SC_2_FORT_DEV`
: Inquire about whether the system has the POSIX.2 Fortran compiler command, `fort77`.

`_SC_2_FORT_RUN`
: Inquire about whether the system has the POSIX.2 `asa` command to interpret Fortran carriage control.

`_SC_2_LOCALEDEF`
: Inquire about whether the system has the POSIX.2 `localedef` command.

`_SC_2_SW_DEV`
: Inquire about whether the system has the POSIX.2 commands `ar`, `make`, and `strip`.

`_SC_BC_BASE_MAX`
: Inquire about the maximum value of `obase` in the `bc` utility.

`_SC_BC_DIM_MAX`
: Inquire about the maximum size of an array in the `bc` utility.

`_SC_BC_SCALE_MAX`
: Inquire about the maximum value of `scale` in the `bc` utility.

`_SC_BC_STRING_MAX`
: Inquire about the maximum size of a string constant in the `bc` utility.

`_SC_COLL_WEIGHTS_MAX`
: Inquire about the maximum number of weights that can necessarily be used in defining the collating sequence for a locale.

`_SC_EXPR_NEST_MAX`
: Inquire about the maximum number of expressions nested within parentheses when using the `expr` utility.

Chapter 27: System Configuration Parameters   505

`_SC_LINE_MAX`
: Inquire about the maximum size of a text line that the POSIX.2 text utilities can handle.

`_SC_EQUIV_CLASS_MAX`
: Inquire about the maximum number of weights that can be assigned to an entry of the `LC_COLLATE` category 'order' keyword in a locale definition. The GNU C library does not presently support locale definitions.

`_SC_VERSION`
: Inquire about the version number of POSIX.1 that the library and kernel support.

`_SC_2_VERSION`
: Inquire about the version number of POSIX.2 that the system utilities support.

`_SC_PAGESIZE`
: Inquire about the virtual memory page size of the machine. `getpagesize` returns the same value.

27.4.3 Examples of `sysconf`

We recommend that you first test for a macro definition for the parameter you are interested in, and call `sysconf` only if the macro is not defined. For example, here is how to test whether job control is supported:

```
int
have_job_control (void)
{
#ifdef _POSIX_JOB_CONTROL
  return 1;
#else
  int value = sysconf (_SC_JOB_CONTROL);
  if (value < 0)
    /* If the system is that badly wedged,
       there's no use trying to go on.  */
    fatal (strerror (errno));
  return value;
#endif
}
```

Here is how to get the value of a numeric limit:

```
int
get_child_max ()
{
#ifdef CHILD_MAX
  return CHILD_MAX;
#else
  int value = sysconf (_SC_CHILD_MAX);
```

```
    if (value < 0)
      fatal (strerror (errno));
    return value;
#endif
  }
```

27.5 Minimum Values for General Capacity Limits

Here are the names for the POSIX minimum upper bounds for the system limit parameters. The significance of these values is that you can safely push to these limits without checking whether the particular system you are using can go that far.

_POSIX_ARG_MAX
> The value of this macro is the most restrictive limit permitted by POSIX for the maximum combined length of the *argv* and *environ* arguments that can be passed to the `exec` functions. Its value is 4096.

_POSIX_CHILD_MAX
> The value of this macro is the most restrictive limit permitted by POSIX for the maximum number of simultaneous processes per real user ID. Its value is 6.

_POSIX_NGROUPS_MAX
> The value of this macro is the most restrictive limit permitted by POSIX for the maximum number of supplementary group IDs per process. Its value is 0.

_POSIX_OPEN_MAX
> The value of this macro is the most restrictive limit permitted by POSIX for the maximum number of files that a single process can have open simultaneously. Its value is 16.

_POSIX_SSIZE_MAX
> The value of this macro is the most restrictive limit permitted by POSIX for the maximum value that can be stored in an object of type `ssize_t`. Its value is 32767.

_POSIX_STREAM_MAX
> The value of this macro is the most restrictive limit permitted by POSIX for the maximum number of streams that a single process can have open simultaneously. Its value is 8.

_POSIX_TZNAME_MAX
> The value of this macro is the most restrictive limit permitted by POSIX for the maximum length of a time zone name. Its value is 3.

`_POSIX2_RE_DUP_MAX`

The value of this macro is the most restrictive limit permitted by POSIX for the numbers used in the '\{*min*,*max*\}' construct in a regular expression. Its value is **255**.

27.6 Limits on File System Capacity

The POSIX.1 standard specifies a number of parameters that describe the limitations of the file system. It's possible for the system to have a fixed, uniform limit for a parameter, but this isn't the usual case. On most systems, it's possible for different file systems (and, for some parameters, even different files) to have different maximum limits. For example, this is very likely if you use NFS to mount some of the file systems from other machines.

Each of the following macros is defined in 'limits.h' only if the system has a fixed, uniform limit for the parameter in question. If the system allows different file systems or files to have different limits, then the macro is undefined; use **pathconf** or **fpathconf** to find out the limit that applies to a particular file. See Section 27.9 [Using "code pathconf], page 510.

Each parameter also has another macro, with a name starting with '**_POSIX**', which gives the lowest value that the limit is allowed to have on *any* POSIX system. See Section 27.8 [Minimum Values for File System Limits], page 509.

int **LINK_MAX**   *Macro*
The uniform system limit (if any) for the number of names for a given file. See Section 9.3 [Hard Links], page 175.

int **MAX_CANON**   *Macro*
The uniform system limit (if any) for the amount of text in a line of input when input editing is enabled. See Section 12.3 [Two Styles of Input: Canonical or Not], page 256.

int **MAX_INPUT**   *Macro*
The uniform system limit (if any) for the total number of characters typed ahead as input. See Section 12.2 [I/O Queues], page 255.

int **NAME_MAX**   *Macro*
The uniform system limit (if any) for the length of a file name component.

int **PATH_MAX**   *Macro*
The uniform system limit (if any) for the length of an entire file name (that is, the argument given to system calls such as **open**).

int PIPE_BUF   Macro
The uniform system limit (if any) for the number of bytes that can be written atomically to a pipe. If multiple processes are writing to the same pipe simultaneously, output from different processes might be interleaved in chunks of this size. See Chapter 10 [Pipes and FIFOs], page 201.

These are alternative macro names for some of the same information.

int MAXNAMLEN   Macro
This is the BSD name for `NAME_MAX`. It is defined in 'dirent.h'.

int FILENAME_MAX   Macro
The value of this macro is an integer constant expression that represents the maximum length of a file name string. It is defined in 'stdio.h'.

Unlike `PATH_MAX`, this macro is defined even if there is no actual limit imposed. In such a case, its value is typically a very large number. **This is always the case on the GNU system.**

Usage Note: Don't use `FILENAME_MAX` as the size of an array in which to store a file name! You can't possibly make an array that big! Use dynamic allocation (see Chapter 3 [Memory Allocation], page 27) instead.

27.7 Optional Features in File Support

POSIX defines certain system-specific options in the system calls for operating on files. Some systems support these options and others do not. Since these options are provided in the kernel, not in the library, simply using the GNU C library does not guarantee any of these features is supported; it depends on the system you are using. They can also vary between file systems on a single machine.

This section describes the macros you can test to determine whether a particular option is supported on your machine. If a given macro is defined in 'unistd.h', then its value says whether the corresponding feature is supported. (A value of -1 indicates no; any other value indicates yes.) If the macro is undefined, it means particular files may or may not support the feature.

Since all the machines that support the GNU C library also support NFS, one can never make a general statement about whether all file systems support the `_POSIX_CHOWN_RESTRICTED` and `_POSIX_NO_TRUNC` features. So these names are never defined as macros in the GNU C library.

int _POSIX_CHOWN_RESTRICTED   Macro
If this option is in effect, the `chown` function is restricted so that the only changes permitted to nonprivileged processes is to change the group owner of a file to either be the effective group ID of the process, or one of its supplementary group IDs. See Section 9.8.4 [File Owner], page 186.

int _POSIX_NO_TRUNC   Macro
If this option is in effect, file name components longer than `NAME_MAX` generate an `ENAMETOOLONG` error. Otherwise, file name components that are too long are silently truncated.

unsigned char _POSIX_VDISABLE   Macro
This option is only meaningful for files that are terminal devices. If it is enabled, then handling for special control characters can be disabled individually. See Section 12.4.9 [Special Characters], page 270.

If one of these macros is undefined, that means that the option might be in effect for some files and not for others. To inquire about a particular file, call `pathconf` or `fpathconf`. See Section 27.9 [Using "code pathconf], page 510.

27.8 Minimum Values for File System Limits

Here are the names for the POSIX minimum upper bounds for some of the above parameters. The significance of these values is that you can safely push to these limits without checking whether the particular system you are using can go that far.

_POSIX_LINK_MAX
: The most restrictive limit permitted by POSIX for the maximum value of a file's link count. The value of this constant is 8; thus, you can always make up to eight names for a file without running into a system limit.

_POSIX_MAX_CANON
: The most restrictive limit permitted by POSIX for the maximum number of bytes in a canonical input line from a terminal device. The value of this constant is 255.

_POSIX_MAX_INPUT
: The most restrictive limit permitted by POSIX for the maximum number of bytes in a terminal device input queue (or typeahead buffer). See Section 12.4.4 [Input Modes], page 261. The value of this constant is 255.

_POSIX_NAME_MAX
> The most restrictive limit permitted by POSIX for the maximum number of bytes in a file name component. The value of this constant is 14.

_POSIX_PATH_MAX
> The most restrictive limit permitted by POSIX for the maximum number of bytes in a file name. The value of this constant is 255.

_POSIX_PIPE_BUF
> The most restrictive limit permitted by POSIX for the maximum number of bytes that can be written atomically to a pipe. The value of this constant is 512.

27.9 Using `pathconf`

When your machine allows different files to have different values for a file system parameter, you can use the functions in this section to find out the value that applies to any particular file.

These functions and the associated constants for the *parameter* argument are declared in the header file 'unistd.h'.

long int pathconf (const char *filename*, int *parameter*) *Function*

This function is used to inquire about the limits that apply to the file named *filename*.

The *parameter* argument should be one of the '_PC_' constants listed below.

The normal return value from `pathconf` is the value you requested. A value of -1 is returned both if the implementation does not impose a limit, and in case of an error. In the former case, `errno` is not set, while in the latter case, `errno` is set to indicate the cause of the problem. So the only way to use this function robustly is to store 0 into `errno` just before calling it.

Besides the usual file name errors (see Section 6.2.3 [File Name Errors], page 79), the following error condition is defined for this function:

> **EINVAL** The value of *parameter* is invalid, or the implementation doesn't support the *parameter* for the specific file.

long int fpathconf (int *filedes*, int *parameter*) *Function*

This is just like `pathconf` except that an open file descriptor is used to specify the file for which information is requested, instead of a file name.

The following `errno` error conditions are defined for this function:

Chapter 27: System Configuration Parameters   511

> EBADF   The *filedes* argument is not a valid file descriptor.
>
> EINVAL   The value of *parameter* is invalid, or the implementation doesn't support the *parameter* for the specific file.

Here are the symbolic constants that you can use as the *parameter* argument to `pathconf` and `fpathconf`. The values are all integer constants.

`_PC_LINK_MAX`
> Inquire about the value of `LINK_MAX`.

`_PC_MAX_CANON`
> Inquire about the value of `MAX_CANON`.

`_PC_MAX_INPUT`
> Inquire about the value of `MAX_INPUT`.

`_PC_NAME_MAX`
> Inquire about the value of `NAME_MAX`.

`_PC_PATH_MAX`
> Inquire about the value of `PATH_MAX`.

`_PC_PIPE_BUF`
> Inquire about the value of `PIPE_BUF`.

`_PC_CHOWN_RESTRICTED`
> Inquire about the value of `_POSIX_CHOWN_RESTRICTED`.

`_PC_NO_TRUNC`
> Inquire about the value of `_POSIX_NO_TRUNC`.

`_PC_VDISABLE`
> Inquire about the value of `_POSIX_VDISABLE`.

27.10 Utility Program Capacity Limits

The POSIX.2 standard specifies certain system limits that you can access through `sysconf` that apply to utility behavior rather than the behavior of the library or the operating system.

The GNU C library defines macros for these limits, and `sysconf` returns values for them if you ask; but these values convey no meaningful information. They are simply the smallest values that POSIX.2 permits.

int **BC_BASE_MAX**   Macro
> The largest value of `obase` that the `bc` utility is guaranteed to support.

int **BC_SCALE_MAX**   Macro
> The largest value of `scale` that the `bc` utility is guaranteed to support.

int BC_DIM_MAX   Macro
The largest number of elements in one array that the `bc` utility is guaranteed to support.

int BC_STRING_MAX   Macro
The largest number of characters in one string constant that the `bc` utility is guaranteed to support.

int BC_DIM_MAX   Macro
The largest number of elements in one array that the `bc` utility is guaranteed to support.

int COLL_WEIGHTS_MAX   Macro
The largest number of weights that can necessarily be used in defining the collating sequence for a locale.

int EXPR_NEST_MAX   Macro
The maximum number of expressions that can be nested within parenthesis by the `expr` utility.

int LINE_MAX   Macro
The largest text line that the text-oriented POSIX.2 utilities can support. (If you are using the GNU versions of these utilities, then there is no actual limit except that imposed by the available virtual memory, but there is no way that the library can tell you this.)

int EQUIV_CLASS_MAX   Macro
The maximum number of weights that can be assigned to an entry of the `LC_COLLATE` category 'order' keyword in a locale definition. The GNU C library does not presently support locale definitions.

27.11 Minimum Values for Utility Limits

_POSIX2_BC_BASE_MAX
> The most restrictive limit permitted by POSIX.2 for the maximum value of `obase` in the `bc` utility. Its value is **99**.

_POSIX2_BC_DIM_MAX
> The most restrictive limit permitted by POSIX.2 for the maximum size of an array in the `bc` utility. Its value is **2048**.

_POSIX2_BC_SCALE_MAX
> The most restrictive limit permitted by POSIX.2 for the maximum value of `scale` in the `bc` utility. Its value is **99**.

_POSIX2_BC_STRING_MAX
The most restrictive limit permitted by POSIX.2 for the maximum size of a string constant in the `bc` utility. Its value is 1000.

_POSIX2_COLL_WEIGHTS_MAX
The most restrictive limit permitted by POSIX.2 for the maximum number of weights that can necessarily be used in defining the collating sequence for a locale. Its value is 2.

_POSIX2_EXPR_NEST_MAX
The most restrictive limit permitted by POSIX.2 for the maximum number of expressions nested within parenthesis when using the `expr` utility. Its value is 32.

_POSIX2_LINE_MAX
The most restrictive limit permitted by POSIX.2 for the maximum size of a text line that the text utilities can handle. Its value is 2048.

_POSIX2_EQUIV_CLASS_MAX
The most restrictive limit permitted by POSIX.2 for the maximum number of weights that can be assigned to an entry of the `LC_COLLATE` category 'order' keyword in a locale definition. Its value is 2. The GNU C library does not presently support locale definitions.

27.12 String-Valued Parameters

POSIX.2 defines a way to get string-valued parameters from the operating system with the function `confstr`:

`size_t` **confstr** (`int` *parameter*, `char` **buf*, `size_t` *len*)   Function

This function reads the value of a string-valued system parameter, storing the string into *len* bytes of memory space starting at *buf*. The *parameter* argument should be one of the '_CS_' symbols listed below.

The normal return value from `confstr` is the length of the string value that you asked for. If you supply a null pointer for *buf*, then `confstr` does not try to store the string; it just returns its length. A value of 0 indicates an error.

If the string you asked for is too long for the buffer (that is, longer than *len* - 1), then `confstr` stores just that much (leaving room for the terminating null character). You can tell that this has happened because `confstr` returns a value greater than or equal to *len*.

The following `errno` error conditions are defined for this function:

EINVAL   The value of the *parameter* is invalid.

Currently there is just one parameter you can read with `confstr`:

_CS_PATH   This parameter's value is the recommended default path for searching for executable files. This is the path that a user has by default just after logging in.

The way to use `confstr` without any arbitrary limit on string size is to call it twice: first call it to get the length, allocate the buffer accordingly, and then call `confstr` again to fill the buffer, like this:

```
char *
get_default_path (void)
{
  size_t len = confstr (_CS_PATH, NULL, 0);
  char *buffer = (char *) xmalloc (len);

  if (confstr (_CS_PATH, buf, len + 1) == 0)
    {
      free (buffer);
      return NULL;
    }

  return buffer;
}
```

Appendix A C Language Facilities in the Library

Some of the facilities implemented by the C library really should be thought of as parts of the C language itself. These facilities ought to be documented in the C Language Manual, not in the library manual; but since we don't have the language manual yet, and documentation for these features has been written, we are publishing it here.

A.1 Explicitly Checking Internal Consistency

When you're writing a program, it's often a good idea to put in checks at strategic places for "impossible" errors or violations of basic assumptions. These checks are helpful in debugging problems due to misunderstandings between different parts of the program.

The `assert` macro, defined in the header file 'assert.h', provides a convenient way to abort the program while printing a message about where in the program the error was detected.

Once you think your program is debugged, you can disable the error checks performed by the `assert` macro by recompiling with the macro `NDEBUG` defined. This means you don't actually have to change the program source code to disable these checks.

But disabling these consistency checks is undesirable unless they make the program significantly slower. All else being equal, more error checking is good no matter who is running the program. A wise user would rather have a program crash, visibly, than have it return nonsense without indicating anything might be wrong.

`void` **assert** (`int` *expression*)   Macro
: Verify the programmer's belief that *expression* should be nonzero at this point in the program.

  If `NDEBUG` is not defined, `assert` tests the value of *expression*. If it is false (zero), `assert` aborts the program (see Section 22.3.4 [Aborting a Program], page 440) after printing a message of the form:

  '*file*':*linenum*: `Assertion` '*expression*' `failed.`

  on the standard error stream `stderr` (see Section 7.2 [Standard Streams], page 83). The filename and line number are taken from the C preprocessor macros `__FILE__` and `__LINE__` and specify where the call to `assert` was written.

  If the preprocessor macro `NDEBUG` is defined at the point where 'assert.h' is included, the `assert` macro is defined to do absolutely nothing.

Warning: Even the argument expression *expression* is not evaluated if `NDEBUG` is in effect. So never use `assert` with arguments that involve side effects. For example, `assert (++i > 0);` is a bad idea, because `i` will not be incremented if `NDEBUG` is defined.

Usage note: The `assert` facility is designed for detecting *internal inconsistency*; it is not suitable for reporting invalid input or improper usage by *the user* of the program.

The information in the diagnostic messages printed by the `assert` macro is intended to help you, the programmer, track down the cause of a bug, but is not really useful for telling a user of your program why his or her input was invalid or why a command could not be carried out. So you can't use `assert` to print the error messages for these eventualities.

What's more, your program should not abort when given invalid input, as `assert` would do—it should exit with nonzero status (see Section 22.3.2 [Exit Status], page 437) after printing its error messages, or perhaps read another command or move on to the next input file.

See Section 2.3 [Error Messages], page 23, for information on printing error messages for problems that *do not* represent bugs in the program.

A.2 Variadic Functions

ANSI C defines a syntax for declaring a function to take a variable number or type of arguments. (Such functions are referred to as *varargs functions* or *variadic functions*.) However, the language itself provides no mechanism for such functions to access their non-required arguments; instead, you use the variable arguments macros defined in 'stdarg.h'.

This section describes how to declare variadic functions, how to write them, and how to call them properly.

Compatibility Note: Many older C dialects provide a similar, but incompatible, mechanism for defining functions with variable numbers of arguments, using 'varargs.h'.

A.2.1 Why Variadic Functions are Used

Ordinary C functions take a fixed number of arguments. When you define a function, you specify the data type for each argument. Every call to the function should supply the expected number of arguments, with types that can be converted to the specified ones. Thus, if the function 'foo' is declared with `int foo (int, char *);` then you must call it with two arguments, a number (any kind will do) and a string pointer.

But some functions perform operations that can meaningfully accept an unlimited number of arguments.

In some cases a function can handle any number of values by operating on all of them as a block. For example, consider a function that allocates a one-dimensional array with `malloc` to hold a specified set of values. This operation makes sense for any number of values, as long as the length of the array corresponds to that number. Without facilities for variable arguments, you would have to define a separate function for each possible array size.

The library function `printf` (see Section 7.10 [Formatted Output], page 94) is an example of another class of function where variable arguments are useful. This function prints its arguments (which can vary in type as well as number) under the control of a format template string.

These are good reasons to define a *variadic* function which can handle as many arguments as the caller chooses to pass.

Some functions such as `open` take a fixed set of arguments, but occasionally ignore the last few. Strict adherence to ANSI C requires these functions to be defined as variadic; in practice, however, the GNU C compiler and most other C compilers let you define such a function to take a fixed set of arguments—the most it can ever use—and then only *declare* the function as variadic (or not declare its arguments at all!).

A.2.2 How Variadic Functions are Defined and Used

Defining and using a variadic function involves three steps:

- *Define* the function as variadic, using an ellipsis ('...') in the argument list, and using special macros to access the variable arguments. See Section A.2.2.2 [Receiving the Argument Values], page 518.
- *Declare* the function as variadic, using a prototype with an ellipsis ('...'), in all the files which call it. See Section A.2.2.1 [Syntax for Variable Arguments], page 517.
- *Call* the function by writing the fixed arguments followed by the additional variable arguments. See Section A.2.2.4 [Calling Variadic Functions], page 520.

A.2.2.1 Syntax for Variable Arguments

A function that accepts a variable number of arguments must be declared with a prototype that says so. You write the fixed arguments as usual, and then tack on '...' to indicate the possibility of additional arguments. The syntax of ANSI C requires at least one fixed argument before the '...'. For example,

```
int
func (const char *a, int b, ...)
{
   ...
```

}

outlines a definition of a function `func` which returns an `int` and takes two required arguments, a `const char *` and an `int`. These are followed by any number of anonymous arguments.

Portability note: For some C compilers, the last required argument must not be declared `register` in the function definition. Furthermore, this argument's type must be *self-promoting*: that is, the default promotions must not change its type. This rules out array and function types, as well as `float`, `char` (whether signed or not) and `short int` (whether signed or not). This is actually an ANSI C requirement.

A.2.2.2 Receiving the Argument Values

Ordinary fixed arguments have individual names, and you can use these names to access their values. But optional arguments have no names—nothing but '...'. How can you access them?

The only way to access them is sequentially, in the order they were written, and you must use special macros from 'stdarg.h' in the following three step process:

1. You initialize an argument pointer variable of type `va_list` using `va_start`. The argument pointer when initialized points to the first optional argument.

2. You access the optional arguments by successive calls to `va_arg`. The first call to `va_arg` gives you the first optional argument, the next call gives you the second, and so on.

   You can stop at any time if you wish to ignore any remaining optional arguments. It is perfectly all right for a function to access fewer arguments than were supplied in the call, but you will get garbage values if you try to access too many arguments.

3. You indicate that you are finished with the argument pointer variable by calling `va_end`.

   (In practice, with most C compilers, calling `va_end` does nothing and you do not really need to call it. This is always true in the GNU C compiler. But you might as well call `va_end` just in case your program is someday compiled with a peculiar compiler.)

See Section A.2.2.5 [Argument Access Macros], page 520, for the full definitions of `va_start`, `va_arg` and `va_end`.

Steps 1 and 3 must be performed in the function that accepts the optional arguments. However, you can pass the `va_list` variable as an argument to another function and perform all or part of step 2 there.

You can perform the entire sequence of the three steps multiple times within a single function invocation. If you want to ignore the optional arguments, you can do these steps zero times.

You can have more than one argument pointer variable if you like. You can initialize each variable with `va_start` when you wish, and then you can fetch arguments with each argument pointer as you wish. Each argument pointer variable will sequence through the same set of argument values, but at its own pace.

Portability note: With some compilers, once you pass an argument pointer value to a subroutine, you must not keep using the same argument pointer value after that subroutine returns. For full portability, you should just pass it to `va_end`. This is actually an ANSI C requirement, but most ANSI C compilers work happily regardless.

A.2.2.3 How Many Arguments Were Supplied

There is no general way for a function to determine the number and type of the optional arguments it was called with. So whoever designs the function typically designs a convention for the caller to tell it how many arguments it has, and what kind. It is up to you to define an appropriate calling convention for each variadic function, and write all calls accordingly.

One kind of calling convention is to pass the number of optional arguments as one of the fixed arguments. This convention works provided all of the optional arguments are of the same type.

A similar alternative is to have one of the required arguments be a bit mask, with a bit for each possible purpose for which an optional argument might be supplied. You would test the bits in a predefined sequence; if the bit is set, fetch the value of the next argument, otherwise use a default value.

A required argument can be used as a pattern to specify both the number and types of the optional arguments. The format string argument to `printf` is one example of this (see Section 7.10.7 [Formatted Output Functions], page 103).

Another possibility is to pass an "end marker" value as the last optional argument. For example, for a function that manipulates an arbitrary number of pointer arguments, a null pointer might indicate the end of the argument list. (This assumes that a null pointer isn't otherwise meaningful to the function.) The `execl` function works in just this way; see Section 23.5 [Executing a File], page 446.

A.2.2.4 Calling Variadic Functions

You don't have to write anything special when you call a variadic function. Just write the arguments (required arguments, followed by optional ones) inside parentheses, separated by commas, as usual. But you should prepare by declaring the function with a prototype, and you must know how the argument values are converted.

In principle, functions that are *defined* to be variadic must also be *declared* to be variadic using a function prototype whenever you call them. (See Section A.2.2.1 [Syntax for Variable Arguments], page 517, for how.) This is because some C compilers use a different calling convention to pass the same set of argument values to a function depending on whether that function takes variable arguments or fixed arguments.

In practice, the GNU C compiler always passes a given set of argument types in the same way regardless of whether they are optional or required. So, as long as the argument types are self-promoting, you can safely omit declaring them. Usually it is a good idea to declare the argument types for variadic functions, and indeed for all functions. But there are a few functions which it is extremely convenient not to have to declare as variadic—for example, `open` and `printf`.

Since the prototype doesn't specify types for optional arguments, in a call to a variadic function the *default argument promotions* are performed on the optional argument values. This means the objects of type `char` or `short int` (whether signed or not) are promoted to either `int` or `unsigned int`, as appropriate; and that objects of type `float` are promoted to type `double`. So, if the caller passes a `char` as an optional argument, it is promoted to an `int`, and the function should get it with `va_arg (ap, int)`.

Conversion of the required arguments is controlled by the function prototype in the usual way: the argument expression is converted to the declared argument type as if it were being assigned to a variable of that type.

A.2.2.5 Argument Access Macros

Here are descriptions of the macros used to retrieve variable arguments. These macros are defined in the header file 'stdarg.h'.

va_list   Data Type

The type `va_list` is used for argument pointer variables.

void **va_start** (va_list *ap*, *last-required*)   Macro

This macro initializes the argument pointer variable *ap* to point to the first of the optional arguments of the current function; *last-required* must be the last required argument to the function.

See Section A.2.3.1 [Old-Style Variadic Functions], page 522, for an alternate definition of `va_start` found in the header file 'varargs.h'.

Appendix A: C Language Facilities in the Library   521

type **va_arg** (**va_list** *ap*, *type*)   Macro
   The **va_arg** macro returns the value of the next optional argument, and modifies the value of *ap* to point to the subsequent argument. Thus, successive uses of **va_arg** return successive optional arguments.

   The type of the value returned by **va_arg** is *type* as specified in the call. *type* must be a self-promoting type (not **char** or **short int** or **float**) that matches the type of the actual argument.

void va_end (**va_list** *ap*)   Macro
   This ends the use of *ap*. After a **va_end** call, further **va_arg** calls with the same *ap* may not work. You should invoke **va_end** before returning from the function in which **va_start** was invoked with the same *ap* argument.

   In the GNU C library, **va_end** does nothing, and you need not ever use it except for reasons of portability.

A.2.3 Example of a Variadic Function

Here is a complete sample function that accepts a variable number of arguments. The first argument to the function is the count of remaining arguments, which are added up and the result returned. While trivial, this function is sufficient to illustrate how to use the variable arguments facility.

```
#include <stdarg.h>
#include <stdio.h>

int
add_em_up (int count,...)
{
  va_list ap;
  int i, sum;

  va_start (ap, count);         /* Initialize the argument list. */

  sum = 0;
  for (i = 0; i < count; i++)
    sum += va_arg (ap, int);    /* Get the next argument value. */

  va_end (ap);                  /* Clean up. */
  return sum;
}

int
main (void)
{
  /* This call prints 16. */
  printf ("%d\n", add_em_up (3, 5, 5, 6));

  /* This call prints 55. */
```

```
    printf ("%d\n", add_em_up (10, 1, 2, 3, 4, 5, 6, 7, 8, 9, 10));

    return 0;
}
```

A.2.3.1 Old-Style Variadic Functions

Before ANSI C, programmers used a slightly different facility for writing variadic functions. The GNU C compiler still supports it; currently, it is more portable than the ANSI C facility, since support for ANSI C is still not universal. The header file which defines the old-fashioned variadic facility is called 'varargs.h'.

Using 'varargs.h' is almost the same as using 'stdarg.h'. There is no difference in how you call a variadic function; See Section A.2.2.4 [Calling Variadic Functions], page 520. The only difference is in how you define them. First of all, you must use old-style non-prototype syntax, like this:

```
tree
build (va_alist)
     va_dcl
{
```

Secondly, you must give va_start just one argument, like this:

```
va_list p;
va_start (p);
```

These are the special macros used for defining old-style variadic functions:

va_alist   Macro
    This macro stands for the argument name list required in a variadic function.

va_dcl   Macro
    This macro declares the implicit argument or arguments for a variadic function.

void **va_start** (va_list *ap*)   Macro
    This macro, as defined in 'varargs.h', initializes the argument pointer variable *ap* to point to the first argument of the current function.

The other argument macros, va_arg and va_end, are the same in 'varargs.h' as in 'stdarg.h'; see Section A.2.2.5 [Argument Access Macros], page 520 for details.

It does not work to include both 'varargs.h' and 'stdarg.h' in the same compilation; they define va_start in conflicting ways.

A.3 Null Pointer Constant

The null pointer constant is guaranteed not to point to any real object. You can assign it to any pointer variable since it has type `void *`. The preferred way to write a null pointer constant is with `NULL`.

void * NULL   *Macro*
This is a null pointer constant.

You can also use `0` or `(void *)0` as a null pointer constant, but using `NULL` is cleaner because it makes the purpose of the constant more evident.

If you use the null pointer constant as a function argument, then for complete portability you should make sure that the function has a prototype declaration. Otherwise, if the target machine has two different pointer representations, the compiler won't know which representation to use for that argument. You can avoid the problem by explicitly casting the constant to the proper pointer type, but we recommend instead adding a prototype for the function you are calling.

A.4 Important Data Types

The result of subtracting two pointers in C is always an integer, but the precise data type varies from C compiler to C compiler. Likewise, the data type of the result of `sizeof` also varies between compilers. ANSI defines standard aliases for these two types, so you can refer to them in a portable fashion. They are defined in the header file 'stddef.h'.

ptrdiff_t   *Data Type*
This is the signed integer type of the result of subtracting two pointers. For example, with the declaration `char *p1, *p2;`, the expression `p2 - p1` is of type `ptrdiff_t`. This will probably be one of the standard signed integer types (`short int`, `int` or `long int`), but might be a nonstandard type that exists only for this purpose.

size_t   *Data Type*
This is an unsigned integer type used to represent the sizes of objects. The result of the `sizeof` operator is of this type, and functions such as `malloc` (see Section 3.3 [Unconstrained Allocation], page 28) and `memcpy` (see Section 5.4 [Copying and Concatenation], page 61) accept arguments of this type to specify object sizes.

Usage Note: `size_t` is the preferred way to declare any arguments or variables that hold the size of an object.

In the GNU system `size_t` is equivalent to either `unsigned int` or `unsigned long int`. These types have identical properties on the GNU system, and for most purposes, you can use them interchangeably. However, they are distinct as data types, which makes a difference in certain contexts.

For example, when you specify the type of a function argument in a function prototype, it makes a difference which one you use. If the system header files declare `malloc` with an argument of type `size_t` and you declare `malloc` with an argument of type `unsigned int`, you will get a compilation error if `size_t` happens to be `unsigned long int` on your system. To avoid any possibility of error, when a function argument or value is supposed to have type `size_t`, never declare its type in any other way.

Compatibility Note: Implementations of C before the advent of ANSI C generally used `unsigned int` for representing object sizes and `int` for pointer subtraction results. They did not necessarily define either `size_t` or `ptrdiff_t`. Unix systems did define `size_t`, in 'sys/types.h', but the definition was usually a signed type.

A.5 Data Type Measurements

Most of the time, if you choose the proper C data type for each object in your program, you need not be concerned with just how it is represented or how many bits it uses. When you do need such information, the C language itself does not provide a way to get it. The header files 'limits.h' and 'float.h' contain macros which give you this information in full detail.

A.5.1 Computing the Width of an Integer Data Type

The most common reason that a program needs to know how many bits are in an integer type is for using an array of `long int` as a bit vector. You can access the bit at index n with

```
vector[n / LONGBITS] & (1 << (n % LONGBITS))
```

provided you define `LONGBITS` as the number of bits in a `long int`.

There is no operator in the C language that can give you the number of bits in an integer data type. But you can compute it from the macro `CHAR_BIT`, defined in the header file 'limits.h'.

CHAR_BIT   This is the number of bits in a `char`—eight, on most systems. The value has type `int`.

You can compute the number of bits in any data type *type* like this:

```
sizeof (type) * CHAR_BIT
```

A.5.2 Range of an Integer Type

Suppose you need to store an integer value which can range from zero to one million. Which is the smallest type you can use? There is no general rule; it depends on the C compiler and target machine. You can use the 'MIN' and 'MAX' macros in 'limits.h' to determine which type will work.

Each signed integer type has a pair of macros which give the smallest and largest values that it can hold. Each unsigned integer type has one such macro, for the maximum value; the minimum value is, of course, zero.

The values of these macros are all integer constant expressions. The 'MAX' and 'MIN' macros for `char` and `short int` types have values of type `int`. The 'MAX' and 'MIN' macros for the other types have values of the same type described by the macro—thus, `ULONG_MAX` has type `unsigned long int`.

SCHAR_MIN
: This is the minimum value that can be represented by a `signed char`.

SCHAR_MAX
UCHAR_MAX
: These are the maximum values that can be represented by a `signed char` and `unsigned char`, respectively.

CHAR_MIN
: This is the minimum value that can be represented by a `char`. It's equal to `SCHAR_MIN` if `char` is signed, or zero otherwise.

CHAR_MAX
: This is the maximum value that can be represented by a `char`. It's equal to `SCHAR_MAX` if `char` is signed, or `UCHAR_MAX` otherwise.

SHRT_MIN
: This is the minimum value that can be represented by a `signed short int`. On most machines that the GNU C library runs on, `short` integers are 16-bit quantities.

SHRT_MAX
USHRT_MAX
: These are the maximum values that can be represented by a `signed short int` and `unsigned short int`, respectively.

INT_MIN
: This is the minimum value that can be represented by a `signed int`. On most machines that the GNU C system runs on, an `int` is a 32-bit quantity.

`INT_MAX`
`UINT_MAX`
> These are the maximum values that can be represented by, respectively, the type `signed int` and the type `unsigned int`.

`LONG_MIN`
> This is the minimum value that can be represented by a `signed long int`. On most machines that the GNU C system runs on, `long` integers are 32-bit quantities, the same size as `int`.

`LONG_MAX`
`ULONG_MAX`
> These are the maximum values that can be represented by a `signed long int` and `unsigned long int`, respectively.

`LONG_LONG_MIN`
> This is the minimum value that can be represented by a `signed long long int`. On most machines that the GNU C system runs on, `long long` integers are 64-bit quantities.

`LONG_LONG_MAX`
`ULONG_LONG_MAX`
> These are the maximum values that can be represented by a `signed long long int` and `unsigned long long int`, respectively.

`WCHAR_MAX`
> This is the maximum value that can be represented by a `wchar_t`. See Section 18.4 [Wide Character Introduction], page 349.

The header file 'limits.h' also defines some additional constants that parameterize various operating system and file system limits. These constants are described in Chapter 27 [System Configuration Parameters], page 499.

A.5.3 Floating Type Macros

The specific representation of floating point numbers varies from machine to machine. Because floating point numbers are represented internally as approximate quantities, algorithms for manipulating floating point data often need to take account of the precise details of the machine's floating point representation.

Some of the functions in the C library itself need this information; for example, the algorithms for printing and reading floating point numbers (see Chapter 7 [Input/Output on Streams], page 83) and for calculating trigonometric and irrational functions (see Chapter 13 [Mathematics], page 281) use it to avoid round-off error and loss of accuracy. User programs that

Appendix A: C Language Facilities in the Library   527

implement numerical analysis techniques also often need this information in order to minimize or compute error bounds.

The header file 'float.h' describes the format used by your machine.

A.5.3.1 Floating Point Representation Concepts

This section introduces the terminology for describing floating point representations.

You are probably already familiar with most of these concepts in terms of scientific or exponential notation for floating point numbers. For example, the number 123456.0 could be expressed in exponential notation as 1.23456e+05, a shorthand notation indicating that the mantissa 1.23456 is multiplied by the base 10 raised to power 5.

More formally, the internal representation of a floating point number can be characterized in terms of the following parameters:

- The *sign* is either -1 or 1.
- The *base* or *radix* for exponentiation, an integer greater than 1. This is a constant for a particular representation.
- The *exponent* to which the base is raised. The upper and lower bounds of the exponent value are constants for a particular representation.

  Sometimes, in the actual bits representing the floating point number, the exponent is *biased* by adding a constant to it, to make it always be represented as an unsigned quantity. This is only important if you have some reason to pick apart the bit fields making up the floating point number by hand, which is something for which the GNU library provides no support. So this is ignored in the discussion that follows.

- The *mantissa* or *significand*, an unsigned integer which is a part of each floating point number.
- The *precision* of the mantissa. If the base of the representation is b, then the precision is the number of base-b digits in the mantissa. This is a constant for a particular representation.

  Many floating point representations have an implicit *hidden bit* in the mantissa. This is a bit which is present virtually in the mantissa, but not stored in memory because its value is always 1 in a normalized number. The precision figure (see above) includes any hidden bits.

  Again, the GNU library provides no facilities for dealing with such low-level aspects of the representation.

The mantissa of a floating point number actually represents an implicit fraction whose denominator is the base raised to the power of the precision. Since the largest representable mantissa is one less than this denominator, the value of the fraction is always strictly less than 1. The mathematical value of a floating point number is then the product of this fraction, the sign, and the base raised to the exponent.

We say that the floating point number is *normalized* if the fraction is at least $1/b$, where b is the base. In other words, the mantissa would be too large to fit if it were multiplied by the base. Non-normalized numbers are sometimes called *denormal*; they contain less precision than the representation normally can hold.

If the number is not normalized, then you can subtract 1 from the exponent while multiplying the mantissa by the base, and get another floating point number with the same value. *Normalization* consists of doing this repeatedly until the number is normalized. Two distinct normalized floating point numbers cannot be equal in value.

(There is an exception to this rule: if the mantissa is zero, it is considered normalized. Another exception happens on certain machines where the exponent is as small as the representation can hold. Then it is impossible to subtract 1 from the exponent, so a number may be normalized even if its fraction is less than $1/b$.)

A.5.3.2 Floating Point Parameters

These macro definitions can be accessed by including the header file 'float.h' in your program.

Macro names starting with 'FLT_' refer to the float type, while names beginning with 'DBL_' refer to the double type and names beginning with 'LDBL_' refer to the long double type. (Currently GCC does not support long double as a distinct data type, so the values for the 'LDBL_' constants are equal to the corresponding constants for the double type.)

Of these macros, only **FLT_RADIX** is guaranteed to be a constant expression. The other macros listed here cannot be reliably used in places that require constant expressions, such as '#if' preprocessing directives or in the dimensions of static arrays.

Although the ANSI C standard specifies minimum and maximum values for most of these parameters, the GNU C implementation uses whatever values describe the floating point representation of the target machine. So in principle GNU C actually satisfies the ANSI C requirements only if the target machine is suitable. In practice, all the machines currently supported are suitable.

FLT_ROUNDS
This value characterizes the rounding mode for floating point addition. The following values indicate standard rounding modes:

Appendix A: C Language Facilities in the Library

> -1   The mode is indeterminable.
>
> 0   Rounding is towards zero.
>
> 1   Rounding is to the nearest number.
>
> 2   Rounding is towards positive infinity.
>
> 3   Rounding is towards negative infinity.
>
> Any other value represents a machine-dependent nonstandard rounding mode.
>
> On most machines, the value is 1, in accordance with the IEEE standard for floating point.
>
> Here is a table showing how certain values round for each possible value of **FLT_ROUNDS**, if the other aspects of the representation match the IEEE single-precision standard.
>
> | | 0 | 1 | 2 | 3 |
> |---|---|---|---|---|
> | 1.00000003 | 1.0 | 1.0 | 1.00000012 | 1.0 |
> | 1.00000007 | 1.0 | 1.00000012 | 1.00000012 | 1.0 |
> | -1.00000003 | -1.0 | -1.0 | -1.0 | -1.00000012 |
> | -1.00000007 | -1.0 | -1.00000012 | -1.0 | -1.00000012 |

FLT_RADIX
> This is the value of the base, or radix, of exponent representation. This is guaranteed to be a constant expression, unlike the other macros described in this section. The value is 2 on all machines we know of except the IBM 360 and derivatives.

FLT_MANT_DIG
> This is the number of base-**FLT_RADIX** digits in the floating point mantissa for the **float** data type. The following expression yields **1.0** (even though mathematically it should not) due to the limited number of mantissa digits:
>
>   float radix = FLT_RADIX;
>
>   1.0f + 1.0f / radix / radix / ... / radix
>
> where **radix** appears **FLT_MANT_DIG** times.

DBL_MANT_DIG
LDBL_MANT_DIG
> This is the number of base-**FLT_RADIX** digits in the floating point mantissa for the data types **double** and **long double**, respectively.

FLT_DIG
> This is the number of decimal digits of precision for the **float** data type. Technically, if p and b are the precision and base (respectively) for the representation, then the decimal precision q

is the maximum number of decimal digits such that any floating point number with q base 10 digits can be rounded to a floating point number with p base b digits and back again, without change to the q decimal digits.

The value of this macro is supposed to be at least 6, to satisfy ANSI C.

`DBL_DIG`
`LDBL_DIG`

These are similar to `FLT_DIG`, but for the data types **double** and **long double**, respectively. The values of these macros are supposed to be at least 10.

`FLT_MIN_EXP`

This is the smallest possible exponent value for type **float**. More precisely, is the minimum negative integer such that the value `FLT_RADIX` raised to this power minus 1 can be represented as a normalized floating point number of type **float**.

`DBL_MIN_EXP`
`LDBL_MIN_EXP`

These are similar to `FLT_MIN_EXP`, but for the data types **double** and **long double**, respectively.

`FLT_MIN_10_EXP`

This is the minimum negative integer such that 10 raised to this power minus 1 can be represented as a normalized floating point number of type **float**. This is supposed to be -37 or even less.

`DBL_MIN_10_EXP`
`LDBL_MIN_10_EXP`

These are similar to `FLT_MIN_10_EXP`, but for the data types **double** and **long double**, respectively.

`FLT_MAX_EXP`

This is the largest possible exponent value for type **float**. More precisely, this is the maximum positive integer such that value `FLT_RADIX` raised to this power minus 1 can be represented as a floating point number of type **float**.

`DBL_MAX_EXP`
`LDBL_MAX_EXP`

These are similar to `FLT_MAX_EXP`, but for the data types **double** and **long double**, respectively.

`FLT_MAX_10_EXP`

This is the maximum positive integer such that 10 raised to this power minus 1 can be represented as a normalized floating point number of type **float**. This is supposed to be at least 37.

Appendix A: C Language Facilities in the Library 531

`DBL_MAX_10_EXP`
`LDBL_MAX_10_EXP`
>These are similar to `FLT_MAX_10_EXP`, but for the data types `double` and `long double`, respectively.

`FLT_MAX`
>The value of this macro is the maximum number representable in type `float`. It is supposed to be at least 1E+37. The value has type `float`.
>
>The smallest representable number is - `FLT_MAX`.

`DBL_MAX`
`LDBL_MAX`
>These are similar to `FLT_MAX`, but for the data types `double` and `long double`, respectively. The type of the macro's value is the same as the type it describes.

`FLT_MIN`
>The value of this macro is the minimum normalized positive floating point number that is representable in type `float`. It is supposed to be no more than 1E-37.

`DBL_MIN`
`LDBL_MIN`
>These are similar to `FLT_MIN`, but for the data types `double` and `long double`, respectively. The type of the macro's value is the same as the type it describes.

`FLT_EPSILON`
>This is the minimum positive floating point number of type `float` such that 1.0 + FLT_EPSILON != 1.0 is true. It's supposed to be no greater than 1E-5.

`DBL_EPSILON`
`LDBL_EPSILON`
>These are similar to `FLT_EPSILON`, but for the data types `double` and `long double`, respectively. The type of the macro's value is the same as the type it describes. The values are not supposed to be greater than 1E-9.

A.5.3.3 IEEE Floating Point

Here is an example showing how the floating type measurements come out for the most common floating point representation, specified by the *IEEE Standard for Binary Floating Point Arithmetic (ANSI/IEEE Std 754-1985)*. Nearly all computers designed since the 1980s use this format.

The IEEE single-precision float representation uses a base of 2. There is a sign bit, a mantissa with 23 bits plus one hidden bit (so the total precision is 24 base-2 digits), and an 8-bit exponent that can represent values in the range -125 to 128, inclusive.

So, for an implementation that uses this representation for the `float` data type, appropriate values for the corresponding parameters are:

```
FLT_RADIX                           2
FLT_MANT_DIG                       24
FLT_DIG                             6
FLT_MIN_EXP                      -125
FLT_MIN_10_EXP                    -37
FLT_MAX_EXP                       128
FLT_MAX_10_EXP                    +38
FLT_MIN              1.17549435E-38F
FLT_MAX              3.40282347E+38F
FLT_EPSILON          1.19209290E-07F
```

Here are the values for the `double` data type:

```
DBL_MANT_DIG                          53
DBL_DIG                               15
DBL_MIN_EXP                        -1021
DBL_MIN_10_EXP                      -307
DBL_MAX_EXP                         1024
DBL_MAX_10_EXP                       308
DBL_MAX           1.7976931348623157E+308
DBL_MIN           2.2250738585072014E-308
DBL_EPSILON       2.2204460492503131E-016
```

A.5.4 Structure Field Offset Measurement

You can use `offsetof` to measure the location within a structure type of a particular structure member.

size_t offsetof (*type, member*)   Macro
This expands to a integer constant expression that is the offset of the structure member named *member* in a the structure type *type*. For example, `offsetof (struct s, elem)` is the offset, in bytes, of the member `elem` in a `struct s`.

This macro won't work if *member* is a bit field; you get an error from the C compiler in that case.

Appendix B Summary of Library Facilities

This appendix is a complete list of the facilities declared within the header files supplied with the GNU C library. Each entry also lists the standard or other source from which each facility is derived, and tells you where in the manual you can find more information about how to use it.

void abort (void)
: 'stdlib.h' (ANSI): Section 22.3.4 [Aborting a Program], page 440.

int abs (int *number*)
: 'stdlib.h' (ANSI): Section 14.3 [Absolute Value], page 290.

int accept (int *socket*, struct sockaddr **addr*, size_t **length-ptr*)
: 'sys/socket.h' (BSD): Section 11.8.3 [Accepting Connections], page 233.

int access (const char **filename*, int *how*)
: 'unistd.h' (POSIX.1): Section 9.8.8 [Testing Permission to Access a File], page 192.

double acosh (double *x*)
: 'math.h' (BSD): Section 13.5 [Hyperbolic Functions], page 285.

double acos (double *x*)
: 'math.h' (ANSI): Section 13.3 [Inverse Trigonometric Functions], page 282.

int adjtime (const struct timeval **delta*, struct timeval **olddelta*)
: 'sys/time.h' (BSD): Section 17.2.2 [High-Resolution Calendar], page 324.

AF_FILE
: 'sys/socket.h' (GNU): Section 11.3.1 [Address Formats], page 210.

AF_INET
: 'sys/socket.h' (BSD): Section 11.3.1 [Address Formats], page 210.

AF_UNIX
: 'sys/socket.h' (BSD): Section 11.3.1 [Address Formats], page 210.

AF_UNSPEC
: 'sys/socket.h' (BSD): Section 11.3.1 [Address Formats], page 210.

unsigned int alarm (unsigned int *seconds*)
: 'unistd.h' (POSIX.1): Section 17.3 [Setting an Alarm], page 335.

void * alloca (size_t *size*);
: 'stdlib.h' (GNU, BSD): Section 3.5 [Automatic Storage with Variable Size], page 49.

tcflag_t ALTWERASE
: 'termios.h' (BSD): Section 12.4.7 [Local Modes], page 266.

int ARG_MAX
: 'limits.h' (POSIX.1): Section 27.1 [General Capacity Limits], page 499.

char * asctime (const struct tm *brokentime*)
: 'time.h' (ANSI): Section 17.2.4 [Formatting Date and Time], page 329.

double asinh (double *x*)
: 'math.h' (BSD): Section 13.5 [Hyperbolic Functions], page 285.

double asin (double *x*)
: 'math.h' (ANSI): Section 13.3 [Inverse Trigonometric Functions], page 282.

int asprintf (char **ptr*, const char *template*, ...)
: 'stdio.h' (GNU): Section 7.10.8 [Dynamically Allocating Formatted Output], page 104.

void assert (int *expression*)
: 'assert.h' (ANSI): Section A.1 [Explicitly Checking Internal Consistency], page 515.

double atan2 (double *y*, double *x*)
: 'math.h' (ANSI): Section 13.3 [Inverse Trigonometric Functions], page 282.

double atanh (double *x*)
: 'math.h' (BSD): Section 13.5 [Hyperbolic Functions], page 285.

double atan (double *x*)
: 'math.h' (ANSI): Section 13.3 [Inverse Trigonometric Functions], page 282.

int atexit (void (**function*) (void))
: 'stdlib.h' (ANSI): Section 22.3.3 [Cleanups on Exit], page 439.

double atof (const char *string*)
: 'stdlib.h' (ANSI): Section 14.7.2 [Parsing of Floats], page 296.

Appendix B: Summary of Library Facilities

`int atoi (const char *string)`
    'stdlib.h' (ANSI): Section 14.7.1 [Parsing of Integers], page 294.

`long int atol (const char *string)`
    'stdlib.h' (ANSI): Section 14.7.1 [Parsing of Integers], page 294.

B0
    'termios.h' (POSIX.1): Section 12.4.8 [Line Speed], page 268.

B110
    'termios.h' (POSIX.1): Section 12.4.8 [Line Speed], page 268.

B1200
    'termios.h' (POSIX.1): Section 12.4.8 [Line Speed], page 268.

B134
    'termios.h' (POSIX.1): Section 12.4.8 [Line Speed], page 268.

B150
    'termios.h' (POSIX.1): Section 12.4.8 [Line Speed], page 268.

B1800
    'termios.h' (POSIX.1): Section 12.4.8 [Line Speed], page 268.

B19200
    'termios.h' (POSIX.1): Section 12.4.8 [Line Speed], page 268.

B200
    'termios.h' (POSIX.1): Section 12.4.8 [Line Speed], page 268.

B2400
    'termios.h' (POSIX.1): Section 12.4.8 [Line Speed], page 268.

B300
    'termios.h' (POSIX.1): Section 12.4.8 [Line Speed], page 268.

B38400
    'termios.h' (POSIX.1): Section 12.4.8 [Line Speed], page 268.

B4800
    'termios.h' (POSIX.1): Section 12.4.8 [Line Speed], page 268.

B50
    'termios.h' (POSIX.1): Section 12.4.8 [Line Speed], page 268.

B600
    'termios.h' (POSIX.1): Section 12.4.8 [Line Speed], page 268.

B75
> 'termios.h' (POSIX.1): Section 12.4.8 [Line Speed], page 268.

B9600
> 'termios.h' (POSIX.1): Section 12.4.8 [Line Speed], page 268.

int BC_BASE_MAX
> 'limits.h' (POSIX.2): Section 27.10 [Utility Program Capacity Limits], page 511.

int BC_DIM_MAX
> 'limits.h' (POSIX.2): Section 27.10 [Utility Program Capacity Limits], page 511.

int BC_DIM_MAX
> 'limits.h' (POSIX.2): Section 27.10 [Utility Program Capacity Limits], page 511.

int bcmp (const void *a1, const void *a2, size_t size)
> 'string.h' (BSD): Section 5.5 [String/Array Comparison], page 65.

void * bcopy (void *from, const void *to, size_t size)
> 'string.h' (BSD): Section 5.4 [Copying and Concatenation], page 61.

int BC_SCALE_MAX
> 'limits.h' (POSIX.2): Section 27.10 [Utility Program Capacity Limits], page 511.

int BC_STRING_MAX
> 'limits.h' (POSIX.2): Section 27.10 [Utility Program Capacity Limits], page 511.

int bind (int socket, struct sockaddr *addr, size_t length)
> 'sys/socket.h' (BSD): Section 11.3.2 [Setting the Address of a Socket], page 211.

tcflag_t BRKINT
> 'termios.h' (POSIX.1): Section 12.4.4 [Input Modes], page 261.

_BSD_SOURCE
> (GNU): Section 1.3.4 [Feature Test Macros], page 8.

void * bsearch (const void *key, const void *array, size_t count, size_t size, comparison_fn_t compare)
> 'stdlib.h' (ANSI): Section 15.2 [Array Search Function], page 299.

int BUFSIZ
> 'stdio.h' (ANSI): Section 7.17.3 [Controlling Which Kind of Buffering], page 131.

Appendix B: Summary of Library Facilities

void * bzero (void *block, size_t size)
: 'string.h' (BSD): Section 5.4 [Copying and Concatenation], page 61.

double cabs (struct { double real, imag; } z)
: 'math.h' (BSD): Section 14.3 [Absolute Value], page 290.

void * calloc (size_t count, size_t eltsize)
: 'malloc.h', 'stdlib.h' (ANSI): Section 3.3.5 [Allocating Cleared Space], page 32.

double cbrt (double x)
: 'math.h' (BSD): Section 13.4 [Exponentiation and Logarithms], page 283.

cc_t
: 'termios.h' (POSIX.1): Section 12.4.1 [Terminal Mode Data Types], page 257.

tcflag_t CCTS_OFLOW
: 'termios.h' (BSD): Section 12.4.6 [Control Modes], page 264.

double ceil (double x)
: 'math.h' (ANSI): Section 14.5 [Rounding and Remainder Functions], page 292.

speed_t cfgetispeed (const struct termios *termios-p)
: 'termios.h' (POSIX.1): Section 12.4.8 [Line Speed], page 268.

speed_t cfgetospeed (const struct termios *termios-p)
: 'termios.h' (POSIX.1): Section 12.4.8 [Line Speed], page 268.

int cfmakeraw (struct termios *termios-p)
: 'termios.h' (BSD): Section 12.4.10 [Noncanonical Input], page 275.

void cfree (void *ptr)
: 'stdlib.h' (Sun): Section 3.3.3 [Freeing Memory Allocated with "code malloc], page 30.

int cfsetispeed (struct termios *termios-p, speed_t speed)
: 'termios.h' (POSIX.1): Section 12.4.8 [Line Speed], page 268.

int cfsetospeed (struct termios *termios-p, speed_t speed)
: 'termios.h' (POSIX.1): Section 12.4.8 [Line Speed], page 268.

int cfsetspeed (struct termios *termios-p, speed_t speed)
: 'termios.h' (BSD): Section 12.4.8 [Line Speed], page 268.

CHAR_BIT
: 'limits.h' (ANSI): Section A.5.1 [Computing the Width of an Integer Data Type], page 524.

CHAR_MAX
> 'limits.h' (ANSI): Section A.5.2 [Range of an Integer Type], page 525.

CHAR_MIN
> 'limits.h' (ANSI): Section A.5.2 [Range of an Integer Type], page 525.

int chdir (const char *filename)
> 'unistd.h' (POSIX.1): Section 9.1 [Working Directory], page 169.

int CHILD_MAX
> 'limits.h' (POSIX.1): Section 27.1 [General Capacity Limits], page 499.

int chmod (const char *filename, mode_t mode)
> 'sys/stat.h' (POSIX.1): Section 9.8.7 [Assigning File Permissions], page 190.

int chown (const char *filename, uid_t owner, gid_t group)
> 'unistd.h' (POSIX.1): Section 9.8.4 [File Owner], page 186.

tcflag_t CIGNORE
> 'termios.h' (BSD): Section 12.4.6 [Control Modes], page 264.

void clearerr (FILE *stream)
> 'stdio.h' (ANSI): Section 7.13 [End-Of-File and Errors], page 124.

int CLK_TCK
> 'time.h' (POSIX.1): Section 17.1.1 [Basic CPU Time Inquiry], page 321.

tcflag_t CLOCAL
> 'termios.h' (POSIX.1): Section 12.4.6 [Control Modes], page 264.

clock_t clock (void)
> 'time.h' (ANSI): Section 17.1.1 [Basic CPU Time Inquiry], page 321.

int CLOCKS_PER_SEC
> 'time.h' (ANSI): Section 17.1.1 [Basic CPU Time Inquiry], page 321.

clock_t
> 'time.h' (ANSI): Section 17.1.1 [Basic CPU Time Inquiry], page 321.

Appendix B: Summary of Library Facilities

int closedir (DIR *dirstream)
: 'dirent.h' (POSIX.1): Section 9.2.3 [Reading and Closing a Directory Stream], page 173.

int close (int filedes)
: 'unistd.h' (POSIX.1): Section 8.1 [Opening and Closing Files], page 139.

int COLL_WEIGHTS_MAX
: 'limits.h' (POSIX.2): Section 27.10 [Utility Program Capacity Limits], page 511.

size_t confstr (int parameter, char *buf, size_t len)
: 'unistd.h' (POSIX.2): Section 27.12 [String-Valued Parameters], page 513.

int connect (int socket, struct sockaddr *addr, size_t length)
: 'sys/socket.h' (BSD): Section 11.8.1 [Making a Connection], page 231.

cookie_close_function
: 'stdio.h' (GNU): Section 7.18.3.2 [Custom Stream Hook Functions], page 137.

cookie_io_functions_t
: 'stdio.h' (GNU): Section 7.18.3.1 [Custom Streams and Cookies], page 136.

cookie_read_function
: 'stdio.h' (GNU): Section 7.18.3.2 [Custom Stream Hook Functions], page 137.

cookie_seek_function
: 'stdio.h' (GNU): Section 7.18.3.2 [Custom Stream Hook Functions], page 137.

cookie_write_function
: 'stdio.h' (GNU): Section 7.18.3.2 [Custom Stream Hook Functions], page 137.

double copysign (double value, double sign)
: 'math.h' (BSD): Section 14.4 [Normalization Functions], page 291.

double cosh (double x)
: 'math.h' (ANSI): Section 13.5 [Hyperbolic Functions], page 285.

double cos (double x)
: 'math.h' (ANSI): Section 13.2 [Trigonometric Functions], page 282.

tcflag_t CREAD
: 'termios.h' (POSIX.1): Section 12.4.6 [Control Modes], page 264.

int creat (const char *filename, mode_t mode)
: 'fcntl.h' (POSIX.1): Section 8.1 [Opening and Closing Files], page 139.

tcflag_t CRTS_IFLOW
: 'termios.h' (BSD): Section 12.4.6 [Control Modes], page 264.

tcflag_t CS5
: 'termios.h' (POSIX.1): Section 12.4.6 [Control Modes], page 264.

tcflag_t CS6
: 'termios.h' (POSIX.1): Section 12.4.6 [Control Modes], page 264.

tcflag_t CS7
: 'termios.h' (POSIX.1): Section 12.4.6 [Control Modes], page 264.

tcflag_t CS8
: 'termios.h' (POSIX.1): Section 12.4.6 [Control Modes], page 264.

tcflag_t CSIZE
: 'termios.h' (POSIX.1): Section 12.4.6 [Control Modes], page 264.

_CS_PATH
: 'unistd.h' (POSIX.2): Section 27.12 [String-Valued Parameters], page 513.

tcflag_t CSTOPB
: 'termios.h' (POSIX.1): Section 12.4.6 [Control Modes], page 264.

char * ctermid (char *string)
: 'stdio.h' (POSIX.1): Section 24.7.1 [Identifying the Controlling Terminal], page 474.

char * ctime (const time_t *time)
: 'time.h' (ANSI): Section 17.2.4 [Formatting Date and Time], page 329.

char * cuserid (char *string)
: 'stdio.h' (POSIX.1): Section 25.11 [Identifying Who Logged In], page 488.

Appendix B: Summary of Library Facilities 541

`int daylight`
: 'time.h' (SVID): Section 17.2.6 [Functions and Variables for Time Zones], page 334.

`DBL_DIG`
: 'float.h' (ANSI): Section A.5.3.2 [Floating Point Parameters], page 528.

`DBL_EPSILON`
: 'float.h' (ANSI): Section A.5.3.2 [Floating Point Parameters], page 528.

`DBL_MANT_DIG`
: 'float.h' (ANSI): Section A.5.3.2 [Floating Point Parameters], page 528.

`DBL_MAX_10_EXP`
: 'float.h' (ANSI): Section A.5.3.2 [Floating Point Parameters], page 528.

`DBL_MAX_EXP`
: 'float.h' (ANSI): Section A.5.3.2 [Floating Point Parameters], page 528.

`DBL_MAX`
: 'float.h' (ANSI): Section A.5.3.2 [Floating Point Parameters], page 528.

`DBL_MIN_10_EXP`
: 'float.h' (ANSI): Section A.5.3.2 [Floating Point Parameters], page 528.

`DBL_MIN_EXP`
: 'float.h' (ANSI): Section A.5.3.2 [Floating Point Parameters], page 528.

`DBL_MIN`
: 'float.h' (ANSI): Section A.5.3.2 [Floating Point Parameters], page 528.

`dev_t`
: 'sys/types.h' (POSIX.1): Section 9.8.1 [What the File Attribute Values Mean], page 181.

`double difftime (time_t time1, time_t time0)`
: 'time.h' (ANSI): Section 17.2.1 [Simple Calendar Time], page 324.

`DIR`
: 'dirent.h' (POSIX.1): Section 9.2.2 [Opening a Directory Stream], page 172.

div_t div (int *numerator*, int *denominator*)
: 'stdlib.h' (ANSI): Section 14.6 [Integer Division], page 293.

div_t
: 'stdlib.h' (ANSI): Section 14.6 [Integer Division], page 293.

double drem (double *numerator*, double *denominator*)
: 'math.h' (BSD): Section 14.5 [Rounding and Remainder Functions], page 292.

int dup2 (int *old*, int *new*)
: 'unistd.h' (POSIX.1): Section 8.8 [Duplicating Descriptors], page 154.

int dup (int *old*)
: 'unistd.h' (POSIX.1): Section 8.8 [Duplicating Descriptors], page 154.

int E2BIG
: 'errno.h' (POSIX.1: Argument list too long): Section 2.2 [Error Codes], page 14.

int EACCES
: 'errno.h' (POSIX.1: Permission denied): Section 2.2 [Error Codes], page 14.

int EADDRINUSE
: 'errno.h' (BSD: Address already in use): Section 2.2 [Error Codes], page 14.

int EADDRNOTAVAIL
: 'errno.h' (BSD: Can't assign requested address): Section 2.2 [Error Codes], page 14.

int EAFNOSUPPORT
: 'errno.h' (BSD: Address family not supported by protocol family): Section 2.2 [Error Codes], page 14.

int EAGAIN
: 'errno.h' (POSIX.1: Resource temporarily unavailable): Section 2.2 [Error Codes], page 14.

int EALREADY
: 'errno.h' (BSD: Operation already in progress): Section 2.2 [Error Codes], page 14.

int EAUTH
: 'errno.h' (BSD: Authentication error): Section 2.2 [Error Codes], page 14.

Appendix B: Summary of Library Facilities

`int EBACKGROUND`
: 'errno.h' (GNU: Inappropriate operation for background process): Section 2.2 [Error Codes], page 14.

`int EBADF`
: 'errno.h' (POSIX.1: Bad file descriptor): Section 2.2 [Error Codes], page 14.

`int EBADRPC`
: 'errno.h' (BSD: RPC struct is bad): Section 2.2 [Error Codes], page 14.

`int EBUSY`
: 'errno.h' (POSIX.1: Device busy): Section 2.2 [Error Codes], page 14.

`int ECHILD`
: 'errno.h' (POSIX.1: No child processes): Section 2.2 [Error Codes], page 14.

`tcflag_t ECHOCTL`
: 'termios.h' (BSD): Section 12.4.7 [Local Modes], page 266.

`tcflag_t ECHOE`
: 'termios.h' (POSIX.1): Section 12.4.7 [Local Modes], page 266.

`tcflag_t ECHO`
: 'termios.h' (POSIX.1): Section 12.4.7 [Local Modes], page 266.

`tcflag_t ECHOKE`
: 'termios.h' (BSD): Section 12.4.7 [Local Modes], page 266.

`tcflag_t ECHOK`
: 'termios.h' (POSIX.1): Section 12.4.7 [Local Modes], page 266.

`tcflag_t ECHONL`
: 'termios.h' (POSIX.1): Section 12.4.7 [Local Modes], page 266.

`tcflag_t ECHOPRT`
: 'termios.h' (BSD): Section 12.4.7 [Local Modes], page 266.

`int ECONNABORTED`
: 'errno.h' (BSD: Software caused connection abort): Section 2.2 [Error Codes], page 14.

`int ECONNREFUSED`
: 'errno.h' (BSD: Connection refused): Section 2.2 [Error Codes], page 14.

`int ECONNRESET`
: 'errno.h' (BSD: Connection reset by peer): Section 2.2 [Error Codes], page 14.

int EDEADLK

'errno.h' (POSIX.1: Resource deadlock avoided): Section 2.2 [Error Codes], page 14.

int EDESTADDRREQ

'errno.h' (BSD: Destination address required): Section 2.2 [Error Codes], page 14.

int EDIED

'errno.h' (GNU: Translator died): Section 2.2 [Error Codes], page 14.

int ED

'errno.h' (GNU: ?): Section 2.2 [Error Codes], page 14.

int EDOM

'errno.h' (ANSI: Numerical argument out of domain): Section 2.2 [Error Codes], page 14.

int EDQUOT

'errno.h' (BSD: Disc quota exceeded): Section 2.2 [Error Codes], page 14.

int EEXIST

'errno.h' (POSIX.1: File exists): Section 2.2 [Error Codes], page 14.

int EFAULT

'errno.h' (POSIX.1: Bad address): Section 2.2 [Error Codes], page 14.

int EFBIG

'errno.h' (POSIX.1: File too large): Section 2.2 [Error Codes], page 14.

int EFTYPE

'errno.h' (BSD: Inappropriate file type or format): Section 2.2 [Error Codes], page 14.

int EGRATUITOUS

'errno.h' (GNU: Gratuitous error): Section 2.2 [Error Codes], page 14.

int EGREGIOUS

'errno.h' (GNU: You really blew it this time): Section 2.2 [Error Codes], page 14.

int EHOSTDOWN

'errno.h' (BSD: Host is down): Section 2.2 [Error Codes], page 14.

Appendix B: Summary of Library Facilities 545

`int EHOSTUNREACH`
> 'errno.h' (BSD: No route to host): Section 2.2 [Error Codes], page 14.

`int EIEIO`
> 'errno.h' (GNU: Computer bought the farm): Section 2.2 [Error Codes], page 14.

`int EINPROGRESS`
> 'errno.h' (BSD: Operation now in progress): Section 2.2 [Error Codes], page 14.

`int EINTR`
> 'errno.h' (POSIX.1: Interrupted system call): Section 2.2 [Error Codes], page 14.

`int EINVAL`
> 'errno.h' (POSIX.1: Invalid argument): Section 2.2 [Error Codes], page 14.

`int EIO`
> 'errno.h' (POSIX.1: Input/output error): Section 2.2 [Error Codes], page 14.

`int EISCONN`
> 'errno.h' (BSD: Socket is already connected): Section 2.2 [Error Codes], page 14.

`int EISDIR`
> 'errno.h' (POSIX.1: Is a directory): Section 2.2 [Error Codes], page 14.

`int ELOOP`
> 'errno.h' (BSD: Too many levels of symbolic links): Section 2.2 [Error Codes], page 14.

`int EMFILE`
> 'errno.h' (POSIX.1: Too many open files): Section 2.2 [Error Codes], page 14.

`int EMLINK`
> 'errno.h' (POSIX.1: Too many links): Section 2.2 [Error Codes], page 14.

`int EMSGSIZE`
> 'errno.h' (BSD: Message too long): Section 2.2 [Error Codes], page 14.

`int ENAMETOOLONG`
> 'errno.h' (POSIX.1: File name too long): Section 2.2 [Error Codes], page 14.

void endgrent (void)
: 'grp.h' (SVID, BSD): Section 25.13.3 [Scanning the List of All Groups], page 492.

void endhostent ()
: 'netdb.h' (BSD): Section 11.5.2.4 [Host Names], page 219.

void endnetent (void)
: 'netdb.h' (BSD): Section 11.12 [Networks Database], page 252.

void endprotoent (void)
: 'netdb.h' (BSD): Section 11.5.6 [Protocols Database], page 225.

void endpwent (void)
: 'pwd.h' (SVID, BSD): Section 25.12.3 [Scanning the List of All Users], page 490.

void endservent (void)
: 'netdb.h' (BSD): Section 11.5.4 [The Services Database], page 222.

int ENEEDAUTH
: 'errno.h' (BSD: Need authenticator): Section 2.2 [Error Codes], page 14.

int ENETDOWN
: 'errno.h' (BSD: Network is down): Section 2.2 [Error Codes], page 14.

int ENETRESET
: 'errno.h' (BSD: Network dropped connection on reset): Section 2.2 [Error Codes], page 14.

int ENETUNREACH
: 'errno.h' (BSD: Network is unreachable): Section 2.2 [Error Codes], page 14.

int ENFILE
: 'errno.h' (POSIX.1: Too many open files in system): Section 2.2 [Error Codes], page 14.

int ENOBUFS
: 'errno.h' (BSD: No buffer space available): Section 2.2 [Error Codes], page 14.

int ENODEV
: 'errno.h' (POSIX.1: Operation not supported by device): Section 2.2 [Error Codes], page 14.

int ENOENT
: 'errno.h' (POSIX.1: No such file or directory): Section 2.2 [Error Codes], page 14.

Appendix B: Summary of Library Facilities

`int ENOEXEC`
: `'errno.h'` (POSIX.1: Exec format error): Section 2.2 [Error Codes], page 14.

`int ENOLCK`
: `'errno.h'` (POSIX.1: No locks available): Section 2.2 [Error Codes], page 14.

`int ENOMEM`
: `'errno.h'` (POSIX.1: Cannot allocate memory): Section 2.2 [Error Codes], page 14.

`int ENOPROTOOPT`
: `'errno.h'` (BSD: Protocol not available): Section 2.2 [Error Codes], page 14.

`int ENOSPC`
: `'errno.h'` (POSIX.1: No space left on device): Section 2.2 [Error Codes], page 14.

`int ENOSYS`
: `'errno.h'` (POSIX.1: Function not implemented): Section 2.2 [Error Codes], page 14.

`int ENOTBLK`
: `'errno.h'` (BSD: Block device required): Section 2.2 [Error Codes], page 14.

`int ENOTCONN`
: `'errno.h'` (BSD: Socket is not connected): Section 2.2 [Error Codes], page 14.

`int ENOTDIR`
: `'errno.h'` (POSIX.1: Not a directory): Section 2.2 [Error Codes], page 14.

`int ENOTEMPTY`
: `'errno.h'` (POSIX.1: Directory not empty): Section 2.2 [Error Codes], page 14.

`int ENOTSOCK`
: `'errno.h'` (BSD: Socket operation on non-socket): Section 2.2 [Error Codes], page 14.

`int ENOTTY`
: `'errno.h'` (POSIX.1: Inappropriate ioctl for device): Section 2.2 [Error Codes], page 14.

`char ** environ`
: `'unistd.h'` (POSIX.1): Section 22.2.1 [Environment Access], page 434.

int ENXIO
: 'errno.h' (POSIX.1: Device not configured): Section 2.2 [Error Codes], page 14.

int EOF
: 'stdio.h' (ANSI): Section 7.13 [End-Of-File and Errors], page 124.

int EOPNOTSUPP
: 'errno.h' (BSD: Operation not supported): Section 2.2 [Error Codes], page 14.

int EPERM
: 'errno.h' (POSIX.1: Operation not permitted): Section 2.2 [Error Codes], page 14.

int EPFNOSUPPORT
: 'errno.h' (BSD: Protocol family not supported): Section 2.2 [Error Codes], page 14.

int EPIPE
: 'errno.h' (POSIX.1: Broken pipe): Section 2.2 [Error Codes], page 14.

int EPROCLIM
: 'errno.h' (BSD: Too many processes): Section 2.2 [Error Codes], page 14.

int EPROCUNAVAIL
: 'errno.h' (BSD: RPC bad procedure for program): Section 2.2 [Error Codes], page 14.

int EPROGMISMATCH
: 'errno.h' (BSD: RPC program version wrong): Section 2.2 [Error Codes], page 14.

int EPROGUNAVAIL
: 'errno.h' (BSD: RPC program not available): Section 2.2 [Error Codes], page 14.

int EPROTONOSUPPORT
: 'errno.h' (BSD: Protocol not supported): Section 2.2 [Error Codes], page 14.

int EPROTOTYPE
: 'errno.h' (BSD: Protocol wrong type for socket): Section 2.2 [Error Codes], page 14.

int EQUIV_CLASS_MAX
: 'limits.h' (POSIX.2): Section 27.10 [Utility Program Capacity Limits], page 511.

Appendix B: Summary of Library Facilities

`int ERANGE`
> `errno.h` (ANSI: Numerical result out of range): Section 2.2 [Error Codes], page 14.

`int EREMOTE`
> `errno.h` (BSD: Too many levels of remote in path): Section 2.2 [Error Codes], page 14.

`int EROFS`
> `errno.h` (POSIX.1: Read-only file system): Section 2.2 [Error Codes], page 14.

`int ERPCMISMATCH`
> `errno.h` (BSD: RPC version wrong): Section 2.2 [Error Codes], page 14.

`volatile int errno`
> `errno.h` (ANSI): Section 2.1 [Checking for Errors], page 13.

`int ESHUTDOWN`
> `errno.h` (BSD: Can't send after socket shutdown): Section 2.2 [Error Codes], page 14.

`int ESOCKTNOSUPPORT`
> `errno.h` (BSD: Socket type not supported): Section 2.2 [Error Codes], page 14.

`int ESPIPE`
> `errno.h` (POSIX.1: Illegal seek): Section 2.2 [Error Codes], page 14.

`int ESRCH`
> `errno.h` (POSIX.1: No such process): Section 2.2 [Error Codes], page 14.

`int ESTALE`
> `errno.h` (BSD: Stale NFS file handle): Section 2.2 [Error Codes], page 14.

`int ETIMEDOUT`
> `errno.h` (BSD: Connection timed out): Section 2.2 [Error Codes], page 14.

`int ETOOMANYREFS`
> `errno.h` (BSD: Too many references: can't splice): Section 2.2 [Error Codes], page 14.

`int ETXTBSY`
> `errno.h` (BSD: Text file busy): Section 2.2 [Error Codes], page 14.

int EUSERS
: 'errno.h' (BSD: Too many users): Section 2.2 [Error Codes], page 14.

int EWOULDBLOCK
: 'errno.h' (BSD: Operation would block): Section 2.2 [Error Codes], page 14.

int EXDEV
: 'errno.h' (POSIX.1: Invalid cross-device link): Section 2.2 [Error Codes], page 14.

int execle (const char *filename, const char *arg0, char *const env[], ...)
: 'unistd.h' (POSIX.1): Section 23.5 [Executing a File], page 446.

int execl (const char *filename, const char *arg0, ...)
: 'unistd.h' (POSIX.1): Section 23.5 [Executing a File], page 446.

int execlp (const char *filename, const char *arg0, ...)
: 'unistd.h' (POSIX.1): Section 23.5 [Executing a File], page 446.

int execve (const char *filename, char *const argv[], char *const env[])
: 'unistd.h' (POSIX.1): Section 23.5 [Executing a File], page 446.

int execv (const char *filename, char *const argv[])
: 'unistd.h' (POSIX.1): Section 23.5 [Executing a File], page 446.

int execvp (const char *filename, char *const argv[])
: 'unistd.h' (POSIX.1): Section 23.5 [Executing a File], page 446.

int EXIT_FAILURE
: 'stdlib.h' (ANSI): Section 22.3.2 [Exit Status], page 437.

void exit (int status)
: 'stdlib.h' (ANSI): Section 22.3.1 [Normal Termination], page 437.

void _exit (int status)
: 'unistd.h' (POSIX.1): Section 22.3.5 [Termination Internals], page 440.

int EXIT_SUCCESS
: 'stdlib.h' (ANSI): Section 22.3.2 [Exit Status], page 437.

Appendix B: Summary of Library Facilities 551

double exp (double *x*)
> 'math.h' (ANSI): Section 13.4 [Exponentiation and Logarithms], page 283.

double expm1 (double *x*)
> 'math.h' (BSD): Section 13.4 [Exponentiation and Logarithms], page 283.

int EXPR_NEST_MAX
> 'limits.h' (POSIX.2): Section 27.10 [Utility Program Capacity Limits], page 511.

double fabs (double *number*)
> 'math.h' (ANSI): Section 14.3 [Absolute Value], page 290.

int fchmod (int *filedes*, int *mode*)
> 'sys/stat.h' (BSD): Section 9.8.7 [Assigning File Permissions], page 190.

int fchown (int *filedes*, int *owner*, int *group*)
> 'unistd.h' (BSD): Section 9.8.4 [File Owner], page 186.

int fclean (FILE **stream*)
> 'stdio.h' (GNU): Section 8.5.3 [Cleaning Streams], page 149.

int fclose (FILE **stream*)
> 'stdio.h' (ANSI): Section 7.4 [Closing Streams], page 86.

int fcntl (int *filedes*, int *command*, ...)
> 'fcntl.h' (POSIX.1): Section 8.7 [Control Operations on Files], page 153.

int FD_CLOEXEC
> 'fcntl.h' (POSIX.1): Section 8.9 [File Descriptor Flags], page 156.

void FD_CLR (int *filedes*, fd_set **set*)
> 'sys/types.h' (BSD): Section 8.6 [Waiting for Input or Output], page 150.

int FD_ISSET (int *filedes*, fd_set **set*)
> 'sys/types.h' (BSD): Section 8.6 [Waiting for Input or Output], page 150.

FILE * fdopen (int *filedes*, const char **opentype*)
> 'stdio.h' (POSIX.1): Section 8.4 [Descriptors and Streams], page 147.

void FD_SET (int *filedes*, fd_set **set*)
> 'sys/types.h' (BSD): Section 8.6 [Waiting for Input or Output], page 150.

`fd_set`
: 'sys/types.h' (BSD): Section 8.6 [Waiting for Input or Output], page 150.

`int FD_SETSIZE`
: 'sys/types.h' (BSD): Section 8.6 [Waiting for Input or Output], page 150.

`int F_DUPFD`
: 'fcntl.h' (POSIX.1): Section 8.8 [Duplicating Descriptors], page 154.

`void FD_ZERO (fd_set *set)`
: 'sys/types.h' (BSD): Section 8.6 [Waiting for Input or Output], page 150.

`int feof (FILE *stream)`
: 'stdio.h' (ANSI): Section 7.13 [End-Of-File and Errors], page 124.

`int ferror (FILE *stream)`
: 'stdio.h' (ANSI): Section 7.13 [End-Of-File and Errors], page 124.

`int fflush (FILE *stream)`
: 'stdio.h' (ANSI): Section 7.17.2 [Flushing Buffers], page 130.

`int fgetc (FILE *stream)`
: 'stdio.h' (ANSI): Section 7.6 [Character Input], page 88.

`int F_GETFD`
: 'fcntl.h' (POSIX.1): Section 8.9 [File Descriptor Flags], page 156.

`int F_GETFL`
: 'fcntl.h' (POSIX.1): Section 8.10.4 [Getting and Setting File Status Flags], page 162.

`struct group * fgetgrent (FILE *stream)`
: 'grp.h' (SVID): Section 25.13.3 [Scanning the List of All Groups], page 492.

`int F_GETLK`
: 'fcntl.h' (POSIX.1): Section 8.11 [File Locks], page 164.

`int F_GETOWN`
: 'fcntl.h' (BSD): Section 8.12 [Interrupt-Driven Input], page 167.

`int fgetpos (FILE *stream, fpos_t *position)`
: 'stdio.h' (ANSI): Section 7.16 [Portable File-Position Functions], page 128.

Appendix B: Summary of Library Facilities

struct passwd * fgetpwent (FILE *stream)
: 'pwd.h' (SVID): Section 25.12.3 [Scanning the List of All Users], page 490.

char * fgets (char *s, int count, FILE *stream)
: 'stdio.h' (ANSI): Section 7.7 [Line-Oriented Input], page 90.

FILE
: 'stdio.h' (ANSI): Section 7.1 [Streams], page 83.

int FILENAME_MAX
: 'stdio.h' (ANSI): Section 27.6 [Limits on File System Capacity], page 507.

int fileno (FILE *stream)
: 'stdio.h' (POSIX.1): Section 8.4 [Descriptors and Streams], page 147.

int finite (double x)
: 'math.h' (BSD): Section 14.2 [Predicates on Floats], page 289.

double floor (double x)
: 'math.h' (ANSI): Section 14.5 [Rounding and Remainder Functions], page 292.

FLT_DIG
: 'float.h' (ANSI): Section A.5.3.2 [Floating Point Parameters], page 528.

FLT_EPSILON
: 'float.h' (ANSI): Section A.5.3.2 [Floating Point Parameters], page 528.

FLT_MANT_DIG
: 'float.h' (ANSI): Section A.5.3.2 [Floating Point Parameters], page 528.

FLT_MAX_10_EXP
: 'float.h' (ANSI): Section A.5.3.2 [Floating Point Parameters], page 528.

FLT_MAX_EXP
: 'float.h' (ANSI): Section A.5.3.2 [Floating Point Parameters], page 528.

FLT_MAX
: 'float.h' (ANSI): Section A.5.3.2 [Floating Point Parameters], page 528.

FLT_MIN_10_EXP
: 'float.h' (ANSI): Section A.5.3.2 [Floating Point Parameters], page 528.

`FLT_MIN_EXP`
: `'float.h'` (ANSI): Section A.5.3.2 [Floating Point Parameters], page 528.

`FLT_MIN`
: `'float.h'` (ANSI): Section A.5.3.2 [Floating Point Parameters], page 528.

`FLT_RADIX`
: `'float.h'` (ANSI): Section A.5.3.2 [Floating Point Parameters], page 528.

`FLT_ROUNDS`
: `'float.h'` (ANSI): Section A.5.3.2 [Floating Point Parameters], page 528.

`tcflag_t FLUSHO`
: `'termios.h'` (BSD): Section 12.4.7 [Local Modes], page 266.

`FILE * fmemopen (void *buf, size_t size, const char *opentype)`
: `'stdio.h'` (GNU): Section 7.18.1 [String Streams], page 133.

`double fmod (double numerator, double denominator)`
: `'math.h'` (ANSI): Section 14.5 [Rounding and Remainder Functions], page 292.

`int fnmatch (const char *pattern, const char *string, int flags)`
: `'fnmatch.h'` (POSIX.2): Section 16.1 [Wildcard Matching], page 305.

`FNM_CASEFOLD`
: `'fnmatch.h'` (GNU): Section 16.1 [Wildcard Matching], page 305.

`FNM_FILE_NAME`
: `'fnmatch.h'` (GNU): Section 16.1 [Wildcard Matching], page 305.

`FNM_LEADING_DIR`
: `'fnmatch.h'` (GNU): Section 16.1 [Wildcard Matching], page 305.

`FNM_NOESCAPE`
: `'fnmatch.h'` (POSIX.2): Section 16.1 [Wildcard Matching], page 305.

`FNM_PATHNAME`
: `'fnmatch.h'` (POSIX.2): Section 16.1 [Wildcard Matching], page 305.

`FNM_PERIOD`
: `'fnmatch.h'` (POSIX.2): Section 16.1 [Wildcard Matching], page 305.

Appendix B: Summary of Library Facilities   555

int F_OK
: 'unistd.h' (POSIX.1): Section 9.8.8 [Testing Permission to Access a File], page 192.

FILE * fopencookie (void *cookie, const char *opentype, cookie_io_functions_t io-functions)
: 'stdio.h' (GNU): Section 7.18.3.1 [Custom Streams and Cookies], page 136.

FILE * fopen (const char *filename, const char *opentype)
: 'stdio.h' (ANSI): Section 7.3 [Opening Streams], page 84.

int FOPEN_MAX
: 'stdio.h' (ANSI): Section 7.3 [Opening Streams], page 84.

pid_t fork (void)
: 'unistd.h' (POSIX.1): Section 23.4 [Creating a Process], page 445.

long int fpathconf (int filedes, int parameter)
: 'unistd.h' (POSIX.1): Section 27.9 [Using "code pathconf], page 510.

FPE_DECOVF_TRAP
: 'signal.h' (BSD): Section 21.2.1 [Program Error Signals], page 374.

FPE_FLTDIV_FAULT
: 'signal.h' (BSD): Section 21.2.1 [Program Error Signals], page 374.

FPE_FLTDIV_TRAP
: 'signal.h' (BSD): Section 21.2.1 [Program Error Signals], page 374.

FPE_FLTOVF_FAULT
: 'signal.h' (BSD): Section 21.2.1 [Program Error Signals], page 374.

FPE_FLTOVF_TRAP
: 'signal.h' (BSD): Section 21.2.1 [Program Error Signals], page 374.

FPE_FLTUND_FAULT
: 'signal.h' (BSD): Section 21.2.1 [Program Error Signals], page 374.

FPE_FLTUND_TRAP
: 'signal.h' (BSD): Section 21.2.1 [Program Error Signals], page 374.

FPE_INTDIV_TRAP
> 'signal.h' (BSD): Section 21.2.1 [Program Error Signals], page 374.

FPE_INTOVF_TRAP
> 'signal.h' (BSD): Section 21.2.1 [Program Error Signals], page 374.

FPE_SUBRNG_TRAP
> 'signal.h' (BSD): Section 21.2.1 [Program Error Signals], page 374.

fpos_t
> 'stdio.h' (ANSI): Section 7.16 [Portable File-Position Functions], page 128.

int fprintf (FILE *stream, const char *template, ...)
> 'stdio.h' (ANSI): Section 7.10.7 [Formatted Output Functions], page 103.

int fputc (int c, FILE *stream)
> 'stdio.h' (ANSI): Section 7.5 [Simple Output by Characters or Lines], page 87.

int fputs (const char *s, FILE *stream)
> 'stdio.h' (ANSI): Section 7.5 [Simple Output by Characters or Lines], page 87.

F_RDLCK
> 'fcntl.h' (POSIX.1): Section 8.11 [File Locks], page 164.

size_t fread (void *data, size_t size, size_t count, FILE *stream)
> 'stdio.h' (ANSI): Section 7.9 [Block Input/Output], page 93.

__free_hook
> 'malloc.h' (GNU): Section 3.3.9 [Storage Allocation Hooks], page 35.

void free (void *ptr)
> 'malloc.h', 'stdlib.h' (ANSI): Section 3.3.3 [Freeing Memory Allocated with "code malloc], page 30.

FILE * freopen (const char *filename, const char *opentype, FILE *stream)
> 'stdio.h' (ANSI): Section 7.3 [Opening Streams], page 84.

double frexp (double value, int *exponent)
> 'math.h' (ANSI): Section 14.4 [Normalization Functions], page 291.

Appendix B: Summary of Library Facilities   557

`int fscanf (FILE *stream, const char *template, ...)`
> 'stdio.h' (ANSI): Section 7.12.8 [Formatted Input Functions], page 123.

`int fseek (FILE *stream, long int offset, int whence)`
> 'stdio.h' (ANSI): Section 7.15 [File Positioning], page 126.

`int F_SETFD`
> 'fcntl.h' (POSIX.1): Section 8.9 [File Descriptor Flags], page 156.

`int F_SETFL`
> 'fcntl.h' (POSIX.1): Section 8.10.4 [Getting and Setting File Status Flags], page 162.

`int F_SETLK`
> 'fcntl.h' (POSIX.1): Section 8.11 [File Locks], page 164.

`int F_SETLKW`
> 'fcntl.h' (POSIX.1): Section 8.11 [File Locks], page 164.

`int F_SETOWN`
> 'fcntl.h' (BSD): Section 8.12 [Interrupt-Driven Input], page 167.

`int fsetpos (FILE *stream, const fpos_t position)`
> 'stdio.h' (ANSI): Section 7.16 [Portable File-Position Functions], page 128.

`int fstat (int filedes, struct stat *buf)`
> 'sys/stat.h' (POSIX.1): Section 9.8.2 [Reading the Attributes of a File], page 184.

`long int ftell (FILE *stream)`
> 'stdio.h' (ANSI): Section 7.15 [File Positioning], page 126.

`F_UNLCK`
> 'fcntl.h' (POSIX.1): Section 8.11 [File Locks], page 164.

`size_t fwrite (const void *data, size_t size, size_t count, FILE *stream)`
> 'stdio.h' (ANSI): Section 7.9 [Block Input/Output], page 93.

`F_WRLCK`
> 'fcntl.h' (POSIX.1): Section 8.11 [File Locks], page 164.

`int getchar (void)`
> 'stdio.h' (ANSI): Section 7.6 [Character Input], page 88.

`int getc (FILE *stream)`
> 'stdio.h' (ANSI): Section 7.6 [Character Input], page 88.

char * getcwd (char *buffer, size_t size)
: 'unistd.h' (POSIX.1): Section 9.1 [Working Directory], page 169.

ssize_t getdelim (char **lineptr, size_t *n, int delimiter, FILE *stream)
: 'stdio.h' (GNU): Section 7.7 [Line-Oriented Input], page 90.

gid_t getegid (void)
: 'unistd.h' (POSIX.1): Section 25.5 [Reading the Persona of a Process], page 481.

char * getenv (const char *name)
: 'stdlib.h' (ANSI): Section 22.2.1 [Environment Access], page 434.

uid_t geteuid (void)
: 'unistd.h' (POSIX.1): Section 25.5 [Reading the Persona of a Process], page 481.

gid_t getgid (void)
: 'unistd.h' (POSIX.1): Section 25.5 [Reading the Persona of a Process], page 481.

struct group * getgrent (void)
: 'grp.h' (SVID, BSD): Section 25.13.3 [Scanning the List of All Groups], page 492.

struct group * getgrgid (gid_t gid)
: 'grp.h' (POSIX.1): Section 25.13.2 [Looking Up One Group], page 492.

struct group * getgrnam (const char *name)
: 'grp.h' (SVID, BSD): Section 25.13.2 [Looking Up One Group], page 492.

int getgroups (int count, gid_t *groups)
: 'unistd.h' (POSIX.1): Section 25.5 [Reading the Persona of a Process], page 481.

struct hostent * gethostbyaddr (const char *addr, int length, int format)
: 'netdb.h' (BSD): Section 11.5.2.4 [Host Names], page 219.

struct hostent * gethostbyname (const char *name)
: 'netdb.h' (BSD): Section 11.5.2.4 [Host Names], page 219.

struct hostent * gethostent ()
: 'netdb.h' (BSD): Section 11.5.2.4 [Host Names], page 219.

long int gethostid (void)
: 'unistd.h' (BSD): Section 26.1 [Host Identification], page 495.

Appendix B: Summary of Library Facilities

```
int gethostname (char *name, size_t size)
```
'unistd.h' (BSD): Section 26.1 [Host Identification], page 495.

```
int getitimer (int which, struct itimerval *old)
```
'sys/time.h' (BSD): Section 17.3 [Setting an Alarm], page 335.

```
ssize_t getline (char **lineptr, size_t *n, FILE *stream)
```
'stdio.h' (GNU): Section 7.7 [Line-Oriented Input], page 90.

```
char * getlogin (void)
```
'unistd.h' (POSIX.1): Section 25.11 [Identifying Who Logged In], page 488.

```
struct netent * getnetbyaddr (long net, int type)
```
'netdb.h' (BSD): Section 11.12 [Networks Database], page 252.

```
struct netent * getnetbyname (const char *name)
```
'netdb.h' (BSD): Section 11.12 [Networks Database], page 252.

```
struct netent * getnetent (void)
```
'netdb.h' (BSD): Section 11.12 [Networks Database], page 252.

```
int getopt (int argc, char **argv, const char *options)
```
'unistd.h' (POSIX.2): Section 22.1.2 [Parsing Program Options], page 427.

```
int getopt_long (int argc, char **argv, const char *shortopts,
struct option *longopts, int *indexptr)
```
'getopt.h' (GNU): Section 22.1.4 [Parsing Long Options], page 430.

```
int getpeername (int socket, struct sockaddr *addr, size_t
*length-ptr)
```
'sys/socket.h' (BSD): Section 11.8.4 [Who is Connected to Me?], page 234.

```
pid_t getpgrp (pid_t pid)
```
'unistd.h' (BSD): Section 24.7.2 [Process Group Functions], page 475.

```
pid_t getpgrp (void)
```
'unistd.h' (POSIX.1): Section 24.7.2 [Process Group Functions], page 475.

```
pid_t getpid (void)
```
'unistd.h' (POSIX.1): Section 23.3 [Process Identification], page 444.

```
pid_t getppid (void)
```
'unistd.h' (POSIX.1): Section 23.3 [Process Identification], page 444.

`int getpriority (int `*`class`*`, int `*`id`*`)`
: 'sys/resource.h' (BSD): Section 17.7 [Process Priority], page 343.

`struct protoent * getprotobyname (const char *`*`name`*`)`
: 'netdb.h' (BSD): Section 11.5.6 [Protocols Database], page 225.

`struct protoent * getprotobynumber (int `*`protocol`*`)`
: 'netdb.h' (BSD): Section 11.5.6 [Protocols Database], page 225.

`struct protoent * getprotoent (void)`
: 'netdb.h' (BSD): Section 11.5.6 [Protocols Database], page 225.

`struct passwd * getpwent (void)`
: 'pwd.h' (POSIX.1): Section 25.12.3 [Scanning the List of All Users], page 490.

`struct passwd * getpwnam (const char *`*`name`*`)`
: 'pwd.h' (POSIX.1): Section 25.12.2 [Looking Up One User], page 490.

`struct passwd * getpwuid (uid_t `*`uid`*`)`
: 'pwd.h' (POSIX.1): Section 25.12.2 [Looking Up One User], page 490.

`int getrlimit (int `*`resource`*`, struct rlimit *`*`rlp`*`)`
: 'sys/resource.h' (BSD): Section 17.6 [Limiting Resource Usage], page 341.

`int getrusage (int `*`processes`*`, struct rusage *`*`rusage`*`)`
: 'sys/resource.h' (BSD): Section 17.5 [Resource Usage], page 339.

`struct servent * getservbyname (const char *`*`name`*`, const char *`*`proto`*`)`
: 'netdb.h' (BSD): Section 11.5.4 [The Services Database], page 222.

`struct servent * getservbyport (int `*`port`*`, const char *`*`proto`*`)`
: 'netdb.h' (BSD): Section 11.5.4 [The Services Database], page 222.

`struct servent * getservent (void)`
: 'netdb.h' (BSD): Section 11.5.4 [The Services Database], page 222.

`char * gets (char *`*`s`*`)`
: 'stdio.h' (ANSI): Section 7.7 [Line-Oriented Input], page 90.

`int getsockname (int `*`socket`*`, struct sockaddr *`*`addr`*`, size_t *`*`length-ptr`*`)`
: 'sys/socket.h' (BSD): Section 11.3.3 [Reading the Address of a Socket], page 212.

Appendix B: Summary of Library Facilities

`int getsockopt (int` *socket*`, int` *level*`, int` *optname*`, void *`*optval*`, size_t *`*optlen-ptr*`)`
: 'sys/socket.h' (BSD): Section 11.11.1 [Socket Option Functions], page 250.

`int gettimeofday (struct timeval *`*tp*`, struct timezone *`*tzp*`)`
: 'sys/time.h' (BSD): Section 17.2.2 [High-Resolution Calendar], page 324.

`uid_t getuid (void)`
: 'unistd.h' (POSIX.1): Section 25.5 [Reading the Persona of a Process], page 481.

`mode_t getumask (void)`
: 'sys/stat.h' (GNU): Section 9.8.7 [Assigning File Permissions], page 190.

`char * getwd (char *`*buffer*`)`
: 'unistd.h' (BSD): Section 9.1 [Working Directory], page 169.

`int getw (FILE *`*stream*`)`
: 'stdio.h' (SVID): Section 7.6 [Character Input], page 88.

`gid_t`
: 'sys/types.h' (POSIX.1): Section 25.5 [Reading the Persona of a Process], page 481.

GLOB_ABORTED
: 'glob.h' (POSIX.2): Section 16.2.1 [Calling "code glob], page 306.

GLOB_APPEND
: 'glob.h' (POSIX.2): Section 16.2.2 [Flags for Globbing], page 308.

GLOB_DOOFFS
: 'glob.h' (POSIX.2): Section 16.2.2 [Flags for Globbing], page 308.

GLOB_ERR
: 'glob.h' (POSIX.2): Section 16.2.2 [Flags for Globbing], page 308.

`int glob (const char *`*pattern*`, int` *flags*`, int (*`*errfunc*`) (const char *`*filename*`, int` *error-code*`), glob_t *`*vector-ptr*`)`
: 'glob.h' (POSIX.2): Section 16.2.1 [Calling "code glob], page 306.

GLOB_MARK
: 'glob.h' (POSIX.2): Section 16.2.2 [Flags for Globbing], page 308.

GLOB_NOCHECK
: 'glob.h' (POSIX.2): Section 16.2.2 [Flags for Globbing], page 308.

GLOB_NOESCAPE
: 'glob.h' (POSIX.2): Section 16.2.2 [Flags for Globbing], page 308.

GLOB_NOMATCH
: 'glob.h' (POSIX.2): Section 16.2.1 [Calling "code glob], page 306.

GLOB_NOSORT
: 'glob.h' (POSIX.2): Section 16.2.2 [Flags for Globbing], page 308.

GLOB_NOSPACE
: 'glob.h' (POSIX.2): Section 16.2.1 [Calling "code glob], page 306.

glob_t
: 'glob.h' (POSIX.2): Section 16.2.1 [Calling "code glob], page 306.

struct tm * gmtime (const time_t *time)
: 'time.h' (ANSI): Section 17.2.3 [Broken-down Time], page 327.

_GNU_SOURCE
: (GNU): Section 1.3.4 [Feature Test Macros], page 8.

int gsignal (int signum)
: 'signal.h' (SVID): Section 21.6.1 [Signaling Yourself], page 403.

HOST_NOT_FOUND
: 'netdb.h' (BSD): Section 11.5.2.4 [Host Names], page 219.

unsigned long int htonl (unsigned long int hostlong)
: 'netinet/in.h' (BSD): Section 11.5.5 [Byte Order Conversion], page 224.

unsigned short int htons (unsigned short int hostshort)
: 'netinet/in.h' (BSD): Section 11.5.5 [Byte Order Conversion], page 224.

double HUGE_VAL
: 'math.h' (ANSI): Section 13.1 [Domain and Range Errors], page 281.

tcflag_t HUPCL
: 'termios.h' (POSIX.1): Section 12.4.6 [Control Modes], page 264.

Appendix B: Summary of Library Facilities

`double hypot (double x, double y)`
: 'math.h' (BSD): Section 13.4 [Exponentiation and Logarithms], page 283.

`tcflag_t ICANON`
: 'termios.h' (POSIX.1): Section 12.4.7 [Local Modes], page 266.

`tcflag_t ICRNL`
: 'termios.h' (POSIX.1): Section 12.4.4 [Input Modes], page 261.

`tcflag_t IEXTEN`
: 'termios.h' (POSIX.1): Section 12.4.7 [Local Modes], page 266.

`tcflag_t IGNBRK`
: 'termios.h' (POSIX.1): Section 12.4.4 [Input Modes], page 261.

`tcflag_t IGNCR`
: 'termios.h' (POSIX.1): Section 12.4.4 [Input Modes], page 261.

`tcflag_t IGNPAR`
: 'termios.h' (POSIX.1): Section 12.4.4 [Input Modes], page 261.

`tcflag_t IMAXBEL`
: 'termios.h' (BSD): Section 12.4.4 [Input Modes], page 261.

`unsigned long int INADDR_ANY`
: 'netinet/in.h' (BSD): Section 11.5.2.2 [Host Address Data Type], page 217.

`unsigned long int INADDR_BROADCAST`
: 'netinet/in.h' (BSD): Section 11.5.2.2 [Host Address Data Type], page 217.

`unsigned long int INADDR_LOOPBACK`
: 'netinet/in.h' (BSD): Section 11.5.2.2 [Host Address Data Type], page 217.

`unsigned long int INADDR_NONE`
: 'netinet/in.h' (BSD): Section 11.5.2.2 [Host Address Data Type], page 217.

`char * index (const char *string, int c)`
: 'string.h' (BSD): Section 5.7 [Search Functions], page 70.

`unsigned long int inet_addr (const char *name)`
: 'arpa/inet.h' (BSD): Section 11.5.2.3 [Host Address Functions], page 218.

`int inet_aton (const char *name, struct in_addr *addr)`
: 'arpa/inet.h' (BSD): Section 11.5.2.3 [Host Address Functions], page 218.

int inet_lnaof (struct in_addr *addr*)
: 'arpa/inet.h' (BSD): Section 11.5.2.3 [Host Address Functions], page 218.

struct in_addr inet_makeaddr (int *net*, int *local*)
: 'arpa/inet.h' (BSD): Section 11.5.2.3 [Host Address Functions], page 218.

int inet_netof (struct in_addr *addr*)
: 'arpa/inet.h' (BSD): Section 11.5.2.3 [Host Address Functions], page 218.

unsigned long int inet_network (const char *name*)
: 'arpa/inet.h' (BSD): Section 11.5.2.3 [Host Address Functions], page 218.

char * inet_ntoa (struct in_addr *addr*)
: 'arpa/inet.h' (BSD): Section 11.5.2.3 [Host Address Functions], page 218.

double infnan (int *error*)
: 'math.h' (BSD): Section 14.2 [Predicates on Floats], page 289.

int initgroups (const char *user*, gid_t *gid*)
: 'grp.h' (BSD): Section 25.7 [Setting the Group IDs], page 483.

void * initstate (unsigned int *seed*, void *state*, size_t *size*)
: 'stdlib.h' (BSD): Section 13.6.2 [BSD Random Number Functions], page 287.

tcflag_t INLCR
: 'termios.h' (POSIX.1): Section 12.4.4 [Input Modes], page 261.

ino_t
: 'sys/types.h' (POSIX.1): Section 9.8.1 [What the File Attribute Values Mean], page 181.

tcflag_t INPCK
: 'termios.h' (POSIX.1): Section 12.4.4 [Input Modes], page 261.

int RLIM_INFINITY
: 'sys/resource.h' (BSD): Section 17.6 [Limiting Resource Usage], page 341.

INT_MAX
: 'limits.h' (ANSI): Section A.5.2 [Range of an Integer Type], page 525.

INT_MIN
: 'limits.h' (ANSI): Section A.5.2 [Range of an Integer Type], page 525.

Appendix B: Summary of Library Facilities

`int _IOFBF`
> 'stdio.h' (ANSI): Section 7.17.3 [Controlling Which Kind of Buffering], page 131.

`int _IOLBF`
> 'stdio.h' (ANSI): Section 7.17.3 [Controlling Which Kind of Buffering], page 131.

`int _IONBF`
> 'stdio.h' (ANSI): Section 7.17.3 [Controlling Which Kind of Buffering], page 131.

`int IPPORT_RESERVED`
> 'netinet/in.h' (BSD): Section 11.5.3 [Internet Ports], page 221.

`int IPPORT_USERRESERVED`
> 'netinet/in.h' (BSD): Section 11.5.3 [Internet Ports], page 221.

`int isalnum (int c)`
> 'ctype.h' (ANSI): Section 4.1 [Classification of Characters], page 55.

`int isalpha (int c)`
> 'ctype.h' (ANSI): Section 4.1 [Classification of Characters], page 55.

`int isascii (int c)`
> 'ctype.h' (SVID, BSD): Section 4.1 [Classification of Characters], page 55.

`int isatty (int filedes)`
> 'unistd.h' (POSIX.1): Section 12.1 [Identifying Terminals], page 255.

`int isblank (int c)`
> 'ctype.h' (GNU): Section 4.1 [Classification of Characters], page 55.

`int iscntrl (int c)`
> 'ctype.h' (ANSI): Section 4.1 [Classification of Characters], page 55.

`int isdigit (int c)`
> 'ctype.h' (ANSI): Section 4.1 [Classification of Characters], page 55.

`int isgraph (int c)`
> 'ctype.h' (ANSI): Section 4.1 [Classification of Characters], page 55.

`tcflag_t ISIG`
> 'termios.h' (POSIX.1): Section 12.4.7 [Local Modes], page 266.

int isinf (double *x*)
: 'math.h' (BSD): Section 14.2 [Predicates on Floats], page 289.

int islower (int *c*)
: 'ctype.h' (ANSI): Section 4.1 [Classification of Characters], page 55.

int isnan (double *x*)
: 'math.h' (BSD): Section 14.2 [Predicates on Floats], page 289.

int isprint (int *c*)
: 'ctype.h' (ANSI): Section 4.1 [Classification of Characters], page 55.

int ispunct (int *c*)
: 'ctype.h' (ANSI): Section 4.1 [Classification of Characters], page 55.

int isspace (int *c*)
: 'ctype.h' (ANSI): Section 4.1 [Classification of Characters], page 55.

tcflag_t ISTRIP
: 'termios.h' (POSIX.1): Section 12.4.4 [Input Modes], page 261.

int isupper (int *c*)
: 'ctype.h' (ANSI): Section 4.1 [Classification of Characters], page 55.

int isxdigit (int *c*)
: 'ctype.h' (ANSI): Section 4.1 [Classification of Characters], page 55.

char * tzname [2]
: 'time.h' (POSIX.1): Section 17.2.6 [Functions and Variables for Time Zones], page 334.

'fcntl.h' (POSIX.1): Section 8.10.3 [I/O Operating Modes], page 161.

ITIMER_PROF
: 'sys/time.h' (BSD): Section 17.3 [Setting an Alarm], page 335.

ITIMER_REAL
: 'sys/time.h' (BSD): Section 17.3 [Setting an Alarm], page 335.

ITIMER_VIRTUAL
: 'sys/time.h' (BSD): Section 17.3 [Setting an Alarm], page 335.

tcflag_t IXANY
: 'termios.h' (BSD): Section 12.4.4 [Input Modes], page 261.

Appendix B: Summary of Library Facilities

`tcflag_t IXOFF`
: 'termios.h' (POSIX.1): Section 12.4.4 [Input Modes], page 261.

`tcflag_t IXON`
: 'termios.h' (POSIX.1): Section 12.4.4 [Input Modes], page 261.

`jmp_buf`
: 'setjmp.h' (ANSI): Section 20.2 [Details of Non-Local Exits], page 368.

`int kill (pid_t pid, int signum)`
: 'signal.h' (POSIX.1): Section 21.6.2 [Signaling Another Process], page 405.

`int killpg (int pgid, int signum)`
: 'signal.h' (BSD): Section 21.6.2 [Signaling Another Process], page 405.

`long int labs (long int number)`
: 'stdlib.h' (ANSI): Section 14.3 [Absolute Value], page 290.

`LANG`
: 'locale.h' (ANSI): Section 19.3 [Categories of Activities that Locales Affect], page 358.

`LC_ALL`
: 'locale.h' (ANSI): Section 19.3 [Categories of Activities that Locales Affect], page 358.

`LC_COLLATE`
: 'locale.h' (ANSI): Section 19.3 [Categories of Activities that Locales Affect], page 358.

`LC_CTYPE`
: 'locale.h' (ANSI): Section 19.3 [Categories of Activities that Locales Affect], page 358.

`LC_MONETARY`
: 'locale.h' (ANSI): Section 19.3 [Categories of Activities that Locales Affect], page 358.

`LC_NUMERIC`
: 'locale.h' (ANSI): Section 19.3 [Categories of Activities that Locales Affect], page 358.

`LC_RESPONSE`
: 'locale.h' (GNU): Section 19.3 [Categories of Activities that Locales Affect], page 358.

`int L_ctermid`
: 'stdio.h' (POSIX.1): Section 24.7.1 [Identifying the Controlling Terminal], page 474.

LC_TIME
 '`locale.h`' (ANSI): Section 19.3 [Categories of Activities that Locales Affect], page 358.

int L_cuserid
 '`stdio.h`' (POSIX.1): Section 25.11 [Identifying Who Logged In], page 488.

double ldexp (double *value*, int *exponent*)
 '`math.h`' (ANSI): Section 14.4 [Normalization Functions], page 291.

ldiv_t ldiv (long int *numerator*, long int *denominator*)
 '`stdlib.h`' (ANSI): Section 14.6 [Integer Division], page 293.

ldiv_t
 '`stdlib.h`' (ANSI): Section 14.6 [Integer Division], page 293.

L_INCR
 '`sys/file.h`' (BSD): Section 7.15 [File Positioning], page 126.

int LINE_MAX
 '`limits.h`' (POSIX.2): Section 27.10 [Utility Program Capacity Limits], page 511.

int link (const char *oldname, const char *newname)
 '`unistd.h`' (POSIX.1): Section 9.3 [Hard Links], page 175.

int LINK_MAX
 '`limits.h`' (POSIX.1): Section 27.6 [Limits on File System Capacity], page 507.

int listen (int *socket*, unsigned int *n*)
 '`sys/socket.h`' (BSD): Section 11.8.2 [Listening for Connections], page 232.

struct lconv * localeconv (void)
 '`locale.h`' (ANSI): Section 19.6 [Numeric Formatting], page 361.

struct tm * localtime (const time_t *time)
 '`time.h`' (ANSI): Section 17.2.3 [Broken-down Time], page 327.

double log10 (double *x*)
 '`math.h`' (ANSI): Section 13.4 [Exponentiation and Logarithms], page 283.

double log1p (double *x*)
 '`math.h`' (BSD): Section 13.4 [Exponentiation and Logarithms], page 283.

Appendix B: Summary of Library Facilities   569

double logb (double *x***)**
    'math.h' (BSD): Section 14.4 [Normalization Functions], page 291.

double log (double *x***)**
    'math.h' (ANSI): Section 13.4 [Exponentiation and Logarithms], page 283.

void longjmp (jmp_buf *state***, int** *value***)**
    'setjmp.h' (ANSI): Section 20.2 [Details of Non-Local Exits], page 368.

LONG_LONG_MAX
    'limits.h' (GNU): Section A.5.2 [Range of an Integer Type], page 525.

LONG_LONG_MIN
    'limits.h' (GNU): Section A.5.2 [Range of an Integer Type], page 525.

LONG_MAX
    'limits.h' (ANSI): Section A.5.2 [Range of an Integer Type], page 525.

LONG_MIN
    'limits.h' (ANSI): Section A.5.2 [Range of an Integer Type], page 525.

off_t lseek (int *filedes***, off_t** *offset***, int** *whence***)**
    'unistd.h' (POSIX.1): Section 8.3 [Setting the File Position of a Descriptor], page 144.

L_SET
    'sys/file.h' (BSD): Section 7.15 [File Positioning], page 126.

int lstat (const char **filename***, struct stat ****buf***)**
    'sys/stat.h' (BSD): Section 9.8.2 [Reading the Attributes of a File], page 184.

int L_tmpnam
    'stdio.h' (ANSI): Section 9.10 [Temporary Files], page 196.

L_XTND
    'sys/file.h' (BSD): Section 7.15 [File Positioning], page 126.

__malloc_hook
    'malloc.h' (GNU): Section 3.3.9 [Storage Allocation Hooks], page 35.

void * malloc (size_t *size***)**
    'malloc.h', 'stdlib.h' (ANSI): Section 3.3.1 [Basic Storage Allocation], page 28.

int MAX_CANON
: 'limits.h' (POSIX.1): Section 27.6 [Limits on File System Capacity], page 507.

int MAX_INPUT
: 'limits.h' (POSIX.1): Section 27.6 [Limits on File System Capacity], page 507.

int MAXNAMLEN
: 'dirent.h' (BSD): Section 27.6 [Limits on File System Capacity], page 507.

int MB_CUR_MAX
: 'stdlib.h' (ANSI): Section 18.3 [Multibyte Characters], page 346.

int mblen (const char *string, size_t size)
: 'stdlib.h' (ANSI): Section 18.6 [Multibyte Character Length], page 351.

int MB_LEN_MAX
: 'limits.h' (ANSI): Section 18.3 [Multibyte Characters], page 346.

size_t mbstowcs (wchar_t *wstring, const char *string, size_t size)
: 'stdlib.h' (ANSI): Section 18.5 [Conversion of Extended Strings], page 350.

int mbtowc (wchar_t *result, const char *string, size_t size)
: 'stdlib.h' (ANSI): Section 18.7 [Conversion of Extended Characters One by One], page 352.

int mcheck (void (*abortfn) (enum mcheck_status status))
: 'malloc.h' (GNU): Section 3.3.8 [Heap Consistency Checking], page 33.

tcflag_t MDMBUF
: 'termios.h' (BSD): Section 12.4.6 [Control Modes], page 264.

void * memalign (size_t boundary, size_t size)
: 'malloc.h', 'stdlib.h' (BSD): Section 3.3.7 [Allocating Aligned Memory Blocks], page 33.

void * memccpy (void *to, const void *from, int c, size_t size)
: 'string.h' (SVID): Section 5.4 [Copying and Concatenation], page 61.

void * memchr (const void *block, int c, size_t size)
: 'string.h' (ANSI): Section 5.7 [Search Functions], page 70.

int memcmp (const void *a1, const void *a2, size_t size)
: 'string.h' (ANSI): Section 5.5 [String/Array Comparison], page 65.

Appendix B: Summary of Library Facilities 571

`void * memcpy (void *to, const void *from, size_t size)`
> 'string.h' (ANSI): Section 5.4 [Copying and Concatenation], page 61.

`void * memmem (const void *needle, size_t needle-len, const void *haystack, size_t haystack-len)`
> 'string.h' (GNU): Section 5.7 [Search Functions], page 70.

`void * memmove (void *to, const void *from, size_t size)`
> 'string.h' (ANSI): Section 5.4 [Copying and Concatenation], page 61.

`void memory_warnings (void *start, void (*warn-func) (const char *))`
> 'malloc.h' (GNU): Section 3.7 [Memory Usage Warnings], page 53.

`void * memset (void *block, int c, size_t size)`
> 'string.h' (ANSI): Section 5.4 [Copying and Concatenation], page 61.

`int mkdir (const char *filename, mode_t mode)`
> 'sys/stat.h' (POSIX.1): Section 9.7 [Creating Directories], page 180.

`int mkfifo (const char *filename, mode_t mode)`
> 'sys/stat.h' (POSIX.1): Section 10.3 [FIFO Special Files], page 204.

`int mknod (const char *filename, int mode, int dev)`
> 'sys/stat.h' (BSD): Section 9.9 [Making Special Files], page 196.

`int mkstemp (char *template)`
> 'unistd.h' (BSD): Section 9.10 [Temporary Files], page 196.

`char * mktemp (char *template)`
> 'unistd.h' (Unix): Section 9.10 [Temporary Files], page 196.

`time_t mktime (struct tm *brokentime)`
> 'time.h' (ANSI): Section 17.2.3 [Broken-down Time], page 327.

`mode_t`
> 'sys/types.h' (POSIX.1): Section 9.8.1 [What the File Attribute Values Mean], page 181.

`double modf (double value, double *integer-part)`
> 'math.h' (ANSI): Section 14.5 [Rounding and Remainder Functions], page 292.

int MSG_DONTROUTE
: 'sys/socket.h' (BSD): Section 11.8.5.3 [Socket Data Options], page 237.

int MSG_OOB
: 'sys/socket.h' (BSD): Section 11.8.5.3 [Socket Data Options], page 237.

int MSG_PEEK
: 'sys/socket.h' (BSD): Section 11.8.5.3 [Socket Data Options], page 237.

struct mstats mstats (void)
: 'malloc.h' (GNU): Section 3.3.10 [Statistics for Storage Allocation with "code malloc], page 36.

int NAME_MAX
: 'limits.h' (POSIX.1): Section 27.6 [Limits on File System Capacity], page 507.

double NAN
: 'math.h' (GNU): Section 14.1 ["Not a Number Values], page 289.

int NCCS
: 'termios.h' (POSIX.1): Section 12.4.1 [Terminal Mode Data Types], page 257.

int NGROUPS_MAX
: 'limits.h' (POSIX.1): Section 27.1 [General Capacity Limits], page 499.

int nice (int *increment*)
: 'dunno.h' (dunno.h): Section 17.7 [Process Priority], page 343.

nlink_t
: 'sys/types.h' (POSIX.1): Section 9.8.1 [What the File Attribute Values Mean], page 181.

NO_ADDRESS
: 'netdb.h' (BSD): Section 11.5.2.4 [Host Names], page 219.

tcflag_t NOFLSH
: 'termios.h' (POSIX.1): Section 12.4.7 [Local Modes], page 266.

tcflag_t NOKERNINFO
: 'termios.h' (BSD): Section 12.4.7 [Local Modes], page 266.

NO_RECOVERY
: 'netdb.h' (BSD): Section 11.5.2.4 [Host Names], page 219.

int NSIG
: 'signal.h' (BSD): Section 21.2 [Standard Signals], page 373.

Appendix B: Summary of Library Facilities   573

unsigned long int ntohl (unsigned long int *netlong*)
: 'netinet/in.h' (BSD): Section 11.5.5 [Byte Order Conversion], page 224.

unsigned short int ntohs (unsigned short int *netshort*)
: 'netinet/in.h' (BSD): Section 11.5.5 [Byte Order Conversion], page 224.

void * NULL
: 'stddef.h' (ANSI): Section A.3 [Null Pointer Constant], page 523.

int O_ACCMODE
: 'fcntl.h' (POSIX.1): Section 8.10.1 [File Access Modes], page 158.

int O_APPEND
: 'fcntl.h' (POSIX.1): Section 8.10.3 [I/O Operating Modes], page 161.

int O_ASYNC
: 'fcntl.h' (BSD): Section 8.10.3 [I/O Operating Modes], page 161.

void obstack_1grow_fast (struct obstack *obstack-ptr*, char *c*)
: 'obstack.h' (GNU): Section 3.4.7 [Extra Fast Growing Objects], page 44.

void obstack_1grow (struct obstack *obstack-ptr*, char *c*)
: 'obstack.h' (GNU): Section 3.4.6 [Growing Objects], page 42.

int obstack_alignment_mask (struct obstack *obstack-ptr*)
: 'obstack.h' (GNU): Section 3.4.9 [Alignment of Data in Obstacks], page 46.

void * obstack_alloc (struct obstack *obstack-ptr*, int *size*)
: 'obstack.h' (GNU): Section 3.4.3 [Allocation in an Obstack], page 40.

void * obstack_base (struct obstack *obstack-ptr*)
: 'obstack.h' (GNU): Section 3.4.8 [Status of an Obstack], page 45.

void obstack_blank_fast (struct obstack *obstack-ptr*, int *size*)
: 'obstack.h' (GNU): Section 3.4.7 [Extra Fast Growing Objects], page 44.

void obstack_blank (struct obstack *obstack-ptr*, int *size*)
: 'obstack.h' (GNU): Section 3.4.6 [Growing Objects], page 42.

int obstack_chunk_size (struct obstack *obstack-ptr*)
: 'obstack.h' (GNU): Section 3.4.10 [Obstack Chunks], page 47.

void * obstack_copy0 (struct obstack *obstack-ptr, void *address, int size)
: 'obstack.h' (GNU): Section 3.4.3 [Allocation in an Obstack], page 40.

void * obstack_copy (struct obstack *obstack-ptr, void *address, int size)
: 'obstack.h' (GNU): Section 3.4.3 [Allocation in an Obstack], page 40.

void * obstack_finish (struct obstack *obstack-ptr)
: 'obstack.h' (GNU): Section 3.4.6 [Growing Objects], page 42.

void obstack_free (struct obstack *obstack-ptr, void *object)
: 'obstack.h' (GNU): Section 3.4.4 [Freeing Objects in an Obstack], page 41.

void obstack_grow0 (struct obstack *obstack-ptr, void *data, int size)
: 'obstack.h' (GNU): Section 3.4.6 [Growing Objects], page 42.

void obstack_grow (struct obstack *obstack-ptr, void *data, int size)
: 'obstack.h' (GNU): Section 3.4.6 [Growing Objects], page 42.

int obstack_init (struct obstack *obstack-ptr)
: 'obstack.h' (GNU): Section 3.4.2 [Preparing for Using Obstacks], page 39.

void * obstack_next_free (struct obstack *obstack-ptr)
: 'obstack.h' (GNU): Section 3.4.8 [Status of an Obstack], page 45.

int obstack_object_size (struct obstack *obstack-ptr)
: 'obstack.h' (GNU): Section 3.4.6 [Growing Objects], page 42.

int obstack_object_size (struct obstack *obstack-ptr)
: 'obstack.h' (GNU): Section 3.4.8 [Status of an Obstack], page 45.

int obstack_printf (struct obstack *obstack, const char *template, ...)
: 'stdio.h' (GNU): Section 7.10.8 [Dynamically Allocating Formatted Output], page 104.

int obstack_room (struct obstack *obstack-ptr)
: 'obstack.h' (GNU): Section 3.4.7 [Extra Fast Growing Objects], page 44.

Appendix B: Summary of Library Facilities   575

`int obstack_vprintf (struct obstack *obstack, const char *template, va_list ap)`
: 'stdio.h' (GNU): Section 7.10.9 [Variable Arguments Output Functions], page 105.

`int O_CREAT`
: 'fcntl.h' (POSIX.1): Section 8.10.2 [Open-time Flags], page 159.

`int O_EXCL`
: 'fcntl.h' (POSIX.1): Section 8.10.2 [Open-time Flags], page 159.

`int O_EXEC`
: 'fcntl.h' (GNU): Section 8.10.1 [File Access Modes], page 158.

`int O_EXLOCK`
: 'fcntl.h' (BSD): Section 8.10.2 [Open-time Flags], page 159.

`size_t offsetof (type, member)`
: 'stddef.h' (ANSI): Section A.5.4 [Structure Field Offset Measurement], page 532.

`off_t`
: 'sys/types.h' (POSIX.1): Section 8.3 [Setting the File Position of a Descriptor], page 144.

`int O_FSYNC`
: 'fcntl.h' (BSD): Section 8.10.3 [I/O Operating Modes], page 161.

`int O_IGNORE_CTTY`
: 'fcntl.h' (GNU): Section 8.10.2 [Open-time Flags], page 159.

`int O_NDELAY`
: 'fcntl.h' (BSD): Section 8.10.3 [I/O Operating Modes], page 161.

`int on_exit (void (*function)(int status, void *arg), void *arg)`
: 'stdlib.h' (SunOS): Section 22.3.3 [Cleanups on Exit], page 439.

`tcflag_t ONLCR`
: 'termios.h' (BSD): Section 12.4.5 [Output Modes], page 263.

`int O_NOATIME`
: 'fcntl.h' (GNU): Section 8.10.3 [I/O Operating Modes], page 161.

`int O_NOCTTY`
: 'fcntl.h' (POSIX.1): Section 8.10.2 [Open-time Flags], page 159.

`tcflag_t ONOEOT`
: 'termios.h' (BSD): Section 12.4.5 [Output Modes], page 263.

`int O_NOLINK`
: 'fcntl.h' (GNU): Section 8.10.2 [Open-time Flags], page 159.

`int O_NONBLOCK`
: 'fcntl.h' (POSIX.1): Section 8.10.2 [Open-time Flags], page 159.

`int O_NOTRANS`
: 'fcntl.h' (GNU): Section 8.10.2 [Open-time Flags], page 159.

`DIR * opendir (const char *dirname)`
: 'dirent.h' (POSIX.1): Section 9.2.2 [Opening a Directory Stream], page 172.

`int open (const char *filename, int flags[, mode_t mode])`
: 'fcntl.h' (POSIX.1): Section 8.1 [Opening and Closing Files], page 139.

`int OPEN_MAX`
: 'limits.h' (POSIX.1): Section 27.1 [General Capacity Limits], page 499.

`FILE * open_memstream (char **ptr, size_t *sizeloc)`
: 'stdio.h' (GNU): Section 7.18.1 [String Streams], page 133.

`FILE * open_obstack_stream (struct obstack *obstack)`
: 'stdio.h' (GNU): Section 7.18.2 [Obstack Streams], page 135.

`tcflag_t OPOST`
: 'termios.h' (POSIX.1): Section 12.4.5 [Output Modes], page 263.

`char * optarg`
: 'unistd.h' (POSIX.2): Section 22.1.2 [Parsing Program Options], page 427.

`int opterr`
: 'unistd.h' (POSIX.2): Section 22.1.2 [Parsing Program Options], page 427.

`int optind`
: 'unistd.h' (POSIX.2): Section 22.1.2 [Parsing Program Options], page 427.

`int optopt`
: 'unistd.h' (POSIX.2): Section 22.1.2 [Parsing Program Options], page 427.

Appendix B: Summary of Library Facilities

`int O_RDONLY`
: 'fcntl.h' (POSIX.1): Section 8.10.1 [File Access Modes], page 158.

`int O_RDWR`
: 'fcntl.h' (POSIX.1): Section 8.10.1 [File Access Modes], page 158.

`int O_READ`
: 'fcntl.h' (GNU): Section 8.10.1 [File Access Modes], page 158.

`int O_SHLOCK`
: 'fcntl.h' (BSD): Section 8.10.2 [Open-time Flags], page 159.

`int O_SYNC`
: 'fcntl.h' (BSD): Section 8.10.3 [I/O Operating Modes], page 161.

`int O_TRUNC`
: 'fcntl.h' (POSIX.1): Section 8.10.2 [Open-time Flags], page 159.

`int O_WRITE`
: 'fcntl.h' (GNU): Section 8.10.1 [File Access Modes], page 158.

`int O_WRONLY`
: 'fcntl.h' (POSIX.1): Section 8.10.1 [File Access Modes], page 158.

`tcflag_t OXTABS`
: 'termios.h' (BSD): Section 12.4.5 [Output Modes], page 263.

`PA_CHAR`
: 'printf.h' (GNU): Section 7.10.10 [Parsing a Template String], page 107.

`PA_DOUBLE`
: 'printf.h' (GNU): Section 7.10.10 [Parsing a Template String], page 107.

`PA_FLAG_LONG_DOUBLE`
: 'printf.h' (GNU): Section 7.10.10 [Parsing a Template String], page 107.

`PA_FLAG_LONG`
: 'printf.h' (GNU): Section 7.10.10 [Parsing a Template String], page 107.

`PA_FLAG_LONG_LONG`
: 'printf.h' (GNU): Section 7.10.10 [Parsing a Template String], page 107.

int PA_FLAG_MASK

'printf.h' (GNU): Section 7.10.10 [Parsing a Template String], page 107.

PA_FLAG_PTR

'printf.h' (GNU): Section 7.10.10 [Parsing a Template String], page 107.

PA_FLAG_SHORT

'printf.h' (GNU): Section 7.10.10 [Parsing a Template String], page 107.

PA_FLOAT

'printf.h' (GNU): Section 7.10.10 [Parsing a Template String], page 107.

PA_INT

'printf.h' (GNU): Section 7.10.10 [Parsing a Template String], page 107.

PA_LAST

'printf.h' (GNU): Section 7.10.10 [Parsing a Template String], page 107.

PA_POINTER

'printf.h' (GNU): Section 7.10.10 [Parsing a Template String], page 107.

tcflag_t PARENB

'termios.h' (POSIX.1): Section 12.4.6 [Control Modes], page 264.

tcflag_t PARMRK

'termios.h' (POSIX.1): Section 12.4.4 [Input Modes], page 261.

tcflag_t PARODD

'termios.h' (POSIX.1): Section 12.4.6 [Control Modes], page 264.

size_t parse_printf_format (const char *template, size_t n, int *argtypes)

'printf.h' (GNU): Section 7.10.10 [Parsing a Template String], page 107.

PA_STRING

'printf.h' (GNU): Section 7.10.10 [Parsing a Template String], page 107.

long int pathconf (const char *filename, int parameter)

'unistd.h' (POSIX.1): Section 27.9 [Using "code pathconf], page 510.

Appendix B: Summary of Library Facilities

int PATH_MAX
: 'limits.h' (POSIX.1): Section 27.6 [Limits on File System Capacity], page 507.

int pause ()
: 'unistd.h' (POSIX.1): Section 21.8.1 [Using "code pause], page 416.

_PC_CHOWN_RESTRICTED
: 'unistd.h' (POSIX.1): Section 27.9 [Using "code pathconf], page 510.

_PC_LINK_MAX
: 'unistd.h' (POSIX.1): Section 27.9 [Using "code pathconf], page 510.

int pclose (FILE *stream)
: 'stdio.h' (POSIX.2, SVID, BSD): Section 10.2 [Pipe to a Subprocess], page 203.

_PC_MAX_CANON
: 'unistd.h' (POSIX.1): Section 27.9 [Using "code pathconf], page 510.

_PC_MAX_INPUT
: 'unistd.h' (POSIX.1): Section 27.9 [Using "code pathconf], page 510.

_PC_NAME_MAX
: 'unistd.h' (POSIX.1): Section 27.9 [Using "code pathconf], page 510.

_PC_NO_TRUNC
: 'unistd.h' (POSIX.1): Section 27.9 [Using "code pathconf], page 510.

_PC_PATH_MAX
: 'unistd.h' (POSIX.1): Section 27.9 [Using "code pathconf], page 510.

_PC_PIPE_BUF
: 'unistd.h' (POSIX.1): Section 27.9 [Using "code pathconf], page 510.

_PC_VDISABLE
: 'unistd.h' (POSIX.1): Section 27.9 [Using "code pathconf], page 510.

tcflag_t PENDIN
: 'termios.h' (BSD): Section 12.4.7 [Local Modes], page 266.

void perror (const char *message)
    'stdio.h' (ANSI): Section 2.3 [Error Messages], page 23.

int PF_FILE
    'sys/socket.h' (GNU): Section 11.4.2 [Details of File Namespace], page 213.

int PF_INET
    'sys/socket.h' (BSD): Section 11.5 [The Internet Namespace], page 215.

int PF_UNIX
    'sys/socket.h' (BSD): Section 11.4.2 [Details of File Namespace], page 213.

pid_t
    'sys/types.h' (POSIX.1): Section 23.3 [Process Identification], page 444.

int PIPE_BUF
    'limits.h' (POSIX.1): Section 27.6 [Limits on File System Capacity], page 507.

int pipe (int filedes[2])
    'unistd.h' (POSIX.1): Section 10.1 [Creating a Pipe], page 201.

FILE * popen (const char *command, const char *mode)
    'stdio.h' (POSIX.2, SVID, BSD): Section 10.2 [Pipe to a Subprocess], page 203.

_POSIX2_BC_BASE_MAX
    'limits.h' (POSIX.2): Section 27.11 [Minimum Values for Utility Limits], page 512.

_POSIX2_BC_DIM_MAX
    'limits.h' (POSIX.2): Section 27.11 [Minimum Values for Utility Limits], page 512.

_POSIX2_BC_SCALE_MAX
    'limits.h' (POSIX.2): Section 27.11 [Minimum Values for Utility Limits], page 512.

_POSIX2_BC_STRING_MAX
    'limits.h' (POSIX.2): Section 27.11 [Minimum Values for Utility Limits], page 512.

int _POSIX2_C_DEV
    'unistd.h' (POSIX.2): Section 27.2 [Overall System Options], page 500.

Appendix B: Summary of Library Facilities 581

`_POSIX2_COLL_WEIGHTS_MAX`
'`limits.h`' (POSIX.2): Section 27.11 [Minimum Values for Utility Limits], page 512.

`long int _POSIX2_C_VERSION`
'`unistd.h`' (POSIX.2): Section 27.3 [Which Version of POSIX is Supported], page 502.

`_POSIX2_EQUIV_CLASS_MAX`
'`limits.h`' (POSIX.2): Section 27.11 [Minimum Values for Utility Limits], page 512.

`_POSIX2_EXPR_NEST_MAX`
'`limits.h`' (POSIX.2): Section 27.11 [Minimum Values for Utility Limits], page 512.

`int _POSIX2_FORT_DEV`
'`unistd.h`' (POSIX.2): Section 27.2 [Overall System Options], page 500.

`int _POSIX2_FORT_RUN`
'`unistd.h`' (POSIX.2): Section 27.2 [Overall System Options], page 500.

`_POSIX2_LINE_MAX`
'`limits.h`' (POSIX.2): Section 27.11 [Minimum Values for Utility Limits], page 512.

`int _POSIX2_LOCALEDEF`
'`unistd.h`' (POSIX.2): Section 27.2 [Overall System Options], page 500.

`_POSIX2_RE_DUP_MAX`
'`limits.h`' (POSIX.2): Section 27.5 [Minimum Values for General Capacity Limits], page 506.

`int _POSIX2_SW_DEV`
'`unistd.h`' (POSIX.2): Section 27.2 [Overall System Options], page 500.

`_POSIX_ARG_MAX`
'`limits.h`' (POSIX.1): Section 27.5 [Minimum Values for General Capacity Limits], page 506.

`_POSIX_CHILD_MAX`
'`limits.h`' (POSIX.1): Section 27.5 [Minimum Values for General Capacity Limits], page 506.

`int _POSIX_CHOWN_RESTRICTED`
'`unistd.h`' (POSIX.1): Section 27.7 [Optional Features in File Support], page 508.

`_POSIX_C_SOURCE`
: (POSIX.2): Section 1.3.4 [Feature Test Macros], page 8.

`int _POSIX_JOB_CONTROL`
: 'unistd.h' (POSIX.1): Section 27.2 [Overall System Options], page 500.

`_POSIX_LINK_MAX`
: 'limits.h' (POSIX.1): Section 27.8 [Minimum Values for File System Limits], page 509.

`_POSIX_MAX_CANON`
: 'limits.h' (POSIX.1): Section 27.8 [Minimum Values for File System Limits], page 509.

`_POSIX_MAX_INPUT`
: 'limits.h' (POSIX.1): Section 27.8 [Minimum Values for File System Limits], page 509.

`_POSIX_NAME_MAX`
: 'limits.h' (POSIX.1): Section 27.8 [Minimum Values for File System Limits], page 509.

`_POSIX_NGROUPS_MAX`
: 'limits.h' (POSIX.1): Section 27.5 [Minimum Values for General Capacity Limits], page 506.

`int _POSIX_NO_TRUNC`
: 'unistd.h' (POSIX.1): Section 27.7 [Optional Features in File Support], page 508.

`_POSIX_OPEN_MAX`
: 'limits.h' (POSIX.1): Section 27.5 [Minimum Values for General Capacity Limits], page 506.

`_POSIX_PATH_MAX`
: 'limits.h' (POSIX.1): Section 27.8 [Minimum Values for File System Limits], page 509.

`_POSIX_PIPE_BUF`
: 'limits.h' (POSIX.1): Section 27.8 [Minimum Values for File System Limits], page 509.

`int _POSIX_SAVED_IDS`
: 'unistd.h' (POSIX.1): Section 27.2 [Overall System Options], page 500.

`_POSIX_SOURCE`
: (POSIX.1): Section 1.3.4 [Feature Test Macros], page 8.

`_POSIX_SSIZE_MAX`
: 'limits.h' (POSIX.1): Section 27.5 [Minimum Values for General Capacity Limits], page 506.

Appendix B: Summary of Library Facilities

`_POSIX_STREAM_MAX`
: 'limits.h' (POSIX.1): Section 27.5 [Minimum Values for General Capacity Limits], page 506.

`_POSIX_TZNAME_MAX`
: 'limits.h' (POSIX.1): Section 27.5 [Minimum Values for General Capacity Limits], page 506.

`unsigned char _POSIX_VDISABLE`
: 'unistd.h' (POSIX.1): Section 27.7 [Optional Features in File Support], page 508.

`long int _POSIX_VERSION`
: 'unistd.h' (POSIX.1): Section 27.3 [Which Version of POSIX is Supported], page 502.

`double pow (double base, double power)`
: 'math.h' (ANSI): Section 13.4 [Exponentiation and Logarithms], page 283.

`printf_arginfo_function`
: 'printf.h' (GNU): Section 7.11.3 [Defining the Output Handler], page 113.

`printf_function`
: 'printf.h' (GNU): Section 7.11.3 [Defining the Output Handler], page 113.

`int printf (const char *template, ...)`
: 'stdio.h' (ANSI): Section 7.10.7 [Formatted Output Functions], page 103.

`PRIO_MAX`
: 'sys/resource.h' (BSD): Section 17.7 [Process Priority], page 343.

`PRIO_MIN`
: 'sys/resource.h' (BSD): Section 17.7 [Process Priority], page 343.

`PRIO_PGRP`
: 'sys/resource.h' (BSD): Section 17.7 [Process Priority], page 343.

`PRIO_PROCESS`
: 'sys/resource.h' (BSD): Section 17.7 [Process Priority], page 343.

`PRIO_USER`
: 'sys/resource.h' (BSD): Section 17.7 [Process Priority], page 343.

char * program_invocation_name
: 'errno.h' (GNU): Section 2.3 [Error Messages], page 23.

char * program_invocation_short_name
: 'errno.h' (GNU): Section 2.3 [Error Messages], page 23.

void psignal (int *signum*, const char **message*)
: 'signal.h' (BSD): Section 21.2.8 [Signal Messages], page 383.

char * P_tmpdir
: 'stdio.h' (SVID): Section 9.10 [Temporary Files], page 196.

ptrdiff_t
: 'stddef.h' (ANSI): Section A.4 [Important Data Types], page 523.

int putchar (int *c*)
: 'stdio.h' (ANSI): Section 7.5 [Simple Output by Characters or Lines], page 87.

int putc (int *c*, FILE **stream*)
: 'stdio.h' (ANSI): Section 7.5 [Simple Output by Characters or Lines], page 87.

int putenv (const char **string*)
: 'stdlib.h' (SVID): Section 22.2.1 [Environment Access], page 434.

int putpwent (const struct passwd **p*, FILE **stream*)
: 'pwd.h' (SVID): Section 25.12.4 [Writing a User Entry], page 491.

int puts (const char **s*)
: 'stdio.h' (ANSI): Section 7.5 [Simple Output by Characters or Lines], page 87.

int putw (int *w*, FILE **stream*)
: 'stdio.h' (SVID): Section 7.5 [Simple Output by Characters or Lines], page 87.

void qsort (void **array*, size_t *count*, size_t *size*, comparison_fn_t *compare*)
: 'stdlib.h' (ANSI): Section 15.3 [Array Sort Function], page 300.

int raise (int *signum*)
: 'signal.h' (ANSI): Section 21.6.1 [Signaling Yourself], page 403.

void r_alloc_free (void ***handleptr*)
: 'malloc.h' (GNU): Section 3.6.2 [Allocating and Freeing Relocatable Blocks], page 53.

Appendix B: Summary of Library Facilities

`void * r_alloc (void **`*handleptr*`, size_t `*size*`)`
: 'malloc.h' (GNU): Section 3.6.2 [Allocating and Freeing Relocatable Blocks], page 53.

`int rand ()`
: 'stdlib.h' (ANSI): Section 13.6.1 [ANSI C Random Number Functions], page 286.

`int RAND_MAX`
: 'stdlib.h' (ANSI): Section 13.6.1 [ANSI C Random Number Functions], page 286.

`long int random ()`
: 'stdlib.h' (BSD): Section 13.6.2 [BSD Random Number Functions], page 287.

`struct dirent * readdir (DIR *`*dirstream*`)`
: 'dirent.h' (POSIX.1): Section 9.2.3 [Reading and Closing a Directory Stream], page 173.

`ssize_t read (int `*filedes*`, void *`*buffer*`, size_t `*size*`)`
: 'unistd.h' (POSIX.1): Section 8.2 [Input and Output Primitives], page 141.

`int readlink (const char *`*filename*`, char *`*buffer*`, size_t `*size*`)`
: 'unistd.h' (BSD): Section 9.4 [Symbolic Links], page 176.

`__realloc_hook`
: 'malloc.h' (GNU): Section 3.3.9 [Storage Allocation Hooks], page 35.

`void * realloc (void *`*ptr*`, size_t `*newsize*`)`
: 'malloc.h', 'stdlib.h' (ANSI): Section 3.3.4 [Changing the Size of a Block], page 31.

`int recvfrom (int `*socket*`, void *`*buffer*`, size_t `*size*`, int `*flags*`, struct sockaddr *`*addr*`, size_t *`*length-ptr*`)`
: 'sys/socket.h' (BSD): Section 11.9.2 [Receiving Datagrams], page 244.

`int recv (int `*socket*`, void *`*buffer*`, size_t `*size*`, int `*flags*`)`
: 'sys/socket.h' (BSD): Section 11.8.5.2 [Receiving Data], page 236.

`int recvmsg (int `*socket*`, struct msghdr *`*message*`, int `*flags*`)`
: 'sys/socket.h' (BSD): Section 11.9.2 [Receiving Datagrams], page 244.

`int RE_DUP_MAX`
: 'limits.h' (POSIX.2): Section 27.1 [General Capacity Limits], page 499.

`REG_BADBR`
: 'regex.h' (POSIX.2): Section 16.3.1 [POSIX Regular Expression Compilation], page 309.

`REG_BADPAT`
: 'regex.h' (POSIX.2): Section 16.3.1 [POSIX Regular Expression Compilation], page 309.

`REG_BADRPT`
: 'regex.h' (POSIX.2): Section 16.3.1 [POSIX Regular Expression Compilation], page 309.

`int regcomp (regex_t *compiled, const char *pattern, int cflags)`
: 'regex.h' (POSIX.2): Section 16.3.1 [POSIX Regular Expression Compilation], page 309.

`REG_EBRACE`
: 'regex.h' (POSIX.2): Section 16.3.1 [POSIX Regular Expression Compilation], page 309.

`REG_EBRACK`
: 'regex.h' (POSIX.2): Section 16.3.1 [POSIX Regular Expression Compilation], page 309.

`REG_ECOLLATE`
: 'regex.h' (POSIX.2): Section 16.3.1 [POSIX Regular Expression Compilation], page 309.

`REG_ECTYPE`
: 'regex.h' (POSIX.2): Section 16.3.1 [POSIX Regular Expression Compilation], page 309.

`REG_EESCAPE`
: 'regex.h' (POSIX.2): Section 16.3.1 [POSIX Regular Expression Compilation], page 309.

`REG_EPAREN`
: 'regex.h' (POSIX.2): Section 16.3.1 [POSIX Regular Expression Compilation], page 309.

`REG_ERANGE`
: 'regex.h' (POSIX.2): Section 16.3.1 [POSIX Regular Expression Compilation], page 309.

`size_t regerror (int errcode, regex_t *compiled, char *buffer, size_t length)`
: 'regex.h' (POSIX.2): Section 16.3.6 [POSIX Regexp Matching Cleanup], page 314.

`REG_ESPACE`
: 'regex.h' (POSIX.2): Section 16.3.3 [Matching a Compiled POSIX Regular Expression], page 312.

Appendix B: Summary of Library Facilities   587

`REG_ESPACE`
> 'regex.h' (POSIX.2): Section 16.3.1 [POSIX Regular Expression Compilation], page 309.

`REG_ESUBREG`
> 'regex.h' (POSIX.2): Section 16.3.1 [POSIX Regular Expression Compilation], page 309.

`int regexec (regex_t *compiled, char *string, size_t nmatch, regmatch_t matchptr [], int eflags)`
> 'regex.h' (POSIX.2): Section 16.3.3 [Matching a Compiled POSIX Regular Expression], page 312.

`REG_EXTENDED`
> 'regex.h' (POSIX.2): Section 16.3.2 [Flags for POSIX Regular Expressions], page 311.

`regex_t`
> 'regex.h' (POSIX.2): Section 16.3.1 [POSIX Regular Expression Compilation], page 309.

`void regfree (regex_t *compiled)`
> 'regex.h' (POSIX.2): Section 16.3.6 [POSIX Regexp Matching Cleanup], page 314.

`REG_ICASE`
> 'regex.h' (POSIX.2): Section 16.3.2 [Flags for POSIX Regular Expressions], page 311.

`int register_printf_function (int spec, printf_function handler-function, printf_arginfo_function arginfo-function)`
> 'printf.h' (GNU): Section 7.11.1 [Registering New Conversions], page 111.

`regmatch_t`
> 'regex.h' (POSIX.2): Section 16.3.4 [Match Results with Subexpressions], page 313.

`REG_NEWLINE`
> 'regex.h' (POSIX.2): Section 16.3.2 [Flags for POSIX Regular Expressions], page 311.

`REG_NOMATCH`
> 'regex.h' (POSIX.2): Section 16.3.3 [Matching a Compiled POSIX Regular Expression], page 312.

`REG_NOSUB`
> 'regex.h' (POSIX.2): Section 16.3.2 [Flags for POSIX Regular Expressions], page 311.

`REG_NOTBOL`
: 'regex.h' (POSIX.2): Section 16.3.3 [Matching a Compiled POSIX Regular Expression], page 312.

`REG_NOTEOL`
: 'regex.h' (POSIX.2): Section 16.3.3 [Matching a Compiled POSIX Regular Expression], page 312.

`regoff_t`
: 'regex.h' (POSIX.2): Section 16.3.4 [Match Results with Subexpressions], page 313.

`int remove (const char *filename)`
: 'stdio.h' (ANSI): Section 9.5 [Deleting Files], page 178.

`int rename (const char *oldname, const char *newname)`
: 'stdio.h' (ANSI): Section 9.6 [Renaming Files], page 179.

`void rewinddir (DIR *dirstream)`
: 'dirent.h' (POSIX.1): Section 9.2.5 [Random Access in a Directory Stream], page 174.

`void rewind (FILE *stream)`
: 'stdio.h' (ANSI): Section 7.15 [File Positioning], page 126.

`char * rindex (const char *string, int c)`
: 'string.h' (BSD): Section 5.7 [Search Functions], page 70.

`double rint (double x)`
: 'math.h' (BSD): Section 14.5 [Rounding and Remainder Functions], page 292.

`RLIMIT_CORE`
: 'sys/resource.h' (BSD): Section 17.6 [Limiting Resource Usage], page 341.

`RLIMIT_CPU`
: 'sys/resource.h' (BSD): Section 17.6 [Limiting Resource Usage], page 341.

`RLIMIT_DATA`
: 'sys/resource.h' (BSD): Section 17.6 [Limiting Resource Usage], page 341.

`RLIMIT_FSIZE`
: 'sys/resource.h' (BSD): Section 17.6 [Limiting Resource Usage], page 341.

`RLIMIT_MEMLOCK`
: 'sys/resource.h' (BSD): Section 17.6 [Limiting Resource Usage], page 341.

Appendix B: Summary of Library Facilities 589

RLIMIT_NOFILE
: 'sys/resource.h' (BSD): Section 17.6 [Limiting Resource Usage], page 341.

RLIMIT_NPROC
: 'sys/resource.h' (BSD): Section 17.6 [Limiting Resource Usage], page 341.

RLIMIT_RSS
: 'sys/resource.h' (BSD): Section 17.6 [Limiting Resource Usage], page 341.

RLIMIT_STACK
: 'sys/resource.h' (BSD): Section 17.6 [Limiting Resource Usage], page 341.

RLIM_NLIMITS
: 'sys/resource.h' (BSD): Section 17.6 [Limiting Resource Usage], page 341.

int rmdir (const char *filename)
: 'unistd.h' (POSIX.1): Section 9.5 [Deleting Files], page 178.

int R_OK
: 'unistd.h' (POSIX.1): Section 9.8.8 [Testing Permission to Access a File], page 192.

void * r_re_alloc (void **handleptr, size_t size)
: 'malloc.h' (GNU): Section 3.6.2 [Allocating and Freeing Relocatable Blocks], page 53.

RUSAGE_CHILDREN
: 'sys/resource.h' (BSD): Section 17.5 [Resource Usage], page 339.

RUSAGE_SELF
: 'sys/resource.h' (BSD): Section 17.5 [Resource Usage], page 339.

int SA_NOCLDSTOP
: 'signal.h' (POSIX.1): Section 21.3.5 [Flags for "code sigaction], page 389.

int SA_ONSTACK
: 'signal.h' (BSD): Section 21.3.5 [Flags for "code sigaction], page 389.

int SA_RESTART
: 'signal.h' (BSD): Section 21.3.5 [Flags for "code sigaction], page 389.

`_SC_2_C_DEV`
: 'unistd.h' (POSIX.2): Section 27.4.2 [Constants for "code sysconf Parameters], page 503.

`_SC_2_FORT_DEV`
: 'unistd.h' (POSIX.2): Section 27.4.2 [Constants for "code sysconf Parameters], page 503.

`_SC_2_FORT_RUN`
: 'unistd.h' (POSIX.2): Section 27.4.2 [Constants for "code sysconf Parameters], page 503.

`_SC_2_LOCALEDEF`
: 'unistd.h' (POSIX.2): Section 27.4.2 [Constants for "code sysconf Parameters], page 503.

`_SC_2_SW_DEV`
: 'unistd.h' (POSIX.2): Section 27.4.2 [Constants for "code sysconf Parameters], page 503.

`_SC_2_VERSION`
: 'unistd.h' (POSIX.2): Section 27.4.2 [Constants for "code sysconf Parameters], page 503.

`double scalb (double value, int exponent)`
: 'math.h' (BSD): Section 14.4 [Normalization Functions], page 291.

`int scanf (const char *template, ...)`
: 'stdio.h' (ANSI): Section 7.12.8 [Formatted Input Functions], page 123.

`_SC_ARG_MAX`
: 'unistd.h' (POSIX.1): Section 27.4.2 [Constants for "code sysconf Parameters], page 503.

`_SC_BC_BASE_MAX`
: 'unistd.h' (POSIX.2): Section 27.4.2 [Constants for "code sysconf Parameters], page 503.

`_SC_BC_DIM_MAX`
: 'unistd.h' (POSIX.2): Section 27.4.2 [Constants for "code sysconf Parameters], page 503.

`_SC_BC_SCALE_MAX`
: 'unistd.h' (POSIX.2): Section 27.4.2 [Constants for "code sysconf Parameters], page 503.

`_SC_BC_STRING_MAX`
: 'unistd.h' (POSIX.2): Section 27.4.2 [Constants for "code sysconf Parameters], page 503.

Appendix B: Summary of Library Facilities

`_SC_CHILD_MAX`
: 'unistd.h' (POSIX.1): Section 27.4.2 [Constants for "code sysconf Parameters], page 503.

`_SC_CLK_TCK`
: 'unistd.h' (POSIX.1): Section 27.4.2 [Constants for "code sysconf Parameters], page 503.

`_SC_COLL_WEIGHTS_MAX`
: 'unistd.h' (POSIX.2): Section 27.4.2 [Constants for "code sysconf Parameters], page 503.

`_SC_EQUIV_CLASS_MAX`
: 'unistd.h' (POSIX.2): Section 27.4.2 [Constants for "code sysconf Parameters], page 503.

`_SC_EXPR_NEST_MAX`
: 'unistd.h' (POSIX.2): Section 27.4.2 [Constants for "code sysconf Parameters], page 503.

`SCHAR_MAX`
: 'limits.h' (ANSI): Section A.5.2 [Range of an Integer Type], page 525.

`SCHAR_MIN`
: 'limits.h' (ANSI): Section A.5.2 [Range of an Integer Type], page 525.

`_SC_JOB_CONTROL`
: 'unistd.h' (POSIX.1): Section 27.4.2 [Constants for "code sysconf Parameters], page 503.

`_SC_LINE_MAX`
: 'unistd.h' (POSIX.2): Section 27.4.2 [Constants for "code sysconf Parameters], page 503.

`_SC_NGROUPS_MAX`
: 'unistd.h' (POSIX.1): Section 27.4.2 [Constants for "code sysconf Parameters], page 503.

`_SC_OPEN_MAX`
: 'unistd.h' (POSIX.1): Section 27.4.2 [Constants for "code sysconf Parameters], page 503.

`_SC_PAGESIZE`
: 'unistd.h' (GNU): Section 27.4.2 [Constants for "code sysconf Parameters], page 503.

`_SC_SAVED_IDS`
: 'unistd.h' (POSIX.1): Section 27.4.2 [Constants for "code sysconf Parameters], page 503.

_SC_STREAM_MAX
'unistd.h' (POSIX.1): Section 27.4.2 [Constants for "code sysconf Parameters], page 503.

_SC_TZNAME_MAX
'unistd.h' (POSIX.1): Section 27.4.2 [Constants for "code sysconf Parameters], page 503.

_SC_VERSION
'unistd.h' (POSIX.1): Section 27.4.2 [Constants for "code sysconf Parameters], page 503.

_SC_VERSION
'unistd.h' (POSIX.2): Section 27.4.2 [Constants for "code sysconf Parameters], page 503.

int SEEK_CUR
'stdio.h' (ANSI): Section 7.15 [File Positioning], page 126.

void seekdir (DIR *dirstream, off_t pos)
'dirent.h' (BSD): Section 9.2.5 [Random Access in a Directory Stream], page 174.

int SEEK_END
'stdio.h' (ANSI): Section 7.15 [File Positioning], page 126.

int SEEK_SET
'stdio.h' (ANSI): Section 7.15 [File Positioning], page 126.

int select (int nfds, fd_set *read-fds, fd_set *write-fds, fd_set *except-fds, struct timeval *timeout)
'sys/types.h' (BSD): Section 8.6 [Waiting for Input or Output], page 150.

int send (int socket, void *buffer, size_t size, int flags)
'sys/socket.h' (BSD): Section 11.8.5.1 [Sending Data], page 235.

int sendmsg (int socket, const struct msghdr *message, int flags)
'sys/socket.h' (BSD): Section 11.9.2 [Receiving Datagrams], page 244.

int sendto (int socket, void *buffer. size_t size, int flags, struct sockaddr *addr, size_t length)
'sys/socket.h' (BSD): Section 11.9.1 [Sending Datagrams], page 244.

void setbuffer (FILE *stream, char *buf, size_t size)
'stdio.h' (BSD): Section 7.17.3 [Controlling Which Kind of Buffering], page 131.

Appendix B: Summary of Library Facilities

void setbuf (FILE *stream, char *buf)
: 'stdio.h' (ANSI): Section 7.17.3 [Controlling Which Kind of Buffering], page 131.

int setgid (gid_t newgid)
: 'unistd.h' (POSIX.1): Section 25.7 [Setting the Group IDs], page 483.

void setgrent (void)
: 'grp.h' (SVID, BSD): Section 25.13.3 [Scanning the List of All Groups], page 492.

int setgroups (size_t count, gid_t *groups)
: 'grp.h' (BSD): Section 25.7 [Setting the Group IDs], page 483.

void sethostent (int stayopen)
: 'netdb.h' (BSD): Section 11.5.2.4 [Host Names], page 219.

int sethostid (long int id)
: 'unistd.h' (BSD): Section 26.1 [Host Identification], page 495.

int sethostname (const char *name, size_t length)
: 'unistd.h' (BSD): Section 26.1 [Host Identification], page 495.

int setitimer (int which, struct itimerval *new, struct itimerval *old)
: 'sys/time.h' (BSD): Section 17.3 [Setting an Alarm], page 335.

int setjmp (jmp_buf state)
: 'setjmp.h' (ANSI): Section 20.2 [Details of Non-Local Exits], page 368.

void setlinebuf (FILE *stream)
: 'stdio.h' (BSD): Section 7.17.3 [Controlling Which Kind of Buffering], page 131.

char * setlocale (int category, const char *locale)
: 'locale.h' (ANSI): Section 19.4 [How Programs Set the Locale], page 359.

void setnetent (int stayopen)
: 'netdb.h' (BSD): Section 11.12 [Networks Database], page 252.

int setpgid (pid_t pid, pid_t pgid)
: 'unistd.h' (POSIX.1): Section 24.7.2 [Process Group Functions], page 475.

int setpgrp (pid_t pid, pid_t pgid)
: 'unistd.h' (BSD): Section 24.7.2 [Process Group Functions], page 475.

int setpriority (int *class*, int *id*, int *priority*)
: 'sys/resource.h' (BSD): Section 17.7 [Process Priority], page 343.

void setprotoent (int *stayopen*)
: 'netdb.h' (BSD): Section 11.5.6 [Protocols Database], page 225.

void setpwent (void)
: 'pwd.h' (SVID, BSD): Section 25.12.3 [Scanning the List of All Users], page 490.

int setregid (gid_t *rgid*, fid_t *egid*)
: 'unistd.h' (BSD): Section 25.7 [Setting the Group IDs], page 483.

int setreuid (uid_t *ruid*, uid_t *euid*)
: 'unistd.h' (BSD): Section 25.6 [Setting the User ID], page 482.

int setrlimit (int *resource*, struct rlimit **rlp*)
: 'sys/resource.h' (BSD): Section 17.6 [Limiting Resource Usage], page 341.

void setservent (int *stayopen*)
: 'netdb.h' (BSD): Section 11.5.4 [The Services Database], page 222.

pid_t setsid (void)
: 'unistd.h' (POSIX.1): Section 24.7.2 [Process Group Functions], page 475.

int setsockopt (int *socket*, int *level*, int *optname*, void **optval*, size_t *optlen*)
: 'sys/socket.h' (BSD): Section 11.11.1 [Socket Option Functions], page 250.

void * setstate (void **state*)
: 'stdlib.h' (BSD): Section 13.6.2 [BSD Random Number Functions], page 287.

int settimeofday (const struct timeval **tp*, const struct timezone **tzp*)
: 'sys/time.h' (BSD): Section 17.2.2 [High-Resolution Calendar], page 324.

int setuid (uid_t *newuid*)
: 'unistd.h' (POSIX.1): Section 25.6 [Setting the User ID], page 482.

int setvbuf (FILE **stream*, char **buf*, int *mode*, size_t *size*)
: 'stdio.h' (ANSI): Section 7.17.3 [Controlling Which Kind of Buffering], page 131.

Appendix B: Summary of Library Facilities 595

SHRT_MAX
: 'limits.h' (ANSI): Section A.5.2 [Range of an Integer Type], page 525.

SHRT_MIN
: 'limits.h' (ANSI): Section A.5.2 [Range of an Integer Type], page 525.

int shutdown (int *socket*, int *how*)
: 'sys/socket.h' (BSD): Section 11.7.2 [Closing a Socket], page 229.

S_IEXEC
: 'sys/stat.h' (BSD): Section 9.8.5 [The Mode Bits for Access Permission], page 188.

S_IFBLK
: 'sys/stat.h' (BSD): Section 9.8.3 [Testing the Type of a File], page 185.

S_IFCHR
: 'sys/stat.h' (BSD): Section 9.8.3 [Testing the Type of a File], page 185.

S_IFDIR
: 'sys/stat.h' (BSD): Section 9.8.3 [Testing the Type of a File], page 185.

S_IFIFO
: 'sys/stat.h' (BSD): Section 9.8.3 [Testing the Type of a File], page 185.

S_IFLNK
: 'sys/stat.h' (BSD): Section 9.8.3 [Testing the Type of a File], page 185.

int S_IFMT
: 'sys/stat.h' (BSD): Section 9.8.3 [Testing the Type of a File], page 185.

S_IFREG
: 'sys/stat.h' (BSD): Section 9.8.3 [Testing the Type of a File], page 185.

S_IFSOCK
: 'sys/stat.h' (BSD): Section 9.8.3 [Testing the Type of a File], page 185.

int SIGABRT
: 'signal.h' (ANSI): Section 21.2.1 [Program Error Signals], page 374.

int sigaction (int *signum*, const struct sigaction *action*, struct sigaction *old-action*)
: 'signal.h' (POSIX.1): Section 21.3.2 [Advanced Signal Handling], page 386.

int sigaddset (sigset_t *set*, int *signum*)
: 'signal.h' (POSIX.1): Section 21.7.2 [Signal Sets], page 409.

int SIGALRM
: 'signal.h' (POSIX.1): Section 21.2.3 [Alarm Signals], page 379.

int sigaltstack (const struct sigaltstack *stack*, struct sigaltstack *oldstack*)
: 'signal.h' (BSD): Section 21.9 [Using a Separate Signal Stack], page 418.

sig_atomic_t
: 'signal.h' (ANSI): Section 21.4.7.2 [Atomic Types], page 401.

int sigblock (int *mask*)
: 'signal.h' (BSD): Section 21.10.2 [BSD Functions for Blocking Signals], page 422.

SIG_BLOCK
: 'signal.h' (POSIX.1): Section 21.7.3 [Process Signal Mask], page 410.

int SIGBUS
: 'signal.h' (BSD): Section 21.2.1 [Program Error Signals], page 374.

int SIGCHLD
: 'signal.h' (POSIX.1): Section 21.2.5 [Job Control Signals], page 380.

int SIGCLD
: 'signal.h' (SVID): Section 21.2.5 [Job Control Signals], page 380.

int SIGCONT
: 'signal.h' (POSIX.1): Section 21.2.5 [Job Control Signals], page 380.

int sigdelset (sigset_t *set*, int *signum*)
: 'signal.h' (POSIX.1): Section 21.7.2 [Signal Sets], page 409.

int sigemptyset (sigset_t *set*)
: 'signal.h' (POSIX.1): Section 21.7.2 [Signal Sets], page 409.

Appendix B: Summary of Library Facilities   597

`int SIGEMT`
> `signal.h` (BSD): Section 21.2.1 [Program Error Signals], page 374.

`sighandler_t SIG_ERR`
> `signal.h` (ANSI): Section 21.3.1 [Basic Signal Handling], page 384.

`int sigfillset (sigset_t *set)`
> `signal.h` (POSIX.1): Section 21.7.2 [Signal Sets], page 409.

`int SIGFPE`
> `signal.h` (ANSI): Section 21.2.1 [Program Error Signals], page 374.

`sighandler_t`
> `signal.h` (GNU): Section 21.3.1 [Basic Signal Handling], page 384.

`int SIGHUP`
> `signal.h` (POSIX.1): Section 21.2.2 [Termination Signals], page 377.

`int SIGILL`
> `signal.h` (ANSI): Section 21.2.1 [Program Error Signals], page 374.

`int SIGINFO`
> `signal.h` (BSD): Section 21.2.7 [Miscellaneous Signals], page 382.

`int siginterrupt (int signum, int failflag)`
> `signal.h` (BSD): Section 21.10.1 [BSD Function to Establish a Handler], page 421.

`int SIGINT`
> `signal.h` (ANSI): Section 21.2.2 [Termination Signals], page 377.

`int SIGIO`
> `signal.h` (BSD): Section 21.2.4 [Asynchronous I/O Signals], page 379.

`int SIGIOT`
> `signal.h` (Unix): Section 21.2.1 [Program Error Signals], page 374.

`int sigismember (const sigset_t *set, int signum)`
> `signal.h` (POSIX.1): Section 21.7.2 [Signal Sets], page 409.

`sigjmp_buf`
: 'setjmp.h' (POSIX.1): Section 20.3 [Non-Local Exits and Signals], page 370.

`int SIGKILL`
: 'signal.h' (POSIX.1): Section 21.2.2 [Termination Signals], page 377.

`void siglongjmp (sigjmp_buf` *state*`, int` *value*`)`
: 'setjmp.h' (POSIX.1): Section 20.3 [Non-Local Exits and Signals], page 370.

`int SIGLOST`
: 'signal.h' (GNU): Section 21.2.6 [Operation Error Signals], page 382.

`int sigmask (int` *signum*`)`
: 'signal.h' (BSD): Section 21.10.2 [BSD Functions for Blocking Signals], page 422.

`sighandler_t signal (int` *signum*`, sighandler_t` *action*`)`
: 'signal.h' (ANSI): Section 21.3.1 [Basic Signal Handling], page 384.

`int sigpause (int` *mask*`)`
: 'signal.h' (BSD): Section 21.10.2 [BSD Functions for Blocking Signals], page 422.

`int sigpending (sigset_t *`*set*`)`
: 'signal.h' (POSIX.1): Section 21.7.6 [Checking for Pending Signals], page 413.

`int SIGPIPE`
: 'signal.h' (POSIX.1): Section 21.2.6 [Operation Error Signals], page 382.

`int SIGPOLL`
: 'signal.h' (SVID): Section 21.2.4 [Asynchronous I/O Signals], page 379.

`int sigprocmask (int` *how*`, const sigset_t *`*set*`, sigset_t *`*oldset*`)`
: 'signal.h' (POSIX.1): Section 21.7.3 [Process Signal Mask], page 410.

`int SIGPROF`
: 'signal.h' (BSD): Section 21.2.3 [Alarm Signals], page 379.

`int SIGQUIT`
: 'signal.h' (POSIX.1): Section 21.2.2 [Termination Signals], page 377.

Appendix B: Summary of Library Facilities 599

`int SIGSEGV`
: 'signal.h' (ANSI): Section 21.2.1 [Program Error Signals], page 374.

`int sigsetjmp (sigjmp_buf` *state*`, int` *savesigs*`)`
: 'setjmp.h' (POSIX.1): Section 20.3 [Non-Local Exits and Signals], page 370.

`int sigsetmask (int` *mask*`)`
: 'signal.h' (BSD): Section 21.10.2 [BSD Functions for Blocking Signals], page 422.

`SIG_SETMASK`
: 'signal.h' (POSIX.1): Section 21.7.3 [Process Signal Mask], page 410.

`sigset_t`
: 'signal.h' (POSIX.1): Section 21.7.2 [Signal Sets], page 409.

`int sigstack (const struct sigstack *`*stack*`, struct sigstack *`*oldstack*`)`
: 'signal.h' (BSD): Section 21.9 [Using a Separate Signal Stack], page 418.

`int SIGSTOP`
: 'signal.h' (POSIX.1): Section 21.2.5 [Job Control Signals], page 380.

`int sigsuspend (const sigset_t *`*set*`)`
: 'signal.h' (POSIX.1): Section 21.8.3 [Using "code sigsuspend], page 417.

`int SIGSYS`
: 'signal.h' (Unix): Section 21.2.1 [Program Error Signals], page 374.

`int SIGTERM`
: 'signal.h' (ANSI): Section 21.2.2 [Termination Signals], page 377.

`int SIGTRAP`
: 'signal.h' (BSD): Section 21.2.1 [Program Error Signals], page 374.

`int SIGTSTP`
: 'signal.h' (POSIX.1): Section 21.2.5 [Job Control Signals], page 380.

`int SIGTTIN`
: 'signal.h' (POSIX.1): Section 21.2.5 [Job Control Signals], page 380.

`int SIGTTOU`
> 'signal.h' (POSIX.1): Section 21.2.5 [Job Control Signals], page 380.

`SIG_UNBLOCK`
> 'signal.h' (POSIX.1): Section 21.7.3 [Process Signal Mask], page 410.

`int SIGURG`
> 'signal.h' (BSD): Section 21.2.4 [Asynchronous I/O Signals], page 379.

`int SIGUSR1`
> 'signal.h' (POSIX.1): Section 21.2.7 [Miscellaneous Signals], page 382.

`int SIGUSR2`
> 'signal.h' (POSIX.1): Section 21.2.7 [Miscellaneous Signals], page 382.

`int sigvec (int` *signum*`, const struct sigvec *`*action*`, struct sigvec *`*old-action*`)`
> 'signal.h' (BSD): Section 21.10.1 [BSD Function to Establish a Handler], page 421.

`int SIGVTALRM`
> 'signal.h' (BSD): Section 21.2.3 [Alarm Signals], page 379.

`int SIGWINCH`
> 'signal.h' (BSD): Section 21.2.7 [Miscellaneous Signals], page 382.

`int SIGXCPU`
> 'signal.h' (BSD): Section 21.2.6 [Operation Error Signals], page 382.

`int SIGXFSZ`
> 'signal.h' (BSD): Section 21.2.6 [Operation Error Signals], page 382.

`double sinh (double` *x*`)`
> 'math.h' (ANSI): Section 13.5 [Hyperbolic Functions], page 285.

`double sin (double` *x*`)`
> 'math.h' (ANSI): Section 13.2 [Trigonometric Functions], page 282.

`S_IREAD`
> 'sys/stat.h' (BSD): Section 9.8.5 [The Mode Bits for Access Permission], page 188.

Appendix B: Summary of Library Facilities

S_IRGRP
> 'sys/stat.h' (POSIX.1): Section 9.8.5 [The Mode Bits for Access Permission], page 188.

S_IROTH
> 'sys/stat.h' (POSIX.1): Section 9.8.5 [The Mode Bits for Access Permission], page 188.

S_IRUSR
> 'sys/stat.h' (POSIX.1): Section 9.8.5 [The Mode Bits for Access Permission], page 188.

S_IRWXG
> 'sys/stat.h' (POSIX.1): Section 9.8.5 [The Mode Bits for Access Permission], page 188.

S_IRWXO
> 'sys/stat.h' (POSIX.1): Section 9.8.5 [The Mode Bits for Access Permission], page 188.

S_IRWXU
> 'sys/stat.h' (POSIX.1): Section 9.8.5 [The Mode Bits for Access Permission], page 188.

int S_ISBLK (mode_t *m*)
> 'sys/stat.h' (POSIX): Section 9.8.3 [Testing the Type of a File], page 185.

int S_ISCHR (mode_t *m*)
> 'sys/stat.h' (POSIX): Section 9.8.3 [Testing the Type of a File], page 185.

int S_ISDIR (mode_t *m*)
> 'sys/stat.h' (POSIX): Section 9.8.3 [Testing the Type of a File], page 185.

int S_ISFIFO (mode_t *m*)
> 'sys/stat.h' (POSIX): Section 9.8.3 [Testing the Type of a File], page 185.

S_ISGID
> 'sys/stat.h' (POSIX): Section 9.8.5 [The Mode Bits for Access Permission], page 188.

int S_ISLNK (mode_t *m*)
> 'sys/stat.h' (GNU): Section 9.8.3 [Testing the Type of a File], page 185.

int S_ISREG (mode_t *m*)
: 'sys/stat.h' (POSIX): Section 9.8.3 [Testing the Type of a File], page 185.

int S_ISSOCK (mode_t *m*)
: 'sys/stat.h' (GNU): Section 9.8.3 [Testing the Type of a File], page 185.

S_ISUID
: 'sys/stat.h' (POSIX): Section 9.8.5 [The Mode Bits for Access Permission], page 188.

S_ISVTX
: 'sys/stat.h' (BSD): Section 9.8.5 [The Mode Bits for Access Permission], page 188.

S_IWGRP
: 'sys/stat.h' (POSIX.1): Section 9.8.5 [The Mode Bits for Access Permission], page 188.

S_IWOTH
: 'sys/stat.h' (POSIX.1): Section 9.8.5 [The Mode Bits for Access Permission], page 188.

S_IWRITE
: 'sys/stat.h' (BSD): Section 9.8.5 [The Mode Bits for Access Permission], page 188.

S_IWUSR
: 'sys/stat.h' (POSIX.1): Section 9.8.5 [The Mode Bits for Access Permission], page 188.

S_IXGRP
: 'sys/stat.h' (POSIX.1): Section 9.8.5 [The Mode Bits for Access Permission], page 188.

S_IXOTH
: 'sys/stat.h' (POSIX.1): Section 9.8.5 [The Mode Bits for Access Permission], page 188.

S_IXUSR
: 'sys/stat.h' (POSIX.1): Section 9.8.5 [The Mode Bits for Access Permission], page 188.

size_t
: 'stddef.h' (ANSI): Section A.4 [Important Data Types], page 523.

unsigned int sleep (unsigned int *seconds*)
: 'unistd.h' (POSIX.1): Section 17.4 [Sleeping], page 338.

int snprintf (char *s, size_t *size*, const char **template*, ...)
: 'stdio.h' (GNU): Section 7.10.7 [Formatted Output Functions], page 103.

SO_BROADCAST
: 'sys/socket.h' (BSD): Section 11.11.2 [Socket-Level Options], page 250.

int SOCK_DGRAM
: 'sys/socket.h' (BSD): Section 11.2 [Communication Styles], page 208.

int socket (int *namespace*, int *style*, int *protocol*)
: 'sys/socket.h' (BSD): Section 11.7.1 [Creating a Socket], page 228.

int socketpair (int *namespace*, int *style*, int *protocol*, int *filedes*[2])
: 'sys/socket.h' (BSD): Section 11.7.3 [Socket Pairs], page 229.

int SOCK_RAW
: 'sys/socket.h' (BSD): Section 11.2 [Communication Styles], page 208.

int SOCK_RDM
: 'sys/socket.h' (BSD): Section 11.2 [Communication Styles], page 208.

int SOCK_SEQPACKET
: 'sys/socket.h' (BSD): Section 11.2 [Communication Styles], page 208.

int SOCK_STREAM
: 'sys/socket.h' (BSD): Section 11.2 [Communication Styles], page 208.

SO_DEBUG
: 'sys/socket.h' (BSD): Section 11.11.2 [Socket-Level Options], page 250.

SO_DONTROUTE
: 'sys/socket.h' (BSD): Section 11.11.2 [Socket-Level Options], page 250.

SO_ERROR
: 'sys/socket.h' (BSD): Section 11.11.2 [Socket-Level Options], page 250.

SO_KEEPALIVE
: 'sys/socket.h' (BSD): Section 11.11.2 [Socket-Level Options], page 250.

SO_LINGER
: 'sys/socket.h' (BSD): Section 11.11.2 [Socket-Level Options], page 250.

int SOL_SOCKET
: 'sys/socket.h' (BSD): Section 11.11.2 [Socket-Level Options], page 250.

SO_OOBINLINE
: 'sys/socket.h' (BSD): Section 11.11.2 [Socket-Level Options], page 250.

SO_RCVBUF
: 'sys/socket.h' (BSD): Section 11.11.2 [Socket-Level Options], page 250.

SO_REUSEADDR
: 'sys/socket.h' (BSD): Section 11.11.2 [Socket-Level Options], page 250.

SO_SNDBUF
: 'sys/socket.h' (BSD): Section 11.11.2 [Socket-Level Options], page 250.

SO_STYLE
: 'sys/socket.h' (GNU): Section 11.11.2 [Socket-Level Options], page 250.

SO_TYPE
: 'sys/socket.h' (BSD): Section 11.11.2 [Socket-Level Options], page 250.

speed_t
: 'termios.h' (POSIX.1): Section 12.4.8 [Line Speed], page 268.

int sprintf (char *s, const char *template, ...)
: 'stdio.h' (ANSI): Section 7.10.7 [Formatted Output Functions], page 103.

double sqrt (double x)
: 'math.h' (ANSI): Section 13.4 [Exponentiation and Logarithms], page 283.

void srand (unsigned int seed)
: 'stdlib.h' (ANSI): Section 13.6.1 [ANSI C Random Number Functions], page 286.

Appendix B: Summary of Library Facilities

void srandom (unsigned int *seed*)
: 'stdlib.h' (BSD): Section 13.6.2 [BSD Random Number Functions], page 287.

int sscanf (const char *s, const char **template*, ...)
: 'stdio.h' (ANSI): Section 7.12.8 [Formatted Input Functions], page 123.

sighandler_t ssignal (int *signum*, sighandler_t *action*)
: 'signal.h' (SVID): Section 21.3.1 [Basic Signal Handling], page 384.

int SSIZE_MAX
: 'limits.h' (POSIX.1): Section 27.1 [General Capacity Limits], page 499.

ssize_t
: 'unistd.h' (POSIX.1): Section 8.2 [Input and Output Primitives], page 141.

int stat (const char **filename*, struct stat **buf*)
: 'sys/stat.h' (POSIX.1): Section 9.8.2 [Reading the Attributes of a File], page 184.

STDERR_FILENO
: 'unistd.h' (POSIX.1): Section 8.4 [Descriptors and Streams], page 147.

FILE * stderr
: 'stdio.h' (ANSI): Section 7.2 [Standard Streams], page 83.

STDIN_FILENO
: 'unistd.h' (POSIX.1): Section 8.4 [Descriptors and Streams], page 147.

FILE * stdin
: 'stdio.h' (ANSI): Section 7.2 [Standard Streams], page 83.

STDOUT_FILENO
: 'unistd.h' (POSIX.1): Section 8.4 [Descriptors and Streams], page 147.

FILE * stdout
: 'stdio.h' (ANSI): Section 7.2 [Standard Streams], page 83.

char * stpcpy (char **to*, const char **from*)
: 'string.h' (Unknown origin): Section 5.4 [Copying and Concatenation], page 61.

int strcasecmp (const char **s1*, const char **s2*)
: 'string.h' (BSD): Section 5.5 [String/Array Comparison], page 65.

char * strcat (char *to, const char *from)
: 'string.h' (ANSI): Section 5.4 [Copying and Concatenation], page 61.

char * strchr (const char *string, int c)
: 'string.h' (ANSI): Section 5.7 [Search Functions], page 70.

int strcmp (const char *s1, const char *s2)
: 'string.h' (ANSI): Section 5.5 [String/Array Comparison], page 65.

int strcoll (const char *s1, const char *s2)
: 'string.h' (ANSI): Section 5.6 [Collation Functions], page 67.

char * strcpy (char *to, const char *from)
: 'string.h' (ANSI): Section 5.4 [Copying and Concatenation], page 61.

size_t strcspn (const char *string, const char *stopset)
: 'string.h' (ANSI): Section 5.7 [Search Functions], page 70.

char * strdup (const char *s)
: 'string.h' (SVID): Section 5.4 [Copying and Concatenation], page 61.

int STREAM_MAX
: 'limits.h' (POSIX.1): Section 27.1 [General Capacity Limits], page 499.

char * strerror (int errnum)
: 'string.h' (ANSI): Section 2.3 [Error Messages], page 23.

size_t strftime (char *s, size_t size, const char *template, const struct tm *brokentime)
: 'time.h' (ANSI): Section 17.2.4 [Formatting Date and Time], page 329.

size_t strlen (const char *s)
: 'string.h' (ANSI): Section 5.3 [String Length], page 61.

int strncasecmp (const char *s1, const char *s2, size_t n)
: 'string.h' (BSD): Section 5.5 [String/Array Comparison], page 65.

char * strncat (char *to, const char *from, size_t size)
: 'string.h' (ANSI): Section 5.4 [Copying and Concatenation], page 61.

int strncmp (const char *s1, const char *s2, size_t size)
: 'string.h' (ANSI): Section 5.5 [String/Array Comparison], page 65.

char * strncpy (char *to, const char *from, size_t size)
: 'string.h' (ANSI): Section 5.4 [Copying and Concatenation], page 61.

char * strpbrk (const char *string, const char *stopset)
: 'string.h' (ANSI): Section 5.7 [Search Functions], page 70.

char * strrchr (const char *string, int c)
: 'string.h' (ANSI): Section 5.7 [Search Functions], page 70.

char * strsignal (int signum)
: 'string.h' (GNU): Section 21.2.8 [Signal Messages], page 383.

size_t strspn (const char *string, const char *skipset)
: 'string.h' (ANSI): Section 5.7 [Search Functions], page 70.

char * strstr (const char *haystack, const char *needle)
: 'string.h' (ANSI): Section 5.7 [Search Functions], page 70.

double strtod (const char *string, char **tailptr)
: 'stdlib.h' (ANSI): Section 14.7.2 [Parsing of Floats], page 296.

char * strtok (char *newstring, const char *delimiters)
: 'string.h' (ANSI): Section 5.8 [Finding Tokens in a String], page 72.

long int strtol (const char *string, char **tailptr, int base)
: 'stdlib.h' (ANSI): Section 14.7.1 [Parsing of Integers], page 294.

unsigned long int strtoul (const char *string, char **tailptr, int base)
: 'stdlib.h' (ANSI): Section 14.7.1 [Parsing of Integers], page 294.

struct dirent
: 'dirent.h' (POSIX.1): Section 9.2.1 [Format of a Directory Entry], page 171.

struct flock
: 'fcntl.h' (POSIX.1): Section 8.11 [File Locks], page 164.

struct group
: 'grp.h' (POSIX.1): Section 25.13.1 [The Data Structure for a Group], page 491.

struct hostent
: 'netdb.h' (BSD): Section 11.5.2.4 [Host Names], page 219.

struct in_addr
: 'netinet/in.h' (BSD): Section 11.5.2.2 [Host Address Data Type], page 217.

struct itimerval
: 'sys/time.h' (BSD): Section 17.3 [Setting an Alarm], page 335.

struct lconv
: 'locale.h' (ANSI): Section 19.6 [Numeric Formatting], page 361.

struct linger
: 'sys/socket.h' (BSD): Section 11.11.2 [Socket-Level Options], page 250.

struct msghdr
: 'sys/socket.h' (BSD): Section 11.9.2 [Receiving Datagrams], page 244.

struct mstats
: 'malloc.h' (GNU): Section 3.3.10 [Statistics for Storage Allocation with "code malloc], page 36.

struct netent
: 'netdb.h' (BSD): Section 11.12 [Networks Database], page 252.

struct obstack
: 'obstack.h' (GNU): Section 3.4.1 [Creating Obstacks], page 38.

struct option
: 'getopt.h' (GNU): Section 22.1.4 [Parsing Long Options], page 430.

struct passwd
: 'pwd.h' (POSIX.1): Section 25.12.1 [The Data Structure that Describes a User], page 489.

struct printf_info
: 'printf.h' (GNU): Section 7.11.2 [Conversion Specifier Options], page 112.

struct protoent
: 'netdb.h' (BSD): Section 11.5.6 [Protocols Database], page 225.

struct rlimit
: 'sys/resource.h' (BSD): Section 17.6 [Limiting Resource Usage], page 341.

struct rusage
: 'sys/resource.h' (BSD): Section 17.5 [Resource Usage], page 339.

struct servent
: 'netdb.h' (BSD): Section 11.5.4 [The Services Database], page 222.

Appendix B: Summary of Library Facilities

`struct sigaction`
: 'signal.h' (POSIX.1): Section 21.3.2 [Advanced Signal Handling], page 386.

`struct sigaltstack`
: 'signal.h' (BSD): Section 21.9 [Using a Separate Signal Stack], page 418.

`struct sigstack`
: 'signal.h' (BSD): Section 21.9 [Using a Separate Signal Stack], page 418.

`struct sigvec`
: 'signal.h' (BSD): Section 21.10.1 [BSD Function to Establish a Handler], page 421.

`struct sockaddr`
: 'sys/socket.h' (BSD): Section 11.3.1 [Address Formats], page 210.

`struct sockaddr_in`
: 'netinet/in.h' (BSD): Section 11.5.1 [Internet Socket Address Format], page 215.

`struct sockaddr_un`
: 'sys/un.h' (BSD): Section 11.4.2 [Details of File Namespace], page 213.

`struct stat`
: 'sys/stat.h' (POSIX.1): Section 9.8.1 [What the File Attribute Values Mean], page 181.

`struct termios`
: 'termios.h' (POSIX.1): Section 12.4.1 [Terminal Mode Data Types], page 257.

`struct timeval`
: 'sys/time.h' (BSD): Section 17.2.2 [High-Resolution Calendar], page 324.

`struct timezone`
: 'sys/time.h' (BSD): Section 17.2.2 [High-Resolution Calendar], page 324.

`struct tm`
: 'time.h' (ANSI): Section 17.2.3 [Broken-down Time], page 327.

`struct tms`
: 'sys/times.h' (POSIX.1): Section 17.1.2 [Detailed Elapsed CPU Time Inquiry], page 322.

`struct utimbuf`
> 'time.h' (POSIX.1): Section 9.8.9 [File Times], page 194.

`struct utsname`
> 'sys/utsname.h' (POSIX.1): Section 26.2 [Hardware/Software Type Identification], page 496.

`size_t strxfrm (char *to, const char *from, size_t size)`
> 'string.h' (ANSI): Section 5.6 [Collation Functions], page 67.

`_SVID_SOURCE`
> (GNU): Section 1.3.4 [Feature Test Macros], page 8.

`int SV_INTERRUPT`
> 'signal.h' (BSD): Section 21.10.1 [BSD Function to Establish a Handler], page 421.

`int SV_ONSTACK`
> 'signal.h' (BSD): Section 21.10.1 [BSD Function to Establish a Handler], page 421.

`int SV_RESETHAND`
> 'signal.h' (Sun): Section 21.10.1 [BSD Function to Establish a Handler], page 421.

`int symlink (const char *oldname, const char *newname)`
> 'unistd.h' (BSD): Section 9.4 [Symbolic Links], page 176.

`long int sysconf (int parameter)`
> 'unistd.h' (POSIX.1): Section 27.4.1 [Definition of "code sysconf], page 503.

`int system (const char *command)`
> 'stdlib.h' (ANSI): Section 23.1 [Running a Command], page 443.

`double tanh (double x)`
> 'math.h' (ANSI): Section 13.5 [Hyperbolic Functions], page 285.

`double tan (double x)`
> 'math.h' (ANSI): Section 13.2 [Trigonometric Functions], page 282.

`int tcdrain (int filedes)`
> 'termios.h' (POSIX.1): Section 12.5 [Line Control Functions], page 277.

`tcflag_t`
> 'termios.h' (POSIX.1): Section 12.4.1 [Terminal Mode Data Types], page 257.

Appendix B: Summary of Library Facilities

`int tcflow (int `*filedes*`, int `*action*`)`
: 'termios.h' (POSIX.1): Section 12.5 [Line Control Functions], page 277.

`int tcflush (int `*filedes*`, int `*queue*`)`
: 'termios.h' (POSIX.1): Section 12.5 [Line Control Functions], page 277.

`int tcgetattr (int `*filedes*`, struct termios *`*termios-p*`)`
: 'termios.h' (POSIX.1): Section 12.4.2 [Terminal Mode Functions], page 258.

`pid_t tcgetpgrp (int `*filedes*`)`
: 'unistd.h' (POSIX.1): Section 24.7.3 [Functions for Controlling Terminal Access], page 476.

TCSADRAIN
: 'termios.h' (POSIX.1): Section 12.4.2 [Terminal Mode Functions], page 258.

TCSAFLUSH
: 'termios.h' (POSIX.1): Section 12.4.2 [Terminal Mode Functions], page 258.

TCSANOW
: 'termios.h' (POSIX.1): Section 12.4.2 [Terminal Mode Functions], page 258.

TCSASOFT
: 'termios.h' (BSD): Section 12.4.2 [Terminal Mode Functions], page 258.

`int tcsendbreak (int `*filedes*`, int `*duration*`)`
: 'termios.h' (POSIX.1): Section 12.5 [Line Control Functions], page 277.

`int tcsetattr (int `*filedes*`, int `*when*`, const struct termios *`*termios-p*`)`
: 'termios.h' (POSIX.1): Section 12.4.2 [Terminal Mode Functions], page 258.

`int tcsetpgrp (int `*filedes*`, pid_t `*pgid*`)`
: 'unistd.h' (POSIX.1): Section 24.7.3 [Functions for Controlling Terminal Access], page 476.

`off_t telldir (DIR *`*dirstream*`)`
: 'dirent.h' (BSD): Section 9.2.5 [Random Access in a Directory Stream], page 174.

`TEMP_FAILURE_RETRY (`*expression*`)`
: 'unistd.h' (GNU): Section 21.5 [Primitives Interrupted by Signals], page 402.

char * tempnam (const char *dir***, const char** *prefix***)**
> 'stdio.h' (SVID): Section 9.10 [Temporary Files], page 196.

time_t time (time_t *result***)**
> 'time.h' (ANSI): Section 17.2.1 [Simple Calendar Time], page 324.

clock_t times (struct tms **buffer***)**
> 'sys/times.h' (POSIX.1): Section 17.1.2 [Detailed Elapsed CPU Time Inquiry], page 322.

time_t
> 'time.h' (ANSI): Section 17.2.1 [Simple Calendar Time], page 324.

long int timezone
> 'time.h' (SVID): Section 17.2.6 [Functions and Variables for Time Zones], page 334.

FILE * tmpfile (void)
> 'stdio.h' (ANSI): Section 9.10 [Temporary Files], page 196.

int TMP_MAX
> 'stdio.h' (ANSI): Section 9.10 [Temporary Files], page 196.

char * tmpnam (char **result***)**
> 'stdio.h' (ANSI): Section 9.10 [Temporary Files], page 196.

int toascii (int *c***)**
> 'ctype.h' (SVID, BSD): Section 4.2 [Case Conversion], page 57.

int tolower (int *c***)**
> 'ctype.h' (ANSI): Section 4.2 [Case Conversion], page 57.

int _tolower (int *c***)**
> 'ctype.h' (SVID): Section 4.2 [Case Conversion], page 57.

tcflag_t TOSTOP
> 'termios.h' (POSIX.1): Section 12.4.7 [Local Modes], page 266.

int toupper (int *c***)**
> 'ctype.h' (ANSI): Section 4.2 [Case Conversion], page 57.

int _toupper (int *c***)**
> 'ctype.h' (SVID): Section 4.2 [Case Conversion], page 57.

TRY_AGAIN
> 'netdb.h' (BSD): Section 11.5.2.4 [Host Names], page 219.

char * ttyname (int *filedes***)**
> 'unistd.h' (POSIX.1): Section 12.1 [Identifying Terminals], page 255.

Appendix B: Summary of Library Facilities 613

int TZNAME_MAX
: 'limits.h' (POSIX.1): Section 27.1 [General Capacity Limits], page 499.

void tzset (void)
: 'time.h' (POSIX.1): Section 17.2.6 [Functions and Variables for Time Zones], page 334.

UCHAR_MAX
: 'limits.h' (ANSI): Section A.5.2 [Range of an Integer Type], page 525.

uid_t
: 'sys/types.h' (POSIX.1): Section 25.5 [Reading the Persona of a Process], page 481.

UINT_MAX
: 'limits.h' (ANSI): Section A.5.2 [Range of an Integer Type], page 525.

ULONG_LONG_MAX
: 'limits.h' (ANSI): Section A.5.2 [Range of an Integer Type], page 525.

ULONG_MAX
: 'limits.h' (ANSI): Section A.5.2 [Range of an Integer Type], page 525.

mode_t umask (mode_t *mask*)
: 'sys/stat.h' (POSIX.1): Section 9.8.7 [Assigning File Permissions], page 190.

int uname (struct utsname *info*)
: 'sys/utsname.h' (POSIX.1): Section 26.2 [Hardware/Software Type Identification], page 496.

int ungetc (int *c*, FILE *stream*)
: 'stdio.h' (ANSI): Section 7.8.2 [Using "code ungetc To Do Unreading], page 92.

union wait
: 'sys/wait.h' (BSD): Section 23.8 [BSD Process Wait Functions], page 453.

int unlink (const char *filename*)
: 'unistd.h' (POSIX.1): Section 9.5 [Deleting Files], page 178.

USHRT_MAX
: 'limits.h' (ANSI): Section A.5.2 [Range of an Integer Type], page 525.

int utime (const char *filename, const struct utimbuf *times)
: 'time.h' (POSIX.1): Section 9.8.9 [File Times], page 194.

int utimes (const char *filename, struct timeval tvp[2])
: 'sys/time.h' (BSD): Section 9.8.9 [File Times], page 194.

va_alist
: 'varargs.h' (Unix): Section A.2.3.1 [Old-Style Variadic Functions], page 522.

type va_arg (va_list ap, type)
: 'stdarg.h' (ANSI): Section A.2.2.5 [Argument Access Macros], page 520.

va_dcl
: 'varargs.h' (Unix): Section A.2.3.1 [Old-Style Variadic Functions], page 522.

void va_end (va_list ap)
: 'stdarg.h' (ANSI): Section A.2.2.5 [Argument Access Macros], page 520.

va_list
: 'stdarg.h' (ANSI): Section A.2.2.5 [Argument Access Macros], page 520.

void * valloc (size_t size)
: 'malloc.h', 'stdlib.h' (BSD): Section 3.3.7 [Allocating Aligned Memory Blocks], page 33.

int vasprintf (char **ptr, const char *template, va_list ap)
: 'stdio.h' (GNU): Section 7.10.9 [Variable Arguments Output Functions], page 105.

void va_start (va_list ap)
: 'varargs.h' (Unix): Section A.2.3.1 [Old-Style Variadic Functions], page 522.

void va_start (va_list ap, last-required)
: 'stdarg.h' (ANSI): Section A.2.2.5 [Argument Access Macros], page 520.

int VDISCARD
: 'termios.h' (BSD): Section 12.4.9.4 [Other Special Characters], page 274.

int VDSUSP
: 'termios.h' (BSD): Section 12.4.9.2 [Characters that Cause Signals], page 272.

Appendix B: Summary of Library Facilities 615

`int VEOF`
> `termios.h` (POSIX.1): Section 12.4.9.1 [Characters for Input Editing], page 271.

`int VEOL2`
> `termios.h` (BSD): Section 12.4.9.1 [Characters for Input Editing], page 271.

`int VEOL`
> `termios.h` (POSIX.1): Section 12.4.9.1 [Characters for Input Editing], page 271.

`int VERASE`
> `termios.h` (POSIX.1): Section 12.4.9.1 [Characters for Input Editing], page 271.

`pid_t vfork (void)`
> `unistd.h` (BSD): Section 23.4 [Creating a Process], page 445.

`int vfprintf (FILE *stream, const char *template, va_list ap)`
> `stdio.h` (ANSI): Section 7.10.9 [Variable Arguments Output Functions], page 105.

`int vfscanf (FILE *stream, const char *template, va_list ap)`
> `stdio.h` (GNU): Section 7.12.9 [Variable Arguments Input Functions], page 123.

`int VINTR`
> `termios.h` (POSIX.1): Section 12.4.9.2 [Characters that Cause Signals], page 272.

`int VKILL`
> `termios.h` (POSIX.1): Section 12.4.9.1 [Characters for Input Editing], page 271.

`int VLNEXT`
> `termios.h` (BSD): Section 12.4.9.4 [Other Special Characters], page 274.

`int VMIN`
> `termios.h` (POSIX.1): Section 12.4.10 [Noncanonical Input], page 275.

`int vprintf (const char *template, va_list ap)`
> `stdio.h` (ANSI): Section 7.10.9 [Variable Arguments Output Functions], page 105.

`int VQUIT`
> `termios.h` (POSIX.1): Section 12.4.9.2 [Characters that Cause Signals], page 272.

`int VREPRINT`
> 'termios.h' (BSD): Section 12.4.9.1 [Characters for Input Editing], page 271.

`int vscanf (const char *template, va_list ap)`
> 'stdio.h' (GNU): Section 7.12.9 [Variable Arguments Input Functions], page 123.

`int vsnprintf (char *s, size_t size, const char *template, va_list ap)`
> 'stdio.h' (GNU): Section 7.10.9 [Variable Arguments Output Functions], page 105.

`int vsprintf (char *s, const char *template, va_list ap)`
> 'stdio.h' (ANSI): Section 7.10.9 [Variable Arguments Output Functions], page 105.

`int vsscanf (const char *s, const char *template, va_list ap)`
> 'stdio.h' (GNU): Section 7.12.9 [Variable Arguments Input Functions], page 123.

`int VSTART`
> 'termios.h' (POSIX.1): Section 12.4.9.3 [Special Characters for Flow Control], page 274.

`int VSTATUS`
> 'termios.h' (BSD): Section 12.4.9.4 [Other Special Characters], page 274.

`int VSTOP`
> 'termios.h' (POSIX.1): Section 12.4.9.3 [Special Characters for Flow Control], page 274.

`int VSUSP`
> 'termios.h' (POSIX.1): Section 12.4.9.2 [Characters that Cause Signals], page 272.

`int VTIME`
> 'termios.h' (POSIX.1): Section 12.4.10 [Noncanonical Input], page 275.

`int VWERASE`
> 'termios.h' (BSD): Section 12.4.9.1 [Characters for Input Editing], page 271.

`pid_t wait3 (union wait *status-ptr, int options, struct rusage *usage)`
> 'sys/wait.h' (BSD): Section 23.8 [BSD Process Wait Functions], page 453.

Appendix B: Summary of Library Facilities

`pid_t wait4 (pid_t `*pid*`, int *`*status-ptr*`, int `*options*`, struct rusage *`*usage*`)`
: 'sys/wait.h' (BSD): Section 23.6 [Process Completion], page 449.

`pid_t wait (int *`*status-ptr*`)`
: 'sys/wait.h' (POSIX.1): Section 23.6 [Process Completion], page 449.

`pid_t waitpid (pid_t `*pid*`, int *`*status-ptr*`, int `*options*`)`
: 'sys/wait.h' (POSIX.1): Section 23.6 [Process Completion], page 449.

WCHAR_MAX
: 'limits.h' (GNU): Section A.5.2 [Range of an Integer Type], page 525.

wchar_t
: 'stddef.h' (ANSI): Section 18.4 [Wide Character Introduction], page 349.

`int WCOREDUMP (int `*status*`)`
: 'sys/wait.h' (BSD): Section 23.7 [Process Completion Status], page 452.

`size_t wcstombs (char *`*string*`, const wchar_t `*wstring*`, size_t `*size*`)`
: 'stdlib.h' (ANSI): Section 18.5 [Conversion of Extended Strings], page 350.

`int wctomb (char *`*string*`, wchar_t `*wchar*`)`
: 'stdlib.h' (ANSI): Section 18.7 [Conversion of Extended Characters One by One], page 352.

`int WEXITSTATUS (int `*status*`)`
: 'sys/wait.h' (POSIX.1): Section 23.7 [Process Completion Status], page 452.

`int WIFEXITED (int `*status*`)`
: 'sys/wait.h' (POSIX.1): Section 23.7 [Process Completion Status], page 452.

`int WIFSIGNALED (int `*status*`)`
: 'sys/wait.h' (POSIX.1): Section 23.7 [Process Completion Status], page 452.

`int WIFSTOPPED (int `*status*`)`
: 'sys/wait.h' (POSIX.1): Section 23.7 [Process Completion Status], page 452.

`int W_OK`
: 'unistd.h' (POSIX.1): Section 9.8.8 [Testing Permission to Access a File], page 192.

`int wordexp (const char *words, wordexp_t *word-vector-ptr, int flags)`
: 'wordexp.h' (POSIX.2): Section 16.4.2 [Calling "code wordexp], page 316.

`wordexp_t`
: 'wordexp.h' (POSIX.2): Section 16.4.2 [Calling "code wordexp], page 316.

`void wordfree (wordexp_t *word-vector-ptr)`
: 'wordexp.h' (POSIX.2): Section 16.4.2 [Calling "code wordexp], page 316.

`WRDE_APPEND`
: 'wordexp.h' (POSIX.2): Section 16.4.3 [Flags for Word Expansion], page 318.

`WRDE_BADCHAR`
: 'wordexp.h' (POSIX.2): Section 16.4.2 [Calling "code wordexp], page 316.

`WRDE_BADVAL`
: 'wordexp.h' (POSIX.2): Section 16.4.2 [Calling "code wordexp], page 316.

`WRDE_CMDSUB`
: 'wordexp.h' (POSIX.2): Section 16.4.2 [Calling "code wordexp], page 316.

`WRDE_DOOFFS`
: 'wordexp.h' (POSIX.2): Section 16.4.3 [Flags for Word Expansion], page 318.

`WRDE_NOCMD`
: 'wordexp.h' (POSIX.2): Section 16.4.3 [Flags for Word Expansion], page 318.

`WRDE_NOSPACE`
: 'wordexp.h' (POSIX.2): Section 16.4.2 [Calling "code wordexp], page 316.

`WRDE_REUSE`
: 'wordexp.h' (POSIX.2): Section 16.4.3 [Flags for Word Expansion], page 318.

`WRDE_SHOWERR`
: 'wordexp.h' (POSIX.2): Section 16.4.3 [Flags for Word Expansion], page 318.

`WRDE_SYNTAX`
: 'wordexp.h' (POSIX.2): Section 16.4.2 [Calling "code wordexp], page 316.

Appendix B: Summary of Library Facilities

WRDE_UNDEF
: 'wordexp.h' (POSIX.2): Section 16.4.3 [Flags for Word Expansion], page 318.

ssize_t write (int *filedes***, const void ****buffer***, size_t** *size***)**
: 'unistd.h' (POSIX.1): Section 8.2 [Input and Output Primitives], page 141.

int WSTOPSIG (int *status***)**
: 'sys/wait.h' (POSIX.1): Section 23.7 [Process Completion Status], page 452.

int WTERMSIG (int *status***)**
: 'sys/wait.h' (POSIX.1): Section 23.7 [Process Completion Status], page 452.

int X_OK
: 'unistd.h' (POSIX.1): Section 9.8.8 [Testing Permission to Access a File], page 192.

Appendix C Library Maintenance

C.1 How to Install the GNU C Library

Installation of the GNU C library is relatively simple, but usually requires several GNU tools to be installed already. (see Section C.1.1 [Recommended Tools to Install the GNU C Library], page 627, below.)

To configure the GNU C library for your system, run the shell script 'configure' with sh. Use an argument which is the conventional GNU name for your system configuration—for example, 'sparc-sun-sunos4.1', for a Sun 4 running SunOS 4.1. See section "Installing GNU CC" in *Using and Porting GNU CC*, for a full description of standard GNU configuration names. If you omit the configuration name, 'configure' will try to guess one for you by inspecting the system it is running on. It may or may not be able to come up with a guess, and the its guess might be wrong. 'configure' will tell you the canonical name of the chosen configuration before proceeding.

Here are some options that you should specify (if appropriate) when you run configure:

'--with-gnu-ld'
: Use this option if you plan to use GNU ld to link programs with the GNU C Library. (We strongly recommend that you do.) This option enables use of features that exist only in GNU ld; so if you configure for GNU ld you must use GNU ld *every time* you link with the GNU C Library, and when building it.

'--with-gnu-as'
: Use this option if you plan to use the GNU assembler, gas, when building the GNU C Library. On some systems, the library may not build properly if you do *not* use gas.

'--with-gnu-binutils'
: This option implies both '--with-gnu-ld' and '--with-gnu-as'. On systems where GNU tools are the system tools, there is no need to specify this option. These include GNU, GNU/Linux, and free BSD systems.

'--without-fp'
'--nfp'
: Use this option if your computer lacks hardware floating-point support.

'--prefix=*directory*'
: Install machine-independent data files in subdirectories of '*directory*'. (You can also set this in 'configparms'; see below.)

'`--exec-prefix=`*directory*'
: Install the library and other machine-dependent files in subdirectories of '*directory*'. (You can also set this in '`configparms`'; see below.)

'`--enable-shared`'
'`--disable-shared`'
: Enable or disable building of an ELF shared library on systems that support it. The default is to build the shared library on systems using ELF when the GNU `binutils` are available.

'`--enable-profile`'
'`--disable-profile`'
: Enable or disable building of the profiled C library, '`-lc_p`'. The default is to build the profiled library. You may wish to disable it if you don't plan to do profiling, because it doubles the build time of compiling just the unprofiled static library.

'`--enable-omitfp`'
: Enable building a highly-optimized but possibly undebuggable static C library. This causes the normal static and shared (if enabled) C libraries to be compiled with maximal optimization, including the '`-fomit-frame-pointer`' switch that makes debugging impossible on many machines, and without debugging information (which makes the binaries substantially smaller). An additional static library is compiled with no optimization and full debugging information, and installed as '`-lc_g`'.

The simplest way to run `configure` is to do it in the directory that contains the library sources. This prepares to build the library in that very directory.

You can prepare to build the library in some other directory by going to that other directory to run `configure`. In order to run configure, you will have to specify a directory for it, like this:

```
mkdir sun4
cd sun4
../configure sparc-sun-sunos4.1
```

`configure` looks for the sources in whatever directory you specified for finding `configure` itself. It does not matter where in the file system the source and build directories are—as long as you specify the source directory when you run `configure`, you will get the proper results.

This feature lets you keep sources and binaries in different directories, and that makes it easy to build the library for several different machines from the same set of sources. Simply create a build directory for each target machine, and run `configure` in that directory specifying the target machine's configuration name.

Appendix C: Library Maintenance

The library has a number of special-purpose configuration parameters. These are defined in the file 'Makeconfig'; see the comments in that file for the details.

But don't edit the file 'Makeconfig' yourself—instead, create a file 'configparms' in the directory where you are building the library, and define in that file the parameters you want to specify. 'configparms' should **not** be an edited copy of 'Makeconfig'; specify only the parameters that you want to override. To see how to set these parameters, find the section of 'Makeconfig' that says "These are the configuration variables." Then for each parameter that you want to change, copy the definition from 'Makeconfig' to your new 'configparms' file, and change the value as appropriate for your system.

It is easy to configure the GNU C library for cross-compilation by setting a few variables in 'configparms'. Set CC to the cross-compiler for the target you configured the library for; it is important to use this same CC value when running configure, like this: 'CC=*target*-gcc configure *target*'. Set BUILD_CC to the compiler to use for for programs run on the build system as part of compiling the library. You may need to set AR and RANLIB to cross-compiling versions of ar and ranlib if the native tools are not configured to work with object files for the target you configured for.

Some of the machine-dependent code for some machines uses extensions in the GNU C compiler, so you may need to compile the library with GCC. (In fact, all of the existing complete ports require GCC.)

To build the library and related programs, type make. This will produce a lot of output, some of which may look like errors from make (but isn't). Look for error messages from make containing '***'. Those indicate that something is really wrong.

To build and run some test programs which exercise some of the library facilities, type make check. This will produce several files with names like '*program*.out'.

To format the *GNU C Library Reference Manual* for printing, type make dvi.

To install the library and its header files, and the Info files of the manual, type make install. This will build things if necessary, before installing them.

C.1.1 Recommended Tools to Install the GNU C Library

We recommend installing the following GNU tools before attempting to build the GNU C library:

- `make` 3.75

    You need the latest version of GNU `make`. Modifying the GNU C Library to work with other `make` programs would be so hard that we recommend you port GNU `make` instead. **Really.** We recommend version GNU `make` version 3.75 or later.

- GCC 2.7.2

    On most platforms, the GNU C library can only be compiled with the GNU C compiler. We recommend GCC version 2.7.2 or later; earlier versions may have problems.

- `binutils` 2.6

    Using the GNU `binutils` (assembler, linker, and related tools) is preferable when possible, and they are required to build an ELF shared C library. We recommend `binutils` version 2.6 or later; earlier versions are known to have problems.

C.1.2 Supported Configurations

The GNU C Library currently supports configurations that match the following patterns:

```
alpha-dec-osf1
ix86-anything-bsd4.3
ix86-anything-gnu
ix86-anything-isc2.2
ix86-anything-isc3.n
ix86-anything-linux
ix86-anything-sco3.2
ix86-anything-sco3.2v4
ix86-anything-sysv
ix86-anything-sysv4
ix86-force_cpu386-none
ix86-sequent-bsd
i960-nindy960-none
m68k-hp-bsd4.3
m68k-mvme135-none
m68k-mvme136-none
m68k-sony-newsos3
m68k-sony-newsos4
m68k-sun-sunos4.n
mips-dec-ultrix4.n
mips-sgi-irix4.n
sparc-sun-solaris2.n
sparc-sun-sunos4.n
```

Each case of 'ix86' can be 'i386', 'i486', or 'i586'. All of those configurations produce a library that can run on any of these processors. The library will be optimized for the specified processor, but will not use instructions not available on all of them.

Appendix C: Library Maintenance   625

   While no other configurations are supported, there are handy aliases for
these few. (These aliases work in other GNU software as well.)
```
decstation
hp320-bsd4.3 hp300bsd
i486-gnu
i586-linux
i386-sco
i386-sco3.2v4
i386-sequent-dynix
i386-svr4
news
sun3-sunos4.n sun3
sun4-solaris2.n sun4-sunos5.n
sun4-sunos4.n sun4
```

C.2 Reporting Bugs

   There are probably bugs in the GNU C library. There are certainly errors
and omissions in this manual. If you report them, they will get fixed. If you
don't, no one will ever know about them and they will remain unfixed for
all eternity, if not longer.

   To report a bug, first you must find it. Hopefully, this will be the hard
part. Once you've found a bug, make sure it's really a bug. A good way to
do this is to see if the GNU C library behaves the same way some other C
library does. If so, probably you are wrong and the libraries are right (but
not necessarily). If not, one of the libraries is probably wrong.

   Once you're sure you've found a bug, try to narrow it down to the smallest
test case that reproduces the problem. In the case of a C library, you really
only need to narrow it down to one library function call, if possible. This
should not be too difficult.

   The final step when you have a simple test case is to report the bug.
When reporting a bug, send your test case, the results you got, the results
you expected, what you think the problem might be (if you've thought of
anything), your system type, and the version of the GNU C library which you
are using. Also include the files 'config.status' and 'config.make' which
are created by running 'configure'; they will be in whatever directory was
current when you ran 'configure'.

   If you think you have found some way in which the GNU C library does
not conform to the ANSI and POSIX standards (see Section 1.2 [Standards
and Portability], page 1), that is definitely a bug. Report it!

   Send bug reports to the Internet address 'bug-glibc@prep.ai.mit.edu'
or the UUCP path 'mit-eddie!prep.ai.mit.edu!bug-glibc'. If you have
other problems with installation or use, please report those as well.

If you are not sure how a function should behave, and this manual doesn't tell you, that's a bug in the manual. Report that too! If the function's behavior disagrees with the manual, then either the library or the manual has a bug, so report the disagreement. If you find any errors or omissions in this manual, please report them to the Internet address 'bug-glibc-manual@prep.ai.mit.edu' or the UUCP path 'mit-eddie!prep.ai.mit.edu!bug-glibc-manual'.

C.3 Adding New Functions

The process of building the library is driven by the makefiles, which make heavy use of special features of GNU `make`. The makefiles are very complex, and you probably don't want to try to understand them. But what they do is fairly straightforward, and only requires that you define a few variables in the right places.

The library sources are divided into subdirectories, grouped by topic. The '`string`' subdirectory has all the string-manipulation functions, '`stdio`' has all the standard I/O functions, etc.

Each subdirectory contains a simple makefile, called '`Makefile`', which defines a few `make` variables and then includes the global makefile '`Rules`' with a line like:

```
include ../Rules
```

The basic variables that a subdirectory makefile defines are:

`subdir` The name of the subdirectory, for example '`stdio`'. This variable **must** be defined.

`headers` The names of the header files in this section of the library, such as '`stdio.h`'.

`routines`
`aux`   The names of the modules (source files) in this section of the library. These should be simple names, such as '`strlen`' (rather than complete file names, such as '`strlen.c`'). Use `routines` for modules that define functions in the library, and `aux` for auxiliary modules containing things like data definitions. But the values of `routines` and `aux` are just concatenated, so there really is no practical difference.

`tests`   The names of test programs for this section of the library. These should be simple names, such as '`tester`' (rather than complete file names, such as '`tester.c`'). '`make tests`' will build and run all the test programs. If a test program needs input, put the test data in a file called '*test-program*`.input`'; it will be given to the test program on its standard input. If a test program wants to

Appendix C: Library Maintenance 627

`others` be run with arguments, put the arguments (all on a single line) in a file called '*test-program*.`args`'.

`others` The names of "other" programs associated with this section of the library. These are programs which are not tests per se, but are other small programs included with the library. They are built by '`make others`'.

`install-lib`
`install-data`
`install` Files to be installed by '`make install`'. Files listed in '`install-lib`' are installed in the directory specified by '`libdir`' in '`configparms`' or '`Makeconfig`' (see Section C.1 [How to Install the GNU C Library], page 625). Files listed in `install-data` are installed in the directory specified by '`datadir`' in '`configparms`' or '`Makeconfig`'. Files listed in `install` are installed in the directory specified by '`bindir`' in '`configparms`' or '`Makeconfig`'.

`distribute`
  Other files from this subdirectory which should be put into a distribution tar file. You need not list here the makefile itself or the source and header files listed in the other standard variables. Only define `distribute` if there are files used in an unusual way that should go into the distribution.

`generated`
  Files which are generated by '`Makefile`' in this subdirectory. These files will be removed by '`make clean`', and they will never go into a distribution.

`extra-objs`
  Extra object files which are built by '`Makefile`' in this subdirectory. This should be a list of file names like '`foo.o`'; the files will actually be found in whatever directory object files are being built in. These files will be removed by '`make clean`'. This variable is used for secondary object files needed to build `others` or `tests`.

C.4 Porting the GNU C Library

The GNU C library is written to be easily portable to a variety of machines and operating systems. Machine- and operating system-dependent functions are well separated to make it easy to add implementations for new machines or operating systems. This section describes the layout of the library source tree and explains the mechanisms used to select machine-dependent code to use.

All the machine-dependent and operating system-dependent files in the library are in the subdirectory 'sysdeps' under the top-level library source directory. This directory contains a hierarchy of subdirectories (see Section C.4.1 [Layout of the "file sysdeps Directory Hierarchy], page 634).

Each subdirectory of 'sysdeps' contains source files for a particular machine or operating system, or for a class of machine or operating system (for example, systems by a particular vendor, or all machines that use IEEE 754 floating-point format). A configuration specifies an ordered list of these subdirectories. Each subdirectory implicitly appends its parent directory to the list. For example, specifying the list 'unix/bsd/vax' is equivalent to specifying the list 'unix/bsd/vax unix/bsd unix'. A subdirectory can also specify that it implies other subdirectories which are not directly above it in the directory hierarchy. If the file 'Implies' exists in a subdirectory, it lists other subdirectories of 'sysdeps' which are appended to the list, appearing after the subdirectory containing the 'Implies' file. Lines in an 'Implies' file that begin with a '#' character are ignored as comments. For example, 'unix/bsd/Implies' contains:

```
# BSD has Internet-related things.
unix/inet
```

and 'unix/Implies' contains:

```
posix
```

So the final list is 'unix/bsd/vax unix/bsd unix/inet unix posix'.

'sysdeps' has two "special" subdirectories, called 'generic' and 'stub'. These two are always implicitly appended to the list of subdirectories (in that order), so you needn't put them in an 'Implies' file, and you should not create any subdirectories under them. 'generic' is for things that can be implemented in machine-independent C, using only other machine-independent functions in the C library. 'stub' is for *stub* versions of functions which cannot be implemented on a particular machine or operating system. The stub functions always return an error, and set errno to ENOSYS (Function not implemented). See Chapter 2 [Error Reporting], page 13.

A source file is known to be system-dependent by its having a version in 'generic' or 'stub'; every system-dependent function should have either a generic or stub implementation (there is no point in having both).

If you come across a file that is in one of the main source directories ('string', 'stdio', etc.), and you want to write a machine- or operating system-dependent version of it, move the file into 'sysdeps/generic' and write your new implementation in the appropriate system-specific subdirectory. Note that if a file is to be system-dependent, it **must not** appear in one of the main source directories.

There are a few special files that may exist in each subdirectory of 'sysdeps':

Appendix C: Library Maintenance 629

'`Makefile`'
: A makefile for this machine or operating system, or class of machine or operating system. This file is included by the library makefile '`Makerules`', which is used by the top-level makefile and the subdirectory makefiles. It can change the variables set in the including makefile or add new rules. It can use GNU `make` conditional directives based on the variable '`subdir`' (see above) to select different sets of variables and rules for different sections of the library. It can also set the `make` variable '`sysdep-routines`', to specify extra modules to be included in the library. You should use '`sysdep-routines`' rather than adding modules to '`routines`' because the latter is used in determining what to distribute for each subdirectory of the main source tree.

   Each makefile in a subdirectory in the ordered list of subdirectories to be searched is included in order. Since several system-dependent makefiles may be included, each should append to '`sysdep-routines`' rather than simply setting it:

   ```
   sysdep-routines := $(sysdep-routines) foo bar
   ```

'`Subdirs`'
: This file contains the names of new whole subdirectories under the top-level library source tree that should be included for this system. These subdirectories are treated just like the system-independent subdirectories in the library source tree, such as '`stdio`' and '`math`'.

   Use this when there are completely new sets of functions and header files that should go into the library for the system this subdirectory of '`sysdeps`' implements. For example, '`sysdeps/unix/inet/Subdirs`' contains '`inet`'; the '`inet`' directory contains various network-oriented operations which only make sense to put in the library on systems that support the Internet.

'`Dist`'
: This file contains the names of files (relative to the subdirectory of '`sysdeps`' in which it appears) which should be included in the distribution. List any new files used by rules in the '`Makefile`' in the same directory, or header files used by the source files in that directory. You don't need to list files that are implementations (either C or assembly source) of routines whose names are given in the machine-independent makefiles in the main source tree.

'`configure`'
: This file is a shell script fragment to be run at configuration time. The top-level '`configure`' script uses the shell . command

to read the 'configure' file in each system-dependent directory chosen, in order. The 'configure' files are often generated from 'configure.in' files using Autoconf.

A system-dependent 'configure' script will usually add things to the shell variables 'DEFS' and 'config_vars'; see the top-level 'configure' script for details. The script can check for '--with-*package*' options that were passed to the top-level 'configure'. For an option '--with-*package*=*value*' 'configure' sets the shell variable 'with_*package*' (with any dashes in *package* converted to underscores) to *value*; if the option is just '--with-*package*' (no argument), then it sets 'with_*package*' to 'yes'.

'configure.in'
: This file is an Autoconf input fragment to be processed into the file 'configure' in this subdirectory. See section "Introduction" in *Autoconf: Generating Automatic Configuration Scripts*, for a description of Autoconf. You should write either 'configure' or 'configure.in', but not both. The first line of 'configure.in' should invoke the m4 macro 'GLIBC_PROVIDES'. This macro does several AC_PROVIDE calls for Autoconf macros which are used by the top-level 'configure' script; without this, those macros might be invoked again unnecessarily by Autoconf.

That is the general system for how system-dependencies are isolated. The next section explains how to decide what directories in 'sysdeps' to use. Section C.4.2 [Porting the GNU C Library to Unix Systems], page 637, has some tips on porting the library to Unix variants.

C.4.1 Layout of the 'sysdeps' Directory Hierarchy

A GNU configuration name has three parts: the CPU type, the manufacturer's name, and the operating system. 'configure' uses these to pick the list of system-dependent directories to look for. If the '--nfp' option is *not* passed to 'configure', the directory '*machine*/fpu' is also used. The operating system often has a *base operating system*; for example, if the operating system is 'sunos4.1', the base operating system is 'unix/bsd'. The algorithm used to pick the list of directories is simple: 'configure' makes a list of the base operating system, manufacturer, CPU type, and operating system, in that order. It then concatenates all these together with slashes in between, to produce a directory name; for example, the configuration 'sparc-sun-sunos4.1' results in 'unix/bsd/sun/sparc/sunos4.1'. 'configure' then tries removing each element of the list in turn, so 'unix/bsd/sparc' and 'sun/sparc' are also tried, among others. Since the precise version number of the operating sys-

Appendix C: Library Maintenance 631

tem is often not important, and it would be very inconvenient, for example, to have identical 'sunos4.1.1' and 'sunos4.1.2' directories, 'configure' tries successively less specific operating system names by removing trailing suffixes starting with a period.

As an example, here is the complete list of directories that would be tried for the configuration 'sparc-sun-sunos4.1' (without the '--nfp' option):

```
sparc/fpu
unix/bsd/sun/sunos4.1/sparc
unix/bsd/sun/sunos4.1
unix/bsd/sun/sunos4/sparc
unix/bsd/sun/sunos4
unix/bsd/sun/sunos/sparc
unix/bsd/sun/sunos
unix/bsd/sun/sparc
unix/bsd/sun
unix/bsd/sunos4.1/sparc
unix/bsd/sunos4.1
unix/bsd/sunos4/sparc
unix/bsd/sunos4
unix/bsd/sunos/sparc
unix/bsd/sunos
unix/bsd/sparc
unix/bsd
unix/sun/sunos4.1/sparc
unix/sun/sunos4.1
unix/sun/sunos4/sparc
unix/sun/sunos4
unix/sun/sunos/sparc
unix/sun/sunos
unix/sun/sparc
unix/sun
unix/sunos4.1/sparc
unix/sunos4.1
unix/sunos4/sparc
unix/sunos4
unix/sunos/sparc
unix/sunos
unix/sparc
unix
sun/sunos4.1/sparc
sun/sunos4.1
sun/sunos4/sparc
sun/sunos4
sun/sunos/sparc
sun/sunos
sun/sparc
sun
sunos4.1/sparc
sunos4.1
sunos4/sparc
sunos4
sunos/sparc
```

```
sunos
sparc
```

Different machine architectures are conventionally subdirectories at the top level of the 'sysdeps' directory tree. For example, 'sysdeps/sparc' and 'sysdeps/m68k'. These contain files specific to those machine architectures, but not specific to any particular operating system. There might be subdirectories for specializations of those architectures, such as 'sysdeps/m68k/68020'. Code which is specific to the floating-point coprocessor used with a particular machine should go in 'sysdeps/*machine*/fpu'.

There are a few directories at the top level of the 'sysdeps' hierarchy that are not for particular machine architectures.

'generic'
'stub'   As described above (see Section C.4 [Porting the GNU C Library], page 631), these are the two subdirectories that every configuration implicitly uses after all others.

'ieee754' This directory is for code using the IEEE 754 floating-point format, where the C type `float` is IEEE 754 single-precision format, and `double` is IEEE 754 double-precision format. Usually this directory is referred to in the 'Implies' file in a machine architecture-specific directory, such as 'm68k/Implies'.

'posix' This directory contains implementations of things in the library in terms of POSIX.1 functions. This includes some of the POSIX.1 functions themselves. Of course, POSIX.1 cannot be completely implemented in terms of itself, so a configuration using just 'posix' cannot be complete.

'unix'   This is the directory for Unix-like things. See Section C.4.2 [Porting the GNU C Library to Unix Systems], page 637. 'unix' implies 'posix'. There are some special-purpose subdirectories of 'unix':

'unix/common'
   This directory is for things common to both BSD and System V release 4. Both 'unix/bsd' and 'unix/sysv/sysv4' imply 'unix/common'.

'unix/inet'
   This directory is for `socket` and related functions on Unix systems. The 'inet' top-level subdirectory is enabled by 'unix/inet/Subdirs'. 'unix/common' implies 'unix/inet'.

'mach'   This is the directory for things based on the Mach microkernel from CMU (including the GNU operating system). Other basic operating systems (VMS, for example) would have their own

Appendix C: Library Maintenance 633

directories at the top level of the 'sysdeps' hierarchy, parallel to 'unix' and 'mach'.

C.4.2 Porting the GNU C Library to Unix Systems

Most Unix systems are fundamentally very similar. There are variations between different machines, and variations in what facilities are provided by the kernel. But the interface to the operating system facilities is, for the most part, pretty uniform and simple.

The code for Unix systems is in the directory 'unix', at the top level of the 'sysdeps' hierarchy. This directory contains subdirectories (and subdirectory trees) for various Unix variants.

The functions which are system calls in most Unix systems are implemented in assembly code in files in 'sysdeps/unix'. These files are named with a suffix of '.S'; for example, '__open.S'. Files ending in '.S' are run through the C preprocessor before being fed to the assembler.

These files all use a set of macros that should be defined in 'sysdep.h'. The 'sysdep.h' file in 'sysdeps/unix' partially defines them; a 'sysdep.h' file in another directory must finish defining them for the particular machine and operating system variant. See 'sysdeps/unix/sysdep.h' and the machine-specific 'sysdep.h' implementations to see what these macros are and what they should do.

The system-specific makefile for the 'unix' directory (that is, the file 'sysdeps/unix/Makefile') gives rules to generate several files from the Unix system you are building the library on (which is assumed to be the target system you are building the library *for*). All the generated files are put in the directory where the object files are kept; they should not affect the source tree itself. The files generated are 'ioctls.h', 'errnos.h', 'sys/param.h', and 'errlist.c' (for the 'stdio' section of the library).

C.5 Contributors to the GNU C Library

The GNU C library was written originally by Roland McGrath. Some parts of the library were contributed or worked on by other people.

- The getopt function and related code were written by Richard Stallman, David J. MacKenzie, and Roland McGrath.
- The merge sort function qsort was written by Michael J. Haertel.
- The quick sort function used as a fallback by qsort was written by Douglas C. Schmidt.
- The memory allocation functions malloc, realloc and free and related code were written by Michael J. Haertel.

- Fast implementations of many of the string functions (`memcpy`, `strlen`, etc.) were written by Torbjörn Granlund.
- The '`tar.h`' header file was written by David J. MacKenzie.
- The port to the MIPS DECStation running Ultrix 4 (`mips-dec-ultrix4`) was contributed by Brendan Kehoe and Ian Lance Taylor.
- The DES encryption function `crypt` and related functions were contributed by Michael Glad.
- The `ftw` function was contributed by Ian Lance Taylor.
- The startup code to support SunOS shared libraries was contributed by Tom Quinn.
- The `mktime` function was contributed by Paul Eggert.
- The port to the Sequent Symmetry running Dynix version 3 (`i386-sequent-bsd`) was contributed by Jason Merrill.
- The timezone support code is derived from the public-domain timezone package by Arthur David Olson and his many contributors.
- The port to the DEC Alpha running OSF/1 (`alpha-dec-osf1`) was contributed by Brendan Kehoe, using some code written by Roland McGrath.
- The port to SGI machines running Irix 4 (`mips-sgi-irix4`) was contributed by Tom Quinn.
- The port of the Mach and Hurd code to the MIPS architecture (`mips-anything-gnu`) was contributed by Kazumoto Kojima.
- The floating-point printing function used by `printf` and friends and the floating-point reading function used by `scanf`, `strtod` and friends were written by Ulrich Drepper. The multi-precision integer functions used in those functions are taken from GNU MP, which was contributed by Torbjörn Granlund.
- The internationalization support in the library, and the support programs `locale` and `localedef`, were written by Ulrich Drepper. Ulrich Drepper adapted the support code for message catalogs ('`libintl.h`', etc.) from the GNU `gettext` package, which he also wrote. He also contributed the entire suite of multi-byte and wide-character support functions ('`wctype.h`', '`wchar.h`', etc.).
- The port to Linux i386/ELF (`i386-anything-linux`) was contributed by Ulrich Drepper, based in large part on work done in Hongjiu Lu's Linux version of the GNU C Library.
- The port to Linux/m68k (`m68k-anything-linux`) was contributed by Andreas Schwab.
- Stephen R. van den Berg contributed a highly-optimized `strstr` function.

Appendix C: Library Maintenance

- Ulrich Drepper contributed the `hsearch` and `drand48` families of functions; reentrant '..._r' versions of the `random` family; System V shared memory and IPC support code; and several highly-optimized string functions for ix86 processors.
- The math functions are taken from `fdlibm-5.1` by Sun Microsystems, as modified by J.T. Conklin and Ian Lance Taylor.
- The Internet-related code (most of the 'inet' subdirectory) and several other miscellaneous functions and header files have been included from 4.4 BSD with little or no modification.

All code incorporated from 4.4 BSD is under the following copyright:

> Copyright © 1991 Regents of the University of California. All rights reserved.

Redistribution and use in source and binary forms, with or without modification, are permitted provided that the following conditions are met:

1. Redistributions of source code must retain the above copyright notice, this list of conditions and the following disclaimer.
2. Redistributions in binary form must reproduce the above copyright notice, this list of conditions and the following disclaimer in the documentation and/or other materials provided with the distribution.
3. All advertising materials mentioning features or use of this software must display the following acknowledgement:

   > This product includes software developed by the University of California, Berkeley and its contributors.

4. Neither the name of the University nor the names of its contributors may be used to endorse or promote products derived from this software without specific prior written permission.

THIS SOFTWARE IS PROVIDED BY THE REGENTS AND CONTRIBUTORS "AS IS" AND ANY EXPRESS OR IMPLIED WARRANTIES, INCLUDING, BUT NOT LIMITED TO, THE IMPLIED WARRANTIES OF MERCHANTABILITY AND FITNESS FOR A PARTICULAR PURPOSE ARE DISCLAIMED. IN NO EVENT SHALL THE REGENTS OR CONTRIBUTORS BE LIABLE FOR ANY DIRECT, INDIRECT, INCIDENTAL, SPECIAL, EXEMPLARY, OR CONSEQUENTIAL DAMAGES (INCLUDING, BUT NOT LIMITED TO, PROCUREMENT OF SUBSTITUTE GOODS OR SERVICES;

LOSS OF USE, DATA, OR PROFITS; OR BUSINESS INTERRUPTION) HOWEVER CAUSED AND ON ANY THEORY OF LIABILITY, WHETHER IN CONTRACT, STRICT LIABILITY, OR TORT (INCLUDING NEGLIGENCE OR OTHERWISE) ARISING IN ANY WAY OUT OF THE USE OF THIS SOFTWARE, EVEN IF ADVISED OF THE POSSIBILITY OF SUCH DAMAGE.

- The random number generation functions `random`, `srandom`, `setstate` and `initstate`, which are also the basis for the `rand` and `srand` functions, were written by Earl T. Cohen for the University of California at Berkeley and are copyrighted by the Regents of the University of California. They have undergone minor changes to fit into the GNU C library and to fit the ANSI C standard, but the functional code is Berkeley's.

- The Internet resolver code is taken directly from BIND 4.9.3, which is under both the Berkeley copyright above and also:

  Portions Copyright © 1993 by Digital Equipment Corporation.

  Permission to use, copy, modify, and distribute this software for any purpose with or without fee is hereby granted, provided that the above copyright notice and this permission notice appear in all copies, and that the name of Digital Equipment Corporation not be used in advertising or publicity pertaining to distribution of the document or software without specific, written prior permission.

  THE SOFTWARE IS PROVIDED "AS IS" AND DIGITAL EQUIPMENT CORP. DISCLAIMS ALL WARRANTIES WITH REGARD TO THIS SOFTWARE, INCLUDING ALL IMPLIED WARRANTIES OF MERCHANTABILITY AND FITNESS. IN NO EVENT SHALL DIGITAL EQUIPMENT CORPORATION BE LIABLE FOR ANY SPECIAL, DIRECT, INDIRECT, OR CONSEQUENTIAL DAMAGES OR ANY DAMAGES WHATSOEVER RESULTING FROM LOSS OF USE, DATA OR PROFITS, WHETHER IN AN ACTION OF CONTRACT, NEGLIGENCE OR OTHER TORTIOUS ACTION, ARISING OUT OF OR IN CONNECTION WITH THE USE OR PERFORMANCE OF THIS SOFTWARE.

- The code to support Sun RPC is taken verbatim from Sun's RPCSRC-4.0 distribution, and is covered by this copyright:

  Copyright © 1984, Sun Microsystems, Inc.

  Sun RPC is a product of Sun Microsystems, Inc. and is provided for unrestricted use provided that this legend is included on all tape media and as a part of the software program in whole or part. Users may copy or modify Sun RPC without charge, but are not authorized to license or distribute it to

Appendix C: Library Maintenance

anyone else except as part of a product or program developed by the user.

SUN RPC IS PROVIDED AS IS WITH NO WARRANTIES OF ANY KIND INCLUDING THE WARRANTIES OF DESIGN, MERCHANTIBILITY AND FITNESS FOR A PARTICULAR PURPOSE, OR ARISING FROM A COURSE OF DEALING, USAGE OR TRADE PRACTICE.

Sun RPC is provided with no support and without any obligation on the part of Sun Microsystems, Inc. to assist in its use, correction, modification or enhancement.

SUN MICROSYSTEMS, INC. SHALL HAVE NO LIABILITY WITH RESPECT TO THE INFRINGEMENT OF COPYRIGHTS, TRADE SECRETS OR ANY PATENTS BY SUN RPC OR ANY PART THEREOF.

In no event will Sun Microsystems, Inc. be liable for any lost revenue or profits or other special, indirect and consequential damages, even if Sun has been advised of the possibility of such damages.

> Sun Microsystems, Inc.
> 2550 Garcia Avenue
> Mountain View, California 94043

- Some of the support code for Mach is taken from Mach 3.0 by CMU, and is under the following copyright terms:

  > Mach Operating System
  > Copyright © 1991,1990,1989 Carnegie Mellon University
  > All Rights Reserved.

  Permission to use, copy, modify and distribute this software and its documentation is hereby granted, provided that both the copyright notice and this permission notice appear in all copies of the software, derivative works or modified versions, and any portions thereof, and that both notices appear in supporting documentation.

  CARNEGIE MELLON ALLOWS FREE USE OF THIS SOFTWARE IN ITS "AS IS" CONDITION. CARNEGIE MELLON DISCLAIMS ANY LIABILITY OF ANY KIND FOR ANY DAMAGES WHATSOEVER RESULTING FROM THE USE OF THIS SOFTWARE.

  Carnegie Mellon requests users of this software to return to

  > Software Distribution Coordinator
  > School of Computer Science
  > Carnegie Mellon University
  > Pittsburgh PA 15213-3890

or '`Software.Distribution@CS.CMU.EDU`' any improvements or extensions that they make and grant Carnegie Mellon the rights to redistribute these changes.

Appendix D GNU LIBRARY GENERAL PUBLIC LICENSE

Version 2, June 1991

Copyright © 1991 Free Software Foundation, Inc.
675 Mass Ave, Cambridge, MA 02139, USA
Everyone is permitted to copy and distribute verbatim copies
of this license document, but changing it is not allowed.

[This is the first released version of the library GPL. It is
numbered 2 because it goes with version 2 of the ordinary GPL.]

Preamble

The licenses for most software are designed to take away your freedom to share and change it. By contrast, the GNU General Public Licenses are intended to guarantee your freedom to share and change free software—to make sure the software is free for all its users.

This license, the Library General Public License, applies to some specially designated Free Software Foundation software, and to any other libraries whose authors decide to use it. You can use it for your libraries, too.

When we speak of free software, we are referring to freedom, not price. Our General Public Licenses are designed to make sure that you have the freedom to distribute copies of free software (and charge for this service if you wish), that you receive source code or can get it if you want it, that you can change the software or use pieces of it in new free programs; and that you know you can do these things.

To protect your rights, we need to make restrictions that forbid anyone to deny you these rights or to ask you to surrender the rights. These restrictions translate to certain responsibilities for you if you distribute copies of the library, or if you modify it.

For example, if you distribute copies of the library, whether gratis or for a fee, you must give the recipients all the rights that we gave you. You must make sure that they, too, receive or can get the source code. If you link a program with the library, you must provide complete object files to the recipients so that they can relink them with the library, after making changes to the library and recompiling it. And you must show them these terms so they know their rights.

Our method of protecting your rights has two steps: (1) copyright the library, and (2) offer you this license which gives you legal permission to copy, distribute and/or modify the library.

Also, for each distributor's protection, we want to make certain that everyone understands that there is no warranty for this free library. If the library is modified by someone else and passed on, we want its recipients to know that what they have is not the original version, so that any problems introduced by others will not reflect on the original authors' reputations.

Finally, any free program is threatened constantly by software patents. We wish to avoid the danger that companies distributing free software will individually obtain patent licenses, thus in effect transforming the program into proprietary software. To prevent this, we have made it clear that any patent must be licensed for everyone's free use or not licensed at all.

Most GNU software, including some libraries, is covered by the ordinary GNU General Public License, which was designed for utility programs. This license, the GNU Library General Public License, applies to certain designated libraries. This license is quite different from the ordinary one; be sure to read it in full, and don't assume that anything in it is the same as in the ordinary license.

The reason we have a separate public license for some libraries is that they blur the distinction we usually make between modifying or adding to a program and simply using it. Linking a program with a library, without changing the library, is in some sense simply using the library, and is analogous to running a utility program or application program. However, in a textual and legal sense, the linked executable is a combined work, a derivative of the original library, and the ordinary General Public License treats it as such.

Because of this blurred distinction, using the ordinary General Public License for libraries did not effectively promote software sharing, because most developers did not use the libraries. We concluded that weaker conditions might promote sharing better.

However, unrestricted linking of non-free programs would deprive the users of those programs of all benefit from the free status of the libraries themselves. This Library General Public License is intended to permit developers of non-free programs to use free libraries, while preserving your freedom as a user of such programs to change the free libraries that are incorporated in them. (We have not seen how to achieve this as regards changes in header files, but we have achieved it as regards changes in the actual functions of the Library.) The hope is that this will lead to faster development of free libraries.

The precise terms and conditions for copying, distribution and modification follow. Pay close attention to the difference between a "work based on the library" and a "work that uses the library". The former contains code derived from the library, while the latter only works together with the library.

Appendix D: GNU LIBRARY GENERAL PUBLIC LICENSE

Note that it is possible for a library to be covered by the ordinary General Public License rather than by this special one.

TERMS AND CONDITIONS FOR COPYING, DISTRIBUTION AND MODIFICATION

0. This License Agreement applies to any software library which contains a notice placed by the copyright holder or other authorized party saying it may be distributed under the terms of this Library General Public License (also called "this License"). Each licensee is addressed as "you".

   A "library" means a collection of software functions and/or data prepared so as to be conveniently linked with application programs (which use some of those functions and data) to form executables.

   The "Library", below, refers to any such software library or work which has been distributed under these terms. A "work based on the Library" means either the Library or any derivative work under copyright law: that is to say, a work containing the Library or a portion of it, either verbatim or with modifications and/or translated straightforwardly into another language. (Hereinafter, translation is included without limitation in the term "modification".)

   "Source code" for a work means the preferred form of the work for making modifications to it. For a library, complete source code means all the source code for all modules it contains, plus any associated interface definition files, plus the scripts used to control compilation and installation of the library.

   Activities other than copying, distribution and modification are not covered by this License; they are outside its scope. The act of running a program using the Library is not restricted, and output from such a program is covered only if its contents constitute a work based on the Library (independent of the use of the Library in a tool for writing it). Whether that is true depends on what the Library does and what the program that uses the Library does.

1. You may copy and distribute verbatim copies of the Library's complete source code as you receive it, in any medium, provided that you conspicuously and appropriately publish on each copy an appropriate copyright notice and disclaimer of warranty; keep intact all the notices that refer to this License and to the absence of any warranty; and distribute a copy of this License along with the Library.

   You may charge a fee for the physical act of transferring a copy, and you may at your option offer warranty protection in exchange for a fee.

2. You may modify your copy or copies of the Library or any portion of it, thus forming a work based on the Library, and copy and distribute such

modifications or work under the terms of Section 1 above, provided that you also meet all of these conditions:

a. The modified work must itself be a software library.

b. You must cause the files modified to carry prominent notices stating that you changed the files and the date of any change.

c. You must cause the whole of the work to be licensed at no charge to all third parties under the terms of this License.

d. If a facility in the modified Library refers to a function or a table of data to be supplied by an application program that uses the facility, other than as an argument passed when the facility is invoked, then you must make a good faith effort to ensure that, in the event an application does not supply such function or table, the facility still operates, and performs whatever part of its purpose remains meaningful.

(For example, a function in a library to compute square roots has a purpose that is entirely well-defined independent of the application. Therefore, Subsection 2d requires that any application-supplied function or table used by this function must be optional: if the application does not supply it, the square root function must still compute square roots.)

These requirements apply to the modified work as a whole. If identifiable sections of that work are not derived from the Library, and can be reasonably considered independent and separate works in themselves, then this License, and its terms, do not apply to those sections when you distribute them as separate works. But when you distribute the same sections as part of a whole which is a work based on the Library, the distribution of the whole must be on the terms of this License, whose permissions for other licensees extend to the entire whole, and thus to each and every part regardless of who wrote it.

Thus, it is not the intent of this section to claim rights or contest your rights to work written entirely by you; rather, the intent is to exercise the right to control the distribution of derivative or collective works based on the Library.

In addition, mere aggregation of another work not based on the Library with the Library (or with a work based on the Library) on a volume of a storage or distribution medium does not bring the other work under the scope of this License.

3. You may opt to apply the terms of the ordinary GNU General Public License instead of this License to a given copy of the Library. To do this, you must alter all the notices that refer to this License, so that they refer to the ordinary GNU General Public License, version 2, instead of to this License. (If a newer version than version 2 of the ordinary GNU

Appendix D: GNU LIBRARY GENERAL PUBLIC LICENSE   643

General Public License has appeared, then you can specify that version instead if you wish.) Do not make any other change in these notices.

Once this change is made in a given copy, it is irreversible for that copy, so the ordinary GNU General Public License applies to all subsequent copies and derivative works made from that copy.

This option is useful when you wish to copy part of the code of the Library into a program that is not a library.

4. You may copy and distribute the Library (or a portion or derivative of it, under Section 2) in object code or executable form under the terms of Sections 1 and 2 above provided that you accompany it with the complete corresponding machine-readable source code, which must be distributed under the terms of Sections 1 and 2 above on a medium customarily used for software interchange.

   If distribution of object code is made by offering access to copy from a designated place, then offering equivalent access to copy the source code from the same place satisfies the requirement to distribute the source code, even though third parties are not compelled to copy the source along with the object code.

5. A program that contains no derivative of any portion of the Library, but is designed to work with the Library by being compiled or linked with it, is called a "work that uses the Library". Such a work, in isolation, is not a derivative work of the Library, and therefore falls outside the scope of this License.

   However, linking a "work that uses the Library" with the Library creates an executable that is a derivative of the Library (because it contains portions of the Library), rather than a "work that uses the library". The executable is therefore covered by this License. Section 6 states terms for distribution of such executables.

   When a "work that uses the Library" uses material from a header file that is part of the Library, the object code for the work may be a derivative work of the Library even though the source code is not. Whether this is true is especially significant if the work can be linked without the Library, or if the work is itself a library. The threshold for this to be true is not precisely defined by law.

   If such an object file uses only numerical parameters, data structure layouts and accessors, and small macros and small inline functions (ten lines or less in length), then the use of the object file is unrestricted, regardless of whether it is legally a derivative work. (Executables containing this object code plus portions of the Library will still fall under Section 6.)

   Otherwise, if the work is a derivative of the Library, you may distribute the object code for the work under the terms of Section 6. Any executables containing that work also fall under Section 6, whether or not they are linked directly with the Library itself.

6. As an exception to the Sections above, you may also compile or link a "work that uses the Library" with the Library to produce a work containing portions of the Library, and distribute that work under terms of your choice, provided that the terms permit modification of the work for the customer's own use and reverse engineering for debugging such modifications.

You must give prominent notice with each copy of the work that the Library is used in it and that the Library and its use are covered by this License. You must supply a copy of this License. If the work during execution displays copyright notices, you must include the copyright notice for the Library among them, as well as a reference directing the user to the copy of this License. Also, you must do one of these things:

    a. Accompany the work with the complete corresponding machine-readable source code for the Library including whatever changes were used in the work (which must be distributed under Sections 1 and 2 above); and, if the work is an executable linked with the Library, with the complete machine-readable "work that uses the Library", as object code and/or source code, so that the user can modify the Library and then relink to produce a modified executable containing the modified Library. (It is understood that the user who changes the contents of definitions files in the Library will not necessarily be able to recompile the application to use the modified definitions.)

    b. Accompany the work with a written offer, valid for at least three years, to give the same user the materials specified in Subsection 6a, above, for a charge no more than the cost of performing this distribution.

    c. If distribution of the work is made by offering access to copy from a designated place, offer equivalent access to copy the above specified materials from the same place.

    d. Verify that the user has already received a copy of these materials or that you have already sent this user a copy.

For an executable, the required form of the "work that uses the Library" must include any data and utility programs needed for reproducing the executable from it. However, as a special exception, the source code distributed need not include anything that is normally distributed (in either source or binary form) with the major components (compiler, kernel, and so on) of the operating system on which the executable runs, unless that component itself accompanies the executable.

It may happen that this requirement contradicts the license restrictions of other proprietary libraries that do not normally accompany the op-

Appendix D: GNU LIBRARY GENERAL PUBLIC LICENSE 645

erating system. Such a contradiction means you cannot use both them and the Library together in an executable that you distribute.

7. You may place library facilities that are a work based on the Library side-by-side in a single library together with other library facilities not covered by this License, and distribute such a combined library, provided that the separate distribution of the work based on the Library and of the other library facilities is otherwise permitted, and provided that you do these two things:
   a. Accompany the combined library with a copy of the same work based on the Library, uncombined with any other library facilities. This must be distributed under the terms of the Sections above.
   b. Give prominent notice with the combined library of the fact that part of it is a work based on the Library, and explaining where to find the accompanying uncombined form of the same work.

8. You may not copy, modify, sublicense, link with, or distribute the Library except as expressly provided under this License. Any attempt otherwise to copy, modify, sublicense, link with, or distribute the Library is void, and will automatically terminate your rights under this License. However, parties who have received copies, or rights, from you under this License will not have their licenses terminated so long as such parties remain in full compliance.

9. You are not required to accept this License, since you have not signed it. However, nothing else grants you permission to modify or distribute the Library or its derivative works. These actions are prohibited by law if you do not accept this License. Therefore, by modifying or distributing the Library (or any work based on the Library), you indicate your acceptance of this License to do so, and all its terms and conditions for copying, distributing or modifying the Library or works based on it.

10. Each time you redistribute the Library (or any work based on the Library), the recipient automatically receives a license from the original licensor to copy, distribute, link with or modify the Library subject to these terms and conditions. You may not impose any further restrictions on the recipients' exercise of the rights granted herein. You are not responsible for enforcing compliance by third parties to this License.

11. If, as a consequence of a court judgment or allegation of patent infringement or for any other reason (not limited to patent issues), conditions are imposed on you (whether by court order, agreement or otherwise) that contradict the conditions of this License, they do not excuse you from the conditions of this License. If you cannot distribute so as to satisfy simultaneously your obligations under this License and any other pertinent obligations, then as a consequence you may not distribute the Library at all. For example, if a patent license would not permit royalty-free redistribution of the Library by all those who receive copies directly

or indirectly through you, then the only way you could satisfy both it and this License would be to refrain entirely from distribution of the Library.

If any portion of this section is held invalid or unenforceable under any particular circumstance, the balance of the section is intended to apply, and the section as a whole is intended to apply in other circumstances.

It is not the purpose of this section to induce you to infringe any patents or other property right claims or to contest validity of any such claims; this section has the sole purpose of protecting the integrity of the free software distribution system which is implemented by public license practices. Many people have made generous contributions to the wide range of software distributed through that system in reliance on consistent application of that system; it is up to the author/donor to decide if he or she is willing to distribute software through any other system and a licensee cannot impose that choice.

This section is intended to make thoroughly clear what is believed to be a consequence of the rest of this License.

12. If the distribution and/or use of the Library is restricted in certain countries either by patents or by copyrighted interfaces, the original copyright holder who places the Library under this License may add an explicit geographical distribution limitation excluding those countries, so that distribution is permitted only in or among countries not thus excluded. In such case, this License incorporates the limitation as if written in the body of this License.

13. The Free Software Foundation may publish revised and/or new versions of the Library General Public License from time to time. Such new versions will be similar in spirit to the present version, but may differ in detail to address new problems or concerns.

    Each version is given a distinguishing version number. If the Library specifies a version number of this License which applies to it and "any later version", you have the option of following the terms and conditions either of that version or of any later version published by the Free Software Foundation. If the Library does not specify a license version number, you may choose any version ever published by the Free Software Foundation.

14. If you wish to incorporate parts of the Library into other free programs whose distribution conditions are incompatible with these, write to the author to ask for permission. For software which is copyrighted by the Free Software Foundation, write to the Free Software Foundation; we sometimes make exceptions for this. Our decision will be guided by the two goals of preserving the free status of all derivatives of our free software and of promoting the sharing and reuse of software generally.

Appendix D: GNU LIBRARY GENERAL PUBLIC LICENSE

NO WARRANTY

15. BECAUSE THE LIBRARY IS LICENSED FREE OF CHARGE, THERE IS NO WARRANTY FOR THE LIBRARY, TO THE EXTENT PERMITTED BY APPLICABLE LAW. EXCEPT WHEN OTHERWISE STATED IN WRITING THE COPYRIGHT HOLDERS AND/OR OTHER PARTIES PROVIDE THE LIBRARY "AS IS" WITHOUT WARRANTY OF ANY KIND, EITHER EXPRESSED OR IMPLIED, INCLUDING, BUT NOT LIMITED TO, THE IMPLIED WARRANTIES OF MERCHANTABILITY AND FITNESS FOR A PARTICULAR PURPOSE. THE ENTIRE RISK AS TO THE QUALITY AND PERFORMANCE OF THE LIBRARY IS WITH YOU. SHOULD THE LIBRARY PROVE DEFECTIVE, YOU ASSUME THE COST OF ALL NECESSARY SERVICING, REPAIR OR CORRECTION.

16. IN NO EVENT UNLESS REQUIRED BY APPLICABLE LAW OR AGREED TO IN WRITING WILL ANY COPYRIGHT HOLDER, OR ANY OTHER PARTY WHO MAY MODIFY AND/OR REDISTRIBUTE THE LIBRARY AS PERMITTED ABOVE, BE LIABLE TO YOU FOR DAMAGES, INCLUDING ANY GENERAL, SPECIAL, INCIDENTAL OR CONSEQUENTIAL DAMAGES ARISING OUT OF THE USE OR INABILITY TO USE THE LIBRARY (INCLUDING BUT NOT LIMITED TO LOSS OF DATA OR DATA BEING RENDERED INACCURATE OR LOSSES SUSTAINED BY YOU OR THIRD PARTIES OR A FAILURE OF THE LIBRARY TO OPERATE WITH ANY OTHER SOFTWARE), EVEN IF SUCH HOLDER OR OTHER PARTY HAS BEEN ADVISED OF THE POSSIBILITY OF SUCH DAMAGES.

END OF TERMS AND CONDITIONS

How to Apply These Terms to Your New Libraries

If you develop a new library, and you want it to be of the greatest possible use to the public, we recommend making it free software that everyone can redistribute and change. You can do so by permitting redistribution under these terms (or, alternatively, under the terms of the ordinary General Public License).

To apply these terms, attach the following notices to the library. It is safest to attach them to the start of each source file to most effectively convey the exclusion of warranty; and each file should have at least the "copyright" line and a pointer to where the full notice is found.

```
one line to give the library's name and an idea of what it does.
Copyright (C) year   name of author

This library is free software; you can redistribute it and/or modify it
under the terms of the GNU Library General Public License as published
by the Free Software Foundation; either version 2 of the License, or (at
your option) any later version.

This library is distributed in the hope that it will be useful, but
WITHOUT ANY WARRANTY; without even the implied warranty of
MERCHANTABILITY or FITNESS FOR A PARTICULAR PURPOSE.  See the GNU
Library General Public License for more details.

You should have received a copy of the GNU Library General Public
License along with this library; if not, write to the Free Software
Foundation, Inc., 675 Mass Ave, Cambridge, MA 02139, USA.
```

Also add information on how to contact you by electronic and paper mail.

You should also get your employer (if you work as a programmer) or your school, if any, to sign a "copyright disclaimer" for the library, if necessary. Here is a sample; alter the names:

```
Yoyodyne, Inc., hereby disclaims all copyright interest in the library
'Frob' (a library for tweaking knobs) written by James Random Hacker.
```

signature of Ty Coon, 1 April 1990
`Ty Coon, President of Vice`

That's all there is to it!

Concept Index

–
_POSIX_OPTION_ORDER environment variable 437

4
4.n BSD Unix 3

A
abort signal 376
aborting a program 440
absolute file name 78
absolute value functions 290
accepting connections 233
access permission for a file 190
access, testing for 192
accessing directories 171
address of socket 209
alarm signal 379
alarms, setting 335
alignment (in obstacks) 46
alignment (with `malloc`) 33
`alloca` disadvantages 51
`alloca` function 49
allocation (obstacks) 40
allocation hooks, for `malloc` 35
allocation of memory with `malloc` 28
allocation size of string 60
allocation statistics 36
alphabetic character 55
alphanumeric character 56
ANSI C 2
append-access files 77
argc (program argument count) 425
argument promotion 520
arguments (variadic functions) 518
arguments, how many 519
arguments, to program 425
argv (program argument vector) 425
arithmetic expansion 316
array comparison functions 65
array copy functions 61
array search function 299

array sort function 300
ASCII character 57
assertions 515
attributes of a file 181
automatic allocation 27
automatic freeing 49
automatic storage with variable size ... 49

B
background job 458
background job, launching 468
base (of floating point number) 527
basic byte sequence 346
baud rate 268
Berkeley Unix 3
bias (of floating point number exponent)
.... 527
big-endian 224
binary I/O to a stream 93
binary search function (for arrays) 299
binary stream 125
binding a socket address 209
blank character 56
block I/O to a stream 93
blocked signals 372
blocked signals, checking for 413
blocking signals 408
blocking signals, in a handler 412
break condition, detecting 262
break condition, generating 277
breaking a string into tokens 72
broken pipe signal 382
broken-down time 323, 327
BSD compatibility library 475
BSD compatibility library 9
BSD Unix 3
buffering of streams 129
buffering, controlling 131
bugs, reporting 629
bus error 376
byte order conversion, for socket 224
byte stream 207

C

calendar time 323
calendar time and broken-down time
    327
calling variadic functions 520
canonical input processing............ 256
capacity limits, POSIX............... 499
carrier detect 264
case conversion of characters 57
catching signals...................... 373
categories for locales 358
change working directory............. 169
changing the locale................... 359
changing the size of a block (`malloc`).. 31
changing the size of a block (obstacks)
    42
channels............................. 148
character case conversion.............. 57
character code 349
character predicates.................. 55
character testing 55
checking for pending signals.......... 413
child process 443, 444
child process signal................... 380
chunks............................... 47
classification of characters 55
cleaning up a stream 148
clearing terminal input queue 278
client 230
clock ticks 321
close-on-exec (file descriptor flag)..... 157
closing a file descriptor............... 139
closing a socket 229
closing a stream...................... 86
code, character...................... 349
collating strings...................... 67
combining locales 358
command argument syntax........... 426
command arguments, parsing......... 427
command line arguments............. 425
command substitution 316
communication style (of a socket) 207
comparing strings and arrays.......... 65
Comparison Function 299
concatenating strings.................. 61
configurations, all supported 628
connecting a socket 231
connection 230

consistency checking 515
consistency checking, of heap.......... 33
continue signal....................... 380
control character..................... 56
control operations on files............ 153
controlling process 459
controlling terminal.................. 458
controlling terminal, access to 459
controlling terminal, determining..... 474
controlling terminal, setting.......... 160
conversion specifications (`printf`) 95
conversion specifications (`scanf`) 116
converting byte order 224
converting case of characters 57
converting extended characters....... 352
converting extended strings 350
converting file descriptor to stream ... 147
converting floats to integers 292
converting group ID to group name... 492
converting group name to group ID... 492
converting host address to name...... 219
converting host name to address...... 219
converting network name to network
    number........................... 252
converting network number to network
    name............................ 252
converting port number to service name
    222
converting service name to port number
    222
converting string to collation order 68
converting strings to numbers 294
converting user ID to user name...... 490
converting user name to user ID...... 490
cookie, for custom stream 136
copying strings and arrays............ 61
CPU time........................... 321
create on open (file status flag)....... 160
creating a directory 180
creating a FIFO special file........... 204
creating a pipe....................... 201
creating a pipe to a subprocess....... 203
creating a process.................... 444
creating a socket 228
creating a socket pair 229
creating special files.................. 196
cube root function 284
currency symbols 363

Concept Index

current working directory 169
custom streams 136
customizing `printf` 110

D

data loss on sockets 207
datagram socket 243
datagrams, transmitting 244
date and time 323
Daylight Saving Time 328
decimal digit character 55
decimal-point separator 362
declaration (compared to definition) 4
declaring variadic functions 520
default action (for a signal) 373
default action for a signal 385
default argument promotions 520
defining new `printf` conversions 110
definition (compared to declaration) 4
delayed suspend character 273
deleting a directory 178
deleting a file 178
delivery of signals 372
descriptors and streams 148
digit character 55
directories, accessing 171
directories, creating 180
directories, deleting 178
directory 78
directory entry 78
directory stream 171
disadvantages of `alloca` 51
DISCARD character 275
domain (of socket) 207
domain error 281
dot notation, for Internet addresses ... 217
DSUSP character 273
duplicating file descriptors 154
dynamic allocation 27

E

echo of terminal input 266
effective group ID 479
effective user ID 479
efficiency and `malloc` 32
efficiency and obstacks 44
efficiency of chunks 47

EINTR, and restarting interrupted
  primitives 403
end of file, on a stream 124
end-of-file, on a file descriptor 141
environment 434
environment access 434
environment representation 434
environment variable 433
EOF character 271
EOL character 271
EOL2 character 271
epoch 324
ERASE character 271
error codes 13
error reporting 13
establishing a handler 384
exception 375
exclusive lock 164
`exec` functions 446
executing a file 446
exit status 437
exit status value 437
expansion of shell words 315
exponent (of floating point number) .. 527
exponentiation functions 283
extended character sets 345
extended characters, converting 352
extended strings, converting
  representations 350
extending `printf` 110
extracting file descriptor from stream
  147

F

`fcntl` function 153
feature test macros 8
field splitting 316
FIFO special file 201
file access permission 190
file access time 194
file attribute modification time 194
file attributes 181
file creation mask 190
file descriptor flags 156
file descriptor sets, for `select` 150
file descriptors, standard 147
file locks 164
file modification time 194

file name 77
file name component 78
file name errors 79
file name resolution 78
file name translation flags 159
file names, multiple 175
file namespace, for sockets............ 212
file owner 186
file permission bits 188
file pointer 83
file position 77
file positioning on a file descriptor 145
file positioning on a stream........... 126
file status flags 158
filtering i/o through subprocess....... 203
flag character (`printf`) 96
flag character (`scanf`) 117
flags for `sigaction`................... 389
flags, file name translation 159
flags, open-time action 159
floating point, IEEE 531
floating type measurements 526
floating-point exception 375
flow control, terminal 278
flushing a stream..................... 130
flushing terminal output queue 277
foreground job 458
foreground job, launching 467
forking a process..................... 444
format string, for `printf` 94
format string, for `scanf` 115
formatted input from a stream 115
formatted output to a stream.......... 94
freeing (obstacks) 41
freeing memory allocated with `malloc`
  30
fully buffered stream 129
function prototypes (variadic) 517

G

generation of signals 372
globbing.............................. 306
graphic character..................... 56
Gregorian calendar................... 323
group database 491
group ID............................. 479
group name........................... 479
group owner of a file 186

grouping of digits 362
growing objects (in obstacks).......... 42

H

handle 52
handling multiple signals............. 395
hangup signal 378
hard limit............................ 342
hard link............................. 175
header files........................... 4
heap consistency checking 33
heap, dynamic allocation from......... 28
heap, freeing memory from 30
hexadecimal digit character 56
hidden bit (of floating point number
  mantissa)......................... 527
high-priority data.................... 241
high-resolution time.................. 323
holes in files 145
home directory....................... 435
HOME environment variable 435
hook functions (of custom streams)... 137
host address, Internet 216
hosts database 219
how many arguments 519
hyperbolic functions.................. 285

I

identifying terminals 255
IEEE floating point 289
IEEE floating point representation ... 531
IEEE Std 1003.1 2
IEEE Std 1003.2 2
ignore action for a signal 385
illegal instruction 376
impossible events 515
independent channels 149
initial signal actions.................. 390
inode number 183
input available signal................. 379
input conversions, for `scanf` 118
input from multiple files.............. 150
installation tools 627
installing the library 625
integer division functions............. 293
integer type range.................... 525
integer type width 524

Concept Index 653

interactive signals, from terminal 267
interactive stop signal 381
internationalization 357
Internet host address 216
Internet namespace, for sockets 215
interprocess communication, with FIFO
   204
interprocess communication, with pipes
   201
interprocess communication, with signals
   407
interprocess communication, with sockets
   207
interrupt character 272
interrupt signal 377
interrupt-driven input 167
interrupting primitives 403
interval timer, setting 335
INTR character 272
inverse hyperbolic functions 285
inverse trigonmetric functions 282
invocation of program 425

J

job 457
job control 457
job control functions 474
job control is optional 458
job control signals 380
job control, enabling 462

K

Kermit the frog 302
KILL character 272
kill signal 378
killing a process 405

L

LANG environment variable 436
launching jobs 464
LC_COLLATE environment variable
   436
LC_CTYPE environment variable 436
LC_MONETARY environment variable
   436
LC_NUMERIC environment variable
   436

LC_TIME environment variable 436
leap second 327
length of multibyte character 351
length of string 60
level, for socket options 249
library 1
limits on resource usage 341
limits, file name length 507
limits, floating types 526
limits, integer types 525
limits, link count of files 507
limits, number of open files 499
limits, number of processes 499
limits, number of supplementary group
   IDs 500
limits, pipe buffer size 507
limits, POSIX 499
limits, program argument size 499
limits, terminal input queue 507
limits, time zone name length 500
line buffered stream 129
line speed 268
lines (in a text file) 125
link 78
link, hard 175
link, soft 176
link, symbolic 176
linked channels 148
listening (sockets) 232
little-endian 224
LNEXT character 274
local network address number 216
local time 323
locale categories 358
locale, changing 359
locales 357
logarithm functions 283
login name 479
login name, determining 488
LOGNAME environment variable 435
long jumps 367
long-named options 426
longjmp 51
loss of data on sockets 207
lost resource signal 382
lower-case character 55

M

macros	41
`main` function	425
`malloc` function	28
mantissa (of floating point number)	527
matching failure, in `scanf`	116
maximum field width (`scanf`)	117
measurements of floating types	526
memory allocation	27
memory usage warnings	53
merging of signals	395
MIN termios slot	275
minimum field width (`printf`)	96
mixing descriptors and streams	148
modem disconnect	264
modem status lines	264
monetary value formatting	361
multibyte character, length of	351
multibyte characters	346
multiple names for one file	175
multiplexing input	150

N

name of running program	24
name of socket	209
name space	6
names of signals	373
namespace (of socket)	207
NaN	289
network byte order	224
network number	216
network protocol	208
networks database	252
non-blocking open	160
non-local exit, from signal handler	393
non-local exits	367
noncanonical input processing	256
normalization functions (floating-point)	291
normalized floating point number	528
not a number	289
null character	59
null pointer constant	523
number of arguments passed	519
number syntax, parsing	294
numeric value formatting	361

O

obstack status	45
obstacks	38
open-time action flags	159
opening a file	75
opening a file descriptor	139
opening a pipe	201
opening a socket	228
opening a socket pair	229
opening a stream	84
optional arguments	516
optional POSIX features	500
orphaned process group	459
out-of-band data	241
output conversions, for `printf`	97
output possible signal	379
owner of a file	186

P

packet	207
page boundary	33
parent directory	79
parent process	443, 444
parity checking	261
parsing a template string	107
parsing numbers (in formatted input)	294
parsing program arguments	427
parsing tokens from a string	72
password database	489
PATH environment variable	435
`pause` function	416
peeking at input	91
pending signals	372
pending signals, checking for	413
permission to access a file	190
persona	479
pi (trigonometric constant)	282
pipe	201
pipe signal	382
pipe to a subprocess	203
port number	221
positioning a file descriptor	145
positioning a stream	126
POSIX	2
POSIX capacity limits	499
POSIX optional features	500
POSIX.1	2

Concept Index

POSIX.2 2
power functions 283
precision (of floating point number) .. 527
precision (`printf`) 96
predicates on arrays 65
predicates on characters 55
predicates on strings 65
primitives, interrupting 403
printing character 56
priority of a process 343
process 425, 443
process completion 449
process group functions 474
process group ID 464
process group leader 464
process groups 457
process ID 444
process image 444
process lifetime 444
process priority 343
process signal mask 410
process termination 437
processor time 321
profiling alarm signal 379
profiling timer 336
program argument syntax 426
program arguments 425
program arguments, parsing 427
program error signals 374
program name 24
program startup 425
program termination 437
program termination signals 377
programming your own streams 136
protocol (of socket) 208
protocol family 208
protocols database 225
prototypes for variadic functions 517
pseudo-random numbers 285
punctuation character 56
pushing input back 91

Q

quick sort function (for arrays) 300
QUIT character 273
quit signal 378
quote removal 316

R

race conditions, relating to job control
 464
race conditions, relating to signals 395
radix (of floating point number) 527
raising signals 403
random numbers 285
random-access files 77
range error 281
range of integer type 525
read lock 164
reading from a directory 171
reading from a file descriptor 141
reading from a socket 235
reading from a stream, by blocks 93
reading from a stream, by characters .. 88
reading from a stream, formatted 115
real group ID 480
real user ID 480
real-time timer 336
receiving datagrams 244
record locking 164
redirecting input and output 154
reentrant functions 398
relative file name 78
relocating memory allocator 52
remainder functions 292
removal of quotes 316
removing a file 178
removing macros that shadow functions
 5
renaming a file 179
reporting bugs 629
reporting errors 13
REPRINT character 272
reserved names 6
resource limits 341
restarting interrupted primitives 403
restrictions on signal handler functions
 398
root directory 78
rounding functions 292
running a command 443

S

scanning the group list 492
scanning the user list 490
search function (for arrays) 299

search functions (for strings) 70	socket protocol 208
seed (for random numbers) 285	socket shutdown 229
seeking on a file descriptor 145	socket, client actions 231
seeking on a stream 126	socket, closing 229
segmentation violation 376	socket, connecting 231
sending a datagram 244	socket, creating 228
sending signals 403	socket, initiating a connection 231
sequential-access files 77	sockets, accepting connections 233
server 230	sockets, listening 232
services database 222	sockets, server actions 232
session 457	soft limit 341
session leader 457	soft link 176
setting an alarm 335	sort function (for arrays) 300
`setuid` programs 481	sparse files 145
setuid programs and file access 192	special files 196
shadowing functions with macros 5	specified action (for a signal) 373
shared lock 164	square root function 284
shell 457	stable sorting 300
shrinking objects 44	standard dot notation, for Internet
shutting down a socket 229	addresses 217
`sigaction` flags 389	standard environment variables 435
`sigaction` function 386	standard error file descriptor 148
SIGCHLD, handling of 469	standard error stream 84
sign (of floating point number) 527	standard file descriptors 147
signal 371	standard input file descriptor 148
signal action 373	standard input stream 83
signal actions 384	standard output file descriptor 148
signal flags 389	standard output stream 84
`signal` function 384	standard streams 83
signal handler function 391	standards 1
signal mask 410	START character 274
signal messages 383	startup of program 425
signal names 373	static allocation 27
signal number 373	STATUS character 275
signal set 409	status codes 13
signals, generating 403	status of a file 181
significand (of floating point number)	status of obstack 45
.... 527	sticky bit 189
SIGTTIN, from background job 459	STOP character 274
SIGTTOU, from background job 459	stop signal 380
size of string 60	stopped job 458
socket 207	stopped jobs, continuing 472
socket address (name) binding 209	stopped jobs, detecting 469
socket domain 207	storage allocation 27
socket namespace 207	stream (sockets) 207
socket option level 249	stream, for I/O to a string 133
socket options 249	streams and descriptors 148
socket pair 229	streams, and file descriptors 147

Concept Index

streams, standard 83
string 59
string allocation 60
string collation functions 67
string comparison functions 65
string concatenation functions 61
string copy functions 61
string length 60
string literal 59
string search functions 70
string stream 133
string, representation of 59
style of communication (of a socket) .. 207
subshell 462
substitution of variables and commands
     316
successive signals 395
summer time 328
SunOS 3
supplementary group IDs 480
SUSP character 273
suspend character 273
SVID 3
symbolic link 176
symbolic link, opening 160
syntax, for program arguments 426
syntax, for reading numbers 294
System V Unix 3

T

TCP (Internet protocol) 225
template, for `printf` 94
template, for `scanf` 115
TERM environment variable 436
terminal flow control 278
terminal identification 255
terminal input queue 255
terminal input queue, clearing 278
terminal input signal 381
terminal line control functions 277
terminal line speed 268
terminal mode data types 257
terminal mode functions 258
terminal output queue 256
terminal output queue, flushing 277
terminal output signal 381
terminated jobs, detecting 469

termination signal 377
testing access permission 192
testing exit status of child process 449
text stream 125
ticks, clock 321
tilde expansion 316
TIME termios slot 276
time zone 332
time zone database 334
time, calendar 323
time, elapsed CPU 321
timer, profiling 336
timer, real-time 336
timer, virtual 336
timers, setting 335
timing error in signal handling 415
TMPDIR environment variable 198
tokenizing strings 72
tools, for installing library 627
transmitting datagrams 244
trigonometric functions 282
type measurements, floating 526
type measurements, integer 524
type modifier character (`printf`) ... 96
type modifier character (`scanf`) ... 117
typeahead buffer 255
TZ environment variable 436

U

umask 190
unbuffered stream 129
unconstrained storage allocation 28
undefining macros that shadow functions
     5
Unix, Berkeley 3
Unix, System V 3
unlinking a file 178
unreading characters 91
upper-case character 55
urgent data signal 379
urgent socket condition 241
usage limits 341
user database 489
user ID 479
user ID, determining 488
user name 479
user signals 383
usual file name errors 79

V

variable number of arguments 516
variable substitution 316
variable-sized arrays.................. 52
variadic function argument access 518
variadic function prototypes.......... 517
variadic functions 516
variadic functions, calling 520
virtual time alarm signal 379
virtual timer 336
`volatile` declarations 398

W

waiting for a signal................... 416
waiting for completion of child process
.... 449
waiting for input or output 150
warnings of memory almost full 53
WERASE character 272
whitespace character 56
wide characters 345
width of integer type................. 524
wildcard expansion................... 316
word expansion 315
working directory 169
write lock........................... 164
writing to a file descriptor............ 143
writing to a socket 235
writing to a stream, by blocks 93
writing to a stream, by characters 87
writing to a stream, formatted......... 94

Type Index

C

cc_t	258
clock_t	322
comparison_fn_t	299
cookie_close_function	138
cookie_io_functions_t	136
cookie_read_function	138
cookie_seek_function	138
cookie_write_function	138

D

dev_t	184
DIR	172
div_t	293

E

enum mcheck_status	34

F

fd_set	151
FILE	83
fpos_t	128

G

gid_t	481
glob_t	306

I

ino_t	183

J

jmp_buf	369

L

ldiv_t	294

M

mode_t	183

N

nlink_t	184

O

off_t	146

P

pid_t	444
printf_arginfo_function	114
printf_function	114
ptrdiff_t	523

R

regex_t	310
regmatch_t	313
regoff_t	313

S

sig_atomic_t	401
sighandler_t	384
sigjmp_buf	370
sigset_t	409
size_t	523
speed_t	270
ssize_t	141
struct dirent	171
struct flock	164
struct group	492
struct hostent	219
struct in_addr	217
struct itimerval	336
struct lconv	362
struct linger	251
struct mstats	36
struct netent	252
struct obstack	38
struct option	430
struct passwd	489
struct printf_info	112
struct protoent	225
struct rlimit	341
struct rusage	339

struct servent 222
struct sigaction 387
struct sigaltstack 419
struct sigstack 420
struct sigvec 421
struct sockaddr 210
struct sockaddr_in 215
struct sockaddr_un 213
struct stat 181
struct termios 257
struct timeval 324
struct timezone 325
struct tm 327
struct tms 322
struct utimbuf 194
struct utsname 496

T

tcflag_t 258
time_t 324

U

uid_t 481
union wait 453

V

va_list 520

W

wchar_t 349
wordexp_t 317

Function and Macro Index

—
_exit 440
_tolower 57
_toupper 57

A
abort 440
abs 290
accept 233
access 193
acos 283
acosh 285
adjtime 326
alarm 337
alloca 50
asctime 329
asin 283
asinh 285
asprintf 104
assert 515
atan 283
atan2 283
atanh 285
atexit 439
atof 297
atoi 296
atol 295

B
bcmp 67
bcopy 64
bind 211
bsearch 299
bzero 65

C
cabs 290
calloc 32
cbrt 284
ceil 292
cfgetispeed 269
cfgetospeed 269
cfmakeraw 277
cfree 30
cfsetispeed 269
cfsetospeed 269
cfsetspeed 269
chdir 170
chmod 190, 191
chown 187
clearerr 124
clock 322
close 141
closedir 173
confstr 513
connect 231
copysign 292
cos 282
cosh 285
creat 140
ctermid 474
ctime 330
cuserid 488

D
difftime 324
div 293
drem 293
DTTOIF 172
dup 155
dup2 155

E
endgrent 493
endhostent 221
endnetent 253
endprotoent 226
endpwent 491
endservent 223
execl 447
execle 447
execlp 448
execv 446
execve 447
execvp 447

exit 437
exp 283
expm1 284

F

fabs 290
fchmod 192
fchown 187
fclean 149
fclose 86
fcntl 154
FD_CLR 151
FD_ISSET 151
FD_SET 151
FD_ZERO 151
fdopen 147
feof 125
ferror 125
fflush 130
fgetc 88
fgetgrent 492
fgetpos 128
fgetpwent 490
fgets 91
fileno 147
finite 290
floor 292
fmemopen 133
fmod 293
fnmatch 305
fopen 84
fopencookie 137
fork 445
fpathconf 510
fprintf 103
fputc 87
fputs 87
fread 94
free 30
freopen 86
frexp 291
fscanf 123
fseek 126
fsetpos 129
fstat 184
ftell 126
fwrite 94

G

getc 89
getchar 89
getcwd 169
getdelim 90
getegid 482
getenv 434
geteuid 482
getgid 481
getgrent 493
getgrgid 492
getgrnam 492
getgroups 482
gethostbyaddr 220
gethostbyname 220
gethostent 221
gethostid 496
gethostname 495
getitimer 337
getline 90
getlogin 488
getnetbyaddr 253
getnetbyname 253
getnetent 253
getopt 427
getopt_long 431
getpeername 234
getpgrp 475
getpid 445
getppid 445
getpriority 343
getprotobyname 225
getprotobynumber 226
getprotoent 226
getpwent 491
getpwnam 490
getpwuid 490
getrlimit 341
getrusage 339
gets 91
getservbyname 223
getservbyport 223
getservent 223
getsockname 212
getsockopt 250
gettimeofday 326
getuid 481
getumask 191

Function and Macro Index

getw 89
getwd 170
glob 307
gmtime 329
gsignal 404

H

htonl 224
htons 224
hypot 284

I

IFTODT 172
index 71
inet_addr 218
inet_aton 218
inet_lnaof 219
inet_makeaddr 219
inet_netof 219
inet_network 219
inet_ntoa 219
infnan 290
initgroups 484
initstate 287
isalnum 56
isalpha 55
isascii 57
isatty 255
isblank 56
iscntrl 57
isdigit 56
isgraph 56
isinf 289
islower 55
isnan 289
isprint 56
ispunct 56
isspace 56
isupper 55
isxdigit 56
ITIMER_PROF 337
ITIMER_REAL 337
ITIMER_VIRTUAL 337

K

kill 405
killpg 406

L

labs 290
ldexp 291
ldiv 294
link 175
listen 232
localeconv 361
localtime 328
log 284
log10 284
log1p 285
logb 291
longjmp 369
lseek 145
lstat 184

M

main 425
malloc 28
mblen 351
mbstowcs 350
mbtowc 352
mcheck 34
memalign 33
memccpy 62
memchr 70
memcmp 65
memcpy 62
memmem 71
memmove 62
memory_warnings 53
memset 62
mkdir 180
mkfifo 205
mknod 196
mkstemp 198
mktemp 198
mktime 329
modf 292
mprobe 34
mstats 37

N

nice 344
ntohl 224
ntohs 224

O

obstack_1grow	43
obstack_1grow_fast	44
obstack_alignment_mask	46
obstack_alloc	40
obstack_base	45
obstack_blank	43
obstack_blank_fast	44
obstack_chunk_alloc	39
obstack_chunk_free	39
obstack_chunk_size	47
obstack_copy	40
obstack_copy0	41
obstack_finish	43
obstack_free	41
obstack_grow	43
obstack_grow0	43
obstack_init	39
obstack_next_free	46
obstack_object_size	43, 46
obstack_printf	105
obstack_room	44
obstack_vprintf	106
offsetof	532
on_exit	439
open	139
open_memstream	134
open_obstack_stream	135
opendir	172

P

parse_printf_format	108
pathconf	510
pause	416
pclose	204
perror	24
pipe	201
popen	203
pow	284
printf	103
psignal	384
putc	87
putchar	87
putenv	434
putpwent	491
puts	88
putw	88

Q

qsort	300

R

r_alloc	53
r_alloc_free	53
r_re_alloc	53
raise	404
rand	286
random	287
read	141
readdir	173
readlink	177
realloc	31
recv	236
recvfrom	245
regcomp	310
regerror	315
regexec	312
regfree	315
register_printf_function	111
remove	179
rename	179
rewind	127
rewinddir	174
rindex	71
rint	292
rmdir	178

S

S_ISBLK	185
S_ISCHR	185
S_ISDIR	185
S_ISFIFO	185
S_ISLNK	185
S_ISREG	185
S_ISSOCK	185
scalb	291
scanf	123
seekdir	175
select	151
send	235
sendto	244
setbuf	132
setbuffer	132
setgid	483
setgrent	493

Function and Macro Index

setgroups	484	snprintf	103
sethostent	221	socket	228
sethostid	496	socketpair	230
sethostname	495	sprintf	103
setitimer	336	sqrt	284
setjmp	369	srand	286
setlinebuf	132	srandom	287
setlocale	359	sscanf	123
setnetent	253	ssignal	386
setpgid	476	stat	184
setpgrp	476	stpcpy	63
setpriority	344	strcasecmp	66
setprotoent	226	strcat	63
setpwent	491	strchr	70
setregid	483	strcmp	66
setreuid	483	strcoll	68
setrlimit	341	strcpy	62
setservent	223	strcspn	71
setsid	475	strdup	63
setsockopt	250	strerror	24
setstate	287	strftime	330
settimeofday	326	strlen	61
setuid	482	strncasecmp	66
setvbuf	131	strncat	64
shutdown	229	strncmp	66
sigaction	387	strncpy	62
sigaddset	410	strpbrk	72
sigaltstack	420	strrchr	71
sigblock	422	strsignal	383
sigdelset	410	strspn	71
sigemptyset	409	strstr	71
sigfillset	409	strtod	296
siginterrupt	422	strtok	72
sigismember	410	strtol	294
siglongjmp	370	strtoul	295
sigmask	422	strxfrm	68
signal	384	symlink	176
sigpause	423	sysconf	503
sigpending	413	system	443
sigprocmask	410		
sigsetjmp	370	**T**	
sigsetmask	423	tan	282
sigstack	420	tanh	285
sigsuspend	417	tcdrain	277
sigvec	422	tcflow	278
sin	282	tcflush	278
sinh	285	tcgetattr	258
sleep	338	tcgetpgrp	476

tcsendbreak	277	va_start	520, 522
tcsetattr	258	valloc	33
tcsetpgrp	477	vasprintf	106
telldir	174	vfork	446
TEMP_FAILURE_RETRY	402	vfprintf	106
tempnam	197	vfscanf	124
time	324	vprintf	106
times	323	vscanf	124
tmpfile	197	vsnprintf	106
tmpnam	197	vsprintf	106
toascii	57	vsscanf	124
tolower	57		
toupper	57		

W

ttyname	255	wait	451
tzset	334	wait3	453
		wait4	451

U

		waitpid	449
umask	191	WCOREDUMP	452
uname	497	wcstombs	351
ungetc	92	wctomb	352
unlink	178	WEXITSTATUS	452
utime	195	WIFEXITED	452
utimes	195	WIFSIGNALED	452
		WIFSTOPPED	453

V

		wordexp	317
va_alist	522	wordfree	318
va_arg	521	write	143
va_dcl	522	WSTOPSIG	453
va_end	521	WTERMSIG	452

Variable and Constant Macro Index

*

* tzname [2] 334

_

__free_hook 35
__malloc_hook 35
__realloc_hook 35
_BSD_SOURCE 8
_GNU_SOURCE 9
_IOFBF 131
_IOLBF 131
_IONBF 131
_POSIX_C_SOURCE 8
_POSIX_CHOWN_RESTRICTED 508
_POSIX_JOB_CONTROL 501
_POSIX_NO_TRUNC 508
_POSIX_SAVED_IDS 501
_POSIX_SOURCE 8
_POSIX_VDISABLE 270
_POSIX_VDISABLE 509
_POSIX_VERSION 502
_POSIX2_C_DEV 501
_POSIX2_C_VERSION 502
_POSIX2_FORT_DEV 501
_POSIX2_FORT_RUN 501
_POSIX2_LOCALEDEF 501
_POSIX2_SW_DEV 502
_SVID_SOURCE 9

A

AF_FILE 210
AF_INET 210
AF_UNIX 210
AF_UNSPEC 211
ALTWERASE 268
ARG_MAX 499

B

B0 270
B110 270
B1200 270
B134 270
B150 270
B1800 270
B19200 270
B200 270
B2400 270
B300 270
B38400 270
B4800 270
B50 270
B600 270
B75 270
B9600 270
BC_BASE_MAX 511
BC_DIM_MAX 511, 512
BC_SCALE_MAX 511
BC_STRING_MAX 511
bit that enables nonblocking mode for the file. If this bit is set, ... 162
BRKINT 262
BUFSIZ 132

C

CCTS_OFLOW 265
CHILD_MAX 499
CIGNORE 265
CLK_TCK 322
CLOCAL 264
CLOCKS_PER_SEC 322
COLL_WEIGHTS_MAX 512
COREFILE 374
CREAD 264
CRTS_IFLOW 265
CS5 265
CS6 265
CS7 265
CS8 265
CSIZE 265
CSTOPB 264

D

daylight 335

E

E2BIG	15
EACCES	16
EADDRINUSE	20
EADDRNOTAVAIL	20
EAFNOSUPPORT	20
EAGAIN	18
EALREADY	19
EAUTH	22
EBACKGROUND	23
EBADF	279
EBADF	15
EBADRPC	22
EBUSY	16
ECHILD	15
ECHO	266
ECHOCTL	267
ECHOE	266
ECHOK	266
ECHOKE	267
ECHONL	267
ECHOPRT	266
ECONNABORTED	20
ECONNREFUSED	21
ECONNRESET	20
ED	23
EDEADLK	15
EDESTADDRREQ	21
EDIED	23
EDOM	18
EDQUOT	22
EEXIST	16
EFAULT	16
EFBIG	17
EFTYPE	22
EGRATUITOUS	23
EGREGIOUS	23
EHOSTDOWN	21
EHOSTUNREACH	21
EIEIO	23
EILSEQ	23
EINPROGRESS	19
EINTR	15
EINVAL	279
EINVAL	17
EIO	15
EISCONN	20
EISDIR	16
ELOOP	21
EMFILE	17
EMLINK	17
EMSGSIZE	19
ENAMETOOLONG	21
ENEEDAUTH	22
ENETDOWN	20
ENETRESET	20
ENETUNREACH	20
ENFILE	17
ENOBUFS	20
ENODEV	16
ENOENT	15
ENOEXEC	15
ENOLCK	22
ENOMEM	16
ENOPROTOOPT	19
ENOSPC	17
ENOSYS	23
ENOTBLK	16
ENOTCONN	20
ENOTDIR	16
ENOTEMPTY	21
ENOTSOCK	19
ENOTTY	279
ENOTTY	17
environ	434
ENXIO	15
EOF	124
EOPNOTSUPP	19
EPERM	14
EPFNOSUPPORT	20
EPIPE	18
EPROCLIM	21
EPROCUNAVAIL	22
EPROGMISMATCH	22
EPROGUNAVAIL	22
EPROTONOSUPPORT	19
EPROTOTYPE	19
EQUIV_CLASS_MAX	512
ERANGE	18
EREMOTE	22
EROFS	17
ERPCMISMATCH	22
errno	13
ESHUTDOWN	21
ESOCKTNOSUPPORT	19
ESPIPE	17

Variable and Constant Macro Index

ESRCH 15
ESTALE 22
ETIMEDOUT 21
ETOOMANYREFS 21
ETXTBSY 17
EUSERS 21
EWOULDBLOCK 18
EXDEV 16
EXIT_FAILURE 438
EXIT_SUCCESS 438
EXPR_NEST_MAX 512
EXTA 270
EXTB 270

F

F_DUPFD 155
F_GETFD 156
F_GETFL 162
F_GETLK 165
F_GETOWN 168
F_OK 194
F_RDLCK 167
F_SETFD 157
F_SETFL 163
F_SETLK 165
F_SETLKW 166
F_SETOWN 168
F_UNLCK 167
F_WRLCK 167
FD_CLOEXEC 157
FD_SETSIZE 151
FILENAME_MAX 508
FLUSHO 268
FOPEN_MAX 86
FPE_DECOVF_TRAP 375
FPE_FLTDIV_TRAP 375
FPE_FLTOVF_TRAP 375
FPE_FLTUND_TRAP 375
FPE_INTDIV_TRAP 375
FPE_INTOVF_TRAP 375
FPE_SUBRNG_TRAP 375

H

h_errno 221
HOST_NOT_FOUND 221
HUGE_VAL 282
HUPCL 264

I

ICANON 266
ICRNL 262
IEXTEN 267
IGNBRK 262
IGNCR 262
IGNPAR 261
IMAXBEL 263
INADDR_ANY 218
INADDR_BROADCAST 218
INADDR_LOOPBACK 218
INADDR_NONE 218
INLCR 262
INPCK 261
int 343
IPPORT_RESERVED 222
IPPORT_USERRESERVED 222
ISIG 267
ISTRIP 261
IXANY 262
IXOFF 262
IXON 262

L

L_ctermid 475
L_cuserid 489
L_INCR 127
L_SET 127
L_tmpnam 197
L_XTND 127
LANG 359
LC_ALL 359
LC_COLLATE 358
LC_CTYPE 358
LC_MONETARY 359
LC_NUMERIC 359
LC_TIME 359
LINE_MAX 512
LINK_MAX 507

M

MAX_CANON 507
MAX_INPUT 507
MAXNAMLEN 508
MB_CUR_MAX 348
MB_LEN_MAX 348
MDMBUF 265
MINSIGSTKSZ 419

MSG_DONTROUTE	237
MSG_OOB	237
MSG_PEEK	237

N

NAME_MAX	507
NAN	289
NCCS	258
NDEBUG	515
NGROUPS_MAX	500
NO_ADDRESS	221
NO_RECOVERY	221
NOFLSH	268
NOKERNINFO	268
NSIG	374
NULL	523

O

O_ACCMODE	159
O_APPEND	161
O_ASYNC	162
O_CREAT	160
O_EXCL	160
O_EXEC	159
O_EXLOCK	161
O_FSYNC	162
O_IGNORE_CTTY	160
O_NDELAY	162
O_NOATIME	162
O_NOCTTY	160
O_NOLINK	160
O_NONBLOCK	160
O_NOTRANS	161
O_RDONLY	158
O_RDWR	158
O_READ	159
O_SHLOCK	161
O_SYNC	162
O_TRUNC	161
O_WRITE	159
O_WRONLY	158
ONLCR	263
ONOEOT	263
OPEN_MAX	499
OPOST	263
optarg	427
opterr	427
optind	427
optopt	427
OXTABS	263

P

P_tmpdir	198
PA_CHAR	108
PA_DOUBLE	108
PA_FLAG_LONG	109
PA_FLAG_LONG_DOUBLE	109
PA_FLAG_LONG_LONG	109
PA_FLAG_MASK	108
PA_FLAG_PTR	109
PA_FLAG_SHORT	109
PA_FLOAT	108
PA_INT	108
PA_LAST	108
PA_POINTER	108
PA_STRING	108
PARENB	264
PARMRK	261
PARODD	265
PATH_MAX	507
PENDIN	268
PF_CCITT	228
PF_FILE	213
PF_IMPLINK	228
PF_INET	215
PF_ISO	228
PF_NS	228
PF_ROUTE	228
PF_UNIX	213
PIPE_BUF	507
PRIO_MAX	343
PRIO_MIN	343
PRIO_PGRP	344
PRIO_PROCESS	344
PRIO_USER	344
program_invocation_name	24
program_invocation_short_name	24

R

R_OK	193
RAND_MAX	286
RE_DUP_MAX	500
RLIM_NLIMITS	343
RLIMIT_CORE	342
RLIMIT_CPU	342

Variable and Constant Macro Index

RLIMIT_DATA 342
RLIMIT_FSIZE 342
RLIMIT_NOFILE 343
RLIMIT_OFILE 343
RLIMIT_RSS 342
RLIMIT_STACK 342

S

S_IEXEC 188
S_IFBLK 186
S_IFCHR 186
S_IFDIR 186
S_IFIFO 186
S_IFLNK 186
S_IFMT 186
S_IFREG 186
S_IFSOCK 186
S_IREAD 188
S_IRGRP 188
S_IROTH 188
S_IRUSR 188
S_IRWXG 188
S_IRWXO 188
S_IRWXU 188
S_ISGID 189
S_ISUID 189
S_ISVTX 189
S_IWGRP 188
S_IWOTH 188
S_IWRITE 188
S_IWUSR 188
S_IXGRP 188
S_IXOTH 188
S_IXUSR 188
SA_DISABLE 419
SA_NOCLDSTOP 390
SA_ONSTACK 419
SA_ONSTACK 390
SA_RESTART 390
SEEK_CUR 127
SEEK_END 127
SEEK_SET 127
SIG_BLOCK 410
SIG_DFL 385
SIG_ERR 386
SIG_IGN 385
SIG_SETMASK 410
SIG_UNBLOCK 410

SIGABRT 376
SIGALRM 379
SIGBUS 376
SIGCHLD 380
SIGCLD 380
SIGCONT 380
SIGEMT 377
SIGFPE 375
SIGHUP 378
SIGILL 376
SIGINFO 383
SIGINT 377
SIGIO 379
SIGIOT 376
SIGKILL 378
SIGLOST 382
SIGPIPE 382
SIGPOLL 380
SIGPROF 379
SIGQUIT 378
SIGSEGV 376
SIGSTKSZ 419
SIGSTOP 380
SIGSYS 377
SIGTERM 377
SIGTRAP 377
SIGTSTP 380
SIGTTIN 381
SIGTTOU 381
SIGURG 379
SIGUSR1 382
SIGUSR2 383
SIGVTALRM 379
SIGWINCH 383
SIGXCPU 382
SIGXFSZ 382
SOCK_DGRAM 208
SOCK_RAW 209
SOCK_STREAM 208
SOL_SOCKET 250
SSIZE_MAX 500
stderr 84
STDERR_FILENO 148
stdin 83
STDIN_FILENO 148
stdout 83
STDOUT_FILENO 148
STREAM_MAX 499

SV_INTERRUPT	422	VDSUSP	273
SV_ONSTACK	422	VEOF	271
SV_RESETHAND	422	VEOL	271
sys_siglist	384	VEOL2	271
		VERASE	271

T

		VINTR	272
		VKILL	272
TCIFLUSH	278	VLNEXT	274
TCIOFF	278	VMIN	275
TCIOFLUSH	278	VQUIT	273
TCION	279	VREPRINT	272
TCOFLUSH	278	VSTART	274
TCOOFF	278	VSTATUS	275
TCOON	278	VSTOP	274
TCSADRAIN	258	VSUSP	273
TCSAFLUSH	259	VTIME	276
TCSANOW	258	VWERASE	272
TCSASOFT	259		
timezone	334		
TMP_MAX	197		

W

TOSTOP	268		
TRY_AGAIN	221	W_OK	194
TZNAME_MAX	500		

V

X

VDISCARD	275	X_OK	194

Program and File Index

-
-lbsd-compat 9, 475

/
/etc/group 491
/etc/hosts 219
/etc/localtime 333
/etc/networks 252
/etc/passwd 489
/etc/protocols 225
/etc/services 222
/share/lib/zoneinfo 334

A
arpa/inet.h 218
assert.h 515

B
bsd-compat 9, 475

C
cd 169
chgrp 187
chown 187
ctype.h 55, 57

D
dirent.h 7, 171, 172, 173, 174

E
errno.h 13, 14

F
fcntl.h . . . 8, 139, 153, 155, 156, 158, 164, 168
float.h 528
fnmatch.h 305

G
gcc 2

grp.h 8, 484, 491

H
hostid 495
hostname 495

K
kill 377

L
limits.h 8, 348, 499, 507, 524
locale.h 359, 361
localtime 333
ls 181

M
malloc.c 53
malloc.h 33, 35, 36, 53
math.h 281, 289, 290, 291, 292
mkdir 180

N
netdb.h 219, 222, 225, 252
netinet/in.h 215, 217, 222, 224

O
obstack.h 38

P
printf.h 111, 112
pwd.h 8, 489

S
setjmp.h 368, 370
sh 443
signal.h 8, 373, 384, 386, 390, 403, 405, 409, 410, 413, 421
stdarg.h 518, 520
stddef.h 349, 523

stdio.h 83, 84, 87, 88, 94, 103, 106, 123, 124, 126, 128, 130, 131, 133, 136, 147, 179, 197, 384, 474, 488
stdlib.h 28, 30, 31, 32, 33, 50, 286, 287, 290, 293, 294, 296, 299, 300, 348, 350, 351, 352, 434, 438, 440, 443
string.h 61, 65, 67, 70, 72, 383
sys/param.h 495
sys/resource.h 339, 341, 343
sys/socket.h 208, 210, 211, 212, 213, 215, 228, 229, 235, 236, 237, 244, 250
sys/stat.h 8, 181, 185, 188, 191, 196, 205
sys/time.h 195, 324, 336
sys/times.h 8, 322
sys/types.h 150, 444, 475, 476, 481, 482, 483
sys/un.h 213
sys/utsname.h 496
sys/wait.h 449, 452, 453

T

termios.h 8, 257
time.h 194, 321, 324, 329, 332

U

umask 191
unistd.h 139, 141, 147, 155, 169, 175, 176, 178, 179, 187, 193, 201, 255, 336, 427, 440, 444, 445, 446, 475, 476, 481, 482, 483, 488, 495, 500, 508, 509
utime.h 194

V

varargs.h 522

Z

zoneinfo 334

C Library Reference Manual

The C language provides no built-in facilities for performing such common operations as input/output, memory management, string manipulation, and the like. Instead, these facilities are defined in a standard library, which you compile and link with your programs.

The GNU C library, described in this manual, defines all of the library functions that are specified by the ANSI C standard, as well as additional features specific to POSIX and other derivatives of the Unix operating system, and extensions specific to the GNU system.

Specifically, the GNU C library supports ANSI C-1989, POSIX 1003.1-1990 and most of the functions in POSIX 1003.2-1992. It is upwardly compatible with 4.4BSD and includes many System V functions, plus GNU extensions.

This manual tells you how to use the facilities of the GNU library, including both what Unix refers to as "library functions" and "system calls."

Since the library is under continuing development, we are printing limited, copier-duplicated runs of this manual until it becomes more stable.

ISBN 1-882114-53-1

55000>

9 781882 114535

FSF • US$50.00 • Printed in USA